TENTH EDITION

AMERICAN HISTORY

A Survey

Volume I: To 1877

Alan Brinkley

Columbia University

 **McGraw-Hill College**

Boston   Burr Ridge, IL   Dubuque, IA   Madison, WI   New York   San Francisco   St. Louis
Bangkok   Bogotá   Caracas   Lisbon   London   Madrid
Mexico City   Milan   New Delhi   Seoul   Singapore   Sydney   Taipei   Toronto

McGraw-Hill College

A Division of The McGraw·Hill Companies

AMERICAN HISTORY: A SURVEY, VOLUME I: TO 1877, TENTH EDITION

This book is printed on acid-free paper.

1 2 3 4 5 6 7 8 9 0 VNH/VNH 9 3 2 1 0 9 8

ISBN 0-07-303391-X

Editorial director: *Jane E. Vaicunas*
Sponsoring editor: *Lyn Uhl*
Developmental editor: *Monica Freedman/Jane Tufts*
Senior marketing manager: *Suzanne Daghlian*
Senior project manager: *Jayne Klein*
Production supervisor: *Laura Fuller*
Cover designer: *Gino Cieslik*
Senior photo research coordinator: *Carrie K. Burger*
Art editor: *Joyce Watters*
Supplement Coordinator: *Tammy Juran*
Compositor: *Shepherd, Inc.*
Typeface: *10/12 Garamond*
Printer: *Von Hoffman Press, Inc.*

Interior designer: *Maureen McCutcheon*
Cover photos: (top) **Principal Front of the Capitol Washington,**
Robert Brandard after William Henry Bartlett, *American Scenery,* 1839.
Hand-colored steel engraving. Courtesy U.S. Senate Collection.
(bottom): **Column of the Court Room, North Wing of the Capitol,**
Benjamin Henry Latrobe, 1817. Ink and watercolor on paper.
Courtesy Architect of the Capitol.
Photo research: *Deborah Bull/PhotoSearch, Inc.; Vicki Gold Levi*
Maps by: *Magellan Geographix*

The Library of Congress has cataloged the complete edition as follows

Brinkley, Alan.
    American history : a survey / Alan Brinkley. — 10th ed.
      p.   cm.
    Includes bibliographical references and index.
    Contents: v. 1. To 1877.
    ISBN 0-07-303391-X (v. 1)
    1. United States—History. I. Title.
E178.1.B826   1999
  973—dc21
                                              98-15454
                                               CIP

www.mhhe.com

About the Author

Alan Brinkley is the Allan Nevins Professor of History at Columbia University. He is the author of *Voices of Protest: Huey Long, Father Coughlin, and the Great Depression*, which won the 1983 American Book Award; *The Unfinished Nation: A Concise History of the American People*; *The End of Reform: New Deal Liberalism in Recession and War*; and *Liberalism and its Discontents.* He is the co-author of *Eyes of the Nation: A Visual History of the United States and New Federalist Papers.* He was educated at Princeton and Harvard and has taught at M. I. T., Harvard (where he received the Joseph R. Levenson Memorial Teaching Prize), Princeton, the City University of New York Graduate School, and Oxford University, where he was the Harmsworth Professor of American History in 1998–99. His articles, essays, and reviews have appeared in *The American Historical Review, the Journal of American History, The New York Review of Books, The New Yorker, The New York Times Magazine and Book Review, The New Republic, The Times Literary Supplement*, and other journals.

Contents

Chapter Three

SOCIETY AND CULTURE IN PROVINCIAL AMERICA   75

Chapter Four

THE EMPIRE UNDER STRAIN   117

Chapter Five

THE AMERICAN REVOLUTION   151

Chapter Six

THE CONSTITUTION AND THE NEW REPUBLIC   193

Chapter Seven

THE JEFFERSONIAN ERA   221

Chapter Ten

AMERICA'S ECONOMIC REVOLUTION   325

Chapter Eleven

COTTON, SLAVERY, AND THE OLD SOUTH   371

Chapter Twelve

ANTEBELLUM CULTURE AND REFORM   399

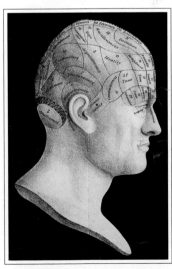

Chapter Fifteen

RECONSTRUCTION AND THE NEW SOUTH   507

Appendices A-1

MAPS

DOCUMENTS AND TABLES

Preface

The past, of course, can never change. But our understanding of the past changes constantly. There may be no time in which that was more evident than in the last several decades, when historical scholarship experienced something close to a revolution.

Once, historians viewed the past largely as the experiences of great men and the unfolding of great public events. Today, they attempt to tell a much more complicated story—one that includes private as well as public lives, ordinary people as well as celebrated ones, difference as well as unity. The new history seems fragmented at times, because it attempts to embrace so many more areas of human experience than the older narrative. It is often disturbing, because it reveals failures and injustices as well as triumphs. But it is also richer, fuller, and better suited to helping us understand our own diverse and contentious world.

This book began its life several decades ago; and like most general American histories of its time, it concentrated at first primarily on America's political and economic development, and on its expanding role in the world. This tenth edition continues to tell those important stories, but it tells many other stories as well. This newest version, the result of a continuing process of change stretching now over more than twenty years, attempts to present both the traditional stories of great public events and the newer stories that historians have more recently revealed. In particular, this tenth edition includes a greatly expanded treatment of the history of American culture,

both through the integration of much new cultural history into the text and through the addition of a series of several dozen new essays, "Patterns of Popular Culture," that examine in depth ways in which men and women throughout American history have diverted, informed, and entertained themselves.

Despite many changes, I have tried to retain what I believe has long been the principal strength of this book: a balanced picture of the American past that connects the new histories of society and culture with the more traditional stories of politics, diplomacy, and great events. The United States is a society of extraordinary diversity, and we cannot hope to understand its history without understanding the experiences of the many different groups that have shaped it. But America is also a nation, whose people share a common political system, a connection to a national economy, and a familiarity with a shared and, in modern times, enormously powerful popular culture. To understand the American past, therefore, it is necessary to examine both the nation's considerable diversity and the powerful forces that have drawn it together and allowed it to survive and flourish.

In addition to its expanded attention to cultural history, the tenth edition incorporates substantial new material in other areas. It has new "Where Historians Disagree" essays in Chapter 1 (one on the nature of historical disagreement, and the other on the size of the pre-Columbian population). "The American Environment" essays have been revised and repositioned to be more immediately accessible within the text.

The book has also been substantially redesigned, with a significantly enhanced and expanded illustration program and with revitalized maps and charts, now with explanatory captions. There are also new summary conclusions for each chapter. The bibliographies have been greatly enhanced as well. In addition to the comprehensive list of books by topic that has appeared in previous editions, this edition includes a short, annotated list of particularly useful books as well as a list of films suitable for teachers and students and a list of significant historical websites.

* * *

As always, I am grateful to many people for their help in producing this new edition. I was particularly blessed to have the help of several gifted research assistants—Thaddeus Russell, Adam Rothman, Charles Forcey, and Sharon Musher—who contributed enormously to the new material in this edition as well as the revision of existing sections. I appreciate the very helpful reviews of this book submitted by a group of talented scholars and teachers; since most of them chose to remain anonymous,

I will list none of them here by name. I am grateful as well to the many people at McGraw-Hill who worked so hard on this new edition: Lyn Uhl and Monica Freedman, who patiently supervised the project from Boston; Jayne Klein, who skillfully managed the production of the book; Kris Queck, the careful and talented copy editor; Carrie Burger, who adeptly managed the illustrations; and Gino Cieslik, who is responsible for the attractive new design of the book. I was fortunate, as well, to have the assistance of three gifted photo researchers: Elyse Rieder, Deborah Bull, and Vicki Gold Levi. My wife, Evangeline Morphos, helped me, as always, in many ways; and my daughter Elly took a particular interest in my forays into popular culture and was directly responsible for the essay in Chapter 30.

Finally, I am grateful to the students, teachers, and other readers of this book who have sent me unsolicited, but always welcome, comments, criticisms, and corrections. I hope they will continue to offer their reactions by sending them to me in care of the Department of History, Columbia University, New York, NY 10027; or by E-mail to ab65@columbia.edu.

Alan Brinkley

AMERICAN HISTORY

A Survey

Chapter One

THE MEETING OF CULTURES

The discovery of America did not begin with Christopher Columbus. It began many thousands of years earlier when human beings first crossed an ancient land bridge over the Bering Strait into what is now Alaska and—almost certainly without realizing it—began to people a new continent. No one is certain when these migrations began; recent estimates suggest between 12,000 and 14,000 years ago, but some scholars believe the first crossings were much earlier. They were probably a result of the development of new stone tools—spears and other hunting implements—with which it became possible to pursue the large animals that regularly crossed between Asia and North America. Year after year, a few at a time, these nomadic peoples—all of them apparently from a Mongolian stock similar to that of modern-day eastern Siberia—entered the new

continent and moved ever deeper into its heart. Ultimately, perhaps as early as 9,000 B.C., the migrations reached the southern tip of South America. By the end of the fifteenth century A.D., when the first important contact with Europeans occurred, America was the home of many millions of men and women. Scholars estimate that more than 50 million people—and perhaps as many as 75 million, more than lived in Europe—lived in the Americas by 1500 and that as many as 10 million lived in the territory that now constitutes the United States.

AMERICA BEFORE COLUMBUS

As settlement spread, the peoples of the different regions of America began to adapt themselves to their surroundings. For many centuries, they lived primarily in small nomadic bands, subsisting through hunting, fishing, and occasionally primitive agriculture, depending on the resources of the lands in which they lived. Gradually, however, they developed substantial civilizations—some of them of vast size and power. There was as much variety among the civilizations of the Americas as among the civilizations of Europe, Asia, and Africa.

The Civilizations of the South

The most elaborate of these societies emerged in South and Central America and in Mexico. In Peru, the Incas created a powerful empire of perhaps 6 million people. They developed a complex political system

■ **THE SPANISH IN MEXICO**
These images by native Mexicans—encouraged by the Dominican friar Diego Duran and added in the 1560s and 1570s to what is known as the *Duran Codex*—recorded the Indians' vision of the Spanish conquest of their land. The painting combines Mexican images and styles with European and Christian influences, which were already transforming the culture and outlook of the natives. *(Oronoz)*

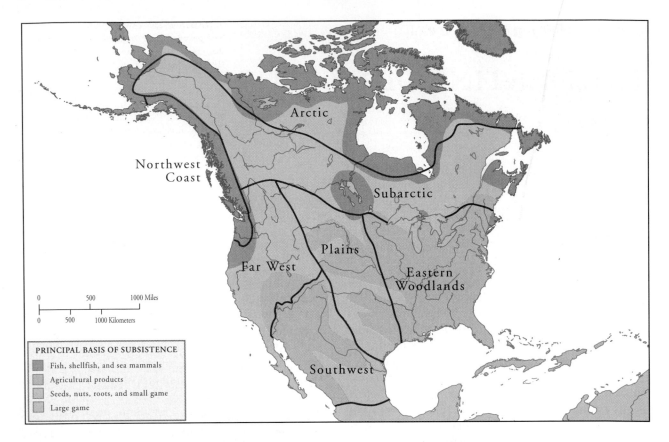

Arctic

Northwest
Coast

Subarctic

Plains

Far West

Eastern
Woodlands

Southwest

| 0 | 500 | 1000 Miles |
| 0 | 500 | 1000 Kilometers |

PRINCIPAL BASIS OF SUBSISTENCE

- Fish, shellfish, and sea mammals
- Agricultural products
- Seeds, nuts, roots, and small game
- Large game

■ **PRINCIPAL SUBSISTENCE PATTERNS OF EARLY NATIVE PEOPLES OF NORTH AMERICA**
North American Indians built complex civilizations of great variety. Native people relied on diverse forms of economic organization. For
instance, coastal tribes in the upper northeast and the northwest relied on fishing for their livelihood, while the Eastern Woodland Indians
throughout the forestland of North America combined farming, hunting, gathering, and fishing.

and a large network of paved roads that welded together the populations of many tribes under a single
rule. In Central America and on the Yucatán peninsula
of Mexico, the Mayas built a sophisticated culture
with a written language, a numerical system similar to
the Arabic (and superior to the Roman), an accurate
calendar, and an advanced agricultural system. They
were succeeded by the Aztecs, a once-nomadic warrior tribe from the north. In the late thirteenth century, the Aztecs established a precarious rule over
much of central and southern Mexico and built elaborate administrative, educational, and medical systems
comparable to the most advanced in Europe at the
time. The Aztecs also developed a harsh religion that
required human sacrifice. Their Spanish conquerors
discovered the skulls of 100,000 victims in one location when they arrived in 1519. That was one reason
why many Europeans came to consider the Aztecs
"savages" despite their impressive accomplishments
(and despite the holy wars and witch burnings in the

Christian world, which show that the Aztecs were not
alone in finding religious justification for killing).

The economies of these societies were based primarily on agriculture, but there were also substantial
cities. In them lived, among others, many of the warriors and priests who ruled the empires and formed
their hereditary elites. Some of these cities were as
large as the greatest capitals of Europe. Tenochtitlán,
the Aztec capital built on the site of present-day Mexico City, had a population of over 100,000 in 1500 and
an impressive complex of majestic public buildings—
including temples equal in size to the great pyramids
of Egypt. The Mayas (at Mayapán and elsewhere) and
the Incas (in such cities as Cuzco and Machu Picchu)
produced similarly elaborate settlements with striking
religious and ceremonial structures of their own.
These achievements are all the more remarkable for
their having been attained without some of the important technologies that Asian and European civilizations
possessed. The Incas, for example, never had any sys-

tem of writing or any equivalent for paper. And as late as the sixteenth century, no American society had yet developed wheeled vehicles.

The Civilizations of the North

The peoples north of Mexico—in the lands that became the United States and Canada—did not develop empires as large or political systems as elaborate as those of the Incas, Mayas, and Aztecs. They did, however, build complex civilizations of great variety. Societies that subsisted on hunting, gathering, fishing, or some combination of the three emerged in the northern regions of the continent. The Eskimos of the Arctic Circle fished and hunted seals; their civilization spanned thousands of miles of largely frozen land, which they traversed by dogsled. The big-game hunters of the northern forests led nomadic lives based on pursuit of moose and caribou. The tribes of the Pacific Northwest, whose principal occupation was salmon fishing, created substantial permanent settlements along the coast and engaged in constant and often violent competition with one another for access to natural resources.

Another group of tribes spread through relatively arid regions of the Far West and developed successful communities—many of them quite wealthy and densely populated—based on fishing, hunting small game, and gathering. Other societies in North America were primarily agricultural. Among the most elaborate were those in the Southwest. The people of

that region built large irrigation systems to allow farming on their relatively dry land, and they constructed substantial towns that became centers of trade, crafts, and religious and civic ritual. Their densely populated settlements at Chaco Canyon and elsewhere consisted of stone and adobe terraced structures, known today as pueblos, many of which resembled the large apartment buildings of later eras in size and design. In the Great Plains region, too, most tribes were engaged in sedentary farming (corn and other grains) and lived in substantial permanent settlements, although there were some small nomadic tribes that subsisted by hunting buffalo. (Only in the eighteenth century, after Europeans had introduced the horse to North America, did buffalo hunting begin to support a large population in the region; at that point, many once-sedentary farmers left the land to pursue the great migratory buffalo herds.)

The eastern third of what is now the United States—much of it covered with forests and inhabited by people who have thus become known as the Woodland Indians—had the greatest food resources of any region of the continent. Many tribes lived there, and most of them engaged simultaneously in farming, hunting, gathering, and fishing. In the South there were for a time substantial permanent settlements and large trading networks based on the corn and other grains grown in the rich lands of the Mississippi River valley. As in the Southwest, cities emerged as trading and political centers. Among them was Cahokia (near present-day St. Louis),

■ **CAHOKIA INDIAN MOUNDS**
The great earthen mounds constructed by the Cahokia Indians near present-day St. Louis have endured into modern times as part of the Missouri landscape. One of them is pictured here, rising above a farm field. *(Missouri Historical Society)*

which at its peak in 1200 A.D. had a population of 40,000 and contained a great complex of large earthen mounds.

The agricultural societies of the Northeast were more mobile than those in other regions. Farming techniques there were designed to exploit the land quickly rather than to develop permanent settlements. Natives often cleared the land by setting forest fires or cutting into trees to kill them. They then planted crops—corn, beans, squash, pumpkins, and others—among the dead or blackened trunks. After a few years, when the land became exhausted or the filth from a settlement began to accumulate, they moved on and established themselves elsewhere. In some parts of eastern North America, villages dispersed every winter and families foraged for themselves in the wilderness until warm weather returned; those who survived then reassembled to begin farming again. Many of the tribes living east of the Mississippi River were linked together loosely by common linguistic roots. The largest of the language groups was the Algonquin tribes, which lived along the Atlantic seaboard from Canada to Virginia. More elaborately organized was the Iroquois Confederation, which emerged in the mid-fifteenth century, centered in what is now upstate New York. The Iroquois included at least five distinct northern "nations"—the Seneca, Cayuga, Onondaga, Oneida, and Mohawk—and had links as well with the Cherokees and the Tuscaroras farther south, in the Carolinas

and Georgia. The third largest language group—the Muskogean—included the tribes in the southernmost region of the eastern seaboard: the Chickasaws, Choctaws, Creeks, and Seminoles. Alliances among the various Indian societies (even among those with common languages) were fragile, since the peoples of the Americas did not think of themselves as members of a single civilization. When Europeans arrived and began to threaten their way of life, Indians generally viewed the threat in terms of how it affected their own community and tribe, not how it affected any larger "Indian nation." Only rarely did tribes unite in opposition to challenges from whites.

Tribal Cultures

The enormous diversity of economic, social, and political structures among the North American Indians makes large generalizations about their cultures difficult. In the last centuries before the arrival of Europeans, however, Native Americans—like peoples in other areas of the world—were experiencing an agricultural revolution. In all regions of the United States (if in varying degrees from place to place), tribes were becoming more sedentary and were developing new sources of food, clothing, and shelter. Most regions were experiencing significant population growth. Virtually all were developing the sorts of elaborate social customs and rituals that only relatively stationary societies can produce. Religion was

■ IROQUOIS WOMEN
This 1734 French engraving shows Iroquois women at work in a settlement somewhere in what is now upstate New York. In the foreground, women are cooking. Others are working in the fields. Men spent much of their time hunting and soldiering, leaving the women to govern and dominate the internal lives of the villages. Property in Iroquois society was inherited through the mother, and women occupied positions of great honor and authority within the tribes. *(Library of Congress)*

■ THE INDIAN VILLAGE OF SECOTON (C. 1585), BY JOHN WHITE
John White created this illustration of life among the Eastern Woodland Indians in coastal North Carolina. It shows the diversified agriculture practiced by the natives: squash, tobacco, and three varieties of corn. The hunters shown in nearby woods suggest another element of the native economy. At bottom right, Indians perform a religious ritual, which White described as "strange gestures and songs." *(British Museum)*

as important to Indian society as it was to most other cultures and was usually closely bound up with the natural world on which the tribes depended. Native Americans worshipped many gods, whom they associated variously with crops, game, forests, rivers, and other elements of nature. Some tribes created elaborate, brightly colored totems as part of their religious ritual; most staged large festivals on such important occasions as harvests or major hunts.

As in other parts of the world, the societies of North America tended to divide tasks according to gender. All tribes assigned women the jobs of caring for children, preparing meals, and gathering certain foods. But the allocation of other tasks varied from one society to another. Some tribal groups (notably the Pueblos of the Southwest) reserved farming tasks almost entirely for men. Among others (including the Algonquins, the Iroquois, and the Muskogees), women tended the fields, while men engaged in hunting, warfare, or clearing land. Iroquois women and children were often left alone for extended periods while men were away hunting or fighting battles. As a result, women tended to control the social and economic organization of the settlements and played powerful roles within families (which in many tribes were traced back "matrilineally," or through the mother's line).

WHY DO HISTORIANS SO OFTEN DIFFER?

There was a time, early in the twentieth century, while the professional study of history was still relatively new, when many historians believed that questions about the past could be answered with the same certainty and precision that questions in other, more scientific fields could be answered. By using scientific methods of research and analysis, and by deploying armies of scholars to sift through available records and produce careful, closely argued accounts of the past, it would be possible to create something close to definitive histories that would survive without controversy for many generations. Scholars who believed this were known as "positivists," and they shared the views of such European thinkers as Auguste Comte and Thomas Henry Huxley that real knowledge can only be derived from direct, scientific, empirical observation. Historians, therefore, set out to answer questions for which extensive archival or statistical evidence was available.

Although a vigorous debate continues to this day over whether historical research can or should be truly objective, almost no historian any longer accepts the "positivist" claim that history could ever be anything like an exact science. Disagreement about the past is, in fact, at the very heart of the effort to understand history—just as disagreement about the present is at the heart of efforts to understand our own time. Critics of contemporary historical scholarship often denounce the way historians are constantly revising earlier interpretations; some denounce the act of interpretation itself. History, they claim, is "what happened." Historians should "stick to the facts." That scholars almost always find it impossible to do so helps account for the many controversies surrounding the historical profession today.

(British Museum)

Historians differ with one another both because the "facts" are seldom as straightforward as their critics claim, and because facts by themselves mean almost nothing without an effort to assign meaning to them. There are, of course, some historical "facts" that are not in dispute. Everyone agrees, for example, that the Japanese bombed Pearl Harbor on December 7, 1941, or that Thomas Jefferson was elected president in 1800. But many other "facts" are much harder to determine—among them, for example, the question of how large the American population was before the arrival of Columbus, which is discussed later in this chapter. How many slaves resisted slavery?

This sounds like a reasonably straightforward question, but it is almost impossible to answer with any certainty —in part because the records of slave resistance are spotty, and in part because the definition of "resistance" is a matter of considerable dispute.

Even when a set of facts is reasonably clear and straightforward, historians disagree—sometimes quite radically—over what they mean. Those disagreements can be the result of political and ideological disagreements. Some of the most vigorous debates in recent decades have been between scholars influenced by Marxist ideas who are convinced that economic interests and class divisions are the key to understanding the past, and those committed to other assumptions who believe that ideas and culture are at least as important as material interests. The disagreements can be a result of the particular perspectives that people of different backgrounds bring to the study of the past. Whites and people of color, men and women, people from the American South and people from the North, young people and older people: these and many other points of difference find their way into scholarly disagreements. And debates can be a result as well of differences over methodology—differences, for example, between those who believe that quantitative studies can answer important historical questions and those who believe that other, less precise methods come closer to the truth.

Most of all, perhaps, historical interpretation changes in response to the nature of the time in which it is written. Historians may strive to be "objective" in their work, but no one can be entirely free from the assumptions and concerns of the present. In the 1950s, the omnipresent shadow of the Cold War had a profound effect on the way most historians viewed the past and produced much work that seemed to validate the American democratic experience in contrast to the new and dangerous alternatives challenging it at the time. In the 1960s, concerns about racial justice and disillusionment with the Vietnam War

(Library of Congress)

altered the way many historians thought, introducing a much more critical tone to scholarship and turning the attention of scholars away from politics and government and toward the study of society and culture.

Many areas of scholarship in the late twentieth century are embroiled in a profound debate over whether there is such a thing as "truth." The world, some scholars argue, is simply a series of "narratives" constructed by people who view life in very different and often highly personal ways. "Facts" do not really exist. Everything is interpretation. Not many historians embrace such radical ideas; most would agree that interpretations, to be of any value, must rest on a solid foundation of observable facts. But historians do recognize that even the most compelling facts are subject to many different interpretations and that the process of understanding the past is a forever continuing—and forever contested—process.

THE AMERICAN POPULATION BEFORE COLUMBUS

No one knows how many people lived in the Americas in the centuries before Columbus. But scholars, and others, have spent more than a century, and have written many thousands of pages, debating the question nevertheless. Interest in this question survives, despite the near impossibility of answering it, because the debate over the pre-Columbian population is closely connected to the much larger debate over the consequences of European settlement of the Western Hemisphere.

Throughout the nineteenth century, Native Americans—in the midst of their many losing battles against the spread of white civilization—spoke often of the great days before Columbus when there were many more people in their tribes. They drew from their own rich tradition of oral history handed down through storytelling from one generation to another. The painter and ethnographer George Catlin, who spent much time among the tribes in the 1830s painting portraits of a race that he feared was "fast passing to extinction," listened to these oral legends and estimated that there had been 16 million Indians in North America before the Europeans came. Most other white Americans who thought about this issue dismissed such claims as preposterous and insisted that the native population could not have been even as large as a million. Indian civilization was far too primitive, they claimed, to have been able to sustain so large a population.

In the early twentieth century, an ethnologist at the Smithsonian Institution, James Mooney, set out to find a method of estimating the early North American population that would be more scientific than the methods of the previous century, which were essentially guesses. He drew from early accounts of soldiers and missionaries in the sixteenth century and in 1928 came up with the implausibly precise figure of 1.15 million natives who lived north of Mexico in the early sixteenth century. That was a larger figure than nineteenth-century writers had suggested, but still much smaller than the Indians themselves claimed. A few years later, the anthropologist Alfred Kroeber used many of Mooney's methods to come up with an estimate of the population of the entire Western Hemisphere—considerably larger than Mooney's, but much lower than Catlin's. He concluded in 1934 that there were 8.4 million people in the Americas in 1492, half in North America and half in the Caribbean and South America. His conclusions remained largely uncontested until the 1960s.

These low early estimates reflected, more than anything else, an assumption that the arrival of the Europeans did not much reduce the native population. Given that assumption, it seemed reasonable to assume that the relatively low numbers of Indians that Europeans encountered in the late sixteenth and seventeenth centuries reflected the numbers of natives living in the Americas in earlier centuries as well. A dramatic change in the scholarly approach to the early population came as a result of the discovery by a number of scholars in the 1960s and 1970s that the early tribes had been catastrophically decimated by European plagues not long after the ar-

(Library of Congress)

rival of Columbus—meaning that the numbers Europeans observed even in the late 1500s were already dramatically smaller than the numbers in 1492. Drawing on early work by anthropologists and others who discovered evidence of widespread deaths by disease, historians such as William McNeill in 1976 and Alfred Crosby a decade later produced powerful accounts of the near extinction of some tribes and the dramatic depopulation of others in a pestilential holocaust with few parallels in history. Almost all scholars now accept that much, perhaps most, of the native population was wiped out by disease—smallpox, measles, tuberculosis, and other plagues imported from Europe—before white settlers began serious efforts to count.

The belief that the native population was much bigger in 1492 than it would be a few decades later has helped spur much larger estimates of how many people were in America before Columbus. Henry Dobyns, an anthropologist who was one of the earliest scholars to challenge Kroeber and the early, low estimates, claimed in 1966 that there were between 10 and 12 million people north of Mexico in 1492, and between 90 and 112 million in all of the Americas. He reached those figures by concluding that epidemics had destroyed 95 percent of the pre-Columbian population. He then took the best information on the population after Columbus and multiplied it by 20. No subsequent scholar has made so high a claim, and most historians have concluded that the 95 percent figure of deaths by disease is too high except for a few, relatively isolated areas such as Hispaniola. But most subsequent estimates have been much closer to Dobyns's than to Kroeber's. The geographer William M. Denevan, for example, argued in 1976 that the American population in 1492 was around 55 million and that the population north of Mexico was under 4 million. Those are among the lowest of modern estimates, but still dramatically higher than the nineteenth-century numbers.

The vehemence with which scholars, and at times the larger public, have debated these figures is not just because of the difficulty inherent in the effort to determine population size. It is also because the debate over the population is part of the debate over whether the arrival of Columbus—and the millions of Europeans who followed him—was a great advance in the history of civilization (as most Americans believed in 1892 when they joyously celebrated the 400th anniversary of Columbus's voyage) or an unparalleled catastrophe that virtually exterminated a large and flourishing native population (as some Americans and Europeans argued during the far more somber commemoration of the 500th anniversary in 1992). How to balance the many achievements of European civilization in the New World after 1492 against the terrible destruction of native peoples that accompanied it is, in the end, less a historical question, perhaps, than a moral one.

EUROPE LOOKS WESTWARD

Europeans were almost entirely unaware of the existence of the Americas before the fifteenth century. A few early wanderers—Leif Eriksson, an eleventh-century Norse seaman, and perhaps others—had glimpsed parts of the New World and had demonstrated that Europeans were capable of crossing the ocean to reach it. But even if their discoveries had become common knowledge (and they did not), there would have been little incentive for others to follow. Europe in the Middle Ages (roughly 500–1500 A.D.) was not an adventurous civilization. Divided into innumerable small duchies and kingdoms, its outlook was overwhelmingly provincial. Subsistence agriculture predominated, and commerce was limited; few merchants looked beyond the boundaries of their own regions. The Roman Catholic Church exercised a measure of spiritual authority over most of the continent, and the Holy Roman Empire provided at least a nominal political center. Even so, real power was for the most part widely dispersed; only rarely could a single leader launch a great venture. Gradually, however, conditions in Europe changed so that by the late fifteenth century interest in overseas exploration had grown.

Commerce and Nationalism

Two important and related changes provided the first incentive for Europeans to look toward new lands. One was a result of the significant growth in Europe's population in the fifteenth century. The Black Death, a catastrophic epidemic of the bubonic plague that began in Constantinople in 1347, had decimated Europe, killing (according to some estimates) more than a third of the people of the continent and debilitating its already limited economy. But a century and a half later, the population had rebounded. With that growth came a rise in land values, a reawakening of commerce, and a general increase in prosperity. Affluent landlords were becoming eager to purchase goods from distant regions, and a new merchant class was emerging to meet their demand. As trade increased, and as advances in navigation and shipbuilding made long-distance sea travel more feasible, interest in developing new markets, finding new products, and opening new trade routes rapidly increased.

Paralleling the rise of commerce in Europe, and in part responsible for it, was the rise of new governments that were more united and powerful than the feeble political entities of the feudal past. In the western areas of Europe, the authority of the distant pope and the even more distant Holy Roman Emperor was necessarily weak. As a result, strong new monarchs were emerging there and creating centralized nation-states, with national courts, national armies, and—perhaps most important—national tax systems. As these ambitious kings and queens consolidated their power and increased their wealth, they became eager to enhance the commercial growth of their nations.

Ever since the early fourteenth century, when Marco Polo and other adventurers had returned from Asia bearing exotic goods (spices, fabrics, dyes) and even more exotic tales, Europeans who hoped for commercial glory had dreamed above all of trade with the East. For two centuries, that trade had been limited by the difficulties of the long, arduous overland journey to the Asian courts. But in the fourteenth century, as the maritime capabilities of several western European societies increased, there began to be serious talk of finding a faster, safer sea route to Asia. Such dreams gradually found a receptive audience in the courts of the new monarchs. By the late fifteenth century, some of them were ready to finance daring voyages of exploration.

The first to do so were the Portuguese. They were the preeminent maritime power in the fifteenth century, in large part because of the work of one man, Prince Henry the Navigator. Henry's own principal interest was not in finding a sea route to Asia, but in exploring the western coast of Africa. He dreamed of establishing a Christian empire there to aid in his country's wars against the Moors of northern Africa; and he hoped to find new stores of gold. The explorations he began did not fulfill his own hopes, but they ultimately led farther than he had dreamed. Some of Henry's mariners went as far south as Cape Verde, on Africa's west coast. In 1486 (six years after Henry's death), Bartholomeu Dias rounded the southern tip of Africa (the Cape of Good Hope); and in 1497–1498 Vasco da Gama proceeded all the way around the cape to India. In 1500, the next fleet bound for India, under the command of Pedro Cabral, was blown westward off its southerly course and happened upon the coast of Brazil. But by then another man, in the service of another country, had already encountered the New World.

Christopher Columbus

Christopher Columbus, who was born and reared in Genoa, Italy, obtained most of his early seafaring experience in the service of the Portuguese. As a young man, he became intrigued with the possibility, already under discussion in many seafaring circles, of reaching Asia by going not east but west. Columbus's hopes rested on several basic misconceptions. He believed that the world was far smaller than it actually is. He also believed that the Asian continent extended farther eastward than it actually does. He assumed, therefore, that the Atlantic was narrow enough to be crossed on a relatively brief voyage. It did not occur to him that anything lay to the west between Europe and Asia.

Columbus failed to win support for his plan in Portugal, so he turned to Spain. The Spaniards were not yet as advanced a maritime people as the Portuguese, but they were at least as energetic and ambitious. And in the fifteenth century, the marriage of Spain's two most powerful regional rulers, Ferdinand of Aragon and Isabella of Castile, had produced the strongest monarchy in Europe. Like other young monarchies, it soon grew eager to demonstrate its strength by sponsoring new commercial ventures.

Columbus appealed to Queen Isabella for support for his proposed westward voyage. In 1492, having consolidated the monarchy's position within Spain itself, Isabella agreed to Columbus's request. Commanding ninety men and three ships—the *Niña*, the *Pinta*, and the *Santa María*—Columbus left Spain in August 1492 and sailed west into the Atlantic on what he thought was a straight course for Japan. Ten weeks later, he sighted land and assumed he had reached his target. In fact, he had landed on an island in the Bahamas. When he pushed on and encountered Cuba, he assumed he had reached China. He returned to Spain in triumph, bringing with him several captured natives as evidence of his achievement. (He called the natives "Indians" because he believed they were from the East Indies in the Pacific.)

But Columbus had not, of course, encountered the court of the great khan in China or the fabled wealth of the Indies. A year later, therefore, he tried again, this time with a much larger expedition. As be-

■ CHRISTOPHER COLUMBUS
In this somewhat idealized drawing, created several years after Christopher Columbus's historic voyage to the New World, Columbus stands in the bow of his ship, a suit of armor ready at his feet, approaching a shore in the New World that he believed was in fact part of Asia. *(Library of Congress)*

fore, he headed into the Caribbean, discovering several other islands and leaving a small and short-lived colony on Hispaniola. On a third voyage, in 1498, he finally reached the mainland and cruised along the northern coast of South America. When he passed the mouth of the Orinoco River (in present-day Venezuela), he concluded for the first time that what he had discovered was not in fact an island off the coast of China, as he had assumed, but a separate continent; such a large freshwater stream, he realized, could emerge only from a large body of land. Still, he remained convinced that Asia was only a short distance away. And although he failed in his

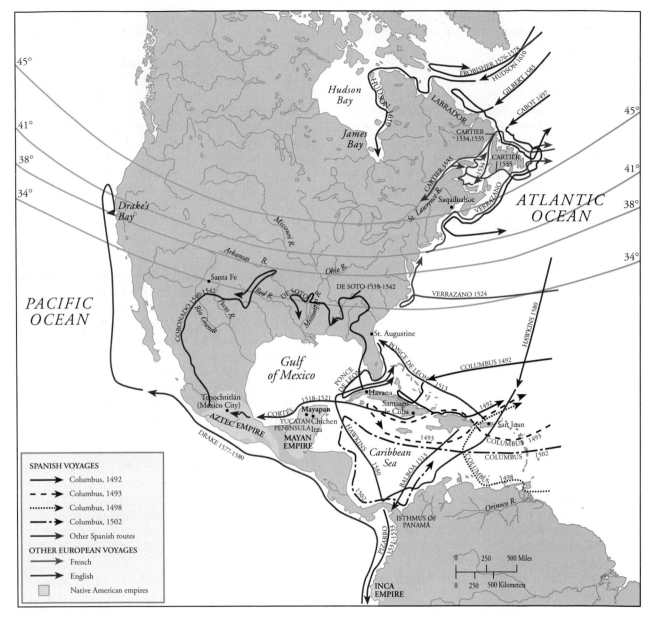

■ EUROPEAN JOURNEYS OF EXPLORATION AND CONQUEST, 1492-1583
By the late fifteenth century, European interest in overseas exploration had grown, led by Spain and Portugal. Christopher Columbus led several voyages to the Caribbean in the 1490s, finally reaching the mainland of North America in 1498. While Spanish exploration and conquest focused on the Gulf of Mexico and South America, the French and English sent exploratory expeditions to the northern coasts of the American continent.

efforts to sail around the northeastern coast of South America to the Indies (he was blocked by the Isthmus of Panama), he returned to Spain believing that he had explored at least the fringes of the Far East. He continued to believe that until he died.

Columbus's celebrated accomplishments made him a popular hero for a time, but he ended his life in obscurity. When Europeans at last gave a name to the New World, they ignored him. The distinction went instead to a Florentine merchant, Amerigo

■ BALBOA DISCOVERING THE PACIFIC
The Spanish historian Herrera created this engraving to
commemorate Vasco de Balboa's discovery of the Pacific Ocean,
which he encountered after fighting his way across the Isthmus of
Panama. Balboa's contemporaries called the Pacific *"El Mar del
Sur,"* the "South Sea." *(Bettmann)*

Vespucci, a member of a later Portuguese expedition
to the New World who wrote a series of vivid descriptions of the lands he visited and who recognized
the Americas as new continents.

Columbus has been celebrated for centuries as the
"Admiral of the Ocean Sea" (a title he struggled to
have officially bestowed on him during his lifetime)
and as a representative of the new, secular, scientific
impulses of Renaissance Europe. But Columbus was
also a deeply religious man, even something of a mystic. His voyages were inspired as much by his conviction that he was fulfilling a divine mission as by his
interest in geography and trade. A strong believer in
biblical prophecies, he came to see himself as a man
destined to advance the coming of the millennium.
"God made me the messenger of the new heaven and
the new earth," he wrote near the end of his life,
"and he showed me the spot where to find it." A similar combination of worldly and religious passions lay
behind many subsequent efforts at exploration and
settlement of the New World.

Partly as a result of Columbus's initiative, Spain
began to devote greater resources and energy to maritime exploration and gradually replaced Portugal as
the leading seafaring nation. The Spaniard Vasco de
Balboa fought his way across the Isthmus of Panama
in 1513 and became the first known European to
gaze westward upon the great ocean that separated
America from China and the Indies. Seeking access to

that ocean, Ferdinand Magellan, a Portuguese in the
employ of the Spanish, found the strait that now
bears his name at the southern end of South America,
struggled through the stormy narrows and into the
ocean (so calm by contrast that he christened it the
"Pacific"), then proceeded to the Philippines. There
Magellan died in a conflict with the natives, but his
expedition went on to complete the first known cir-
cumnavigation of the globe (1519–1522). By 1550,
Spaniards had explored the coasts of North America
as far north as Oregon in the west and Labrador in
the east, as well as some of the interior regions of the
continent.

The Conquistadores

In time, Spanish explorers in the New World
stopped thinking of America simply as an obstacle to
their search for a route to the East. They began instead to consider it a possible source of wealth rivaling and even surpassing the original Indies. On the
basis of Columbus's discoveries, the Spanish claimed
for themselves the whole of the New World, except
for a piece of it (today's Brazil) that was reserved by
a papal decree for the Portuguese. By the mid-
sixteenth century, the Spanish were well on their
way to establishing a substantial American empire.

The early Spanish colonists, beginning with those
Columbus brought on his second voyage, settled on
the islands of the Caribbean, where they tried to enslave the Indians and find gold. They had little luck in
either effort. But then, in 1518, Hernando Cortés led
a small military expedition of about 600 men into
Mexico. Cortés had been a Spanish government official in Cuba for fourteen years and to that point had
achieved little success. But when he heard stories of
great treasures in Mexico, he decided to go in search
of them. He met strong and resourceful resistance
from the Aztecs and their powerful emperor, Montezuma. The first Spanish assault on Tenochtitlán, the
Aztec capital, failed. But Cortés and his army had, un-
knowingly, unleashed an assault on the Aztecs far
more devastating than military attack: they had exposed the natives to smallpox. A smallpox epidemic
decimated the population and made it possible for
the Spanish to triumph in their second attempt at
conquest. Through his ruthless suppression of the
surviving natives, Cortés established a lasting reputation as the most brutal of the Spanish *conquistadores* (conquerors).

■ **THE MEXICANS STRIKE BACK**
In this vivid scene from the Duran Codex, Mexican artists illustrate a rare moment in which Mexican warriors gained the upper hand over the Spanish invaders. Driven back by native fighters, the Spanish have taken refuge in a room in the royal palace in Tenochtitlán while brightly attired Mexican warriors besiege them. Although the Mexicans gained a temporary advantage in this battle, the drawing illustrates one of the reasons for their inability to withstand the Spanish in the longer term. The Spanish soldiers are armed with rifles and crossbows, while the Indians carry only spears and shields. *(Oronoz)*

The news that silver was to be found in Mexico attracted the attention of other Spaniards. From the island colonies and from Spain itself, a wave of conquistadores descended on the mainland in search of fortune—a movement comparable in some ways to the nineteenth-century gold rushes elsewhere in the world, but far more vicious. Francisco Pizarro, who conquered Peru (1532–1538) and revealed to Europeans the wealth of the Incas, opened the way for other advances into South America. His one-time deputy Hernando de Soto, in a futile search for gold, silver, and jewels, led several expeditions (1539–1541) through Florida west into the continent and became the first white man known to have crossed the Mississippi River. Francisco Coronado traveled north from Mexico (1540–1542) into what is now New Mexico in a similarly fruitless search for gold and jewels; in the process, he helped open the Southwest of what is now the United States to Spanish settlement.

■ **PIZARRO IN PERU**
A European artist depicted Pizarro's arrival on the coast of Peru in the early 1530s, where he was greeted by crowds of hostile Indians. By 1538, Pizarro had conquered the empire of the Incas. *(British Museum)*

■ **DE SOTO IN NORTH AMERICA**
This gruesome drawing portrays Spanish troops under Hernando de Soto massacring a group of Mobile Indians in what is now Alabama, in the winter of 1540–1541. De Soto had been governor of Cuba, but in 1539 he sailed to Florida with 600 troops and for the next several years traveled through large areas of what would later become the southern United States until dying of fever in 1542. Here, as elsewhere, his troops dealt with the Indian tribes they encountered along the way with unrestrained brutality. *(Rare Books and Special Collections, Library of Congress)*

The story of the Spanish warriors is one of great military daring and achievement. It is also a story of remarkable brutality and greed. The conquistadores subjugated and, in some areas (through a combination of warfare and disease), almost exterminated the native populations. In this horrible way, they made possible the creation of a vast Spanish empire in the New World.

The Spanish Empire

Spanish exploration, conquest, and colonization in America was primarily a work of private enterprise, carried on by individual leaders, with little direct support from the government at home. Those who wished to launch expeditions to the New World had first to get licenses from the crown. Those who obtained licenses *(encomiendas)* were permitted to exact labor and tribute from the natives in specific areas, a system the Spanish had first used in dealing with the Moors in Spain itself. Settlers did not receive actual land grants, but the control of the labor in a territory in effect gave them control of the land.

A license did no more than confer rights; colonizers had to equip and finance their expeditions on their own and assume the full risk of loss or ruin. They might succeed and make a fortune; they might fail—through shipwreck, natural disaster, incompetence, or bad luck—and lose everything, including their lives, as many adventurers did. The New World did not always attract good or intelligent immigrants, but in the beginning it seldom attracted the fainthearted.

OUTPOSTS ON THE NORTHERN
FRONTIER OF NEW SPAIN
(Not simultaneous; through
the 18th century)

• Missions
• Forts (Sometimes with missions)
• Settlements

LOUISIANA
(Spanish 1763-1800)

UNITED
STATES
(from 1783)

San Francisco (1776)
Monterey (1770)
San Luis Obispo (1772)
Los Angeles (1781)
San Juan Capistrano (1776)
San Diego de Alcala (1769)
Tucson (1709)

Taos (1609)
Santa Fe (1607)

Red R.
Mississippi R.
Rio Grande

SPANISH
FLORIDA
(to 1819)

St. Augustine (1565)

Gulf of
Mexico

VICEROYALTY OF

Culiacán (1531)

Bahamas
(to Britain 1646)

La Habana (1515)

Cuba
(1492)

Tampico

Yucatan
Peninsula

Santiago (1514)

Espanola
(1492)

Puerto Rico
(1502)

ATLANTIC OCEAN

Mexico City
(Tenochtitlan)
(1325)

Veracruz (1519)

NEW SPAIN

Guatemala
(1519)

Jamaica
(to Britain
1655)

HAITI
(French
after 1697)

Santo
Domingo
(1496)

World divided into
Spanish and
Portuguese hemispheres:
Treaty of Tordesillas
(1494)

Caribbean Sea

Panama
(1519)

Caracas
(1567)

Trinidad
(1498)

Orinoco R.

SURINAM
(Dutch)
(1625)

FRENCH
GUIANA
(1626)

Santa Fe de Bogotá
(1538)

VICEROYALTY OF
NEW GRANADA

Quito
(1534)

Guayaquil
(1535)

Amazon R.

PACIFIC OCEAN

Cuidad de los
Reyes (Lima)
(1535)

Cuzco
(1535)

La Paz
(1548)

VICEROYALTY
OF
NEW CASTILIA
(Peru)

VICEROYALTY
OF
LA PLATA

Valparaiso
(1544)

Santiago (1541)

PORTUGUESE BRAZIL

Parana R.

Paraguay R.

Rio de
Janeiro
(1567)

São Paulo
(1554)

Montevideo
(1724)

Buenos Aires
(1580)

Rio de
la Plata

Straits of
Magellan

Tierra del
Fuego

0   1000   2000 Miles

0   1000   2000 Kilometers

Aztec Empire at the time of Spanish Conquest

Inca Empire at the time of Spanish Conquest

Colonial boundaries and provincial names
are for the late 18th century

■ SPANISH AMERICA

Lured by dreams of treasure, Spanish explorers, conquistadores, and colonists established a vast empire for Spain in the New World. New European diseases and Spanish military power forced the previously powerful Aztec and Incan empires into submission. Catholic missionaries also established a network of religious outposts in the New World with hopes of converting the indigenous peoples to Christianity. After the 1540s, the missionary impulse became one of the principal motives for European emigration to America.

The first Spaniards to arrive in the New World, the conquistadores, were interested in only one thing: getting rich. And in that they were fabulously successful. For 300 years, beginning in the sixteenth century, the mines in Spanish America yielded more than ten times as much gold and silver as the rest of the world's mines put together. These riches made Spain for a time the wealthiest and most powerful nation on earth.

After the first wave of conquest, however, most Spanish settlers in America traveled to the New World for other reasons. Many went in hopes of creating a profitable agricultural economy. Unlike the conquistadores, who left little but destruction behind them, these settlers helped establish elements of European civilization in America that permanently altered both the landscape and the social structure. Other Spaniards went to America to spread the Christian religion. Indeed, after the era of the conquistadores came to a close in the 1540s, the missionary impulse became one of the principal motives for European emigration to America. Priests or friars accompanied all colonizing ventures. Through the work of zealous missionaries, the gospel of the Catholic Church ultimately extended throughout South and Central America, Mexico, and into the South and Southwest of the present United States.

Northern Outposts

The Spanish fort established in 1565 at St. Augustine, Florida, became the first permanent European settlement in the present-day United States. But it was little more than a military outpost and a headquarters for unsuccessful campaigns among North American natives that were ultimately abandoned. It did not mark the beginning of a substantial effort at colonization in the region.

A more substantial colonizing venture began thirty years later in the Southwest. In 1598, Don Juan de Oñate traveled north from Mexico with a party of 500 men and claimed for Spain some of the lands of the Pueblo Indians that Coronado had passed through over fifty years before. The Spanish migrants began to establish a colony, modeled roughly on those the Spanish had created farther south, in what is now New Mexico. Oñate distributed *encomiendas,* and the Spanish began demanding tribute from the local Indians (and at times commandeering them as laborers). Spanish colonists founded Santa Fe in 1609.

Oñate's harsh treatment of the natives (who greatly outnumbered the small Spanish population) threatened the stability of the new colony and led to his removal as governor in 1606. Over time, relations between the Spanish and the Pueblos improved. Substantial numbers of Pueblos converted to Christianity under the influence of Spanish missionaries. Others entered into important trading relationships with the Spanish. The colony remained precarious nevertheless because of the danger from Apache and Navajo raiders, who threatened the Spanish and Pueblos alike. Even so, the New Mexico settlement continued to grow. By 1680, there were over 2,000 Spanish colonists living among about 30,000 Pueblos. The economic heart of the colony was not the gold and precious metals the early Spanish explorers had tried in vain to find. It was cattle and sheep, raised on the *ranchos* that stretched out around the small towns Spanish settlers established.

In 1680, the colony was nearly destroyed when the Pueblos rose in revolt. Despite the widespread conversions to Catholicism, most natives (including the converts) continued to practice their own religious rituals—rituals that sustained their sense of tribal identity. In 1680, Spanish priests and the colonial government, which was closely tied to the missionaries, launched one of their periodic efforts to suppress these rituals. In response, an Indian religious leader named Pope led an uprising that killed hundreds of European settlers (including twenty-one priests), captured Santa Fe, and drove the Spanish temporarily from the region. But twelve years later the Spanish returned, resumed seizing Pueblo lands, and crushed a last revolt in 1696.

Spanish exploitation of the Pueblos did not end. But after the revolts, many Spanish colonists realized that they could not prosper in New Mexico if they remained constantly in conflict with a native population that greatly outnumbered them. They tried to solve the problem in two ways. On the one hand, the Spanish intensified their efforts to assimilate the Indians—baptizing Indian children at birth and enforcing observance of Catholic rituals. On the other hand, they now permitted the Pueblos to own land; they stopped commandeering Indian labor; they replaced the encomienda system with a less demanding and oppressive one; and they tacitly tolerated the practice of tribal religious rituals.

These efforts were at least partially successful. After a while, there was significant intermarriage between Europeans and Indians. Increasingly, the Pueblos came to consider the Spanish their allies in the continuing battles with the Apaches and Navajos. By 1750, the Spanish population had grown modestly to about 4,000. The Pueblo population had declined (through disease, war, and migration) to about 13,000, less than half what it had been in 1680. New Mexico had by then become a reasonably stable but still weak and isolated outpost of the Spanish empire.

The Empire at High Tide

By the end of the sixteenth century, the Spanish empire had become one of the largest in the history of the world. It included the islands of the Caribbean and the coastal areas of South America that had been the first targets of the Spanish expeditions. It extended to Mexico and southern North America, where a second wave of colonizers had established outposts. Most of all, the empire spread southward and westward into the vast landmass of South America—the areas that are now Chile, Argentina, and Peru. In 1580, when the Spanish and Portuguese monarchies temporarily united, Brazil came under Spanish jurisdiction as well.

It was, however, a colonial empire very different politically from the one the English would establish in North America beginning in the early seventeenth century. Although the earliest Spanish ventures in the New World had been largely independent of the throne, by the end of the sixteenth century the monarchy had extended its authority directly into the governance of local communities. Colonists had few opportunities to establish political institutions independent of the crown.

There was also a significant economic difference between the Spanish empire and the later British one. The Spanish were far more successful than the British would be in extracting great surface wealth—gold and silver—from their American colonies. But for the same reason, they concentrated relatively less energy on making agriculture and commerce profitable in their colonies. The strict and inflexible commercial policies of the Spanish government made things worse. To enforce the collection of duties and to provide protection against pirates, the government established rigid and restrictive regulations. They required all trade with the colonies to go through a single Spanish port and only a few colonial ports, in fleets making but two voyages a year. The system stifled the economic development of the Spanish areas of the New World.

There was also an important difference between the character of the population in the Spanish empire and that of the colonies to the north. Almost from the beginning, the English, Dutch, and French colonies in North America concentrated on establishing permanent settlement and family life in the New World. The Europeans in North America reproduced rapidly after their first difficult years and in time came to outnumber the natives. The Spanish, by contrast, ruled their empire but did not people it. In the first century of settlement, fewer than 250,000 settlers in the Spanish colonies were from Spain itself or from any other European country. Only about 200,000 more arrived in the first half of the seventeenth century. Some additional settlers came from various outposts of Spanish civilization in the Atlantic—the Azores, the Cape Verde Islands, and elsewhere; but even with these other sources, the number of European settlers in Spanish America remained very small relative to the native population. Despite the ravages of disease and war, the vast majority of the population of the Spanish Empire continued to consist of natives. The Spanish, in other words, imposed a small ruling class upon a much larger existing population; they did not create a self-contained European society in the New World as the English would attempt to do in the north. The story of the Spanish Empire, therefore, is the story of a collision between two cultures that had been developing for centuries along completely different lines followed by a partial fusion of those cultures.

Biological and Cultural Exchanges

The lines separating the races in the Spanish Empire gradually grew less distinct than they would be in the English colonies to the north, but European and native cultures never entirely merged. Indeed, significant differences remain today between European and Indian cultures throughout South and Central America. Nevertheless, the arrival of whites launched a process of interaction between different peoples that left no one unchanged.

Europeans would not have been exploring the Americas at all without their early contacts with the natives. From them, they first learned of the rich deposits of gold and silver. After that, the history of the Americas became one of increasing levels of exchanges—some beneficial, some catastrophic—among different peoples and cultures.

The first and perhaps most profound result of this exchange was the importation of European diseases to the New World. It would be difficult to exaggerate the consequences of the exposure of Native Americans to such illnesses as influenza, measles, chicken pox, mumps, typhus, and above all smallpox—diseases to which Europeans had over time developed at least a partial immunity but to which Native Americans were tragically vulnerable. Millions died.

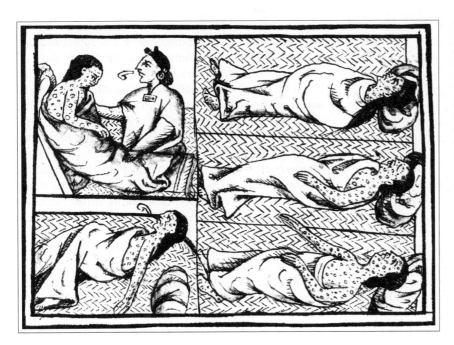

■ **SMALLPOX AMONG THE INDIANS**
Far more devastating to the Indians of America than the military ventures of Europeans were deadly diseases carried to the New World by invaders from the old. Natives had developed no immunity to the infectious diseases of Europe, and they died by the hundreds of thousands from such epidemics as measles, influenza, and (as depicted here by a European artist) smallpox.
(Biblioteca Mediceo Laurenxiana, Firenze/IKONA, Rome)

Native groups inhabiting some of the large Caribbean islands and some areas of Mexico were virtually extinct within fifty years of their first contact with whites. On Hispaniola—where the Dominican Republic and Haiti are today and where Columbus landed and established a small, short-lived colony in the 1490s—the native population quickly declined from approximately 1 million to about 500. In the Mayan areas of Mexico, as much as 95 percent of the population perished within a few years of their first contact with the Spanish. Some groups fared better than others; some (although far from all) of the tribes north of Mexico, whose contact with European settlers came later and was often less intimate, were spared the worst of the epidemics. But most areas of the New World experienced a demographic catastrophe at least as grave as, and in many places far worse than, the Black Death that had killed at least a third of the population of Europe two centuries before.

The decimation of native populations in the southern regions of the Americas was not, however, purely a result of this inadvertent exposure to infection. It was also a result of the conquistadores' quite deliberate policy of subjugation and extermination. Their brutality was in part a reflection of the ruthlessness with which Europeans waged war in all parts of the world. It was also a result of their conviction that the natives were "savages"—uncivilized peoples whom they considered somehow not fully human. Paradoxically, the brutality was also a consequence of the high level of development of some native societies. Had the natives truly been as primitive as Europeans wanted to believe, there would have been little need to destroy them. But organized into substantial empires, they posed a threat to the conquistadores' ambitions.

That, more than anything else, accounts for the thoroughness with which the Spanish set about obliterating native cultures. They razed cities and dismantled temples and monuments. They destroyed records and documents (one reason why modern scholars have been able to learn so little about the histories of these native societies). They systematically killed Indian warriors, leaders, and priests. They tried, in short, to eliminate the underpinnings of existing native civilizations so as to bring the Indian population fully under Spanish control and to remove all obstacles to the spread of Christianity. By the 1540s, the combined effects of European diseases and European military brutality had all but destroyed the empires of Mexico and South America and had largely eliminated native resistance to the Spanish.

Not all aspects of the exchange were so disastrous to the natives. The Europeans introduced to America important new crops (among them sugar and bananas), domestic livestock (cattle, pigs, and sheep), and perhaps most significantly the horse, which had disappeared from the Western Hemisphere in the Ice Age and now returned aboard Spanish ships in the sixteenth century. The Europeans imported these things for their own use. But Indian tribes soon learned to cultivate the new crops, and European livestock proliferated rapidly and spread widely among natives. In the past, most tribes had possessed no domesticated animals at all other than dogs. The horse, in particular, became central to the lives of many natives and transformed their societies.

The exchange was at least as important (and more beneficial) to the Europeans. In both North and South America, the arriving white peoples learned new agricultural techniques from the natives, techniques often better adapted to the character of the new land than those they had brought with them from Europe. They discovered new crops, above all maize (corn), which became an important staple among the settlers. Columbus took it back to Europe from his first trip to America, and it soon spread through much of Europe as well. Such American foods as squash, pumpkins, beans, sweet potatoes, tomatoes, peppers, and potatoes also found their way back to Europe and in the process revolutionized European agriculture. Agricultural discoveries ultimately proved more important to the future of Europe than the gold and silver the conquistadores valued so highly.

In South America, Central America, and Mexico, a society emerged in which Europeans and natives lived in intimate, if unequal, contact with one another. As a result, Indians adopted many features of European civilization, although those features seldom survived the transfer to America unchanged. Many natives gradually came to learn Spanish or Portuguese, but in the process they created a range of dialects, combining the European languages with their own. European missionaries—through both persuasion and coercion—spread Catholicism through most areas of the Spanish Empire. But native Christians tended to connect the new creed with features of their old religions, creating a hybrid of faiths that were, while essentially Christian, nevertheless distinctively American.

Colonial officials were expected to take their wives with them to America, but among the ordinary settlers—the majority—European men outnumbered European women by at least ten to one. Not surprisingly, therefore, the Spanish immigrants had substantial sexual contact with native women. Intermarriage became frequent, and before long the population of the colonies came to be dominated (numerically, at least) by people of mixed race, or *mestizos.* Through much of the Spanish Empire, as a result, an elaborate racial hierarchy developed, with Spanish at the top, natives at the bottom, and people of mixed races distributed in between. Racial categories, however, were much more fluid than the Spanish wanted to believe and could not long remain fixed. Over time, the wealth and influence of a family often came to define its place in the "racial" hierarchy more decisively than race itself. A successful or powerful person could become "Spanish" regardless of his or her actual racial ancestry.

The frequency of intermarriage suggests a great deal about how the society of the Spanish Empire was taking shape. It reveals, of course, that men living alone in a strange land craved female companionship and the satisfactions of family life and that they sought those things in the only places they could—among the native population. It shows the desperate need for labor among the white settlers, including the domestic labor that native wives could provide; in some cases, intermarriage was a form of labor recruitment. Finally, it suggests why the lines separating the races in the areas of Spanish settlement did not remain as distinct as they did in the later English colonies, which were peopled largely by families and in which intermarriage with natives was consequently rare.

Intermarriage was not, however, just a result of the needs and desires of white men. Some Indian women entered marriages to white men only under coercion, but the extent of intermarriage suggests that not all women resisted. Native women might have seen some advantage in marrying Spanish men because the male populations of their tribes were so depleted by warfare or enslavement by the Spaniards. There were also long-established customs of intermarriage among some Indian tribes as a way of forming or cementing alliances. Since many Indians considered the white settlers little more foreign than some rival native groups, that custom probably contributed to the frequency of intermarriage as well.

Natives were the principal labor source for the Europeans. Virtually all the commercial, agricultural, and mining enterprises of the Spanish and Portuguese colonists depended on an Indian work force.

Different labor systems emerged in different areas of the empire. In some places, Indians were sold into slavery. More often, colonists used a wage system closely related, but not identical, to slavery, by which Indians were forced to work in the mines and on the plantations for fixed periods, unable to leave without the consent of their employers. Such work forces survived in some areas of South American mainland for many centuries. So great was the need for native labor that European settlers were less interested in acquiring land than they were in gaining control over Indian villages, which could become a source of labor and tribute to landlords.

Even so, the native population could not meet all the labor needs of the colonists—particularly since the native population had declined (and in some places virtually vanished) because of disease and war. As early as 1502, therefore, European settlers began importing slaves from Africa.

Africa and America

Most of the black men and women who were forcibly taken to America came from a large region in west Africa below the Sahara Desert, known as Guinea. It was the home of a wide variety of peoples and cultures. Since over half of all the new arrivals in the New World between 1500 and 1800 were Africans, those cultures, too, greatly affected the character of American civilization. Europeans and white Americans came to portray African society as primitive and uncivilized (in part to justify the en-

slavement of Africa's people). But most Africans were, in fact, civilized peoples with well-developed economies and political systems.

Humans began settling in west Africa at least 10,000 years ago. By the fifteenth century A.D., they had developed extensive civilizations and complex political systems. The residents of upper Guinea had substantial commercial contact with the Mediterranean world—trading ivory, gold, and slaves for finished goods. Largely as a result, they became early converts to Islam. After the collapse of the ancient kingdom of Ghana around 1100 A.D., the even larger empire of Mali emerged and survived well into the fifteenth century. Its great city, Timbuktu, became fabled as a trading center and a seat of education.

Africans further south were more isolated from Europe and the Mediterranean. They were also more politically fragmented. The central social unit in much of the south was the village, which usually consisted of members of an extended family group. Some groups of villages united in small kingdoms—among them Benin, Congo, and Songhay. But no large empires emerged in the south comparable to the Ghana and Mali kingdoms farther north. Nevertheless, these southern societies developed extensive trade—in woven fabrics, ceramics, and wooden and iron goods, as well as crops and livestock—both among themselves and, to a lesser degree, with the outside world.

The African civilizations naturally developed economies that reflected the climates and resources of their lands. In upper Guinea, fishing and rice cultivation, supplemented by the extensive trade with

Mediterranean lands, were the foundation of the economy. Farther south, Africans grew wheat and other food crops, raised livestock, and fished. There were some more nomadic tribes in the interior, which subsisted largely on hunting and gathering and developed less elaborate social systems. But most Africans were sedentary people, linked together by elaborate political, economic, and familial relationships.

Like many Native American societies, but unlike those in Europe, African societies tended to be matrilineal—which means that people traced their heredity through, and inherited property from, their mothers rather than their fathers. When a couple married, the husband left his own family to join the family of his wife. Like most other peoples, Africans divided work by gender, but the nature of that division varied greatly from place to place. Women played a major role, often the dominant role, in trade; in many areas they were the principal farmers (while the men hunted, fished, and raised livestock); everywhere, they managed child care and food preparation. Most tribes also divided political power by gender, with men choosing leaders and systems for managing what they defined as male affairs and women choosing parallel leaders to handle female matters. Tribal chiefs generally were men (although in some places there was a female counterpart), but the position customarily passed down not to the chief's son but to the son of the chief's eldest sister. African societies, in short, were characterized by a greater degree of sexual equality than those of most other parts of the world.

In those areas of west Africa where indigenous religions had survived the spread of Islam (which included most of the lands south of the empire of Mali), people worshipped many gods, whom they associated with various aspects of the natural world and whose spirits they believed lived in trees, rocks, forests, and streams. Most Africans also developed forms of ancestor worship and took great care in tracing family lineage; the most revered priests (who were often also important social and political leaders as well) were generally the oldest people.

African societies had elaborate systems of social ranks (or hierarchies). Small elites of priests and nobles stood at the top. Most people belonged to a large middle group of farmers, traders, crafts workers, and others. At the bottom of society were slaves—men and women who were put into bondage after being captured in wars or because of criminal behavior or unpaid debts. Slavery was not usually permanent; people were generally placed in bondage for a fixed period and in the meantime retained certain legal protections (including the right to marry). Their children, moreover, did not inherit their parents' condition of bondage. The slavery that Africans would experience at the hands of the Europeans was to be very different; but the existence of slavery among Africans themselves helped make their enslavement by Europeans easier.

The African slave trade began long before the European migration to the New World. As early as the eighth century A.D., west Africans began selling slaves to traders from the Mediterranean. They were responding to a demand from affluent families who wanted black men and women as domestic servants. They were also responding to more general labor shortages in some areas of Europe and North Africa. When Portuguese sailors began exploring the coast of Africa in the fifteenth century, they too bought slaves—usually criminals and people captured in war—and took them back to Portugal, where there was a small but steady demand.

In the sixteenth century, however, the market for slaves grew dramatically as a result of the rising European demand for sugar cane. The small areas of sugar cultivation in the Mediterranean were proving inadequate, and production soon moved to the island of Madeira off the African coast, which became a Portuguese colony. Not long after that, it moved to the Caribbean islands and Brazil. Sugar was a labor-intensive crop, and the demand for workers in these new areas increased rapidly. European slave traders responded to that demand by increasing the recruitment of workers from along the coast of west Africa (and from some areas of east Africa as well). As the demand increased, African kingdoms warred with one another in an effort to capture potential slaves to exchange for European goods. At first the slave traders were overwhelmingly Portuguese and, to a lesser extent, Spanish. By the seventeenth century, the Dutch had won control of most of the slave market. In the eighteenth century, the English dominated it. (Despite some recent claims, Jews were never significantly involved in the slave trade.) By 1700 slavery had begun to spread well beyond its original locations in the Caribbean and South America and into the English colonies to the north.

THE ARRIVAL OF THE ENGLISH

England's first documented contact with the New World came only five years after Spain's. In 1497, John Cabot (like Columbus a native of Genoa) sailed to the northeastern coast of North America on an expedition sponsored by King Henry VII. Other English navigators continued Cabot's unsuccessful search for a northwest passage through the New World to the Orient. They explored other areas of North America during the sixteenth century. But even though England claimed dominion over the lands its explorers surveyed, nearly a century passed before the English made any serious efforts to establish colonies there. Like other European nations, England had to experience an internal transformation before it could begin settling new lands. That transformation occurred in the sixteenth century.

The Commercial Incentive

Part of the attraction of the New World to the English was its newness, its contrast to their own troubled land. America seemed a place where human settlement could start anew, where a perfect society could be created without the flaws and inequities of the Old World. Such dreams began to emerge in England only a few years after Columbus's voyages. They found classic expression in Sir Thomas More's *Utopia* (published in Latin in 1516, translated into English thirty-five years later), which described a mythical and nearly perfect society on an imaginary island supposedly discovered by a companion of Amerigo Vespucci in the waters of the New World.

More's picture of an ideal community was, among other things, a comment on the social and economic ills of the England of his own time. The people of Tudor England suffered from frequent and costly European wars, from almost constant religious strife, and above all from a harsh economic transformation of the countryside. Because the worldwide demand for wool was growing rapidly, many landowners were finding it profitable to convert their land from fields for crops to pastures for sheep. The result was a significant growth in the wool trade. But that meant land worked at one time by serfs and later by rent-paying tenants was steadily enclosed for sheep runs and taken away from the farmers. Thousands of evicted tenants roamed the countryside in gangs, begging from (and at times robbing) the more fortunate householders through whose communities they passed.

The government passed various laws designed to halt enclosures, relieve the worthy poor, and compel the able-bodied or "sturdy beggars" to work. Such laws had little effect. The enclosure movement continued unabated, and relatively few of the dislocated farmers could find reemployment in raising sheep or manufacturing wool. By removing land from cultivation, the enclosure movement also limited England's ability to feed its population, which grew from 3 million in 1485 to 4 million in 1603. Both because of the dislocation of farmers and the restriction of the food supply, therefore, the nation had a serious problem of surplus population.

Amid this growing distress, a rising class of merchant capitalists was prospering from the expansion of foreign trade. At first, England had exported little except raw wool; but new merchant capitalists helped create a domestic cloth industry that allowed them to begin marketing finished goods at home and abroad. At first, most exporters did business almost entirely as individuals. In time, however, some merchants joined forces and formed chartered companies. Each such enterprise operated on the basis of a charter acquired from the monarch, which gave the company a monopoly for trading in a particular region. Among the first of these were the Muscovy Company (1555), the Levant Company (1581), the Barbary Company (1585), the Guinea Company (1588), and the East India Company (1600). Investors in these companies often made fantastic profits from the exchange of English manufactures, especially woolens, for exotic goods; and they felt a powerful urge to continue the expansion of their profitable trade.

Central to this drive was the emergence of a new concept of economic life known as mercantilism, which was gaining favor throughout Europe. Mercantilism rested on the assumption that the nation as a whole was the principal actor in the economy, not the individuals within it. The goal of economic activity should be to increase the nation's total wealth. Mercantilists believed that the world's wealth was finite. One person or nation could grow rich only at the expense of another. A nation's economic health depended, therefore, on extracting as much wealth as possible from foreign lands and exporting as little wealth as possible from home.

■ **THE DOCKS OF BRISTOL, ENGLAND**
By the eighteenth century, when this scene was painted, Bristol had become one of the principal English ports serving the so-called triangular trade among the American colonies, the West Indies, and Africa. The lucrativeness of that trade is evident in the bustle and obvious prosperity of the town. Even earlier, however, Bristol was an important port of embarkation for the thousands of English settlers migrating to the New World. *(Docks and Quay. English School (18th Century). City of Bristol Museum and Art Gallery/The Bridgeman Art Library, London)*

The principles of mercantilism guided the economic policies of virtually all the European nation-states in the sixteenth and seventeenth centuries. Mercantilism greatly enhanced the position of the new merchant capitalists, whose overseas ventures were thought to benefit the entire nation and to be worthy of government assistance. It also increased competition among nations. Every European state was trying to find markets for its exports while trying to limit its imports. One result was the increased attractiveness of acquiring colonies, which could become the source of goods that a country might otherwise have to buy from other nations.

In England, the mercantilistic program thrived at first on the basis of the flourishing wool trade with the European continent, and particularly with the great cloth market in Antwerp. Beginning in the 1550s, however, that glutted market collapsed, and English merchants found themselves obliged to look elsewhere for overseas trade. The establishment of colonies seemed to be a ready answer to that and other problems. Richard Hakluyt, an Oxford clergyman and the outstanding English propagandist for colonization, argued that colonies would not only create new markets for English goods, they would also help alleviate poverty and unemployment by siphoning off the surplus population. For the poor who remained in England "idly to the annoy of the whole state," there would be new work as a result of the prosperity the colonies would create. Perhaps most important, colonial commerce would allow England to acquire products from its own new territories for which the nation had previously been dependent on foreign rivals—products such as lumber, naval stores, and, above all, silver and gold.

The Religious Incentive

In addition to these economic motives for colonization, there were also religious ones, rooted in the events of the European and English Reformations. The Protestant Reformation began in Germany in 1517, when Martin Luther openly challenged some of the basic practices and beliefs of the Roman Catholic Church—until then, the supreme religious authority and also one of the strongest political authorities throughout western Europe. Luther, an Augustinian monk and ordained priest, challenged the Catholic belief that salvation could be achieved through good works or through loyalty (or payments) to the church itself. He denied the church's claim that God communicated to the world through the pope and the clergy. The Bible, not the church, was the authentic voice of God, Luther claimed, and salvation was to be found not through "works" or through the formal practice of religion, but through faith alone. Luther's challenge quickly won him a wide following among ordinary men and women in northern Europe. He himself insisted that he was not revolting against the church, that his purpose was to reform it from within. But when the pope excommunicated him in 1520, Luther defied him and began to lead his followers out of the Catholic Church entirely. A schism within European Christianity had begun that was never to be healed.

As the spirit of the Reformation spread rapidly throughout Europe, creating intellectual ferment and (in some places) war, other dissidents began offering alternatives to orthodox Catholicism. The Swiss theologian John Calvin was, after Luther, the most influential reformer and went even further than Luther had in rejecting the Catholic belief that human institutions could affect an individual's prospects for salvation. Calvin introduced the doctrine of predestination. God "elected" some people to be saved and condemned others to damnation; each person's destiny was determined before birth, and no one could change that predetermined fate. But while individuals could not alter their destinies, they could strive to know them. Calvinists believed that the way people led their lives might reveal to them their chances of salvation. A wicked or useless existence would be a sign of damnation; saintliness, diligence, and success could be signs of grace. Calvinism created anxieties among its followers, to be sure; but it also produced a strong incentive to lead virtuous, productive lives. The new creed spread rapidly throughout northern Europe and produced (among other groups) the Huguenots in France and the Puritans in England.

The English Reformation began, however, more because of a political dispute between the king and the pope than as a result of these doctrinal revolts. In 1529 King Henry VIII became angered by the pope's refusal to grant him a divorce from his Spanish wife (who had failed to bear him the son he desperately wanted). In response, he broke England's ties with the Catholic Church and established himself as the head of the Christian faith in his country. He made relatively few other changes in English Christianity, however, and after his death the survival of Protestantism remained in doubt for a time. When Henry's Catholic daughter Mary ascended the throne, she quickly restored England's allegiance to Rome and harshly persecuted those who refused to return to the Catholic fold. Many Protestants were executed (the origin of the queen's enduring nickname, "Bloody Mary"); others fled to the European continent, where they came into contact with the most radical ideas of the Reformation. Mary died in 1558, and her half-sister, Elizabeth, became England's sovereign. Elizabeth once again severed the nation's connection with the Catholic Church (and, along with it, an alliance with Spain that Mary had forged).

The Church of England, as the official religion was now known, satisfied the political objectives of the queen, but it failed to satisfy the religious desires of many English Christians. Large groups of Catholics continued to claim allegiance to the pope. Others, affected by the teachings of the European Reformation, believed the new Church of England had abandoned Rome without abandoning Rome's offensive beliefs and practices. Under Elizabeth, the church began to incorporate some of the tenets of Calvinism, but never enough to satisfy its critics—particularly the many exiles who had fled the country under Mary and who now returned, bringing their new, more

■ JOHN CALVIN
Next to Martin Luther, John Calvin was the most important figure
of the European Reformation. His belief in predestination was
central to the Puritan faith of early New England. *(Bettmann)*

radical religious ideas with them. They continued to
clamor for reforms that would "purify" the church;
as a result, they became known as "Puritans."

A few Puritans took what were, by the standards
of the time, genuinely radical positions. They were
known as Separatists, and they were determined to
worship as they pleased in their own independent
congregations. That determination flew in the face of
English law—which outlawed unauthorized religious
meetings, required all subjects to attend regular Anglican services, and levied taxes to support the established church. The radicalism of the Separatists was
visible in other ways as well, including their rejection
of prevailing assumptions about the proper religious
roles of women. Many Separatist sects, perhaps most
prominently the Quakers, permitted women to serve
as preachers and to assume a prominence in other religious matters that would have been impossible in
the established church.

Most Puritans resisted separatism. Still, their demands were by no means modest. They wanted to
simplify Anglican forms of worship. They wanted to
reduce the power of the bishops, who were appointed by the crown and who were, in many cases,
openly corrupt and highly extravagant. Perhaps
above all they wanted to reform the local clergy, a
group composed in large part of greedy, uneducated
men with little interest in (or knowledge of) theology. The more moderate Puritans wished, in short, to
see the church give more attention to its spiritual
role and less to its worldly ambitions. No less than
the Separatists, they grew increasingly frustrated by
the refusal of either the political or ecclesiastical
leaders of the nation to respond to their demands.

Puritan discontent, already festering, grew rapidly
after the death of Elizabeth, the last of the Tudors,
and the accession to the throne of James I, a Scots-
man and the first of the Stuarts, in 1603. James believed kings ruled by divine right, and he felt no
obligation to compromise with his opponents. He
quickly antagonized the Puritans, a group that included most of the rising businessmen, by resorting
to arbitrary taxation, by favoring English Catholics in
the granting of charters and other favors, and by supporting "high church" forms of ceremony. By the
early seventeenth century, some religious noncon-
formists were beginning to look for places of refuge
outside the kingdom. Along with the other economic
and social incentives for colonization, such religious
discontent helped turn England's gaze to distant
lands.

The English in Ireland

England's first experience with colonization came
not in the New World, but in a land separated from
Britain only by a narrow stretch of sea: Ireland. The
English had long laid claim to the island and had for
many years maintained small settlements in the area
around Dublin. Only in the second half of the sixteenth century, however, did serious efforts at large-
scale colonization begin. Through the 1560s and
1570s, would-be colonists moved through Ireland,
capturing territory and attempting to subdue the native population. In the process they developed many
of the assumptions that would guide later English
colonists in America.

The most important of these assumptions was
that the native population of Ireland—approximately

THE MEETING OF CULTURES

■ ELIZABETH I
The flemish artist Marcus Gheeraerts the younger moved to
England in 1568 (along with his father, also a painter) as a
Protestant refugee from his homeland. In approximately 1593 he
painted this portrait of the English queen, portraying her as she
was seen by many of her contemporaries: a strong, confident ruler
presiding over an ambitious, expansionist nation. She stands here
on a map of England. *(National Portrait Gallery, London)*

1 million people, loyal to the Catholic Church, with
their own language (Gaelic) and their own
culture—was a collection of wild, vicious, and ignorant "savages." The Irish lived in ways the English
considered crude and wasteful ("like beasts"), and
they fought back against the intruders with a ferocity that the English considered barbaric. Such people could not be tamed, the English concluded.
They certainly could not be assimilated into English
society. They must, therefore, be suppressed, isolated, and if necessary destroyed. Eventually, they
might be "civilized," but only after they were thoroughly subordinated.

Whatever barbarities the Irish may have inflicted
on the colonizers, the English more than matched in

return. Sir Humphrey Gilbert, who was later to establish the first British colony in the New World (an unsuccessful venture in Newfoundland), served for a
time as governor of one Irish district and suppressed
native rebellions with extraordinary viciousness.
Gilbert was an educated and supposedly civilized
man. But he considered the natives somehow less
than human, and therefore not entitled to whatever
decencies civilized people reserved for their treatment of one another. As a result, he managed to justify, both to himself and to others, such atrocities as
beheading Irish soldiers after they were killed in battle. Gilbert himself, Sir Walter Raleigh, Sir Richard
Grenville, and others active in Ireland in the mid-
sixteenth century derived from their experiences
there an outlook they would take to America, where
they made similarly vicious efforts to subdue and sub-
jugate the natives.

The Irish experience led the English to another
important (and related) assumption about colonization: that English settlements in distant lands must retain a rigid separation from the native populations. In
Ireland, English colonizers established what they
called "plantations," transplantations of English society in a foreign land. Unlike the Spanish in America,
the English in Ireland did not try simply to rule a subdued native population; they tried to build a complete society of their own, peopled with emigrants
from England itself. The new society would exist
within a "pale of settlement," an area physically separated from the natives. That concept, too, they
would take with them to the New World, even
though in Ireland, as later in America, the separation
of peoples and the preservation of "pure" English
culture proved impossible.

The French and the Dutch in America

English settlers in North America, unlike those in Ireland, were to encounter not only natives but also
other Europeans who were, like them, driven by
mercantilist ideas to establish economic outposts
abroad. To the south and southwest was the Spanish
Empire. Spanish ships continued to threaten English
settlements along the coast for years. But except for
Mexico and scattered outposts such as those in
Florida and New Mexico, the Spanish made little serious effort to colonize North America.

England's more formidable North American rivals
in the early sixteenth century were the French.

France founded its first permanent settlement in America at Quebec in 1608, less than a year after the English started their first colony at Jamestown. The French colony's population grew very slowly. Few French Catholics felt any inclination to leave their homeland, and French Protestants who might have wished to emigrate were excluded from the colony. The French, however, exercised an influence in the New World disproportionate to their numbers, largely because of their relationships with Native Americans. Unlike the English, who for many years hugged the coastline and traded with the Indians of the interior through intermediaries, the French forged close, direct ties with natives deep inside the continent. French Jesuit missionaries were among the first to penetrate Indian societies, and they established some of the first contacts between the two peoples. More important still were the *coureurs de bois*—adventurous fur traders and trappers—who also penetrated far into the wilderness and developed an extensive trade that became one of the underpinnings of the French colonial economy.

The fur trade was, in fact, more an Indian than a French enterprise. The *coureurs de bois* were, in many ways, little more than agents for the Algonquins and the Hurons, who were the principal fur traders among the Indians of the region and from whom the French purchased their pelts. The French traders were able to function only to the degree that they could form partnerships with the Indians. Successful partnerships often resulted from their ability to become virtually a part of native society, living among the Indians and at times marrying Indian women. The fur trade helped open the way for the other elements of the French presence in North America—the agricultural estates (or *seignuries*) along the St. Lawrence River, the development of trade and military centers at Quebec and Montreal, and the creation of an alliance with the Algonquins and others—that enabled the French to compete with the more numerous British in the contest for control of North America. That alliance also brought the French into conflict with the Iroquois, the Algonquins' ancient enemies, who assumed the central role in the English fur trade. An early result of these tensions was a 1609 attack led by Samuel de Champlain, the founder of Quebec, on a band of Mohawks, apparently at the instigation of his Algonquin trading partners.

The Dutch, too, were establishing a presence in North America. Holland had won its independence from Spain in the early seventeenth century and was one of the leading trading nations of the world. Its merchant fleet was larger than England's, and its traders were active not only in Europe but also in Africa, Asia, and—increasingly—America. In 1609 an English explorer in the employ of the Dutch, Henry Hudson, sailed up the river that was to be named for him in what is now New York State. Because the river was so wide, he believed for a time that he had found the long-sought water route through the continent to the Pacific. He was wrong, of course, but his explorations led to a Dutch claim on territory in America and to the establishment of a permanent Dutch presence in the New World.

For more than a decade after Hudson's voyage, the Dutch maintained an active trade in furs in and around New York. In 1624, the Dutch West India Company established a series of permanent trading posts on the Hudson, Delaware, and Connecticut Rivers. The company actively encouraged settlement of the region—not just from Holland itself, but from such other parts of northern Europe as Germany, Sweden, and Finland. It transported whole families to the New World and granted vast feudal estates to landlords (known as "patroons") on condition that they bring still more immigrants to America. The result was the colony of New Netherland and its principal town, New Amsterdam, on Manhattan Island. Its population, diverse as it was, remained relatively small; the colony was only loosely united, with chronically weak leadership.

The First English Settlements

The first permanent English settlement in the New World was established at Jamestown, in Virginia, in 1607. But for nearly thirty years before that, English merchants and adventurers had been engaged in a series of failed efforts to create colonies in America. Through much of the sixteenth century, the English had mixed feelings about the New World. They knew of its existence and were intrigued by its possibilities. Under the strong leadership of Elizabeth I, they were developing a powerful sense of nationalism that encouraged dreams of expansion. At the same time, however, England was leery of Spain, which remained the dominant force in America and, it seemed, the dominant naval power in Europe.

■ **NEW AMSTERDAM**
Dutch settlers in the colony of New Amsterdam (later New York), constructed high narrow houses that looked much like those they had known in Holland. This row of brick houses was built in Fort Orange, which later became Albany. *(Library of Congress)*

But much changed in the 1570s and 1580s. English "sea dogs" such as Sir Francis Drake staged successful raids on Spanish merchant ships and built confidence in England's ability to challenge Spanish sea power. More important was the attempted invasion of England by the Spanish Armada in 1588. Philip II, the powerful Spanish king, had recently united his nation with Portugal. He was now determined to end England's challenges to Spanish commercial supremacy and to bring the English back into the Catholic Church. He assembled one of the largest military fleets in the history of warfare—known to history as the "Spanish Armada"—to carry his troops across the English Channel and into England itself. Philip's bold venture turned into a fiasco when the smaller English fleet dispersed the Armada and, in a single stroke, ended Spain's domination of the Atlantic. The English now felt much freer to establish themselves in the New World.

The pioneers of English colonization were Sir Humphrey Gilbert and his half-brother Sir Walter Raleigh—both friends of Queen Elizabeth, and both veterans of the earlier colonial efforts in Ireland. In 1578 Gilbert obtained from Elizabeth a patent granting him the exclusive right for six years "to inhabit and possess at his choice all remote and heathen lands not in the actual possession of any Christian prince."

After numerous setbacks, Gilbert led an expedition to Newfoundland in 1583 and took possession of it in the queen's name. He proceeded southward along the coast, looking for a good place to build a military outpost that might eventually grow into a profitable colony. But a storm sank his ship, and he was lost at sea.

Roanoke

Raleigh was undeterred by Gilbert's misfortune. The next year, he secured from Elizabeth a six-year grant similar to Gilbert's and sent a small group of men on an expedition to explore the North American coast. They returned with two captive Indians and glowing reports of what they had seen. They were particularly enthusiastic about an island the natives called Roanoke and about the area of the mainland just beyond it (in what is now North Carolina). Raleigh asked the queen for permission to name the entire region "Virginia" in honor of Elizabeth, "the Virgin Queen." But while Elizabeth granted the permission, she did not offer the financial assistance Raleigh had hoped his flattery would produce. So he turned to private investors to finance another expedition.

In 1585 Raleigh recruited his cousin, Sir Richard Grenville, to lead a group of men (most of them from

■ **ROANOKE**
A drawing by one of the English colonists in the ill-fated Roanoke expedition of 1585 became the basis for this engraving by Theodore DeBry, published in England in 1590. A small European ship carrying settlers approaches the island of Roanoke, at left. The wreckage of several larger vessels farther out to sea and the presence of Indian settlements on the mainland and on Roanoke itself suggest some of the perils the settlers encountered. *(New York Public Library)*

the English plantations in Ireland) to Roanoke to establish a colony. Grenville deposited the settlers on the island, remained long enough to antagonize the natives by razing an Indian village as retaliation for a minor theft, and returned to England. The following spring, Sir Francis Drake unexpectedly arrived in Roanoke. With supplies and reinforcements from England long overdue, the beleaguered colonists boarded Drake's ships and left.

Raleigh tried again in 1587, sending an expedition carrying ninety-one men, seventeen women (two of them pregnant), and nine children—the nucleus, he hoped, of a viable "plantation." The settlers landed on Roanoke and attempted to take up where the first group of colonists had left off. (Shortly after arriving,

one of the women—the daughter of the commander of the expedition, John White—gave birth to a daughter, Virginia Dare, the first American-born child of English parents.) White returned to England after several weeks (leaving his daughter and granddaughter behind) in search of supplies and additional settlers; he hoped to return in a few months. But the hostilities with Spain intervened, and White did not return to the island for three years. When he did, in 1590, he found the island utterly deserted, with no clue to the settlers' fate other than the cryptic inscription "Croatoan" carved on a post. Some have argued that the colonists were slaughtered by the Indians in retaliation for Grenville's (and perhaps their own) hostilities. Others have contended that they left their settle-

BIBLIOGRAPHY

Pre-Columbian America and Indian Societies
James Axtell, *The European and the Indian: Essays in the Ethnohistory of Colonial North America* (1981); *The Invasion Within: The Contest of Cultures in Colonial North America* (1985); *After Columbus: Essays in the Ethnohistory of Colonial North America* (1988). *John Bierhorst, The Mythology of North America* (1985). Henry Warner Bowden, *American Indians and Christian Missions* (1982). Alfred M. Crosby, *Ecological Imperialism: The Biological Expansion of Europe, 900–1900* (1986). Carol Devens, *Countering Colonization: Native American Women and Great Lakes Missions, 1630–1900* (1992). Harold E. Driver, *Indians of North America,* 2nd ed. (1969). Stuart Fiedel, *The Prehistory of the Americas* (1987). Robert S. Grumet, *Historic Contact: Indian People and Colonists in Today's Northeastern United States in the Sixteenth through Eighteenth Centuries* (1995). Francisco Guerra, *The Pre-Columbian Mind* (1971). Ake Hultkrantz, *The Religions of the American Indians* (1979). Francis Jennings, *The Founders of America* (1993); *The Invasion of America: Indians, Colonialism, and the Cant of Conquest* (1975). J. D. Jennings, ed., *Ancient North America* (1983). Alvin M. Josephy, Jr., *The Indian Heritage of America* (1968). James H. Merrell, *The Indians' New World* (1989). Christopher L. Miller, *Prophetic Worlds: Indians and Whites on the Columbia Plateau,* (1985). Neal Salisbury, *Manitou and Providence: Indians, Europeans, and the Making of New England* (1982). Carl Sauer, *Sixteenth-Century North America* (1985). R. F. Spencer et al., *The Native Americans* (1978). William C. Sturtevant et. al., eds., *Handbook of North American Indians* (1986). Bruce G. Trigger, *Natives and Newcomers* (1985). Bruce G. Trigger and Wilcomb Washburn, eds., *Cambridge History of the Native Peoples of the New World, vol. 3: North America* (1993). Nathan Wachtel, *The Vision of the Vanquished* (1977). Wilcomb E. Washburn, *The Indian in America* (1975).

European Explorations and Spanish America
James Axtell, *Beyond 1492: Encounters in Colonial North America* (1992). Claudia Bushman, *America Discovers Columbus: How an Italian Explorer Became an American Hero* (1992). H. Elliott, *The Old World and the New, 1492–1650* (1970). Charles Gibson, *Spain in America* (1966). Thomas D. Hall, *Social Change in the Southwest, 1350–1880* (1989). Robert Jackson and Edward Castillo, *Indians, Franciscans, and Spanish Colonization* (1995). Andrew Knaut, *The Pueblo Revolt of 1680* (1995). James Lang, *Conquest and Commerce: Spain and England in the Americas* (1975). James Lockhart, *Spanish Peru, 1532–1560: A Colonial Society* (1968). Samuel Eliot Morison, *Admiral of the Ocean Sea,* 2 vols. (1942); *The European Discovery of America: The Northern Voyages* (1971); *The European Discovery of America: The Southern Voyages* (1974). Anthony Pagden, *European Encounters with the New World: From Renaissance to Romanticism* (1993). J. H. Parry, The *Age of Reconnaissance* (1963). William H. Prescott, *History of the Conquest of Mexico,* 3 vols. (1843). David B. Quinn, *North America from Earliest Discovery to First Settlements* (1977). Kirkpatrick Sale, *The Conquest of Paradise: Christopher Columbus and the Columbian Legacy* (1990). Richard C. Trexler, *Sexual Conquest: Gendered Violence, Political Order and the European Conquest of the Americas* (1995). David J. Weber, *The Spanish Frontier in North America* (1992). Donald J. Weber, *The Spanish Empire in North America* (1992). Eric Wolf, *Europe and the People Without History* (1982).

Africa and America   J. F. A. Ajayi and Michael Crowder, eds., *History of West Africa,* vol. 1 (1972). J. S. Fage, *A History of Africa* (1978). Patrick Manning, *Slavery and African Life: Occidental, Oriental, and African Slave Trades* (1990). Walter Rodney, *A History of the Upper Guinea Coast* (1970). Barbara L. Solow, *Slavery and the Rise of the Atlantic System* (1991). Hugh Thomas, *The Slave Trade* (1997). John Thornton, *Africa and Africans in the Making of the Atlantic World, 1400–1680* (1992).

England Looks West   Carl Bridenbaugh, *Vexed and Troubled Englishmen, 1590–1642* (1968). Nicholas Canny, *The Elizabethan Conquest of Ireland* (1976); *Kingdom and Colony: Ireland in the Atlantic World* (1988). Patrick Collinson, *The Elizabethan Puritan Movement* (1967). C. H. George and Katherine George, *The Protestant Mind of the English Reformation* (1961). Christopher Hill, *The Century of Revolution, 1603–1714* (1961). Peter Laslett, *The World We Have Lost* (1965). W. H. McNeill, *The Rise of the West* (1963). Wallace Notestein, *The English People on the Eve of Colonization, 1603–1630* (1954). J. H. Parry, *Europe and the New World, 1415–1715* (1949); *The Age of Reconnaissance* (1963). David B. Quinn, *The Elizabethans and the Irish* (1966); *North America from Earliest Discoveries to First Settlements* (1977). Margaret Spufford, *Contrasting Communities* (1974). Lawrence Stone, *The Crisis of the Aristocracy* (1965). Keith Thomas, *Religion and the Decline of Magic* (1971). David Underdown, *Pride's Purge* (1985). Michael Walzer, *The Revolution of the Saints* (1965).

First English Colonies   Karen Ordahl Kupperman, *Roanoke: The Abandoned Colony* (1984). David B. Quinn, *The Roanoke Voyages, 1584–1590,* 2 vols. (1955); *Raleigh and the British Empire* (1947); *Set Fair for Roanoke* (1985). Keith Wrightson, *English Society, 1580–1680* (1982).

THE INCONVENIENCIES
THAT HAVE HAPPENED TO SOME PER-
SONS WHICH HAVE TRANSPORTED THEMSELVES

from *England* to *Virginia*, vvithout prouisions necessary to suftaine themselues, hath
greatly hindred the Progresse of that noble *Plantation*: For preuention of the like disorders
heereafter, that no man suffer, either through ignorance or misinformation; it is thought requisite to publish this short declaration: wherein is contained a particular of such neces-
saries, as either priuate families or single persons shall haue cause to furnish themselues with, for their better
support at their first landing in *Virginia*; whereby also greater numbers may receiue in part,
directions how to prouide themselues.

Apparrell.	li.	s.	d.
One Monmouth Cap	00	01	10
Three falling bands	—	01	03
Three shirts	—	07	06
One waste-coate	—	02	02
One suite of Canuase	—	07	06
One suite of Frize	—	10	00
One suite of Cloth	—	15	00
Three paire of Irish stockins	—	04	00
Foure paire of shooes	—	08	08
One paire of garters	—	00	10
One doozen of points	—	00	03
One paire of Canuase sheets	—	08	00
Seuen ells of Canuase, to make a bed and boulster, to be filled in *Virginia* 8.s. One Rug for a bed 8.s. which with the bed seruing for two men, halfe is	—	08	00
Fiue ells coorse Canuase, to make a bed at Sea for two men, to be filled with straw, iiij.s. One coorse Rug at Sea for two men, will cost vj.s. is for one	—	05	00
	04	00	00

Apparrell for one man, and so after the rate for more.

Victuall.			
Eight bushels of Meale	02	00	00
Two bushels of pease at 3.s.	—	06	00
Two bushels of Oatemeale 4.s. 6.d.	—	09	00
One gallon of *Aquauitae*	—	02	06
One gallon of Oyle	—	03	06
Two gallons of Vineger 1.s.	—	02	00
	03	03	00

For a whole yeere for one man, and so for more after the rate.

Armes.			
One Armour compleat, light	—	17	00
One long Peece, fiue foot or fiue and a halfe, neere Musket bore	01	02	00
One sword	—	05	00
One belt	—	01	00
One bandaleere	—	01	06
Twenty pound of powder	—	18	00
Sixty pound of shot or lead, Pistoll and Goose shot	—	05	00
	03	09	06

For one man, but if halfe of your men haue armour it is sufficient so that all haue Peeces and swords.

For a family of 6. persons and so after the rate for more.

Tooles.	li.	s.	d.
Fiue broad howes at 2.s. a piece	—	10	00
Fiue narrow howes at 16.d. a piece	—	06	08
Two broad Axes at 3.s. 8.d. a piece	—	07	04
Fiue felling Axes at 18.d. a piece	—	07	06
Two steele hand sawes at 16.d. a piece	—	02	08
Two two-hand sawes at 5.s. a piece	—	10	00
One whip-saw, set and filed with box, file, and wrest	—	10	00
Two hammers 12.d. a piece	—	02	00
Three shouels 18.d. a piece	—	04	06
Two spades at 18.d. a piece	—	03	00
Two augers 6.d. a piece	—	01	00
Six chissels 6.d. a piece	—	03	00
Two percers stocked 4.d. a piece	—	00	08
Three gimlets 2.d. a piece	—	00	06
Two hatchets 21.d. a piece	—	03	06
Two froues to cleaue pale 18.d.	—	03	00
Two hand bills 20. a piece	—	03	04
One grindlestone 4.s.	—	04	00
Nailes of all sorts to the value of	02	00	00
Two Pickaxes	—	03	00
	06	02	08

Houshold Implements.			
One Iron Pot	00	07	00
One kettle	—	06	00
One large frying pan	—	02	06
One gridiron	—	01	06
Two skillets	—	05	00
One spit	—	02	00
Platters, dishes, spoones of wood	—	04	00
	01	08	00

For a family of 6. persons, and so for more or lesse after the rate.

For Suger, Spice, and fruit, and at Sea for 6. men — 00 | 12 | 06

So the full charge of Apparrell, Victuall, Armes, Tooles, and houshold stuffe, and after this rate for each person, will amount vnto about the summe of — 12 | 10 | 00
The passage of each man is — 06 | 00 | 00
The fraight of these prouisions for a man, will bee about halfe a Tun, which is — 01 | 10 | 00

So the whole charge will amount to about — 20 | 00 | 00

Nets, hookes, lines, and a tent must be added, if the number of people be greater, as also some kine.

And this is the vsuall proportion that the *Virginia Company* doe
bestow vpon their Tenants which they send.

Whosoeuer transports himselfe or any other at his owne charge vnto *Virginia*, shall for each person so transported before Midsummer 1625.
haue to him and his heires for euer fifty Acres of Land vpon a first, and fifty Acres vpon a second diuision.

Imprinted at London by FELIX KYNGSTON. 1622.

Chapter Two

THE ENGLISH "TRANSPLANTATIONS"

The Roanoke fiasco dampened the colonizing enthusiasm in England—for a time. But the lures of the New World—the presumably vast riches, the abundant land, the opportunities for religious freedom, the chance to begin anew—were too strong to be suppressed for very long. Propagandizers such as Richard Hakluyt kept the image of America alive in English society. By the early seventeenth century, the effort to establish permanent colonies in the New World resumed.

The first of these new efforts were much like the earlier, failed ones. They were largely private ventures, with little planning or direction from the English government. They were small, fragile settlements, and generally unprepared for the hardships they were to face. They met with terrible disasters.

Three things characterized these first permanent English settlements. First, the colonies were business enterprises. They were financed by private companies, and, in most cases, they were expected to produce a profit. Second, as in Ireland, there were few efforts to blend English society with the society of the natives. The Europeans attempted, as best they could, to isolate themselves from the Indians and create enclosed societies that would be entirely their own—"transplantations" of the English world they had left behind. Third, almost nothing worked out as they had planned.

Most colonies made few if any profits for their corporate sponsors until years, even decades, after their founding; and when they did, the profits usually came from sources no one had anticipated. European settlers generally found it impossible to isolate themselves entirely from the native population; their lives were shaped in crucial ways by their relationships with Indians, and the tribes were transformed in turn by their relationships with the white immigrants. However much the settlers tried to re-create English society in the New World, American society very quickly began to develop its own habits and institutions.

THE EARLY CHESAPEAKE

After James I issued his 1606 charters to the London and Plymouth Companies, the principal obstacle to founding new American colonies was, as usual, money. The Plymouth group made an early, unsuccessful attempt to establish a colony at Sagadoahoc, on the coast of Maine; but in the aftermath of that failure, it largely abandoned its colonizing efforts. The London Company, by contrast, moved quickly and decisively. Only a few months after receiving its charter, it launched a colonizing expedition headed for Virginia—a party of 144 men aboard three ships: the *Godspeed,* the *Discovery,* and the *Susan Constant.*

The Founding of Jamestown

Only 104 men survived the journey. They reached the American coast in the spring of 1607, sailed into the Chesapeake Bay and up a river they named the James, and established their colony on a peninsula extending from the river's northern bank. They called it Jamestown. The colonists had chosen their site poorly. In an effort to avoid the mistakes of Roanoke (whose residents were assumed to have been killed by Indians), they selected what they believed to be an easily defended location—an inland setting that they believed would offer them security. But the site was low and swampy, hot and humid in the summer, and prey to outbreaks of malaria. It was surrounded by thick woods, which were difficult to clear for cultivation. And it lay within the territories of powerful local Indians, a confederation led by the imperial chief Powhatan.

The result could hardly have been more disastrous. For seventeen years, one wave of English settlers after another attempted to make Jamestown a habitable and profitable colony. Every effort failed. The town became instead a place of misery and death; and the London Company, which had sponsored it in the hope of vast profits, saw itself drained of funds and saddled with seemingly endless losses. All that could be said of Jamestown at the end of this first period of its existence was that it had survived.

The initial colonists, too many of whom were adventurous gentlemen and too few of whom were willing laborers, ran into serious difficulties from the moment they landed. Much like the Indians to the south who had succumbed quickly to European diseases when first exposed to them, these English settlers had had no prior exposure, and thus no immunity, to the infections of the new land. Malaria, in particular, debilitated the colony, killing some and weakening others so they could do virtually no work. Because the promoters in London demanded a quick return on their investment, the colonists spent much of their limited and dwindling energy on futile searches for gold. They made only slightly more successful efforts to pile up lumber, tar, pitch, and iron for export. Growing food was a low priority.

The London Company promoters had little interest in creating a family-centered community, and at first they sent no women to Jamestown. The absence of English women made it difficult for the settlers to establish any semblance of a "society." The colonists were seldom able (and also seldom willing) to intermarry with native women, and hence Jamestown was at first an entirely male settlement. Without women, settlers could not establish real households, could not order their domestic lives, and had difficulty feeling any sense of a permanent stake in the community.

Greed and rootlessness contributed to the failure to grow sufficient food; inadequate diets contributed to the colonists' vulnerability to disease; the ravages of disease made it difficult for the settlers to recover from their early mistakes. The result was a community without the means to sustain itself. By January 1608, when ships appeared with additional men and supplies, all but 38 of the first 104 colonists were dead. Jamestown, now facing extinction, survived the crisis largely because of the efforts of twenty-seven-year-old Captain John Smith. He was already a famous world traveler, the hero of implausible travel narratives he had written and published. But he was also a capable organizer. Leadership in the colony had been divided among the several members of a council who quarreled continually. In the fall of 1608, however, Smith became council president and asserted his will. He imposed work and order on the community. He also organized raids on neighboring Indian villages to steal food and kidnap natives. During the colony's second winter, fewer than a dozen (in a population of about 200) died. By the summer of 1609, when Smith was deposed from the council and returned to England to receive treatment for a serious powder burn, the colony was showing promise of survival.

Reorganization

The London Company (now calling itself the Virginia Company) was, in the meantime, dreaming of bigger things. In 1609 it obtained a new charter from the king, which increased its power over the colony and enlarged the area of land to which it had title. The company raised additional capital by selling stock to "adventurers" who would remain in England but share in future profits. It attracted new settlers by offering additional stock to "planters" who were willing to migrate at their own expense. And it provided free passage to Virginia for poorer people who would agree to serve the company for seven years. In the spring of 1609, confident that it was now poised to transform Jamestown into a vibrant, successful venture, the company launched a "great fleet" of nine vessels with about 600 people (including some women and children) aboard—headed for Virginia.

More disaster followed. One of the Virginia-bound ships was lost at sea in a hurricane. Another ran aground on one of the Bermuda islands and was unable to free itself for months. Many of those who reached Jamestown, still weak from their long and stormy voyage, succumbed to fevers before the cold weather came. The winter of 1609–1610 became known as the "starving time," a period worse than anything before. The local Indians, antagonized by John Smith's raids and other hostile actions by the early English settlers, killed off the livestock in the woods and kept the colonists barricaded within their palisade. The Europeans lived on what they could find: "dogs, cats, rats, snakes, toadstools, horsehides," and even the "corpses of dead men," as one survivor recalled. The following May, the migrants who had run aground and been stranded on Bermuda finally arrived in Jamestown. They found only about 60 people (out of 500 residents the previous summer) still alive—and those so weakened by the ordeal that they seemed scarcely human. There seemed no point in staying on. The new arrivals took the survivors onto their ship, abandoned the settlement, and sailed downriver for home.

That might have been the end of Jamestown had it not been for an extraordinary twist of fate. As the refugees proceeded down the James toward the Chesapeake Bay, they met an English ship coming up the river—part of a fleet bringing supplies and the colony's first governor, Lord De La Warr. The departing settlers agreed to turn around and return to Jamestown. New relief expeditions with hundreds of colonists soon began to arrive, and the effort to turn a profit in Jamestown resumed.

De La Warr and his successors (Sir Thomas Dale and Sir Thomas Gates) imposed a harsh and rigid discipline on the colony. They organized settlers into work gangs. They sentenced offenders to be flogged, hanged, or broken on the wheel. But this communal system of labor did not function effectively for long. Settlers often evaded work, "presuming that howsoever the harvest prospered, the general store must

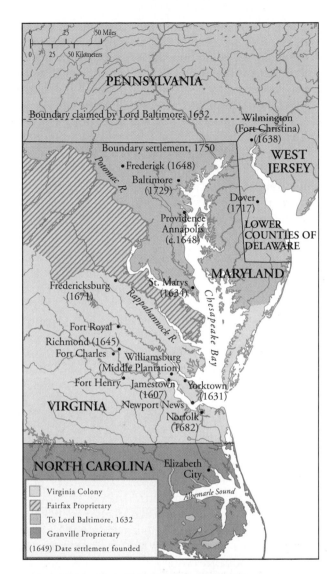

■ **GROWTH OF THE CHESAPEAKE, 1607–1750**
Virginia was founded by private investors chartered by the English crown and interested in making money. The profits generated by tobacco cultivation provided the main impetus for population growth and geographic expansion in the Chesapeake region. George Calvert, the first proprietor of Maryland, envisioned his new colony both as a great speculative venture and as a retreat for English Catholics who felt oppressed by the Anglican establishment in England.

maintain them." Governor Dale soon concluded that the colony would fare better if the colonists had personal incentives to work. He began to permit the private ownership and cultivation of land. Landowners would repay the company with part-time work and contributions of grain to its storehouses.

Under the leadership of these first, harsh governors, Virginia was not always a happy place. But it survived and even expanded. New settlements began lining the river above and below Jamestown. The expansion was partly a result of the order and discipline the governors at times managed to impose. It was a partly a product of increased military assaults on the local Indian tribes, which provided protection for the new settlements. But it also occurred because the colonists had at last discovered a marketable crop: tobacco.

Tobacco

Europeans had become aware of tobacco soon after Columbus's first return from the West Indies, where he had seen the Cuban natives smoking small cigars *(tabacos),* which they inserted in the nostril. By the early seventeenth century, tobacco from the Spanish colonies was already in wide use in Europe. Some critics denounced it as a poisonous weed, the cause of many diseases. King James I himself led the attack with *A Counterblaste to Tobacco* (1604), in which he urged his people not to imitate "the barbarous and beastly manners of the wild, godless, and slavish Indians, especially in so vile and stinking a custom." Other critics were concerned because England's tobacco purchases from the Spanish colonies meant a drain of English gold to the Spanish importers. Still, the demand for tobacco soared.

Then in 1612, the Jamestown planter John Rolfe began to experiment in Virginia with a harsh strain of tobacco that local Indians had been growing for years. He produced crops of high quality, and he found ready buyers in England. Tobacco cultivation quickly spread up and down the James. The character of this tobacco economy—its profitability, its uncertainty, its land and labor demands—transformed Chesapeake society in fundamental ways.

Of most immediate importance, perhaps, was the pressure tobacco cultivation created for territorial expansion. Tobacco growers needed large areas of farmland to grow their crops; and because tobacco exhausted the soil after only a few years, the demand for land increased even more. English farmers began establishing plantations deeper and deeper in the interior, isolating themselves from the center of European settlement at Jamestown and encroaching on territory the natives considered their own.

Expansion

Even the discovery of tobacco cultivation was not enough to help the Virginia Company. By 1616, there were still no profits, only land and debts. Nevertheless, the promoters continued to hope that the tobacco trade would allow them finally to turn the corner. In 1618, they launched a last great campaign to attract settlers and make the colony profitable.

Part of that campaign was an effort to recruit new settlers and workers to the colony. The company established what they called the "headright" system. Headrights were fifty-acre grants of land, which new settlers could acquire in a variety of ways. Those who already lived in the colony received 100 acres apiece. Each new settler received a single headright for himself or herself. This system encouraged family groups to migrate together, since the more family members traveled to America, the larger the landholding the family would receive. In addition, anyone (new settler or old) who paid for the passage of other immigrants to Virginia would receive an additional headright for each new arrival—thus, it was hoped, inducing the prosperous to import new laborers to America. Some colonists were able to assemble sizable plantations with the combined headrights they received for their families and their servants. In return, they contributed a small quitrent (one shilling a year for each headright) to the company.

The company added other incentives as well. To diversify the colonial economy, it transported ironworkers and other skilled craftsmen to Virginia. In 1619, it sent 100 Englishwomen to the colony (which was still overwhelmingly male) to become the wives of male colonists. (The women could be purchased for 120 pounds of tobacco and enjoyed a status somewhere between indentured servants and free people, depending on the good will—or lack of it—of their husbands.) It promised the colonists the full rights of Englishmen (as provided in the original charter of 1606), an end to the strict and arbitrary rule of the communal years, and even a share in self-government. On July 30, 1619, in the Jamestown church, delegates from the various communities met as the House of Burgesses. It was the first meeting of an elected legislature, a representative assembly, within what was to become the United States.

A month later, another event in Virginia established a very different but no less momentous precedent. As John Rolfe recorded, "about the latter end of August" a Dutch ship brought in "20 and odd Ne-

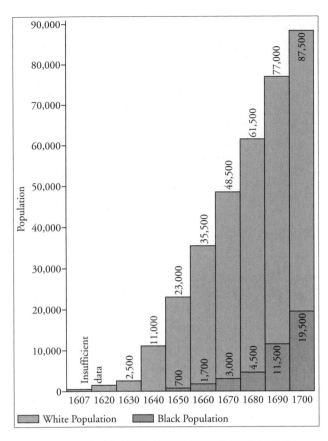

■ THE NON-INDIAN POPULATION OF THE CHESAPEAKE, 1607–1700

In the seventeenth century, the European population of the Chesapeake grew rapidly, although the rate of growth slowed over time. In both Virginia and Maryland, the headright system—through which settlers received a tract of land for every person in their household—provided an incentive for prosperous colonists to promote immigration from Europe. As this graph indicates, slaves imported from Africa and the Caribbean accounted for a growing proportion of population growth in the region beginning in the 1680s.

■ TOBACCO CULTIVATION IN VIRGINIA

This series of drawings, published in England in 1800 as "An Historical and Practical Essay on the Culture of Tobacco," illustrates the various processes by which early tobacco growers in the New World dried, bundled, stored, and sold their crops in the late seventeenth century. *(Colonial Williamsburg Foundation)*

groes." The status and fate of these first Africans in the English colonies remains obscure. There is some reason to believe that the colonists did not consider them slaves, that they thought of them as servants to be held for a term of years and then freed, like the white servants with whom the planters were already familiar. For a time, moreover, the use of black labor remained limited. Although Africans continued to trickle steadily into the colony, planters continued to prefer European indentured servants until at least the 1670s, when such servants began to become scarce and expensive. But whether or not anyone realized it at the time, the small group of black people who arrived in 1619 marked a first step toward the enslavement of Africans within what was to be the American republic.

The expansion of the colony was able to proceed only because of effective suppression of the local Indians, who resisted the expanding English presence. For two years, Sir Thomas Dale led unrelenting assaults against the Powhatan Indians and in the process kidnapped the great chief Powhatan's daughter Pocahontas. When Powhatan refused to ransom her, she converted to Christianity and in 1614 married John Rolfe. (Pocahontas accompanied her husband back to England, where, as a Christian convert and a gracious woman, she stirred interest in projects to "civilize" the Indians. She died while abroad.) At that point, Powhatan ceased his attacks on the English in the face of overwhelming odds. But after his death several years later, his brother, Opechancanough, became head of the native confederacy and resumed the effort to defend tribal lands from European encroachments. On a March morning in 1622, tribesmen called on the white settlements as if to offer goods for sale, then suddenly attacked. Not until 347 whites of both sexes and all ages (including John Rolfe) lay dead or dying were the Indian warriors finally forced to retreat. The surviving English struck back mercilessly at the Indians and turned back the threat for a time. Only after Opechancanough led another unsuccessful uprising in 1644 did the Powhatans finally cease to challenge the eastern regions of the colony.

By then the Virginia Company in London was defunct. The company had poured virtually all its funds into its profitless Jamestown venture and in the aftermath of the 1622 Indian uprising faced imminent bankruptcy. In 1624, James I revoked the company's charter, and the colony came under the control of the crown. It would remain so until 1776.

Maryland and the Calverts

Maryland was founded under circumstances very different from those of Virginia, but it nonetheless developed in ways markedly similar to its neighbor to the south. The new colony was the dream of George Calvert, the first Lord Baltimore, a recent convert to Catholicism and a shrewd businessman. Calvert envisioned establishing a colony both as a great speculative venture in real estate and as a retreat for English Catholics, many of whom felt oppressed by the Anglican establishment at home. He died before he could receive a charter from the king. But in 1632, his son Cecilius, the second Lord Baltimore, received a charter remarkable not only for the extent of the territory it granted him—an area that encompassed parts of what are now Pennsylvania, Delaware, and Virginia, in addition to present-day Maryland—but also for the powers it bestowed on him. He and his heirs were to hold their province as "true and ab-

■ **THE MARYLAND PROPRIETOR, C. 1670**
In a detail of a portrait by the court painter to King Charles II, the young Cecilius Calvert reaches for a map of Maryland. His grandfather and namesake, the second Lord Baltimore (1606–1675), holds it out to him. George Calvert, the father of the elder Cecilius, began negotiations to win a royal charter for Maryland; his son completed them in 1632 and became the first proprietor of the colony. He published the map shown here in 1635 as part of an effort to attract settlers to the colony. By the time this portrait was painted, Lord Baltimore's son, Charles, was governor of Maryland. The boy Cecilius, the heir apparent, died in 1681 before he could assume his title. *(Enoch Pratt Free Library)*

solute lords and proprietaries," and were to acknowledge the ultimate sovereignty of the king only by paying an annual fee to the crown.

Lord Baltimore named his brother, Leonard Calvert, governor and sent him with another brother to oversee the settlement of the province. In March 1634, two ships—the *Ark* and the *Dove*—bearing 200 to 300 passengers entered the Potomac River and turned into one of its eastern tributaries. On a high and dry bluff, these first arrivals laid out the village of St. Mary's (named, diplomatically, for the queen). The neighboring Indians, who were more worried about rival tribes in the region than they were about the new arrivals, befriended the settlers, provided them with temporary shelter, sold them land, and supplied them with corn. Unlike the Virginians, the early Marylanders experienced no Indian assaults, no plagues, no starving time.

The Calverts had invested heavily in their American possessions, and they needed to attract many settlers to make the effort profitable. As a result, they had to encourage the immigration of Protestants as well as their fellow English Catholics, who were both relatively few in number (about 2 percent of the population of England) and generally reluctant to emigrate. The Protestant settlers (mostly Anglicans) outnumbered the Catholics from the start, and the Calverts quickly realized that Catholics would always be a minority in the colony. They prudently adopted a policy of religious toleration. To appease the non-Catholic majority, Calvert appointed a Protestant as governor in 1648. A year later, he sent from England the draft of an "Act Concerning Religion," which assured freedom of worship to all Christians.

Nevertheless, politics in Maryland remained plagued for years by tensions between the Catholic minority (which included the proprietor) and the Protestant majority. Zealous Jesuits and crusading Puritans frightened and antagonized their opponents with their efforts to establish the dominance of their own religion. At one point, the Protestant majority barred Catholics from voting and repealed the Toleration Act. There was frequent violence, and in 1655 a civil war temporarily unseated the proprietary government and replaced it with one dominated by Protestants. The English in Maryland were spared serious conflict with Indians, but they made up for that by inflicting decades of conflict and instability on themselves.

Although Maryland's government ultimately came to resemble those of other American colonies, with a two-house assembly and a governor appointed from abroad, the distribution of real power in the colony differed sharply from that in other parts of English America. The proprietor retained absolute authority to distribute land as he wished. Lord Baltimore initially granted large estates to his relatives and to other English aristocrats, so that a landed aristocracy quickly established itself in Maryland. By 1640, a severe labor shortage in the colony had forced a change in the land grant procedure; and Maryland, like Virginia, adopted a "headright" system—a grant of 100 acres to each male settler, another 100 for his wife and each servant, and 50 for each of his children. But the great landlords of the colony's earliest years remained powerful even as the population grew larger and more diverse. Like Virginia, Maryland became a center of tobacco cultivation; and like Virginia, planters worked their land with the aid, first, of indentured servants imported from England and then, beginning late in the seventeenth century, with slaves imported from Africa. Settlement and trade remained dispersed, centered on scattered large plantations, and few towns of any significance emerged.

Turbulent Virginia

By the mid-seventeenth century, the Virginia colony had survived its early disasters, and both its population and the complexity and profitability of its economy were increasing. It was also growing more politically contentious, as emerging factions within the province began to compete for the favor of the government. Perhaps the most important dispute involved policy toward the natives. As settlement moved west, further into Indian lands, border conflicts grew increasingly frequent. Much of the tension within English Virginia in the late seventeenth century revolved around how to respond to those conflicts.

Sir William Berkeley arrived in Virginia in 1642 at the age of thirty-six, appointed governor by King Charles I. With but one interruption he remained in control of the government until the 1670s. Berkeley was popular at first as he sent explorers across the Blue Ridge Mountains to open up the western interior of Virginia. He organized the force that put down the 1644 Indian uprising, captured Opechancanough, and (against Berkeley's orders) shot and killed him. The defeated Indians ceded a large area of land to the English, but Berkeley agreed to prohibit white settlement west of a line he negotiated with the tribes.

This attempt to protect Indian territory—like many such attempts later in American history—was a failure from the start, largely because of the rapid growth of the Virginia population. Oliver Cromwell's victory in 1649 in the English Civil War (see p. 59) and the flight of many of his defeated opponents to the colony contributed to what was already a substantial population increase. Between 1640 and 1650, Virginia's population doubled from 8,000 to 16,000. By 1660, it had more than doubled again, to 40,000. As the choice lands along the tidewater became scarce, new arrivals and indentured servants completing their terms or escaping from their masters pressed westward into the piedmont. By 1652, English settlers had established three counties in the territory promised to the Indians. Unsurprisingly, there were frequent clashes between natives and whites.

By the 1660s, Berkeley had become a virtual autocrat in the colony. When the first burgesses were elected in 1619, all men aged seventeen or older were entitled to vote. By 1670, the vote was restricted to landowners, and elections were rare. The same burgesses, loyal and subservient to the governor, remained in office year after year. Each county continued to have only two representatives, even though some of the new counties of the interior contained many more people than the older ones of the tidewater area. Thus the more recent settlers in the "backcountry" were underrepresented or (if living in areas not yet formally organized as counties) not represented at all.

Bacon's Rebellion

In 1676, backcountry unrest and political rivalries combined to create a major conflict. Nathaniel Bacon, a wealthy young graduate of Cambridge University, arrived in Virginia in 1673. He purchased a substantial farm in the west and won a seat on the governor's council. He established himself, in other words, as a member of the backcountry gentry—one of the influential, propertied landowners who were emerging in the western region of the state and becoming leaders in their areas.

But the new backcountry gentry was squabbling with the leaders of the tidewater region in the east. They disagreed on many issues, but above all on policies toward the natives. The backcountry settlements were in constant danger of attack from Indians, because many of these settlements were being established on lands reserved for the tribes by treaty. White settlers in western Virginia had long resented the governor's attempts to hold the line of settlement steady so as to avoid antagonizing the natives. That policy was, they believed, an effort by the eastern aristocracy to protect its dominance by holding down the white population in the west. (In reality, the policy was at least as much an effort by

Berkeley to protect his own lucrative fur trade with the Indians.)

Bacon, an aristocratic man with great political ambitions, had additional reasons for unhappiness with Berkeley. He resented his exclusion from the inner circle of the governor's council (the so-called Green Spring group, whose members enjoyed special access to patronage). Bacon also fumed about Berkeley's refusal to allow him a piece of the Indian fur trade. He was developing grievances that made him a natural leader of an opposing faction.

Bloody events thrust him into that role. In 1675, some Doeg Indians—angry about the European intrusions into their lands—raided a western plantation and killed a white servant. Bands of local whites struck back angrily and haphazardly, attacking not only the small Doeg tribe but the powerful Susquehannock as well. The Indians responded with more raids on plantations and killed many more white settlers. As the fighting escalated, Bacon and other concerned landholders—unhappy with the governor's cautious response to their demand for help—defied Berkeley and struck out on their own against the Indians. Berkeley dismissed Bacon from the governor's council and proclaimed him and his men rebels. At that point what had started as an unauthorized assault on the Indians became a military challenge to the colonial government, a conflict known as Bacon's Rebellion. It was the largest and most powerful insurrection against established authority in the history of the colonies, one that would not be surpassed until the Revolution.

Twice, Bacon led his army east to Jamestown. The first time he won a temporary pardon from the governor; the second time, after the governor reneged on the agreement, he burned the city and drove the governor into exile. In the midst of widespread social turmoil throughout the colony, Bacon stood on the verge of taking command of Virginia. Instead, he died suddenly of dysentery; and Berkeley, his position bolstered by the arrival of British troops, soon managed to regain control. In 1677, the Indians (aware of their inability to defeat the white forces militarily) reluctantly signed a new treaty that opened additional lands to white settlement.

Bacon's Rebellion was significant for several reasons. It was part of the continuing struggle to define the boundary between Indian and white lands in Virginia; it showed how unwilling the English settlers were to abide by earlier agreements with the natives, and how unwilling the Indians were to tolerate further white movement into their territory. It revealed the bitterness of the competition among eastern and western landowners. But it also revealed something that Bacon himself had never intended to unleash: the potential for instability in the colony's large population of free, landless men. These men—most of them former indentured servants, propertyless, unemployed, with no real prospects—had formed the bulk of Bacon's constituency during the rebellion. They had become a large, unstable, floating population eager above all for access to land. Bacon had for a time maintained his popularity among them by exploiting their hatred of Indians. Gradually, however, he found himself unintentionally leading a movement that reflected the animosity of these landless men toward the landed gentry of which Bacon himself was a part.

One result was that landed people in both eastern and western Virginia began to recognize a common interest in preventing social unrest from below. That was one of several reasons that they turned increasingly to the African slave trade to fulfill their need for labor. Enslaved blacks might pose dangers too, but the events of 1676 suggested that the perils of importing a large white subordinate class were even greater.

CARIBBEAN COLONIZATION

The Chesapeake was the site of the first permanent English settlements in the New World. Throughout the first half of the seventeenth century, however, the most important destinations for English immigrants were the islands of the Caribbean and the northern way station of Bermuda. More than half the English migrants to the New World in the early seventeenth century settled on these islands. The island

■ **MAKING MOLASSES IN BARBADOS**
African slaves, who constituted the vast majority of the population of the flourishing sugar-producing island of Barbados, work here in a sugar mill grinding sugar cane and then boiling it to produce refined sugar, molasses, and—after a later distillation process not pictured here—rum. *(Arents Collections, Rare Books Division, New York Public Library. Astor, Lenox and Tilden Foundations)*

societies had close ties to English North America from the beginning and influenced the development of the mainland colonies in several ways.

The West Indies

Most of the Caribbean islands had substantial native populations—the Arawaks, the Caribs, and the Ciboney—before the arrival of the Europeans. But beginning with Christopher Columbus's first visit in 1492, and accelerating after the Spanish established their first colony on Hispaniola in 1496, the native population was all but wiped out by European epidemics. Indians were never an obstacle to European settlement of the Caribbean.

The Spanish Empire claimed title to all the islands in the Caribbean, but there was substantial Spanish settlement only on the largest of them: Cuba, Hispaniola, and Puerto Rico. English, French, and Dutch traders began settling on some of the smaller islands early in the sixteenth century, although these weak colonies were always vulnerable to Spanish attack. After Spain and the Netherlands went to war in 1621 (distracting the Spanish navy and leaving the English in the Caribbean relatively unmolested), the pace of English colonization increased. By mid-century, there were several substantial English settlements on the islands, the most important of them on Antigua, St. Kitts, Jamaica, and Barbados. Even so, through the seventeenth century, the English settlements in the Caribbean were the targets of almost constant attacks and invasions by the Spanish, the Portuguese, the French, the Dutch, and the remaining Indians of the region. The world of the Caribbean was a violent and turbulent place.

The Caribbean colonies built their economies on raising crops for export. In the first years of the seventeenth century, English settlers experimented unsuccessfully with tobacco and cotton. But they soon discovered that the most lucrative crop was sugar, for which there was a substantial and growing market in Europe. Sugar cane could also be distilled into rum, for which there was also a booming market abroad. Within a decade of the introduction of sugar cultivation to the West Indies, planters were devoting almost all of their land to sugar cane. In their appetite for more land for sugar cane, they cut down forests and destroyed the natural habitats of many animals, and greatly reduced the amount of land available for growing food.

Because sugar was a labor-intensive crop, and because the remnant of the native population was too small to provide a work force, English planters quickly found it necessary to import laborers. As in the Chesapeake, they began by bringing indentured servants from England. But the arduous work discouraged white laborers; many found it impossible to adapt to the harsh tropical climate so different from that of England. By mid-century, therefore, the English planters in the Caribbean (like the Spanish colonists who preceded them) were relying more and more heavily on an enslaved African work force, which soon substantially outnumbered them.

On Barbados and other islands where a flourishing sugar economy developed, the English planters were a tough, aggressive, and ambitious breed. Some of them grew enormously wealthy; and since their livelihoods depended on their work forces, they expanded and solidified the system of African slavery there remarkably quickly. By the late seventeenth century, there were four times as many African slaves as there were white settlers. By then the West Indies had ceased to be an attractive destination for ordinary English immigrants; most now went to the colonies on the North American mainland instead.

Masters and Slaves

A small white population, much of it enjoying great economic success, and a large African population, all of it in bondage, was a potentially explosive combination. As in other English colonies in the New World in which Africans came to outnumber Europeans, whites in the Caribbean grew fearful of slave revolts. They had good reason, for there were at least seven major slave revolts in the islands, more than the English colonies of North America experienced in their entire history as slave societies. As a result, white planters monitored their labor forces closely and often harshly. Beginning in the 1660s, all the islands enacted legal codes to regulate relations between masters and slaves and to give white people virtually absolute authority over Africans. A master could even murder a slave with virtual impunity.

There was little in either the law or in the character of the economy to compel planters to pay much attention to the welfare of their workers. Many white slaveowners concluded that it was cheaper to buy new slaves periodically than to protect the well-being of those they already owned, and it was not uncommon for masters literally to work their slaves to death. Few African workers survived more than a decade in the brutal Caribbean working environment—they were either sold to planters in North America or died. Even whites, who worked far less hard than did the slaves, often succumbed to the harsh climate; most died before the age of forty—often from tropical diseases to which they had no immunity.

Establishing a stable society and culture was extremely difficult for people living in such harsh and even deadly conditions. Many of the whites were principally interested in getting rich and had no long-term commitment to the islands. Those who could returned to England with their fortunes and left their estates in the hands of overseers. A large proportion of the European settlers were single men, and many of them either died or left at a young age. Those who remained, many of them common white farmers and laborers living in desperate poverty, were too poor to contribute much to the development of a flourishing society. Europeans in the Caribbean lacked many of the institutions that gave stability to the North American settlements: church, family, community. That was one reason that the white population remained such a small minority on the islands. Like much of the Spanish Empire, the Caribbean colonies of England were governed by a small white ruling class governing a much larger population of Africans and natives. But as in the English colonies on the mainland, there was little intermarriage between whites and blacks.

Africans in the Caribbean faced even greater difficulties, of course, but they managed to create a world of their own despite the hardships. They started families (although many of them were broken up by death or the slave trade); they sustained African religious and social traditions (and resisted Christianity); and within the rigidly controlled world of the sugar plantations, they established patterns of resistance.

The Caribbean settlements were important to the North American colonies in many ways. They were an important part of the Atlantic trading world in which many Americans became involved—a source of sugar and rum and a market for goods made in the mainland colonies and in England. They were the principal source of African slaves for the mainland colonies; fewer than half the slaves in North America came directly from Africa. And because Caribbean

planters established an elaborate plantation system earlier than planters in North America, they provided models that many mainland people consciously or unconsciously copied. In the American South, too, planters grew wealthy at the expense of poor whites and, above all, of African slaves.

THE GROWTH OF NEW ENGLAND

The first enduring settlement in New England—the second in English America—resulted from the discontent of a congregation of Puritan Separatists in England. For years, Separatists had been periodically imprisoned and even executed for defying the government and the Church of England; some of them, as a result, began to contemplate leaving England altogether in search of freedom to worship as they wished.

Plymouth Plantation

It was illegal to leave England without the consent of the king. In 1608, however, a congregation of Separatists from the hamlet of Scrooby began emigrating quietly, a few at a time, to Leyden, Holland, where they could worship without interference. Holland, however, was unsatisfying to them in other ways. As foreigners, they were barred from the Dutch craft guilds and had to work at unskilled and poorly paid jobs. They were also troubled by the effects of the tolerant atmosphere of Dutch society, which seemed to pose as much of a threat to their dream of a close-knit Christian community as had the repression in England. They watched with alarm as their children began to drift away from their families and their church and into Dutch society. As a result, some of the Separatists decided to move again, this time across the Atlantic, where they hoped to create the kind of community they wanted and where they could spread "the gospel of the Kingdom of Christ in those remote parts of the world."

Leaders of the Scrooby group obtained permission from the Virginia Company to settle in Virginia. From the king, they received informal assurances that he would "not molest them, provided they carried themselves peaceably." (This was a historic concession by the crown, for it opened English America to settlement not only by the Scrooby group but by other dissenting Protestants.) Several English merchants agreed to advance the necessary funds in exchange for a share in the profits of the settlement at the end of seven years.

The migrating Puritans "knew they were pilgrims" even before they left Holland, their leader and historian, William Bradford, later wrote. In September 1620 they left the port of Plymouth, on the English coast, in the *Mayflower* with thirty-five "saints" (Puritan Separatists) and sixty-seven "strangers" (people who were not full members of the leaders' church) aboard. By the time they sighted land in November, it was too late in the year to go on. Their original destination was probably the mouth of the Hudson River, in what is now New York. But they found themselves instead on Cape Cod. After exploring the region for a while, they chose a site for their settlement in the area just north of the cape, an area Captain John Smith had named "Plymouth" (after the English port from which the Puritans had sailed) during an exploratory journey some years before. Plymouth lay outside the London Company's territory, and the settlers realized they had no legal basis for settling there. As a result, forty-one of the "saints" signed a document, the Mayflower Compact, which established a civil government and proclaimed their allegiance to the king. Then, on December 21, 1620, the Pilgrims stepped ashore at Plymouth Rock.

They settled on cleared land that had once been an Indian village until, three years earlier, a mysterious epidemic—known as "the plague" and probably brought to the region by earlier European explorers—had swept through the region and substantially depopulated it. The Pilgrims' first winter was a difficult one; half the colonists perished from malnutrition, disease, and exposure. But the colony survived.

The Pilgrims' experience with the Indians was, for a time at least, very different from the experiences of the early English settlers farther south. That was in part because the remaining natives in the region—their numbers thinned by disease—were significantly weaker than their southern neighbors and realized they had to get along with the Europeans. It was also probably because the Pilgrims were less actively hostile to the natives than the colonists in Virginia were. In the end, the survival and growth of the colony depended crucially on the assistance they received from natives. Important Indian friends—Squanto and Samoset, among others—showed them how to gather seafood, cultivate corn, and hunt local animals. Squanto, a Pawtuxet who had earlier been captured by an English explorer and taken to Europe, spoke English and was of particular help to the settlers in forming an alliance with the local Wampanoags, under Chief Massasoit. After the first harvest, in 1621, the settlers marked the alliance by inviting the Indians to join them in an October festival, the first Thanksgiving.

The relationship between settlers and natives was never an equal one. The Pilgrims were few and weak, but the epidemic-ravaged Wampanoags were even weaker, particularly in the face of the firearms the English had brought with them. (They became weaker still sixteen years after the *Mayflower* arrived when a smallpox epidemic—a result of contact with English settlers—swept through the region with devastating consequences.)

The Pilgrims could not hope to create rich farms on the sandy, marshy soil, and their early fishing efforts produced no profits. In 1622, the military officer Miles Standish, one of the leaders of the colony, established a semi-military regime to impose discipline on the settlers. Eventually the Pilgrims began to grow enough corn and other crops to provide them with a modest trading surplus. They also developed a small fur trade with the Abenaki Indians of Maine. From time to time new colonists arrived from England, and in a decade the population reached 300.

The people of "Plymouth Plantation," as they called their settlement, chose William Bradford again and again to be their governor. As early as 1621, he persuaded Council for New England (the successor to the old Plymouth Company, which had charter rights to the territory) to give them legal permission to live there. He ended the communal labor plan Standish had helped create, distributed land among the families, and thus, as he explained it, made "all hands very industrious." He and a group of fellow "undertakers" took over the colony's debt to its original financiers in England and, with earnings from the fur trade, finally paid it off—even though the financiers had repeatedly cheated them and had failed to send them promised supplies.

The Pilgrims were always a poor community. As late as the 1640s, they had only one plow among them. But they clung to the belief that God had put them in the New World to live as a truly Christian community; and they were, on the whole, content to live their lives in what they considered godly ways.

THE OTHER PILGRIMS

The story of the Pilgrims and the first Thanksgiving remains one of the oldest and best known in American history. But there is another pilgrim story that is much less familiar. The colonists at Plymouth, like those up and down the Atlantic seaboard (and like the Spanish and Portugese settlers who preceded them to their south), did not travel alone. They brought with them to America a host of other organisms, plants, and animals that were familiar to Europeans but completely unknown to the Indians. The colonization of America was as much a biological invasion as a cultural one. It helped transform American landscape.

In some respects, the invasion was devastating. The English, like the Spanish, brought with them deadly epidemics such as smallpox and debilitating illnesses such as tuberculosis, previously unknown in North America. Indian immune systems were not equipped with antibodies that could defend against those diseases. Thirteen years after the Pilgrims arrived, a devastating smallpox epidemic wiped out much of the Indian population around Plymouth. The native communities there, as elsewhere in America, experienced population declines of 50 to 90 percent as a result of these epidemics, which would continue for centuries.

The disappearance of so many Indians was itself a profound change in the American landscape. But Indians who survived the epidemics often formed relationships with the colonists in ways that made other profound changes in the environment. The fur trade caused some of the most important of those changes. Indians were eager for goods they could trade with the colonists; and the colonists' demand for furs encouraged some tribes (and some colonists as well) to hunt native animals much more intensively than ever before. Animal populations declined as hunting pressure increased, so much so that areas like New England had lost most of their large mammals—as well as smaller ones such as deer, moose, wild turkeys, and wolves—within two centuries of the first settlements. Their departure made room for the domesticated grazing animals that colonists brought with them: cattle, sheep, hogs, and horses. Most of these animals had been entirely absent from Indian America.

Increasing their livestock became one of the colonists' overriding goals. As the herds expanded, so did the colonists' need for new land. They cut down forests to create new pastures. Cattle and horses enabled the colonists to cultivate much more land than had the tribes, because the animals made it possible to plant crops using plows. Indians had depended on hoes for their farming, which required much more human labor and thus limited the amount of land that one person or family could tend.

Although some of the crops the colonists planted were in fact Indian—corn being the most important—many were brought across the Atlantic as seeds. Wheat, rye, barley, and oats soon appeared in colonists' fields and quickly spread wherever the colonists went. In their gardens, colonial women tended vegetables and herbs that were a mixture of Indian and European crops. Cabbages, peas, and potatoes (a Caribbean plant reimported from Europe) lent variety to the colonial diet. Herbs added flavorings to otherwise bland meals, furnished medicines for healing, and supplied the color in homespun fabrics. In the orchards around their homesteads, colonists planted apples,

(continued)

pears, plums, cherries, and other fruit trees. From apples came one of the colonists' favorite beverages, cider, and from orchards generally came fresh fruit, preserves, and other sweeteners that found their way to colonial tables.

To enable their imported animals and plants to thrive, colonists sought to re-create the ecological conditions under which they had lived on the other side of the Atlantic. They divided their lands into the familiar functional units of a peasant agricultural system: grain fields, pastures, hay meadows, woodlots, orchards, gardens, barnyards. They built fences to separate the places reserved for animals from the places where crops grew. And so

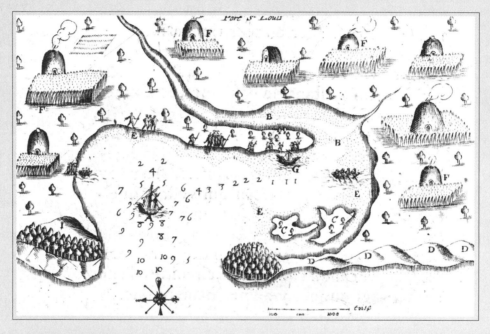

■ **CHAMPLAIN'S MAP OF PLYMOUTH PLANTATION, 1605**
When Samuel de Champlain visited Plymouth, Massachusetts, in 1605, he drew this map of the bay showing numerous Indian settlements in the vicinity. The many cornfields suggest what a prosperous community this was. Fifteen years later, when the Pilgrims arrived, most of these Indians would be dead from European diseases. *(Houghton Library, Harvard University)*

the fence—a construction almost entirely absent from Indian America—became for the colonists a symbol of "improvement," a sign that the landscapes of the New World were becoming more like those of the Old.

When the Pilgrims celebrated their first November harvest, they were partly thanking their Indian neighbors for the corn and wild meat they had shared. But they were also giving thanks for their own crops and animals, on which not just their survival but their sense of safety and familiarity depended. Those other, nonhuman, pilgrims were in fact one of the foundations on which the whole of colonial society would be built.

■ **DOMESTICATED ANIMALS AT PLYMOUTH**
Among the most important Eurasian species that the Pilgrims and other colonists introduced to North America were domesticated grazing animals. Goats ate almost anything and supplied their owners with dairy products; horses, although rare at first, helped pull plows and wagons. Even more important to the colonists were cattle, pigs, and sheep. *(Plimoth Plantation Photo)*

At times, they spoke of serving as a model for other Christians. Governor Bradford wrote in retrospect: "As one small candle may light a thousand, so the light here kindled hath shone to many, yea in some sort to our whole nation." But the Pilgrims were less committed to grand designs, less concerned about how they were viewed by others, than the Puritans who settled the larger and more ambitious English colonies to their north.

The Massachusetts Bay Experiment

Turbulent events in England in the 1620s (combined with the example of the Plymouth colony) created strong interest in colonization among other groups of Puritans. James I had been creating serious tensions for years between himself and Parliament through his effort to claim the divine right of kings and by his harsh, repressive policies toward the Puritans. The situation worsened after his death in 1625, when he was succeeded by his son, Charles I. By trying to restore Roman Catholicism to England and destroy religious nonconformity, he started the nation down the road that in the 1640s would lead to civil war. The Puritans were particular targets of Charles's policies. Some were imprisoned for their beliefs, and many began to consider the climate of England intolerable. The king's disbanding of Parliament in 1629 (it was not to be recalled until 1640) ensured that there would be no political solution to the Puritans' problems.

In the midst of this political and social turmoil, a group of Puritan merchants began organizing a new enterprise designed to take advantage of opportunities in America. At first their interest was largely an economic one. They obtained a grant of land in New England for most of the area now comprising Massachusetts and New Hampshire; they acquired a charter from the king (who was evidently unaware that they were Puritans) allowing them to create the Massachusetts Bay Company and to establish a colony in the New World; and they bought equipment and supplies from a defunct fishing and trading company that had attempted (and failed) to establish a profitable enterprise in North America. In 1629, they were ready to dispatch a substantial group of settlers to New England.

Among the members of the Massachusetts Bay Company, however, were a number of Puritans who saw the enterprise as something more than a

■ PORTRAIT OF A BOSTON WOMAN
Anne Pollard, a member of the original Winthrop expedition to Boston, was 100 years old when this portrait was painted in 1721. In 1643, thirteen years after her arrival in Massachusetts, she married a Boston innkeeper with whom she had 13 children. After her husband's death in 1679, she continued to manage the tavern on her own. When she died in 1725, at the age of 104, she left 130 direct descendants. The artist who painted this early portrait is unknown, but is assumed to be an American working in the relatively primitive style common in New England before the arrival in 1729 of the first academically trained portraitists from England. (*Courtesy of the Massachusetts Historical Society*)

business venture. They began to consider emigrating themselves and creating a haven for Puritans in New England. Members of this faction met secretly in Cambridge in the summer of 1629 and agreed to buy out the other investors and move en masse to America.

As governor, the new owners of the company chose John Winthrop, an affluent, university-educated gentleman with a deep piety and a forceful character. Winthrop had been instrumental in organizing the migration, and he commanded the expedi-

■ BOSTON HARBOR
The founders of Boston (and of the Massachusetts Bay colony, of which it was the capital) envisioned the town as a peaceful, harmonious, religious community. But they also hoped to create a thriving commercial center that would contribute to their own and the empire's prosperity. This early view of Boston harbor, showing the north battery built in 1646, suggests the growing commercial orientation of the city even in its early years. *(Library of Congress)*

tion that sailed for New England in 1630: seventeen ships and 1,000 people (who were, unlike the earlier migrants to Virginia, mostly family groups). It was the largest single migration of its kind in the seventeenth century. Winthrop carried with him the charter of the Massachusetts Bay Company, which meant that the colonists would be responsible to no company officials in England, only to themselves.

Unlike the two previous English settlements in America—Jamestown and Plymouth—the Massachusetts migration quickly produced several different new settlements. The port of Boston, at the mouth of the Charles River, became the company's headquarters and the colony's capital. But in the course of the next decade colonists moved into a number of other new towns in eastern Massachusetts: Charlestown, Newtown (later renamed Cambridge), Roxbury, Dorchester, Watertown, Ipswich, Concord, Sudbury, and others.

The Massachusetts Bay Company soon transformed itself into a colonial government. According to the original company charter, the eight stockholders (or "freemen") were to meet as a general court to choose officers and adopt rules for the corporation. But this commercial definition of government, which concentrated authority in what was in effect a corporate board of directors, quickly gave way to a more genuinely political system. The definition of "freemen" changed to include all male citizens, not just the stockholders. John Winthrop dominated colonial politics just as he had dominated the original corporation, but after 1634 he and most other officers of the colony had to face election each year.

Unlike the Separatist founders of Plymouth, the founders of Massachusetts had no intention of breaking away from the Church of England. Yet if they continued to feel any real attachment to the Anglican establishment, they gave little sign of it in their behavior. In every town, the community church had (in the words of the prominent minister John Cotton) "complete liberty to stand alone," unlike churches in the highly centralized Anglican structure in England. Each congregation chose its own minister and regulated its own affairs. In both Plymouth and Massachusetts, this form of parish organization eventually became known as the Congregational Church.

The Massachusetts Puritans were not grim or joyless, as many observers would later portray them. They were, however, serious and pious people. They strove to lead useful, conscientious lives of thrift and hard work, and they honored material success as evidence of God's favor. "We here enjoy God and Jesus Christ," Winthrop wrote to his wife soon after his arrival; "is this not enough?" He and the other Massachusetts founders believed they were founding a holy commonwealth—a "city upon a hill"—that could serve as a model for the rest of the world.

If Massachusetts was to become a beacon to others, it had first to maintain its own "holiness." The clergy and the government worked closely together to ensure that it did. Ministers had no formal political power, but they exerted great influence on church members, who were the only people who could vote or hold office. The government in turn protected the ministers, taxed the people (members and nonmembers alike) to support the church, and enforced the law requiring attendance at services. Dissidents had no more freedom of worship in America than the Puritans themselves had had in England. Colonial Massachusetts was, in effect, a "theocracy," a society in which the line between the church and the state was hard to see.

Like other new settlements, the Massachusetts Bay colony had early difficulties. During their first winter, an unusually severe one, nearly a third of the colonists died; others left in the spring. But more rapidly than Jamestown or Plymouth, the colony grew and prospered. The Pilgrims and neighboring Indians helped with food and advice. Incoming settlers, many of them affluent, brought needed tools and other goods, which they exchanged for the cattle, corn, and other produce of the established colonists and the natives. The large number of family groups in the colony (a sharp contrast to the early years at Jamestown) helped ensure a feeling of commitment to the community and a sense of order among the settlers. It also allowed the population to reproduce itself more rapidly. The strong religious and political hierarchy ensured a measure of social stability.

The Expansion of New England

As the population grew, more and more people arrived in Massachusetts who did not accept all the religious tenets of the colony's leaders or who were not Puritan "saints" and hence could not vote. The Massachusetts government considered religious dissent as much a threat to the community as heresy or treason. Newcomers had a choice of conforming to the religious practices of the colony or leaving. Many left, helping to begin a process that would spread

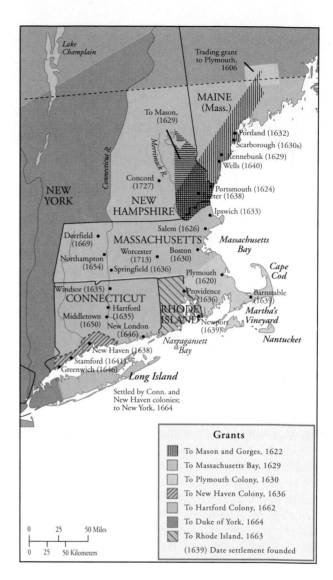

■ **GROWTH OF NEW ENGLAND, 1620–1750**
Economic ambition and religious dissent helped shape the population growth and geographic expansion of European settlement in New England. In the 1630s, colonists settled in the fertile Connecticut River valley, extending English settlement to the west and south of Massachusetts Bay. Some Puritans, distressed by what they saw as religious laxity in Boston, established a more orthodox community in New Haven, while Roger Williams's movement for the separation of church and state led to the founding of Rhode Island.

settlement throughout present-day New England and beyond.

The Connecticut Valley, about 100 miles west of the edge of European settlement around Boston, began attracting English families as early as the 1630s, despite claims to those lands by the Dutch.

The Connecticut settlers were attracted by the valley's fertile lands (a contrast to the stony, unproductive soil around Boston) and by its isolation from the intensely religious character of Massachusetts Bay. The valley appealed in particular to Thomas Hooker, a minister of Newtown (Cambridge), who defied the Massachusetts government in 1635 and led his congregation through the wilds to establish the town of Hartford. Four years later, the people of Hartford and of two other newly founded upriver towns, Windsor and Wethersfield, established a colonial government of their own and adopted a constitution known as the Fundamental Orders of Connecticut. This created a government similar to that of Massachusetts Bay but gave a larger proportion of the men the right to vote and hold office. (Women were barred from voting virtually everywhere.)

Another Connecticut colony, the project of a Puritan minister and a wealthy merchant from England, grew up around New Haven on the Connecticut coast. It reflected impatience not with the orthodoxy of Massachusetts Bay, but with what its founders considered the increasing religious laxity in Boston. The Fundamental Articles of New Haven (1639) established a religious government even stricter than that in Boston. New Haven remained independent until 1662, when a royal charter combined it with Hartford to create the colony of Connecticut.

Rhode Island had its origins in the religious and political dissent of Roger Williams, an engaging but controversial young minister who lived for a time in Salem, Massachusetts. Even John Winthrop, who considered Williams a heretic, called him a "sweet and amiable" man, and William Bradford described him as "a man godly and zealous, having many precious parts." But he was, Bradford added, "very unsettled in judgment." Williams, a confirmed Separatist, argued that the Massachusetts church should abandon all allegiance to the Church of England. More disturbing to the clergy, he called for a complete separation of church and state—to protect the church from the corruption of the secular world. The colonial government, alarmed at this challenge to its spiritual authority, banished him. During the bitter winter of 1635–1636, he took refuge with Narragansett tribesmen; the following spring he bought a tract of land from them and, with a few followers, created the town of Providence on it. Other communities of dissidents followed him to what became Rhode Island, and in 1644 Williams obtained a charter from Parliament permitting him to establish a gov-

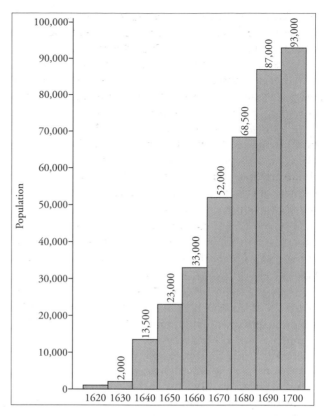

■ **THE WHITE POPULATION OF NEW ENGLAND, 1620–1700**
As in the Chesapeake colonies, the population of New England grew rapidly in the seventeenth century, although the rate of growth slowed over time. Most of the emigrants to New England were Puritans who had no intention of breaking away from the Church of England. Healthier, more self-sufficient, and more stable than the colonies in the Chesapeake (at least until King Philip's War), the population of New England grew through natural reproduction as well as immigration.

ernment. Rhode Island's government gave no support to the church and allowed "liberty in religious concernments." For a time, it was the only colony in which members of all faiths (including Jews) could worship without interference.

An even greater challenge to the established order in Massachusetts Bay emerged in the person of Anne Hutchinson, an intelligent and charismatic woman from a substantial Boston family. Hutchinson had come to Massachusetts with her husband in 1634 as part of a community led by the minister John Cotton. She shared Cotton's belief that only the "elect" were entitled to any religious or political authority. Living a righteous life was not enough to earn a place among the elect; to be a saint, it was necessary to have undergone a conversion experience—something relatively few residents of Massachusetts had done.

Hutchinson antagonized the leaders of the colony by arguing much more vehemently than Cotton that the members of the Massachusetts clergy who were not among the elect had no right to spiritual office. She claimed that her own uninspiring minister was among the nonelect and that he had no right to exercise any authority over his congregation. Over time she made the same claim about many other clergy as well and eventually charged that all the ministers in Massachusetts—with the exception of John Cotton and her own brother-in-law—were not among the elect. Such teachings (which her critics called "Antinomianism," from the Greek meaning "hostile to the law") were a serious threat to the spiritual authority of the established clergy. Hutchinson also created alarm by affronting prevailing assumptions about the proper role of women in Puritan society. She was not a retiring, deferential wife and mother, but a powerful religious figure in her own right.

Hutchinson developed a large following among women, to whom she offered an active role in religious affairs. She also attracted support from others (merchants, young men, and dissidents of many sorts) who resented the oppressive character of the colonial government. As her influence grew, and as she began to deliver open attacks on some members of the clergy, the Massachusetts leadership mobilized to stop her. Hutchinson's followers were numerous and influential enough to prevent Winthrop's reelection as governor in 1636, but the next year he returned to office and put her on trial for heresy. Hutchinson embarrassed her accusers by displaying a remarkable knowledge of theology; but because she continued to defy clerical authority (and because she claimed she had herself communicated directly with the Holy Spirit—a violation of the Puritan belief that the age of such revelations had passed), she was convicted of sedition and banished as "a woman not fit for our society." With her family and some of her followers, she moved to Rhode Island. Later still, she moved south into New Netherland (later New York), where in 1643 she died during an Indian uprising.

Alarmed by Hutchinson's heresy, male clergy began to restrict further the already limited public activities of women within congregations and to con-

■ **ANNE HUTCHINSON PREACHING IN HER HOUSE IN BOSTON**
Anne Hutchinson was alarming to many of Boston's religious leaders not only because she openly challenged the authority of the clergy, but also because she implicitly challenged norms of female behavior in Puritan society. *(Bettmann)*

trol other activities she had inspired. As a result, many of Hutchinson's followers began to migrate out of Massachusetts Bay, especially to New Hampshire and Maine.

Colonies had been established there in 1629 when two English proprietors, Captain John Mason and Sir Ferdinando Gorges, had received a grant from the Council for New England and divided it along the Piscataqua River to create two separate provinces. But despite their lavish promotional efforts, few settlers had moved into these northern regions until the religious disruptions in Massachusetts Bay. In 1639, John Wheelwright, a disciple of Anne Hutchinson, led some of his fellow dissenters to Exeter, New Hampshire. Other groups—of both dissenting and orthodox Puritans—soon followed. New Hampshire became a separate colony in 1679. Maine remained a part of Massachusetts until 1820.

Settlers and Natives

Indians were less powerful rivals to the early New England immigrants than natives were to the English settlers further south. By the mid-1630s, the native population, small to begin with, had been almost extinguished by the epidemics. The surviving Indians sold much of their land to the English (a great boost to settlement, since much of it had already been cleared). Some natives—known as "praying Indians"—even converted to Christianity and joined Puritan communities.

Indians provided crucial assistance to the early settlers as they tried to adapt to the new land. Whites learned from the natives about vital local food crops: corn, beans, pumpkins, and potatoes. They also learned such crucial agricultural techniques as annual burning for fertilization and planting beans to replenish exhausted soil. Natives also served as important trading partners to European immigrants, particularly in the creation of the thriving North American fur trade. They were an important market for such manufactured goods as iron pots, blankets, metal-tipped arrows, eventually guns and rifles, and (often tragically) alcohol. Indeed, commerce with the Indians was responsible for the creation of some of the first great fortunes in British North America and for the emergence of wealthy families who would exercise influence in the colonies (and later the nation) for many generations. The relationship between whites and Indians, in New England as throughout the areas of European settlement in the Americas, was one of constant interaction, in which each group influenced the other in crucial ways.

But as in other areas of white settlement, there were also conflicts; and the early peaceful relations between whites and Indians did not last. Tensions soon developed as a result of the white colonists' enormous appetite for land, an appetite that grew as the white population of the colonies increased. The expanding white demand for land was also a result of a change in the colonists' agrarian economy. As the wild animals of the region began to disappear from overhunting, colonists began to concentrate more and more on raising domesticated animals: cattle, sheep, hogs, horses, and others. Increasing their livestock became one of the colonists' overriding goals. As the herds expanded, so did the colonists' need for new land. As a result, they moved steadily into territories such as the Connecticut Valley, where the natives were more numerous and more powerful than they had been along the Massachusetts coast. White settlers in those areas came into conflict with the local tribes.

The character of those conflicts—and the brutality with which whites assaulted their Indian foes—emerged in part out of changing Puritan attitudes toward the natives. At first, many white New Englanders had looked at the Indians with a slightly condescending admiration. Before long, however, they came to view them primarily as "heathens" and "savages," and hence as a constant threat to the existence of a godly community in the New World. Some Puritans believed the solution to the Indian "problem" was to "civilize" the natives by converting them to Christianity and European ways, and some English missionaries had modest success in producing converts. One such missionary, John Eliot, even translated the Bible into an Algonquian language. Other Puritans, however, envisioned a harsher "solution": displacing or, if that failed, exterminating the natives.

To the natives, the threat from the English was very direct. European settlers were penetrating deeper and deeper into the interior, seizing land, clearing forests, driving away much of the wild game on which the tribes depended for food. English farmers often let their livestock run wild, and the animals often destroyed natives' crops. The Indian population in the region had been declining for years as a result of epidemic diseases. Now land and food shortages worsened their plight. There had been more than 100,000 Indians in New England at the beginning of the seventeenth century; by 1675, only 10,000 remained. This decline created despair among New England natives. It drove some Indians to alcoholism and others to conversion to Christianity. But it also produced conflict.

The first major conflict came in 1637, when hostilities broke out between English settlers in the Connecticut Valley and the Pequot Indians of the region. It was a result of competition between the white settlers and the Pequots over trade with the Dutch in New Netherland and friction over land. In what became known as the Pequot War, English settlers allied with the Mohegan and Narragansett Indians

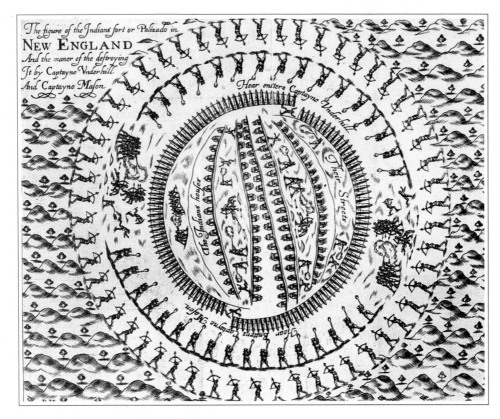

■ **A PEQUOT VILLAGE DESTROYED**
An English artist drew this view of a fortified Pequot village in Connecticut surrounded by English soldiers and their allies from other tribes during the Pequot War in 1637. The invaders massacred more than 600 residents of the settlement. *(Rare Book Division, New York Public Library)*

(who were also rivals of the Pequots). The greatest savagery in the conflict was the work of the English. In the bloodiest act of the war, white raiders under Captain John Mason marched against a palisaded Pequot stronghold and set it afire. Hundreds of Indians died, burned to death in the flaming stockade or killed as they attempted to escape. Those who survived were hunted down, captured, and sold as slaves. The Pequot tribe was almost wiped out.

The most prolonged and deadly encounter between whites and Indians in the seventeenth century began in 1675, a conflict that the English would remember for generations as King Philip's War. As in the earlier Pequot War in Connecticut, an Indian tribe—in this case the Wampanoags, under the leadership of a chieftain known to the white settlers as King Philip and among his own people as Metacomet—rose up to resist English incursions into their lands. The Wampanoags had not always been hostile to the settlers; indeed, Metacomet's grandfather had

once forged an alliance with the English. But by the 1670s, they had become convinced that only armed resistance could protect them from the movement of the English into their lands and, more immediately, from the efforts by the colonial governments to impose English law on the natives. (A court in Plymouth had recently tried and hanged several Wampanoags for murdering a member of their own tribe.)

For three years, the natives—well organized and armed with guns—terrorized a string of Massachusetts towns, destroying twenty of them and causing the deaths of as many as a thousand people (including at least one-sixteenth of the white males in the colony). The war greatly weakened both the society and economy of Massachusetts. But the white settlers fought back and gradually prevailed, beginning in 1676 when Massachusetts leaders joined forces with the Mohawks, long-time rivals of the Wampanoags, and recruited guides, spies, and soldiers from among the so-called praying Indians of the region. While white militiamen attacked Indian villages and destroyed native food supplies, a group of Mohawks ambushed Metacomet and shot and killed him, then bore his severed head to Boston to present to the colonial leaders. After that the fragile alliance that Metacomet had managed to forge among local tribes collapsed. Europeans were soon able to crush the uprising. Some Wampanoag leaders were executed; others were sold into slavery in the West Indies. The Wampanoags and their allies, their populations depleted and their natural resources reduced, were now powerless to resist the English.

Yet these victories by the white colonists did not end the danger to their settlements. This was in part because other Indians in other tribes survived, and were still capable of attacking English settlements. It was also because the New England settlers faced competition not only from the natives but also from the Dutch and the French, who claimed the territory on which some of the outlying settlements were established. The French, in particular, would pose a constant threat to the English through their alliance with the Algonquins. In later years, they would join forces with Indians in their attacks on the New England frontier.

&

THE RESTORATION COLONIES

By the end of the 1630s, English settlers had established the beginnings of what would eventually become six of the thirteen original states of the American republic: Virginia, Massachusetts, Maryland, Connecticut, Rhode Island, and New Hampshire. (Maine remained officially part of Massachusetts until after the American Revolution.) But for nearly thirty years after Lord Baltimore received the charter for Maryland in 1632, the English government launched no additional colonial ventures. It was preoccupied with troubles of its own at home.

The English Civil War

England's problems had begun during the rule of James I, who attracted widespread opposition before he died in 1625 but never openly challenged Parliament. His son, Charles I, was not so prudent. After he dissolved Parliament in 1629 and began ruling as an absolute monarch, he steadily alienated a growing number of his subjects—and the members of the powerful Puritan community above all. Finally, desperately in need of money, Charles called Parliament back into session and asked it to levy new taxes. But he antagonized the members by dismissing them twice in two years. In 1642, some of them organized a military challenge to the king, thus launching the English Civil War.

The conflict between the Cavaliers (the supporters of the king) and the Roundheads (the forces of Parliament, who were mostly Puritans) lasted seven years. Finally, in 1649, the Roundheads defeated the king's forces, captured Charles himself, and—in an action that horrified not only much of continental Europe at the time but also future generations of English men and women—beheaded the monarch. To replace him, they elevated the stern Roundhead leader Oliver Cromwell to the position of "protector," from which he ruled for the next nine years. When Cromwell died in 1658, his son and heir proved unable to maintain his authority. Two years later, King Charles II, son of the beheaded monarch, returned from exile and claimed the throne.

Among the many results of the Stuart Restoration was the resumption of colonization in America. Charles II quickly began to reward faithful courtiers with grants of land in the New World; and in the twenty-five years of his reign, he issued charters for four additional colonies: Carolina, New York, New Jersey, and Pennsylvania. The new colonies were all proprietary ventures (modeled on Maryland rather than on Virginia and Massachusetts), thus exposing an important change in the nature of American settlement. No longer were private companies interested in launching colonies, realizing at last that there were no quick profits to be had in the New World. The goal of the founders of the new colonies was not so much quick commercial success as permanent settlements that would provide proprietors with land and power.

The Carolinas

Carolina (a name derived from the Latinate form of "Charles") was, like Maryland, carved in part from the original Virginia grant. Charles II awarded the territory to a group of eight court favorites, all prominent politicians already active in colonial affairs. In successive charters issued in 1663 and 1665, the

■ **CHARLES TOWN IN 1739**
An English engraver produced this prospect of the harbor at Charles Town (now Charleston), South Carolina, as it looked six decades after the city was founded in 1680. It was by then the principal port of the southern colonies. The city's original waterfront (or battery), pictured here, looks much the same today as it did in the eighteenth century. *(I.N. Phelps Stokes Collection of American Historical Prints, New York Public Library)*

eight proprietors received joint title to a vast territory stretching south to the Florida peninsula and west to the Pacific Ocean. Like Lord Baltimore, they received almost kingly powers over their grant.

Also like Lord Baltimore, they expected to profit as landlords and land speculators. They reserved large estates for themselves, and they proposed to sell or give away the rest in smaller tracts (using a headright system similar to those in Virginia and Maryland) and to collect annual payments ("quitrents") from the settlers. Although committed Anglicans themselves, they welcomed any settlers they could get. The charter of the colony guaranteed religious freedom to everyone who would worship as a Christian. The proprietors also promised a measure of political freedom; laws were to be made by a representative assembly. With these incentives, they hoped to attract settlers from the existing American colonies and thus to avoid the expense of financing expeditions from England.

Their initial efforts failed dismally, and some of the original proprietors gave up. But one man—Anthony Ashley Cooper, soon to become the earl of Shaftesbury—persisted. Cooper convinced his partners to finance migrations to Carolina from England. In the spring of 1670, the first of these expeditions—a party of 300—set out from England. Only 100 people survived the difficult voyage; those who did established a settlement in the Port Royal area of the Carolina coast. Ten years later they founded a city at the junction of the Ashley and Cooper Rivers, which in 1690 became the colonial capital. They called it Charles Town. (It was later renamed Charleston.)

The earl of Shaftesbury, troubled by the instability in England, wanted a planned and well-ordered community. With the aid of the English philosopher John Locke, he drew up the Fundamental Constitution for Carolina in 1669, which created an elaborate system of land distribution and an elaborately designed social order. In fact, however, Carolina developed along lines quite different from the almost utopian vision of Shaftesbury and Locke. For one thing, the colony was never really united in anything more than name. The northern and southern regions remained widely separated and were socially and economically distinct from one another. The northern settlers were mainly backwoods farmers, largely isolated from the outside world, scratching out a meager existence through subsistence agriculture. They developed no important aristocracy and for many years imported virtually no African slaves. In the south, fertile lands and the good harbor at Charles Town promoted a more prosperous economy and a more aristocratic society. Settlements grew up rapidly along the Ashley and Cooper Rivers, and colonists established a flourishing trade in corn, lumber, cattle, pork, and (beginning in the 1690s) rice—which was to become the colony's principal commercial crop. Traders from the interior used Charles Town to market furs and hides they had acquired from Indian trading partners; some also marketed Indian slaves, generally natives captured by rival tribes and sold to the white traders.

Southern Carolina very early developed close ties to the large (and now overpopulated) English colony on the island of Barbados. For many years, Barbados was Carolina's most important trading partner. During the first ten years of settlement, most of the new settlers in Carolina were Barbadians, some of whom arrived with large groups of African workers and established themselves quickly as substantial landlords. African slavery had taken root on Barbados earlier than in any of the mainland colonies (see pp. 45–47); and the white Caribbean migrants—tough, uncompromising profit seekers—established a similar slave-based plantation society in Carolina. (The proprietors, four of whom had a financial interest in the African slave trade, encouraged the importation of Africans.)

For several decades, Carolina remained one of the most unstable of all the English colonies in America. There were tensions between the small farmers of the Albemarle region in the north and the wealthy planters in the south. There were conflicts between the rich Barbadians in southern Carolina and the smaller landowners around them. After Lord Shaftesbury's death, the proprietors proved unable to establish order, and in 1719 the colonists seized control of the colony from them. Ten years later, the king divided the region into two royal colonies, North and South Carolina.

New Netherland, New York, and New Jersey

In 1664, one year after he issued the Carolina charter, Charles II granted to his brother James, the duke of York, all the territory lying between the Connecticut and Delaware Rivers. But much of the territory included in the grant was already claimed by the Dutch, who had established substantial settlements at New Amsterdam and other strategic points beginning in 1624.

The emerging conflict between the English and the Dutch in America was part of a larger commercial rivalry between the two nations in the seventeenth century throughout the world. But the English particularly resented the Dutch presence in America, because it served as a wedge between the northern and southern English colonies and because it provided bases for Dutch smugglers evading English customs laws. And so in 1664, an English fleet under the command of Richard Nicolls sailed into the lightly defended port of New Amsterdam and extracted a surrender from the arbitrary and unpopular Dutch governor, Peter Stuyvesant, who had failed to mobilize resistance to the invasion. Under the Articles of Capitulation, the Dutch colony surrendered to the British and received in return assurances that the Dutch settlers would not be displaced. Several years later, in 1673, the Dutch briefly reconquered New Amsterdam. But they lost it for good in 1674.

James, the duke of York, his title to New Netherland now clear, renamed the colony New York and prepared to govern a colony of extraordinary diversity. New York contained not only Dutch and English, but Scandinavians, Germans, French, Africans (imported as slaves by the Dutch West India Company), and members of several different Indian tribes. There were, of course, many different religious faiths among these groups. James made no effort to impose his own Roman Catholicism on the colony. Like other proprietors before him, he remained in England and delegated powers to a governor and a council. But he provided for no representative assembly, perhaps because a parliament had executed his own father, Charles I. The laws did, however, establish local governments and guarantee religious toleration. Despite these concessions, there were immediate tensions over the distribution of power in the colony. The great Dutch "patroons" (large landowners) survived with their economic

■ NEW AMSTERDAM
The small Dutch settlement on Manhattan Island, known before 1664 as New Amsterdam, fell to the English in 1664. This painting shows buildings clustered at the southern tip of the island, which remained the center of what became New York City until the nineteenth century. *(Bettmann)*

and political power largely intact. James granted large estates as well to some of his own political supporters in an effort to create a class of influential landowners loyal to him. Power in the colony thus remained widely and unequally dispersed—among wealthy English landlords, Dutch patroons, fur traders (who forged important alliances with the Iroquois), and the duke's political appointees. Like Carolina, New York would for many years be a highly factious society.

It was also a growing and generally prosperous colony. By 1685, when the duke of York ascended the English throne as James II, New York contained approximately 30,000 people, about four times as many as when James had received his grant twenty years before. Most of them still lived within the Hudson Valley, close to the river itself, with the largest settlement at its mouth, in the town of New York (formerly New Amsterdam).

Originally, James's claims in America extended south of the Hudson to the Delaware Valley and beyond. But shortly after receiving his charter, he gave a large portion of that land to a pair of political allies, Sir John Berkeley and Sir George Carteret, both of whom were also Carolina proprietors. Carteret named the territory New Jersey, after the island in the English channel on which he had been born. In 1702, after nearly a decade of political squabbling and economic profitlessness, the proprietors ceded control of the territory back to the crown and New Jersey became a royal colony.

Like New York (from which much of the population had come), New Jersey was a place of enormous ethnic and religious diversity. But unlike New York, New Jersey developed no important class of large landowners; most of its residents remained small farmers. Nor did New Jersey (which, unlike New

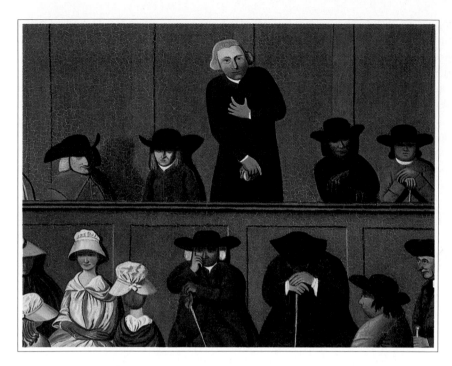

York, had no natural harbor) produce any single important city.

The Quaker Colonies

Pennsylvania, like Massachusetts, was born out of the efforts of dissenting English Protestants to find a home for their own religion and their own distinctive social order. The Society of Friends originated in mid-seventeenth-century England and grew into an important force as a result of the preachings of George Fox, a Nottingham shoemaker, and Margaret Fell. Their followers came to be known as Quakers because Fox urged them to "tremble at the name of the Lord." Unlike the Puritans, Quakers rejected the concepts of predestination and original sin. All people had divinity within themselves (an "Inner Light," which could guide them along the path of righteousness), and all who cultivated that divinity could attain salvation. Also unlike the Puritans, Quakers granted women a position within the church generally equal to that of men. Women and men alike could become preachers and define church doctrine. A symbol of that sexual equality was the longtime partnership between Fox and Fell.

Of all the Protestant sectarians of the time, the Quakers were the most anarchistic and the most democratic. They had no church government, only periodic meetings of representatives from congregations. They had no paid clergy, and in their worship they spoke up one by one as the spirit moved them. Disregarding distinctions of gender and class, they addressed one another with the terms "thee" and "thou," words then commonly used in other parts of English society only in speaking to servants and social inferiors. And as confirmed pacifists, they refused to fight in wars. The Quakers were unpopular enough in England as a result of these beliefs and practices. They increased their unpopularity by occasionally breaking up other religious groups at worship. Many were jailed.

As a result, like the Puritans before them, the Quakers looked to America for asylum. A few went to New England. But except in Rhode Island, they were greeted there with fines, whippings, and banishment; three men and a woman who refused to leave were actually put to death. Others migrated to northern Carolina, and there became the fastest-growing religious community in the region. They were soon influential in colonial politics. But many

Quakers wanted a colony of their own. As a despised sect, they had little chance of getting the necessary royal grant without the aid of someone influential at court. But fortunately for Fox and his followers, a number of wealthy and prominent men had become attracted to the faith. One of them was William Penn—the son of an admiral in the Royal Navy who was a landlord of valuable Irish estates. He had received the gentleman's education expected of a person of his standing, but he resisted his father in being attracted to untraditional religions. Converted to the doctrine of the Inner Light, the younger Penn became an evangelist for Quakerism. With George Fox, he visited the European continent and found Quakers there who, like Quakers in England, longed to emigrate to the New World. He set out to find a place for them to go.

Penn turned his attention first to New Jersey, half of which belonged to two fellow Quakers after 1764. Penn himself became an owner and proprietor of part of the colony. But in 1681, after the death of his father, he received from the king an even more valuable grant of lands. Penn had inherited his father's Irish lands and also his father's claim to a large debt from the king. Charles II, short of cash, paid the debt with a grant of territory between New York and Maryland—an area larger than England and Wales combined and which (unknown to him) contained more valuable soil and minerals than any other province of English America. Penn would have virtually total authority within the province. At the king's insistence, the territory was named Pennsylvania, after Penn's late father.

Like most proprietors, Penn wanted Pennsylvania to be profitable for him and his family. And so he set out to attract settlers from throughout Europe through informative and honest advertising in several languages. Pennsylvania soon became the best known of all the colonies among ordinary people in England and on the continent. It also became the most cosmopolitan. Settlers flocked to the province from throughout Europe, joining several hundred Swedes and Finns who had been living in a small trading colony—New Sweden—established in 1638 at the mouth of the Delaware River. But the colony was never profitable for Penn and his descendants. Indeed, Penn himself, near the end of his life, was imprisoned in England for debt and died in poverty in 1718.

Penn was more than a mere real estate promoter, however, and he sought to create in Pennsylvania what he called a holy experiment. He helped create a liberal Frame of Government with a representative assembly. In 1682, he sailed to America and personally supervised the laying out of a city between the Delaware and the Schuylkill Rivers, which he named Philadelphia ("Brotherly Love"). With its rectangular streets, like those of Charles Town, Philadelphia helped set the pattern for most later cities in America. Penn believed, as had Roger Williams, that the land belonged to the Indians, and he was careful to see that they were reimbursed for it, as well as to see that they were not debauched by the fur traders' alcohol. Indians respected Penn as an honest white man, and during his lifetime the colony had no major conflicts with the natives. More than any other English colony, Pennsylvania prospered from the outset (even if its proprietor did not), because of Penn's successful recruitment of emigrants, his thoughtful planning, and the region's mild climate and fertile soil.

But the colony was not without conflict. By the late 1690s, some residents of Pennsylvania were beginning to resist the nearly absolute power of the proprietor. Residents of the southern areas of the colony, in particular, complained that the government in Philadelphia was unresponsive to their needs. As a result, a substantial opposition emerged to challenge Penn. Pressure from these groups grew to the point that in 1701, shortly before he departed for England for the last time, Penn agreed to a Charter of Liberties for the colony. The charter established a representative assembly (consisting, alone among the English colonies, of only one house), which greatly limited the authority of the proprietor. The charter also permitted "the lower counties" of the colony to establish their own representative assembly. The three counties did so in 1703 and as a result became, in effect, a separate colony: Delaware—although until the American Revolution, it had the same governor as Pennsylvania.

The Founding of Georgia

By the mid-1680s, English settlements extended along the Atlantic Coast from New England to South Carolina. But while the European presence continued to spread steadily westward, there were no attempts to enlarge English North America farther north or south for nearly fifty years. Not until 1733 did another new colony emerge: Georgia, the last

English colony on the mainland of what would become the United States.

Georgia was unique in its origins. Its founders were a group of unpaid trustees led by General James Oglethorpe, a member of Parliament and military hero. They were interested in economic success, but they were driven primarily by military and philanthropic motives. They wanted to erect a military barrier against the Spanish lands on the southern border of English America, and they wanted to provide a refuge for the impoverished, a place where English men and women without prospects at home could begin anew.

The need for a military buffer between South Carolina and the Spanish settlements in Florida was growing urgent in the first years of the eighteenth century. There had been tensions between the English and the Spanish ever since the first settlement at Jamestown. In a 1676 treaty, Spain had recognized England's title to lands already occupied by English settlers. But conflict between the two colonizing powers continued. In 1686, a force of Indians and Creoles from Florida, directed by Spanish agents, attacked and destroyed an outlying South Carolina settlement south of the treaty line. And when hostilities broke out again between Spain and England in 1701 (known in England as Queen Anne's War and on the continent as the War of the Spanish Succession), the fighting renewed in America as well. That war ended in 1713, but another European conflict with similar repercussions for the New World was continually expected.

Oglethorpe, himself a veteran of the most recent Spanish war, was keenly aware of the military advantages of an English colony south of the Carolinas. Yet his interest in settlement rested even more on his philanthropic commitments. As head of a parliamentary committee investigating English prisons, he had grown appalled by the plight of honest debtors rotting in confinement. Such prisoners, and other poor people in danger of succumbing to a similar fate, could, he believed, become the farmer-soldiers of the new colony in America.

In 1732, King George II granted Oglethorpe and his fellow trustees control of the land between the Savannah and Altamaha Rivers. Their colonization policies reflected the vital military purposes of the colony. They limited the size of landholdings to make the settlement compact and easier to defend against Spanish and Indian attacks. They excluded Africans,

free or slave; Oglethorpe feared slave labor would produce internal revolts, and that disaffected slaves might turn to the Spanish as allies. The trustees prohibited rum (both because Oglethorpe disapproved of it on moral grounds and because the trustees feared its effects on the natives). They strictly regulated trade with the Indians, again to limit the possibility of wartime insurrection. They also excluded Catholics for fear they might collude with their coreligionists in the Spanish colonies to the south.

Oglethorpe himself led the first colonial expedition to Georgia, which built a fortified town at the mouth of the Savannah River in 1733 and later constructed additional forts south of the Altamaha. In the end, only a few debtors were released from jail and sent to Georgia. Instead, the trustees brought hundreds of impoverished tradesmen and artisans from England and Scotland and many religious refugees from Switzerland and Germany. Among the immigrants was a small group of Jews. English settlers made up a lower proportion of the European population of Georgia than of any other English colony.

The strict rules governing life in the new colony stifled its early development and ensured the failure of Oglethorpe's vision. Settlers in Georgia—many of whom were engaged in labor-intensive agriculture—needed a work force as much as those in other southern colonies. Almost from the start they began demanding the right to buy slaves. Some opposed the restrictions on the size of individual property holdings. Many resented the nearly absolute political power of Oglethorpe and the trustees. As a result, newcomers to the region generally preferred to settle in South Carolina, where there were fewer restrictive laws.

Oglethorpe (whom some residents of Georgia began calling "our perpetual dictator") at first bitterly resisted the demands of the settlers for social and political reform. Over time, however, he wearied of the conflict in the colony and grew frustrated at its failure to grow. He also suffered military disappointments, such as a 1740 assault on the Spanish outpost at St. Augustine, Florida, which ended in failure. Oglethorpe, now disillusioned with his American venture, began to loosen his grip. Even before the 1740 defeat, the trustees had removed the limitation on individual landholdings. In 1750, they removed the ban on slavery. A year later they ended the prohibition of rum and returned control of the colony to the king, who immediately permitted the summoning of a

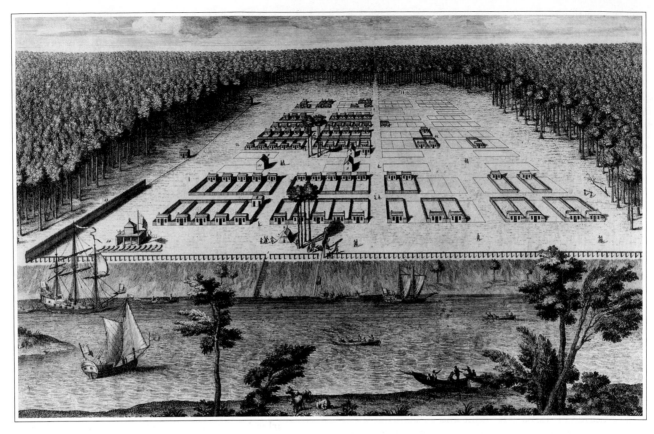

■ **SAVANNAH IN 1734**
This early view of the English settlement at Savannah by an English artist shows the intensely orderly character of Georgia in the early moments of European settlement there. As the colony grew, its residents gradually abandoned the rigid plan created by Georgia's founders. *(I.N. Phelps Stokes Collection of American Historical Prints, New York Public Library)*

representative assembly. Georgia continued to grow more slowly than the other southern colonies, but in other ways it now developed along lines roughly similar to those of South Carolina. By 1770, there were over 20,000 non-Indian residents of the colony, nearly half of them African slaves.

THE DEVELOPMENT OF EMPIRE

The English colonies in America had originated as quite separate projects, and for the most part they grew up independent of one another. But by the mid-seventeenth century, the growing commercial success of the colonial ventures was producing pressure in England for a more rational, uniform structure to the empire.

The Drive for Reorganization

Imperial reorganization, many people in England claimed, would increase the profitability of the colonies and the power of the English government to supervise them. Above all, it would contribute to the success of the mercantile system, the foundation of the English economy. Colonies would provide a market for England's manufactured goods and a source of supply for raw materials it could not produce at home, thus promoting the principal goal of the mercantile system—increasing the total wealth of the nation. But for the new possessions truly to promote mercantilist goals, England would have to exclude foreigners (as Spain had done) from its colonial trade. According to mercantilist theory, any wealth flowing to another nation could come only at the expense of England itself. Hence the

British government sought to monopolize trade relations with its colonies.

In theory, the mercantile system offered benefits to the colonies as well by providing them with a ready market for the raw materials they produced and a source for the manufactured goods they did not. But some colonial goods were not suitable for export to England, which itself produced wheat, flour, and fish and had no interest in obtaining them from America. Colonists also found it more profitable at times to trade with the Spanish, French, or Dutch even in goods that England did import. Thus, a considerable trade soon developed between the English colonies and non-English markets.

For a time, the English government made no serious efforts to restrict this challenge to the principles of mercantilism, but gradually it began passing laws to regulate colonial trade. During Oliver Cromwell's "Protectorate," in 1650 and 1651, Parliament passed laws to keep Dutch ships out of the English colonies. After the Restoration, the government of Charles II adopted three Navigation Acts designed to regulate colonial commerce even more strictly. The first of them, in 1660, closed the colonies to all trade except that carried in English ships. This law also required the colonists to export certain items, among them tobacco, only to England or English possessions. The second act, in 1663, provided that all goods being shipped from Europe to the colonies had to pass through England on the way; that would make it possible for England to tax them. The third act, in 1673, was a response to the widespread evasion of the first two laws by the colonial shippers, who frequently left port claiming to be heading for another English colony but then sailed to a foreign port. It imposed duties on the coastal trade among the English colonies, and it provided for the appointment of customs officials to enforce the Navigation Acts. These acts formed the legal basis of England's mercantile system in America for a century.

The system created by the Navigation Acts had obvious advantages for England. But it had some advantages for the colonists as well. By restricting all trade to British ships, the laws encouraged the colonists (who were themselves legally British subjects) to create an important shipbuilding industry of their own. And because the English wanted to import as many goods as possible from their own colonies (as opposed to importing them from other, rival nations), they encouraged—and at times subsidized—the development of American production of goods they needed, among them iron, silk, and lumber. Despite the bitter complaints the laws provoked in America in the late seventeenth century, and the even more bitter conflicts they would help to provoke decades later, the system of the Navigation Acts served the interests of the British and the Americans alike reasonably well through most of the eighteenth century.

The Dominion of New England

Enforcement of the Navigation Acts required not only the stationing of customs officials in America, but the establishment of an agency in England to oversee colonial affairs. In 1679, Charles II attempted to increase his control over Massachusetts (which behaved at times as if its leaders considered it an independent nation) by stripping the colony of its authority over New Hampshire and chartering a separate, royal colony there whose governor he would himself appoint. Five years later, after the Massachusetts General Court defied instructions from Parliament to enforce the Navigation Acts, Charles revoked the Massachusetts corporate charter and made it a royal colony.

Charles II's brother and successor, James II, who came to the throne in 1685, went much further. In 1686, he created a single Dominion of New England, which combined the government of Massachusetts with the governments of the rest of the New England colonies and, in 1688, with those of New York and New Jersey as well. He eliminated the existing assemblies within the new Dominion and appointed a single governor, Sir Edmund Andros, to supervise the entire region from Boston. Andros was an able administrator but a stern and tactless man; his rigid enforcement of the Navigation Acts, his brusque dismissal of the colonists' claims to the "rights of Englishmen," and his crude and arbitrary tactics made him quickly and thoroughly unpopular. He was particularly despised in Massachusetts, where he tried to strengthen the Anglican Church.

The "Glorious Revolution"

James II was not only losing friends in America; he was making powerful enemies in England by attempting to exercise autocratic control over Parliament and the courts. He was also appointing his fellow Catholics to high office, inspiring fears that he would try to reestablish Catholicism as England's official religion. By 1688, his popular support had all but vanished.

Until 1688, James's heirs were two daughters—Mary and Anne—both of whom were Protestant. But in that year the king had a son and made clear that the boy would be raised a Catholic. Some members of Parliament were so alarmed that they invited the king's daughter Mary and her husband, William of Orange, ruler of the Netherlands and Protestant champion of Europe, to assume the throne together. When William and Mary arrived in England with a small army, James II (perhaps remembering what had happened to his father, Charles I) offered no resistance and fled to France. As a result of this bloodless coup, which the English called "the Glorious Revolution," William and Mary became joint sovereigns.

When Bostonians heard of the overthrow of James II, they moved quickly to unseat his unpopular viceroy in New England. Andros managed to escape an angry mob, but he was arrested and imprisoned as he sought to flee the city dressed as a woman. The new sovereigns in England chose not to contest the toppling of Andros and quickly acquiesced in what the colonists had, in effect, already done: abolishing the Dominion of New England and restoring separate colonial governments. They did not, however, accede to all the colonists' desires. In 1691, they combined Massachusetts with Plymouth and made it a royal colony. The new charter restored the General Court, but it gave the crown the right to appoint the governor. It also replaced church membership with property ownership as the basis for voting and office-holding and required the Puritan leaders of the colony to tolerate Anglican worship.

Andros had been governing New York through a lieutenant governor, Captain Francis Nicholson, who enjoyed the support of the wealthy merchants and fur traders of the province—the same groups who had dominated the colony for years. Other, less favored colonists—farmers, mechanics, small traders, and shopkeepers—had a long accumulation of grievances against both Nicholson and his allies. The leader of the New York dissidents was Jacob Leisler, a German immigrant and a prosperous merchant who had married into a prominent Dutch family but had never won acceptance as one of the colony's ruling class. Much like Nathaniel Bacon in Virginia, the ambitious Leisler resented his exclusion and eagerly grasped the opportunity to challenge the colonial elite. In May 1689, when news of the Glorious Revolution in England and the fall of Andros in Boston reached New York, Leisler raised a militia, captured the city fort, drove Nicholson into exile, and proclaimed himself the new head of government in New York. For two years, he tried in vain to stabilize his power in the colony amid fierce factional rivalry. In 1691, when William and Mary appointed a new governor, Leisler briefly resisted this challenge to his authority. Although he soon yielded, his hesitation allowed his many political enemies to charge him with treason. He and one of his sons-in-law were hanged, drawn, and quartered. Fierce rivalry between what became known as the "Leislerians" and the "anti-Leislerians" dominated the politics of New York for many years thereafter.

In Maryland, many people erroneously assumed when they heard news of the Glorious Revolution that their proprietor, the Catholic Lord Baltimore, who was living in England, had sided with the Catholic James II and opposed William and Mary. So in 1689, an old opponent of the proprietor's government, John Coode, started a new revolt as head of an organization calling itself "An Association in Arms for the Defense of the Protestant Religion, and for Asserting the Right of King William and Queen Mary to the Province of Maryland and All the English Dominions." The insurgents drove out Lord Baltimore's officials. Through an elected convention, they chose a committee to run the government and petitioned the crown for a charter as a royal colony. In 1691, William and Mary complied, stripping the proprietor of his authority. The colonial assembly established the Church of England as the colony's official religion and forbade Catholics to hold public office, to vote, or even to practice their religion in public. Maryland became a proprietary colony again in 1715, but only after the fifth Lord Baltimore joined the Anglican Church.

As a result of the Glorious Revolution, the colonies revived their representative assemblies and successfully thwarted the plan for colonial unification. In the process, they legitimized the idea that the colonists had some rights within the empire, that the English government needed to consider their views in making policies that affected them. But the Glorious Revolution in America was not, as many

Significant Events

1607	Jamestown founded
1608	Pilgrims flee to Holland from England
1612	Tobacco production established in Virginia
1619	First African workers arrive in Virginia
	Virginia House of Burgesses meets for first time
1620	Pilgrims found Plymouth colony
1620s	English colonization accelerates in the Caribbean
1622	Powhatan Indians attack English colony in Virginia
1624	Dutch establish settlement on Manhattan Island
1629	New Hampshire and Maine established
1630	Puritans establish Massachusetts Bay colony at Boston
1634	First English settlements founded in Maryland
1635	Hartford settled in Connecticut
1636	Roger Williams founds settlement in Rhode Island
1637	Anne Hutchinson expelled from Massachusetts Bay colony
	Pequot War fought
1638	Swedes and Finns establish New Sweden on the Delaware River
1642–1649	English Civil War
1644	Last major Powhatan uprisings against English settlers in Virginia
1649	Charles I executed
1655	Civil war in Maryland temporarily unseats Catholic proprietor
1660	English Restoration: Charles II becomes king
	First Navigation Act passed
1663	Carolina colony chartered
	Second Navigation Act passed
1664	English capture New Netherland
	New Jersey chartered
1673	Third Navigation Act passed
1675–1676	King Philip's War in New England
1676	Bacon's Rebellion in Virginia
1681	William Penn receives charter for Pennsylvania
1685	James II becomes king
1686	Dominion of New England established
1688	Glorious Revolution in England: William and Mary ascend throne
1689	Glorious Revolution in America: rebellion breaks out against Andros in New England
	Leisler leads rebellion in New York
1732	Georgia chartered

Americans later came to believe, a clear demonstration of American resolve to govern itself or a clear victory for colonial self-rule. In New York and Maryland, in particular, the uprisings had more to do with local factional and religious divisions than with any larger vision of the nature of the empire. And while the insurgencies did succeed in eliminating the short-lived Dominion of New England, their ultimate results were governments that increased the crown's potential authority in many ways. As the first century of English settlement in America came to its end and as colonists celebrated their victories over arbitrary British rule, they were in fact becoming more a part of the imperial system than ever before.

✦

CONCLUSION

The English colonization of North America—which began with several unsuccessful attempts at settlement in the late sixteenth century and started its permanent life in Virginia in 1607—was part of a larger effort by England and other European nations to expand the reach of their increasingly commercial societies. Although some English settlers came to the New World to escape religious or political persecution, most came in hopes of finding opportunities to prosper by serving the needs of the emerging market economies of Europe.

In the South, civilization grew rapidly once the settlers discovered a European market for tobacco. Land was plentiful and cheap, but labor was scarce. So the early settlers relied heavily on indentured white laborers from England. Gradually, however, they turned instead to another source of labor: men and women captured in Africa, carried forcibly to the Americas, and sold into bondage. The white recruitment of African labor gradually evolved into a rigid system of absolute white ownership of blacks—slavery.

In the northern colonies, the economies and the European populations were more diverse—and composed in much greater numbers of religious refugees from England and of immigrants from other European nations as well. There an even more vigorously commercial economy developed that relied heavily on trade with Europe and the Caribbean.

By the early eighteenth century, English settlement had spread from northern New England (in what is now Maine) south into Georgia, while a substantial French empire had developed to the north in Canada. Most of the colonists considered themselves English subjects, with the same rights and privileges as those who lived in England itself. But as time went on, they began to develop social and political traditions very different from those in England—traditions that led to increasing levels of tension and conflict.

✦

FOR FURTHER REFERENCE

Suggested Readings William Cronon, *Changes in the Land: Indians, Colonists, and the Ecology of New England* (1983) examines the social and environmental effects of English settlement in colonial America. Perry Miller, *The New England Mind: From Colony to Province* (1953) is a classic exposition of the Puritan intellectual milieu. Michael Kammen, *Colonial New York* (1975) illuminates the diversity and pluralism of New York under the Dutch and the English. Edmund Morgan, *American Slavery, American Freedom* (1975) is a compelling narrative of political and social development in early Virginia. Peter Wood, *Black Majority* (1974) describes the early importance of slavery in the founding of South Carolina. Richard S. Dunn, *Sugar and Slaves: The Rise of the Planter Class in the English West Indies, 1624–1713* (1972) is important for understanding the origins of British colonial slavery.

Films (The best source for information on how to find these and other films is *Bowker's Complete Video Directory*—3 volumes.) *The Era of Colonization,* Part 2 (1996) explores European settlement from New England to Virginia, and relations between Europeans and Indians from the late sixteenth century through the Seven Years' War. *The Puritan Experience: Forsaking England, and The Puritan Experience: Making of a New World* (1975) follow the Higgins family from England to Massachusetts in the 1630s. *Jamestown: The Beginning* (1992) tells the story of Virginia's first permanent English settlement from the viewpoint of John Leydon, one of the few settlers who managed to survive the early decades of settlement. *Slavery & Freedom,* Part 3 (1996) examines the rise of slavery in the New World. *The Southern Colonies* (1987) analyzes the origins of slavery in colonial Virginia.

Internet Resources (For up-to-date URL addresses and links to these and other websites, consult the McGraw-Hill history site at *http://www.mhhe.com/socscience/history/usa/link/linktop.htm*) *Mayflower Web Pages* includes passenger lists, journals, and historical essays about the founders of Plymouth. *Plymouth-on-Web* contains Plymouth Plantation's living history museum. *APVA Jamestown Rediscovery* is an introduction to the history of Jamestown, and to the ongoing archaeological work conducted by the Association for the Preservation of Virginia Antiquities.

BIBLIOGRAPHY

General Histories   Charles M. Andrews, *The Colonial Period in American History,* 4 vols. (1934-1938). John E. Pomfret and F. M. Shumway, *Founding the American Colonies, 1583-1660* (1970). Clarence L. Ver Steeg, *The Formative Years, 1607-1763* (1964).

Jamestown   Philip L. Barbour, ed., *The Complete Works of Captain John Smith,* 3 vols. (1986); *The Three Worlds of Captain John Smith* (1964). Bradford Smith, *Captain John Smith* (1953). Alden T. Vaughn, *American Genesis* (1975).

The Chesapeake   T. H. Breen, *Tobacco Culture* (1985). T. H. Breen and Stephen Innes, *"Myne Owne Ground": Race and Freedom on Virginia's Eastern Shore, 1640-1676* (1980). Kathleen M. Brown, *Good Wives, Nasty Wenches, and Anxious Patriarchs: Gender, Race and Power in Colonial Virginia* (1996). Lois G. Carr and David W. Jordan, *Maryland's Revolution of Government, 1689-1692* (1974). Jordan Goodman, *Tobacco in History* (1993). James Horn, *Adapting to a New World: English Society in the Seventeenth Century Chesapeake* (1994). David W. Jordan, *Foundations of Representative Government in Maryland, 1632-1715* (1988). Allan Kulikoff, *Tobacco and Slaves: The Development of Southern Cultures in the Chesapeake, 1680-1800* (1986). Aubrey Land et al., *Law, Society, and Politics in Early Maryland* (1977). Suzanne Lebsock, *A Share of Honour* (1984). Gloria L. Main, *Tobacco Colony: Life in Early Maryland, 1650-1720* (1982). Richard L. Morton, *Colonial Virginia,* 2 vols. (1960). James R. Perry, *The Formation of a Society on Virginia's Eastern Shore, 1615-1655* (1990). David B. Quinn, ed., *Early Maryland in a Wider World* (1982). Darrett B. Rutman and Anita H. Rutman, *A Place in Time* (1984). Fredrick F. Siegel, *The Roots of Southern Distinctiveness: Tobacco and Society in Danville, Virginia 1780-1865* (1987). Thad Tate and David L. Ammerman, eds., *The Chesapeake in the Seventeenth Century* (1979). Wilcomb E. Washburn, *The Governor and the Rebel* (1958).

The West Indies   Hilary M. Beckles, *White Servitude and Black Slavery in Barbados, 1627-1715* (1989). Richard B. Sheridan, *Sugar and Slavery: An Economic History of the West Indies* (1973).

Plymouth and Massachusetts Bay   Bernard Bailyn, *The New England Merchants in the Seventeenth Century* (1955). David Cressy, *Coming Over: Migration and Communication Between England and New England in the Seventeenth Century* (1987). John Demos, *A Little Commonwealth* (1970); *The Unredeemed Captive: A Family Story from Early America* (1994). John Frederick Martin, *Profits in the Wilderness: Entrepreneurship and the Founding of New England Towns in the Seventeenth Century* (1991). Edmund S. Morgan, *The Puritan Dilemma: The Story of John Winthrop* (1958). Samuel Eliot Morison, *Builders of the Bay Colony* (1930). Darrett Rutman, *Winthrop's Boston* (1965). Alden T. Vaughn, *New England Frontier: Puritans and Indians* (1965). R. E. Wall, *Massachusetts Bay: The Crucial Decade, 1640-1650* (1972).

New England Puritanism   Sacvan Bercovitch, *The American Jeremiad* (1978); *The Puritan Origins of the American Self* (1975). Andrew Delbanco, *The Puritan Ordeal* (1989). Kai Erikson, *Wayward Puritans* (1966). Stephen Foster, *Their Solitary Way: The Puritan Social Ethic in the First Century of Settlement in New England* (1971); *The Long Argument: English Puritanism and the Shaping of New England Culture, 1570-1700* (1991). Edwin S. Gaustad, *Liberty of Conscience: Roger Williams in America* (1991). Philip F. Gura, *A Glimpse of Sion's Glory* (1984). David Hall, *The Faithful Shepherd* (1972); *Worlds of Wonder, Days of Judgment* (1989). Charles Hambrick-Stowe, *The Practice of Piety* (1982). J. V. James, *Colonial Rhode Island* (1975). M. J. A. Jones, *Congregational Commonwealth: Connecticut, 1636-1662* (1968). Janice Knight, *Orthodoxies in Massachusetts: Rereading American Puritanism* (1994). Paul R. Lucas, *Valley of Discord* (1976). Robert Middlekauff, *The Mathers* (1971). Perry Miller, *The New England Mind: The Seventeenth Century* (1939); *Orthodoxy in Massachusetts* (1933); *Errand into the Wilderness* (1956). Edmund S. Morgan, *Visible Saints* (1963); *The Puritan Family* (1966); *Roger Williams: The Church and the State* (1967). Norman Pettit, *The Heart Prepared: Grace and Conversion in Puritan Spiritual Life* (1989). Kenneth Silverman, *The Life and Times of Cotton Mather* (1984). W. K. B. Stoever, *A Faire and Easy Way to Heaven* (1978). Harry S. Stout, *The New England Soul* (1986). Larzer Ziff, *Puritanism in America* (1973).

The Restoration Colonies   Thomas J. Archdeacon, *New York City, 1664-1710* (1976). Van Cleaf Bachman, *Peltries or Plantations* (1969). Patricia Bonomi, *A Factious People* (1971). Edwin B. Bronner, *William Penn's Holy Experiment* (1962). Kenneth Coleman, *Colonial Georgia* (1976). Thomas J. Condon, *New York Beginnings* (1968). Mary Maples Dunn, *William Penn: Politics and Conscience* (1967). Roger Ekirch, *Poor Carolina* (1981). Christopher Hill, *The World Turned Upside*

Down (1972). James T. Lemmon, *The Best Poor Man's Country* (1972). Barry Levy, *Quakers and the American Family* (1988). H. T. Merrens, *Colonial North Carolina* (1964). Donna Merwick, *Possessing Albany, 1630-1710: The Dutch and English Experiences* (1990). Gary B. Nash, *Quakers and Politics: Pennsylvania, 1681-1726* (1968). Oliver A. Rink, *Holland on Hudson* (1986). Robert C. Ritchie, *The Duke's Province: A Study of New York Politics and Society, 1664-1691* (1977). George L. Smith, *Religion and Trade in New Netherland* (1973). Alan Tully, *William Penn's Legacy* (1977). Clarence L. Ver Steeg, *Origins of a Southern Mosaic* (1975). Robert M. Weir, *Colonial South Carolina* (1983). Peter H. Wood, *Black Majority* (1974).

The Development of Empire   Thomas C. Barrow, *Trade and Empire* (1967). Lawrence Gipson, *The British Empire Before the American Revolution,* 15 vols. (1936-1970). James Henretta, *Salutary Neglect* (1972). Richard R. Johnson, *Adjustment to Empire: The New England Colonies, 1675-1715* (1981). Michael Kammen, *Empire and Interest* (1970). Leonard Labaree, *Royal Government in America* (1964). David S. Lovejoy, *The Glorious Revolution in America* (1972). J. M. Sosin, *English America and the Revolution of 1688* (1982); *English America and the Restoration Monarchy of Charles II* (1980). I. K. Steele, *The Politics of Colonial Policy* (1968). Stephen S. Webb, *The Governors-General* (1979); *1676: The End of American Independence* (1984).

Chapter Three

SOCIETY AND CULTURE IN PROVINCIAL AMERICA

As the European and African populations of North America grew, and as the economies of the colonies began to flourish, several distinctive ways of life emerged. The new American societies differed considerably from the society that many settlers had attempted to re-create in the New World—the society of England. They differed as well from one another.

There were many reasons for the divergence between the cultures of the colonies and that of England. The physical environment was very different—vaster and less tamed. The population was more diverse as well. Beginning with the Dutch settlements in New York, the area that would become the United States was a magnet for immigrants from many lands other than England: Scotland, Ireland, the European continent. And beginning with the first importation of slaves into Virginia, English North America became the destination for thousands of forcibly transplanted Africans.

At least equally important, Europeans and Africans were interacting constantly with a native population that for many years outnumbered them. Despite the efforts of the colonists to isolate themselves from Indian society and create a culture all their own, the European and Native American worlds could not remain entirely separate.

Just as the colonies were becoming increasingly different from England, so were they different from one another. Indeed, the pattern of society in some areas of North America scarcely resembled that of other areas. Although Americans would ultimately discover that they had enough in common to join together to form a single nation, these regional differences continued to affect their society well beyond the colonial period.

☙

THE COLONIAL POPULATION

Not until long after the beginning of European colonization did Europeans and Africans in North America outnumber the native population. But after uncertain beginnings at Jamestown and Plymouth, the non-native population grew rapidly and substantially, through continued immigration and through natural increase, until by the late seventeenth century Europeans and Africans became the dominant population groups along the Atlantic coast.

■ **DETAIL FROM** *THE FISHING LADY,* **C. 1750**
This embroidered sampler depicts scenes of upper-class life in colonial New England. Its style reflects the continuing dominance of English culture and fashions in American life. *(Museum of Fine Arts, Boston)*

The Early Population

A few of the early English settlers were members of the upper classes—usually the younger sons of the lesser gentry, men who stood to inherit no land at home and aspired to establish estates for themselves in America. For the most part, however, the early English population was very unaristocratic. It included some members of the emerging middle class, businessmen who migrated to America for religious or commercial reasons, or (like John Winthrop) both. But the dominant element was English laborers. Some came to the New World independently. The religious dissenters who formed the bulk of the population of early New England, for example, were men and women of modest means who arranged their own passage, brought their families with them, and established themselves immediately on their own land.

Others came as indentured servants. At least three-fourths of the immigrants to the Chesapeake in the seventeenth century, and a majority in the southern and mid-Atlantic colonies as a whole, arrived as indentures. The system of temporary servitude in the New World developed out of existing practices in England. Young men and women bound themselves to masters for a fixed term of servitude (usually four to five years). In return they received passage to America, food, and shelter. Upon completion of their terms of service, male indentures were supposed to receive such benefits as clothing, tools, and occasionally land; in reality, however, many left service with-

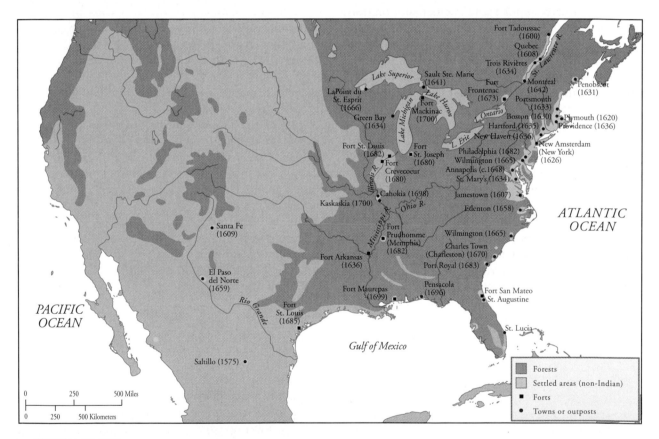

■ **AMERICA IN 1700**

In 1700, European settlement in North America remained mostly confined to the Atlantic seaboard and Gulf Coast, although Spanish and French colonists had penetrated the Rio Grande, Mississippi, and St. Lawrence Rivers as well. The French established a cordon of fortifications extending from Fort Tadoussac at the mouth of the St. Lawrence to Fort Maurepas near the mouth of the Mississippi, thereby commanding river access to the vast interior of North America.

out anything at all, unprepared and unequipped to begin earning livings on their own. Roughly one-fourth of the indentures in the Chesapeake were women, most of whom worked as domestic servants. Because men greatly outnumbered women in the region in the seventeenth century, they could reasonably expect to marry when their terms of servitude expired. Male domestic servants, however, usually had no such options.

Most indentured servants came to the colonies voluntarily, but not all. Beginning as early as 1617, the English government occasionally dumped shiploads of convicts in America to be sold into servitude, although some criminals, according to Captain John Smith, "did chuse to be hanged ere they would go thither, and were." The government also sent prisoners taken in battles with the Scots and the Irish in the 1650s, as well as other groups deemed undesirable: orphans, vagrants, paupers, and those who were "lewd and dangerous." Other involuntary immigrants were neither dangerous nor indigent but simply victims of kidnapping, or "impressment," by aggressive and unscrupulous investors and promoters.

It was not difficult to understand why the system of indentured servitude proved so appealing to those in a position to employ workers and servants in colonial America—particularly once it became clear, as it quickly did, that the Indian population could not easily be transformed into a servile work force. The indenture system provided a means of coping with the severe labor shortage in the New World. In the Chesapeake, the headright system (by which masters received additional land grants for every servant they imported) offered another incentive. For the servants themselves, the attractions were not always so clear. Those who came voluntarily often did so to escape troubles in England; others came in the hope of establishing themselves on land or in trades of their own when their terms of service expired. Yet the reality often differed sharply from the hope.

By the late seventeenth century, indentured servants and people who had begun as indentures had become one of the largest elements of the population. Some former indentures managed to establish themselves successfully as farmers, tradespeople, or artisans. Others (mostly males) found themselves without land, without employment, without families, and without prospects. A large floating population of young

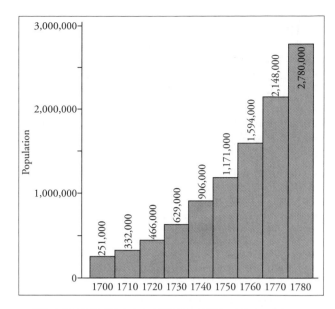

■ **THE NON-INDIAN POPULATION OF THE COLONIES, 1700–1780**
The non-Indian population of the North American colonies expanded more than tenfold between 1700 and 1780. By the eighteenth century, the ability of the colonial population to reproduce itself had replaced immigration as the single largest factor in the growth of the population, although the importance of immigration varied according to regional circumstances. The natural increase in population resulted from improved conditions of settlement and a gradual leveling of the sex ratio within the colonial population.

single men—such as those who supported Bacon's Rebellion—emerged in some areas. They traveled restlessly from place to place in search of work or land and were a potential (and at times actual) source of social unrest, particularly in the Chesapeake. Even free laborers who did find employment or land and settled down with families often did not stay put for very long. The phenomenon of families simply pulling up stakes and moving to another, more promising location every several years was one of the most prominent characteristics of the colonial population.

Indentured servitude remained an important source of population growth well into the eighteenth century, but beginning in the 1670s the flow began to decline substantially. A decrease in the English birth rate and an increase in English prosperity reduced the pressures on many men and women who might otherwise have considered emigrating. After 1700, those

■ SERVANTS FOR SALE
The *South Carolina Gazette* of Charles Town ran this
advertisement in November 1749 to announce the arrival of a
group of English "indentures"—men and women who had
accepted passage to America in exchange for their agreement to
sell themselves as servants for a fixed period of years once they
arrived. Indentures were the most common form of labor in
most of the colonies during much of the seventeenth century,
but by 1749 the system was already beginning to die out—
replaced in the South by the enslavement of Africans. The
appeal at the end of this advertisement for help in capturing
two German indentures who had run away was similar to many
such advertisements in many southern papers over the next
century appealing for help in finding runaway slaves. *(Charleston
Library Society)*

who did travel to America as indentured servants generally avoided the southern colonies, where working
conditions were arduous and prospects for advancement were slim, and settled in the mid-Atlantic
colonies, especially Pennsylvania and New York,
where they could anticipate better opportunities. In
the Chesapeake, landowners themselves began to
find the indenture system less attractive, in part because they were troubled by the instability that former servants created or threatened to create. That
was one reason for the increasing centrality of African
slavery in the southern agricultural economy.

Birth and Death

At first, new arrivals in most colonies, whatever
their background or status, could anticipate great
hardship: inadequate food, frequent epidemics, and
in an appalling number of cases, early death. Gradually, however, conditions of settlement improved
enough to allow the non-Indian population to begin
to expand. By the end of the seventeenth century,
the non-Indian population in the English colonies of
North America had grown to over a quarter of a million, of whom about 25 percent were Africans.

Although immigration remained for a time the
greatest source of population increase, the most important long-range factor in the growth of the non-
Indian colonial population was its ability to reproduce itself. Marked improvement in the reproduction rate began in New England and the mid-Atlantic
colonies in the second half of the seventeenth century, and after the 1650s natural increase became
the most important source of population growth
there. The New England population more than
quadrupled through reproduction alone in the second half of the seventeenth century. This was less a
result of unusual fertility (families in England and in
other colonies were probably equally fertile) than
of exceptional longevity. Indeed, the life spans of
residents of some areas of New England were nearly
equal to those of people in the twentieth century.
In the first generation of American-born colonists,
according to one study, men who survived infancy
lived to an average age of seventy-one, women to
seventy. The next generation's life expectancy declined somewhat—to sixty-five for men who survived infancy—but remained at least ten years
higher than the English equivalent and approximately twenty years higher than life expectancy in
the South. Scholars disagree on the reasons for
these remarkable life spans, but contributing factors
probably include the cool climate and the relatively
disease-free environment it produced, clean water
(a stark contrast to England in these years), and the
absence of large population centers that might
breed epidemics.

Conditions improved much more slowly in the
South. The mortality rates for whites in the Chesapeake region remained markedly higher than those
elsewhere until the mid-eighteenth century (and the
mortality rates for Africans improved much more

slowly still). Throughout the seventeenth century, the average life expectancy for white men in the region was just over forty years, and for white women slightly less. One in four children died in infancy, and fully half died before the age of twenty. The high death rate among adults meant that only about a third of all marriages lasted more than ten years; thus those children who survived infancy often lost one or both of their parents before reaching maturity. Widows, widowers, and orphans formed a substantial proportion of the white population of the Chesapeake. The continuing ravages of disease (particularly malaria) and the prevalence of salt-contaminated water kept the death rate high in the South; only after the settlers developed immunity to the local diseases (a slow process known as "seasoning") did life expectancy increase significantly. Population growth was substantial in the region, but largely as a result of immigration.

Natural increases in the population, wherever they occurred, were in large part a result of a steady improvement in the sex ratio through the seventeenth century. In the early years of settlement, more than three-quarters of the white population of the Chesapeake consisted of men. And even in New England, which from the beginning had attracted more families (and thus more women) than the southern colonies, 60 percent of the white inhabitants in 1650 were male. Gradually, however, more women began to arrive in the colonies; and increasing birth rates, which of course produced roughly equal numbers of males and females, contributed to shifting the sex ratio as well. Not until well into the eighteenth century did the ratio begin to match that in England (where women were a slight majority), but by the late seventeenth century, the proportion of males to females in all the colonies was becoming more balanced.

Women and Families in the Chesapeake

The importance of reproduction in the labor-scarce society of seventeenth-century America had particularly significant effects on women. The high sex ratio meant that few women remained unmarried for long. The average European woman in America married for the first time at twenty or twenty-one years of age, considerably earlier than in England; in some areas of the Chesapeake, the average bride was three to four years younger.

In the Chesapeake, the most important factor affecting women and families remained, until at least the mid-eighteenth century, the extraordinarily high mortality rate. Under those circumstances, the traditional male-centered family structure of England—by which husbands and fathers exercised firm, even dictatorial control over the lives of their wives and children—was difficult to maintain. Because so few families remained intact for long, rigid patterns of male authority were constantly undermined. Standards of sexual behavior were also more flexible in the South than they were in England or other parts of America. Because of the large numbers of indentured servants who were forbidden to marry until their terms of service expired, premarital sexual relationships were frequent. Female servants who became pregnant before the expiration of their terms could expect harsh treatment: heavy fines, whippings if no one could pay the fines, an extra year or two of service added to their contract, and the loss of their children after weaning. Bastard children were themselves bound out as indentures at a very early age. On the other hand, a pregnant woman whose term of service expired before the birth of her child or whose partner was able to buy her remaining time from her master might expect to marry quickly. Over a third of Chesapeake marriages occurred with the bride already pregnant.

Women in the Chesapeake could anticipate a life consumed with childbearing. The average wife became pregnant every two years. Those who lived long enough bore an average of eight children apiece (up to five of whom typically died in infancy or early childhood). Since childbirth was one of the most frequent causes of female death, relatively few women survived to see all their children grow to maturity.

For all the hardships women encountered in the seventeenth-century South, they also enjoyed more power and a greater level of freedom than women in other areas (or than southern women in later years). Because men were plentiful and women scarce, females had considerable latitude in choosing husbands. (They also often had no fathers or other male relatives nearby trying to control their choices.) Because women generally married at a much younger age than men, they also tended to outlive their husbands (even though female life expectancy was somewhat shorter than male). Widows were often left with several children and with responsibility for managing a farm or plantation, a circumstance of enormous hardship but one that also gave them significant economic power.

Widows seldom remained unmarried for long, however. Those who had no grown sons to work the tobacco farms and plantations had particular need for male assistance, and marriage was the surest way to secure it. Since many widows married men who were themselves widowers, complex combinations of households were frequent. With numerous stepchildren, half brothers, and half sisters living together in a single household, women often had to play the role of peacemaker—a role that may have further enhanced their authority within the family.

The high mortality rate in the seventeenth-century Chesapeake also created large numbers of orphans, many with no property and no extended family on which to rely. Much earlier than in England or in the northern American colonies, therefore, Maryland and Virginia created special courts and other institutions to protect and control orphaned children.

By the early eighteenth century, the character of the Chesapeake population was beginning to change, and with it the nature of the typical family. Life expectancy was increasing; indentured servitude was in decline; and natural reproduction was becoming the principal source of white population increase. The sex ratio was becoming more equal. One result of these changes was that life for white people in the region became less perilous and less arduous. Another result was that women lost some of the power that their small numbers had once given them. As families grew more stable, traditional patterns of male authority revived. By the mid-eighteenth century, southern families were becoming highly "patriarchal," that is dominated by the male head of the family.

Women and Families in New England

In New England, where many more immigrants arrived with family members and where death rates declined quickly, family structure was much more stable than it was in the Chesapeake and hence much more traditional. Because the sex ratio was reasonably balanced, most men could expect to marry.

■ **A BOSTON WOMAN AND HER BABY, C. 1674**
This oil portrait by an unknown Boston artist is of Elizabeth Freake and her daughter Mary. The lives of most New England women in the seventeenth century were largely consumed by childbearing and child rearing, although women also performed other important functions in the home-centered economies of the time. *(Worcester Art Museum)*

Women, however, remained in the minority; and as in the Chesapeake, they married young, began producing children early, and continued to do so well into their thirties. In contrast to the South, however, northern children were more likely to survive (the average family raised six to eight children to maturity), and families were more likely to remain intact. Fewer New England women became widows, and those who did generally lost their husbands later in life. Hence women were less often cast in roles independent of their husbands. Young women, moreover, had less control over the conditions of marriage, both because there were fewer unmarried men vying for them and because their fathers were more often alive and able to exercise control over their choice of husbands.

Among other things, increased longevity meant that, unlike in the Chesapeake (where three-fourths of all children lost at least one parent before the age of twenty-one), white parents in New England usually lived to see their children and even their grandchildren grow to maturity. Still, the lives of most New England women were nearly as consumed by childbearing and child rearing as those of women in the Chesapeake. Even women who lived into their sixties spent the vast majority of their mature years with young children in the home. The longer lives in New England also meant that parents continued to control their children far longer than did parents in the South. Although they were less likely than parents in England actually to "arrange" marriages for their children, few sons and daughters could choose spouses entirely independent of their parents' wishes. Men usually depended on their fathers for land—generally a prerequisite for beginning families of their own. Women needed dowries from their parents if they were to attract desirable husbands. Stricter parental supervision of children meant, too, that fewer women became pregnant before marriage than in the South (although even in Puritan New England the premarital pregnancy rate was not insubstantial—as high as 20 percent in some communities).

For New Englanders more than for residents of the Chesapeake, family relationships and the status of women were defined in part by religious belief. In the South, established churches were relatively weak. But in New England the Puritan church was a powerful institutional and social presence. In theory, the Puritan belief that men and women were equal before God and hence equally capable of interpreting the Bible created possibilities for women to emerge as spiritual leaders. But in reality, religious authority remained securely in the hands of men, who used it in part to reinforce a highly patriarchal view of society. The case of Anne Hutchinson—a woman who became an important religious figure only to be disciplined and expelled by the male church hierarchy—is an example of both the possibilities and the limits of female spiritual power.

Puritanism placed a high value on the family, which was not only the principal economic unit but also the principal religious unit within every community. In one sense, then, Puritan women played important roles within their families because their culture valued the position of wife and mother. At the same time, however, Puritanism reinforced the idea of nearly absolute male authority and the assumption of female weakness and inferiority. Women were expected to be modest and submissive. (Such popular girls' names as Prudence, Patience, Chastity, and Comfort suggest something about Puritan expectations of female behavior.) A wife was expected to devote herself almost entirely to serving the needs of her husband and household.

Women were of crucial importance to the New England agricultural economy. Not only did they bear and raise children who at relatively young ages became part of the work force, but they themselves were continuously engaged in tasks vital to the functioning of the farm—gardening, raising poultry, tending cattle, spinning, and weaving, as well as cooking, cleaning, and washing.

The Beginnings of Slavery in British America

Almost from the beginning of European settlement in America, there was a demand for black servants to supplement the always scarce southern labor supply. The demand grew rapidly once tobacco cultivation became a staple of the Chesapeake economy. But the supply of African laborers was limited during much of the seventeenth century, because the Atlantic slave trade did not at first serve the English colonies in America. Portuguese slavers, who had dominated the trade since the sixteenth century, shipped captive men and women from the west coast of Africa to the new European colonies in South America and the Caribbean. Gradually, however, Dutch and French navigators joined the slave trade. A substantial commerce in slaves grew up within the Americas, particularly between the Caribbean islands and the southern colonies of English America. By the late seventeenth century, the supply of black workers in North America was becoming plentiful.

As the commerce in slaves grew more extensive and more sophisticated, it also grew more horrible. Before it ended in the nineteenth century, it was responsible for the forced immigration of as many as 11 million Africans to North and South America and the Caribbean. (Until the late eighteenth century, the number of African immigrants to the Americas was higher than that of Europeans.) Native African chieftains captured members of enemy tribes in battle, tied them together in long lines, or "coffles," and sold them in the flourishing slave marts on the African coast. Then, after some haggling on the

THE ORIGINS OF SLAVERY

The debate among historians over how and why white Americans created a system of slave labor in the seventeenth century—and how and why they determined that people of African descent and no others should populate that system—has been a long and unusually heated one. At its center is the question of whether slavery was a result of white racism or helped to cause it.

In 1950, Oscar and Mary Handlin published an influential article, "Origins of the Southern Labor System," which noted that many residents of the American colonies (and of England) lived in varying degrees of "unfreedom" in the seventeenth century, although none resembling slavery as it came to be known in America. The first Africans who came to America lived for a time in conditions not very different from those of white indentured servants. But slavery came ultimately to differ substantially from other conditions of servitude. It was permanent bondage, and it passed from one generation to the next. That it emerged in America, the Handlins argued, resulted from efforts by colonial legislatures to increase the available labor force. Racism emerged to justify slavery; it did not cause slavery.

In 1959, Carl Degler became the first of a number of important historians to challenge the Handlins. In his essay "Slavery and the Genesis of American Race Prejudice," he argued that Africans had never been like other servants in the Chesapeake; "the Negro was actually never treated as an equal of the white man, servant or free." Racism was strong "long before slavery had come upon the scene." It did not result from slavery, but helped cause it. Nine years later, Winthrop D. Jordan argued similarly that white racism, not economic or legal conditions, produced slavery. In *White Over Black* (1968) and other, earlier writings, Jordan argued that Europeans had long viewed people of color—and black Africans in particular—as inferior beings appropriate for serving whites. Those attitudes migrated with white Europeans to the New World, and white racism shaped the treatment of Africans in America—and the nature of the slave labor system—from the beginning.

George Fredrickson has echoed Jordan's emphasis on the importance of racism as an independent factor reinforcing slavery; but unlike Jordan, he has argued that racism did not precede slavery. "The treatment of blacks," he wrote, "engendered a cul-

(View of Mulberry (House and Street) *by Thomas Coram. Gibbes Museum of Art/Carolina Art Association)*

tural and psycho-social racism that after a certain point took on a life of its own. . . . Racism, although the child of slavery, not only outlived its parent but grew stronger and more independent after slavery's demise."

Peter Wood's *Black Majority* (1974), a study of seventeenth-century South Carolina, moved the debate back away from racism and toward social and economic conditions. Wood demonstrated that blacks and whites often worked together on relatively equal terms in the early years of settlement. But as rice cultivation expanded, finding white laborers willing to do the arduous work became more difficult. The forcible importation of African workers, and the creation of a system of permanent bondage, was a response to a growing demand for labor and to fears among whites that without slavery a black labor force would be difficult to control. Similarly, Edmund Morgan's *American Slavery, American Freedom* (1975) argued that the southern labor system was at first relatively flexible and later grew more rigid. In colonial Virginia, he claimed, white settlers did not at first intend to create a system of permanent bondage. But as the tobacco economy grew and created a high demand for cheap labor, white

(The National Maritime Museum)

landowners began to feel uneasy about their dependence on a large group of dependent white workers, since such workers were difficult to recruit and control. Thus slavery was less a result of racism than of the desire for whites to find a reliable and stable labor force. Racism, Morgan contended, was a result of slavery, an ideology created to justify a system that had been developed to serve other needs. And David Brion Davis, in *The Problem of Slavery in the Age of Revolution* (1975), argued that while prejudice against blacks had a long history, racism as a systematic ideology was crystallized during the American Revolution—as Americans such as Thomas Jefferson struggled to explain the paradox of slavery existing in a republic committed to individual freedom.

Robin Blackburn's *The Making of New World Slavery* (1996) is perhaps the most emphatic statement of the economic underpinnings of slavery. Why, he asks, did the American colonies create a thriving slave labor system at a time when slavery had almost entirely died out in Europe? He concedes that race was a factor; Africans were "different" in appearance, culture, and religion from European colonists, and it was easier to justify enslaving them than it was to justify enslaving English, French, or Spanish workers. But the real reasons for slavery were hardheaded economic decisions by ambitious entrepreneurs, who realized very early that a slave-labor system in the labor-intensive agricultural world of the American South and the Caribbean was more profitable than a free-labor system. Slaveowning planters, he argues, not only enriched themselves; they created wealth that benefited the all of colonial society and provided significant capital for the rapidly developing economy of England. Thus, slavery served the interests of a powerful combination of groups: planters, merchants, governments, industrialists, and consumers. Race may have been a rationale for slavery, allowing planters and traders to justify to themselves the terrible human costs of the system. But the most important reason for the system was not racism, but the pursuit of profit—and the success of the system in producing it. Slavery was not, according to Blackburn, an antiquated remnant of an older world. It was, he concludes uncomfortably, a recognizably modern labor system that, however horrible, served the needs of an emerging market economy.

■ AFRICANS BOUND FOR AMERICA
Shown here are the below-deck slave quarters of a Spanish vessel en route to the West Indies. A British warship captured the slaver, and a young English naval officer (Lt. Francis Meynell) made this watercolor sketch on the spot. The Africans seen in this picture appear somewhat more comfortable than prisoners on some other slave ships, who were often chained and packed together so tightly that they had no room to stand or even sit. *(National Maritime Museum, London)*

docks between the European traders and the African suppliers, the terrified victims were packed into the dark, filthy holds of ships for the horrors of the "middle passage"—the journey to America. For weeks, sometimes even months, the black prisoners remained chained in the bowels of the slave ships. Conditions varied from one ship to another. Some captains took care to see that their potentially valuable cargo remained reasonably healthy. Others accepted the deaths of numerous Africans as inevitable and tried to cram as many as possible into their ships to ensure that enough would survive to yield a profit at journey's end. On such ships, the African prisoners were sometimes packed together in such close quarters that they were unable to stand, hardly able to breathe. Some ships supplied them with only minimal food and water. Women were often victims of rape and other sexual abuse. Those who died en

route were simply thrown overboard. Upon arrival in the New World, slaves were auctioned off to white landowners and transported, frightened and bewildered, to their new homes.

The first black laborers arrived in English North America before 1620, and as English seamen began to establish themselves in the slave trade, the flow of Africans to the colonies gradually increased. But North America was always a much less important market for Africans than were other parts of the New World, especially the Caribbean islands and Brazil, whose labor-intensive sugar economies created an especially large demand for slaves. Fewer than 5 percent of the Africans imported to the Americas went directly to the English colonies on the mainland. Most blacks who ended up in what became the United States spent time first in the West Indies. Not until the 1670s did traders start importing blacks directly from Africa to North America. Even then, however, the flow remained small for a time, mainly because a single group, the Royal African Company of England, maintained a monopoly on trade in the mainland colonies and managed as a result to keep prices high and supplies low.

A turning point in the history of the African population in North America came in the mid-1690s, when the Royal African Company's monopoly was finally broken. With the trade now opened to English and colonial merchants on a competitive basis, prices fell and the number of Africans arriving in North America rapidly increased. By the end of the century, only about one in ten of the residents of the colonies was African (about 25,000 in all). But because Africans were so heavily concentrated in a few southern colonies, they were already beginning to outnumber Europeans in some areas. The high ratio of men to women among African immigrants (there were perhaps two males to one female in most areas) retarded the natural increase of the black population. But in the Chesapeake at least, more new slaves were being born by 1700 than were being imported from Africa. In South Carolina, by contrast, the difficult conditions of rice cultivation—and the high death rates of those who worked in the rice fields— ensured that the black population would barely be able to sustain itself through natural increase until much later.

Between 1700 and 1760, the number of Africans in the colonies increased tenfold to about a quarter of a million. A relatively small number (16,000 in 1763) lived in New England; there were slightly more (29,000) in the middle colonies. The vast majority, however, continued to live in the South. By then the flow of free white laborers to that region had all but stopped, and Africans had become securely established as the basis of the southern work force.

It was not entirely clear at first that the status of black laborers in America would be fundamentally different from that of white indentured servants. In the rugged conditions of the seventeenth-century South, it was often difficult for Europeans and Africans to maintain strictly separate roles. In some areas—South Carolina, for example, where the number of African arrivals swelled more quickly than anywhere else—whites and blacks lived and worked together for a time on terms of relative equality. Some blacks were treated much like white hired servants, and some were freed after a fixed term of servitude.

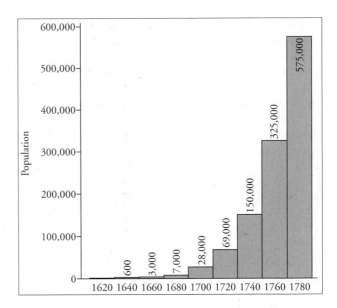

■ **THE BLACK POPULATION OF THE BRITISH COLONIES, 1620–1780**
Beginning in the 1690s, when prices for African slaves fell because of the breakup of the Royal African Company's monopoly, the number of Africans imported into British North America greatly increased. Between 1700 and 1780, the black population increased from 28,000 to 575,000 due to both importation and natural reproduction. Although the black population in 1780 comprised only about 20% of the total non-Indian population, some plantation districts in the southern colonies contained black majorities.

A few Africans themselves became landowners, and some apparently owned slaves of their own.

By the early eighteenth century, however, a rigid distinction had become established between black and white. (See "Where Historians Disagree," pp. 82–83.) Masters were contractually obliged to free white servants after a fixed term of servitude. There was no such necessity to free black workers, and the assumption slowly spread that blacks would remain in service permanently. Another incentive for making the status of Africans rigid was that the children of slaves provided white landowners with a self-perpetuating labor force.

White assumptions about the inferiority of people of color contributed to the growing rigidity of the system. Such assumptions came naturally to the English settlers. They had already defined themselves as a superior race in their relations with the native Indian population (and earlier in their relations with the Irish). The idea of subordinating a supposedly inferior race was, therefore, already established in the

English imagination by the time substantial numbers of Africans appeared in America.

In the early eighteenth century, colonial assemblies began to pass "slave codes," limiting the rights of blacks in law and ensuring almost absolute authority to white masters. One factor, and one factor only, determined whether a person was subject to the slave codes: color. In contrast to the colonial societies of Spanish America, where people of mixed race had a different (and higher) status than pure Africans, English America recognized no such distinctions. Any African ancestry was enough to classify a person as black.

Changing Sources of European Immigration

The diverse character of the early colonial population was a result of the mingling of the English with Indians and Africans. But it was also a result of substantial immigration from other parts of Europe. By the early eighteenth century, the flow of immigrants from England itself began to decline substantially—a result of better economic conditions there and of new government restrictions on emigration in the face of massive depopulation in some regions of the country. But as English immigration declined, French, German, Swiss, Irish, Welsh, Scottish, and Scandinavian immigration continued and increased.

The earliest, although not the most numerous, of these non-English European immigrants were the French Calvinists, or Huguenots. A royal proclamation, the Edict of Nantes of 1598, had allowed them to become practically a state within the state in Roman Catholic France. In 1685, however, the French government revoked the edict. Soon after that, Huguenots began leaving the country. A total of about 300,000 left France in the following decades, and a small proportion of them traveled to the English colonies in North America. Many German Protestants suffered similarly from the arbitrary religious policies of their rulers; and all Germans, Catholics as well as Protestants, suffered from the devastating wars with King Louis XIV of France (the "Sun King"). The Rhineland of southwestern Germany, the area known as the Palatinate, experienced particular hardships. Because it was close to France, its people were particularly exposed to slaughter and their farms to ruin at the hands of invaders. The un-

■ **THE PENNSYLVANIA DUTCH**
This painting of a gentleman in traditional dress was a familiar subject of Pennsylvania Dutch folk art in the eighteenth century. The Pennsylvania Dutch were, in fact, German immigrants. They were known to their neighbors in Pennsylvania as "Dutch" because that was how their native word for their nationality ("Deutsch") sounded to most English-speakers. *(Free Library of Philadelphia)*

usually cold winter of 1708–1709 dealt a final blow to the precarious economy of the region. More than 12,000 Palatinate Germans sought refuge in England, and approximately 3,000 of them soon found their way to America. They arrived in New York and tried at first to make homes in the Mohawk Valley, only to be ousted by the powerful landlords of the region. Some of the Palatines moved farther up the Mohawk, out of reach of the patroons; but most made their way to Pennsylvania, where they received a warm welcome (and where they ultimately became known to English settlers as the "Pennsylvania Dutch," a cor-

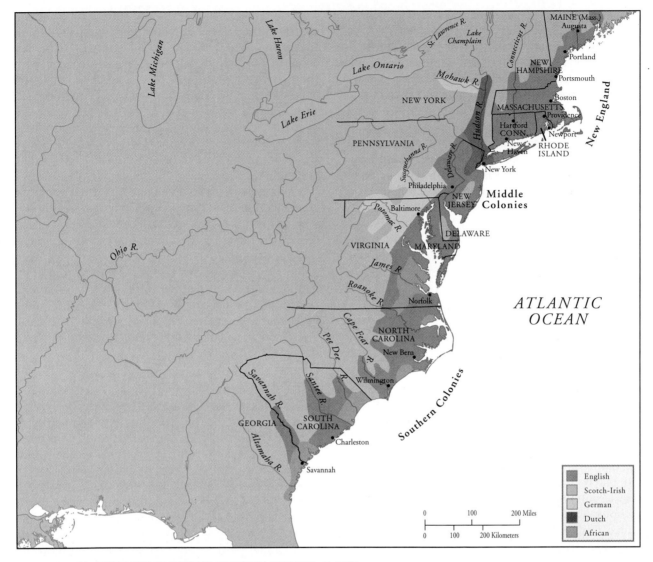

DOMINANT IMMIGRANT GROUPS IN COLONIAL AMERICA, C. 1760
Colonial America was ethnically and racially diverse. In the middle colonies, for instance, Dutch colonists remained prominent in New York City and the Hudson River valley through the eighteenth century, and German immigrants settled large regions of Pennsylvania and Maryland. African slaves were heavily concentrated in the tobacco, rice, and long-staple cotton producing regions of the southern coast, and large numbers of Scotch-Irish settlers moved into the backcountry of Virginia and the Carolinas.

ruption of their own word for "German": "Deutsch"). The Quaker colony became the most common destination for Germans, who came to America in growing numbers. (Among them were Moravians and Mennonites, with religious views similar to those of the Quakers.) Many German Protestants went to North Carolina as well, especially after the founding of New Bern in 1710 by a company of 600 German-speaking Swiss.

The most numerous of the newcomers were the Scotch-Irish—Scottish Presbyterians who had settled in northern Ireland (in the province of Ulster) in the early seventeenth century. The Ulster colonists had prospered for a time despite the barren soil and the constant, never wholly successful, struggle to suppress the Catholic natives. But in the first years of the eighteenth century, Parliament prohibited Ulster from exporting to England the woolens and other products that had become the basis of the northern Irish economy; at the same time, the English government virtually outlawed the practice of the Presbyterian religion in Ulster and insisted on conformity with the Anglican church. After 1710, moreover, the long-term leases of many Scotch-Irish expired; English landlords doubled and even tripled the rents. Thousands of tenants embarked for America.

Often coldly received at the colonial ports, most of the Scotch-Irish pushed out to the edges of European settlement. There they occupied land without much regard for who actually claimed to own it, whether absentee whites, Indians, or the colonial governments. They believed that, as one colonist said "it was against the laws of God and nature that so much land should be idle while so many Christians wanted it to labor on and to raise bread." They were as ruthless in their displacement and suppression of the Indians as they had been with the native Irish Catholics.

Immigrants from Scotland itself and from southern Ireland added other elements to the colonial population. Scottish Highlanders, some of them Roman Catholics who had been defeated in rebellions in 1715 and 1745, immigrated into several colonies, North Carolina above all. Presbyterian Lowlanders, faced in Scotland with high rents in the country and unemployment in the towns, left for America in large numbers shortly before the American Revolution. The Catholic Irish migrated steadily over a long period, and by the time of the Revolution they were almost as numerous as the Scots, although less conspicuous. Many of them had by then abandoned their Roman Catholic religion and with it much of their ethnic identity.

Continuing immigration and natural increase contributed to a rapid population growth in the colonies in the eighteenth century. In 1700, the non-Indian population of the colonies totaled less than 250,000; by 1775, it was over 2 million—a nearly tenfold increase. Throughout the colonial period, the non-Indian population nearly doubled every twenty-five years.

⌒

THE COLONIAL ECONOMIES

To those who remained in Europe, and even to some who settled in North America, the English colonies often appeared so small and isolated as to seem virtu-

ally at the end of the world. But from the beginning, almost all the English colonies were commercial ventures and were tied in crucial ways to other economies. They developed substantial trade with the native population of North America, with the French settlers to the north, and, to a lesser extent, with Spanish colonists to the south and west. And over time they developed an even more substantial trade within the growing Atlantic economy of the sixteenth and seventeenth centuries, of which they became a critical part.

American colonists engaged in a wide range of economic pursuits. But except for a few areas in the West where the small white populations subsisted largely on the fur and skin trade with the Indians, farming dominated all areas of European and African settlement throughout the seventeenth and eighteenth centuries. Some farmers engaged in simple subsistence agriculture; but whenever possible American farmers attempted to grow crops for the local, intercolonial, and export markets.

The Southern Economy

In the Chesapeake region, tobacco early established itself as the basis of the economy. A strong European demand for the crop enabled some planters to grow enormously wealthy and at times allowed the region as a whole to prosper. But production frequently exceeded demand, and as a result the price of tobacco periodically suffered severe declines. The first major bust in the tobacco economy occurred in 1640, and the boom-and-bust pattern continued throughout the colonial period and beyond. Growing more tobacco only made the problem of overproduction worse, but Chesapeake farmers never understood that. Those planters who could afford to do so expanded their landholdings, enlarged their fields, and acquired additional laborers. After 1700, tobacco plantations employing several dozen slaves or more were common.

The staple of the economies of South Carolina and Georgia was rice production. By building dams and dikes along the low-lying coastline with its many tidal rivers, farmers managed to create rice paddies that could be flooded and then drained. Rice cultivation was arduous work, performed standing knee-deep in the mud of malarial swamps under a blazing sun, surrounded by insects. It was a task so difficult and unhealthful that white laborers generally refused to per-

■ **SELLING TOBACCO**
This late-seventeenth-century label was used in the sale of American tobacco in England. The drawing depicts Virginia as a land of bright sunshine, energetic slaves, and prosperous, pipe-smoking planters. *(American Heritage)*

form it. As a result, planters in South Carolina and Georgia were even more dependent than those elsewhere on African slaves. It was not only because Africans could be compelled to perform these difficult tasks that whites found them so valuable. It was also because they were much better at the work than whites. They showed from the beginning a greater resistance than whites to malaria and other local diseases (although the impact of disease on African workers was by no means inconsiderable). And they proved more adept at performing the basic agricultural tasks required, in part because some of them had come from rice-producing regions of west Africa (a fact that has led some historians to argue that Africans were responsible for introducing rice cultivation to America in the early seventeenth century). It was also because most Africans were more accustomed to hot and humid climates such as those of the rice-growing regions than were the Europeans.

In the early 1740s, another staple crop contributed to the South Carolina economy: indigo. Eliza Lucas, a young Antiguan woman who managed her family's North American plantations, experimented with cultivating the West Indian plant (which was the source of a blue dye in great demand in Europe) on the mainland. She discovered that it could grow on the high ground of South Carolina, which was unsuitable for rice planting, and that its harvest came while the rice was still growing. Indigo became an important complement to rice and a popular import in England.

Because of the South's early dependence on large-scale cash crops, the southern colonies developed less of a commercial or industrial economy than the colonies of the North. The trading in tobacco and rice was handled largely by merchants based in London and, later, in the northern colonies. Few cities of more than modest size developed in the South. No substantial local merchant communities emerged. A pattern was established that would characterize the southern economy, and differentiate it from that of other regions, for more than two centuries.

The Northern Economy

The economies of the northern colonies—the settlements stretching from Pennsylvania into Maine—were more varied than those of their southern counterparts. In the North, as in the South, agriculture continued to dominate, but it was agriculture of a more diverse kind. In addition to farming, there gradually emerged an important commercial sector of the economy.

One reason why so many nonagricultural economic activities developed in the North was that conditions for farming were less favorable there than in the South. In most of New England, in particular, colder weather and hard, rocky soil made it difficult for colonists to develop the kind of large-scale commercial farming system that southerners were creating. Instead, most settlers cultivated relatively small areas of land, growing food, raising animals, and in general attempting to serve their own families' needs. Modest cash crops—livestock, apples, and corn—enabled New Englanders to trade for those things they could not grow or make for themselves. But most New Englanders did not produce a staple crop that could become a major export item.

Conditions for agriculture were far better in southern New England and the middle colonies, where the soil was fertile and the weather slightly more temperate. Farmers in New York, Pennsylvania, and the Connecticut River valley cultivated staple crops for sale both at home and abroad. The region was the chief supplier of wheat to much of New England and to parts of the South. In Pennsylvania, in particular, German immigrants succeeded in greatly increasing production by applying methods of intensive cultivation they had practiced in Europe. The sex ratio in the German communities was relatively even, and women commonly worked alongside men in the fields—a practice that other immigrant groups on occasion found appalling.

From time to time, entrepreneurs in New England and the middle colonies (particularly New Jersey and Pennsylvania) attempted to augment their agricultural economy with industrial enterprises. Many such ventures failed (beginning with an unsuccessful ironworks in Saugus, Massachusetts, in the mid-seventeenth century), but the colonists did manage to establish a wide range of industrial activities on a modest scale. At the simplest level, almost every colonist engaged in a certain amount of industry at home. Women, in particular, were active in spinning, weaving, making soap and candles, and other tasks basic to family life. Men engaged in carpentry. Occasionally these home industries provided families with goods they could trade or sell. Beyond these domestic efforts, craftsmen and artisans established themselves in colonial towns as cobblers, blacksmiths, riflemakers, cabinetmakers, silversmiths, and printers. In some areas, entrepreneurs harnessed the water power of the many streams and rivers to run small mills—some for grinding grain, others for processing cloth, still others for milling lumber. In several places, large-scale shipbuilding operations began to flourish.

The largest industrial enterprise anywhere in English North America was that of the German ironmaster Peter Hasenclever in northern New Jersey. Founded in 1764 with British capital, it employed several hundred laborers, many of them imported from ironworks in Germany. There were other, smaller ironmaking enterprises in every northern colony (with particular concentrations in Massachusetts, New Jersey, and Pennsylvania), and in several of the southern colonies as well. But these and other growing industries did not become the basis for the kind of explosive industrial growth that Great Britain experienced in the late eighteenth century. That was in part because of restrictions such as those imposed by the Iron Act of 1750, a measure passed by Parliament that barred the colonists from engaging in metal processing (and thus stifled the development of a steel industry in America). Similar prohibitions applied to the manufacture of woolens (the Woolen Act of 1699) and hats (the Hat Act of 1732), although Americans often disregarded such legislation. The real obstacles to industrialization, however, were more basic: an inadequate labor supply, an inadequate domestic market, and an inadequate infrastructure of transportation facilities, energy supplies, and other ne-

■ **COMMERCE IN NEW ENGLAND**
This late-eighteenth-century painting of the home, wharves, countinghouse, and fleet of a prosperous New England fisherman gives some indication of how commerce was expanding even in such relatively small places as Duxbury, Massachusetts. The owner, Joshua Winsor, was active in the mackerel and cod fishing industry. The painting—evidently an effort to celebrate Winsor's great material success and record it for posterity—was by his son-in-law, Dr. Rufus Hathaway. *(A View of Mr. Joshua Winsor's House, 1793-95. By Rufus Hathaway. Museum of American Folk Art, New York. Promised anonymous gift.)*

cessities. Americans would not overcome such obstacles until the mid-nineteenth century.

More important than manufacturing to the economy of the northern colonies were industries that exploited the natural resources of the continent. The flourishing fur trade of the first decades of settlement did not survive for long; by the mid-seventeenth century, the supply of fur-bearing animals along the Atlantic seaboard had been nearly exhausted, and the interior fur trade was largely in the hands of the Algonquins and their French allies. For the next century and more, the colonists relied instead on lumbering, which took advantage of the vast forests of the New World; mining, which exploited iron and other mineral reserves throughout the colonies; and fishing, particularly in the waters off the New England coast. These extractive industries provided what manufacturing and agriculture often failed to give the northern colonists: commodities that could be exported to England in exchange for manufactured goods. They helped, therefore, to produce the most distinctive feature of the northern economy: a thriving commercial class.

The Rise of Colonial Commerce

Perhaps the most remarkable feature of colonial commerce in the seventeenth century was that it was able to survive at all. American merchants faced such bewildering and intimidating obstacles, and lacked so many of the basic institutions of trade, that they managed to stay afloat only with great difficulty. There was, first, no commonly accepted medium of exchange. The colonies had almost no specie (gold or silver coins). They experimented at times with different forms of paper currency—tobacco certificates, for example, which were secured by tobacco stored in warehouses; or land certificates, secured by property. Such paper was not, however, acceptable as payment for any goods from abroad and it was in any case ultimately outlawed by Parliament. For many years, colonial merchants had to rely on a haphazard barter system or on crude money substitutes such as beaver skins.

A second obstacle was the near impossibility of imposing order on their trade. In the fragmented,

jerry-built commercial world of colonial America, no merchants could be certain that the goods on which their commerce relied would be produced in sufficient quantity; nor could they be certain of finding adequate markets for them. Few channels of information existed to inform traders of what they could expect in foreign ports; vessels sometimes stayed at sea for several years, journeying from one market to another, trading one commodity for another, attempting to find some way to turn a profit. Engaged in this chaotic commerce, moreover, were an enormous number of small, fiercely competitive companies, which made the problem of stabilizing the system even more acute.

Despite these and other problems, commerce in the colonies not only survived but grew. There was an elaborate coastal trade, through which the colonies did business with one another and with the West Indies, largely in such goods as rum, agricultural products, meat, and fish. The mainland colonies received sugar, molasses, and slaves from the Caribbean markets in return. There was as well an expanding transatlantic trade, which linked the North American colonies in an intricate network of commerce with England, continental Europe, and the west coast of Africa. This commerce has often

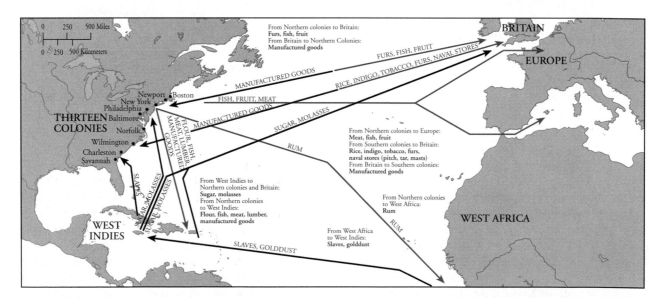

■ **OVERSEAS TRADE DURING THE COLONIAL PERIOD**
The American colonies participated in a dense network of overseas trade with the West Indies, Africa, and Europe, as well as in a lucrative intercolonial coastal trade. The American colonies exported agricultural and manufactured goods to the West Indies, agricultural goods and naval stores to Britain, and rum to Africa. In return, the colonies imported molasses and slaves from the West Indies, and manufactured goods from Britain.

been described, somewhat inaccurately, as the "triangular trade," suggesting a neat process: merchants carried rum and other goods from New England to Africa; exchanged their merchandise for slaves, whom they then transported to the West Indies (hence the term "middle passage" for the dreaded journey—it was the second of the three legs of the voyage); and then exchanged the slaves for sugar and molasses, which they shipped back to New England to be distilled into rum. In fact, the system was almost never so simple. The "triangular" trade in rum, slaves, and sugar was in fact a maze of highly diverse trade routes: between the northern and southern colonies, America and England, America and Africa, the West Indies and Europe, and other combinations.

Out of this complex and highly risky trade emerged a group of adventurous entrepreneurs who by the mid-eighteenth century were beginning to constitute a distinct merchant class. Concentrated in the port cities of the North (above all, Boston, New York, and Philadelphia), they enjoyed protection from foreign competition within the English colonies—the British Navigation Acts had excluded all non-British ships from the colonial carrying trade. They had access to a market in England for such American products as furs, timber, and ships. That did not, however, satisfy all their commercial needs. Many colonial products—fish, flour, wheat, and meat, all of which England could produce for itself—required markets altogether outside the British empire. Ignoring laws restricting colonial trade to England and its possessions, many merchants developed markets in the French, Spanish, and Dutch West Indies, where prices were often higher than in the British colonies. The profits from this commerce enabled the colonies to import the manufactured goods they needed from Europe.

In the course of the eighteenth century, the colonial commercial system began to stabilize. In some cities, the more successful merchants expanded their operations so greatly that they were able to dominate some sectors of trade and curb some of the destabilizing effects of competition. Merchants managed, as well, to make extensive contacts in the English commercial world, securing their positions in certain areas of transatlantic trade. But the commercial sector of the American economy remained open to newcomers, largely because it—and the society on which it was based—was expanding so rapidly.

PATTERNS OF SOCIETY

Although there were sharp social distinctions in the colonies, the well-defined and deeply entrenched class system of England failed to reproduce itself in America. In England, where land was scarce and the population large, the relatively small number of people who owned property had enormous power over the great majority who did not; the imbalance between land and population became a foundation of the English economy and the cornerstone of its class system. In America, the opposite was true. Land was abundant, and people were scarce. Aristocracies emerged in America, to be sure. But they tended to rely less on landownership than on control of a substantial work force, and they were generally less secure and less powerful than their English counterparts. Far more than in England, there were opportunities in America for social mobility—both up and down.

There emerged, too, new forms of community whose structure reflected less the British model than the realities of the American environment. These forms varied greatly from one region to another, but several basic—and distinctly American—types emerged.

The Plantation

The plantation defined a distinctive way of life for many white and black southerners that would survive, in varying forms, until the Civil War. The first plantations emerged in the early settlements of Virginia and Maryland, once tobacco became the economic basis of the Chesapeake.

In a few cases, plantations were of enormous size—much like some of the great estates of England. The Maryland plantation of Charles Carroll of Carrollton, reputedly the wealthiest man in the colonies, covered 40,000 acres and contained 285 slaves. On the whole, however, seventeenth-century colonial plantations were rough and relatively small estates. In the early days in Virginia, they were little more than crude clearings where landowners and indentured servants worked side by side in conditions so horrible that death was an everyday occurrence. Even in later years, when the death rate declined and the landholdings became more established, plantation work forces seldom exceeded thirty people.

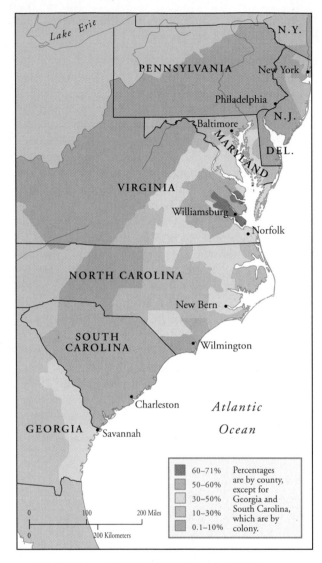

■ **BLACK POPULATION: PROPORTION OF TOTAL
POPULATION, C. 1775**

Blacks were concentrated in the plantation regions of the
southern colonies, where cotton, rice, indigo, and tobacco were
the principal crops. Although most southern farmers did not own
any slaves at all, and most slaveowners only held a few slaves,
most slaves lived on plantations that contained ten slaves or more.
On large plantations, slaves developed a distinctive society and
culture, influenced by their white masters but also partly
independent of them.

Most landowners lived in rough cabins or houses,
with their servants or slaves nearby. Relatively few
lived in anything resembling aristocratic splendor.

The economy of the plantation, like all agricultural
economies, was a precarious one. In good years, successful growers could earn great profits and expand
their operations. But since they could not control
their markets, even the largest planters were constantly at risk. When prices for their crops fell—as tobacco prices did, for example, in the 1660s—they
faced ruin.

Because plantations were often far from cities and
towns—which were, in any case, relatively few in
the South—they tended to become self-contained
communities. Residents lived in close proximity to
one another in a cluster of buildings that included
the "great house" of the planter himself (a house
that was usually, although not always, far from
great), the service buildings, the barns, and the cabins of the slaves. Wealthier planters often created
something approaching a full town on their plantations, with a school (for white children only), a
chapel, and a large population. Smaller planters lived
more modestly, but still in a relatively self-sufficient
world.

On the larger plantations, the presence of a substantial slave work force altered not only the economic, but the family lives of the planter class. Plantation mistresses, unlike the wives of small farmers,
could rely on servants to perform ordinary household chores and could thus devote more time to
their husbands and children than their counterparts
in other parts of colonial society. But there were
also frequent sexual liaisons between their husbands
or sons and black women of the slave community.
Southern women generally learned to pretend not to
notice these relationships, but they were almost certainly a source of anxiety and resentment. Black
women, naturally, had even greater cause to resent
such liaisons.

Southern society was highly stratified. Even
though the fortunes of planters could rise and fall
quickly, at any given time there were always wealthy
landowners who exercised much greater social and
economic influence than their less prosperous neighbors. Within given areas, great landowners controlled not only the lives of those who worked on
their own plantations but also the livelihoods of
small farmers who could not effectively compete
with the wealthy planters and thus depended on
them to market crops and receive credit. Small farmers, working modest plots of land with few or no
slaves to help them, formed the majority of the
southern agrarian population, but it was the planters
who dominated the southern agrarian economy.

■ **MULBERRY PLANTATION, 1770**
This painting of a rice plantation in South Carolina is unusual in placing the slave quarters in the forefront of the picture. The steep roofs of the slave cabins, which were built by the slaves themselves, reflected African architectural styles. The high roofs helped keep the cabins cool by allowing the heat to rise into the rafters. The master's house and adjacent chapel, built in more conventionally European style, is in the background. *(*View of Mulberry (House and Street) *by Thomas Coram. Gibbes Museum of Art/Carolina Art Association)*

Plantation Slavery

African slaves, of course, lived very differently. On the smaller farms with only a handful of slaves, there was not always a rigid social separation between whites and blacks. But by the mid-eighteenth century, over three-fourths of all blacks lived on plantations of at least ten slaves; nearly half lived in communities of fifty slaves or more. In these larger establishments, Africans developed a society and culture of their own—influenced by their white masters, to be sure, but also partly independent of them.

Although whites seldom encouraged formal marriages among slaves, Africans themselves developed a strong and elaborate family structure. Slaves attempted to construct nuclear families, and they managed at times to build stable households, even to work together growing their own food in gardens provided by their masters. But such efforts were in constant jeopardy. Any family member could be sold at any time to another planter, even to one in another colony. As a result, the black family evolved along lines in many ways different from its white counterpart. Africans placed special emphasis on extended kinship networks. They even created surrogate "relatives" for those who were separated entirely from their own families. They adapted themselves, in short, to difficult conditions over which they had limited control.

African workers also developed languages of their own. In South Carolina, for example, the early slaves communicated with one another in Gullah, a hybrid of English and African tongues, that not only reinforced a sense of connection with their African ancestry but enabled them to engage in conversations their white masters could not understand. There emerged, too, a distinctive slave religion, which blended Christianity with African folklore and which became a central element in the emergence of an independent black culture.

Nevertheless, slave society was subject to constant intrusions from and interaction with white society. African house servants, for example, at times lived in what was, by the standards of slavery, great luxury; but they were also isolated from their own community and under constant surveillance from whites. Black women were subject to usually unwanted sexual advances from owners and overseers and hence to bearing mulatto children, who were rarely recognized by their white fathers but who were generally accepted as members of the slave community. On some plantations, African workers received kindness and even affection from their masters and mistresses and at times displayed genuine devotion in return. On others, they encountered physical brutality and occasionally even sadism, against which they were virtually powerless.

There were occasional acts of individual resistance by slaves against masters, and at least twice during the colonial period there were actual slave rebellions. In the most important such revolt, the so-called Stono Rebellion in South Carolina in 1739, about 100 Africans rose up, seized weapons, killed several whites, and attempted to escape south to Florida. Whites quickly crushed the uprising and executed most participants. The most frequent form of resistance was simply running away, but for most slaves that provided no real solution either. There was nowhere to go.

Most slaves, male and female, worked as field hands (with women shouldering the additional burdens of cooking and child rearing). But on the larger plantations that aspired to genuine self-sufficiency, some slaves learned trades and crafts: blacksmithing, carpentry, shoemaking, spinning, weaving, sewing, midwifery, and others. These skilled craftsmen and craftswomen were at times hired out to other planters. Some set up their own establishments in towns or cities and shared their profits with their owners. On occasion, they were able to buy their freedom. There was a small free black population living in southern cities by the time of the Revolution.

The Puritan Community

A very different form of community emerged in Puritan New England, but one that was also distinctively American. The characteristic social unit in New England was not the isolated farm, but the town. Each new settlement drew up a "covenant" among its members, binding all residents together in a religious and social commitment to unity and harmony. Some such settlements consisted of people who had immigrated to America together (occasionally, entire Puritan congregations who had traveled to the New World as a group). More often, they consisted of people who had met during their voyage or after their arrival in America.

The structure of the towns reflected the spirit of the covenant. Colonists laid out a village, with houses and a meetinghouse arranged around a central pasture, or "common." They also divided up the outlying fields and woodlands of the town among the residents; the size and location of a family's field depended on the family's numbers, wealth, and social station. But wherever their lands might lie, families generally lived in the village with their neighbors close by, reinforcing the strong sense of community.

Once established, a town was generally able to run its own affairs, with little interference from the colonial government. Residents held a yearly "town meeting" to decide important questions and to choose a group of "selectmen," who governed until the next meeting. Only adult males were permitted to participate in the meeting. But even among them, important social distinctions remained, the most crucial of which was membership in the church. Only those residents who could give evidence of grace, of being among the elect (the "visible saints") confident of salvation as a result of a conversion experience, were admitted to full membership, although other residents of the town were still required to attend church services.

The English system of primogeniture—the passing of all inherited property to the firstborn son—did not take root in New England. Instead, a father divided up his lands among all his sons. His control of this inheritance was one of the most effective means of exercising power over the male members of his family. Often a son would reach his late twenties before his father would allow him to move into his own household and work his own land. Even then, sons would usually continue to live in close proximity to their fathers. Young women were generally more mobile than their brothers, since they did not stand to inherit land; their dowries and their inheritances consisted instead of movable objects (furniture, household goods, occasionally money or precious objects) and thus did not tie them to a particular place.

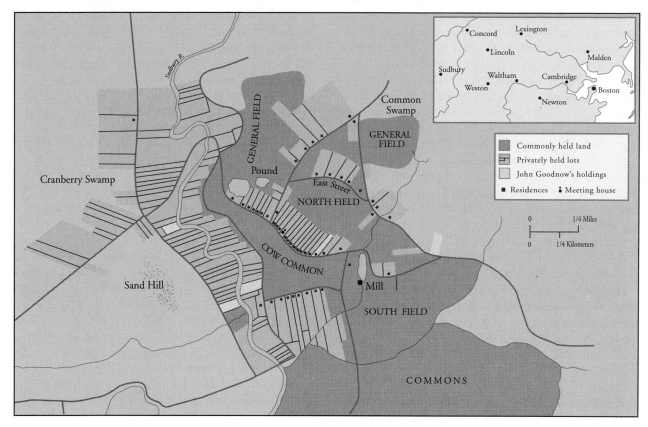

■ **THE NEW ENGLAND TOWN: SUDBURY, MASSACHUSETTS, 17TH CENTURY**
The town was the characteristic social unit of community life in New England. Houses were laid out around a central pasture called a
"common," and the villagers divided up outlying fields and woodlands according to the wealth, status, and size of the different families in
the town. No matter where their lands were, most families lived in close proximity to each other around the common. In this map, the
holdings of one Sudbury man, John Goodnow, are highlighted in yellow to illustrate the way an individual's lands could be scattered in
several different areas, far from his house.

The early Puritan community, in short, was a tightly knit society. The town as a whole was bound together by its initial covenant, by the centralized layout of the village, by the power of the church, and by the town meeting. The family was held together by the rigid patriarchal structure that limited opportunities for younger members (males in particular) to strike out on their own. Yet as the years passed and the communities grew, this communal structure experienced strains. This was partly because of the increasing commercialization of New England society. But it was also a result of other pressures that developed even within purely agricultural communities, pressures that were a result primarily of population growth.

As towns grew larger, residents tended to cultivate lands farther and farther from the community center. Some moved out of the town center to be nearer their lands and thus began to find themselves far away from the church. Some groups of outlying residents would eventually apply for permission to build a church of their own, which was usually the first step toward creation of a wholly new town. Such applications were frequently the occasion for bitter quarrels between the original townspeople and those who proposed to break away.

The practice of distributing land through the patriarchal family structure also helped create tensions in the Puritan community. In the first generations, fathers generally controlled enough land to satisfy the needs of all their sons. After several generations, however, when such lands were being subdivided for the third or fourth time, there was often too little to go around, particularly in communities surrounded by other towns, with no room to expand outward. The result was that in many communities, groups of younger residents began breaking off and moving elsewhere—at times far away—to form towns of their own where land was more plentiful.

Even within the family, economic necessity often undermined the patriarchal model to which most Puritans, in theory at least, subscribed. It was not only the sons who needed their fathers (as a source of land and wealth); fathers needed their sons, as well as their wives and daughters, as a source of labor to keep the farm and the household functioning. Thus, while in theory men had nearly dictatorial control over their wives and children, in reality relationships were more contractual, with the authority of husbands and fathers limited by economic necessity (and, of course, bonds of affection).

The Witchcraft Phenomenon

The gap between the expectation of a cohesive, united community and the reality of an increasingly diverse and fluid one was difficult for early New Englanders to accept. At times, such tensions could produce bizarre and disastrous events. One example was the widespread hysteria in the 1680s and 1690s over supposed witchcraft—the human exercise of Satanic powers—in New England.

The most famous outbreak (although by no means the only one) was in Salem, Massachusetts, where adolescent girls began to exhibit strange behavior and leveled accusations of witchcraft against several West Indian servants steeped in voodoo lore. The hysteria they produced spread throughout the town, and before it was over, hundreds of people (most of them women) were accused of witchcraft. As the crisis in Salem grew, accusations shifted from marginal women like the West Indians to more prominent and substantial people. Nineteen residents of Salem were put to death before the trials finally ended in 1692; the girls who had been the original accusers later recanted and admitted that they had made up the story.

In Salem, at least, the witchcraft crisis seems to have been in part a reflection of social strains peculiar to the community. The character of the accused and the accusers there suggests that the crisis emerged out of tensions between those who were gravitating toward the new commercial economy of the town's thriving seaport and those who remained tied to the languishing agricultural economy of the community's western areas. Residents of the outlying areas of the town resented the favored position of their eastern neighbors. Many of the accusations were made by the relatively isolated and unsuccessful members of the community against people associated with its more prosperous segments—perhaps reflecting a jealousy that could not be openly expressed in a "godly" community and that hence found other, more dangerous expressions.

■ **ACCUSATION OF A WITCH**
This nineteenth-century inlaid wood version of an earlier painting conveys something of the terror that witchcraft accusations produced in Puritan communities in the 1690s and earlier.
(Peabody Essex Museum)

But the Salem experience was only one of many. Accusations of witchcraft spread through many New England towns in the early 1690s (and indeed had emerged regularly in Puritan society for many years before). Research into the background of accused witches reveals that most were middle-aged women, often widowed, with few or no children. Many accused witches were of low social position, were often involved in domestic conflicts, had frequently been accused of other crimes, and were considered abrasive by their neighbors. Others were women who, through inheritance or enterprise, had come into possession of substantial land and property on their own and hence also challenged the gender norms of the community. Puritan society had little tolerance for "independent" women. That so many "witches" were women who were not securely lodged within a male-dominated family structure (and that many seemed openly to defy the passive, submissive norms society had created for them) suggests that tensions over gender roles played a substantial role in generating the crisis.

The witchcraft controversies were also a reflection of the highly religious character of these societies. New Englanders believed in the power of Satan and his ability to assert his power in the world. Belief in witchcraft was not a marginal superstition, rejected by the mainstream. It was a common feature of Puritan religious conviction.

Cities

To call the commercial centers that emerged along the Atlantic coast in the eighteenth century "cities" would be to strain the modern definition of that word. Even the largest colonial community was scarcely bigger than a modern small town. Yet by the standards of the eighteenth century, cities did indeed exist in America. In the 1770s the two largest ports—Philadelphia and New York—had populations of 28,000 and 25,000, respectively, which made them larger than most English urban centers. Boston (16,000), Charles Town (later Charleston), South Carolina (12,000), and Newport, Rhode Island (11,000), were also substantial communities by the standards of the day.

Colonial cities served as trading centers for the farmers of their regions and as marts for international trade. Their leaders were generally merchants who had acquired substantial estates. Disparities of wealth were features of almost all communities in America, but in cities they seemed particularly glaring. Wealthy merchants and their families moved along crowded streets dressed in fine imported clothes, often riding in fancy carriages, coming in and out of large houses with staffs of servants. As time went on, these wealthy elites (like planter elites in the South) began to define their status in their community by the luxuries they were able to gather and the elegance they were able to display in their homes, their clothing, and their social activities.

Moving beside them were the numerous minor tradesmen, workers, and indigents, dressed simply and living in crowded and often filthy conditions. More than in any other area of colonial life (except, of course, in the relationship between masters and slaves), social distinctions were real and visible in urban areas.

There were other distinctive features of urban life as well. Cities were the centers of much of what industry there was in the colonies, such as ironworks and distilleries for turning imported molasses into exportable rum. They were the locations of the most advanced schools and the most sophisticated cultural activities, and of shops where imported goods could be bought. In addition, they were communities with peculiarly urban social problems: crime, vice, pollution, epidemics, traffic. Unlike smaller towns, cities were required to establish elaborate governments. They set up constables' offices and fire departments. They developed systems for supporting the urban poor, whose numbers grew steadily and became especially large in times of economic crisis.

Cities were also particularly vulnerable to fluctuations in trade. When a market for a particular product became glutted and prices fell, the effects on residents of a town—merchants and those whose livelihoods derived from commerce—could be severe. In the countryside, the impact was generally more muted. Finally, and of particular importance for the political future of the colonies, cities became places where new ideas could circulate and be discussed. Because there were printers, it was possible to have regular newspapers. Books and other publications from abroad introduced new intellectual influences. And the taverns and coffeehouses of cities provided forums in which people could gather and debate the issues of the day. It was not surprising that when the revolutionary crisis began to build in the 1760s and 1770s, it was first visible in the cities.

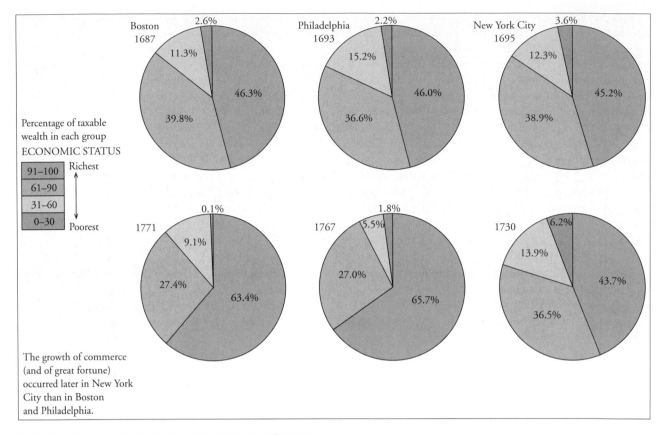

■ **WEALTH DISTRIBUTION IN COLONIAL CITIES, 1687–1771**
In Boston and Philadelphia, the rise of urban commerce in the early eighteenth century produced considerable new wealth, but it also increased economic inequality. In New York, by contrast, the distribution of wealth actually became more equal between 1695 and 1730, in part because of the breakup of some of the great Dutch estates after New York fell to the British. Disparities of wealth within the free population were everywhere more evident in colonial cities than in the countryside.

THE COLONIAL MIND

Two powerful forces were competing in American intellectual life in the eighteenth century. One was the traditional outlook of the sixteenth and seventeenth centuries, with its emphasis on a personal God, intimately involved with the world, keeping watch over individual lives. The other was the new spirit of the Enlightenment, a movement that was sweeping both Europe and America, which stressed the importance of science and human reason. The old views supported such phenomena as the belief in witchcraft, and they placed great value on a stern moral code in which intellect was less important than faith. The Enlightenment, by contrast, suggested that people had substantial control over their own lives and the course of their societies, that the world could be explained and therefore could be structured along rational scientific lines. Much of the intellectual climate of colonial America was shaped by the tension between these two impulses.

The Pattern of Religions

American colonists brought their religions with them from abroad. But like so many other imported institutions, religion took on a new and distinctive pattern in the New World. In part, this was because there were so many different faiths. America was an ecclesiastical patchwork. Toleration of religious diversity, although limited by later standards, flourished to a degree unmatched in any European nation, not because the colonists deliberately sought to produce it, but because conditions virtually required it.

■ BALTIMORE IN 1752
Baltimore remained a small and relatively quiet port even two decades after its founding in 1729. Most Maryland tobacco growers shipped their crops from their own wharves along the river and had little need for a central harbor. *(Maryland Historical Society, Baltimore)*

The experience of the Church of England illustrated how difficult the establishment of a common religion would be in the colonies. Anglicanism was established by law as the official faith in Virginia, Maryland, New York, the Carolinas, and Georgia. In these colonies everyone, regardless of belief or affiliation, was supposed to be taxed for the support of the church. But except in Virginia and Maryland, the Church of England could not protect its position as the established church except in a few localities. To strengthen Anglicanism, in America and elsewhere, the Church of England set up the Society for the Propagation of the Gospel in Foreign Parts (SPG) in 1701; but SPG missionaries never succeeded in making Anglicanism a dominant force in America.

Even in areas where a single faith had once predominated, religious diversity gradually became the norm. In New England, for example, Puritans had believed themselves all to be part of a single faith: Calvinism. In the course of the eighteenth century, however, there was a growing tendency for different congregations to affiliate with different denominations. Some became Congregationalists; others identi-

fied themselves as Presbyterians. In belief, these two groups were largely (although not entirely) the same, but they differed in ecclesiastical organization. Each Congregationalist church was virtually autonomous; the Presbyterians had a more highly centralized government. Difference in church structure helped reinforce other differences in religious practice and even in belief.

In parts of New York and New Jersey, Dutch settlers established their own Calvinist denomination, Dutch Reformed, which survived long after the colonies became part of the British Empire. The American Baptists (of whom Roger Williams is considered the first) were also originally Calvinist in their theology, but gradually diverged from the orthodox teachings of the faith. In Rhode Island and in other colonies, a bewildering variety of Baptist sects sprang up. They had in common a belief that infant baptism did not suffice and that rebaptism, usually by total immersion, was necessary when believers reached maturity. Although some Baptists remained Calvinists, believers in predestination, others came to believe in salvation by free will.

Protestants extended toleration to one another more readily than they did to Roman Catholics. To strict Puritans, the pope seemed no less than the Antichrist. They viewed their Catholic neighbors across the border in New France (Canada) not only as commercial and military rivals, but as agents of the devil bent on frustrating the divine mission of the Puritans in New England. In most of the English colonies, however, Roman Catholics were too small a minority to cause serious conflict. They were most numerous in Maryland, and even there they numbered no more than 3,000. Ironically, they suffered their worst persecution in that colony, which had been founded as a refuge for them and had been distinguished by its Toleration Act of 1649. According to Maryland laws passed after 1691, following the overthrow of the original proprietors, Catholics not only were deprived of political rights but also were forbidden to hold religious services except in private houses. In the American Southwest, still part of the Spanish Empire, Catholicism was considerably stronger, but the small group of Spanish settlers had only partial success in converting the Indian majority to their faith.

Jews in provincial America totaled no more than about 2,000 at any time. The largest community lived in New York City. Smaller groups settled in Newport and Charleston, and there were scattered Jewish families in all the colonies. Nowhere could they vote and hold office. Only in Rhode Island could they practice their religion openly. Such restrictions survived in some communities until after the American Revolution.

Substantial numbers of Americans embraced religious traditions that were not part of the Judeo-Christian tradition. Although some Indians converted to Christianity, most clung to traditional tribal faiths, which deified various elements of nature and placed great importance on tradition and genealogy. African slaves brought their native religious traditions with them to America, traditions similarly rooted in a sensitivity to nature and lineage; and while most African Americans eventually converted to Christianity, elements of African faith remained part of their religious life for generations.

The Decline of Piety

By the beginning of the eighteenth century, some Americans were troubled by the apparent decline in religious piety in their society. In part, this was a re-sult of the rise of denominationalism. With so many diverse sects existing side by side, some people were tempted to doubt whether any particular denomination, even their own, possessed a monopoly on truth and grace.

More important, however, were other changes in colonial society. The populations in many colonies were moving westward, and the wide scattering of settlements caused many communities to lose touch with organized religion. Most of all, colonial culture was growing increasingly secular and materialistic—a result in large part of the rising commercial life in many areas of the New World. In Connecticut, for example, the increased demand for land created great pressure for new sources of credit. The average personal indebtedness more than tripled in the last decades of the seventeenth century; to many Puritans, in particular, debt had long been a sign of sinfulness and sloth. There was also an increase in lawsuits and other signs of decaying communal spirit. New scientific ideas and Enlightenment thought arrived from Europe. They caused at least some colonists to adopt a more rational and skeptical view of the world. They caused others to bemoan the decline of the religious character of their society.

Concerns about excessive worldliness and declining piety surfaced as early as the 1660s in New England. The Puritan oligarchy expressed these concerns by warning of a deterioration in the power of the church. As the first generation of American Puritans died, the number of church members rapidly declined, for few of the second generation seemed to harbor enough religious passion to demonstrate the "saving grace" that was a prerequisite for membership. The children of "saints" had generally been baptized and had attended services, but in the absence of a true "conversion experience," many had never become full members of the church. When these people began to have children of their own, the clergy was faced with a dilemma. Should the infants of these unconverted churchgoers be baptized? In 1662, a conference of ministers attempted to solve the problem by instituting the Halfway Covenant, which gave people of the third and later generations the right to be baptized but not the right to partake of communion or vote in church affairs.

As time passed, this carefully drawn distinction between full and half members was often forgotten, and in many communities the church came to include the families of all who could take part in colonial politics as voters and officeholders. Qualification for membership in the church, in other words, became largely secular. Orthodox Puritans, however, continued to oppose these changes. Sabbath after Sabbath, ministers preached sermons of despair (known as "jeremiads"), deploring the signs of waning piety. "Truly so it is," one minister lamented in 1674, "the very heart of New England is changed and exceedingly corrupted with the sins of the times." Only in relative terms was religious piety actually declining in New England. By the standards of later eras (or by the standards of other societies of the seventeenth century), the Puritan faith remained remarkably strong. So did the communal character of the New England town and the patriarchal character of the Puritan family. But New Englanders measured their faith by their own standards, not by those of other times and places, and to them the "declension" of religious piety was a serious problem.

The Great Awakening

By the early eighteenth century, such concerns were emerging in other regions and among members of other faiths. Everywhere, colonists were coming to believe, religious piety was in decline and opportunities for spiritual regeneration were dwindling. The result was the first great American revival.

It was known as the Great Awakening. Although the first stirrings (or "freshenings") began in some places early in the century, the Great Awakening began in earnest in the 1730s and reached its climax in the 1740s. Then, for a time, a new spirit of religious fervor seemed to reverse the trend away from piety for thousands of Americans.

That the movement was not purely religious in origin is suggested by the identity of those who responded most frequently to it: residents of areas where social and economic tensions were greatest; women (who constituted the majority of converts) frustrated by their social and familial subjugation; younger sons of the third or fourth generation of settlers—those who stood to inherit the least land and who thus faced the most uncertain futures. The social origins of the revival were also evident in much of its rhetoric, which emphasized the potential of every person to break away from the constraints of the past and start anew in his or her relationship to God (and, implicitly, to the world). But social tensions were not alone responsible for the revival. At

■ **GEORGE WHITEFIELD**
Whitefield succeeded John Wesley as leader of the Calvinistic Methodists in Oxford, England. Like Wesley, he was a major force in promoting religious revivalism in both England and America. He made his first missionary journey to the New World in 1738 and returned in the mid-1740s for a celebrated journey through the colonies that helped spark the Great Awakening. *(National Portrait Gallery, London)*

work, too, was a powerful desire among people of all backgrounds for an intense religious experience.

Wandering exhorters from England did much to stimulate the revivalistic spirit. John and Charles Wesley, the founders of Methodism (which had begun as a reform movement within the Church of England), visited Georgia and other colonies in the 1730s with the intention of revitalizing religion and converting Indians and blacks. George Whitefield, a powerful open-air preacher from England and for a time an associate of the Wesleys, made several evangelizing tours through the colonies. Everywhere he went, Whitefield drew tremendous crowds. He understood that many of the men and women who flocked to hear him were torn between their desire to remain loyal to their faith and their equally strong desire to prosper in the secular world. Whitefield offered them relief from their guilt by telling them that they could atone for their sins by admitting them directly to God; that they need not rely on the established clergy to help them gain forgiveness. The promise of exoneration from sin, therefore, joined the promise that individuals could create their own relationships with God, that they could experience faith outside the traditional church.

The Wesleys, Whitefield, and other evangelizers from abroad were ultimately less important than the colonial ministers themselves. Theodore Frelinghuysen, of the Dutch Reformed Church, and Gilbert Tennent, a Presbyterian, were important native voices of evangelism. But the outstanding preacher of the Great Awakening was the New England Congregationalist Jonathan Edwards—a deeply orthodox Puritan but also one of the most original theologians in American history. From his pulpit in Northampton, Massachusetts, Edwards attacked the new doctrines of easy salvation for all. He preached anew the traditional Puritan ideas of the absolute sovereignty of God, the depravity of man, predestination, the necessity of experiencing a sense of election, and salvation by God's grace alone. His vivid descriptions of hell could terrify his listeners. Day after day agonized sinners crowded his parsonage to seek his aid; at least one committed suicide in despair at his inability to experience grace.

The Great Awakening spread over the colonies like a religious epidemic. It created a sharp division in the established denominations between a large and rapidly growing group of revivalistic "New Light" ministers and the traditional "Old Lights." It weakened the authority of established churches and denominations, created increasing hostility to the traditional clergy, and ultimately helped make American religion more open and diverse than it had been before. But it also strengthened the hold of orthodox Calvinist belief on many Americans.

The Enlightenment

The Great Awakening caused one great upheaval in the culture of the colonies. The Enlightenment, a very different—and in many ways competing—phenomenon, caused another. It began in Europe, but it came to America in force in the early eighteenth century, partly as a reaction to the Great Awakening.

The Enlightenment was to a large degree the product of some of the great scientific and intellectual discoveries in Europe in the seventeenth century. As scientists and other thinkers discovered natural laws that they believed regulated the workings of nature, they came to celebrate the power of human reason and scientific inquiry. Enlightenment thinkers argued that reason, not just faith, could create progress and advance knowledge. They argued that humans had a moral sense on which they could rely to tell the difference between right and wrong; that they did not need always to turn to God for guidance in making decisions. They insisted that men and women could, through the power of their own reason, move civilization to ever greater heights.

In celebrating reason, the Enlightenment slowly helped undermine the power of traditional authority—something the Great Awakening did as well. But unlike the Great Awakening, the Enlightenment encouraged men and women to look to themselves—not to God—for guidance as to how to live their lives and to shape society. Enlightenment thought encouraged a new emphasis on education. It helped create a heightened interest in politics and government (for through governments, the believers in reason argued, society had its best chance of bettering itself).

In the early seventeenth century, Enlightenment ideas in America were largely borrowed from Europe—and from such earlier giants as Francis Bacon and John Locke of England, Baruch Spinoza of Amsterdam, and René Descartes of France. Few Americans had yet made important contributions of their own to the new age of science and reason. Later, however, such Americans as Benjamin Franklin, Thomas Jefferson, Thomas Paine, and James Madison made their own vital contributions to the Enlightenment tradition.

Education

Even before Enlightenment ideas became common in America, colonists had placed a high value on education, despite the difficulties they confronted in gaining access to it. Some families tried to teach their children to read and write at home, although the heavy burden of work in most agricultural households limited the time available for schooling. In Massachusetts, a 1647 law required every town to support a public school, and while many communities failed to comply, a modest network of educational establishments emerged as a result. Elsewhere, the Quakers and other sects operated church

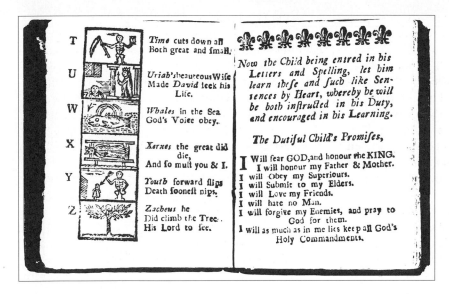

T

U   *Time* cuts down all
      Both great and small.

W   *Uriah's* beauteous Wife
      Made *David* seek his
      Life.

X   *Whales* in the Sea
      God's Voice obey.

Y   *Xerxes* the great did
      die,
      And so must you & I.

Z   *Youth* forward slips
      Death soonest nips.

      Zacheus he
      Did climb the Tree
      His Lord to see.

*Now the Child being entred in his
Letters and Spelling, let him
learn these and such like Sentences by Heart, whereby he will
be both instructed in his Duty,
and encouraged in his Learning.*

The Dutiful Child's Promises,

I Will fear GOD, and honour the KING.
  I will honour my Father & Mother.
I will Obey my Superiours.
I will Submit to my Elders.
I will Love my Friends.
I will hate no Man.
I will forgive my Enemies, and pray to
      God for them.
I will as much as in me lies keep all God's
      Holy Commandments.

■ A "DAME SCHOOL" PRIMER
More than the residents of any other region of North America (and far more than those of most of Europe), the New England colonists strove to educate their children and achieved perhaps the highest level of literacy in the world. Throughout the region, young children attended institutions known as "dame schools" (because the teachers were almost always women) and learned from primers like this one. Puritan education emphasized both basic skills (the alphabet and reading) and moral and religious precepts, as this sample page suggests.
(American Antiquarian Society)

schools. And in some communities, widows or un-married women conducted "dame schools" by holding private classes in their homes. In cities, master craftsmen set up evening schools for their apprentices; at least a hundred such schools appeared between 1723 and 1770.

Only a relatively small number of children received education beyond the primary level; but white male Americans, at least, achieved a high degree of literacy. By the time of the Revolution, well over half of all white men could read and write, a rate substantially higher than in most European countries. The large number of colonists who could read helped create a market for the first widely circulated publications in America other than the Bible: almanacs. (See pp. 106–107.) The literacy rate for women lagged behind that of men until the nineteenth century; and while opportunities for further education were scarce for males, they were almost nonexistent for females. Nevertheless, in their early years colonial girls often received the same home-based education as boys, and their literacy rate too was substantially higher than that of their European counterparts. African slaves had virtually no access to education. Occasionally a master or mistress would teach slave children to read and write, but they had few real incentives to do so. Indeed, as the slave system became more firmly entrenched, strong social (and ultimately legal) sanctions developed to discourage any efforts to promote black literacy, lest it encourage slaves to question their station. Indians, too, remained largely outside the white educational system—to a large degree by choice; most

tribes preferred to educate their children in their own way. But some white missionaries and philanthropists established schools for Native Americans and helped create a small but significant population of Indians literate in spoken and written English.

Nowhere was the intermingling of the influences of traditional religiosity and the new spirit of the Enlightenment clearer than in the colleges and universities that grew up in colonial America. Of the six colleges in operation by 1763, all but two were founded by religious groups primarily for the training of preachers. Yet in almost all, the influences of the new scientific, rational approach to knowledge could be felt. Harvard, the first American college, was established in 1636 by the General Court of Massachusetts at the behest of Puritan theologians, who wanted to create a training center for ministers. Two years later, in 1638, instruction began in Cambridge. The college was named for a Charlestown minister, John Harvard, who had died and left his library and half his estate to the college. Decades later, in 1693, William and Mary College (named for the English king and queen) was established in Williamsburg, Virginia, by Anglicans; like Harvard, it was conceived as an academy to train clergymen. In 1701, conservative Congregationalists, dissatisfied with what they considered the growing religious liberalism of Harvard, founded Yale (named for one of its first benefactors, Elihu Yale) in New Haven, Connecticut. Out of the Great Awakening emerged the College of New Jersey, founded in 1746 and known later as Princeton (after the town in which it is located). One of its first presidents was Jonathan Edwards.

COLONIAL ALMANACS

Books were scarce and expensive in colonial America, and many families owned only one: the Bible. But starting very early in the life of the English colonies, men and women had another important source of information: almanacs, the most popular nonreligious literature in early America.

Almanacs had been popular in Europe since at least the mid-sixteenth century. They first appeared in America in 1638 or 1639 when printers in Cambridge, Massachusetts began publishing the *Philomath Almanac,* which combined an elaborate calendar of religious holidays with information about astronomy, astrology, and, as time went on, other popular interests. By the 1680s, the *Farmer's Almanac* began to rival the *Philomath.* It was a heavily illustrated publication that set a pattern for the future by adding medical advice, practical wisdom, navigational information, and humor. It also indulged in the European custom of prognostication; through a combination of superstition, popular folklore, and astronomical (and astrological) devices, it predicted weather patterns throughout the year, crop yields, and many other things. Almanac predictions were notoriously unreliable; but in the absence of any better alternatives, many people relied on them nevertheless.

By 1700, there were dozens, perhaps hundreds, of almanacs circulating throughout the colonies and even in the sparsely settled lands to the west and north. The most popular almanacs sold tens of thousands of copies every year. Most families had at least one, and many had several. "It is easy to prove," one almanac writer claimed in the mid-eighteenth century, "that no book we read (except the Bible) is so much valued and so serviceable to the community."

America was a multilingual society, and although most almanacs were in English, some appeared in French, Dutch, Hebrew, Norwegian, Spanish, German, and various Indian languages. For five years just after the Revolution, Benjamin Banneker of Maryland was the only African-American almanac writer, pub-

■ **POOR RICHARD'S ALMANACK**

This page from a 1757 edition of *Poor Richard's Almanack* illustrates the wide range of material that almanacs presented to their readers—an uplifting poem, a calendar of holidays and weather predictions, and such scattered pieces of advice and wisdom as "A rich rogue is like a fat hog, who never does good till as dead as a log." *(New York Public Library)*

lishing a book that occasionally included harsh commentary on slavery and the slave trade.

The best-known almanac in the colonies in the years before the American Revolution was published by Benjamin Franklin, a printer's son who ran away from an apprenticeship in his older brother's print shop in Rhode Island and eventually settled in Philadelphia. There, from 1732 to 1758, he published *Poor Richard's Almanac* under the pseudonym Richard Saunders. "I endeavor'd to make it both entertaining and useful," Franklin later wrote in his *Autobiography.* "And observing that it was generally read, . . . I consider'd it as a proper vehicle for conveying instruction among the common people, who bought scarcely any other books." In issue after issue, Franklin accompanied his calendars, astronomical information, and other standard almanac fare with "proverbial sentences, chiefly such as inculcated industry and frugality." One of his favorite proverbs, which he said illustrated how difficult it was for a poor man always to act honestly, was "It is hard for an empty sack to stand upright." Poor Richard's many sayings became among the most familiar passages in America.

Almanacs were virtually the only widely-read publications in America that contained popular humor, and they are one of the best sources today for understanding what early Americans considered funny. Not unlike later generations, they delighted in humor that ridiculed the high and mighty (aristocrats, lawyers, clergymen, politicians), that made fun of relationships between men and women, and that expressed stereotypes about racial and ethnic groups. In the 1760s and 1770s, almanac humor was often used to disguise political ideas, in the way it ridiculed British officials and American Tories. During the war itself, humorous anecdotes about military officers and political leaders reflected the uneasy views of Americans about the long and difficult struggle.

During and after the Revolution, much almanac humor consisted of admiring anecdotes about the man who was by then perhaps the most famous and beloved man in America—Poor Richard himself, Benjamin Franklin. Much less reverential, and probably funnier to readers, was the often ribald ethnic and racial humor in many almanacs. In *Beer's Almanac* of 1801, an Irishman boasted that he had owned a large

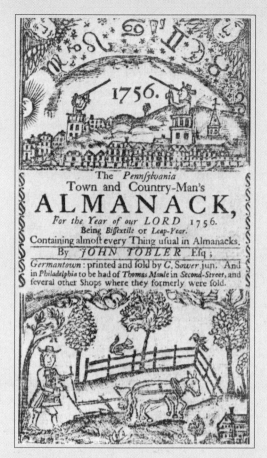

■ **TOWN AND COUNTRY-MAN'S ALMANACK**
As the population of colonial cities and towns grew, almanacs—originally targetted mainly at farmers—began to make explicit appeal to townspeople as well. *(Sinclair Hamilton Collection, Princeton, New Jersey)*

estate in Ireland before leaving for America. Why, he was asked, had he left it to come to the United States? "Ah," he replied, "It was indeed under a small encumbrance; for another man's land lay right a top of it."

Almanacs remained enormously popular throughout the nineteenth century, and some are still published today. But they had their greatest influence in the early years of European settlement when, for thousands of Americans, they were virtually the only source of printed information people had. "A good Almanac," the printer Isaac Briggs wrote in 1798, in a preface to one of his own, "is, like *iron,* far more valuable (although much less valued) than *gold,* if we estimate its value by its *absolute* usefulness to the common purposes of life."

■ **THE MAGNETIC DISPENSARY**
In this 1790 painting, artist Samuel Collings caricatured the popular enthusiasm that Benjamin Franklin and others had produced for scientific experiments. The men and women shown here are rubbing iron rods with silk cloth to produce static electricity. A popular pastime was to place the charged rods over people's heads to watch their hair stand on end. *(Library Company of Philadelphia)*

Despite the religious basis of these colleges, students at most of them could derive something of a liberal education from the curricula, which included not only theology, but logic, ethics, physics, geometry, astronomy, rhetoric, Latin, Hebrew, and Greek. From the beginning, Harvard attempted not only to provide an educated ministry but also to "advance learning and perpetuate it to posterity." King's College, founded in New York in 1754 and later renamed Columbia, was even more devoted to the spread of secular knowledge. It had no theological faculty and was interdenominational from the start. The Academy and College of Philadelphia, which became the University of Pennsylvania, was a completely secular institution, founded in 1755 by a group of laymen under the inspiration of Benjamin Franklin. It offered courses in utilitarian subjects—mechanics, chemistry, agriculture, government, commerce, and modern languages—as well as in the liberal arts.

The Allure of Science

The clearest indication of the spreading influence of the Enlightenment in America was an increasing interest in scientific knowledge. Most of the early colleges established chairs in the natural sciences and introduced some of the advanced scientific theories of Europe, including Copernican astronomy and Newtonian physics, to their students. But the most vigorous promotion of science in these years occurred outside the colleges, through the private efforts of amateurs and the activities of scientific societies. Leading merchants, planters, and even theologians became corresponding members of the Royal Society of London, the leading English scientific organization. Benjamin Franklin, the most cele-brated amateur scientist in America, won interna-tional fame through his experiments with electric-ity (and most notably through his 1752 demonstration, using a kite, that lightning and elec-tricity were the same).

The high value that influential Americans were beginning to place on scientific knowledge was clearly demonstrated by the most daring and contro-versial scientific experiment of the eighteenth cen-tury: inoculation against smallpox. The Puritan the-ologian Cotton Mather had learned of experiments in England by which people had been deliberately infected with mild cases of smallpox in order to im-munize them against the deadly disease. Despite strong opposition from many of his neighbors, he urged inoculation on his fellow Bostonians during an epidemic in the 1720s. The results confirmed the ef-fectiveness of the technique. Other theologians (in-cluding Jonathan Edwards) took up the cause, along with many physicians. By the mid-eighteenth cen-tury, inoculation had become a common medical procedure in America.

■ **PUNISHMENT IN NEW ENGLAND**
New England communities prescribed a wide range of punishments for misconduct and crime in the seventeenth and eighteenth centuries. Among the more common punishments were public humiliations—placing offenders in stocks, forcing them to wear badges of shame, or, as in this woodcut, publicly ducking them in a stream or pond to create both discomfort and embarrassment. (© *The British Museum*)

Concepts of Law and Politics

In seventeenth- and eighteenth-century law and poli-tics, as in other parts of their lives, Americans of Eu-ropean descent believed that they were re-creating in the New World the practices and institutions of the Old. But as in other areas, they managed, without meaning to or even realizing it, to create something very different.

Changes in the law in America resulted in part from the scarcity of English-trained lawyers, who were almost unknown in the colonies until after 1700. Not until well into the eighteenth century did authorities in England try to impose the common law and the statutes of the realm upon the provinces. By then, it was already too late. Although the American legal system adopted most of the es-sential elements of the English system, including such ancient rights as trial by jury, significant differ-ences had already become well established. Plead-ing and court procedures were simpler in America than in England, and punishments were different. Instead of the gallows or prison, colonists more commonly resorted to the whipping post, the branding iron, the stocks, and (for "gossipy"

women) the ducking stool. In a labor-scarce society, it was not in the interests of communities to exe-cute or incarcerate potential workers. Crimes were redefined. In England, a printed attack on a public official, whether true or false, was considered li-belous. In the 1734 trial of the New York publisher John Peter Zenger, who was powerfully defended by the Philadelphia lawyer Andrew Hamilton, the courts ruled that criticisms of the government were not libelous if factually true—a verdict that re-moved some restrictions on the freedom of the press. There was a subtle but decisive transforma-tion in legal philosophy. Some colonists came to think of law as a reflection of the divine will; others saw it as a result of the natural order. In neither case did they consider it an expression of the power of an earthly sovereign.

Even more significant for the future of the rela-tionship between the colonies and England were im-portant emerging differences between the American and British political systems. Because the royal government was so far away, Americans created a group of institutions of their own that gave them—in reality, if not in theory—a large measure of

Significant Events

1636	Harvard College founded in Massachusetts
1640	Instability in tobacco markets begins
1647	Massachusetts law requires a public school in every town
1662	Halfway Covenant established in New England
1650	Population of New England begins to grow by natural increase
1670s	Flow of indentured servants declines
	Slave traders begin importing slaves directly from Africa to North America
1685	Edict of Nantes revoked in France; Huguenots begin migrating to North America
1690s	Rice production becomes central to South Carolina economy
	Slave trade expands as prices decline
1691	Official toleration of Catholics ends in Maryland
1692	Witchcraft trials begin in Salem
1693	College of William and Mary founded in Virginia
1697	Royal African Company monopoly of slave trade broken; slave importations begin to increase
1701	Yale College founded in Connecticut
1708–1709	First major migration of Palatinate Germans to North America begins
1710	Major Scotch-Irish migrations to North America begin
	German Swiss establish settlements in North Carolina
1720	Cotton Mather initiates smallpox inoculations in Massachusetts
1734	Great Awakening begins in Massachusetts
	Zenger tried in New York
1739	George Whitefield arrives in North America
	Great Awakening intensifies
	Stono slave rebellion in South Carolina
1740s	Indigo production begins in South Carolina
1746	College of New Jersey founded at Princeton
1754	King's College (later Columbia University) founded in New York
1755	Academy and College of Philadelphia (later University of Pennsylvania) founded
1764	Major ironworks established in New Jersey

self-government. In most colonies, local communities grew accustomed to running their own affairs with minimal interference from higher authorities. Communities also expected to maintain strict control over their delegates to the colonial assemblies, and those assemblies came to exercise many of the powers that Parliament exercised in England (even though in theory Parliament remained the ultimate authority in America). Provincial governors appointed by the crown had broad powers on paper, but in fact their influence was sharply limited. They lacked control over appointments and contracts; such influence resided largely in England or with local colonial leaders. They could never be certain of their tenure in office; because governorships were patronage appointments, a governor could be removed any time his patron in England lost favor. And in many cases, governors were not even familiar with the colonies they were meant to govern. Some governors were native-born Americans, but most were Englishmen who came to the colonies for the first time to assume their offices. The result of all this was that the focus of politics in the colonies became a local one. The provincial governments became accustomed to acting more or less independently of Parliament, and a set of assumptions and expectations about the rights of the colonists began to take hold in America that policymakers in England did not share. These differences caused few problems before the 1760s, because the British did little to exert the authority they believed they possessed. But when, beginning in 1763, the English government began attempting to tighten its control over the American colonies, a great imperial crisis developed.

CONCLUSION

What began as a few small, isolated, precarious settlements in the wilderness had evolved by the mid-eighteenth century into a large and complex society. The English colonies in America grew steadily between the 1650s and the 1750s: in population, in the size of their economies, and in the sophistication—and diversity—of their cultures. Although most white Americans in the 1750s still believed that they were fully a part of the British Empire, they were in fact living in a world that had become very different from that of England.

Many distinct societies developed in the colonies, but the greatest distinction was between the colonies of the North and those of the South. In the North, society was dominated by relatively small family farms and by towns and cities of growing size. A thriving commercial class was developing, and with it an increasingly elaborate urban culture. In the South, there were many family farms as well. But there were also large plantations cultivating tobacco, rice, indigo, and cotton for export. By the late seven-

teenth century, these plantations were relying heavily on African workers who had been brought to the colonies forcibly as slaves. There were few significant towns and cities in the South, and little commerce other than the marketing of crops.

The colonies did, however, also have much in common. Most white Americans accepted common assumptions about racial inequality. That enabled them to tolerate (and at times celebrate) the enslavement of African men and women and to justify a campaign of displacement and often violence against Native Americans that would continue for two centuries. Most white Americans (and, in different ways, most nonwhite Americans as well) were deeply religious. The Great Awakening, therefore, had a powerful impact throughout the colonies, North and South. And most white colonists shared a belief in certain basic principles of law and politics, which they considered embedded in the English constitution, and which in the years after the 1750s would lead to a great imperial crisis.

FOR FURTHER REFERENCE

Suggested Readings Bernard Bailyn, *Voyagers to the West: A Passage in the Peopling of America on the Eve of the Revolution* (1986) reveals the complexity and scope of European emigration to North America. Bailyn's *The Origin of American Politics* (1968) remains an excellent introduction to colonial politics. David Hackett Fischer, *Albion's Seed* (1989) suggests four major folkways for English migrants to America. Laurel Thatcher Ulrich, *Good Wives: Image and Reality in the Lives of Women in Northern New England, 1650–1750* (1982) offers a typology of women's roles in colonial New England. Kathleen M. Brown, *Good Wives, Nasty Wenches, and Anxious Patriarchs: Gender, Race and Power in Colonial Virginia* (1996) places gender at the center of the development of slavery in the Chesapeake. Rhys Isaac, *The Transformation of Virginia, 1740–1790* (1982) uses the methods of cultural anthropology in an influential study of the world of the colonial Virginia gentry.

Films (The best source for information on how to find these and other films is *Bowker's Complete Video Directory*—3 volumes.) *The Roots of Democracy, 1700s* studies the economic forces and political beliefs that

shaped the British colonies. *Colonial America: Life in the Maturing Colonies* (1991) looks at the lives of New World settlers, and explores their attitudes towards Indians, slaves, and women. *Benjamin Franklin* (1987) looks at the life of one of the leading figures of American colonial history. *Religion in the Colonies* (1994) explores the diversity of religious sects transported from Europe to the American colonies. *Anne Hutchinson* (1983) narrates the life and struggles of an important dissident woman in the Massachusetts Bay colony. *The Salem Witch Trials* introduces the accused "witches," judges, and girls involved in a tragic episode in the history of colonial Massachusetts.

Internet Resources (For up-to-date URL addresses and links to these and other websites, consult the McGraw-Hill history site at *http://www.mhhe.com/socscience/history/usa/link/linktop.htm*) *Archiving Early America* contains primary source documents from eighteenth-century America, including newspapers, maps, and private writings. *Colonial Williamsburg Almanack* provides extensive information about eighteenth-century Williamsburg, Virginia, and the people who lived there. *Rare Map Collection–Colonial America* includes contemporary maps of the colonies.

⌖

BIBLIOGRAPHY

General Social Histories   James A. Henretta and Gregory Nobles, *The Evolution of American Society, 1700-1815,* rev. ed. (1987). Richard Hofstadter, *America at 1750: A Social Portrait* (1971).

Population and Family   Richard Bushman, *The Refinement of America: Persons, Houses, Cities* (1992). John Putnam Demos, *Past, Present, and Personal: The Family and Life Course in American History* (1986). J. William Frost, *The Quaker Family in Colonial America* (1972). Philip Greven, *Four Generations* (1970); *The Protestant Temperament: Patterns of Child-Rearing, Religious Experience, and the Self in Early America* (1977). Christopher Jedrey, *The World of John Cleaveland: Family and Community in Eighteenth-Century New England* (1979). Joan M. Jensen, *Loosening the Bonds: Mid-Atlantic Farm Women, 1750-1850* (1986). Lyle Koehler, *A Search for Power: "The Weaker Sex" in Seventeenth-Century New England* (1982). Judith Walzer Leavitt, *Brought to Bed: Child Bearing in America, 1750-1950* (1986). Edmund S. Morgan, *The Puritan Family* (1966). Daniel K. Richter, *The Ordeal of the Longhouse: The Peoples of the Iroquois League in the Era of European Colonization* (1992). Daniel Blake Smith, *Inside the Great House: Planter Family Life in Eighteenth Century Chesapeake Society* (1980). Roger Thompson, *Women in Stuart England and America* (1974). Robert V. Wells, *The Population of the British Colonies in America Before 1776* (1975). Stephanie Grauman Wolf, *As Various as Their Land: The Everyday Lives of Eighteenth-Century Americans* (1993).

Immigration   Bernard Bailyn, *The Peopling of British North America: An Introduction* (1986). R. J. Dickson, *Ulster Immigration to the United States* (1966). Marcus L. Hanson, *The Atlantic Migration, 1607-1860* (1940). James Kettner, *The Development of American Citizenship* (1978). James G. Leyburn, *The Scotch-Irish: A Social History* (1962).

Society and Slavery in the Colonial South   T. H. Breen, *Tobacco Culture* (1985). T. H. Breen and Stephen Innes, *"Myne Owne Ground": Race and Freedom on Virginia's Eastern Shore* (1980). Jay Coughtry, *The Notorious Triangle: Rhode Island and the African Slave Trade, 1799-1807* (1981). Philip D. Curtin, *The Atlantic Slave Trade* (1969). David Brion Davis, *The Problem of Slavery in Western Culture* (1966). David Eltis, *Economic Growth and the Ending of the Transatlantic Slave Trade* (1987). Jean E. Friedman, *The Enclosed Garden: Women and Community in the Evangelical South* (1985). David W. Galenson, *Traders, Planters, and Slaves: Market Behavior in Early English America* (1986). Eugene Genovese, *From Rebellion to Revolution* (1979). Jack P. Greene, *Pursuits of Happiness: The Social Development of Early Modern British Colonies and the Formation of American Culture* (1988). Gwendolyn Midlo Hall, *Africans in Colonial Louisiana: The Development of Afro-Creole Culture in the Eighteenth Century* (1992). Winthrop D. Jordan, *White over Black* (1968); *The White Man's Burden* (1974). Charles Joyner, *Down by the Riverside: A South Carolina Slave Community* (1984). Marvin L. Michael Kay and Lorin Lee Cary, *Slavery in North Carolina, 1748-1775* (1995). Jack Temple Kirby, *Poquosin* (1995). Peter Kolchin, *American Slavery, 1619-1877* (1993). Allan Kulikoff, *Tobacco and Slaves* (1986). Daniel Littlefield, *Rice and Slaves: Ethnicity and the Slave Trade in Colonial South Carolina* (1981). Edmund S. Morgan, *American Slavery, American Freedom: The Ordeal of Colonial Virginia* (1975). Gerald Mullin, *Flight and Rebellion* (1972). Gary B. Nash, *Red, White, and Black,* rev. ed. (1982). James R. Perry, *Formation of a Society on Virginia's Eastern Shore, 1615-1655* (1990). Darrett B. Rutman and Anita H. Rutman, *A Place in Time: Middlesex County, Virginia, 1659-1750* (1984). Abbot E. Smith, *Colonists in Bondage* (1947). Mechal Sobel, *The World They Made Together: Black and White Values in Eighteenth-Century Virginia* (1987). Julia C. Spruill, *Women's Life and Work in the Southern Colonies* (1972). Hugh Thomas, *The Slave Trade* (1997). James Titus, *The Old Dominion at War: Society, Politics, and Warfare in Late Colonial Virginia* (1991). Daniel H. Usner, Jr., *Indians, Settlers, and Slaves in a Frontier Exchange Economy: The Lower Mississippi Valley Before 1783* (1992). Betty Wood, *Women's Work, Men's Work: The Informal Slave Economies of Lowcountry Georgia* (1995). Peter Wood, *Black Majority* (1974). J. Leitch Wright, Jr., *Anglo-Spanish Rivalry in North America* (1971); *The Only Land They Knew: The Tragic Story of the American Indians of the Old South* (1981).

Society and Town in Colonial New England   Paul Boyer and Stephen Nissenbaum, *Salem Possessed* (1974). Richard Bushman, *From Puritan to Yankee* (1967). John Camp, *Out of the Wilderness: The Emergence of an American Identity in Colonial New England* (1990). David Conroy, *In Public Houses: Drink & the Revolution of Authority in Colonial Massachusetts* (1995). E. M. Cook, Jr., *The Fathers of Towns* (1975). John Putnam Demos, *Entertaining Satan: Witchcraft and the Culture of Early New England* (1982); *The Unredeemed Captive* (1994). Charles Grant, *Democracy in the Connecticut Frontier Town of Kent* (1961). Paul Robert Gross, *The Minutemen and Their World* (1976). David D. Hall, *Worlds of Wonder,*

Engrav'd Printed & Sold by PAUL REVERE BOSTON

Law and Politics   Bernard Bailyn, *The Origins of American Politics* (1968). J. C. D. Clark, *The Language of Liberty, 1660–1832* (1994). Thomas Curry, *The First Freedoms: Church and State in America to the Passage of the First Amendment* (1986). Robert Ferguson, *Law and Letters in American Culture* (1984). Gerald W. Gawalt, *The Promise of Power: The Emergence of the Legal Profession in Massachusetts, 1760–1840* (1979). Jack P. Greene, *The Quest for Power* (1963). Charles Hoffer, *Law and People in Colonial America* (1992). Michael Kammen, *Spheres of Liberty: Changing Perceptions of Liberty in American Culture* (1986). Leonard W. Labaree, *Royal Government in America* (1930). J. G. A. Pocock, *The Machiavellian Moment* (1975). J. R. Pole, *Political Representation in England and the Origins of the American Republic* (1966). A. G. Roeber, *Faithful Magistrates and Republican Lawyers: Creators of Virginia Legal Culture, 1680–1810* (1981). Caroline Robbins, *The Eighteenth-Century Commonwealthman* (1959). Marylynn Salmon, *Women and the Law of Property in Early America* (1986). Alan Tully, *Forming American Politics: Ideals, Interests, and Institutions in Colonial New York and Pennsylvania* (1994). Robert Zemsky, *Merchants, Farmers, and River Gods* (1971). Michael P. Zuckert, *Natural Rights and the New Republicanism* (1994).

Days of Judgment: Popular Religious Belief in Early New England (1990). Karen Hansen, *A Very Social Time: Crafting Community in Antebellum New England* (1994). Carol Karlsen, *The Devil in the Shape of a Woman: Witchcraft in Colonial New England* (1987). Kenneth Lockridge, *A New England Town* (1970). Teresa Anne Murphy, *Ten Hours Labor: Religion, Reform, and Gender in Early New England* (1992). Carla Gardina Pestana, *Quakers and Baptists in Colonial Massachusetts* (1991). Sumner Chilton Powell, *Puritan Village* (1963). Bernard Rosenthal, *Salem Story: Reading the Witch Trials of 1692* (1993). Darrett B. Rutman, *Winthrop's Boston* (1965). Michael Zuckerman, *Peaceable Kingdoms* (1970).

The Colonial Economy Carl Bridenbaugh, *Myths and Realities: Societies of the Colonial South* (1963). Stuart Bruchey, *Roots of American Economic Growth, 1607-1861* (1965). Paul G. E. Clemens, *The Atlantic Economy and Colonial Maryland's Eastern Shore: From Tobacco to Grain* (1980). David W. Galenson, *White Servitude in Colonial America: An Economic Analysis* (1982). Stephen Innes, *Labor in a New Land: Economy and Society in Seventeenth Century Springfield* (1983). Stephen Innes, ed., *Work and Labor in Early America* (1988). Alice Hanson Jones, *Wealth of a Nation to Be* (1980). Jackson Turner Main, *The Social Structure of Revolutionary America* (1965). John J. McCusker and Russell R. Menard, *The Economy of British America, 1607-1787* (1985). Harry R. Merrens, *Colonial North Carolina in the Eighteenth Century* (1964). Edmund S. Morgan, *Virginians at Home* (1952). Edward Price, *Dividing the Land: Early American Beginnings of our Private Property Mosaic* (1995). Jacob M. Price, *France and the Chesapeake*, 2 vols. (1973); *The Tobacco Adventure to Russia* (1961); *Capital and Credit in the British Overseas Trade: The View from the Chesapeake, 1700-1776* (1980). Sharon U. Salinger, *"To Serve Well and Faithfully": Labor and Indentured Servants in Pennsylvania, 1692-1800* (1987).

Cities and Commerce Bernard Bailyn, *The New England Merchants in the Seventeenth Century* (1955). Carl Bridenbaugh, *Cities in the Wilderness* (1938); *Cities in Revolt* (1955). Stuart Bruchey, *The Colonial Merchant* (1966). Thomas M. Doerflinger, *A Vigorous Spirit of Enterprise: Merchants and Economic Development in Revolutionary Philadelphia* (1986). Joyce D. Goodfriend, *Before the Melting Pot: Society and Culture in New York City, 1664-1730* (1992). Arthur Jensen, *The Maritime Commerce of Colonial Philadelphia* (1963). Randolph S. Klein, *Portrait of an Early American Family* (1975). Gary B. Nash, *The Urban Crucible* (1979); *Forging Freedom: The Formation of Philadelphia's Black Community, 1720-1840* (1988). Marcus Rediker, *Between the Devil and the Deep Sea: Merchant Seamen, Pirates, and the Anglo-American Maritime World, 1700-1750* (1987). J. F. Shepherd and G. M. Walton, *The Economic Rise of Early America* (1979). G. B. Warden, *Boston, 1687-1776* (1970). Stephanie G. Wolf, *Urban Village* (1976).

Colonial Religion (For studies of Puritanism, see bibliography for Chapter 2.) Sidney Ahlstrom, *A Religious History of the American People* (1972). Patricia U. Bonomi, *Under the Copy of Heaven: Religion, Society, and Politics in Colonial America* (1986). Carl Bridenbaugh, *Mitre and Sceptre: Transatlantic Faiths, Ideas, Personalities, and Politics, 1689-1775* (1962). J. T. Ellis, *Catholics in America* (1965). J. R. Marcus, *Early American Jewry* (1951). William C. McLoughlin, *New England Dissent, 1630-1833,* 2 vols. (1971). Sidney Mead, *The Lively Experiment: The Shaping of Christianity in America* (1963). W. W. Sweet, *Religion in Colonial America* (1942). Marilyn Westerkamp, *Triumph of Laity* (1988).

The Great Awakening J. M. Bumsted and John E. Van de Wetering, *What Must I Do to Be Saved? The Great Awakening in Colonial America* (1976). J. W. Davidson, *The Logic of Millennial Thought* (1977). Edwin S. Gaustad, *The Great Awakening in New England* (1957). Alan Heimert, *Religion and the American Mind* (1966). Frank Lambert, *"Pedlar in Divinity": George Whitefield and the Transatlantic Revivals, 1737-1770* (1994). Perry Miller, *Jonathan Edwards* (1949). Patricia Tracy, *Jonathan Edwards: Pastor* (1980). Conrad Wright, *The Beginnings of Unitarianism in America* (1955).

Education James Axtell, *The School upon a Hill: Education and Society in Colonial New England* (1974). Bernard Bailyn, *Education in the Forming of American Society* (1960). Lawrence A. Cremin, *American Education: The Colonial Experience, 1607-1783* (1970). Jurgen Herbst, *From Crisis to Crisis* (1982). Kenneth Lockridge, *Literacy in Colonial New England* (1974). Robert Middlekauff, *Ancients and Axioms* (1963). Samuel Eliot Morison, *The Founding of Harvard College* (1935).

Culture and the Enlightenment Jean-Christophe Agnew, *Worlds Apart: The Market and the Theater in Anglo-American Thought, 1550-1750* (1986). Daniel J. Boorstin, *The Americans: The Colonial Experience* (1958). Charles E. Clark, *The Public Prints: The Newspaper in Anglo-American Culture, 1665-1740* (1994). Richard Beale Davis, *Intellectual Life in the Colonial South,* 2 vols. (1978). Brook Hindle, *The Pursuit of Science in Revolutionary America* (1956). Howard Mumford Jones, *O Strange New World* (1964). H. Leventhal, *In the Shadow of Enlightenment* (1976). Henry May, *The Enlightenment in America* (1976). Carl Van Doren, *Benjamin Franklin* (1941).

Chapter Four

THE EMPIRE UNDER STRAIN

As late as the 1750s, few Americans saw any reason to object to their membership in the British Empire. The imperial system provided them with many benefits: opportunities for trade and commerce, military protection, political stability. And those benefits were accompanied by few costs; for the most part, the English government left the colonies alone. While Britain did attempt to regulate the colonists' external trade, those regulations were usually so laxly administered that they could be easily circumvented. Some Americans predicted that the colonies would ultimately develop to a point where greater autonomy would become inevitable. But few expected such a change to occur soon.

■ **THE BOSTON MASSACRE (1770), BY PAUL REVERE**

This is one of many sensationalized engravings, by Revere and others, of the conflict between British troops and Boston laborers that became important propaganda documents for the Patriot cause in the 1770s. Among the victims of the massacre listed by Revere was Crispus Attucks, probably the first black man to die in the struggle for American independence.

(American Antiquarian Society)

By the mid-1770s, however, the relationship between the American colonies and their British rulers had become so strained, so poisoned, so characterized by suspicion and resentment that the once seemingly unbreakable bonds of empire were ready to snap. And in the spring of 1775, the first shots were fired in a war that would ultimately win America its independence.

The revolutionary crisis emerged as a result of both longstanding differences between the colonies and England and particular events in the 1760s and 1770s. Ever since the first days of settlement in North America, the ideas and institutions of the colonies had been diverging from those in England in countless ways. Only because the relationship between America and Britain had been so casual had those differences failed to create serious tensions in the past. Beginning in 1763, however, the British government embarked on a series of new policies toward its colonies—policies dictated by changing international realities and new political circumstances within England itself—that brought the differences between the two societies into sharp focus. In the beginning, most Americans reacted to the changes with relative restraint. Gradually, however, as crisis followed crisis, a large group of Americans found themselves fundamentally disillusioned with the imperial relationship. By 1775, that relationship was, for all practical purposes, damaged beyond repair.

A LOOSENING OF TIES

After the Glorious Revolution of 1688 in England and the collapse of the Dominion of New England in America, the English government (which became the British government after 1707, when a union of England and Scotland created Great Britain) made no serious or sustained effort to tighten its control over the colonies for over seventy years. During those years, it is true, an increasing number of colonies were brought under the direct control of the king. New Jersey in 1702, North and South Carolina in 1729, Georgia in 1754—all became royal colonies, bringing the total to eight; in all of them, the king had the power to appoint the governors and other colonial officials. During those years, Parliament also passed new laws supplementing the original Navigation Acts and strengthening the mercantilist program—laws restricting colonial manufactures, prohibiting paper currency, and regulating trade. On the whole, however, the British government remained uncertain and divided about the extent to which it ought to interfere in colonial affairs. The colonies were left, within broad limits, to go their separate ways.

A Tradition of Neglect

In the fifty years after the Glorious Revolution, the British Parliament established a growing supremacy over the king. During the reigns of George I (1714-1727) and George II (1727-1760), both of whom were German born and unaccustomed to English ways, the prime minister and his fellow cabinet ministers began to become the nation's real executives. They held their positions not by the king's favor but by their ability to control a majority in Parliament.

These parliamentary leaders were less inclined than the seventeenth-century monarchs had been to try to tighten imperial organization. They depended heavily on the support of the great merchants and landholders, most of whom feared that any such experiments would require large expenditures, would increase taxes, and would diminish the profits they were earning from the colonial trade. The first of the modern prime ministers, Robert Walpole, deliberately refrained from strict enforcement of the Navigation Acts, believing that relaxed trading restrictions would stimulate commerce.

Meanwhile, the day-to-day administration of colonial affairs remained decentralized and inefficient. There was no colonial office in London. The nearest equivalent was the Board of Trade and Plantations, established in 1696—a mere advisory body that had little role in any actual decisions. Real authority rested in the Privy Council (the central administrative agency for the government as a whole), the admiralty, and the treasury. But those agencies were responsible for administering laws at home as well as overseas; none could concentrate on colonial affairs alone. To complicate matters further, there was considerable overlapping and confusion of authority among the departments.

Few of the London officials, moreover, had ever visited America; few knew very much about conditions there. What information they did gather came in large part from agents sent to England by the colonial assemblies to lobby for American interests, and these agents, naturally, did nothing to encourage interference with colonial affairs. (The best known of them, Benjamin Franklin, represented not only his own colony, Pennsylvania, but also Georgia, New Jersey, and Massachusetts.)

It was not only the weakness of administrative authority in London and the policy of neglect that weakened England's hold on the colonies. It was also the character of the royal officials in America—among them the governors, the collectors of customs, and naval officers. Some of these officeholders were able and intelligent men; most were not. Appointments generally came as the result of bribery or favoritism, not as a reward for merit. Many appointees remained in England and, with part of their salaries, hired substitutes to take their places in America. Such deputies received paltry wages and thus faced great temptations to augment their incomes with bribes. Few resisted the temptation. Customs collectors, for example, routinely waived duties on goods when merchants paid them to do so. Even honest and well-paid officials usually found it expedient, if they wanted to get along with their neighbors, to yield to the colonists' resistance to trade restrictions.

Resistance to imperial authority centered in the colonial legislatures. By the 1750s the American assemblies had claimed the right to levy taxes, make appropriations, approve appointments, and pass laws for their respective colonies. Their legislation was subject to veto by the governor or the Privy Council. But the assemblies had leverage over the governor through their control of the colonial budget, and they could circumvent the Privy Council by repassing disallowed laws in slightly altered form. The assemblies came to look upon themselves as little parliaments, each practically as sovereign within its colony as Parliament itself was in England. In 1754, the Board of Trade reported to the king, regarding the members of the New York assembly, that they "have wrested from Your Majesty's governor the nomination of all offices of government, the custody and direction of the public military stores, the mustering and direction of troops raised for Your Majesty's service, and in short almost every other part of executive government."

The Colonies Divided

Despite their frequent resistance to the authority of London, the colonists continued to think of themselves as loyal English subjects. In many respects, in fact, they felt stronger ties to England than they did to one another. "Fire and water," an English traveler wrote, "are not more heterogeneous than the different colonies in North America." New Englanders and Virginians viewed each other as something close to foreigners. A Connecticut man denounced the merchants of New York for their "frauds and unfair practices," while a New Yorker condemned Connecticut because of the "low craft and cunning so incident to the people of that country." Only an accident of geography, it seemed, connected these disparate societies to each other.

Yet for all their differences, the colonies could scarcely avoid forging connections with one another. The growth of the colonial population produced an almost continuous line of settlement along the seacoast and led to the gradual construction of roads and the rise of intercolonial trade. The colonial postal service helped increase communication. In 1691, it had operated only from Massachusetts to New York and Pennsylvania. In 1711, it extended to New Hampshire in the North; in 1732, to Virginia in the South; and ultimately, all the way to Georgia.

Still, the colonists were loath to cooperate even when, in 1754, they faced a common threat from their old rivals, the French, and France's Indian allies. A conference of colonial leaders—with delegates from Pennsylvania, Maryland, New York, and New England—was meeting in Albany in that year to negotiate a treaty with the Iroquois, as the British government had advised the colonists to do. The dele-

■ **AN APPEAL FOR COLONIAL UNITY**
This sketch, one of the first American editorial cartoons, appeared in Benjamin Franklin's Philadelphia newspaper, the *Pennsylvania Gazette,* on May 9, 1754. It was meant to illustrate the need for intercolonial unity and, in particular, for the adoption of Franklin's Albany Plan. *(Library Company of Philadelphia)*

gates stayed on to talk about forming a colonial federation for defense against the Indians. Benjamin Franklin proposed, and the delegates tentatively approved, a plan by which Parliament would set up in America "one general government" for all the colonies (except Georgia and Nova Scotia). Each colony would "retain its present constitution," but would grant to the new general government such powers as the authority to govern all relations with the Indians. The central government would have a "president general" appointed and paid by the king (just as colonial governors were) and a legislature (a "grand council") elected by the colonial assemblies.

War with the French and Indians was already beginning when this Albany Plan was presented to the colonial assemblies. None approved it. "Everyone cries, a union is necessary," Franklin wrote to the Massachusetts governor, "but when they come to the manner and form of the union, their weak noodles are perfectly distracted."

THE STRUGGLE FOR THE CONTINENT

In the late 1750s and early 1760s, a great war raged through North America, changing forever the balance of power both within the continent and between it and the rest of the world. In part, the war was simply a part of a larger struggle between England and France for dominance in world trade and naval power. The British victory in that struggle, known in Europe as the Seven Years' War, confirmed England's commercial supremacy and cemented its control of the settled regions of North America.

In another sense, however, the conflict was the final stage in a long battle among the three principal powers in northeastern North America: the English, the French, and the Iroquois. For more than a century prior to the conflict—which was known in America as the French and Indian War—these three groups had maintained an uneasy balance of power. The events of the 1750s upset that balance, produced a prolonged and open conflict, and established a precarious dominance for the English societies throughout the region.

The French and Indian War was important to the English colonists in America for another reason as well. By bringing the Americans into closer contact with British authority than ever before, it raised to the surface some of the underlying tensions in the colonial relationship.

New France and the Iroquois Nation

The French and the English had coexisted relatively peacefully in North America for nearly a century. But by the 1750s, as both English and French settlements expanded, religious and commercial tensions began to produce new frictions and new conflicts. The crisis began in part because of the expansion of the French presence in America in the late seventeenth century—a result of Louis XIV's search for national unity and increased world power. France began to devote new attention to the development of its North American territories, and French settlement rapidly expanded. The lucrative fur trade drew immigrant French peasants deeper into the wilderness. Missionary zeal drew large numbers of French Jesuits into the interior in search of potential converts. The bottomlands of the Mississippi River valley attracted French farmers discouraged by the short growing season in Canada.

By the mid-seventeenth century, the French Empire in America comprised a vast territory. Louis Joliet and Father Jacques Marquette, French explorers of the 1670s, journeyed together by canoe from Green Bay on Lake Michigan as far south as the junction of the Arkansas and Mississippi Rivers. A year later, René Robert Cavelier, Sieur de La Salle, began the explorations that in 1682 took him to the delta of the Mississippi, where he claimed the surrounding country for France and named it Louisiana in the king's honor. Subsequent traders and missionaries wandered to the southwest as far as the Rio Grande; and the explorer Pierre Gaultier de Varennes, Sieur de La Verendrye, pushed westward in 1743 from Lake Superior to a point within sight of the Rocky Mountains. The French had by then revealed the outlines of, and laid claim to, the whole continental interior.

To secure their hold on these enormous claims, they founded a string of widely separated communities, fortresses, missions, and trading posts. Fort Louisbourg, on Cape Breton Island, guarded the approach to the Gulf of St. Lawrence. Would-be feudal lords established large estates (*seigneuries*) along the banks of the St. Lawrence River; and on a high bluff above the river stood the fortified city of Quebec, the center of the French Empire in America. To the south was Montreal, and to the west Sault Sainte Marie and Detroit. On the lower Mississippi emerged plantations much like those in the southern colonies of English America, worked by black slaves and owned by "Creoles" (white immigrants of French descent). New Orleans, founded in 1718 to service the French plantation economy, soon was as big as some of the larger cities of the Atlantic seaboard; Biloxi and Mobile to the east completed the string of French settlement.

But the French were not, of course, alone in the continental interior. They shared their territories with a large and powerful Indian population, and their relations with the natives were crucial to the shaping of their empire. Both the French and the English were aware that the battle for control of North America would be determined in part by which group could best win the allegiance of native tribes—as trading partners and, at times, as military allies. The Indians, for their part, were principally concerned with protecting their independence. Whatever alignments they formed with the European societies growing up around them were generally marriages of convenience, determined by which group offered the most attractive terms.

The English—with their more advanced commercial economy—could usually offer the Indians better and more plentiful goods. But the French offered something that was often more important: tolerance. Unlike the English settlers, most of whom tried to impose their own social norms on the Native Americans they encountered, the French settlers in the interior generally adjusted their own behavior to Indian patterns. French fur traders frequently married Indian women and adopted tribal ways. Jesuit missionaries interacted comfortably with the natives and converted them to Catholicism by the thousands without challenging most of their social customs. By the mid-eighteenth century, therefore, the French had better and closer relations with most of the tribes of the interior than did the English.

The most powerful native group, however, had a rather different relationship with the French. The Iroquois Confederacy—the five Indian nations (Mohawk, Seneca, Cayuga, Onondaga, and Oneida) that had formed a defensive alliance in the fifteenth century—had been the most powerful tribal presence in the Northeast since the 1640s, when they had fought—and won—a bitter war against the Hurons. Once their major competitors were largely gone from the region, the Iroquois forged an important commercial relationship with the English and Dutch along the eastern seaboard—although they continued to trade with the French as well. Indeed, the key to the success of the Iroquois in maintaining their independence was that they avoided too close a relationship with either group and astutely played the French and the English off against each other. As a result, they managed to maintain an uneasy balance of power in the Great Lakes region.

The principal area of conflict among these many groups was the Ohio Valley. The French claimed it. Several competing Indian tribes (many of them refugees from lands farther east, driven into the valley by the English expansion) lived there. English settlement was expanding into it. And the Iroquois were trying to establish a presence there as traders. With so many competing groups jostling for influence, the Ohio Valley quickly became a potential battleground.

Anglo-French Conflicts

As long as England and France remained at peace in Europe, and as long as the precarious balance in the North American interior survived, the tensions among the English, French, and Iroquois remained relatively mild. But after the Glorious Revolution in England, the English throne passed to one of Louis XIV's principal enemies, William III, who was also the stadholder (chief magistrate) of the Netherlands and who had long opposed French expansionism. William's successor, Queen Anne (the daughter of James II), ascended the throne in 1702 and carried on the struggle against France and its new ally, Spain. The result was a series of Anglo-French wars that continued intermittently in Europe for nearly eighty years.

The wars had important repercussions in America. King William's War (1689–1697) produced a few, indecisive clashes between the English and French in northern New England. Queen Anne's War, which began in 1701 and continued for nearly twelve years, generated more substantial conflicts: border fighting with the Spaniards in the South as well as with the French and their Indian allies in the North. The Treaty of Utrecht, which brought the conflict to a close in 1713, transferred substantial areas of French territory in North America to the English, including Acadia (Nova Scotia) and Newfoundland. Two decades later, European rivalries led to still more conflicts in America. Disputes over British trading rights in the Spanish colonies produced a war between England and Spain and led to clashes between the British in Georgia and the Spaniards in Florida. (It was in the context of this conflict that the last English colony in America, Georgia, was founded in 1733; see pp. 118–119.) The Anglo-Spanish conflict soon merged with a much larger European war, in which England and France lined up on opposite sides of a territorial dispute between Frederick the Great of Prussia and Maria Theresa of Austria. (France supported Prussia, in the hope of seizing the Austrian Netherlands; England supported Austria, to keep Holland from the French.) The English colonists in America were soon drawn into the struggle, which they called King George's War; and between 1744 and 1748 they engaged in a series of conflicts with the French. New Englanders captured the French bastion at Louisbourg on Cape Breton Island; but the peace treaty that finally ended the conflict forced them (in bitter disappointment) to abandon it.

In the aftermath of King George's War, relations among the English, French, and Iroquois in North America quickly deteriorated. The Iroquois (in what in retrospect appears a major blunder) began for the first time to grant trading concessions in the interior to English merchants. In the context of the already

■ THE SIEGE OF LOUISBOURG, 1758
The fortress of Louisbourg, on Cape Breton Island in Nova Scotia, was one of the principal French outposts in eastern Canada during the French and Indian War. It took a British fleet of 157 ships nearly two months to force the French garrison to surrender. "We had not had our Batteries against the Town above a Week," wrote a British solder after the victory, "tho we were ashore Seven Weeks; the Badness of the Country prevented our Approaches. It was necessary to make Roads for the Cannon, which was a great Labour, and some Loss of Men; but the spirits the Army was in is capable of doing any Thing." *(New Brunswick Museum)*

tense Anglo-French relationship in America, that decision set in motion a chain of events disastrous for the Iroquois Confederacy. The French feared that the English were using the concessions as a first step toward expansion into French lands (which to some extent they were). They began in 1749 to construct new fortresses in the Ohio Valley. The English interpreted the French activity as a threat to their western settlements. They protested and began making military preparations and building fortresses of their own. The balance of power that the Iroquois had strove to maintain for so long rapidly disintegrated, and the five Indian nations allied themselves with the British and assume an essentially passive role in the conflict that followed.

For the next five years, tensions between the English and the French increased. In the summer of 1754 the governor of Virginia sent a militia force (under the command of an inexperienced young colonel, George Washington) into the Ohio Valley to challenge French expansion. Washington built a crude stockade (Fort Necessity) not far from the larger French outpost, Fort Duquesne, on the site of what is now Pittsburgh. After the Virginians staged an unsuccessful attack on a French detachment, the French countered with an assault on Fort Necessity, trapping Washington and his soldiers inside. After a third of them died in the fighting, Washington surrendered.

That clash marked the beginning of the French and Indian War, the American part of the much larger Seven Years' War that spread through Europe at the same time. It was the climactic event in the long Anglo-French struggle for empire.

The Great War for the Empire

The French and Indian War lasted nearly nine years, and it proceeded in three distinct phases. The first of these phases lasted from the Fort Necessity debacle in 1754 until the expansion of the war to Europe in 1756. It was primarily a local, North American conflict, which the English colonists managed largely on their own.

The British provided modest assistance during this period, but they provided it so ineptly that it had little impact on the struggle. The British fleet failed to prevent the landing of large French reinforcements in Canada; and the newly appointed commander in chief of the British army in America, General Edward Braddock, failed miserably in a major effort in the summer of 1755 to retake the crucial site at the forks of the Ohio River where Washington had lost the battle at Fort Necessity. A French and Indian ambush a few miles from the fort left Braddock dead and what remained of his forces in disarray.

The local colonial forces, meanwhile, were preoccupied with defending themselves against raids on their western settlements by the Indians of the Ohio Valley. Virtually all of them (except the Iroquois) were now allied with the French, having interpreted the defeat of the Virginians at Fort Duquesne as evidence of British weakness. Even the Iroquois, who were nominally allied with the British, remained fearful of antagonizing the French. They engaged in few hostilities and launched no offensive into Canada, even though they had, under heavy English pressure, declared war on the French. By late 1755, many English settlers along the frontier had withdrawn to the east of the Allegheny Mountains to escape the hostilities.

The second phase of the struggle began in 1756, when the governments of France and England formally opened hostilities and a truly international conflict (the Seven Years' War) began. In Europe, the war was marked by a realignment within the complex system of alliances. France allied itself with its former enemy, Austria; England joined France's former ally, Prussia. The fighting now spread to the West Indies, India, and Europe itself. But the principal struggle remained the one in North America, where so far England had suffered nothing but frustration and defeat.

Beginning in 1757, William Pitt, the English secretary of state (and future prime minister), began to transform the war effort in America by bringing it for the first time fully under British control. Pitt himself began planning military strategy for the North American conflict, appointing military commanders, and issuing orders to the colonists. Military recruitment had slowed dramatically in America after the defeat of Braddock. To replenish the army, British commanders began forcibly enlisting colonists (a practice known as "impressment"). Officers also began to seize supplies and equipment from local farmers and tradesmen and compelled colonists to offer shelter to British troops—all generally without compensation. The Americans had long ago become accustomed to running their own affairs and had been fighting for over two years without much assistance or direction from the British. They resented these new impositions and firmly resisted them—at times, as in a 1757 riot in New York City, violently. By early 1758, the friction between the British authorities and the colonists was threatening to bring the war effort to a halt.

Beginning in 1758, therefore, Pitt initiated the third and final phase of the war by relaxing many of the policies that Americans found obnoxious. He agreed to reimburse the colonists for all supplies requisitioned by the army. He returned control over military recruitment to the colonial assemblies (which resulted in an immediate and dramatic increase in enlistments). And he dispatched large numbers of additional troops to America.

Finally, the tide of battle began to turn in England's favor. The French had always been outnumbered by the British colonists; after 1756, they suffered as well from a series of poor harvests. As a result, they were unable to sustain their early military successes. By mid-1758, the British regulars in America (who did the bulk of the actual fighting) and the colonial militias were seizing one French stronghold after another. Two brilliant English generals, Jeffrey Amherst and James Wolfe, captured the fortress at Louisbourg in July 1758; a few months later Fort Duquesne fell without a fight. The next year, at the end of a siege of Quebec, supposedly impregnable atop its towering cliff, the army of General James Wolfe struggled up a hidden ravine under cover of darkness, surprised the larger forces of the Marquis de Montcalm, and defeated them in a battle in which both commanders died. The dramatic fall of Quebec on September 13, 1759, marked the beginning of the end of the American phase of the war. A year later, in September 1760, the French army formally surrendered to Amherst in Montreal.

Not all aspects of the struggle were as romantic as Wolfe's dramatic assault on Quebec. The British resorted at times to such brutal military expedients as population dispersal. In Nova Scotia, for example, they uprooted several thousand French inhabitants, whom they suspected of disloyalty, and scattered them throughout the English colonies. (Some of these Acadians eventually made their way to Louisiana, where they became the ancestors of the present-day Cajuns.) Elsewhere, English and colonial troops inflicted even worse atrocities on the Indian allies of the French—for example, offering "scalp bounties" to those who could bring back evidence of having killed a native. The French and their Indian allies retaliated, and hundreds of families along the English frontier perished in brutal raids on their settlements.

Peace finally came after the accession of George III to the British throne and the resignation of Pitt, who, unlike the new king, wanted to continue hostilities. The British achieved most of Pitt's aims nevertheless in the Peace of Paris, signed in 1763. Under its terms, the French ceded to Great Britain some of their West Indian islands and most of their colonies in India. They also transferred Canada and all other French territory east of the Mississippi, except New Orleans, to Great Britain. They ceded New Orleans and their claims west of the Mississippi to Spain, thus surrendering all title to the mainland of North America.

The French and Indian War had profound effects on the British Empire and the American colonies. It greatly expanded England's territorial claims in the New World. At the same time, it greatly enlarged Britain's debt; financing the vast war had been a major drain on the treasury. It also generated substantial resentment toward the Americans among British leaders. Officials in England were contemptuous of the colonists for what they considered American military ineptitude during the war; they were angry that the colonists had made so few financial contributions to a struggle waged largely for American benefit; they were particularly bitter that some colonial merchants had been selling food and other goods to the French in the West Indies throughout the conflict. All these factors combined to persuade many English leaders that a major reorganization of the empire, giving London increased authority over the colonies, would be necessary in the aftermath of the war.

The war had an equally profound but very different effect on the American colonists. It forced them, for the first time, to act in concert against a common foe. The friction of 1756–1757 over British requisition and impressment policies, and the 1758 return of authority to the colonial assemblies, established an important precedent in the minds of the colonists: it seemed to confirm the illegitimacy of English interference in local affairs. For thousands of Americans—the men who served in the colonial armed forces—the war was an important socializing experience. The colonial troops, unlike the British regiments, generally viewed themselves as part of a "people's army." The relationship of soldiers to their units was, the soldiers believed, in some measure voluntary; their army was a communal, not a coercive or hierarchical, organization. The contrast with the British regulars, whom the colonists widely resented for their arrogance and arbitrary use of power, was striking; and in later years, the memory of that contrast helped to shape the American response to British imperial policies.

For the Indians of the Ohio Valley, the third major party in the French and Indian War, the British victory was disastrous. Those tribes that had allied themselves with the French had earned the enmity of the victorious English. The Iroquois Confederacy, which had allied itself with Britain, fared only slightly better. English officials saw the passivity of the Iroquois during the war (a result of their effort to hedge their bets and avoid antagonizing the French) as evidence of duplicity. In the aftermath of the peace settlement, the Iroquois alliance with the British quickly unraveled, and the Iroquois Confederacy itself began to crumble from within. The Iroquois nations would continue to contest the English for control of the Ohio Valley for another fifty years; but increasingly divided and increasingly outnumbered, they would seldom again be in a position to deal with their white rivals on terms of military or political equality.

THE NEW IMPERIALISM

With the treaty of 1763, England found itself truly at peace for the first time in more than fifty years. But the difficult experiences of the previous decade had convinced many English leaders that they could no longer govern their empire as casually as they had in the past. Saddled with enormous debts from the many years of fighting, England was desperately in need of new revenues from its empire. Responsible for vast new lands in the New World, the imperial government could not long avoid expanding its involvement in its colonies.

Burdens of Empire

The experience of the French and Indian War, however, suggested that such increased involvement would not be easy to achieve. Not only had the colonists proved so resistant to British control that Pitt had been forced to relax his policies in 1758, but the colonial assemblies had continued after that to respond to British needs slowly and grudgingly. Unwilling to be taxed by Parliament to support the war effort, the colonists were generally reluctant to tax themselves as well. Defiance of imperial trade regulations and other British demands continued, and even increased, through the last years of the war.

The problems of managing the empire became more difficult after 1763 because of a basic shift in Britain's imperial design. In the past, the English had viewed their colonial empire primarily in terms of trade; they had opposed acquisition of territory for its own sake. But by the mid-eighteenth century, a growing number of English and American leaders (including both William Pitt and Benjamin Franklin) were beginning to argue that land itself was of value to the empire—because of the population it could support, the taxes it could produce, and the imperial splendor it would confer. The debate between the old commercial imperialists and the new territorial ones came to a head at the conclusion of the French and Indian War. The mercantilists wanted England to return Canada to France in exchange for Guadeloupe, the most commercially valuable of the French "sugar islands" in the West Indies. The territorialists, however, prevailed. The acquisition of the French territories in North America was a victory for, among others, Benjamin Franklin, who had long argued that the American people would need these vast spaces to accommodate their rapid and, he believed, limitless growth. Franklin and his supporters in the colonies were soon to discover, however, that the new acquisitions brought with them unexpected problems.

With the territorial annexations of 1763, the area of the British Empire was suddenly twice as great as it had been, and the problems of governing it were thus considerably more complex. Some argued that the empire should restrain rapid settlement in the western territories. To allow Europeans to move into the new lands too quickly, they warned, would run the risk of stirring up costly conflicts with the Indians. Restricting settlement would also keep the land available for hunting and trapping.

Other colonists wanted to see the new territories opened for immediate development, but they disagreed among themselves about who should control the western lands. Colonial governments made fervent, and often conflicting, claims of jurisdiction. Others argued that control should remain in England, and that the territories should be considered entirely new colonies, unlinked to the existing settlements. There were, in short, a host of problems and pressures that the British could not ignore.

At the same time, the government in London was running out of options in its effort to find a way to deal with its staggering war debt. Landlords and merchants in England itself were objecting strenuously to increases in what they already considered excessively high taxes. The necessity of stationing significant numbers of British troops on the Indian border after 1763 was adding even more to the cost of defending the American settlements. And the halfhearted response of the colonial assemblies to the war effort had suggested that in its search for revenue, England could not rely on any cooperation from the colonial governments. Only a system of taxation administered by London, the leaders of the empire believed, could effectively meet England's needs.

At this crucial moment in Anglo-American relations, with the imperial system in desperate need of redefinition, the English government experienced a series of changes as a result of the accession to the throne of a new king. George III assumed power in 1760 on the death of his grandfather. And he brought two particularly unfortunate qualities to the office. First, he was determined, unlike his two predecessors, to be an active and responsible monarch. In part because of pressure from his ambitious mother, he removed from power the longstanding and relatively stable coalition of Whigs, who had (under Pitt and others) governed the empire for much of the century and whom the new king mistrusted. In their place, he

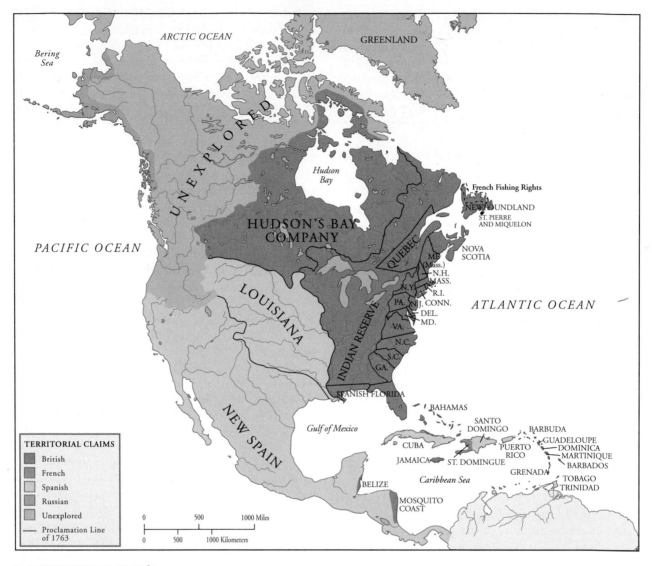

ARCTIC OCEAN

GREENLAND

Bering Sea

Hudson Bay

UNEXPLORED

HUDSON'S BAY COMPANY

French Fishing Rights

NEWFOUNDLAND
ST. PIERRE AND MIQUELON

QUEBEC

NOVA SCOTIA

PACIFIC OCEAN

LOUISIANA

INDIAN RESERVE

ME.
(Mass.)
N.H.
MASS.
N.Y.
R.I.
PA. N.J. CONN.
DEL.
VA. MD.

N.C.

S.C.
GA.

ATLANTIC OCEAN

SPANISH FLORIDA

NEW SPAIN

Gulf of Mexico

BAHAMAS

SANTO DOMINGO

BARBUDA
GUADELOUPE
DOMINICA
MARTINIQUE
BARBADOS

CUBA

PUERTO RICO

JAMAICA   ST. DOMINGUE

GRENADA

TOBAGO
TRINIDAD

BELIZE   *Caribbean Sea*

MOSQUITO COAST

TERRITORIAL CLAIMS

- British
- French
- Spanish
- Russian
- Unexplored
- Proclamation Line of 1763

0   500   1000 Miles

0   500   1000 Kilometers

■ **NORTH AMERICA IN 1763**

The French defeat in the Seven Years' War and the Treaty of Paris that ended it reshaped the map of colonial North America. Britain obtained Canada and all other French territory east of the Mississippi, thereby doubling the extent of the British Empire in North America. Hoping to control the expansion of white colonists into lands west of the Applachian Mountains, the British government issued the Proclamation of 1763, forbidding settlers to advance west of the red line seen on this map.

created a new coalition of his own through patronage and bribes and gained an uneasy control of Parliament. The new ministries that emerged as a result of these changes were inherently unstable, each lasting in office an average of only about two years.

The king had serious intellectual and psychological limitations that compounded his political difficul-

ties. He suffered, apparently, from a rare disease that produced intermittent bouts of insanity. (Indeed, in the last years of his long reign he was, according to most accounts, a virtual lunatic, confined to the palace and unable to perform any official functions.) Yet even when George III was lucid and rational, which in the 1760s and 1770s was most of the time, he was painfully immature (he was only twenty-two

■ **GEORGE III**
This portrait by the Scottish artist Allan Ramsay shows the twenty-two-year-old English king in his coronation robes as he ascended the throne in 1760. American patriots during the long revolutionary crisis came to consider George III a vicious and brutal tyrant. In reality, the king was a man of limited ability who tried desperately, stubbornly, and generally unsuccessfully to play a role for which he was fundamentally ill-suited. As early as 1780, he began to suffer intermittently from insanity. After 1810, he was blind and permanently deranged and spent the last decade of his sixty-year reign as an invalid, barred from all official business by the Regency Act of 1811. His son (later King George IV) served as regent in those years. *(Colonial Williamsburg Foundation)*

when he ascended the throne) and insecure—striving constantly to prove his fitness for his position but time and again finding himself ill equipped to handle the challenges he seized for himself. The king's personality, therefore, contributed to both the instability and the intransigence of the British government during these critical years.

More immediately responsible for the problems that soon emerged with the colonies, however, was George Grenville, whom the king made prime minister in 1763. Grenville, a brother-in-law of William

Pitt, did not share Pitt's sympathy with the American point of view. He agreed instead with the prevailing opinion within Britain that the colonists had been too long indulged and that they should be compelled to obey the laws and to pay a part of the cost of defending and administering the empire. He promptly began trying to impose a new system of control upon what had been a loose collection of colonial possessions in America.

The British and the Tribes

The western problem was the most urgent. With the departure of the French, settlers and traders from the English colonies had begun immediately to move over the mountains and into the upper Ohio Valley. The Indians of the region objected to this intrusion into their land and commerce; and an alliance of tribes, under the Ottawa chieftain Pontiac, struck back. To prevent an escalation of the fighting that might threaten western trade, the British government issued a ruling—the Proclamation of 1763—forbidding settlers to advance beyond a line drawn along the Appalachian Mountains.

The Proclamation of 1763 was appealing to the British for several reasons. It would allow London, rather than the provincial governments and their land-hungry constituents, to control the westward movement of the white population. Hence, westward expansion would proceed in an orderly manner, and conflicts with the tribes, which were both militarily costly and dangerous to trade, might be limited. Slower western settlement would also slow the population exodus from the coastal colonies, where England's most important markets and investments were. And it would reserve opportunities for land speculation and fur trading for English rather than colonial entrepreneurs.

Although the tribes were not enthusiastic about the Proclamation, which required them to cede still more land to the white settlers, many tribal groups supported the agreement as the best bargain available to them. The Cherokee, in particular, worked actively to hasten the drawing of the boundary, hoping to put an end to white encroachments for good. Relations between the western tribes and the British improved in at least some areas after the Proclamation, partly as a result of the work of the Indian superintendents the British appointed. John Stuart was in charge of Indian affairs in the southern colonies and Sir William Johnson in the northern ones. Both were sympathetic to Native American needs and lived among the tribes; Johnson married a Mohawk woman, Mary Brant, who was later to play an important role in the American Revolution.

In the end, however, the Proclamation of 1763 failed to meet even the modest expectations of the Native Americans. It had some effect in limiting colonial land speculation in the West and in controlling the fur trade, but on the crucial point of the line of settlement it was almost completely ineffective. White settlers continued to swarm across the boundary and to claim lands farther and farther into the Ohio Valley. The British authorities tried repeatedly to establish limits to the expansion. In 1768, Stuart and Johnson negotiated new agreements with the western tribes creating a supposedly permanent boundary (which, as always, increased the area of white settlement at the expense of Native Americans). But these treaties (signed respectively at Hard Labor Creek, South Carolina, and Fort Stanwix, New York) also failed to stop the white advance. Within a few years, the 1768 agreements were replaced with new ones, which pushed the line of settlement still farther west.

The Colonial Response

The Grenville ministry soon moved to increase its authority in the colonies in more direct ways. Regular British troops, London announced, would now be stationed permanently in America; and under the Mutiny Act of 1765 the colonists were required to assist in provisioning and maintaining the army. Ships of the British navy were assigned to patrol American waters and search for smugglers. The customs service was reorganized and enlarged. Royal officials were ordered to take up their colonial posts in person instead of sending substitutes. Colonial manufacturing was to be restricted, so that it would not compete with the rapidly expanding industry of Great Britain.

The Sugar Act of 1764, designed in part to eliminate the illegal sugar trade between the continental colonies and the French and Spanish West Indies, raised the duty on sugar (while lowering the duty on molasses, further damaging the market for sugar grown in the colonies). It also established new vice-admiralty courts in America to try accused smugglers—thus depriving them of the benefit of sympathetic local juries. The Currency Act of 1764 required the colonial assemblies to stop issuing paper money (a widespread practice during the war) and to retire on schedule all the paper money already in circulation. Most momentous of all, the Stamp Act of 1765 imposed a tax on most printed documents in the colonies: newspapers, almanacs, pamphlets, deeds, wills, licenses.

The new imperial program was an effort to reapply to the colonies the old principles of mercantilism. And in some ways, it proved highly effective. British officials were soon collecting more than ten times as much annual revenue from America as before 1763. But the new policies created many more problems than they solved.

The colonists may have resented the new imperial regulations, but at first they found it difficult to resist them effectively. For one thing, Americans continued to harbor as many grievances against one another as against the authorities in London. Often, the conflicts centered around tensions between the established societies of the Atlantic coast and the newer, more precarious areas of white settlement further west—areas often known as the "backcountry." Residents of the backcountry often felt isolated from, and underrepresented in, the colonial governments. They sometimes felt beleaguered because they lived closer to the worlds of the Indian tribes than the societies of the East. In 1763, for example, a band of people from western Pennsylvania known as the Paxton Boys descended on Philadelphia with demands for relief from colonial (not British) taxes and for money to help them defend themselves against Indians; the colonial government averted bloodshed only by making concessions to them.

In 1771, a small-scale civil war broke out as a result of the so-called Regulator movement in North Carolina. The Regulators were farmers of the Carolina upcountry who organized in opposition to the high taxes that local sheriffs (appointed by the colonial governor) collected. The western counties were badly underrepresented in the colonial assembly, and the Regulators failed to win redress of their grievances there. Finally they armed themselves and began resisting tax collections by force. To suppress the revolt, Governor William Tryon raised an army of militiamen, mostly from the eastern counties, who defeated a band of 2,000 Regulators in the Battle of Alamance. Nine on each side were killed, and many

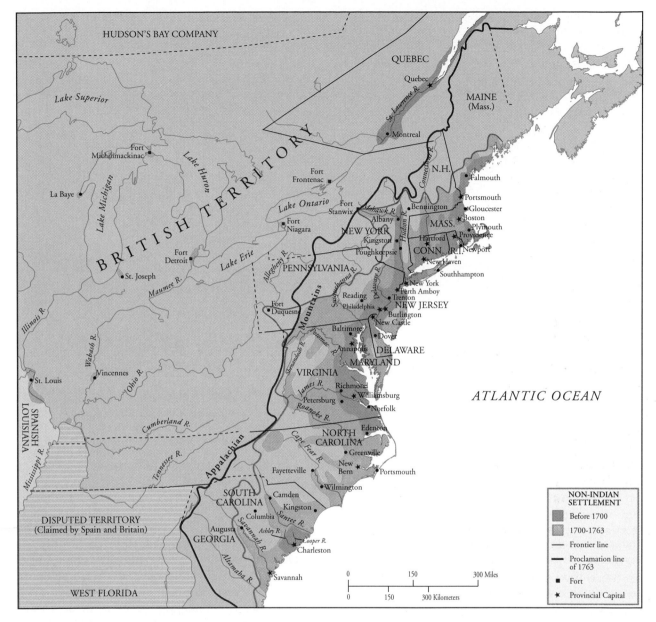

■ THE THIRTEEN COLONIES IN 1736
After 1700, settlement in the British colonies began to move westward. The complex relationship between the French, Indians, and British in the backcountry made the frontier a crucial battleground during the Seven Years' War. The defeat of the French and their Indian allies in 1763 weakened groups like the Iroquois Confederation, enabling settlers from the British colonies to settle the Ohio River valley despite attempts by the British government to restrain them.

others were wounded. Afterward, six Regulators were hanged for treason.

The bloodshed was exceptional, but bitter conflicts within the colonies were not. After 1763, however, the new policies of the British government began to create common grievances among virtually all colonists that to some degree counterbalanced these internal divisions. For under the Grenville program, as the Americans saw it, all people—in all classes, in all colonies—would suffer.

Indeed, there was something in the Grenville program to antagonize virtually everyone. Northern

■ PREPARING TO MEET THE PAXTON BOYS
The "Paxton Boys" were residents of western Pennsylvania who were declared outlaws by the assembly in Philadelphia after they launched an unauthorized attack on neighboring Conestoga Indians. Instead of surrendering, they armed themselves and marched on Philadelphia. This engraving satirizes the haphazard military preparations in the city for the expected invasion. An accompanying poem, expressing the contempt some colonists felt toward the urbanized, pacifist Quakers of Philadelphia, commented: "To kill the Paxtonians, they then did Advance, With Guns on their Shoulders, but how did they Prance." Benjamin Franklin finally persuaded the Paxton rebels not to attack in return for greater representation in the legislature. *(Library Company of Philadelphia)*

merchants believed they would suffer from restraints on their commerce, from the closing of opportunities for manufacturing, and from the increased burden of taxation. Settlers in the northern backcountry resented the closing of the West to land speculation and fur trading. Southern planters, in debt to English merchants, feared having to pay additional taxes and losing their ability to ease their debts by speculating in western land. Professionals—ministers, lawyers, professors, and others—depended on merchants and planters for their livelihood and thus shared their concerns about the effects of English law. Small farmers, the largest group in the colonies, believed they would suffer from increased taxes and from the abolition of paper money, which had enabled them to pay their loans. Workers in towns opposed the restraints on manufacturing.

The new restrictions came, moreover, at the beginning of an economic depression. The British government, by pouring money into the colonies to finance the fighting, had stimulated a wartime boom; that flow of funds stopped after the peace in 1763, precipitating an economic bust. Now the authorities in London proposed to aggravate the problem by taking money out of the colonies. The imperial policies would, many colonists feared, doom them to permanent economic stagnation and a declining standard of living.

In reality, most Americans soon found ways to live with (or circumvent) the new British policies. The American economy was not, in fact, being destroyed. But economic anxieties were rising in the colonies nevertheless, and they created a growing sense of unease, particularly in the cities—the places most directly affected by British policies and the places where resistance first arose. Urban Americans were worried about the periodic economic slumps that were occurring with greater and greater frequency. They had been shocked by the frightening depression of the early 1760s. They were alarmed by the growth of a large group within the population who were unemployed or semi-employed, and who were in either case a destabilizing element in the community. The result of all these anxieties was a feeling in some colonial cities—and particularly in Boston, the city suffering the worst economic problems—that something was deeply amiss.

Whatever the economic consequences of the British government's programs, the political consequences were—in the eyes of the colonists, at least—far worse. Perhaps nowhere else in the late-eighteenth-century world did so large a proportion of the people take an active interest in public affairs. That was partly because Anglo-Americans were accustomed (and deeply attached) to very broad powers of self-government; and the colonists were determined to protect those powers. The keys to self-government, they believed, were the provincial assemblies; and the key to the power of the provincial assemblies was their long-established right to give or withhold appropriations for the colonial governments. By attempting to circumvent the colonial assemblies, raise extensive revenues directly from the public, and provide salaries directly and unconditionally to royal officials in America, the British government was challenging the basis of colonial political power: control over public finance. Home rule, therefore, was not something new and different that the colonists were striving to attain. It was something old and familiar that they desired to keep. The movement to resist the new imperial policies, a movement for which many would ultimately fight and die, was thus at the same time democratic and conservative. It was a movement to conserve liberties Americans believed they already possessed.

STIRRINGS OF REVOLT

By the mid-1760s, therefore, a hardening of positions had begun in both England and America that would bring the colonies into increasing conflict with the mother country. The victorious war for empire had given the colonists a heightened sense of their own importance and a renewed commitment to protecting their political autonomy. It had given the British a strengthened belief in the need to tighten administration of the empire and a strong desire to use the colonies as a source of revenue. The result was a series of events that, more rapidly than anyone could imagine, shattered the English Empire in America.

The Stamp Act Crisis

Even if he had tried, Prime Minister Grenville could not have devised a better method for antagonizing and unifying the colonies than the Stamp Act of 1765. The Sugar Act of a year earlier had affected few people other than the New England merchants whose trade it hampered. But the new tax fell on all Americans, of whatever section, colony, or class. And it evoked particular opposition from some of the most powerful members of the population. Merchants and lawyers were obliged to buy stamps for ships' papers and legal documents. Tavern owners, often the political leaders of their neighborhoods, were required to buy stamps for their licenses. Printers—the most influential group in distributing information and ideas in colonial society—had to buy stamps for their newspapers and other publications.

The actual economic burdens of the Stamp Act were, in the end, relatively light; the stamps were not very expensive. What made the law obnoxious to the colonists was not so much its immediate cost as the precedent it seemed to set. In the past, Americans had rationalized the taxes and duties on colonial trade as measures to regulate commerce, not raise money. Some Americans had even managed to persuade themselves that the Sugar Act, which was in fact designed primarily to raise money, was not fundamentally different from the traditional imperial duties. The Stamp Act, however, they could interpret in only one way. It was a direct attempt by England to raise revenue in the colonies without the consent of the colonial assemblies. If this new tax passed without resistance, the door would be open for more burdensome taxation in the future.

Few colonists believed that they could do anything more than grumble and buy the stamps—until the Virginia House of Burgesses sounded what one colonist called a "trumpet of sedition" that aroused Americans to action almost everywhere. The "trumpet" was the collective voice of a group of young

■ **PATRICK HENRY AND THE PARSON'S CAUSE, 1763**
A dispute over ministerial salaries in the 1750s and early 1760s, known as the "Parson's Cause," became the occasion for some of the earliest colonial challenges to British authority. In 1759 the Privy Council in England responded to appeals from Anglican ministers in Virginia and overturned a colonial law regulating (and limiting) their salaries. As a result, ministers were able to sue for back pay. In a 1763 trial in Hanover County, the young Virginia attorney Patrick Henry persuaded a jury to rule against the Rev. James Maury in one such suit on the grounds that the king and his government had exceeded their authority. This painting by George Cooke (c. 1830) portrays Henry addressing the court as a large crowd of onlookers presses at the doors. *(Virginia Historical Society)*

Virginia aristocrats. They hoped, among other things, to challenge the power of tidewater planters who (in alliance with the royal governor) dominated Virginia politics. Foremost among the malcontents was Patrick Henry, who had already achieved fame for his fiery oratory and his occasional defiance of British authority. Henry made a dramatic speech to the House of Burgesses in May 1765, concluding with a vague prediction that if present policies were not revised, George III, like earlier tyrants, might lose his head. There were shocked cries of "Treason!" and, according to one witness, an immediate apology from Henry (although many years later he was quoted as having made the defiant reply: "If this be treason, make the most of it").

Henry introduced a set of resolutions declaring that Americans possessed the same rights as the English, especially the right to be taxed only by their own representatives; that Virginians should pay no taxes except those voted by the Virginia assembly; and that anyone advocating the right of Parliament to tax Virginians should be deemed an enemy of the colony. The House of Burgesses defeated the most extreme of Henry's resolutions, but all of them were printed and circulated as the "Virginia Resolves" (creating an impression in other colonies that the people of Virginia were more militant than they actually were).

In Massachusetts at about the same time, James Otis persuaded his fellow members of the colonial assembly to call an intercolonial congress for action against the new tax. In October 1765, the Stamp Act Congress met in New York with delegates from nine colonies and decided to petition the king and the two houses of Parliament. Their petition conceded that Americans owed to Parliament "all due subordination," but it denied that the colonies could rightfully be taxed except through their own provincial assemblies.

Meanwhile, in several colonial cities mobs began taking the law into their own hands. During the summer of 1765 serious riots broke out up and down the coast, the largest of them in Boston. Men belonging to the newly organized Sons of Liberty terrorized stamp agents and burned the stamps. The agents, themselves Americans, hastily resigned; and the sale of stamps in the continental colonies virtually ceased. In Boston, a mob also attacked such pro-British "aristocrats" as the lieutenant governor, Thomas Hutchinson (who had privately opposed passage of the Stamp Act but who, as an officer of the crown, felt obliged to support it once it became law). The protestors pillaged Hutchinson's elegant house and virtually destroyed it.

The action of the Stamp Act mobs raises the question of whether the protests in the colonies represented more than opposition to British policy. That the mobs seemed often to target symbols of affluence (such as Hutchinson's lavish home) as well as symbols of authority suggests that resentment of disparities of wealth (which had grown increasingly visible in colonial cities) played at least some role in fueling the anger among ordinary citizens. But opposition to British policy and protests against it were widespread, embracing rich and poor alike. Whatever basis in class resentments there may have been to the protests was almost certainly less important in the end than the larger political and ideological foundation.

The Stamp Act crisis was a dangerous moment in the relationship between the colonies and the British government. But the crisis subsided, largely because England backed down. The authorities in London did not relent because of the resolutions by the colonial assemblies, the petitions from the Stamp Act Congress, or the riots in American cities. They changed their attitude because of economic pressure. Even before the Stamp Act, many New Englanders had stopped buying English goods to protest the Sugar Act of 1764. Now the colonial boycott spread, and

■ **"THE TORY'S DAY OF JUDGMENT"**
A mob of American Patriots hoists a Loyalist neighbor up a flagpole in this woodcut, which is obviously sympathetic to the victim. The crowd is shown as fat, rowdy, and drunken. Public humiliations of Tories were not infrequent during the war. More common, however, was seizure of their property. *(Library of Congress)*

the Sons of Liberty intimidated those colonists who were reluctant to participate in it. The merchants of England, feeling the loss of much of their colonial market, begged Parliament to repeal the Stamp Act; and stories of unemployment, poverty, and discontent arose from English seaports and manufacturing towns.

The Marquis of Rockingham, who succeeded Grenville as prime minister in July 1765, tried to appease both the English merchants and the American colonists, and he finally convinced the king to kill the Stamp Act. On March 18, 1766, Parliament repealed it. Rockingham's opponents were strong and vociferous, and they insisted that unless England compelled the colonists to obey the Stamp Act, they would soon cease to obey any laws of Parliament. So on the same day, to satisfy such critics, Parliament passed the Declaratory Act, asserting Parliament's authority over the colonies "in all cases whatsoever." In their rejoicing over the repeal of the Stamp Act, most Americans paid little attention to this sweeping declaration of power.

The Townshend Program

The reaction in England to the Rockingham government's policy of appeasement was less enthusiastic than it was in America. English landlords, a powerful political force, angrily protested that the government had "sacrificed the landed gentlemen to the interests of traders and colonists." They feared that backing down from taxing the colonies would lead the government to increase taxes on them. The king finally bowed to their pressure and dismissed the Rockingham ministry. To replace it, he called upon the aging but still powerful William Pitt to form a government. Pitt had been a strong critic of the Stamp Act and had a reputation in America as a friend of the colonists (even though his acceptance of a peerage in 1766 had disillusioned some of his American admirers). Once in office, however, Pitt (now Lord Chatham) was so hobbled by gout and at times so incapacitated by mental illness that the actual leadership of his administration fell to the chancellor of the exchequer, Charles Townshend—a brilliant, flamboyant, and at times reckless politician known to his contemporaries variously as "the Weathercock" and "Champagne Charlie."

Among Townshend's first challenges was dealing with the continuing American grievances against Parliament. The greatest of them, now that the Stamp Act had failed, involved the Mutiny (or Quartering) Act of 1765, which required the colonists to provide quarters and supplies for the British troops in America. The British considered this a reasonable requirement. The troops were stationed in North America to protect the colonists from Indian or French attack and to defend the frontiers; lodging the troops in coastal cities was simply a way to reduce the costs to England of supplying them. To the colonists, however, the law was another assault on their liberties.

They did not so much object to quartering the troops or providing them with supplies; they had been doing that voluntarily ever since the last years of the French and Indian War. They resented that these contributions were now mandatory, and they considered it another form of taxation without consent. They responded with defiance. The Massachusetts Assembly refused to vote the mandated supplies to the troops. The New York Assembly soon did likewise, posing an even greater challenge to imperial authority, since the army headquarters were in New York City.

To enforce the law and to try again to raise revenues in the colonies, Townshend steered two measures through Parliament in 1767. The first disbanded the New York Assembly until the colonists agreed to obey the Mutiny Act. (By singling out New York, Townshend thought he would avoid Grenville's mistake of arousing all the colonies at once.) The second levied new taxes (known as the Townshend Duties) on various goods imported to the colonies from England—lead, paint, paper, and tea. The colonists could not logically object to taxation of this kind, Townshend reasoned, because it met standards they themselves had accepted. Benjamin Franklin, as a colonial agent in London trying to prevent the passage of the Stamp Act, had long ago argued for the distinction between "internal" and "external" taxes and had denounced the stamp duties as internal taxation. Townshend himself had considered the distinction laughable; but he was nevertheless imposing duties on what he believed were clearly external transactions.

Townshend's efforts to satisfy colonial grievances were to no avail. The new duties were no more acceptable to Americans than the stamp tax. Townshend might call them external taxes, but colonial merchants and, indirectly, colonial consumers would have to pay them. Their purpose, Americans believed, was the same as that of the Stamp Act: to raise revenue from the colonists without their consent. And the suspension of the New York Assembly, far from isolating New York, aroused the resentment of all the colonies. They considered this assault on the rights of one provincial government a precedent for the annihilation of the rights of all of them.

The Massachusetts Assembly took the lead in opposing the new measures by circulating a letter to all the colonial governments urging them to stand up against every tax, external or internal, imposed by

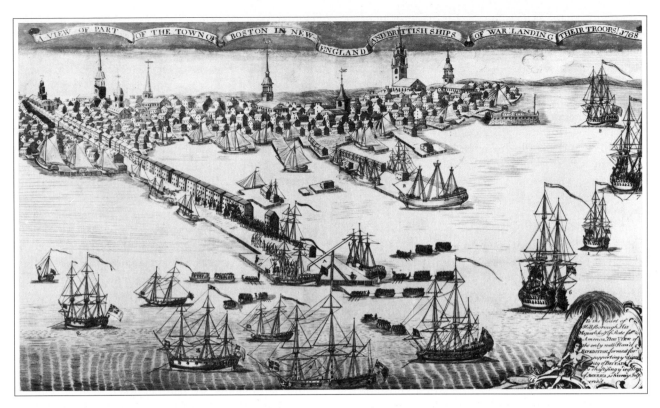

A VIEW OF PART OF THE TOWN OF BOSTON IN NEW ENGLAND AND BRITTISH SHIPS OF WAR LANDING THEIR TROOPS! 1768

■ **THE BRITISH IN BOSTON, 1768**
British troops arrived in Boston on September 30, 1768, marched into the city, and pitched tents on the Boston common. The solders were charged with ensuring the safety of British customs officers, who three months earlier had been driven from the city by local residents and had appealed to England for protection. The presence of the troops became a continuing irritant in relations between the colonists and the British government. This 1770 engraving by Paul Revere shows troops embarking from British naval vessels at Long Wharf and marching "with insolent Parade" up King Street into the city. *(Henry Francis du Point Winterthur Museum)*

Parliament. At first, the circular evoked little response in some of the legislatures (and ran into strong opposition in Pennsylvania's). Then Lord Hillsborough, secretary of state for the colonies, issued a circular letter of his own from London in which he warned that assemblies endorsing the Massachusetts letter would be dissolved. Massachusetts defiantly reaffirmed its support for the circular. (The vote in the Assembly was 92 to 17, and for a time "ninety-two" became a patriotic rallying cry throughout British America.) The other colonies, including Pennsylvania, promptly rallied to the support of Massachusetts.

In addition to his other unpopular measures, Townshend tried to strengthen enforcement of commercial regulations in the colonies by, among other things, establishing a new board of customs commissioners in America. Townshend hoped the new board would stop the rampant corruption in the colonial customs houses, and to some extent his hopes were fulfilled. The new commissioners virtually ended smuggling in Boston, their headquarters, although smugglers continued to carry on a busy trade in other colonial seaports.

The Boston merchants—accustomed, like all colonial merchants, to loose enforcement of the Navigation Acts and doubly aggrieved now that the new commission was diverting the lucrative smuggling trade elsewhere—were indignant, and they took the lead in organizing another boycott. In 1768, the merchants of Philadelphia and New York joined them in a nonimportation agreement, and later some southern merchants and planters also agreed to cooperate. Colonists boycotted British goods subject to the Townshend Duties; and throughout the colonies, American homespun and other domestic products became suddenly fashionable, while English luxuries fell from favor.

Late in 1767, Charles Townshend suddenly died—before the consequences of his ill-conceived program had become fully apparent. The question of dealing with colonial resistance to the Townshend Duties fell, therefore, to the new prime minister, Lord North. Hoping to break the nonimportation agreement and divide the colonists, Lord North secured the repeal of all the Townshend Duties except the tax on tea in March 1770.

The Boston Massacre

The withdrawal of the Townshend Duties never had a chance to pacify colonial opinion. Before news of the repeal reached America, an event in Massachusetts raised colonial resentment to a new level of intensity. The colonists' harassment of the new customs commissioners in Boston had grown so intense that the British government had placed four regiments of regular troops inside the city. The presence of the "redcoats" was a constant affront to the colonists' sense of independence and a constant reminder of what they considered British oppression. Everywhere they went, Bostonians encountered British soldiers—often arrogant and intrusive, sometimes coarse and provocative. There was particular tension between the redcoats and Boston laborers. Many British soldiers, poorly paid and poorly treated by the army, wanted jobs in their off-duty hours; and they competed with local workers in an already tight market. Clashes between them were frequent.

On the night of March 5, 1770, a few days after a particularly intense skirmish between workers at a ship-rigging factory and British soldiers who were trying to find work there, a mob of dockworkers, "liberty boys," and others began pelting the sentries at the customs house with rocks and snowballs. Hastily, Captain Thomas Preston of the British regiment lined up several of his men in front of the building to protect it. There was some scuffling; one of the soldiers was knocked down; and in the midst of it all, apparently, several British soldiers fired into the crowd, killing five people (among them a mulatto sailor, Crispus Attucks).

This murky incident, almost certainly the result of panic and confusion, was quickly transformed by local resistance leaders into the "Boston Massacre"—a graphic symbol of British oppression and brutality.

The victims became popular martyrs; the event became the subject of such lurid (and inaccurate) accounts as the widely circulated pamphlet *Innocent Blood Crying to God from the Streets of Boston*. A famous engraving by Paul Revere, widely reproduced and circulated, portrayed the massacre as a carefully organized, calculated assault on a peaceful crowd. A jury of Massachusetts colonists found the British soldiers guilty of manslaughter and sentenced them to a token punishment. Colonial pamphlets and newspapers, however, convinced many Americans that the soldiers were guilty of official murder. Year after year, resistance leaders marked the anniversary of the massacre with demonstrations and speeches. The leading figure in fomenting public outrage over the Boston Massacre was Samuel Adams, the most effective radical in the colonies. Adams (a distant cousin of John Adams, second president of the United States) was born in 1722 and was thus somewhat older than other leaders of colonial protest. As a member of an earlier generation with strong ties to New England's Puritan past, he was particularly inclined to view public events in stern moral terms. A failure in business, he had occupied several political and governmental positions. His real importance, however, was as an unflagging voice expressing outrage at British oppression. England, he argued, had become a morass of sin and corruption; only in America did public virtue survive. He spoke frequently at Boston town meetings; and as one unpopular English policy followed another—the Townshend Duties, the placement of customs commissioners in Boston, the stationing of British troops in the city (with its violent results)—his message attracted increasing support. In 1772, he proposed the creation of a "committee of correspondence" in Boston to publicize the grievances against England throughout the colony. He became its first head. Other colonies followed Massachusetts's lead, and there grew up a loose network of political organizations that kept the spirit of dissent alive through the 1770s.

The Philosophy of Revolt

"The Revolution was effected before the war commenced," John Adams later remarked. "The Revolution was in the minds and hearts of the people." Adams exaggerated. Few Americans were willing to consider complete independence from England until after the war had begun, and even those few (among them Samuel Adams) generally denied that independence was their goal. But John Adams was certainly correct in arguing that well before the fighting began in 1775, a profound ideological shift had occurred in the way many Americans viewed the British government and their own.

The ideas that would support the Revolution emerged from many sources. Some were indigenous to America, drawn from religious (particularly Puritan) sources or from the political experiences of the colonies. But powerful arguments from abroad enriched and enlarged these native ideas. Particularly important were the "radical" ideas of those in Great Britain who stood in opposition to their government. Some were Scots, who viewed the English government as tyrannical. Others were embittered "country Whigs," who considered the existing system (from which they were largely excluded) corrupt and oppressive. Drawing from some of the great philosophical minds of earlier generations—among them John Locke—these English dissidents framed a powerful argument against their government; and while that argument had only limited appeal in England, it found a ready audience in the troubled colonies. Central to this argument was a new concept of what government should be. Because humans were inherently corrupt and selfish, government was necessary to protect individuals from the evil in one another. But corruptible people ran government; and so government too needed safeguards against abuses of power.

In the eyes of most Englishmen and most Americans, the English constitution was the best system ever devised to meet these necessities. By distributing power among the three elements of society—the monarch, the aristocracy, and the common people—the English political system ensured that no individual or group could exercise authority unchecked by another. By the mid-seventeenth century, however, dissidents in both England and America were becoming convinced that this noble constitution was in danger. The king and his ministers were exercising such corrupt and autocratic authority that they were undermining the independence of the various elements of government. A single center of power was emerging, and the system was thus threatening to become a dangerous tyranny.

The English constitution was not a written document. Nor was it a fixed set of unchangeable rules. It was—and remains—a general (and flexible) sense of the "way things are done." Americans, however, thought of a constitution in terms of their colonial charters, which set out permanently, on paper, the shape and powers of government. They had difficulty accepting the idea of a flexible, changing set of basic principles. Many argued that the English constitution should itself be written down, to prevent fallible politicians from tampering with its essence.

Part of that essence, Americans believed, was their right to be taxed only with their own consent. When Townshend levied his "external" duties, the Philadelphia lawyer John Dickinson published a widely circulated pamphlet, *Letters of a Pennsylvania Farmer,* which argued that even external taxation was legal only to regulate trade, not to raise revenue. Gradually, most Americans ceased to accept even that distinction and took an unqualified stand: "No taxation without representation." Whatever the nature of a tax—whether internal or external, whether designed to raise revenue or to control trade—Parliament could not levy it without the consent of the colonists themselves.

This clamor about "representation" made little sense to the English. Only about 4 percent of the population of Great Britain could vote for members of Parliament, and some populous boroughs in England had no representatives at all. According to the prevailing English theory, such apparent inequities were of no importance. Members of Parliament did not represent individuals or particular geographical areas. Instead, each member represented the interests of the whole nation and indeed the whole empire, no matter where he happened to come from. The unenfranchised boroughs of England, the whole of Ireland, and the colonies thousands of miles away—all were thus represented in the Parliament at London, even though they elected no representatives of their own.

This was the theory of "virtual" representation. But Americans, drawing from their experiences with their town meetings and their colonial assemblies, believed in "actual" representation. Every community was entitled to its own representative, elected by the people of that community and directly responsible to them. Since Americans had no representatives of their own in Parliament, it followed that they were not represented there. But even having representatives in Parliament, many believed, would not resolve the problem, because their delegates would be outnumbered and outvoted and would be so isolated from the people who had elected them that they would not be able to perform as true representatives. Thus most colonists reverted to the argument that they could be fairly represented only in their own colonial assemblies.

According to the emerging American view of the empire, these assemblies played the same role within the colonies—had the same powers, enjoyed the same rights—that Parliament did within England. By the mid-1770s, some Americans were arguing that the empire was a sort of federation of commonwealths, each with its own legislative body, all tied together by common loyalty to the king (a view that suggested the structure of the British Commonwealth in the twentieth century). This concept allowed them to vent their anger not at the empire itself, but at the English Parliament, which was presumptuously exerting authority over the colonies to which it was not entitled. Not until very late did Americans begin to criticize the king himself. And not until the colonies were ready to declare their independence in 1776 were they ready to repudiate the English constitution.

What may have made the conflict between England and America ultimately insoluble was a fundamental difference of opinion over the nature of sovereignty. By arguing that Parliament had the right to legislate for England and for the empire as a whole, but that only the provincial assemblies could legislate for the individual colonies, Americans were in effect arguing for a division of sovereignty. Parliament would be sovereign in some matters; the assemblies would be sovereign in others. To the British, such an argument was untenable and absurd. Sovereignty, they believed, was by definition unitary. In any system of government there must be a single, ultimate authority. Since the empire was, in their view, a single, undivided unit, there could be only one authority within it: the English government of king and Parliament. As a result, the Anglo-American crisis ultimately presented the colonists with a stark choice. In the eyes of the English, there was, in effect, no middle ground between complete subordination (at least in theory) and complete independence. Slowly, cautiously, Americans found themselves moving toward independence.

That movement began with resistance, not open revolt. Opposition to British policies in the 1760s had taken the form of refusal to obey certain unjust laws. Colonists justified that resistance by citing biblical and Lockean justifications for opposing tyranny. But those justifications included within them a rationale for actual rebellion as well. The Bible suggested that people had a right not only to resist but to overthrow unjust rulers. And Locke had argued that if a government should persist in exceeding its rightful powers, the people would be free not only from their obligation to obey particular laws but from their obligation to obey the government at all. They would have the right to dissolve the "compact" and make a new one, to establish another government. The right to resist was, in other words, only the first step. If resistance proved ineffective, if a government proved to be so thoroughly corrupt and tyrannical that it could not be reformed, then citizens were entitled to revolt against it. They had a "right of revolution."

By the early 1770s, the relationship between America and England had become poisoned by resentment and mutual suspicion. Many Americans had become convinced that a "conspiracy against liberty" existed within the British government. They had articulated a philosophy that seemed to them to justify whatever measures might be necessary to protect themselves from that conspiracy. Only a small distance remained between resistance and revolution, before the colonists would be ready to break their ties with the empire. They crossed that distance quickly, beginning in 1773, when a new set of British policies shattered the imperial relationship forever.

The Tea Excitement

An apparent calm in America in the first years of the 1770s disguised a growing sense of resentment at the increasingly heavy-handed British enforcement of the Navigation Acts. The customs commissioners, who remained in the colonies despite the repeal of the Townshend Acts, were mostly clumsy, intrusive, and arrogant officials. They harassed colonial merchants and seamen constantly with petty restrictions, and they also enriched themselves through graft and through illegal seizures of merchandise.

Colonists also kept revolutionary sentiment alive through writing and talking. Dissenting leaflets, pamphlets, and books circulated widely through the colonies. In towns and cities, men gathered in churches, schools, town squares, and above all in taverns to discuss politics and express their growing dis-

Monday Morning, December 27, 1773.
THE Tea-Ship being arrived, every Inhabitant who will to preserve the Liberty of America, is defired to meet the STATE-HOUSE, This Morning, precifely at TEN o'Clock, advife what is beft to be done on this alarming Crifis.

To the PUBLIC.

THE Senfe of the City relative to the Landing the India Company's Tea, being fignified to Captain Lockyer, by the Committee, neverthelefs, it is the Defire of a Number of the Citizens, that at his Departure from hence, he fhould fee, with his own Eyes, their Deteftation of the Meafures purfued by the Miniftry and the India Company, to enflave this Country. This will be declared by the Convention of the People at his Departure from this City; which will be on next Saturday Morning, about nine o'Clock, when no Doubt, every Friend to this Country will attend. The Bells will give the Notice about an Hour before he embarks from Murray's Wharf.
By Order of the COMMITTEE.
NEW YORK, APRIL 21 st, 1774.

■ **THE BOSTON TEA PARTY**
The artist Ramberg produced this wash drawing of the Boston Tea Party in 1773. A handbill in a Philadelphia newspaper ten days later and another distributed in New York the following April illustrate how quickly the spirit of resistance spread to other colonies. *(Left, Metropolitan Museum of Art;* Upper Right, *Chicago Historical Society;* Bottom Right, *Bettmann)*

enchantment with English policy. The rise of revolutionary ideology was not simply a result of the ideas of intellectuals. It was also a product of a social process by which ordinary people heard, discussed, and absorbed new ideas.

The popular anger lying just beneath the surface was also visible in occasional acts of rebellion. At one point, colonists seized a British revenue ship on the lower Delaware River. And in 1772, angry residents of Rhode Island boarded the British schooner *Gaspée,* set it afire, and sank it in Narragansett Bay. The British response to the *Gaspée* affair further inflamed American opinion. Instead of putting the accused attackers on trial in colonial courts, the British sent a special commission to America with power to send the defendants back to England for trial.

What finally revived the revolutionary fervor of the 1760s, however, was a new act of Parliament—one that the English government had expected to be relatively uncontroversial. It involved the business of selling tea. In 1773, Britain's East India Company (which had an official monopoly on trade with the Far East) was sitting on large stocks of tea that it could not sell in England. It was on the verge of bankruptcy. In an effort to save the company, the

government passed the Tea Act of 1773, which gave the company the right to export its merchandise directly to the colonies without paying any of the regular taxes that were imposed on the colonial merchants, who had traditionally served as the middlemen in such transactions. With these privileges, the East India Company could undersell American merchants and monopolize the colonial tea trade.

The act angered many colonists for several reasons. First, it enraged influential colonial merchants, who feared being replaced and bankrupted by a powerful monopoly. The East India Company's decision to grant franchises to certain American merchants for the sale of their tea created further resentments among those excluded from this lucrative trade. More important, however, the Tea Act revived American passions about the issue of taxation without representation. The law provided no new tax on tea. But the original Townshend duty on the commodity—the only one of the original duties that had not been repealed—survived. It was the East India Company's exemption from that duty that put the colonial merchants at such a grave competitive disadvantage. Lord North assumed that most colonists

TAVERNS IN REVOLUTIONARY MASSACHUSETTS

In colonial Massachusetts, as in many other American colonies in the 1760s and 1770s, taverns (or "public houses," as they were often known) were crucial to the development of popular resistance to British rule. The Puritan culture of New England created some resistance to taverns, and there were continuing efforts by reformers to regulate or close them to reduce the problems caused by "public drunkenness," "lewd behavior," and anarchy. But as the commercial life of the colonies expanded, and as increasing numbers of people began living in towns and cities, taverns became a central institution in American social life—and eventually in its political life as well.

Taverns were appealing, of course, because they provided alcoholic drinks in a culture where the craving for alcohol—and the extent of drunkenness—was very high. But taverns had other attractions as well. There were few other places where people could meet and talk openly in public, and to many colonists the life of the tavern came to seem the only vaguely democratic experience available to them. Gradually, many came to see the attacks on the public houses as efforts to increase the power of existing elites and suppress the freedoms of ordinary people. The tavern was a mostly male institu-

■ **THE SCALES OF JUSTICE**
This sign for a Hartford tavern promises hospitality (from "the charming Patroness") and "entertainment" as well as food and drink. *(The Connecticut Historical Society, Hartford)*

would welcome the new law because it would reduce the price of tea to consumers by removing the middlemen. But resistance leaders in America argued that it was another insidious example of the results of an unconstitutional tax. Many colonists responded by boycotting tea.

The boycott was an important event in the history of colonial resistance. Unlike earlier protests, most of which had involved relatively small numbers of people, the boycott mobilized large segments of the population. It also helped link the colonies together in a common experience of mass popular protest. Partic-

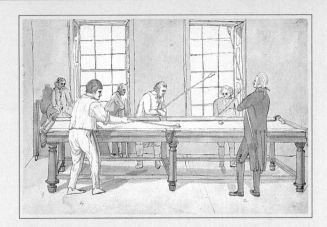

■ **TAVERN BILLIARDS**
Gentlemen in Hanover Town, Virginia gather for a game of
billiards in a local tavern in this 1797 drawing by Benjamin
Henry Latrobe. *(Maryland Historical Society, Baltimore)*

tion, just as politics was considered a mostly
male concern. And so the fusion of male cama-
raderie and political discourse emerged naturally
out of the tavern culture.

As the revolutionary crisis deepened, taverns
and pubs became the central meeting places for
discussions of the ideas that fueled resistance to
British polices. Educated and uneducated men
alike joined in animated discussions of events.
Those who could not read—and there were
many—could learn about the contents of revolutionary pamphlets from listening to tavern discussions. They could join in the discussion of the
new republican ideas emerging in the Americas
by participating in tavern celebrations of, for ex-

ample, the anniversaries of resistance to the
Stamp Act. Those anniversaries inspired elaborate
toasts in public houses throughout the colonies.
Such toasts were the equivalents of political
speeches, and illiterate men could learn much
from them about the political concepts that were
circulating through the colonies.

Taverns were important sources of information in an age before any wide distribution of
newspapers. Tavernkeepers were often trusted
informants and confidants to the Sons of Liberty
and other activists, and they were fountains of
information about the political and social turmoil
of the time. Taverns were also the settings for
political events. In 1770, for example, a report
circulated through the taverns of Danvers, Massachusetts about a local man who was continuing
to sell tea despite the colonial boycott. The Sons
of Liberty brought the seller to the Bell Tavern
and persuaded him to sign a confession and
apology before a crowd of defiant men in the
public room.

Almost all politicians found it necessary to
visit taverns in colonial Massachusetts if they
wanted any real contact with the public. Samuel
Adams spent considerable time in the public
houses of Boston, where he sought to encourage
resistance to British rule while taking care to
drink moderately so as not to erode his stature
as a leader. His cousin John Adams was somewhat more skeptical of taverns, more sensitive to
the vices they encouraged. But he, too, recognized their political value. In taverns, he once
said, "bastards, and legislatores are frequently
begotten."

ularly important to the movement were the activities
of colonial women, who were among the principal
consumers of tea and now became leaders of the effort to boycott it.

Women had played a significant role in resistance
activities from the beginning. Several women (most

prominently Mercy Otis Warren) had been important
in writing the dissident literature—in Warren's case
satirical plays—that did much to fan colonial resentments in the 1760s. Women had participated actively
in anti-British riots and crowd activities in the 1760s;
they had formed an informal organization—the

Daughters of Liberty—that occasionally mocked their male counterparts as insufficiently militant. The Sons of Liberty, they wrote in a 1768 poem, were "Supinely asleep, and depriv'd of their Sight . . . strip'd of their Freedom, and rob'd of their Right." Now, as the sentiment for a boycott grew, some women mobilized as never before, determined (as the Daughters of Liberty had written) "that rather than Freedom, we'll part with our Tea."

In the last weeks of 1773, with strong popular support, leaders in various colonies made plans to prevent the East India Company from landing its cargoes in colonial ports. In Philadelphia and New York, determined colonists kept the tea from leaving the company's ships. In Charleston, they stored it away in a public warehouse. In Boston, after failing to turn back the three ships in the harbor, local patriots staged a spectacular drama. On the evening of December 16, 1773, three companies of fifty men each, masquerading as Mohawks, passed through a tremendous crowd of spectators (which served to protect them from official interference), went aboard the three ships, broke open the tea chests, and heaved them into the harbor. As the electrifying news of the Boston "tea party" spread, other seaports followed the example and staged similar acts of resistance of their own.

When the Bostonians refused to pay for the property they had destroyed, George III and Lord North decided on a policy of coercion, to be applied only against Massachusetts—the chief center of resistance. In four acts of 1774, Parliament closed the port of Boston, drastically reduced the powers of self-government in the colony, permitted royal officers to be tried in other colonies or in England when accused of crimes, and provided for the quartering of troops in the colonists' barns and empty houses.

Parliament followed these Coercive Acts—or, as they were more widely known in America, Intolerable Acts—with the Quebec Act, which was separate from them in origin and quite different in purpose. Its object was to provide a civil government for the French-speaking Roman Catholic inhabitants of Canada and the Illinois country. The law extended the boundaries of Quebec to include the French communities between the Ohio and Mississippi Rivers. It also granted political rights to Roman Catholics and recognized the legality of the Roman Catholic Church within the enlarged province. In many ways it was a tolerant and long overdue piece of legislation. But in the inflamed atmosphere of the time, many people in

■ **PAYING THE EXCISEMAN**
This eighteenth-century satirical drawing by a British artist depicts Bostonians forcing tea down the throat of a customs official, whom they have tarred and feathered. In the background, colonists are dumping tea into the harbor (presumably a representation of the 1773 Boston Tea Party); and on the tree at right is a symbol of the Stamp Act, which the colonists had defied eight years earlier. (*Metropolitan Museum of Art*)

the thirteen English-speaking colonies considered it a threat. They were already alarmed by rumors that the Church of England was scheming to appoint a bishop for America who would impose Anglican authority on all the various sects. Since the line between the Church of England and the Church of Rome had always seemed to many Americans dangerously thin, the passage of the Quebec Act convinced some of them that a plot was afoot in London to subject Americans to the tyranny of the pope. Those interested in western lands, moreover, believed that the act would hinder westward expansion.

The Coercive Acts, far from isolating Massachusetts, made it a martyr to residents of other colonies and sparked new resistance up and down the coast. Colonial legislatures passed a series of resolves supporting

Massachusetts. Women's groups throughout the colonies mobilized to extend the boycotts of British goods and to create substitutes for the tea, textiles, and other commodities they were shunning. In Edenton, North Carolina, fifty-one women signed an agreement in October 1774 declaring their "sincere adherence" to the anti-British resolutions of their provincial assembly and proclaiming their duty to do "every thing as far as lies in our power" to support the "publick good."

✑ COOPERATION AND WAR

Revolutions do not simply happen. They need organizers and leaders. Beginning in 1765, colonial leaders developed a variety of organizations for converting popular discontent into direct action—organizations that in time formed the basis for an independent government.

New Sources of Authority

The passage of authority from the royal government to the colonists themselves began on the local level, where the tradition of autonomy was already strong. In colony after colony, local institutions responded to the resistance movement by simply seizing authority on their own. At times, entirely new, extralegal bodies emerged semi-spontaneously and began to perform some of the functions of government. In Massachusetts in 1768, for example, Samuel Adams called a convention of delegates from the towns of the colony to sit in place of the General Court, which the governor had dissolved. The Sons of Liberty, which Adams had helped organize in Massachusetts and which sprang up elsewhere as well, became another source of power. Its members at times formed disciplined bands of vigilantes who made certain that all colonists respected the boycotts and other forms of popular resistance. And in most colonies, committees of prominent citizens began meeting to perform additional political functions.

The most effective of these new groups were the committees of correspondence, which Adams had inaugurated in Massachusetts in 1772. Virginia later established the first intercolonial committees of correspondence, which made possible continuous cooperation among the colonies. Virginia also took the greatest step of all toward united action in 1774

when, after the royal governor dissolved the assembly, a rump session met in the Raleigh Tavern at Williamsburg, declared that the Intolerable Acts menaced the liberties of every colony, and issued a call for a Continental Congress.

Variously elected by the assemblies and by extralegal meetings, delegates from all the thirteen colonies except Georgia were present when, in September 1774, the First Continental Congress convened in Carpenter's Hall in Philadelphia. They made five major decisions. First, in a very close vote, they rejected a plan (proposed by Joseph Galloway of Pennsylvania) for a colonial union under British authority (much like the earlier Albany Plan). Second, they endorsed a statement of grievances, whose tortured language reflected the conflicts among the delegates between moderates and extremists. The statement reflected the influence of the moderates by seeming to concede Parliament's right to regulate colonial trade and by addressing the king as "Most Gracious Sovereign"; but it also included a more extreme demand for the repeal of all the oppressive legislation passed since 1763. Third, they approved a series of resolutions that a Suffolk County, Massachusetts, convention had passed, recommending, among other things, that the colonists make military preparations for defense against possible attack by the British troops in Boston. Fourth, they agreed to nonimportation, nonexportation, and nonconsumption as means of stopping all trade with Great Britain, and they formed a "Continental Association" to enforce the agreements. And fifth, when the delegates adjourned, they agreed to meet again the next spring, thus indicating that they considered the Continental Congress a continuing organization.

Through their representatives in Philadelphia the colonies had, in effect, reaffirmed their autonomous status within the empire and declared something close to economic war to maintain that position. The more optimistic of the Americans hoped that this economic warfare alone would win a quick and bloodless victory, but the more pessimistic had their doubts. "I expect no redress, but, on the contrary, increased resentment and double vengeance," John Adams wrote to Patrick Henry; "we must fight." And Henry replied, "By God, I am of your opinion."

During the winter, the Parliament in London debated proposals for conciliating the colonists. Lord Chatham (William Pitt), the former prime minister,

■ **RECRUITING PATRIOTS**

This Revolutionary War recruiting poster tries to attract recruits by appealing to their patriotism (asking them to defend "the liberties and independence of the United States"), their vanity (by showing the "handsome clothing" and impressive bearing of soldiers), and their greed (by offering them "a bounty of twelve dollars" and "sixty dollars a year"). *(Library of Congress)*

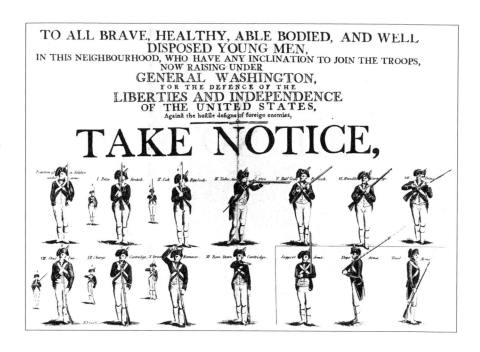

urged the withdrawal of troops from America. Edmund Burke called for the repeal of the Coercive Acts. But their efforts were in vain. Lord North finally won approval early in 1775 for a series of measures known as the Conciliatory Propositions, but they were in fact far less conciliatory than the approaches Burke or Chatham had urged. Parliament now proposed that the colonies, instead of being taxed directly by Parliament, would tax themselves at Parliament's demand. With this offer, Lord North hoped to divide the American moderates, who he believed represented the views of the majority, from the extremist minority. But his offer was probably too little and, in any case, too late. It did not reach America until after the first shots of war had been fired.

Lexington and Concord

For months, the farmers and townspeople of Massachusetts had been gathering arms and ammunition and training as "minutemen," preparing to fight on a minute's notice. The Continental Congress had approved preparations for a defensive war, and the citizen-soldiers awaited an aggressive move by the British regulars in Boston.

In Boston, General Thomas Gage, commanding the British garrison, knew of the military preparations in the countryside but considered his army too small to do anything until reinforcements arrived. He resisted the advice of less cautious officers, who assured him that the Americans would never dare actually to fight, that they would back down quickly before any show of British force. Major John Pitcairn, for example, insisted that a single "small action," such as the burning of a few towns, would "set everything to rights."

When General Gage received orders from England to arrest the rebel leaders Sam Adams and John Hancock, known to be in the vicinity of Lexington, he still hesitated. But when he heard that the minutemen had stored a large supply of gunpowder in Concord (eighteen miles from Boston), he at last decided to act. On the night of April 18, 1775, he sent a detachment of about 1,000 soldiers out from Boston on the road to Lexington and Concord. He intended to surprise the colonials and seize the illegal supplies without bloodshed.

But patriots in Boston were watching the British movements closely, and during the night two horsemen, William Dawes and Paul Revere, rode out to warn the villages and farms. When the British troops arrived in Lexington the next day, several dozen minutemen awaited them on the town common. Shots were fired and minutemen fell; eight of them were killed and ten more wounded. Advancing to Concord, the British discovered that the Americans had hastily removed most of the powder supply, but the

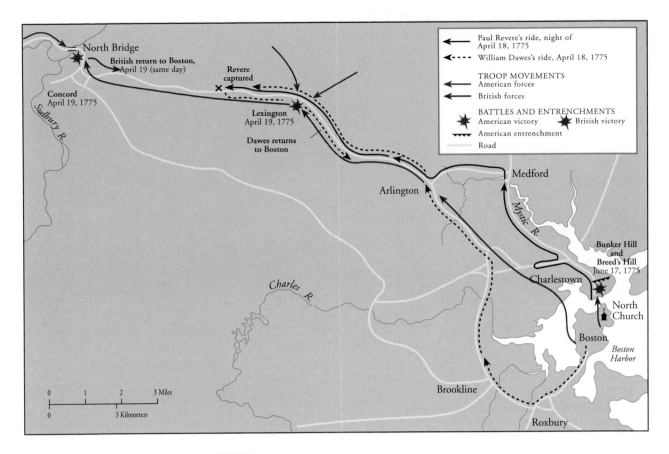

Paul Revere's ride, night of April 18, 1775
William Dawes's ride, April 18, 1775

TROOP MOVEMENTS
American forces
British forces

BATTLES AND ENTRENCHMENTS
American victory   British victory
American entrenchment
Road

North Bridge

British return to Boston, April 19 (same day)

Revere captured

Concord April 19, 1775

Sudbury R.

Lexington April 19, 1775

Dawes returns to Boston

Arlington

Medford

Mystic R.

Bunker Hill and Breed's Hill June 17, 1775

Charlestown

North Church

Boston

Boston Harbor

Charles R.

Brookline

Roxbury

0   1   2   3 Miles
0   3 Kilometers

■ THE FIRST BATTLES OF THE REVOLUTION

On April 18, 1775, General Thomas Gage sent about 1,000 soldiers from the British garrison in Boston to Lexington and Concord, where the Massachusetts minutemen were reported to be storing a large supply of gunpowder. Thanks to the midnight heroics of Patriot leaders William Dawes and Paul Revere, who rode from Boston the night before to warn the minutemen of the British plans, Gage's troops met armed resistance at Lexington, and were harassed by continual gunfire all along the road from Concord back to Boston. These skirmishes rallied thousands of colonists to the rebel cause.

British burned what was left of it. All along the road from Concord back to Boston, farmers hiding behind trees, rocks, and stone fences harassed the British with continual gunfire. By the end of the day, the British had lost almost three times as many men as the Americans.

The first shots—the "shots heard round the world," as Americans later called them—had been fired. But who had fired them? According to one of the minutemen at Lexington, Major Pitcairn had shouted to the colonists on his arrival, "Disperse, ye rebels!" When the Americans ignored the command, he had given the order to fire. British officers and soldiers told a different story. They claimed that the minutemen had fired first, that only after seeing the flash of American guns

had the British begun to shoot. Whatever the truth, the rebels succeeded in circulating their account well ahead of the British version, adorning it with lurid tales of British atrocities. The effect was to rally to the rebel cause thousands of colonists, north and south, who previously had had little enthusiasm for it.

It was not immediately clear to the British, and even to many Americans, that the skirmishes at Lexington and Concord were the first battles of a war. Many saw them as simply another example of the tensions that had been afflicting Anglo-American relations for years. But whether they recognized it at the time or not, the British and the Americans had taken a decisive step. The War for Independence had begun.

■ THE BRITISH RETREAT FROM CONCORD, 1775

This American cartoon satirizes the retreat of British forces from Concord after the battle there on April 19, 1775. Patriot forces are lined up on the left, and the retreating British forces (portrayed with dog heads, perhaps because many of the soldiers were "wild" Irish) straggle off at right—some fleeing in panic, others gloating over the booty they have plundered from the burning homes above. In its crude and exaggerated way, the cartoon depicts the success of Patriot forces at the Old North Bridge in Concord in repulsing a British contingent under the command of Lord Percy. As the redcoats retreated to Lexington and then to Boston, they continued to encounter fire from colonial forces, not arrayed in battle lines as shown here, but hidden along the road. One British soldier described the nightmarish withdrawal: "We were fired on from Houses and behind Trees . . . the Country was . . . full of Hills, Woods, stone Walls . . . which the Rebels did not fail to take advantage of." *(Brown University Library)*

CONCLUSION

When the French and Indian War ended in 1763, it might have seemed reasonable to expect that relations between the English colonists in America and Great Britain itself would have been cemented more firmly than ever. America and Britain had fought together in a great war against the French and their Indian allies. They had won impressive victories. They had vastly expanded the size of the British Empire.

But in fact the end of the French and Indian War altered the imperial relationship forever, in ways that ultimately drove Americans to rebel against English rule and begin a war for independence. To the British, the lesson of the war was that the colonies in America needed firmer control from London. The empire was now much bigger, and it needed better administration. The war had produced great debts, and the Americans—among the principal beneficiaries of the war—should help pay them. And so for more than a decade after the end of the fighting, the British tried one strategy after another to tighten control over and extract money from the colonies, all of them in the end failures.

To the colonists, this effort to tighten imperial rule was both a betrayal of the sacrifices they had

Significant Events

1713	Treaty of Utrecht concludes Queen Anne's War
1718	New Orleans founded to serve French plantation economy in Louisiana
1744–1748	King George's War
1749	French construct fortresses in Ohio Valley
1754	Albany Plan for intercolonial cooperation rejected
	Battle of Fort Duquesne begins French and Indian War
1756	Seven Years' War begins in Europe
1757	British policies provoke riots in New York
1758	Pitt returns authority to colonial assemblies
	British capture Louisbourg fortress and Fort Duquesne
1759	British forces under Wolfe capture Quebec
1760	George III becomes king
	French army surrenders to Amherst at Montreal
1763	Peace of Paris ends Seven Years' (and French and Indian) War
	Grenville becomes prime minister
	Proclamation of 1763 restricts western settlement
	Paxton uprising in Pennsylvania
1764	Sugar Act passed
	Currency Act passed
1765	Stamp Act crisis
	Mutiny Act passed
1766	Stamp Act repealed
	Declaratory Act passed
1767	Townshend duties imposed
1768	Boston, New York, and Philadelphia merchants make nonimportation agreement
1770	Boston Massacre
	Most Townshend Duties repealed
1771	Regulator movement quelled in North Carolina
1772	Committees of correspondence established in Boston
	Gaspée incident in Rhode Island
1773	Tea Act passed
	Bostonians stage tea party
1774	Intolerable Acts passed
	First Continental Congress meets at Philadelphia
	North Carolina women sign Edenton Proclamation calling for boycott of British goods
1775	Clashes at Lexington and Concord begin American Revolution

made in the war and a challenge to their long-developing assumptions about the rights of English people to rule themselves. Gradually, white Americans came to see in the British policies evidence of a conspiracy to establish tyranny in the New World. And so throughout the 1760s and 1770s, the colonists developed ever more overt and effective forms of resistance. By the time the first shots were fired in the American Revolution in 1775, Britain and America—not long before bonded so closely to one another that most white Americans considered themselves as English as any resident of London—had come to view each other as two very different societies. Their differences, which came to seem irreconcilable, propelled them into a war that would change the course of history.

FOR FURTHER REFERENCE

Suggested Readings   Richard White, *The Middle Ground: Indians, Empires, and Republics in the Great Lakes Region, 1650–1815* (1991) argues that Indians in the Great Lakes regions were able to take advantage of European rivalries for much of the eighteenth century. Francis Jennings, *The Ambiguous Iroquois Empire* (1984) makes a similar point. Richard Bushman, *King and People in Colonial Massachusetts* (1987) traces the fracture between Massachusetts colonists and the imperial government. Gary Nash, *The Urban Crucible: The Northern Seaports and the Origins of the American Revolution* (1979) argues that increasing class stratification in northern cities contributed to the coming of the American Revolution. Robert R. Palmer, *The Age of Democratic Revolution: Vol. 1, The Challenge* (1959) and J.G.A. Pocock, *The Machiavellian Moment* (1975) both place the American Revolution in the context of a transatlantic political culture. Bernard Bailyn, *The Ideological Origins of the American Revolution* (1967) was one of the first works by an American historian to emphasize the importance of English republican political thought for the revolutionary ideology of the American colonists.

Films   (The best source for information on how to find these and other films is *Bowker's Complete Video Directory*—3 volumes.) *The American Story, No. 1: Road to Revolution* (1985) reviews the events, beginning with the Stamp Act crisis, that led the American colonies to the brink of open rebellion. *Colonial America in the Seventeen Sixties* (1967) examines the conflicts between the colonies and Britain in the crucial years after 1763. *Colonial America: The Roots of Revolution 1607–1775* (1979) uses full costume recreations to help explain the economic, cultural, and religious reasons for revolution. *Paul Revere* (1996) is a biography of one of America's most celebrated patriots. *Lexington, Concord, & Independence* (1967) narrates the first battles of the American Revolution. *Patrick Henry: Virginia Patriot* (1990) documents the life and achievements of the man whose words "Give Me Liberty or Give Me Death" became a rallying cry of the Revolution.

Internet Resources   (For up-to-date URL addresses and links to these and other websites, consult the McGraw-Hill history site at *http://www.mmhe.com/socscience/history/usa/link/linktop.htm*) *The Avalon Project at the Yale Law School: 18th Century Documents* assembles political documents relating to American independence, from the Albany Plan of Union to the Jay Treaty. *The French and Indian War* provides information on the confrontation between English and French power in North America.

BIBLIOGRAPHY

General Histories   J. R. Alden, *A History of the American Revolution* (1969). Charles M. Andrews, *The Colonial Background of the American Revolution* (1924, rev. 1931). Ian R. Christie, *Crisis of Empire* (1966). Ian R. Christie and Benjamin W. Labaree, *Empire or Independence, 1760–1776* (1976). Edward Countryman, *The American Revolution* (1985). Lawrence Henry Gipson, *The Coming of the Revolution, 1763–1775* (1954). Merill Jensen, *The Founding of a Nation* (1968). Robert Middlekauff, *The Glorious Cause: The American Revolution, 1763–1789* (1982). Edmund S. Morgan, *The Birth of the Republic* (1956). Alfred E. Young, Jr., ed., *The American Revolution* (1976).

The British Imperial System   John Brewer, *Party Ideology and Popular Politics at the Accession of George III* (1967). John Brooke, *King George III* (1972). Richard L. Bushman, *King and People in Colonial Massachusetts* (1987). Robert Calhoon, *Dominion and Liberty: Ideology in the Anglo-American World* (1994).

J.C.D. Clark, *The Language of Liberty, 1660–1832* (1994). Sylvia R. Frey, *The British Soldier in America* (1981). Lawrence Henry Gipson, *The British Empire Before the American Revolution*, 15 vols. (1936–1970). Michael Kammen, *A Rope of Sand* (1968). Lewis B. Namier, *England in the Age of the American Revolution*, rev. ed. (1961); *The Structure of Politics at the Accession of George III*, rev. ed. (1961). Alison Gilbert Olson, *Making the Empire Work: London and American Interest Groups, 1690–1790* (1992). Howard H. Peckham, *The Colonial Wars, 1689–1762* (1963). Alan Rogers, *Empire and Liberty* (1974). John Shy, *Toward Lexington: The Role of the British Army in the Coming of the American Revolution* (1965).

The French and the Indians   Fred Anderson, *A People's Army: Massachusetts Soldiers and Society in the Seven Year's War* (1984). David H. Corkran, *The Cherokee Frontier* (1962); *The Creek Frontier* (1967). Gregory Evans Dowd, *A Spirited Resistance: The North American*

Indian Struggle for Unity, 1745–1815 (1992). Francis Jennings, *Empire of Fortune* (1988). William Pencak, *War, Politics, and Revolution in Provincial Massachusetts* (1981). Harold E. Selesky, *War and Society in Early Connecticut* (1990). J. M. Sosin, *Whitehall and the Wilderness* (1961).

Merchants and the Empire   Thomas C. Barrow, *Trade and Empire: The British Customs Service in Colonial America* (1967). John Crowley, *The Privileges of Independence: Neomercantilism and the American Revolution* (1993). Thomas Doerflinger, *A Vigorous Spirit of Enterprise: Merchants and Economic Development in Revolutionary Philadelphia* (1986). Joseph Ernst, *Money and Politics in America, 1755–1775* (1973). Michael Kammen, *Empire and Interest: The American Colonies and the Politics of Mercantilism* (1970). Arthur M. Schlesinger, *The Colonial Merchants and the American Revolution* (1917). John W. Tyler, *Smugglers and Patriots: Boston Merchants and the Advent of the American Revolution* (1986).

American Resistance   David Ammerman, *In the Common Cause* (1974). Marc Egnal, *A Mighty Empire: The Origins of the American Revolution* (1988). Paul A. Gilje, *The Road to Mobocracy: Popular Disorder in New York City, 1763–1834* (1987). Dirk Hoerder, *Crowd Action in Revolutionary Massachusetts* (1977). Peter C. Hoffer, *Revolution and Regeneration: Life Cycle and the Historical Vision of the Generation of 1776* (1983). Benjamin W. Labaree, *The Boston Tea Party* (1964). Pauline Maier, *From Resistance to Revolution* (1972). Edmund S. Morgan and Helen M. Morgan, *The Stamp Act Crisis,* rev. ed. (1953). Peter D. G. Thomas, *The Townshend Duties Crisis* (1987). Hiller B. Zobel, *The Boston Massacre* (1970).

Revolutionary Ideology   Ian R. Christie, *Wilkes, Wyvil, and Reform* (1962). Nathan Hatch, *The Sacred Cause of Liberty* (1977). Rhys Isaac, *The Transformation of Virginia, 1740–1790* (1982). Isaac Kramnick, *Bolingbroke and His Circle* (1968). Richard Merritt, *Symbols of American Community, 1735–1775* (1966). George Rudé, *Wilkes and Liberty* (1962).

Revolutionary Politics   Carl Becker, *The History of Political Parties in the Province of New York* (1909). R. E. Brown and B. K. Brown, *Virginia, 1705–1786* (1964). Richard D. Brown, *Revolutionary Politics in Massachusetts* (1970). L. R. Gerlach, *Prologue to Independence* (1976). Ronald Hoffman, *A Spirit of Dissension* (1973). Neil R. Stout, *The Perfect Crisis: The Beginning of the Revolutionary War* (1976).

Chapter Five

THE AMERICAN REVOLUTION

Two struggles occurred simultaneously during the seven years of war that began in April 1775. One was the military conflict with Great Britain. The second was a political struggle within America. The two struggles had profound effects on each other.

The military conflict was, by the standards of later wars, a relatively modest one. Battle deaths on the American side totaled fewer than 5,000. The technology of warfare was so crude that cannons and rifles were effective only at very close range, and fighting of any kind was virtually out of the question in bad weather. Yet the war in America was, by the standards of its own day, an unusually savage conflict, pitting not only army against army, but at times the population at large against a powerful external force. This shift of the war from a traditional, conventional struggle to a new kind of conflict—a revolutionary war for liberation—made it possible for the new American army finally to defeat the vastly more powerful British.

At the same time, Americans were wrestling with the great political questions the conflict necessarily produced: first, whether to demand independence from Britain; then, how to structure the new nation they had proclaimed. Only the first of these questions had been resolved when the British surrendered at Yorktown in 1781. But by then the United States had already established itself—both in its own mind and in the mind of much of the rest of the world—as a new kind of nation, one with a special mission and dedicated to enlightened ideals. Thomas Paine, an important figure in shaping the Revolution, reflected the opinion of many when he claimed that the American War for Independence had "contributed more to enlighten the world, and diffuse a spirit of freedom and liberality among mankind, than any human event . . . that ever preceded it." And if the subsequent history of the United States did not always fulfill those ideals, the belief that the nation should try to do so exercised a continuing influence on the nation's behavior.

■ **PULLING DOWN THE KING'S STATUE**
American Patriots tear down a statue of King George III from its pedestal in New York City's Bowling Green in 1776 to demonstrate their new independence from England—much as demonstrators tore down statues of Lenin and others in eastern Europe in 1989 as they overthrew communist governments there. *(Pulling down the statue of George III at Bowling Green [Detail]. By William Walcutt) (Lafayette College Art Collection, Easton, Pennsylvania)*

THE STATES UNITED

Although many Americans had been expecting a military conflict with Britain for months, even years, the actual beginning of hostilities in 1775 found the colonies generally unprepared for the enormous challenges awaiting them. America was an unformed nation, with a population less than a third as large as the 9 million of Great Britain, and with vastly inferior economic and military resources. It faced the task of mobilizing for war against the world's greatest armed power. Americans faced that task, moreover, deeply divided about what they were fighting for.

Defining American War Aims

Three weeks after the battles of Lexington and Concord, the Second Continental Congress met in the State House in Philadelphia, with delegates from every colony except Georgia, which sent no representative until the following autumn. The members agreed to support the war. But they disagreed, at times profoundly, about its purpose.

At one pole was a group led by the Adams cousins (John and Samuel), Richard Henry Lee of Virginia, and others, who favored complete independence from Great Britain. At the other pole was a group led by such moderates as John Dickinson of Pennsylvania, who hoped for modest reforms in the imperial relationship that would permit an early reconciliation with Great Britain. Most of the delegates tried to find some middle ground between these positions. They demonstrated their uncertainty in two very different declarations, which they adopted in quick succession. They approved one last, conciliatory appeal to the king, the "Olive Branch Petition." Then, on July 6, 1775, they adopted a more antagonistic "Declaration of the Causes and Necessity of Taking Up Arms." It proclaimed that the British government had left the American people with only two alternatives, "unconditional submission to the tyranny of irritated ministers or resistance by force."

The attitude of much of the public mirrored that of the Congress. At first, most Americans believed they were fighting not for independence but for a redress of grievances within the British Empire. During the first year of fighting, however, many of them began to change their minds, for several reasons. First, the costs of the war—human and financial—were so high

that the original war aims began to seem too modest to justify them. Second, what lingering affection American Patriots retained for England greatly diminished when the British began trying to recruit Indians, African slaves, and foreign mercenaries (the hated "Hessians") against them. Third, and most important, colonists came to believe that the British government was forcing them toward independence by rejecting the Olive Branch Petition and instead enacting a "Prohibitory Act," which closed the colonies to all overseas trade and made no concessions to American demands except an offer to pardon repentant rebels. The British enforced the Prohibitory Act with a naval blockade of colonial ports.

But the growing support for independence remained to a large degree unspoken until January 1776, when an impassioned pamphlet appeared that galvanized many Americans. It was called, simply, *Common Sense*. Its author, unmentioned on the title page, was Thomas Paine, who had emigrated from England to America less than two years before (with letters of introduction from Benjamin Franklin, whom he had met in London). Long a failure in various trades, Paine now proved a brilliant success as a revolutionary propagandist. His pamphlet helped change the American outlook toward the war. Paine wished to expose the folly of continuing to believe reconciliation with Britain was possible. He wanted to turn the anger of Americans away from the specific parliamentary measures they were resisting and toward what he considered the root of the problem—the English constitution itself. It was not enough, he argued, for Americans to continue blaming their problems on particular ministers, or even on Parliament. It was the king, and the system that permitted him to rule, that was to blame. It was, he argued, simple common sense for Americans to break completely with a government that could produce so corrupt a monarch as George III, a government that could inflict such brutality on its own people, a government that could drag Americans into wars in which America had no interest. The island kingdom of England was no more fit to rule the American continent, he claimed, than a satellite was fit to rule the sun.

The Decision for Independence

Common Sense sold more than 100,000 copies in its first few months. (Given the size of the American population at the time, that would be the equivalent

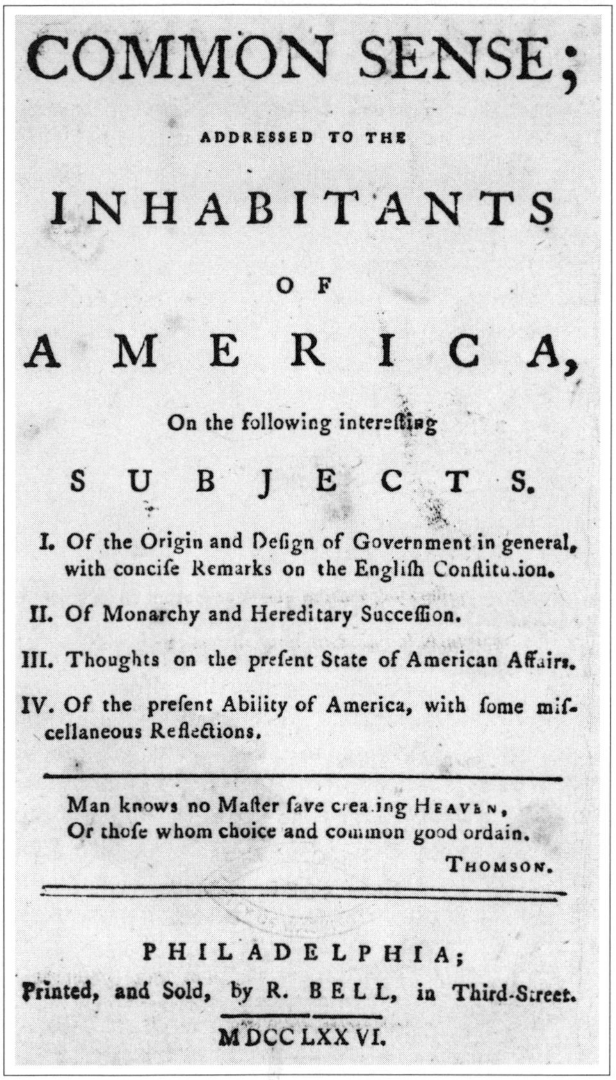

COMMON SENSE;

ADDRESSED TO THE

INHABITANTS

O F

AMERICA,

On the following interesting

SUBJECTS.

I. Of the Origin and Defign of Government in general,
with concife Remarks on the Englifh Conftitution.

II. Of Monarchy and Hereditary Succeffion.

III. Thoughts on the prefent State of American Affairs.

IV. Of the prefent Ability of America, with fome mif-
cellaneous Reflections.

Man knows no Mafter fave creating HEAVEN,
Or thofe whom choice and common good ordain.
THOMSON.

PHILADELPHIA;

Printed, and Sold, by R. BELL, in Third-Street.

MDCCLXXVI.

■ *COMMON SENSE*
Shown here is the title page of the first edition of Thomas Paine's influential pamphlet, published anonymously in Philadelphia on January 10, 1776. Paine served in Washington's army during the campaigns in New Jersey and at the same time wrote a series of essays designed to arouse support for the Patriot cause. They were collectively titled *The Crisis* (the first of them contains the famous phrase "These are the times that try men's souls"). In later years Paine took an active part in the French Revolution, on behalf of which he published *The Rights of Man* (1791–1792). He also wrote *The Age of Reason* (1794–1796), which attacked conventional Christian beliefs and promoted his own "deist" philosophy. He returned to America in 1802 and spent the last years before his death in 1809 in poverty and obscurity. *(Library of Congress)*

of selling 8 million copies today.) To many of its readers it was a revelation. Although sentiment for independence remained far from unanimous, support for the idea grew rapidly in the first months of 1776.

In the midst of all this, the Continental Congress (meeting again in Philadelphia) was moving slowly and tentatively toward a final break with England. It declared American ports open to the ships of all nations except Great Britain. It entered into communication with foreign powers. It recommended to the various colonies that they establish new governments independent of the British Empire, as in fact most already were doing. Congress also appointed a committee to draft a formal declaration of independence. On July 2, 1776, it adopted a resolution: "That these United Colonies are, and, of right, ought to be, free and independent states; that they are absolved from all allegiance to the British crown, and that all political connexion between them and the state of Great Britain is, and ought to be, totally dissolved." Two days later, on July 4, Congress approved the Declaration of Independence itself, which provided the formal justifications for the actions the delegates had in fact taken two days earlier.

Thomas Jefferson, a thirty-three-year-old delegate from Virginia, wrote most of the Declaration, with help from Benjamin Franklin and John Adams. As Adams later observed, Jefferson said little in the document that was new. Its virtue lay in the eloquence with which it expressed beliefs already widespread in America. In particular, it expressed ideas that had been voiced throughout the colonies in the preceding months in the form of at least ninety other, local "declarations of independence"—declarations drafted up and down the coast by town meetings, artisan and militia organizations, county officials, grand juries, Sons of Liberty, and colonial assemblies. Jefferson borrowed heavily from these texts, both for the ideas he expressed and, to some extent, for the precise language he used.

The document was in two parts. In the first, the Declaration restated the familiar contract theory of John Locke: that governments were formed to protect the rights of life, liberty, and property; Jefferson gave the theory a more idealistic tone by referring instead to the rights of "life, liberty and the pursuit of happiness." In the second part, the Declaration listed the alleged crimes of the king, who, with the backing of Parliament, had violated his "contract"

THE AMERICAN REVOLUTION

Through most of its long life, the debate over the origins of the American Revolution has tended to reflect two broad schools of interpretation. One sees the Revolution largely as a political and intellectual event and argues that the revolt against Britain was part of a defense of ideals and principles. The other views the Revolution as a social and economic phenomenon and contends that material interests were at its heart.

The Revolutionary generation itself portrayed the conflict as a struggle over ideals, and their interpretation prevailed through most of the nineteenth century. For example, George Bancroft wrote in 1876 that the Revolution "was most radical in its character, yet achieved with such benign tranquillity that even conservatism hesitated to censure." Its aim, he argued, was to "preserve liberty" against British tyranny.

But in the early twentieth century, historians influenced by the reform currents of the progressive era began to identify social and economic forces that they believed had contributed to the rebellion. In a 1909 study of New York, Carl Becker wrote that two questions had shaped the Revolution: "The first was the question of home rule; the second was the question . . . of who should rule at home." The colonists were not only fighting the British; they were also engaged in a kind of civil war, a contest for power between radicals and conservatives that led to the "democratization of American politics and society."

Other "progressive" historians elaborated on Becker's thesis. In *The American Revolution Considered as a Social Movement* (1926), J. Franklin Jameson argued that "the stream of revolution, once started, could not be confined within narrow banks, but spread abroad upon the land. . . . Many economic desires, many social aspirations, were set free by the political struggle, many aspects of society profoundly altered by the

(Brown University Library)

forces thus let loose." In a 1917 book, Arthur M. Schlesinger maintained that colonial merchants, motivated by their own interest in escaping the restrictive policies of British mercantilism, aroused American resistance in the 1760s and 1770s.

Beginning in the 1950s, a new generation of scholars began to re-emphasize the role of ideology and to de-emphasize the role of economic interests. Robert E. Brown (in 1955) and Edmund S. Morgan (in 1956) both argued that most eighteenth-century white Americans, regardless of station, shared basic political principles and that the social and economic conflicts the progressives had identified were not severe. The rhetoric of the Revolution, they suggested, was not propaganda, but a real reflection of the colonists' ideas. Bernard Bailyn, in *The Ideological Origins of the American Revolution* (1967), demonstrated the complex roots of the ideas behind the Revolution and argued that this carefully constructed political stance was not a disguise for economic interests but a genuine ideology that itself motivated the colonists to act. The Revolution, he claimed, "was above all else an ideological, constitutional, political struggle and not primarily a controversy between social groups undertaken to force changes in the organization of the society or the economy."

By the late 1960s, however, a group of younger historians—many of them influenced by the New Left—were challenging the ideological interpretation again by illuminating social and economic tensions within colonial society that they claimed helped shape the Revolutionary struggle. Jesse Lemisch and Dirk Hoerder pointed to the actions of mobs in colonial cities as evidence of popular resentment of both American and British elites. Joseph Ernst re-emphasized the significance of economic pressures on colonial merchants and tradesmen. Gary Nash, in *The Urban Crucible* (1979), emphasized the role of growing economic distress in colonial cities in creating a climate in which Revolutionary sentiment could flourish. Edward Countryman and Rhys Isaac both pointed to changes in the nature of colonial society and culture, and in the relationship between classes in eighteenth-century America, as a crucial prerequisite for the growth of the Revolutionary movement.

Some newer social interpretations of the Revolution attempt to break free of the old debate pitting ideas against interests. The two things are not in competition with, but rather reinforce one another, more recent scholars argue. "Everyone has economic interests," Gary Nash has written, "and everyone . . . has an ideology." Only by exploring the relationships between the two can historians

(National Gallery of Art, Washington)

hope fully to understand either. Also, as Linda Kerber has written, newer interpretations have "reinvigorated the Progressive focus on social conflict between classes and extended it to include the experience not only of rich and poor but of a wide variety of interest groups, marginal communities, and social outsiders." That extension of focus to previously little-studied groups includes work by Mary Beth Norton on women, Silvia Frey on slaves, and Colin Calloway on Native Americans.

Finally, Gordon Wood, in *The Radicalism of the American Revolution* (1992), helped revive an interpretation of the Revolution that few historians have embraced in recent decades: that it was a genuinely radical event, which led to the breakdown of such longstanding patterns of society as deference, patriarchy, and traditional gender relations. Class conflict and radical goals may not have caused the Revolution; but the Revolution had a profound, even radical, impact on society nevertheless.

■ **VOTING FOR INDEPENDENCE**
The Continental Congress actually voted in favor of independence from Great Britain on July 2, 1776. July 4, the date Americans now celebrate as Independence Day, is when the Congress formally approved the Declaration of Independence. This painting by Edgar Pine-Savage re-creates the scene in Philadelphia as delegates from the various colonies made their momentous decision. *(Historical Society of Pennsylvania)*

with the colonists and thus had forfeited all claim to their loyalty.

The Declaration's ringing endorsement of the idea that "all men are created equal"—a phrase borrowed from an earlier document by Jefferson's fellow Virginian George Mason—later helped movements of liberation and reform of many kinds in the United States and abroad. It helped inspire, among other things, the French Revolution's own Declaration of the Rights of Man. More immediately, the Declaration—and its bold claim that the American colonies were now a sovereign nation, "The United States of America"—led to increased foreign aid for the struggling rebels and prepared the way for France's intervention on their side. The Declaration also encouraged American Patri-

ots, as those opposing the British called themselves, to fight on and to reject the idea of a peace that stopped short of winning independence. At the same time it created deep divisions within American society.

Responses to Independence

At the news of the Declaration of Independence, crowds in Philadelphia, Boston, and other places gathered to cheer, fire guns and cannons, and ring church bells. But there were many in America who did not rejoice. Some had disapproved of the war from the beginning. Others had been willing to support it only so long as its aims did not conflict with their basic loyalty to the king. Such people were a minority, but a substantial one. They called themselves Loyalists; supporters of independence called them Tories.

In the aftermath of the Declaration of Independence, the colonies began to call themselves states—a reflection of their belief that each province was now in some respects a separate and sovereign entity. And as states, they had to create new governments to replace the royal governments that independence had repudiated. By 1781, most states had produced written constitutions that established republican governments; some of these constitutions survived, with only minor changes, for decades to come.

At the national level, however, the process of forming a government was more halting and less successful. For a time, Americans were uncertain whether they even wanted a real national government; the Continental Congress had not been much more than a coordinating mechanism, and virtually everyone considered the individual colonies (now states) the real centers of authority. Yet fighting a war required a certain amount of central direction. Americans began almost immediately to do something they would continue to do for more than two centuries: balance the commitment to state and local autonomy against the need for some centralized authority.

In November 1777, Congress adopted the Articles of Confederation (which were not finally ratified until 1781). They did little more than confirm the weak, decentralized system already in operation. The Continental Congress would survive as the chief coordinating agency of the war effort. Its powers over the individual states would be very limited. Indeed, the Articles did not make it entirely clear that the Congress was to be a real government at all. As a result, the new nation had to fight a war for its own survival with a weak and uncertain central government, never sure of its own legitimacy.

Mobilizing for War

The new governments of the states and the nation faced a series of overwhelming challenges: raising and organizing armies, providing them with the supplies and equipment they needed, and finding a way to pay for it all. Without access to the British markets on which the colonies had come to depend, finding necessary supplies was exceptionally difficult. Shortages persisted to the end.

America had many gunsmiths, but they could not come close to meeting the wartime demand for guns and ammunition, let alone the demand for heavy arms. Although Congress created a government arsenal at Springfield, Massachusetts, in 1777, the Americans managed to manufacture only a small fraction of the equipment they used. They relied heavily on weapons and materiel they were able to capture from the British. But they got most of their war supplies from European nations, mainly from France.

Financing the war proved in many ways the most nettlesome problem. Congress had no authority to levy taxes directly on the people; it had to requisition funds from the state governments. But hard money was scarce in America, and the states were little better equipped to raise it than Congress was. None of them contributed more than a small part of their expected share. Congress tried to raise money by selling long-term bonds, but few Americans could afford them and those who could generally preferred to invest in more profitable ventures, such as privateering. In the end, the government had no choice but to issue paper money. Continental currency came from the printing presses in large and repeated batches. The states printed sizable amounts of paper currency of their own.

The result, predictably, was inflation. Prices rose to fantastic heights, and the value of paper money plummeted. Many American farmers and merchants began to prefer doing business with the British, who could pay for goods in gold or silver coin. (That was one reason why George Washington's troops suffered from severe food shortages at Valley Forge in the winter of 1777–1778; many Philadelphia merchants would not sell to them.) Congress tried repeatedly to stem the inflationary spiral. All such efforts failed. In the end, the new American government was able to finance the war effort only by borrowing heavily from other nations.

After the first great surge of patriotism faded in 1775, few Americans volunteered for military service. As a result, the states had to resort to persuasion and force: to paying bounties to attract new

■ **REVOLUTIONARY SOLDIERS**
Jean Baptiste de Verger, a French officer serving in America during the Revolution, kept a journal of his experiences illustrated with watercolors. Here he portrays four American soldiers carrying different kinds of arms: a black infantryman with a light rifle, a musketman, a rifleman, and an artilleryman. *(Brown University Library)*

recruits and to drafting them. Even when it was possible to recruit substantial numbers of militiamen, they remained under the control of their respective states. Congress quickly recognized the disadvantages of this decentralized system and tried, with some success, to correct it. In the spring of 1775, it created a Continental army with a single commander in chief. George Washington, the forty-three-year-old Virginia planter-aristocrat who had commanded colonial forces during the French and Indian War, possessed more experience than any other American-born officer available. He had also been an early advocate of independence. Above all, he was admired, respected, and trusted by nearly all Patriots. He was the unanimous choice of the delegates, and he took command in June 1775.

Congress had chosen well. Throughout the war, Washington kept faithfully at his task, despite difficulties and discouragements that would have daunted a lesser man. He had to deal with serious problems of morale among soldiers who consistently received short rations and low pay; open mutinies broke out in 1781 among the Pennsylvania and New Jersey troops. The Continental Congress, Washington's "employers," always seemed too little interested in supplying him with manpower and equipment and too much interested in interfering with his conduct of military operations. During the discouraging winter of Valley Forge, some congressmen and army officers apparently even conspired unsuccessfully (in the so-called Conway Cabal, named for Thomas Conway, one of its alleged leaders) to replace Washington as commander in chief.

■ **BATTLE OF GERMANTOWN**
On October 4, 1777, Washington launched an attack on General Howe's camp at Germantown, near Philadelphia. Although the Patriots were successful in the first hours of the battle, a heavy fog confused them and allowed the British finally to force them to retreat. This 1782 painting re-creates a part of the battle: an attack by American forces led by "Mad Anthony" Wayne. *(Valley Forge Historical Society)*

Washington was not without shortcomings as a military commander. But he was, in the end, a great war leader. With the aid of foreign military experts such as the Marquis de Lafayette from France and Baron von Steuben from Prussia, he succeeded in building and holding together an army of fewer than 10,000 men that, along with state militias, ultimately prevailed against the greatest military power in the world. Even more important, perhaps, in a new nation still unsure of either its purposes or its structure, with a central government both weak and divided, Washington provided the army—and the people— with a symbol of stability around which they could rally. He may not have been the most brilliant of the country's early leaders, but in the crucial years of the war, at least, he was the most successful in holding the new nation together.

THE WAR FOR INDEPENDENCE

On the surface, at least, all the advantages in the military struggle between America and Great Britain appeared to lie with the British. They possessed the greatest navy and the best-equipped army in the world. They had access to the resources of an empire. They had a coherent structure of command. The Americans, by contrast, were struggling to create a new army and a new government at the same time that they were trying to fight a war.

Yet the United States had advantages that were not at first apparent. Americans were fighting on their own ground, while the English were far from their own land (and their own resources). The American Patriots were, on the whole, deeply committed

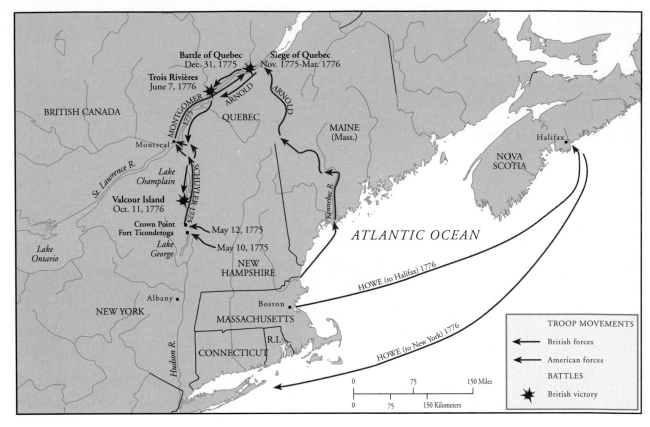

■ **THE REVOLUTION IN THE NORTH, 1775–1776**
The military phase of the American Revolution began in Massachusetts in 1775, but quickly spread. The American rebels attacked Fort Ticonderoga in May 1775 and moved up Lake Champlain to threaten Quebec. The invasion of Canada proved unsuccessful, but combined with Patriot agitation in the South, it convinced the British that the colonial revolt was not a local phenomenon in the area around Boston. After the British evacuated Boston, the focus of the war moved to New York and Pennsylvania.

to the conflict; the British people only halfheartedly supported the war. Beginning in 1777, moreover, the Americans had the benefit of substantial aid from abroad, when the American war became part of a larger world contest in which Great Britain faced the strongest powers of Europe—most notably France—in a struggle for imperial supremacy.

The American victory was not, however, simply the result of these advantages. It was not simply a result, either, of the remarkable spirit and resourcefulness of the people and the army. It was a result, too, of a series of egregious blunders and miscalculations by the British in the early stages of the fighting, when England could (and probably should) have won. And it was, finally, a result of the transformation of the war—which proceeded in three different phases—into a new kind of conflict that the British military, for all its strength, could not win.

The First Phase: New England

For the first year of the fighting—from the spring of 1775 to the spring of 1776—the British remained uncertain about whether or not they were actually engaged in a war. Many English authorities continued to believe that what was happening in America was a limited, local conflict and that British forces were simply attempting to quell pockets of rebellion in the contentious area around Boston. Gradually, however, colonial forces took the offensive and made almost the entire territory of the American colonies a battleground.

■ THE BATTLE OF BUNKER HILL, 1775
British troops face Patriot forces outside Boston on June 17, 1775, in the first great battle of the American Revolution. The British ultimately drove the Americans from their positions on Breed's Hill and Bunker Hill, but only after suffering enormous casualties. General Gage, the British commander, reported to his superiors in London after the battle: "These people show a spirit and conduct against us they never showed against the French." This anonymous painting reveals the array of British troops and naval support and also shows the bombardment and burning of Charlestown from artillery in Boston. *(National Gallery of Art, Washington)*

After the British withdrawal from Concord and Lexington in April 1775, American forces besieged the army of General Thomas Gage in Boston. The Patriots suffered severe casualties in the Battle of Bunker Hill (actually fought on Breed's Hill) on June 17, 1775, and were ultimately driven from their position there. But they inflicted much greater losses on the enemy than the enemy inflicted on them. Indeed, the British suffered their heaviest casualties of the entire war at Bunker Hill. After the battle, the Patriots continued to tighten the siege.

By the first months of 1776, the British had concluded that Boston was not the best place from which to wage war. Not only was it in the center of the most fervently anti-British region of the colonies, it was also tactically indefensible—a narrow neck of land, easily isolated and besieged. By late winter, in fact, Patriot forces had surrounded the city and occupied strategic positions on the heights. On March 17, 1776 (a date still celebrated in Boston as Evacuation Day), the British departed Boston for Halifax in Nova Scotia with hundreds of Loyalist refugees. Less than a year after the firing of the first shots, the Massachusetts colonists had driven the British—temporarily—from American soil.

Elsewhere, the war proceeded fitfully and inconclusively. To the south, at Moore's Creek Bridge in North Carolina, a band of Patriots crushed an uprising of Loyalists on February 27, 1776, and in the process discouraged a British plan to invade the southern states. The British had expected substantial aid from local Tories in the South; they realized now that such aid might not be as effective as they had hoped. To the north, Americans launched an invasion of Canada—hoping to remove the British threat and win the Canadians to their cause. Benedict Arnold, the commander of a small American force, threatened Quebec in late 1775 and early 1776 after a winter march of incredible hardship. Richard Montgomery, coming to his assistance, combined his forces with Arnold's and took command of both. Montgomery died in the assault on the city; and although a wounded Arnold kept up the siege for a time, the Quebec campaign ended in frustration. Congress sent a civilian commission to Canada, headed by the seventy-year-old Benjamin Franklin. But Franklin also failed to win the allegiance of the northern colonists. Canada was not to become part of the new nation.

The British evacuation of Boston in 1776 was not, therefore, so much a victory for the Americans as a reflection of changing English assumptions about the war. By the spring of 1776, it had become clear to the British that the conflict was not a local phenomenon in the area around Boston. The American campaigns in Canada, the agitation in the South, and the growing evidence of colonial unity all suggested that England must be prepared to fight a much larger conflict. The departure of the British, therefore, marked a shift in strategy more than an admission of defeat. It signaled the beginning of a new phase in the war.

The Second Phase: The Mid-Atlantic Region

The next phase of the war, which lasted from 1776 until early 1778, was when the British were in the best position to win. Indeed, had it not been for a series of blunders and misfortunes, they probably would have crushed the rebellion then. During this period the struggle became, for the most part, a traditional, conventional war. And in that, the Americans were woefully overmatched.

The British regrouped quickly after their retreat from Boston. During the summer of 1776, in the weeks immediately following the Declaration of Independence, the waters around New York City grew crowded with the most formidable military force Great Britain had ever sent abroad. Hundreds of men-of-war and troopships and 32,000 disciplined soldiers arrived, under the command of the affable

William Howe. Howe felt no particular hostility toward the Americans. He hoped to awe them into submission rather than fight them, and he believed that most of them, if given a chance, would show their loyalty to the king. In a meeting with commissioners from Congress, he offered them a choice between submission with royal pardon and a battle against overwhelming odds.

To oppose Howe's impressive array, Washington could muster only about 19,000 poorly armed and trained soldiers, even after combining the Continental army with state militias; he had no navy at all. Even so, the Americans quickly rejected Howe's offer and chose to continue the war—a decision that led inevitably to a succession of rapid defeats. The British pushed the defenders off Long Island, compelled them to abandon Manhattan, and then drove them in slow retreat over the plains of New Jersey, across the Delaware River, and into Pennsylvania.

For eighteenth-century Europeans, warfare was a seasonal activity. Fighting generally stopped in cold weather. The British settled down for the winter at various points in New Jersey, leaving an outpost of Hessians (German mercenaries) at Trenton on the Delaware River. But Washington did not sit still. On Christmas night 1776, he boldly recrossed the icy river, surprised and scattered the Hessians, and occupied the town. Then he advanced to Princeton and drove a British force from their base in the college there. But Washington was unable to hold either Princeton or Trenton, and he finally took refuge for the rest of the winter in the hills around Morristown, New Jersey.

For their campaigns of 1777 the British devised a strategy to cut the United States in two. Howe would move north from New York City up the Hudson to Albany, while another British force would come south from Canada to meet him. One of the younger British officers, the dashing John Burgoyne, secured command of this northern force and planned a two-pronged attack along both the Mohawk and the upper Hudson approaches to Albany.

But after setting this plan in motion, Howe himself abandoned it. He decided instead to launch an assault on the rebel capital Philadelphia—an assault that would, he hoped, discourage the Patriots, rally the Loyalists, and bring the war to a speedy conclusion. He removed the bulk of his forces from New York by sea, landed at the head of the Chesapeake Bay, brushed Washington aside at the Battle of

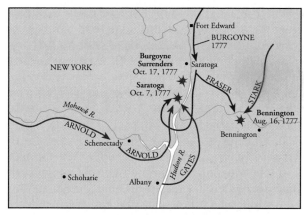

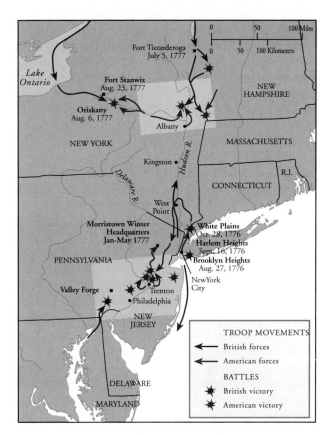

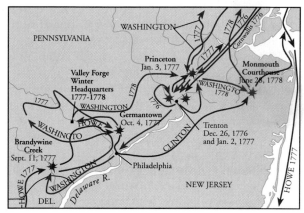

■ **THE REVOLUTION IN THE MIDDLE COLONIES, 1776-1778**
From 1776 to 1778, the military conflict between the British and the rebellious American colonists centered on New York and Pennsylvania. During this period, this struggle turned into a conventional war in which the Americans were woefully overmatched. Had it not been for a series of British blunders and misfortunes, the British might have suppressed the colonial rebellion during this phase of the conflict. Particularly important was the stunning American victory in upstate New York in the fall of 1777.

Brandywine Creek on September 11, and proceeded north to Philadelphia, which he was able to occupy with little resistance. Meanwhile, Washington, after an unsuccessful October 4 attack at Germantown (just outside Philadelphia), went into winter quarters at Valley Forge. The Continental Congress, now dislodged from its capital, reassembled at York, Pennsylvania.

Howe's move to Philadelphia left Burgoyne to carry out the campaign in the north alone. Burgoyne sent Colonel Barry St. Leger up the St. Lawrence River toward Lake Ontario and the headwaters of the Mohawk, while Burgoyne himself advanced directly down the upper Hudson Valley. He got off to a flying start. He seized Fort Ticonderoga easily and with it

an enormous store of powder and supplies; this caused such dismay in Congress that the delegates removed General Philip Schuyler from command of American forces in the north and replaced him with Horatio Gates.

By the time Gates took command, Burgoyne had already experienced two staggering defeats. In one of them—at Oriskany, New York, on August 6—a Patriot band of German farmers led by Nicholas Herkimer held off a force of Indians and Tories commanded by St. Leger. That gave Benedict Arnold time to go to the relief of Fort Stanwix and close off the Mohawk Valley to St. Leger's advance.

In the other battle—at Bennington, Vermont, on August 16—New England militiamen under the

Bunker Hill veteran John Stark severely mauled a British detachment that Burgoyne had sent out to seek supplies. Short of materials, with all help cut off, Burgoyne fought several costly engagements and then withdrew to Saratoga, where Gates surrounded him. On October 17, 1777, Burgoyne ordered what was left of his army, nearly 5,000 men, to surrender to the Americans.

To the Patriots, the New York campaign was a remarkable victory. News of it reverberated throughout the new nation and through Europe as well. The British surrender at Saratoga became a major turning point in the war—above all, perhaps, because it led directly to an alliance between the United States and France.

The British failure to win the war during this period, a period in which they had overwhelming advantages, was in large part a result of their own mistakes. And in assessing them, the role of William Howe looms large. He abandoned his own most important strategic initiative—the northern campaign—leaving Burgoyne to fight alone. And even in the south, where he chose to engage the enemy, he refrained from moving in for a final attack on the weakened Continental army, even though he had several opportunities. Instead, he repeatedly allowed Washington to retreat and regroup; and he permitted the American army to spend a long winter unmolested in Valley Forge, where—weak and hungry—they might have been easy prey for British attack. Some believed that Howe did not want to win the war, that he was secretly in sympathy with the American cause. His family had close ties to the colonies, and he himself was linked politically to those forces within the British government that opposed the war. Others pointed to personal weaknesses: Howe's apparent alcoholism, his romantic attachment (he spent the winter of 1777-1778 in Philadelphia with his mistress when many were urging him to move elsewhere). But the most important problem, it seems clear, was lack of judgment.

The Iroquois and the British

The campaign in upstate New York was not just a British defeat. It was a setback for the ambitious efforts of several Iroquois leaders, who hoped to involve Indian forces in the English military effort, believing that a British victory would help stem white movement onto tribal lands. The Iroquois Confederacy had declared itself a neutral in the war in 1776, but not all its members were content to remain passive in the northern campaign. Among those who worked to expand the Native American role in the war were a Mohawk brother and sister, Joseph and Mary Brant. Both were people of stature within the Mohawk nation: Joseph was a celebrated warrior; Mary was a magnetic woman and the widow of Sir William Johnson, the British superintendent of Indians, who had achieved wide popularity among the tribes. The Brants persuaded their own tribe to contribute to the British cause and attracted the support of the Seneca and Cayuga as well. They played an important role in Burgoyne's unsuccessful campaigns in the north.

But the alliance was also a sign of the growing divisions within the Iroquois Confederacy. Only three of the six nations of the Confederacy supported the British. The Oneida and the Tuscarora backed the Americans; the Onondaga split into several factions. The three-century-old Confederacy, weakened by the aftermath of the French and Indian War, continued to unravel.

The alliance had other unhappy consequences for the Iroquois. A year after Oriskany, Indians joined British troops in a series of raids on outlying white settlements in upstate New York. Months later, Patriot forces under the command of General John Sullivan harshly retaliated, wreaking such destruction on tribal settlements that large groups of Iroquois fled north into Canada to seek refuge. Many never returned.

Securing Aid from Abroad

The failure of the British to crush the Continental army in the mid-Atlantic states, combined with the stunning American victory at Saratoga, was a turning point in the war. It transformed the conflict and ushered it into a new and final phase.

Central to this transformation of the war was American success in winning support from abroad—indirect support from several European nations, and direct support from France. Even before the Declaration of Independence, Congress dispatched representatives to the capitals of Europe to negotiate commercial treaties with the governments there; if America was to leave the British Empire, it would need to cultivate new trading partners. Such treaties would, of course, require European governments to recognize the United States as an independent nation. John Adams called the early American representatives abroad "militia diplomats." Unlike the diplomatic regulars of Europe, they had little experience with the formal art and etiquette of Old World diplomacy. Since transatlantic communication was slow and uncertain (it took from one to three months for a message to cross the Atlantic), they had to interpret the instructions of Congress very freely and make crucial decisions entirely on their own.

The most promising potential ally for the United States was France. King Louis XVI, who had come to the throne in 1774, and his astute foreign minister, the Count de Vergennes, were eager to see Britain lose a crucial part of its empire. Through a series of covert bargains, facilitated by the creation of a fictional trading firm and the use of secret agents on both sides (among them the famed French dramatist Caron de Beaumarchais), France began supplying the Americans large quantities of much-needed supplies. But the French government remained reluctant to provide the United States with what it most wanted: diplomatic recognition.

Finally, Benjamin Franklin himself went to France to represent the United States. A natural diplomat, Franklin became a popular hero among the French—aristocrats and common people alike. His popularity there greatly helped the American cause. Of even greater help was the news of the American victory at Saratoga, which arrived in London on December 2, 1777, and in Paris two days later. On February 6, 1778—in part to forestall a British peace offensive that Vergennes feared might persuade the Americans to abandon the war—France formally recognized the United States as a sovereign nation and laid the groundwork for greatly expanded assistance to the American war effort.

France's intervention made the war an international conflict. In the course of the next two years, France, Spain, and the Netherlands all drifted into another general war with Great Britain in Europe, and all contributed both directly and indirectly to the ultimate American victory. But France was America's truly indispensable ally. Not only did it furnish the new nation with most of its money and munitions; it also provided a navy and an expeditionary force that proved invaluable in the decisive phase of the revolutionary conflict.

The Final Phase: The South

The last phase of the military struggle in America was very different from either of the first two. The British government had never been fully united behind the war in the first place; after the defeat at Saratoga and the intervention of the French, it imposed new limits on its commitment to the conflict. Instead of a full-scale military struggle against the American army, therefore, the British decided to try to enlist the support of those elements of the American population—a majority, they continued to believe—who were still loyal to the crown; in other words, they would work to undermine the Revolution from within. Since the British believed Loyalist sentiment was strongest in the southern colonies (despite their earlier failure to enlist Loyalist support in North Carolina), the main focus of their effort shifted there; and so it was in the South, for the most part, that the final stages of the war occurred.

The new strategy was a dismal failure. British forces spent three years (from 1778 to 1781) moving through the South, fighting small battles and large, and attempting to neutralize the territory through which they traveled. All such efforts ended in frustration. The British badly overestimated the extent of Loyalist sentiment. There were many Tories in Georgia and the Carolinas, some of them disgruntled members of the Regulator movement. But there were also many more Patriots than the British had believed. In Virginia, support for independence was as fervent as in Massachusetts. And even in the lower South, Loyalists often refused to aid the British because they feared reprisals from the Patriots around them. The British also faced severe logistical problems in the South. Patriot forces could move at will throughout the region, living off the resources of the countryside, blending in with the civilian population and leaving the British unable to distinguish friend from foe. The British, by contrast, suffered all the disadvantages of an army in hostile territory.

It was this phase of the conflict that made the war truly "revolutionary"—not only because it introduced a new kind of combat, but also because it had the effect of mobilizing and politicizing large groups of the population who had previously remained aloof from the struggle. With the war expanding into previously isolated communities, with many civilians forced to involve themselves whether they liked it or not, the political climate of the United States grew more

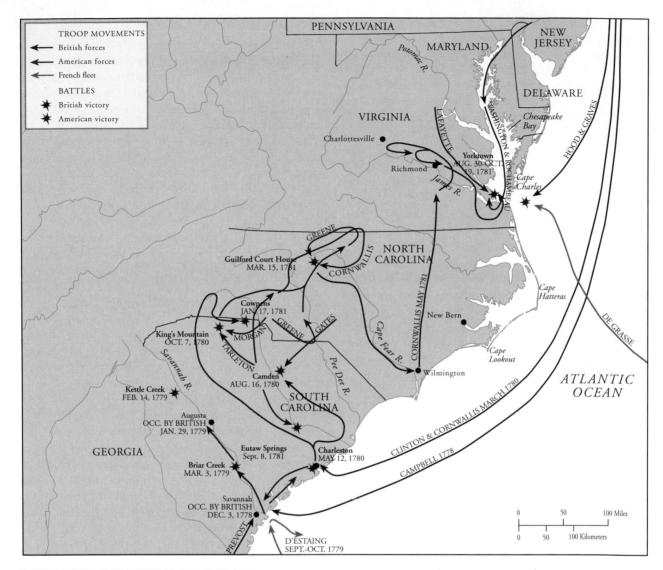

TROOP MOVEMENTS
→ British forces
← American forces
← French fleet

BATTLES
★ British victory
★ American victory

■ **THE REVOLUTION IN THE SOUTH, 1778–1781**

Hoping to rely on the support of Loyalists in the colonies, the British turned their attention to the South. British forces spent three long and frustrating years in the southern colonies. The British command overestimated Loyalist power and encountered a new and baffling form of guerrilla warfare in the southern countryside. Despite significant victories at Savannah and Charleston, the British commander Lord Cornwallis was forced to surrender the bulk of the British troops at Yorktown on October 17, 1781.

heated than ever. And support for independence, far from being crushed as the British had hoped, greatly increased.

That was the context in which the important military encounters of the last years of the war occurred. In the North, where significant numbers of British troops remained, the fighting settled into a relatively quiet stalemate. Sir Henry Clinton replaced the hapless William Howe in 1778 and moved what had

been Howe's army from Philadelphia back to New York. There the British troops stayed for more than a year, with Washington using his army to keep watch around them. The American forces in New York did so little fighting in this period that Washington sent some troops west to fight hostile Indians who had been attacking white settlers. In that same winter, George Rogers Clark, under orders from the state of Virginia—not from either Washington or Congress—

■ **THE BRITISH ON THE HUDSON, 1776**

In one of the largest troop movements of the Revolution, English commanders send 13,000 British and Hessian troops up the Hudson River to drive George Washington and his Patriot army from strongholds in the palisades above the river. The British took nearly 3,000 prisoners when the Patriots surrendered on November 16, 1776. Thomas Davies painted this watercolor of the British landing at the time. *(Emmet Collection. Miriam & Ira D. Wallach Division of Art, Prints & Photographs, The New York Public Library, Astor, Lenox and Tilden Foundations)*

led a daring expedition over the mountains and captured settlements in the Illinois country from the British and their Indian allies.

During this period of relative calm, General Benedict Arnold shocked the American forces—and Washington in particular—by becoming a traitor. Arnold had been one of the early heroes of the war, but now, convinced that the American cause was hopeless, he conspired with British agents to betray the Patriot stronghold at West Point on the Hudson River. The scheme unraveled before Arnold could complete it, and he fled to the safety of the British camp, where he spent the rest of the war.

In the meantime, decisive fighting was in progress in the South. The British did have some significant military successes during this period. On December 29, 1778, they captured Savannah, on the coast of

Georgia; and on May 12, 1780, they took the port of Charleston, South Carolina. They also inspired some Loyalists to take up arms and advance with them into the interior. But although the British were able to win conventional battles, they were constantly harassed as they moved through the countryside by Patriot guerrillas led by such resourceful fighters as Thomas Sumter, Andrew Pickens, and Francis Marion, the "Swamp Fox."

Moving inland to Camden, South Carolina, Lord Cornwallis (Clinton's choice as British commander in the South) met and crushed a Patriot force under Horatio Gates on August 16, 1780. Congress recalled Gates, and Washington gave the southern command to Nathanael Greene, a former Quaker blacksmith from Rhode Island and probably the ablest of all the American generals of the time next to Washington himself.

Even before Greene joined the southern army, the tide of battle began to turn against Cornwallis. At King's Mountain (near the North Carolina–South Carolina border) on October 7, 1780, a band of Patriot riflemen from the backwoods killed, wounded, or captured an entire force of 1,100 New York and South Carolina Tories that Cornwallis was using as auxiliaries. Once Greene arrived, he confused and exasperated Cornwallis further by dividing the American forces into small, fast-moving contingents and refraining from a showdown in open battle. One of the contingents inflicted what Cornwallis admitted was "a very unexpected and severe blow" at Cowpens on January 17, 1781. Finally, after receiving reinforcements, Greene combined all his forces and maneuvered to meet the British on ground of his own choosing, at Guilford Court House, North Carolina. After a hard-fought battle there on March 15, 1781, Greene withdrew from the field; but Cornwallis had lost so many men that he decided at last to abandon the Carolina campaign.

Cornwallis withdrew to the port town of Wilmington, North Carolina, to receive supplies being sent to him by sea; later he moved north to launch raids in the interior of Virginia. But Clinton, concerned for the army's safety, ordered him to take up a position on the peninsula between the York and James Rivers and wait for ships to carry his troops to New York or Charleston. So Cornwallis retreated to Yorktown and began to build fortifications there.

George Washington—along with the Count Jean Baptiste de Rochambeau, commander of the French expeditionary force in America, and Admiral François Joseph Paul de Grasse, commander of the French fleet in American waters—set out to trap Cornwallis at Yorktown. Washington and Rochambeau marched a French-American army from New York to join other French forces under Lafayette in Virginia, while de Grasse sailed with additional troops for Chesapeake Bay and the York River. These joint operations, perfectly timed and executed, caught Cornwallis between land and sea. After a few shows of resistance, he capitulated on October 17, 1781 (four years to the day after the surrender of Burgoyne at Saratoga). Two days later, as a military band played the old tune "The World Turn'd Upside Down," he formally surrendered his army of more than 7,000 men.

Except for a few skirmishes, the fighting was now over; but the United States had not yet won the war.

British forces continued to hold the seaports of Savannah, Charleston, Wilmington, and New York. Before long, a British fleet met and defeated Admiral de Grasse's fleet in the West Indies, ending Washington's hopes for further French naval assistance. For more than a year, although there was no significant further combat between British and American forces, it remained possible that the war might resume and the struggle for independence might still be lost.

Winning the Peace

Cornwallis's defeat provoked outcries in England against continuing the war. Lord North resigned as prime minister; Lord Shelburne emerged from the political wreckage to succeed him; and British emissaries appeared in France to talk informally with the American diplomats there, of whom the three principals were Benjamin Franklin, John Adams, and John Jay.

The Americans were under instructions to cooperate fully with France in their negotiations with England. But Vergennes insisted that France could not agree to any settlement of the war with England until its ally Spain had achieved its principal war aim: winning back Gibraltar from the British. There was no real prospect of that happening soon, and the Americans began to fear that the alliance with France might keep them at war indefinitely. As a result, Franklin, Jay, and Adams began proceeding on their own, without informing Vergennes, and signed a preliminary treaty with Great Britain on November 30, 1782. Franklin, in the meantime, skillfully pacified Vergennes and avoided an immediate rift in the French-American alliance.

The British and Americans reached a final settlement—the Treaty of Paris—on September 3, 1783, when both Spain and France agreed to end hostilities. It was, on the whole, remarkably favorable to the United States in granting a clear-cut recognition of its independence and a generous, though ambiguous cession of territory—from the southern boundary of Canada to the northern boundary of Florida and from the Atlantic to the Mississippi. With good reason Americans celebrated in the fall of 1783 as the last of the British occupation forces embarked from New York and General Washington, at the head of his troops, rode triumphantly into the city.

WAR AND SOCIETY

Historians have long debated whether the American Revolution was a social as well as a political revolution. Some have argued that the colonists were struggling not only over the question of home rule, but over "who should rule at home." Others claim that domestic social and economic concerns had little to do with the conflict. (See "Where Historians Disagree," pp. 154–155.) Whatever the motivations of Americans, however, there can be little doubt that the War for Independence had important effects on the nature of American society.

Loyalists and Minorities

The losers in the American Revolution included not only the British but also American Loyalists. There is no way to be sure how many Americans remained loyal to England during the Revolution, but it is clear that there were many—at least a fifth (and some estimate as much as a third) of the white population. Their motivations were varied. Some were officeholders in the imperial government, who stood to lose their positions as a result of the Revolution. Others were merchants engaged in trade closely tied to the imperial system. (Most merchants, however, supported the Revolution.) Still others were people who lived in relative isolation and who thus had not been exposed to the wave of discontent that had turned so many Americans against Britain; they had simply retained their traditional loyalties. There were cultural and ethnic minorities who feared that an independent America would not offer them sufficient protection. And there were those who, expecting the British to win the war, were simply currying favor with the anticipated victors.

What happened to these men and women during the war is a turbulent and at times tragic story. Hounded by Patriots in their communities, harassed by legislative and judicial actions, the position of many Loyalists became intolerable. Up to 100,000 fled the country. Those who could afford to—for example, the hated Tory governor of Massachusetts, Thomas Hutchinson—moved to England, where many lived in difficult and lonely exile. Others of more modest means moved to Canada, establishing the first English-speaking community in the province of Quebec. Some returned to America after the war and, as the earlier passions and resentments faded, managed to reenter the life of the nation. Others remained abroad for the rest of their lives.

Most Loyalists were people of average means, but a substantial minority consisted of men and women of wealth. They left behind large estates and vacated important positions of social and economic leadership. Even some who remained in the country saw their property confiscated and their positions forfeited. The result was new opportunities for Patriots to acquire land and influence, a situation that produced significant social changes in many communities.

It would be an exaggeration, however, to claim that the departure of the Loyalists was responsible for anything approaching a social revolution or that the Revolution created a general assault on the wealthy and powerful in America. When the war ended, those who had been wealthy at its beginning were, for the most part, still wealthy. Most of those who had wielded social and political influence continued to wield it. Indeed, the distribution of wealth and power changed more rapidly after the war than it had changed during it.

The war had a significant effect on other minorities as well, and on certain religious groups in particular. No sect suffered more than the Anglicans, many of whose members were Loyalists and all of whom Patriots identified with England. In Virginia and Maryland, where the colonial governments had recognized Anglicanism as the official religion and had imposed a tax for its maintenance, the new Revolutionary regimes disestablished the church and eliminated the subsidy. In other states, Anglicans had received aid from England, which also ceased with the outbreak of war. By the time the fighting ended, many Anglican parishes no longer even had clergymen, for there were few ministers to take the place of those who had died or who had left the country as Loyalist refugees. Anglicanism survived in America, but the losses during the Revolution permanently weakened it. The Revolution also weakened the Quakers in Pennsylvania and elsewhere. They incurred widespread unpopularity because of their pacifism. Their refusal to support the war destroyed much of the social and political prestige they had once enjoyed, and the church never fully recovered.

While the war was weakening the Anglicans and the Quakers, it was improving the position of the Roman Catholic Church. On the advice of Charles

Carroll of Carrollton, a Maryland statesman and Catholic lay leader, most American Catholics supported the Patriot cause during the war. The French alliance brought Catholic troops and chaplains to the country, and the gratitude with which most Americans greeted them did much to erode old hostilities toward Catholics, whom Americans had in the past often denounced as agents of the devil. The church did not greatly increase its numbers as a result of the Revolution, but it did gain considerable strength as an institution. Not long after the end of the war, the Vatican provided the United States with its own Catholic hierarchy. (Until then, Catholic bishops in England had controlled the American church.) Father John Carroll (also of Maryland) was named head of Catholic missions in America in 1784 and, in 1789, the first American bishop. In 1808 he became archbishop of Baltimore.

For the largest of America's minorities—the African-American population—the war had limited, but nevertheless profound, significance. For some, it meant freedom. Because so much of the fighting occurred in the South during the last years of the war, many slaves came into contact with the British army, which—in the interests of disrupting and weakening the American cause—emancipated thousands of slaves and led them out of the country. For other African Americans, the Revolution meant an increased exposure to the concept, although seldom to the reality, of liberty. Most black Americans could not read, but few could avoid exposure to the new and exciting ideas circulating through the towns and cities where many of them lived. At times, they attempted to apply those ideas to themselves. The results included incidents in several communities in which African Americans engaged in open resistance to white control. In Charleston, South Carolina, for example, Thomas Jeremiah, a free black, was executed after white authorities learned of elaborate plans for a slave uprising.

That was one reason why revolutionary sentiment was more restrained in South Carolina and Georgia than in other colonies. Slaves constituted a majority in South Carolina and almost half the population in Georgia, and whites in both places feared that revolution would foment slave rebellions. The same fears helped prevent English colonists in the Caribbean islands (who were far more greatly outnumbered by African slaves) from joining with the continental Americans in the revolt against Britain.

Native Americans and the Revolution

Most Indians viewed the American Revolution with considerable uncertainty. The American Patriots tried to persuade them to remain neutral in the conflict, which they described as a "family quarrel" between the colonists and Britain that had nothing to do with the tribes. The British, too, generally sought to maintain Indian neutrality, fearing that native allies would prove unreliable and uncontrollable. Most tribes ultimately chose to stay out of the war.

To some Indians, however, the Revolution threatened to replace a ruling group in which they had developed at least some measure of trust (the British) with one they considered generally hostile to them (the Patriots). The British had consistently sought to limit the expansion of white settlement into Indian land (even if unsuccessfully); the Americans had spearheaded the encroachments. Thus some Native Americans, among them those Iroquois who participated in the Burgoyne campaign in upper New York, chose to join the English cause. Still others took advantage of the conflict to launch attacks of their own.

In the western Carolinas and Virginia, the Cherokee, led by Chief Dragging Canoe, launched a series of attacks on outlying white settlements in the summer of 1776. Patriot militias responded with overwhelming force, ravaging Cherokee lands and forcing the chief and many of his followers to flee west across the Tennessee River. Those Cherokee who remained behind agreed to a new treaty by which they gave up still more land. Not all Native American military efforts were so unsuccessful. Some Iroquois, despite the setbacks at Oriskany, continued to wage war against white Americans in the West and caused widespread destruction in large agricultural areas of New York and Pennsylvania—areas whose crops were of crucial importance to the Patriot cause. And although the retaliating United States armies inflicted heavy losses on the Indians, the attacks continued throughout the war.

In the end, however, the Revolution generally weakened the position of Native Americans in several ways. The Patriot victory increased the white demand for western lands; many American whites associated restrictions on settlement with British oppression and expected the new nation to remove the obstacles. At the same time, white attitudes toward the tribes, seldom friendly in the best of times, took a turn for the worse. Many whites deeply resented the assistance the Mohawk and other Indian nations had given the British and insisted on treating them as conquered people. Others adopted a paternalistic view of the tribes that was only slightly less dangerous to them. Thomas Jefferson, for example, came to view the Native Americans as "noble savages" uncivilized in their present state but redeemable if they were willing to adapt to the norms of white society.

Among the tribes themselves, the Revolution both revealed and increased the deep divisions that made it difficult for them to form a common front to resist the growing power of whites. In 1774, for example, the Shawnee Indians in western Virginia had attempted to lead an uprising against white settlers moving into the lands that would later become Kentucky. They attracted virtually no allies and (in a conflict known as Lord Dunmore's War) were defeated by the colonial militia and forced to cede more land to white settlers. The Cherokee generated little support from surrounding tribes in their 1776 battles. And the Iroquois, whose power had been eroding since the end of the French and Indian War, were unable to act in unison in the Revolution. The Iroquois nations that chose to support the British attracted little support from tribes outside the Confederacy (many of whom resented the long Iroquois domination of the interior) and even from other tribes within the Iroquois nation.

Nor did the conclusion of the Revolutionary War end the fighting between white Americans and Indians. Bands of Native Americans continued to launch raids against white settlers on the frontier. White militias, often using such raids as pretexts, continued to attack Indian tribes who stood in the way of expansion. Perhaps the most vicious massacre of the era occurred in 1782, after the British surrender, when white militias slaughtered a peaceful band of Delaware Indians at Gnadenhuetten in Ohio. They claimed to be retaliating for the killing of a white family several days before, but few believed this band of Delaware (who were both Christian converts and pacifists) had played any role in the earlier attack. The white soldiers killed ninety-six people, including many women and children. Such massacres did not become the norm of Indian-white relations. But they did reveal how little the Revolution had done to settle the basic conflict between the two peoples.

Women's Rights and Women's Roles

The long Revolutionary War, which touched the lives of almost every region, naturally had a significant effect on American women. The departure of so many men to fight in the Patriot armies left wives, mothers, sisters, and daughters in charge of farms and businesses. Some women handled these tasks with great success. In other cases, inexperience, inflation, the unavailability of male labor, or the threat of enemy troops led to failures and dislocations. Some women whose husbands or fathers went off to war did not have even a farm or shop to fall back on. Many cities and towns developed significant populations of impoverished women, who on occasion led popular protests against price increases. On a few occasions, hungry women rioted and looted for food. On several other occasions (in New Jersey and Staten Island), women launched attacks on occupying British troops, whom they were required to house and feed at considerable expense.

Not all women, however, stayed behind when the men went off to war. Sometimes by choice, but more often out of economic necessity or because they had been driven from their homes by the enemy (and by the smallpox and dysentery the British army carried with it), women flocked in increasing numbers to the camps of the Patriot armies to join their male relatives. George Washington looked askance at these female "camp followers," convinced that they were disruptive and distracting (even though his own wife, Martha, spent the winter of 1778–1779 with him at Valley Forge). Other officers were even more hostile, voicing complaints that reflected a high level of anxiety over this seeming violation of traditional gender roles (and also, perhaps, over the generally lower-class backgrounds of the camp women). One described them in decidedly hostile terms: "their hair falling, their brows beady with the heat, their belongings slung over one shoulder, chattering and yelling in sluttish shrills as they went and spitting in the gutters." In fact, however, the women were of significant value to the new army. It had not yet developed an adequate system of supply and auxiliary services, and it profited greatly from the presence of women. They increased army morale, and they performed such necessary tasks as cooking, laundry, and nursing.

But female activity did not always remain restricted to "women's" tasks. In the rough environment of the camps, traditional gender distinctions proved difficult to maintain. Considerable numbers of women became involved, at least intermittently, in combat—including the legendary "Molly Pitcher" (so named because she carried pitchers of water to soldiers on the battlefield). Molly Pitcher watched her husband fall during one encounter and immediately took his place at a field gun. A few women even disguised themselves as men so as to be able to fight.

After the war, of course, the soldiers and the female camp followers returned home. The experience of combat had little visible impact on how society (or on how women themselves) defined female roles in peacetime. The Revolution did, however, call certain assumptions about women into question in other ways. The emphasis on liberty and the "rights of man" led some women to begin to question their position in society as well. "By the way," Abigail Adams wrote to her husband John Adams in 1776, "in the new code of laws which I suppose it will be necessary for you to make, I desire you would remember the ladies and be more generous and favorable to them than your ancestors. Do not put such unlimited power into the hands of the Husbands."

Adams was calling for a very modest expansion of women's rights. She wanted new protections against abusive and tyrannical men. A few women, however, went further. Judith Sargent Murray, one of the leading essayists of the late eighteenth century, wrote in 1779 that women's minds were as good as men's and that girls as well as boys therefore deserved access to education. Murray later became one of the leading defenders of the works of the English feminist Mary Wollstonecraft, whose *Vindication of the Rights of Women* was published in the United States in 1792. After reading it, Murray rejoiced that Americans were beginning to understand "the Rights of Women" and that future generations of women would inaugurate "a new era in female history."

In most respects, however, the new era did not arrive. Some political leaders—among them Benjamin Franklin and Benjamin Rush—voiced support for the education of women and for other feminist reforms. Yale students in the 1780s debated the question "Whether women ought to be admitted into the mag-

■ **NANCY HART, THE "WAR WOMAN"**
This nineteenth-century engraving, based on an earlier painting, portrays a legendary event of the Revolutionary war in Georgia. Six Tories attempted to raid the cabin of Nancy Hart, a six-foot-tall Patriot woman, who reportedly shot one dead, held the others at bay at rifle point, and waited for her husband to return home to help her hang the rest.
(Library of Congress)

istracy and government of empires and republics." And there was for a time wide discussion of the future role of women in a new republic that had broken with so many other traditions already. But few concrete reforms became either law or common social practice.

In colonial society, under the doctrines of English common law, an unmarried woman had some legal rights (to own property, to enter contracts, and others), but a married woman had virtually no rights at all. She could own no property and earn no independent wages; everything she owned and everything she earned belonged to her husband. She had no legal authority over her children; the father was, in the eyes of the law, the autocrat of the family. Because a married woman had no property rights, she could not engage in any legal transactions (buying or selling, suing or being sued, writing wills). She could not vote. Nor could she obtain a divorce; that, too, was a right reserved almost exclusively for men. That was what Abigail Adams (who herself enjoyed a very happy marriage) meant when she appealed to her husband not to put "such unlimited power into the hands of the Husbands."

The Revolution did little to change any of these legal customs. In some states, it did become easier for women to obtain divorces. And in New Jersey, women obtained the right to vote (although that right was repealed in 1807). Otherwise, there were few advances and some setbacks—including widows' loss of the right to regain their dowries from their husbands' estates. That change left many widows without any means of support and was one of the reasons for the increased agitation for female education: such women needed a way to support themselves.

The Revolution, in other words, far from challenging the patriarchal structure of American society, actually confirmed and strengthened it. Few American women challenged the belief that they occupied a special sphere distinct from men. Most accepted that their place remained in the family. Abigail Adams, in the same letter in which she asked her husband to "remember the ladies," urged him to "regard us then as Beings placed by providence under your protection and in imitation of the Supreme Being make use of that power only for our happiness." Nevertheless, the revolutionary experience did contribute to a subtle but important alteration of women's expectations of their status within the family. In the past, they had often been little better than servants in their husbands' homes; men and women both had generally viewed the wife as a clear subordinate, performing functions in the family of much less importance than those of the husband. But the Revolution encouraged people of both genders to reevaluate the contribution of women to the family and the society.

One reason for this was the participation of women in the revolutionary struggle itself. And part was a result of the reevaluation of American life during and after the revolutionary struggle. As the republic searched for a cultural identity for itself, it began to place additional value on the role of women as mothers. The new nation was, many Americans liked to believe, producing a new kind of citizen, steeped in the principles of liberty. Mothers had a particularly important task, therefore, in instructing their children in the virtues the republican citizenry was expected now to possess. Wives were still far from equal partners in marriage, but their ideas, interests, and domestic roles received increased respect.

The War Economy

Inevitably, the Revolution produced important changes in the structure of the American economy. After more than a century of dependence on the British imperial system, American trade suddenly found itself on its own. No longer did it have the protection of the great British navy; on the contrary, English ships now attempted to drive American vessels from the seas. No longer did American merchants have access to the markets of the empire; those markets were now hostile ports—including, of course, the most important source of American trade: England itself.

Yet while the Revolution disrupted traditional economic patterns, in the long run it strengthened the American economy. Well before the war was over, American ships had learned to evade the British navy with light, fast, easily maneuverable vessels. Indeed, the Yankees began to prey on British commerce with hundreds of privateers. For many shipowners, privateering proved to be more profitable than ordinary peacetime trade. More important in the long run, the end of imperial restrictions on American shipping opened up enormous new areas of trade to the nation. Colonial merchants had been violating British regulations for years, but the rules of empire had nevertheless inhibited American exploration of many markets. Now, enterprising merchants in New England and elsewhere began to develop new commerce in the Caribbean and in South America. By the mid-1780s, American merchants were developing an important new pattern of trade with Asia; and by the end of that decade, Yankee ships were regularly sailing from the eastern seaboard around Cape Horn to California, there exchanging manufactured goods for hides and furs, and then proceeding across the Pacific to barter for goods in China. There was also a substantial increase in trade among the American states.

When English imports to America were cut off—first by the prewar boycott, then by the war itself—there were desperate efforts throughout the states to stimulate domestic manufacturing of certain necessities. No great industrial expansion resulted, but there were several signs of the economic growth that was to come in the next century. Americans began to make their own cloth—"homespun," which became both patriotic and fashionable—to replace the now unobtainable British fabrics. It would be some time before a large domestic textile industry would emerge, but the nation was never again to rely exclusively on foreign sources for its cloth. There was, of course, pressure to build factories for the manufacture of guns and ammunition. And there was a growing general awareness that America need

■ **BANNER OF THE SOCIETY OF PEWTERERS**
Members of the American Society of Pewterers carried this patriotic banner when they marched in a New York City parade in July 1788. Its inscription celebrates the adoption of the new federal Constitution and predicts a future of prosperity and freedom in "Columbia's Land." The banner also suggests the growing importance of American manufacturing, which had received an important boost during the Revolution when British imports became unavailable. *(New York Historical Society)*

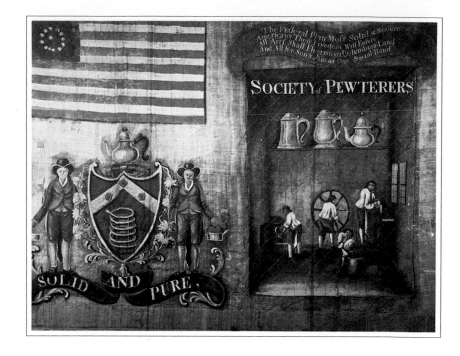

not forever be dependent on other nations for manufactured goods.

The war stopped well short of revolutionizing the American economy—not until the nineteenth century would that begin to occur. But it did serve to release a wide range of entrepreneurial energies that, despite the temporary dislocations, encouraged growth and diversification.

☙
THE CREATION OF STATE GOVERNMENTS

At the same time that Americans were struggling to win their independence on the battlefield, they were also struggling to create new institutions of government for themselves, to replace the British system they had repudiated. That effort continued for more than fifteen years, culminating in the federal Constitution of 1789. But its most crucial phase occurred during the war itself, and at the state, not the national, level.

The formation of state governments began early in 1776, even before the adoption of the Declaration of Independence. At first, the new state constitutions reflected primarily the fear of bloated executive power that had become so pronounced during the 1760s and early 1770s. Gradually, however, Americans began to become equally concerned about the instability of a government too responsive to the popular will. In a second phase of state constitution writing, therefore, they gave renewed attention to the idea of balance in government.

The Assumptions of Republicanism

If Americans agreed on nothing else when they began to build new governments for themselves, they agreed that those governments would be republican. To them, that meant a political system in which all power came directly from the people, rather than from some supreme authority (such as a king) standing above them. The success of any government, therefore, depended on the nature of its citizenry. If the population consisted of sturdy, virtuous, independent property owners, then the republic could survive. If it consisted of a few powerful aristocrats and a great mass of dependent workers, then it would be in danger. From the beginning, therefore, the ideal of the small "freeholder" became basic to American political ideology.

Another crucial part of that ideology was the concept of equality. The Declaration of Independence had given voice to that idea in its most ringing phrase: "all men are created equal." It was a belief that stood in direct contrast to the old European assumption of an inherited aristocracy. Every citizen, Americans believed, was born in a position of equality with every other citizen. The innate talents and energies of individuals would determine their roles in society, not their position at birth. The republican vision did not, in other words, envision a society without social gradations. Some people would inevitably be wealthier and more powerful than others. But all people would have to earn their success. There would be no equality of condition, but there would be full equality of opportunity.

In reality, of course, these assumptions could not always be sustained. The United States was never to become a nation in which all (or even most) people were independent property holders. From the beginning, there was a large dependent labor force—of which the white members were allowed many of the privileges of citizenship and the black members had virtually no rights at all. American women remained both politically and economically subordinate, with few opportunities for advancement independent of their husbands. Native Americans were systematically exploited and displaced by whites hungry for land and impatient with legalities. Nor was it possible to ensure full equality of opportunity. American society was more open and more fluid than that of most European nations, but it remained true that wealth and privilege were often passed from one generation to another. The conditions of a person's birth survived as a crucial determinant of success.

Nevertheless, in embracing the assumptions of republicanism, Americans were adopting a powerful, even revolutionary new ideology, one that would enable them to create a form of government never before seen in the world. Their experiment in statecraft became a model for many other countries and made the United States the most admired and studied nation on earth.

The First State Constitutions

Two of the original thirteen states saw no need to produce new constitutions. Connecticut and Rhode Island already had corporate charters that provided them with governments that were republican in all but name; they simply deleted references to England and the king from their charters and adopted them as constitutions. The other eleven states, however, chose to create entirely new governments. In doing so, they set out to avoid the problems of the British system they were repudiating.

The first and perhaps most basic decision was that the American constitutions, unlike the English one, were to be written down. Americans believed that the vagueness of the English system had opened the way to the corruption of the British government. To avoid a similar fate, they insisted that their own governments rest on clearly stated and permanently inscribed laws, so that no individual or group could pervert them.

The second decision was that the power of the executive, which Americans believed had grown bloated and threatening in England (and even, at times, in the colonies), must be limited. One state—Pennsylvania—went so far as to eliminate the executive altogether. But most states inserted provisions sharply limiting the power of the governor over appointments, reducing or eliminating his right to veto bills, and preventing him from dismissing or otherwise interfering with the legislature. Above all, every state forbade the governor or any other executive officer from holding a seat in the legislature, thus ensuring that (unlike in England) the two branches of government would remain wholly separate. The constitutions also added provisions protecting the judiciary from executive control, although in most states the courts did not yet emerge as fully autonomous branches of government.

In limiting the executive and expanding the power of the legislature, the new constitutions were moving in the direction of direct popular rule. They did not, however, move all the way. Only in Georgia and Pennsylvania did the legislature consist of one house. In all the other states there was an upper and a lower chamber, and in most cases, the upper chamber was designed to represent the "higher orders" of society. In all states, there were property requirements for voters—in some states, only the modest amount that would qualify a person as a taxpayer, in other states somewhat greater requirements. Universal suffrage (even among white men) was not yet an accepted part of American government.

The initial phase of constitution writing proceeded rapidly. Ten of the states completed the process before the end of 1776. Only Georgia, New York, and Massachusetts delayed. Georgia and New York completed the task by the end of the following year, but Massachusetts did not finally adopt its version until 1780. By then, the construction of state governments had moved into a new phase.

Revising State Governments

By the late 1770s, Americans were already growing concerned about what they perceived as the excessive fractiousness and instability of their new state governments. Legislatures were the scene of constant squabbling. Governors were unable to exercise sufficient power to provide any real leadership. It was proving extraordinarily difficult to get the new governments to accomplish anything at all. Many observers began to believe that the problem was one of too much democracy. By placing so much power in the hands of the people (and their elected representatives in the legislature), the state constitutions were inviting disorder and political turbulence. As a result, most of the states began to revise their constitutions to cope with what they considered to be their problems. Massachusetts—which had waited until 1780 to ratify its first constitution—became the first state to act on these new concerns. It produced a constitution that was to serve as a model for the efforts of others.

Two changes in particular characterized the Massachusetts and later constitutions. The first was a change in the process of constitution writing itself. In the first phase, the documents had usually been written by state legislatures. As a result, they could easily be amended (or violated) by those same bodies. By 1780, sentiment was growing to find a way to protect the constitutions from the people who had written them, to make it difficult to change the documents once they were approved. The solution was the constitutional convention: a special assembly of the people that would meet only for the purpose of writing the constitution and that would never (except under extraordinary circumstances) meet again. The constitution would, therefore, be the product of the popular will; but once approved, it would be protected from the whims of public opinion and from the political moods of the legislature.

The second change was also a reflection of the new concerns about excessive popular power: a significant strengthening of the executive. In Massachusetts, the governor under the 1780 constitution became one of the strongest in any state. He was to be elected directly by the people; he was to have a fixed salary (in other words, he would not be dependent on the good will of the legislature each year for his wages); he would have expanded powers of appointment; and he would be able to veto legislation. Other states soon followed. Those states that had weak or nonexistent upper houses strengthened or created them. Most states increased the powers of the governor; and Pennsylvania, which at first had no executive at all, now produced a strong one. By the late 1780s, almost every state had either revised its constitution or drawn up an entirely new one to accommodate the belief in the need for stability.

Toleration and Slavery

The new states moved far and quickly in the direction of complete religious freedom. Most Americans continued to believe religion should play some role in government, but they did not wish to give special powers to any particular denomination. So they stripped away the privileges they had once given particular churches. New York and the southern states, in which the Church of England had received public support, disestablished the church. The New England states stripped the Congregational Church of its special status. Boldest of all was Virginia. In 1786, it enacted a Statute of Religious Freedom, written by Thomas Jefferson, which called for the complete separation of church and state.

More difficult to resolve was the question of slavery. In areas where slavery was weak—in New England, where there had never been many slaves, and in Pennsylvania, where the Quakers were outspoken in their opposition to slavery—state governments abolished it. Pennsylvania passed a general gradual-emancipation act in 1780, and the supreme court of Massachusetts ruled in 1783 that the ownership of slaves was impermissible under the state's bill of rights. Even in the South, there were some pressures to amend the institution (a result, in part, of the activities of the first antislavery society in America, founded in 1775). Every state but South Carolina and Georgia prohibited the further importation of slaves from abroad, and even South Carolina placed a temporary wartime ban on the slave trade. Virginia passed a law encouraging manumission (the freeing of slaves), and other states encountered growing political pressures to change the institution.

In the end, however, slavery survived in all the southern and border states, for several reasons: racist assumptions about the natural inferiority of African Americans; the enormous economic investments many white southerners had in their black laborers, investments they were unwilling to give up; and the inability of most southerners—including such men as Washington and Jefferson, who expressed deep moral misgivings about slavery—to envision any alternative to it. If slavery were abolished, what would happen to the African people in America? Returning the slaves to Africa, as some urged, was clearly unrealistic; the black population was too large, and many slaves felt little identification with Africa and had no wish to go there. Few whites believed that Africans could be integrated into American society as equals. In maintaining slavery, Jefferson once remarked, Americans were holding a "wolf by the ears." However unappealing it was to hold on to it, letting go would be even worse. Jefferson himself, for all his qualms, never did let go. He continued to own slaves until he died, and unlike George Washington, he made no provision for their freedom on his death—in part because he died so deeply in debt that he could not afford to liberate them.

There was, finally, a more subtle obstacle to the elimination of slavery. The economy of the South depended, most southerners believed, on a large, servile labor force. Yet the ideals of republicanism required a homogeneous population of independent, property-owning citizens. Were slavery to be abolished, the South would have to recruit a labor force that would consist of unpropertied free people; and whether that class were black or white, its existence would raise troubling implications for the future of democracy. The social tensions that would inevitably result from such class divisions within white society would, southerners feared, ultimately destroy the democratic quality—and the stability—of the region. African Americans lived in positions of complete unfreedom in part to protect the freedoms of white southerners.

■ **A FREE BLACK MAN**
John Singleton Copley, the great American portraitist of the Revolutionary age, painted this picture of a young African American in 1777–78. He was probably a worker on New England fishing boats who appeared in another Copley painting ("Watson and the Shark"). It is one of a relatively small number of portrayals of the free blacks in the North in this era, and one of even a smaller number that portrays them realistically and seriously. (Head of a Negro, 1777-1778. *By John Singleton Copley. Oil on canvas, 53.3 x 41.3 cm) (Founders Society Purchase, Gibbs-Williams Fund. Photograph © 1986 The Detroit Institute of Arts)*

‿➂
THE SEARCH FOR A NATIONAL GOVERNMENT

Americans were much quicker to agree on the proper shape of their state institutions than they were to decide on the form of their national government. At first, most believed that the central government should remain relatively weak and unimportant. Each state would be virtually a sovereign nation, and national institutions would serve only as loose, coordinating mechanisms, with little independent authority. Such beliefs reflected the assumption that a republic operated best in a relatively limited, homogeneous area; that were a republican government to attempt to administer too large and diverse a nation, it would flounder. It was in response to such ideas that the Articles of Confederation emerged.

The Confederation

No sooner did the Continental Congress appoint a committee to draft a declaration of independence in 1776 than it appointed another to draft a plan of union. After much debate and many revisions, the Congress adopted the committee's proposal in November 1777 as the Articles of Confederation.

The Articles provided for a national political structure very similar to the one already in operation. Congress was to survive as the central—indeed the only—institution of national authority. But its powers were to be somewhat expanded. It was to have the authority to conduct wars and foreign relations, and to appropriate, borrow, and issue money. But it could not regulate trade, draft troops, or levy taxes directly on the people. For troops and taxes it would have to make formal requests to the state legislatures, which could and often did refuse them. There was to be no separate executive (the "president of the United States" was merely the presiding officer at the sessions of Congress). Each state would have a single vote in Congress, and at least nine of the states would have to approve any important measure. All thirteen state legislatures would have to approve the Articles before they could be ratified or amended.

The ratification process revealed broad disagreements over the plan. The small states had insisted on equal state representation, but the larger states wanted representation based on population. More important, the states claiming western lands wished to keep them, but the rest of the states demanded that all such territory be turned over to the Confederation government. When New York and Virginia finally agreed to give up their western claims, Maryland (the only state still holding out) approved the Articles of Confederation. They went into effect in 1781.

The Confederation, which existed from 1781 until 1789, was not the complete failure that subsequent accounts often described. But it was far from a success. Lacking adequate powers to deal with interstate issues or to enforce its will on the states, and lacking sufficient stature in the eyes of the world to be able to negotiate effectively, it suffered a series of damaging setbacks.

Diplomatic Failures

Evidence of the low esteem in which the rest of the world held the Confederation made it difficult to persuade Great Britain (and, to a lesser extent, Spain) to live up to the terms of the peace treaty of 1783.

The British had promised to evacuate American soil, but British forces continued to occupy a string of frontier posts along the Great Lakes within the United States. Nor did the British honor their agreement to make restitution to slaveowners whose slaves the British army had confiscated. There were also disputes over the northeastern boundary of the new nation and over the border between the United States and Florida, which Britain had ceded back to Spain in the treaty. And there were diplomatic problems involving American commerce. Freed from imperial regulations, it was expanding in new directions, but most American trade remained within the British Empire. Americans wanted full access to British markets; England, however, placed sharp postwar restrictions on that access.

In 1784, Congress sent John Adams as minister to London to resolve these differences, but Adams made no headway with the English, who could never be sure whether he represented a single nation or thirteen different ones. Throughout the 1780s, the British government refused even to return the courtesy of sending a minister to the American capital.

In dealing with the Spanish government, the Confederation demonstrated similar weakness. Its diplomats agreed to a treaty with Spain in 1786 that accepted the American interpretation of the Florida boundary in return for American recognition of Spanish possessions in North America and an agreement that the United States would limit its right to navigate the Mississippi for twenty years. But the southern states, incensed at the idea of giving up their access to the Mississippi, blocked ratification.

The Confederation and the Northwest

The Confederation's most important accomplishment was its resolution of some of the controversies involving the western lands—although even this was a partial and ambiguous achievement.

When the Revolution began, only a few thousand whites lived west of the Appalachian divide; by 1790 their numbers had increased to 120,000. The Confederation had to find a way to include these new settlements in the political structure of the new nation. The western settlers were already often in conflict with the established centers of the East over Indian policies, trade provisions, and taxes. At times, in fact (as with the Paxton Boys uprising in Pennsylvania in 1763 and the Regulator movements in North Carolina in 1771), there had been overt hostilities between eastern and western peoples. Congress faced the additional difficulty of competing with state governments for jurisdiction over the trans-Appalachian region. When Virginia first ceded its western terri-

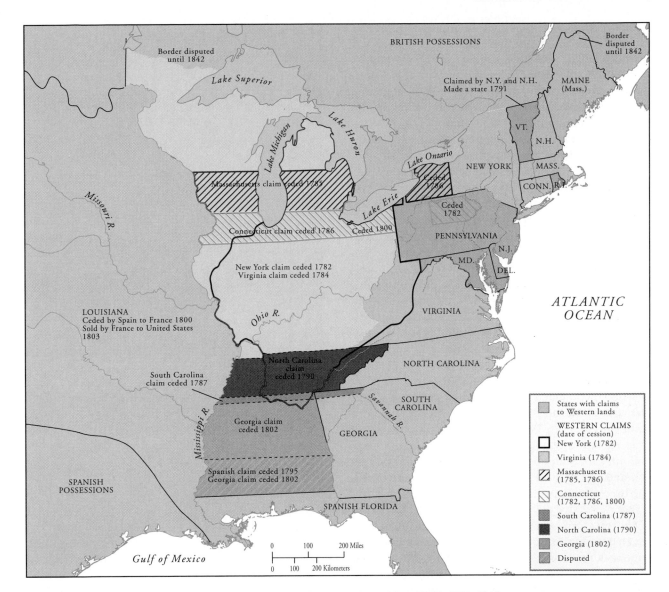

■ **STATE CLAIMS TO WESTERN LANDS AND CESSIONS TO NATIONAL GOVERNMENT, 1782–1802**
Most of the original thirteen colonies claimed extensive tracts of western lands. After the American Revolution, the new national government induced most of the states to give up their claims to these lands. By 1784, the states had ceded enough land to the Confederation to permit Congress to begin making policy for the national domain. The Ordinances of 1784 and 1785 began the process of organizing, surveying, and selling the western lands that were now in the possession of the federal government.

tory to Congress in 1781 (a cession not finally concluded until 1784), the other land-rich states began to yield their claims to the Confederation as well. By 1784 the states had ceded enough land to the Confederation to permit Congress to begin making policy for the national domain.

The Ordinance of 1784, based on a proposal by Thomas Jefferson, divided the western territory into ten self-governing districts, each of which could petition Congress for statehood when its population equaled the number of free inhabitants of the smallest existing state. Then, in the Ordinance of 1785, Congress created a system for surveying and selling the western lands. The territory north of the Ohio River would be surveyed and marked off into neat rectangular townships. (This grid system established a pattern that would leave an indelible mark on the American landscape and, through it, the American economy. (See "The American Environment," pp. 188–189.) In every township four of 36 sections would be reserved for the national government; the revenue from the sale of one of the others would support the creation of a public school (the first example of federal aid to education). Sections were to be sold at auction for no less than one dollar an acre. Since there were 640 acres in a section, the prospective buyer of government land had to have at least $640—a very large sum by the standards of the day. The original ordinances proved highly favorable to land speculators and less so to ordinary settlers, many of whom could not afford to buy the land. Congress compounded the problem by selling much of the best land to the Ohio and Scioto companies (land speculation operations) before making it available to anyone else. Criticism of these policies led to the passage in 1787 of another law governing western settlement—legislation that became known as the "Northwest Ordinance."

The new ordinance abandoned the ten districts established in 1784 and created a single Northwest Territory out of the lands north of the Ohio; the territory might subsequently be divided into three to five territories. It also specified a population of 60,000 as a minimum for statehood, guaranteed freedom of religion and the right of trial by jury to residents of the Northwest, and prohibited slavery throughout the territory.

The western lands south of the Ohio River received less attention from Congress, and development was more chaotic there. The region that became Kentucky and Tennessee developed rapidly in the late 1770s, and in the 1780s speculators and settlers began setting up governments and asking for recognition as states. The Confederation Congress was never able to resolve the conflicting claims in that region successfully. But in the Northwest Territory, the western land policies of the

■ **LAND SURVEY: ORDINANCE OF 1785**

In 1785, Congress established a system for surveying and selling the western lands. The Ordinance of 1785 organized the territory north of the Ohio River in a Cartesian grid pattern, imposing a semblance of rationality and order on the physical geography of the American landscape. The grid system simplified the problem of determining property boundaries, and made it easier for settlers and speculators to select and identify the lands they wished to purchase.

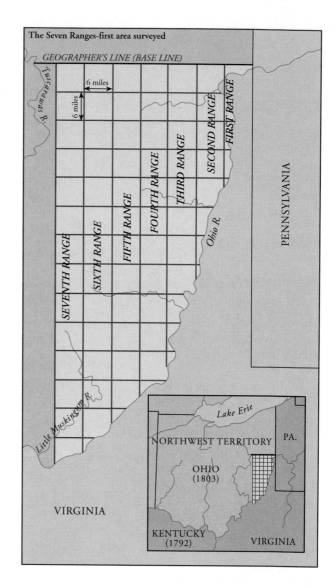

The Seven Ranges-first area surveyed

GEOGRAPHER'S LINE (BASE LINE)

6 miles

6 miles

Tuscarawas R.

SEVENTH RANGE   SIXTH RANGE   FIFTH RANGE   FOURTH RANGE   THIRD RANGE   SECOND RANGE   FIRST RANGE

Ohio R.

PENNSYLVANIA

Little Muskingum R.

VIRGINIA

Lake Erie

NORTHWEST TERRITORY   PA.

OHIO (1803)

KENTUCKY (1792)   VIRGINIA

* Four sections reserved for subsequent sales

Section 16 reserved for school funds

36	30	24	18	12	6
35	29*	23	17	11*	5
34	28	22	16	10	4
33	27	21	15	9	3
32	26*	20	14	8*	2
31	25	19	13	7	1

A

B   C   D   E

6 miles

1 mile

One Section = 640 acres (1 mile square)
A Half section = 320 acres
B Quarter section =160 acres
C Half-quarter section = 80 acres
D & E Quarter-quarter section = 40 acres

One township (six miles square)

Confederation created a system that—on paper at least—brought order and stability to the process of white settlement.

Indians and the Western Lands

That order and stability came slowly, and at great cost. That was because the lands the Confederation was taking from the states, neatly subdividing, and offering for sale consisted in large part of territory the Indians of the region already occupied. Congress tried to resolve that problem in 1784, 1785, and 1786 by pressuring Iroquois, Choctaw, Chickasaw, and Cherokee leaders to sign several treaties surrendering substantial western lands in the North and South to the United States. But those agreements proved largely ineffective. Even the Indian nations that agreed to the treaties did so unwillingly.

In 1786, the leadership of the Iroquois Confederacy repudiated the treaty it had signed two years earlier and threatened to attack white settlements in the disputed lands (although by then the Six Nations were too weak and divided to mount an effective resistance). Other tribes had never agreed to the treaties affecting them. One of those tribes, the Creek, strenuously resisted white movement into their lands in Georgia and South Carolina for five years until 1790 when their leader, Alexander McGillivray (who had fought with the British during the Revolution), negotiated a treaty with the federal government settling the dispute for a time. Other tribes—among them the Miami, Shawnee, Delaware, Ottawa, and Chippewa—some of whom had once been represented in negotiations with whites by the Iroquois, formed new confederations of their own in an effort to strengthen their hand in dealings with the United States government.

Violence between whites and Indians on the Northwest frontier reached a crescendo in the early 1790s. The first governor of the new Northwest Territory, General Arthur St. Clair, tried and failed in 1789 to force an agreement on the Miami, Shawnee, and Delaware, whose refusal to hand over their lands threatened plans by the Ohio Company and others to extend white settlement north of the Ohio River. In 1790 and again in 1791, the Miami, led by the famed warrior Little Turtle, defeated United States forces in two major battles near what is now the western border of Ohio; in the second of those battles, on November 4, 1791, 630 white Americans died in fight-

■ **LITTLE TURTLE**
Little Turtle led the Miami confederacy in its wars with the United States in what is now Ohio and Indiana in the early 1790s. For a time he seemed almost invincible, but in 1794 Little Turtle was defeated in the Battle of Fallen Timbers. In this sketch (a rough copy of a painting attributed to Gilbert Stuart), Little Turtle wears a medal bearing the likeness of George Washington, awarded him by the United States after the signing of the Treaty of Greenville. *(Bettmann)*

ing at the Wabash River—the greatest military victory Indians had ever or would ever achieve in their battles with whites. Efforts to negotiate a settlement foundered on the Miami insistence that no treaty was possible that did not forbid white settlement west of the Ohio River.

In 1794, General Anthony Wayne cautiously moved 4,000 soldiers into the Ohio Valley toward the Maumee River, building forts as he went. British officials in Canada, who were providing supplies to the tribes, themselves constructed a fort about twenty miles from the mouth of the river, well within the boundaries of the United States. In the

THE GRID

Among the many environmental changes that people have wrought upon the American landscape is one so familiar that we seldom notice it—except, perhaps, when we look down upon the land from the air and see, in almost all regions of the nation, the unmistakable square and rectangular patterns that make up the most characteristic of American geographical forms: the grid. The grid did not come naturally to America. It was imposed upon the land—but not until after several centuries of European settlement in the New World and several experiments with other systems.

Methods of dividing up land into specific pieces of property that individuals can own or control are known as "cadastral" systems. Several different versions of them emerged in the Americas. The Spanish, for instance, had given a few of their most prominent colonists in New Mexico, Texas, and California vast estates *(encomiendas),* which were defined less by the actual boundaries of the land—which remained somewhat informal and undefined—than by the right of the owners to claim payments in labor or crops from the people who lived there. The Dutch created a similar land system along the banks of the Hudson River in New York, where most of the tenants were European immigrants rather than Indians. The cadastral systems of the Spanish and the Dutch encouraged and reinforced social hierarchy—giving great power to large landholders at the expense of those who worked the land—and discouraged social fluidity.

The English colonies had at least two major cadastral systems. One was the New England town system, in which a large tract of land was granted by charter to a small group of proprietors, who then divided it up for the benefit of individual settlers. All original colonists were given house lots near the church and meetinghouse in the center of town,

but each also received tracts of land for traditional agricultural uses, often widely scattered in different parts of the town. In the South, land was surveyed according to a much more informal system called "metes and bounds"—which in practice amounted to virtually no system at all. People wanting to buy land went to the county courthouse and purchased a claim to a given number of acres. They then went more or less wherever they chose and marked out the allotted number of acres. The result was a crazy-quilt pattern of properties, many of them overlapping because many owners did not know of a prior claim to the land they were surveying. The southern system was cheap and at first easy to administer, but it produced so many conflicts over who owned what land that claimants were often forced to battle one another in court for decades. Prior to the Revolution, in short, there were highly variable methods for dividing up land in America, most of them loose, informal, and unstable.

When the new government of the United States met in the wake of the Revolution to settle various problems of the new nation, one of their most important tasks was to decide which cadastral system was most appropriate for the republic—and particularly for the vast western territories ceded to the national government by the states in 1781 that became known as the "public domain." Clearly, a semifeudal system of large land estates like that of the Spanish or Dutch was inappropriate for a republic like the United States. Members of Congress were also eager to avoid the random irregularities and legal conflicts associated with southern metes and bounds. They therefore turned to a modified version of the New England town system. Shortly after the end of the Revolution, they passed what would become one of the great founding laws in American history, the Land Ordinance of 1785. This act was as important to

The lack of a standardized survey system in the southern colonies produced crazy-quilt field patterns that persist to this day. The irregular fence lines and property boundaries one sees when flying over the southern landscape reflect the metes and bounds surveys that were made centuries ago. *(Comstock)*

the future shape of the American landscape as the Constitution was to the future shape of American government.

The Ordinance originally applied only to what was then called the Northwest Territory—present-day Ohio, Indiana, Michigan, Illinois, and Wisconsin—but it became a model for all subsequent land systems administered by the federal government. One of its most important features was its requirement that lands be surveyed before they could be purchased, thus circumventing the problems of the southern system. To make sure that surveyed tracts did not overlap, the authors of the ordinance turned to a familiar Enlightenment symbol of rationality and order: the Cartesian coordinate plane that René Descartes had offered as a foundation for his new mathematics—in other words, a grid composed of square or rectangular areas.

Lands west of the Ohio River were divided into square townships six miles to a side, each containing thirty-six square miles, or "sections." Surveyors walked along each side of a section and located its four corners to eliminate confusion about where one section ended and another began. Townships were sold in two ways: either as thirty-six-square-mile units to large proprietors who broke them up and resold them as speculations, or as one-square-mile sections to smaller landowners.

The environmental effects of the 1785 Ordinance are almost impossible to exaggerate. The modern landscape of the West and Midwest would be unrecognizable without it. As one flies today from Pennsylvania to Ohio, one instantly recognizes the shift from random field shapes near the Atlantic coast to the rigid north-south, east-west rectilinear patterns of the grid further inland. Except for modern interstate highways,

(continued)

■ **THE GRID, ILLINOIS**
Starting at the point where the Ohio River crosses the Pennsylvania-Ohio border, government
surveyors applied the Land Ordinance of 1785 to most parts of the United States. The uniform
checkerboard pattern of the national grid is visible to any traveler who flies or drives across this
terrain. (*Comstock*)

most roads still follow the edges of the original
section lines. Farmers still plow their fields
within the boundaries set by the original surveyors and still preserve many of the old
gnarled "witness trees" the surveyors used to
mark section corners. American cities and
towns—from New York to Seattle—mimic the
national grid in the rectangular layout of their
streets and lots. We live in a rectilinear world.

The 1785 Ordinance accomplished its goals
with great success. It surveyed the public domain according to a regular system, prevented
unnecessary litigation over property rights, and
speeded the development of western lands. But
it was not without problems. It encouraged a
dispersed form of settlement—each farm family
often a half mile or more from its neighbors—
that undermined the community ideals that the

Ordinance's model, the New England town system, had sought to promote. It led people to
arrange their fields and roads according to a
rigid north-south, east-west alignment, regardless of local topography. Finally, when the surveyors eventually reached the arid West, where
a dry climate made traditional eastern farming
impossible, the square mile units of the grid
proved inappropriate both for livestock raising
and for irrigation.

Despite these social and environmental problems, however, the grid is here to stay. Once
drawn, property boundaries can survive for
centuries and even millennia after the society
that originally drew them has disappeared. In
writing the 1785 Ordinance, members of Congress made an indelible mark on the American
landscape.

summer of 1794, Wayne met and decisively defeated the Indians in a battle fought near the British fort: the Battle of Fallen Timbers (so named because it occurred at a place where trees had been blown over by a windstorm). The British garrison prudently stayed out of the fight. A year later, the Miami unhappily signed the Treaty of Greenville. It ceded substantial new lands to the United States. In exchange, the Miami received a formal acknowledgment of their claim to the territory they retained. This was the first recognition by the United States government of the sovereignty of Indian nations; in doing so, the United States was repudiating its earlier position (that the tribes had no binding legal claim to land) and affirming that Indian lands could be ceded only by the tribes themselves. That hard-won assurance, however, proved a frail protection against the pressure for white expansion westward in later years.

The conflicts in the Ohio Valley in the aftermath of the Northwest Ordinance suggested the continuing tenuousness of the American claim to control of its western territories. Large areas of the region remained highly unstable, and hence unreceptive to white settlement, until the first decades of the nineteenth century.

Debts, Taxes, and Daniel Shays

At the end of the Revolutionary War, foreign ships crowded into American seaports with cargoes of all kinds, and the American people bought extravagantly with cash or credit—satisfying a desire for foreign goods that had found few outlets during the Revolution. As a result, there was a rapid and substantial flow of hard currency out of the country. Consumer indebtedness to importing merchants increased greatly, which intensified an already severe postwar depression that had begun in 1784 and lasted until 1787. The depression increased the perennial American problem of an inadequate money supply, a problem that bore particularly heavily on debtors. It was in dealing with this increasingly serious problem of debts that the Confederation Congress failed most conspicuously.

The Confederation itself had an enormous outstanding debt, and few means with which to pay it. It had borrowed large sums of money from American citizens and foreign governments during the war, and it owed back pay to its Revolutionary soldiers. Its

powers of taxation, in the meantime, were limited; Congress received only about one-sixth of the money it requisitioned from the states—barely enough to meet the government's ordinary operating expenses. The nation was faced with the prospect of defaulting on its obligations, a possibility that threatened to destroy the fragile new government.

This alarming prospect brought to the fore a group of leaders who would play a crucial role in the shaping of the republic for the next several decades. Committed nationalists, they were looking for ways to increase the powers of the central government and to permit it to meet its financial obligations. Robert Morris, the head of the Confederation's treasury; Alexander Hamilton, his young protégé; James Madison of Virginia; and others were soon lobbying for a "continental impost"—a 5 percent duty on imported goods, to be levied by Congress and used to fund the debt. The impost, the nationalists believed, would not only preserve the financial integrity of the new nation; it would strengthen the national government by making it principally responsible for the nation's debts.

But their proposals encountered substantial opposition. Many Americans feared that the impost plan was the first step toward the creation of a corrupt center of privilege, that it would concentrate too much financial power in the hands of Robert Morris and his allies in Philadelphia. The first effort to secure the impost, in 1781, received the approval of twelve state delegations in Congress, but Rhode Island's refusal to agree killed the plan. A second effort in 1783 also failed to win the necessary unanimous approval. Angry and discouraged, the nationalists largely withdrew from any active involvement in the Confederation.

In the absence of effective action by Congress, the domestic debt problem remained in the hands of the states, which generally relied on increased taxation to deal with their financial difficulties. To the state creditors—that is, the bondholders—this was sound, honest public finance, which protected their legitimate interests. But poor farmers, already burdened by debt and now burdened again by taxes on their lands, considered such policies unfair, even tyrannical. They demanded that the state governments issue paper currency to increase the money supply and make it easier for them to meet their obligations. Resentment ran especially high among farmers in New England, who

■ **DANIEL SHAYS AND JOB SHATTUCK**
Shays and Shattuck were the principal leaders of the 1786
uprising by poor farmers in Massachusetts demanding relief
from their indebtedness. Shattuck led an insurrection in the
east, which collapsed when he was captured on November 30.
Shays organized the rebellion in the west, which continued
until finally dispersed by state militia in late February 1787. The
following year, state authorities pardoned Shays; even before
that, the legislature responded to the rebellion by providing
some relief to the impoverished farmers. These drawings are
part of a hostile account of the rebellion published in 1787 in a
Boston almanac. *(National Portrait Gallery, Smithsonian
Institution/Art Resource, NY)*

felt that the states were extorting money from
them to swell the coffers of wealthy bondholders
in Boston and other towns. Debtors who failed to
pay their taxes found their mortgages foreclosed
and their property seized; sometimes they found
themselves in jail.

Throughout the late 1780s, therefore, mobs of
distressed farmers rioted periodically in various parts
of New England. They caused the most serious trouble in Massachusetts. Dissidents in the Connecticut
Valley and the Berkshire Hills, many of them Revolu-

tionary veterans, rallied behind Daniel Shays, himself
a former captain in the Continental army. Shays demanded paper money, tax relief, a moratorium on
debts, the relocation of the state capital from Boston
to the interior, and the abolition of imprisonment
for debt. He organized his followers into a military
force. During the summer of 1786, the Shaysites
concentrated on preventing the collection of debts,
private or public, and traveled from place to place in
armed bands to keep courts from sitting and to prevent sheriffs from selling confiscated property. In
Boston, members of the legislature, including
Samuel Adams, denounced Shays and his men as
rebels and traitors.

When winter came, the rebels advanced on
Springfield hoping to seize weapons from the arsenal there. An army of state militiamen, financed by
a loan from wealthy merchants who feared a new
revolution, set out from Boston to confront them.
In January 1787, this army met Shays's ragged
troops, killed several of them, captured many
more, and scattered the rest to the hills in a blind-
ing snowstorm.

As a military enterprise, Shays's Rebellion was a
fiasco. But it had important consequences for the
future of the United States. In Massachusetts, it resulted in a few immediate gains for the discon-
tented groups. Shays and his lieutenants, at first sentenced to death, soon received pardons and even
some economic concessions: tax relief and post-
ponement of debt payments. Much more significant, however, the rebellion added urgency to a
movement already gathering support throughout
the new nation—the movement to produce a new,
national constitution.

CONCLUSION

Between a small, inconclusive battle on a village
green in New England in 1775 and a momentous surrender at Yorktown in 1781, the American people
fought a great and terrible war against the mightiest
military nation in the world. No one outside America,
and few within it, would have predicted in 1775 that
the makeshift armies of the colonies could withstand
the armies and navies of the British empire. But a
combination of luck, brilliance, determination, and

timely aid from abroad allowed the Patriots, as they
began to call themselves, to make full use of the advantages of fighting on their home soil and to frustrate British designs time and again.

The war was not just a historic military event. It
was also a great political one, for it propelled the
colonies to unite, to organize, and—in July 1776—to
declare their independence. Having done so, they
fought with even greater determination, defending

Significant Events

1774	Shawnee defeated by Virginia militia in Lord Dunmore's War
1775	Second Continental Congress meets
	George Washington appointed to command American forces
	Battle of Bunker Hill
	Montgomery assault on Quebec fails
1776	Thomas Paine's *Common Sense* published
	British troops leave Boston
	Declaration of Independence debated and signed (July 2–4)
	Howe routs Americans on Long Island
	Battle of Trenton
	First state constitutions written
1777	Articles of Confederation adopted
	Battles of Princeton, Brandywine, and Germantown
	Howe occupies Philadelphia
	Washington camps at Valley Forge for winter
	Burgoyne surrenders to Gates at Saratoga
1778	French-American alliance established
	Clinton replaces Howe
	British leave Philadelphia
	War shifts to the South
	British capture Savannah
1780	British capture Charleston
	Cornwallis defeats Gates at Camden, South Carolina
	Patriots defeat Tories at King's Mountain, South Carolina
	Massachusetts constitution ratified
	Slavery abolished in Pennsylvania
1781	Battles of Cowpens and Guilford Court House
	Cornwallis surrenders at Yorktown
	Articles of Confederation ratified
	Continental impost proposed
1782	American militiamen massacre Delaware Indians in Ohio
1781–1784	States cede western lands to Confederation
1783	Treaty of Paris with Great Britain recognizes American independence
	Slavery abolished in Massachusetts
1784	Postwar depression begins, aggravating currency problems
1784–1785	First ordinances establishing procedures for settling western lands enacted
1786	Virginia Statute of Religious Freedom passed
1786–1787	Shays's Rebellion in Massachusetts
1787	Northwest Ordinance enacted
1789	John Carroll named first bishop of Catholic Church of United States
1792	Mary Wollstonecraft's *Vindication of the Rights of Women* published in the United States
1794	Anthony Wayne defeats Indians in Ohio

now not just a set of principles, but an actual, fledgling nation. By the end of the war, they had created new governments at both the state and national level and had begun experimenting with new political forms that would distinguish the United States from any previous nation in history.

The war was also important for its effects on American society—for the way it shook (although never overturned) the existing social order; for the way it caused women to question (although seldom openly to challenge) their place in society; and for the way it spread notions of liberty and freedom throughout a society that in the past had often been rigidly hierarchical and highly deferential. Even African-American slaves absorbed some of the ideas of the Revolution, although it would be many years before they would be in any position to make very much use of them.

Victory in the American Revolution solved many of the problems of the new nation, but it also produced others. What should the United States do about its relations with the Indians and with its neighbors to the north and south? What should it do about the distribution of western lands? What should it do about slavery? How should it balance its commitment to liberty with its need for order? These questions bedeviled the new national government in its first years of existence and ultimately led Americans to create a new political order.

FOR FURTHER REFERENCE

Suggested Readings Edward Countryman, *The American Revolution* (1985) is a useful overview. Gordon Wood, *The Radicalism of the American Revolution* (1992) emphasizes the profound political change that the Revolution entailed. Charles Royster, *A Revolutionary People at War: The Continental Army and American Character* (1979) suggests the importance of military service for American men. Mary Beth Norton, *Liberty's Daughters: The Revolutionary Experience of American Women, 1750-1800* (1980) demonstrates that the Revolution had a significant impact on the lives of American women as well. Eric Foner, *Tom Paine and Revolutionary America* (1976) connects the leading pamphleteer of the Revolution with urban radicalism in Philadelphia. Pauline Maier, *American Scripture* (1997) is a penetrating study of the making of the Declaration of Independence, and of its impact on subsequent generations of Americans. Colin Calloway, *The American Revolution in Indian Country* (1995) is a new and important study on an often neglected aspect of the war. Sylvia R. Frey, *Water from the Rock: Black Resistance in a Revolutionary Age* (1991), argues that the American Revolution was a major turning point in the history of slavery in the American South.

Films (The best source for information on how to find these and other films is *Bowker's Complete Video Directory*—3 volumes.) *Liberty* (1997) is a compelling six-hour PBS documentary history of the American Revolution, from its early origins in the 1760s. *The American Revolution Collector's Edition* is a comprehensive (five hours) and riveting documentary produced by the Arts & Entertainment Network. *The American Story, No. 2: Declaring Independence* (1985) features the writing, consequences, and significance of the Declaration of Independence. *The Early Campaigns of Francis Marion and the Loyalists in the South* explores key battles of the American Revolution in the southern colonies. *Thomas Jefferson: Philosopher of Freedom* (1996) is a biography of America's leading revolutionary from the Arts & Entertainment Network. *The Battle of Yorktown* (1983) examines the climactic battles of the American Revolution.

Internet Resources (For up-to-date URL addresses and links to these and other websites, consult the McGraw-Hill history site at *http://www.mmhe.com/socscience/history/usa/link/linktop.htm*) *Liberty!: The American Revolution* is a companion to the six-hour PBS documentary on the American Revolution from the French and Indian War to the ratification of the Constitution. *Rare Map Collection—Revolutionary America* includes contemporary maps of the American Revolution. *The Benjamin Marston Diaries Project* makes available the diary of a Massachusetts Loyalist who fled to Canada. *Letters from an American Farmer* is Crevecoeur's famous description of rural life in 1782.

⌀

BIBLIOGRAPHY

General Studies   Theodore Draper, *A Struggle for Power: The American Revolution* (1996). Jack P. Greene, ed., *The American Revolution: Its Character and Limits* (1987). Merrill Jensen, *The Founding of a Nation, A History of the American Revolution, 1763–1789* (1968). Michael Kammen, *A Season of Youth: The American Revolution and the Historical Imagination* (1978). Robert Middlekauff, *The Glorious Cause: The American Revolution, 1763–1789* (1985). Edmund S. Morgan, *The Birth of the Republic, 1763–1789* (1956). Gordon S. Wood, *The Radicalism of the American Revolution* (1992). Alfred E. Young, Jr., ed., *The American Revolution* (1976).

The Road to Independence   Carl Becker, *The Declaration of Independence* (1922). David Hawke, *Paine* (1974). John R. Howe, Jr., *The Changing Political Thought of John Adams* (1966). Edmund S. Morgan, *The Meaning of Independence* (1976). Peter Shaw, *The Character of John Adams* (1976); *American Patriots and the Rituals of Revolution* (1981). Morton White, *The Philosophy of the American Revolution*(1978). Gary Willis, *Inventing America: Jefferson's Declaration of Independence* (1978).

The War   John R. Alden, *The American Revolution* (1964). Richard Buel, Jr., *Dear Liberty: Connecticut's Mobilization for the Revolutionary War* (1980). E. Wayne Carp, *To Starve the Army at Pleasure: Continental Army Administration and American Political Culture, 1775–1783* (1984). Lawrence D. Cress, *Citizens in Arms: The Army and the Militia in American Society to the War of 1812* (1982). David Hackett Fischer, *Paul Revere's Ride* (1994). James T. Flexner, *George Washington in the American Revolution* (1968). Douglas Southall Freeman, *George Washington,* 7 vols. (1948–1957). Ronald Hoffman and Thad W. Tate, eds., *An Uncivil War: The Southern Backcountry During the American Revolution* (1985). Don Higginbotham, *The War of American Independence* (1983); *George Washington and the American Military Tradition* (1985). Piers Mackesy, *The War for America* (1964). Samuel Eliot Morison, *John Paul Jones* (1959). Howard H. Peckham, *The War for Independence* (1958). Steven Rosswurm, *Arms, Country, and Class: The Philadelphia Militia and the "Lower Sort" in the Era of the American Revolution* (1987). Charles Royster, *Light-Horse Larry Lee and the Legacy of the American Revolution* (1981). John Shy, *A People Numerous and Armed* (1976); *The American Revolution* (1973). Willard Wallace, *Appeal to Arms* (1950).

Revolutionary Diplomacy   Samuel F. Bemis, *The Diplomacy of the American Revolution* (1935). Jonathan R. Dull, *A Diplomatic History of the American Revolution* (1985). E. J. Ferguson, *The Power of the Purse* (1961). L. S. Kaplan, *Colonies into Nation: American Diplomacy, 1763–1801* (1972). Richard B. Morris, *The Peacemakers* (1965). Gerald Stourzh, *Benjamin Franklin and American Foreign Policy,* rev. ed. (1969).

The Loyalists   Bernard Bailyn, *The Ordeal of Thomas Hutchinson* (1974). Wallace Brown, *The King's Friends* (1965). Robert M. Calhoon, *The Loyalists in Revolutionary America* (1973). Mary Beth Norton, *The British Americans: The Loyalist Exiles in England 1774–1789* (1972). Anne M. Ousterhout, *A State Divided: Opposition in Pennsylvania to the American Revolution* (1987). Paul H. Smith, *Loyalists and Redcoats* (1964). James W. St. G. Walker, *The Black Loyalists* (1976).

Women, Family, and the Revolution   Joy Day Buel and Richard Buel, Jr., *The Way of Duty: A Woman and Her Life in Revolutionary America* (1984). Linda Grant DePauw, *Founding Fathers* (1975). Ronald Hoffman and Peter J. Albert, eds., *Women in the Age of the American Revolution* (1989). Joan Jensen, *Loosening the Bonds: Mid-Atlantic Farm Women, 1750–1850* (1986). Susan Juster, *Disorderly Women: Sexual Politics & Evangelicalism in Revolutionary New England* (1994). Linda K. Kerber, *Women of the Republic: Intellect and Ideology in Revolutionary America* (1980).

Indians and Blacks in the Revolution   Ira Berlin and Ronald Hoffman, eds., *Slavery in the Revolutionary Era* (1982). David Brion Davis, *The Problem of Slavery in the Age of Revolution* (1975). Barbara Graymount, *The Iroquois in the American Revolution* (1973). Isabel T. Kelsay, *Joseph Brant, 1743–1807* (1984). Duncan McLeod, *Slavery, Race and the American Revolution* (1974). Edmund S. Morgan, *American Slavery American Freedom: The Ordeal of Colonial Virginia* (1975). Gary B. Nash, *Race and Revolution* (1990). Gary B. Nash and Jean R. Soderlund, *Freedom by Degrees: Emancipation in Pennsylvania and Its Aftermath* (1991). James H. O'Donnell, III, *Southern Indians in the American Revolution* (1973).

Benjamin Quarles, *The Negro in the American Revolution* (1961). Bruce A. Ragsdale, *A Planter's Republic: The Search for Economic Independence in Revolutionary Virginia* (1996) Anthony F. C. Wallace, *The Death and Rebirth of the Seneca* (1969). Arthur Zilversmit, *The First Emancipation* (1967).

Social and Economic Effects   Edward Countryman, *A People in Revolution* (1981). Jeffrey J. Crow and Larry E. Tise, *The Southern Experience in the American Revolution* (1978). Robert Gross, *The Minutemen and Their World* (1976). J. F. Jameson, *The American Revolution Considered as a Social Movement* (1962). Merrill Jensen, *The American Revolution Within America* (1974). Rachel N. Klein, *Unification of a Slave State: The Rise of the Planter Class in the South Carolina Backcountry, 1760-1808* (1990). Jean B. Lee, *The Price of Nationhood: The American Revolution in Charles County* (1994). Staughton Lynd, *Class Conflict, Slavery and the United States Constitution* (1968). Jackson Turner Main, *The Social Structure of Revolutionary America* (1965). Cathy D. Matson and Peter S. Onuf, *Union of Interests: Political and Economic Thought in Revolutionary America* (1990). Jerome J. Nadlehaft, *The Disorders of War: The Revolution in South Carolina* (1981). Billy G. Smith, *"The Lower Sort": Philadelphia's Laboring People, 1750-1800* (1990). Charles G. Steffen, *The Mechanics of Baltimore: Workers and Politics in the Age of Revolution, 1763-1812* (1984). Gordon S. Wood, *The Radicalism of the American Revolution* (1992).

State Governments   Willi Paul Adams, *The First American Constitutions* (1980). Richard Beeman et al., eds., *Beyond Confederation: Origins of the Constitution and American National Identity* (1987). Donald S. Lutz, *Origins of American Constitutionalism* (1988). Jackson Turner Main, *Political Parties Before the Constitution* (1973); *The Sovereign States, 1775-1783* (1973); *The Upper House in Revolutionary America, 1763-1788* (1967). Stephen E. Patterson, *Political Parties in Revolutionary Massachusetts* (1973). Irwin Polishook, *Rhode Island and the Union, 1774-1795* (1969). Gordon S. Wood, *The Creation of the American Republic* (1969).

The Articles of Confederation   Andrew R. L. Cayton, *The Frontier Republic: Ideology and Politics in the Ohio Country, 1780-1825* (1986). Jack Eblen, *The First and Second United States Empires* (1968). John Fiske, *The Critical Period of American History, 1783-1789* (1883). H. James Henderson, *Party Politics in the Continental Congress* (1974). Merrill Jensen, *The New Nation* (1950); *The Articles of Confederation,* rev. ed. (1959). Calvin Jillson and Rick Wilson, *Congressional Dynamics: Structure, Coordination and Choice in the First American Congress, 1774-1789* (1994). Jack N. Rakove, *The Beginnings of National Politics* (1979). David Szatmary, *Shays' Rebellion: The Making of an Agrarian Insurrection* (1980). Steven Watts, *The Republic Reborn: War and the Making of Liberal America, 1790-1800* (1987).

THE AMERICAN STAR

GEN: GEO: WASHINGTON

First in War,
First in Peace,
First in defence
of
our Country.

Independence
of
AMERICA
July 4th 1776

Chapter Six

THE CONSTITUTION AND THE NEW REPUBLIC

By the late 1780s, most Americans had grown deeply dissatisfied with the deficiencies of the Confederation: with the government's apparent inability to deal with factiousness and instability; with its failure to handle economic problems effectively; and perhaps most of all with the frightening powerlessness it had displayed in the face of Shays's Rebellion. A decade earlier, Americans had deliberately avoided creating a genuine national government, fearing that it would encroach on the sovereignty of the individual states. Now they reconsidered. In 1787, they created a new government defined by the Constitution of the United States.

The American Constitution derived most of its principles from the state documents that had preceded it. But it was also a remarkable achievement in its own right. Out of the contentious atmosphere of a fragile new nation, Americans fashioned a system of government that has survived for more than two centuries as one of the stablest and most successful in the world. William Gladstone, the great nineteenth-century British statesman, once called the Constitution the "most wonderful work ever struck off at a given time by the brain and purpose of man." The American people in the years to come generally agreed. Indeed, to them the Constitution took on some of the characteristics of a sacred document, a holy mystery. Later generations viewed its framers as men almost godlike in their wisdom. Many considered its provisions an unassailable "fundamental law," from which all public policies, all political principles, all solutions of controversies must spring.

The adoption of the Constitution did not complete the creation of the republic. It only defined the terms in which debate over the future of government would continue. Americans may have agreed that the Constitution was a nearly perfect document, but they disagreed—at times fundamentally—on what that document meant. They still do. Out of such disagreements emerged the first great political battles of the new nation.

FRAMING A NEW GOVERNMENT

So unpopular and ineffectual had the Confederation Congress become by the mid-1780s that it began to lead an almost waiflike existence. In 1783, its members timidly withdrew from Philadelphia to escape from the clamor of army veterans demanding back pay. They took refuge for a while in Princeton, New Jersey, then moved to Annapolis, and in 1785 settled in New York. Through all of this, the delegates were

■ **THE AMERICAN STAR**
Frederick Kemmelmeyer painted this tribute to George Washington sometime in the 1790s. It was one of many efforts by artists and others to create an iconography for the new republic.
(Metropolitan Museum of Art)

■ **GEORGE WASHINGTON AT MOUNT VERNON**
Washington was in his first term as president in 1790 when an anonymous folk artist painted this view of his home at Mount Vernon, Virginia. Washington appears in uniform, along with members of his family, on the lawn. After he retired from office in 1797, Washington returned happily to his plantation and spent the two years before his death in 1799 "amusing myself in agricultural and rural pursuits." He also played host to an endless stream of visitors from throughout the country and Europe. *(National Gallery of Art, Washington)*

often conspicuous largely by their absence. Only with great difficulty did Congress secure a quorum to ratify the treaty with Great Britain ending the Revolutionary War. Eighteen members, representing only eight states, voted on the Confederation's most important piece of legislation, the Northwest Ordinance. In the meantime, a major public debate was beginning over the future of the Confederation.

Advocates of Centralization

Weak and unpopular though the Confederation was, it had for a time satisfied a great many—probably a majority—of the people. They believed they had fought the Revolutionary War to avert the danger of what they considered remote and tyrannical authority; now they wanted to keep political power centered in the states, where they could carefully and closely control it.

But during the 1780s, some of the wealthiest and most powerful groups in the country began to clamor for a more genuinely national government capable of dealing with the nation's problems—particularly the economic problems that most directly afflicted them. Some military men, many of them members of the exclusive and hereditary Society of the Cincinnati (formed by Revolutionary army officers in 1783), were disgruntled at the refusal of Congress to fund their pensions. They began aspiring to influence and invigorate the national government; some even envisioned a form of military dictatorship and flirted briefly (in 1783, in the so-called Newburgh Conspiracy) with a direct challenge to Congress, until George Washington intervened and blocked the potential rebellion.

American manufacturers—the artisans and "mechanics" of the nation's cities and towns—wanted to replace the various state tariffs with a uniformly high national duty. Merchants and shippers wanted to replace the thirteen different (and largely ineffective) state commercial policies with a single, national one. Land speculators wanted the "Indian menace" finally removed from their western tracts. People who were owed money wanted to stop the states from issuing paper money, which would lower the value of what they received in payment. Investors in Confederation securities wanted the government to fund the debt and thus enhance the value of their securities. Large property owners looked for protection from the threat of mobs, a threat that seemed particularly menacing in light of such episodes as Shays's Rebellion. By 1786, these diverse demands had grown so powerful that the issue was no longer whether the Confederation should be changed but how drastic the changes should be. Even the defenders of the existing system reluctantly came to agree that the government needed strengthening at its weakest point—its lack of power to tax.

The most resourceful of the reformers was Alexander Hamilton, political genius, New York lawyer, one-time military aide to General Washington, and illegitimate son of a Scottish merchant in the West Indies. From the beginning, Hamilton had been unhappy with the Articles of Confederation and the weak central government they had created. He now called for a national convention to overhaul the entire document. He found an important ally in James Madison of Virginia, who persuaded the Virginia legislature to convene an interstate conference on commercial questions. Only five states sent delegates to the meeting, held in Annapolis, Maryland, in 1786; but the delegates approved a proposal drafted by Hamilton (who was representing New York) recommending that Congress call a convention of special delegates from all the states to gather in Philadelphia the next year and consider ways to "render the constitution of the Federal government adequate to the exigencies of the union."

At that moment, in 1786, there seemed little possibility that the Philadelphia convention would attract any more interest than the meeting at Annapolis had attracted. Only by winning the support of George Washington, the centralizers believed, could they hope to prevail. But Washington at first showed little interest in joining the cause. Then, early in 1787, the news of Shays's Rebellion spread throughout the nation. Thomas Jefferson, then the American minister in Paris, was not alarmed. "I hold," he confided in a

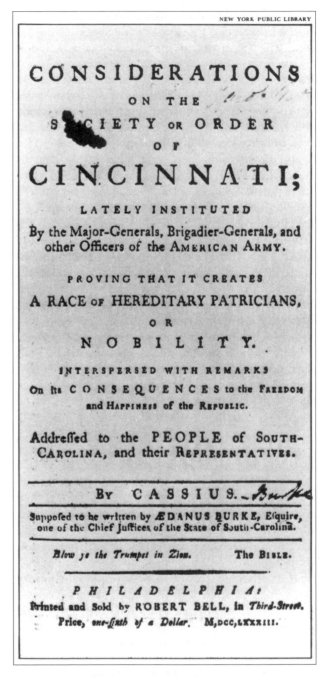

■ A BROADSIDE AGAINST "NOBILITY"
This 1783 pamphlet was one of many expressions of the broad democratic sentiment that the Revolution unleashed in American society. The Society of the Cincinnati was an organization created shortly after the Revolution by men who had served as high-ranking officers in the Patriot Army. To many Americans, however, the Society—membership in which was to be hereditary—looked suspiciously like the inherited aristocracies of England. This pamphlet, printed in Philadelphia but intended for South Carolinians, warns of the dangers the Society supposedly posed to the "Freedom and Happiness of the Republic." *(New York Public Library)*

letter to James Madison, "that a little rebellion, now and then, is a good thing, and as necessary in the political world as storms in the physical." But Washington took the news less calmly. "There are combustibles in every State which a spark might set fire to," he exclaimed. "I feel infinitely more than I can express for the disorders which have arisen. Good God!" In May, he left his home at Mount Vernon in Virginia for the Constitutional Convention in Philadelphia. His support gave the meeting immediate credibility.

A Divided Convention

Fifty-five men, representing all the states except Rhode Island, attended one or more sessions of the convention that sat in the Philadelphia State House from May to September 1787. These "Founding Fathers," as they would later become known, were on the whole relatively young men; their average age was forty-four, and only one delegate (Benjamin Franklin, then eighty-one) was of advanced age. They were well educated by the standards of their time. Most represented the great propertied interests of the country, and many feared what one of them called the "turbulence and follies" of democracy. Yet all were also products of the American Revolution and retained the Revolutionary suspicion of concentrated power.

The convention unanimously chose Washington to preside over its sessions and then closed its business to the public and the press. The members then ruled that each state delegation would have a single vote. Major decisions would not require unanimity, as they did in Congress, but only a simple majority. Virginia, the most populous state, sent the best-prepared delegation to Philadelphia. James Madison (thirty-six years old) was its intellectual leader. He had devised a detailed plan for a new "national" government, and the Virginians used it to control the agenda from the moment the convention began.

Edmund Randolph of Virginia began the discussion by proposing that "a national government ought to be established, consisting of a supreme Legislative, Executive, and Judiciary." Despite its vagueness, it was a drastic proposal. It called for the creation of a government very different from the existing Confederation, which, among other things, had no executive branch. But so committed were the delegates to fundamental reform that they approved this resolu-

tion after only perfunctory debate. Then Randolph introduced the details of Madison's plan. The Virginia Plan (as it came to be known) called for a new national legislature consisting of two houses. In the lower house, the states would be represented in proportion to their population; thus the largest state (Virginia) would have about ten times as many representatives as the smallest (Delaware). Members of the upper house were to be elected by the lower house under no rigid system of representation; thus some of the smaller states might at times have no members at all in the upper house.

The proposal aroused immediate opposition among delegates from Delaware, New Jersey, and other small states. Some responded by arguing that Congress had called the convention "for the sole and express purpose of revising the Articles of Confederation" and had no authority to do more than that. Eventually, however, William Paterson of New Jersey submitted a substantive alternative to the Virginia Plan, a proposal for a "federal" as opposed to a "national" government. The New Jersey Plan preserved the existing one-house legislature, in which each state had equal representation, but it gave Congress expanded powers to tax and to regulate commerce. The delegates voted to table Paterson's proposal, but not without taking note of the substantial support for it among small-state representatives.

The Virginia Plan remained the basis for discussion. But its supporters realized they would have to make concessions to the small states if the convention was ever to reach a general agreement. They soon conceded an important point by agreeing to permit the members of the upper house to be elected by the state legislatures rather than by the lower house of the national legislature. Thus each state would be sure of always having at least one member in the upper house.

But many questions remained. Would the states be equally represented in the upper house, or would the large states have more members than the small ones? Would slaves (who could not vote) be counted as part of the population in determining the size of a state's representation in Congress, or were they to be considered simple property? Delegates from states with large and apparently permanent slave populations—especially those from South Carolina—wanted to have it both ways. They argued that slaves should be considered persons in determining representation. But they wanted slaves to be considered property if the new government were to levy taxes on each state on the basis of population. Representatives from states where slavery had disappeared or was expected soon to disappear argued that slaves should be included in calculating taxation but not representation. No one argued seriously for giving slaves citizenship or the right to vote.

Compromise

The delegates bickered for weeks. By the end of June, as both temperature and tempers rose to uncomfortable heights, the convention seemed in danger of collapsing. Benjamin Franklin, who remained a calm voice of conciliation through the summer, warned that if they failed, the delegates would "become a reproach and by-word down to future ages. And what is worse, mankind may hereafter, from this unfortunate instance, despair of establishing governments by human wisdom, and leave it to chance, war and conquest." Partly because of Franklin's soothing presence, the delegates refused to give up.

Finally, on July 2, the convention agreed to create a "grand committee," with a single delegate from each state (and with Franklin as chairman), to resolve the disagreements. The committee produced a proposal that became the basis of the "Great Compromise." Its most important achievement was resolving the difficult problem of representation. The proposal called for a legislature in which the states would be represented in the lower house on the basis of population, with each slave counted as three-fifths of a free person in determining the basis for both representation and direct taxation. (The three-fifths formula was based on the false assumption that a slave was three-fifths as productive as a free worker and thus contributed only three-fifths as much wealth to the state.) The committee proposed that in the upper house, the states should be represented equally with two members apiece. The proposal broke the deadlock. On July 16, 1787, the convention voted to accept the compromise.

Over the next few weeks, while several committees worked on the details of various parts of the emerging constitution, the convention as a whole agreed to another important compromise on the explosive issue of slavery. The representatives of the southern states feared that the power to regulate trade might interfere the cotton economy, which relied heavily on sales abroad, and with slavery. In re-

sponse, the convention agreed that the new legislature would not be permitted to tax exports; Congress would also be forbidden to impose a duty of more than $10 a head on imported slaves, and it would have no authority to stop the slave trade for twenty years. To those delegates who viewed the continued existence of slavery as an affront to the principles of the new nation, this was a large and difficult concession. They agreed to it because they feared that without it the Constitution would fail.

The convention disposed of other differences of opinion it was unable to harmonize by evasion or omission—leaving important questions alive that would surface again in later years. The Constitution provided no definition of citizenship. Most important was the absence of a list of individual rights, which would restrain the powers of the national government in the way that bills of rights restrained the state governments. Madison opposed the idea, arguing that specifying rights that were reserved to the people would, in effect, limit those rights. Others, however, feared that without such protections the national government might abuse its new authority.

The Constitution of 1787

Many people contributed to the creation of the American Constitution, but the single most important of them was James Madison—the most creative political thinker of his generation. Madison created the Virginia Plan, from which the final document ultimately emerged, and he did most of the drafting of the Constitution itself. But Madison's most important achievement was in helping resolve two important philosophical questions that had served as obstacles to the creation of an effective national government: the question of sovereignty and the question of limiting power.

The question of sovereignty had been one of the chief sources of friction between the colonies and Great Britain, and it continued to trouble Americans as they attempted to create their own government. How could both the national government and the state governments exercise sovereignty at the same time? Where did ultimate sovereignty lie? The answer, Madison and his contemporaries decided, was that all power, at all levels of government, flowed ultimately from the people. Thus neither the federal government nor the state governments were truly sovereign. All of them derived their authority from

■ **THE CONVENTION AT PHILADELPHIA**
This engraving of delegates at work, created in 1823, is one of countless efforts in the early nineteenth century to imaginatively re-create the great constitutional convention in Philadelphia in 1787. It appeared in an early *History of the United States of America* by Rev. Charles A. Goodrich. *(General Research Division, New York Public Library, Astor, Lenox and Tilden Foundations)*

below. The opening phrase of the Constitution (devised by Robert Morris) was "We the people of the United States"—an expression of the belief that the new government derived its power not from the states but from its citizens.

Resolving the problem of sovereignty made possible one of the distinctive features of the Constitution—its distribution of powers between the national and state governments. It was, Madison wrote at the time, "in strictness, neither a national nor a federal Constitution, but a composition of both." The Constitution and the government it created were to be the "supreme law" of the land; no state would have the authority to defy it. The federal government was to have broad powers, including the power to tax, to regulate commerce, to control the currency, and to pass such laws as would be "necessary and proper" for carrying out its other responsibilities. Gone was the stipulation of the Articles that "each State shall retain every power, jurisdiction, and right not expressly delegated to the United States in Congress assembled." On the other hand, the Constitution accepted the existence of separate states and left important powers in their hands.

In addition to solving the question of sovereignty, the Constitution produced a solution to a problem

that was particularly troubling to Americans: the problem of concentrated authority. Nothing so frightened the leaders of the new nation as the prospect of creating a tyrannical government. Indeed, that fear had been one of the chief obstacles to the creation of a national government at all. Drawing from the ideas of the French philosopher Baron de Montesquieu, most Americans had long believed that the best way, perhaps the only way, to avoid tyranny was to keep government close to the people. A republic, they thought, must remain confined to a relatively small area; a large nation would breed corruption and despotism because the rulers would be so distant from most of the people that there would be no way to control them. In the first years of the new American nation, these assumptions had led to the belief that the individual states must remain sovereign and that a strong national government would be dangerous.

Madison, however, helped break the grip of these assumptions by arguing that a large republic would be less, not more, likely to produce tyranny, because it would contain so many different factions that no single group would ever be able to dominate it. (In this, he drew from—among other sources—the Scottish philosopher David Hume.) This idea of many centers of power "checking each other" and preventing any single, despotic authority from emerging not only made possible the idea of a large republic, but also helped shape the internal structure of the federal government. The Constitution's most distinctive feature was its "separation of powers" within the government, its creation of "checks and balances" among the legislative, executive, and judicial branches. The array of forces within the government would constantly compete with (and often frustrate) one another. Congress would have two chambers, the Senate and the House of Representatives, each with members elected in a different way and for different terms, and each checking the other, since both would have to agree before any law could be passed. The president would have the power to veto acts of Congress. The federal courts would have protection from both the executive and the legislature because judges and justices, once appointed by the president and confirmed by the Senate, would serve for life.

The "federal" structure of the government, which divided power between the states and the nation, and the system of "checks and balances," which

THE BACKGROUND OF THE CONSTITUTION

The Constitution—America's most powerful symbol of national identity and the nation's most important source of authority—has inspired debate from the moment it was drafted. Today, as throughout American national history, views of the Constitution reflect the political views of those who seek to interpret it. Some argue that the Constitution is a flexible document intended to evolve in response to society's evolution. Others argue that it has a fixed meaning, rooted in the "original intent" of the framers and that to move beyond that is to deny its value.

Historians, too, disagree about why the Constitution was written and what it meant; and their debate has also reflected contemporary beliefs about what the Constitution should mean. To some scholars, the creation of the federal system was an effort to preserve the ideals of the Revolution by eliminating the disorder and contention that threatened the new nation; it was an effort to create a strong national government capable of exercising real authority. To others, the Constitution was an effort to protect the economic interests of existing elites, even at the cost of betraying the principles of the Revolution. And to still others, the Constitution was designed to protect individual freedom and to limit the power of the federal government.

The first influential exponent of the heroic view of the Constitution as the culmination of the Revolution was John Fiske, whose book *The Critical Period of American History* (1888) painted a grim picture of political life under the Articles of Confederation. The nation, Fiske argued, was reeling under the impact of a business depression; the weakness and ineptitude of the national government; the threats to American territory from Great Britain and Spain; the inability of either the Congress or the state governments to make good their debts; the interstate jealousies and barriers to trade; the widespread use of inflation-producing paper money; and the lawlessness that culminated in Shays's Rebellion. Only the timely adoption of the Constitution, Fiske claimed, saved the young republic from disaster.

Fiske's view met with little dissent until 1913, when Charles A. Beard published a powerful challenge to it in *An Economic Interpretation of the Constitution of the United States.* According to Beard, the 1780s had been a "critical period" not for the nation as a whole but only for certain conservative business interests who feared that the decentralized political structure of the republic imperiled their financial position. Such men, he claimed, wanted a government able to promote industry and trade, protect private property, and perhaps most of all, make good the public debt—much of which was owed to them. The Constitution was, Beard claimed, "an economic document drawn with superb skill by men whose property interests were immediately at stake" and who won its ratification over the opposition of a majority of the people. Were it not for their impatience and determination, he argued in a later book (1927), the Articles of Confederation might have formed a perfectly satisfactory, permanent form of government. The Beardian view of the Constitution influenced more than a generation of historians. As late as the 1950s, for example, Merrill Jensen argued in *The New Nation* (1950) that the 1780s were not years of chaos and despair, but a time of hopeful striving. He agreed with Beard that only the economic interests of a small group of wealthy men could account for the creation of

(*continued*)

the Constitution. To them, the Constitution was notable chiefly for the way it abridged the democratic possibilities of the new nation.

But in the 1950s—in the aftermath of a great world crisis that many scholars believed called into question the desirability of giving free reign to popular passions—a series of powerful challenges to the Beard thesis emerged. The Constitution was not an effort to preserve property, but an enlightened effort to ensure stability and order. Robert E. Brown, for example, argued in 1956 that "absolutely no correlation" could be shown between the wealth of the delegates to the Constitutional Convention and their position on the Constitution. Forrest McDonald, in *We the People* (1958), looked beyond the convention itself to the debate between the Federalists and the Antifederalists and concluded similarly that there was no consistent relationship between wealth and property and support for the Constitution. Instead, opinion on the new system was far more likely to reflect local and regional interests. Areas suffering social and economic distress were likely to support the Constitution; states that were stable and prosperous were likely to oppose it. There was no intercolonial class of monied interests operating in concert to produce the Constitution. The cumulative effect of these attacks greatly weakened Beard's argument; few historians any longer accepted his thesis without reservation.

(General Research Division, New York Public Library, Astor, Lenox and Tilden Foundations)

In the 1960s, a new group of scholars began to revive an economic interpretation of the Constitution—one that differed from Beard's in important ways but that nevertheless emphasized social and economic factors as motives for supporting the federal system. Jackson Turner Main argued, in *The Anti-federalists* (1961), that supporters of the Constitution, while not perhaps the united creditor class that Beard described, were nevertheless economically distinct from critics of the document. The Federalists, he argued, were "cosmopolitan commercialists," eager to advance the

divided power among various elements within the national government itself, were designed to protect the United States from the kind of despotism Americans believed had emerged in England. But they were also designed to protect the nation from another kind of despotism, perhaps equally menacing: the tyranny of the people. Fear of the "mob," of an "excess of democracy," was at least as important to the framers as fear of a single tyrant. Shays's Rebellion had been only one example, they believed, of

what could happen if a nation did not defend itself against the unchecked exercise of popular will. Thus in the new government, only the members of the House of Representatives would be elected directly by the people. Senators, the president, and federal judges would be insulated in varying degrees from the public.

On September 17, 1787, thirty-nine delegates signed the Constitution, doubtless sharing the feelings that Benjamin Franklin expressed at the end: "Thus I

economic development of the nation; the Antifederalists, by contrast, were "agrarian localists," fearful of centralization. Gordon Wood's important study, *The Creation of the American Republic* (1969), de-emphasized economic grievances but nevertheless suggested that the debate over the state constitutions in the 1770s and 1780s reflected profound social divisions and that those same divisions helped shape the argument over the federal Constitution. The Federalists, he suggested, were largely traditional aristocrats. They had become deeply concerned by the instability of life under the Articles of Confederation and were particularly alarmed by the decline in popular deference toward social elites. The creation of the Constitution was part of a larger search to create a legitimate political leadership based on the existing social hierarchy; it reflected the efforts of elites to contain what they considered the excesses of democracy.

In more recent years, as contemporary debates over the Constitution have intensified, historians have continued to examine the question of "intent." Did the framers intend a strong, centralized political system; or did they intend to create a decentralized system with a heavy emphasis on individual rights. The answer, according to Jack Rakove's *Original Meanings* (1996), is both—and many other things as well. The Constitution, he argues, was not the product of a single intelligence or of a broad consensus. It was the result of a long and vigorous debate through which the views of many different groups found their way into the document. James Madison, generally known as the father of the Constitution, was a strong nationalist, who believed that only a powerful central government could preserve stability in a large nation and keep narrow factionalism in check. Alexander Hamilton, Madison's ally in the battle, also saw the Constitution as a way to protect order and property, as a way to defend the nation against the dangers of too much liberty. But if Madison and Hamilton feared too much liberty, they also feared too little. And that made them receptive to the vigorous demands of the "anti-Federalists" for protections of individual rights, which culminated in the Bill of Rights. The framers differed as well in their views of the proper relationship between the federal government and the state governments. Madison favored unquestioned federal supremacy, and even tried to insert a clause in the Constitution giving Congress the right to invalidate state laws. Many others involved in the debate wanted to preserve the rights of the states and saw in the federal system—and in its unusual division of sovereignty among different levels and branches of government—a guarantee against too much national power. The Constitution is not, Rakove argues, "infinitely malleable." But neither does it have a fixed meaning that can be a reliable guide to how we interpret it today.

consent, Sir, to this Constitution, because I expect no better, and because I am not sure it is not the best."

Federalists and Antifederalists

The delegates at Philadelphia had greatly exceeded their instructions from Congress and the states. Instead of making simple revisions to the Articles of Confederation, they had produced a plan for a completely different form of government. They feared, therefore, that the Constitution might never be ratified under the rules of the Articles of Confederation, which required unanimous approval by the state legislatures. So the convention changed the rules. The Constitution specified that the new government would come into existence among the ratifying states when any nine of the thirteen had ratified it. The delegates recommended to Congress that special state conventions, not state legislatures, consider the document.

The old Confederation Congress, now overshadowed by the events in Philadelphia, passively accepted the convention's work and submitted it to the states for approval. All the state legislatures except Rhode Island's elected delegates to ratifying conventions, most of which began meeting by early 1788. Even before the ratifying conventions convened, however, a great national debate on the new Constitution had begun—in the state legislatures, in mass meetings, in the columns of newspapers, and in ordinary conversations. Occasionally, passions rose to the point that opposing factions came to blows. In at least one place—Albany, New York—such clashes resulted in injuries and death.

Supporters of the Constitution had a number of advantages. They were better organized than their opponents, and they had the support of the two most eminent men in America, Franklin and Washington. (Washington, for example, had declared that the nation faced a choice between the Constitution and disunion.) And they seized an appealing label for themselves: "Federalists"—the term that opponents of centralization had once used to describe themselves—thus implying that they were less committed to a "nationalist" government than in fact they were. The Federalists also had the support of the ablest political philosophers of their time: Alexander Hamilton, James Madison, and John Jay. Those three men, under the joint pseudonym "Publius," wrote a series of essays—widely published in newspapers throughout the nation—explaining the meaning and virtues of the Constitution. The essays were later issued as a book, and they are known today as *The Federalist Papers*. They are among the greatest American contributions to political theory.

The Federalists called their critics "Antifederalists," implying that their rivals had nothing to offer except opposition and chaos. But the Antifederalists had serious and intelligent arguments of their own. They presented themselves as the defenders of the true principles of the Revolution. The Constitution, they believed, would betray those principles by establishing a strong, potentially tyrannical, center of power in the new national government. The new government, they claimed, would increase taxes, obliterate the states, wield dictatorial powers, favor the "well born" over the common people, and put an end to individual liberty. But their biggest complaint was that the Constitution lacked a bill of rights, a

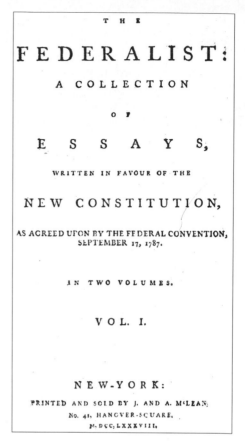

■ **THE FEDERALIST PAPERS**
James Madison, John Jay, and Alexander Hamilton would later become antagonists. But in 1788, they collaborated on one of the most important political documents ever created by Americans—a defense of and justification for the new federal Constitution. Originally published as separate essays in newspapers around the new nation, the *Federalist* was published as a book later the same year. *(New York Public Library)*

concern that revealed one of the most important sources of their opposition: a basic mistrust of human nature and of the capacity of human beings to wield power. (Some contemporaries, and some later scholars, described them as "men of little faith.") The Antifederalists argued that any government that centralized authority would inevitably produce despotism. Their demand for a bill of rights was a product of this belief: no government could be trusted to protect the liberties of its citizens; only by enumerating the natural rights of the people could there be any assurance that those rights would be preserved.

At its heart, then, the debate between the Federalists and the Antifederalists was a battle between two fears. The Federalists were afraid, above all, of disorder, anarchy, chaos; they feared the unchecked power of the masses, and they sought in the Constitution to create a government that would function at some distance from popular passions and that would be strong enough to act against threats to order and stability. The Antifederalists were not anarchists. They too recognized the need for an effective government. But they were much more afraid of the state than they were of the people, much more concerned about the dangers of concentrated power than about the dangers of popular will. They opposed the Constitution for some of the same reasons the Federalists supported it: because it placed obstacles between the people and the exercise of power.

Despite the Antifederalist efforts, ratification proceeded quickly (although not without occasional difficulty) during the winter of 1787–1788. The Delaware convention was the first to act, when it ratified the Constitution unanimously. The New Jersey and Georgia conventions did the same. In the larger states of Pennsylvania and Massachusetts, the Antifederalists put up a more determined struggle but lost in the final vote. New Hampshire ratified the document in June 1788—the ninth state to do so. It was now theoretically possible for the Constitution to go into effect.

A new government could not hope to flourish, however, without the participation of Virginia and New York, the two biggest states, whose conventions remained closely divided. By the end of June, first Virginia and then New York had consented to the Constitution by narrow margins. The New York convention yielded to expediency—even some of the most staunchly Antifederalist delegates feared that the state's commercial interests would suffer if, once the other states gathered under the "New Roof," New York were to remain outside. Massachusetts, Virginia, and New York all ratified, on the assumption that a bill of rights would be added to the Constitution. The North Carolina convention adjourned without taking action, waiting to see what happened to the amendments. Rhode Island, whose leaders had opposed the Constitution almost from the start, did not even call a convention to consider ratification.

Completing the Structure

The first elections under the Constitution took place in the early months of 1789. Almost all the newly elected congressmen and senators had favored ratification, and many had served as delegates to the Philadelphia convention. There was never any real doubt about who would be the first president. George Washington had presided at the Constitutional Convention, and many who had favored ratification did so only because they expected him to preside over the new government as well. Washington received the votes of all the presidential electors. John Adams, a leading Federalist, became vice president. After a journey from Mount Vernon marked by elaborate celebrations along the way, Washington was inaugurated in New York—the national capital for the time being—on April 30, 1789.

The first Congress served in many ways almost as a continuation of the Constitutional Convention, because its principal responsibility was filling in the various gaps in the Constitution. Its most important task was drafting a bill of rights. By early 1789, even Madison had come to agree that some sort of bill of rights was essential to legitimize the new government in the eyes of its opponents. Congress approved twelve amendments on September 25, 1789; ten of them were ratified by the states by the end of 1791. What we know as the Bill of Rights is these first ten amendments to the Constitution. Nine of them placed limitations on Congress by forbidding it to infringe on certain basic rights: freedom of religion, speech, and the press; immunity from arbitrary arrest; trial by jury; and others. The Tenth Amendment reserved to the states all powers except those specifically withheld from them or delegated to the federal government.

On the subject of the federal courts, the Constitution said only: "The judicial power of the United States shall be vested in one Supreme Court, and in such inferior courts as the Congress may from time to time ordain and establish." It was left to Congress to determine the number of Supreme Court judges to be appointed and the kinds of lower courts to be organized. In the Judiciary Act of 1789, Congress provided for a Supreme Court of six members, with a chief justice and five associate justices; thirteen district courts with one judge apiece; and three circuit courts of appeal, each to consist of one of the district judges sitting with two of the Supreme Court justices. In the same act, Congress gave the Supreme Court the power to make the final decision in cases involving the constitutionality of state laws.

The Constitution referred indirectly to executive departments but did not specify what or how many there should be. The first Congress created three such departments—state, treasury, and war—and also established the offices of the attorney general and postmaster general. To the office of secretary of the treasury, Washington appointed Alexander Hamilton of New York, who at age thirty-two was an acknowledged expert in public finance. For secretary of war he chose a Massachusetts Federalist, General Henry Knox. As attorney general he named Edmund Randolph of Virginia, sponsor of the plan on which the Constitution had been based. As secretary of state he chose another Virginian, Thomas Jefferson, who had recently served as minister to France.

FEDERALISTS AND REPUBLICANS

The resolution of these initial issues, however, did not resolve the deep disagreements about the nature of the new government. On the contrary, for the first twelve years under the Constitution, American politics was characterized by a level of acrimony seldom matched in any period since. The framers of the Constitution had dealt with many disagreements not by solving them but by papering them over with a series of vague compromises; as a result, the conflicts survived to plague the new government.

At the heart of the controversies of the 1790s was the same basic difference in philosophy that had been at the heart of the debate over the Constitution. On one side stood a powerful group that believed America required a strong, national government: that the country's mission was to become a genuine nation-state, with centralized authority, a complex commercial economy, and a proud standing in world affairs. On the other side stood another group—a minority at first, but one that gained strength during the decade—that envisioned a far more modest central government. American society should not, this group believed, aspire to be highly commercial or urban. It should remain predominantly rural and agrarian, and it should have a central government of modest size

and powers that would leave most power in the hands of the states and the people. The centralizers became known as the Federalists and gravitated to the leadership of Alexander Hamilton. Their opponents took the name Republicans and gathered under the leadership of James Madison and Thomas Jefferson.

Hamilton and the Federalists

For twelve years, control of the new government remained firmly in the hands of the Federalists. That was in part because George Washington had always envisioned a strong national government and as president had quietly supported those who were attempting to create one. His enormous prestige throughout the nation was one of the Federalists' greatest assets. But Washington also believed that the presidency should remain above political controversies, and so he avoided any personal involvement in the deliberations of Congress. As a result, the dominant figure in his administration became his talented secretary of the treasury, Alexander Hamilton, who exerted more influence on domestic and foreign policy than anyone else both during his term of office and, to an almost equal extent, after his resignation in 1794.

Of all the national leaders of his time, Hamilton was one of the most aristocratic in personal tastes and political philosophy—ironically, perhaps, since his own origins as an illegitimate child in the Caribbean had been so humble. Far from embracing the republican ideals of the virtue of the people, he believed that a stable and effective government required an enlightened ruling class. Thus, the new government needed the support of the wealthy and powerful; and to get that support it needed to give those elites a stake in its success. Hamilton proposed, therefore, that the new government take responsibility for the existing public debt. Many of the miscellaneous, uncertain, depreciated certificates of indebtedness that the old Congress had issued during and after the Revolution were now in the hands of wealthy speculators; the government should call them in and exchange them for uniform, interest-bearing bonds, payable at definite dates. (This policy was known as "funding" the debt.) He also recommended that the federal government "assume" (or take over) the debts the states had accumulated during the Revolution; this assumption policy would encourage state as well as federal bondholders to look

■ **BANK NOTE**
How to create a stable currency was one of the greatest challenges facing the new American nation. This fifty dollar bank note illustrates the principal form paper money assumed in the early republic. It was issued in 1797 by a bank in Philadelphia, and its value was directly tied to the stability of the bank itself. Only many years later did the national government assume control of printing and distributing currency. *(Eric P. Newman Numismatic Education Society)*

to the central government for eventual payment. Hamilton did not, in other words, envision paying off and thus eliminating the debt. He wanted instead to create a large and permanent national debt, with new bonds being issued as old ones were paid off. The result, he believed, would be that creditors—the wealthy classes most likely to lend money to the government—would have a permanent stake in seeing the government survive.

Hamilton also wanted to create a national bank. At the time, there were only a few banks in the country, located principally in Boston, Philadelphia, and New York. A new, national bank would help fill the void that the absence of a well-developed banking system had created. It would provide loans and currency to businesses. It would give the government a safe place to deposit federal funds. It would help collect taxes and disburse the government's expenditures. It would keep up the price of government bonds through judicious bond purchases. The bank would be chartered by the federal government, would have a monopoly of the government's own banking business, and would be controlled by directors, of whom one-fifth would be appointed by the government. It would provide a stable center to the nation's small and feeble banking system.

The funding and assumption of debts would require new sources of revenue, since the government would now have to pay interest on the loans it was accepting. Up to now, most government revenues had come from the sale of public lands in the West. Hamilton proposed two new kinds of taxes. One was an excise to be paid by distillers of alcoholic liquors, a tax that would fall most heavily on the whiskey distillers of the backcountry, especially in Pennsylvania,

Virginia, and North Carolina—small farmers who converted part of their corn and rye crop into whiskey. The other was a tariff on imports, which not only would raise revenue but would also protect American manufacturing from foreign competition. In his famous "Report on Manufactures" of 1791, he laid out a grand scheme for stimulating the growth of industry in the United States and wrote glowingly of the advantages to the nation of a healthy manufacturing base.

The Federalists, in short, offered more than a vision of how to stabilize the new government. They offered a vision of the sort of nation America should become—a nation with a wealthy, enlightened ruling class, a vigorous, independent commercial economy, and a thriving industrial sector; a nation able to play a prominent role in world economic affairs.

Enacting the Federalist Program

Few members of Congress objected to Hamilton's plan for funding the national debt, but many did oppose his proposal to accept the debt "at par," that is at face value. The old certificates had been issued to merchants and farmers in payment for war supplies during the Revolution, or to officers and soldiers of the Revolutionary army in payment for their services. But many of these original holders had sold their bonds during the hard times of the 1780s to speculators, who had bought them at a fraction of their face value. Many members of Congress believed if the federal government was to assume responsibility for these bonds, some of them should be returned to the original purchasers. James Madison, now a representative from Virginia, proposed dividing the federally-funded bonds between the original purchasers and the speculators. But Hamilton's allies insisted that such a plan was impractical and that the honor of the government required that it pay the bondholders themselves, not the original lenders who had sold their bonds of their own accord. Congress finally passed the funding bill Hamilton wanted.

Hamilton's proposal that the federal government assume the state debts encountered greater difficulty. His opponents argued that if the federal government took over the state debts, the people of states with few debts would have to pay taxes to service the larger debts of other states. Massachusetts, for example, owed far more money than did Virginia. Hamilton and his supporters struck a bargain with the Virginians to win passage of the bill.

The deal involved the location of the national capital. The capital had moved from New York back to Philadelphia in 1790. But the Virginians wanted a new capital near them in the South. Hamilton met with Thomas Jefferson (after Jefferson's return from France) and agreed over dinner to provide northern support for placing the capital in the South in exchange for Virginia's votes for the assumption bill. The bargain called for the construction of a new capital city on the banks of the Potomac River, which divided Virginia and Maryland, on land to be selected by Washington himself. The government would move there by the beginning of the new century.

Hamilton's bank bill sparked the most heated debate, the first of many on this controversial issue. Hamilton argued that creation of a national bank was compatible with the intent of the Constitution, even though the document did not explicitly authorize it. But Madison, Jefferson, Randolph, and others argued that Congress should exercise no powers that the Constitution had not clearly assigned it. Nevertheless, both the House and the Senate finally agreed to Hamilton's bill. Washington displayed some uncertainty about its legality at first, but he finally signed it. The Bank of the United States began operations in 1791, under a charter that granted it the right to continue for twenty years.

Hamilton also had his way with the excise tax, although protests from farmers later forced revisions to reduce the burden on the smaller distillers. He won passage, too, of a new tariff in 1792, although it raised rates less than he had wished.

Once enacted, Hamilton's program had many of the effects he had intended and won the support of influential segments of the population. It quickly restored public credit; the bonds of the United States were soon selling at home and abroad at prices even above their par value. Speculators (among them many members of Congress) reaped large profits as a result. Manufacturers profited from the tariffs, and merchants in the seaports benefited from the new banking system.

Others, however, found the Hamilton program less appealing. Small farmers, who formed the vast majority of the population, complained that they had to bear a disproportionate tax burden. Not only did they have to pay property taxes to their state governments, but they bore the brunt of the excise tax on distilleries and, indirectly, the tariff. A feeling grew among many Americans that the Federalist program served the interests not of the people but of small, wealthy elites. Out of this feeling an organized political opposition arose.

The Republican Opposition

The Constitution had made no reference to political parties, and the omission was not an oversight. Most of the framers—and George Washington in particular—believed that organized parties were dangerous and should be avoided. Disagreement on particular issues was inevitable, but most of the founders believed that such disagreements need not and should not lead to the formation of permanent factions. "The public good is disregarded in the conflicts of rival parties," Madison had written in *The Federalist Papers* (in Number 10, perhaps the most influential of all the essays), "and . . . measures are too often decided, not according to the rules of justice and the rights of the minor party, but by the superior force of an interested and overbearing majority."

Yet within just a few years after ratification of the Constitution, Madison and others became convinced that Hamilton and his followers had become just such an "interested and overbearing majority." Not only had the Federalists enacted a program that many of these leaders opposed. More ominously, Hamilton himself had, in their eyes, worked to establish a national network of influence that embodied all the worst features of a party. The Federalists had used their control over appointments and the awarding of government franchises, and all the other powers of their offices, to reward their supporters and win additional allies. They had encouraged the formation of local associations—largely aristocratic in nature—to strengthen their standing in local communities. They were doing many of the same things, their opponents believed, that the corrupt British governments of the early eighteenth century had done.

Because the Federalists appeared to be creating such a menacing and tyrannical structure of power, their critics felt, there was no alternative but to organize a vigorous opposition. The result was the emergence of an alternative political organization, which called itself the Republican Party. (This first "Republican" Party is not a direct ancestor of the modern Republican Party, which was born in the 1850s.) By the late 1790s, the Republicans were going to even greater lengths than the Federalists to create an apparatus of partisan influence. In every state they formed committees, societies, and caucuses. Republican groups were corresponding with one another across state lines. They were banding together to influence state and local elections. And they were justifying their actions by claiming that they and they alone represented the true interests of the nation—that they were fighting to defend the people against a corrupt conspiracy by the Federalists. Just as Hamil-

ton believed that the network of supporters he was creating represented the only legitimate interest group in the nation, so the Republicans believed that their party organization represented the best interests of the people. Neither side was willing to admit that it was acting as a party; neither would concede the right of the other to exist. This institutionalized factionalism is known to scholars as the "first party system."

From the beginning, the preeminent figures among the Republicans were Thomas Jefferson and James Madison. Indeed, the two men were such intimate collaborators with such similar political philosophies that it is sometimes difficult to distinguish the contributions of one from those of the other. But Jefferson, the more magnetic personality of the two, gradually emerged as the most prominent spokesman for the Republicans. Jefferson considered himself a farmer. (He was, in fact, a substantial planter; but he had spent relatively little time in recent years at his estate in Virginia.) He believed in an agrarian republic, most of whose citizens would be sturdy, independent farmer-citizens tilling their own soil.

■ **THE JEFFERSONIAN IDYLL**
American artists in the early nineteenth century were drawn to tranquil rural scenes, symbolic of the Jeffersonian vision of a nation of small, independent farmers. By 1822, when Francis Alexander painted this pastoral landscape, the simple agrarian republic it depicts was already being transformed by rapid economic growth. *(National Gallery of Art, Washington)*

Jefferson did not scorn commercial activity; he assumed farmers would market their crops in the national and even international markets. Nor did he oppose industry; he believed the United States should develop some manufacturing capacity. But he was suspicious of large cities, feared urban mobs as "sores upon the body politic," and opposed the development of an advanced industrial economy because it would, he feared, increase the number of propertyless workers packed in cities. In short, Jefferson envisioned a decentralized society, dominated by small property owners engaged largely in agrarian activities.

The difference between the Federalist and Republican social philosophies was visible in, among other things, reactions to the French Revolution. As that revolution grew increasingly radical in the 1790s, with its attacks on organized religion, the overthrow of the monarchy, and eventually the execution of the king and queen, the Federalists expressed horror. But the Republicans generally applauded the democratic, anti-aristocratic spirit they believed the French Revolution embodied. Some even imitated the French radicals (the Jacobins) by cutting their hair short, wearing pantaloons, and addressing one another as "Citizen" and "Citizeness."

Although both parties had supporters in all parts of the country and among all classes, there were regional and economic differences. The Federalists were most numerous in the commercial centers of the Northeast and in such southern seaports as Charleston; the Republicans were most numerous in the rural areas of the South and the West.

As the 1792 presidential election—the nation's second—approached, both Jefferson and Hamilton urged Washington to run for another term. The president reluctantly agreed. But while most Americans considered Washington above the partisan battle, he was actually much more in sympathy with the Federalists than with the Republicans. And during his presidency, Hamilton remained the dominant figure in government.

ESTABLISHING NATIONAL SOVEREIGNTY

The Federalists consolidated their position—and attracted wide public support for the new national government—by dealing effectively with two problems the old Confederation had been unable fully to resolve. They helped stabilize the nation's western lands, and they strengthened America's international position.

Securing the Frontier

Despite the Northwest Ordinance, the Confederation Congress had largely failed to tie the outlying western areas of the country firmly to the government. Farmers in western Massachusetts had risen in revolt; settlers in Vermont, Kentucky, and Tennessee had toyed with the idea of separating from the Union. At first, the new government under the Constitution faced similar problems.

In 1794, farmers in western Pennsylvania raised a major challenge to federal authority when they refused to pay a whiskey excise tax and began terrorizing the tax collectors (much as colonists had done at the time of the Stamp Act). But the federal government did not leave settlement of the so-called Whiskey Rebellion to Pennsylvania, as the Confederation Congress had left Shays's Rebellion to Massachusetts. At Hamilton's urging, Washington called out the militias of three states, raised an army of nearly 15,000 (a larger force than he had commanded against the British during most of the Revolution), and personally led the troops into Pennsylvania. As the militiamen approached Pittsburgh, the center of the resistance, the rebellion quickly collapsed.

The federal government won the allegiance of the whiskey rebels by intimidating them. It won the loyalties of other frontier people by accepting their territories as new states in the Union. The last of the original thirteen colonies joined the Union once the Bill of Rights had been appended to the Constitution—North Carolina in 1789 and Rhode Island in 1790. Then Vermont, which had had its own state government since the Revolution, became the fourteenth state in 1791 after New York and New Hampshire finally agreed to give up their claims to it. Next came Kentucky, in 1792, when Virginia gave up its claim to that region. After North Carolina finally ceded its western lands to the Union, Tennessee became first a territory and, in 1796, a state.

Native Americans and the New Nation

The new government faced a greater challenge, inherited from the Confederation, in the more distant areas of the Northwest and the Southwest, where In-

AN EXCISEMAN. *Carrying off two Kegs of Whiskey, is pursued by two farmers, intending to tar and feather him. he runs to*...

dians (occasionally in alliance with the British and Spanish) continued to challenge the republic's claim to tribal lands. The ordinances of 1784–1787, establishing the terms of white settlement in the West, had produced a series of border conflicts with Indian tribes resisting white settlement in their lands. The new government inherited these clashes, which continued with few interruptions for nearly a decade. Although the United States eventually defeated virtually every Indian challenge (if often at great cost), it was clear that the larger question of who was to control the lands of the West—the United States or the Indian nations—remained unanswered.

These clashes revealed another issue the Constitution had done little to resolve: the place of the Indian nations within the new federal structure. The Constitution barely mentioned Native Americans. Article I excluded "Indians not taxed" from being counted in the population totals that determined the number of seats states would receive in the House of Representatives; and it gave Congress the power to "regulate Commerce with foreign Nations, and among the several States, and with the Indian tribes." Article VI bound the new government to respect treaties negotiated by the Confederation, most of which had been with the tribes. But none of this did very much to clarify the precise legal standing of Indians or Indian nations within the United States.

On the one hand, the Constitution seemed to recognize the existence of the tribes as legal entities. On the other hand, it made clear that they were not

"foreign Nations" (in the same sense that European countries were); nor were their members citizens of the United States. The tribes received no direct representation in the new government. Above all, the Constitution did not address the major issue that would govern relations between whites and Indians: land. Indian nations lived within the boundaries of the United States, yet they claimed (and the white government at times agreed) that they had some measure of sovereignty within their own lands. But neither the Constitution nor common law offered any clear guide to the rights of a "nation within a nation" or to the precise nature of tribal sovereignty, which ultimately depended on control of land. Thus, the relationship between the tribes and the United States remained to be determined by a series of treaties, agreements, and judicial decisions in a process that has continued for two centuries.

Maintaining Neutrality

Not until 1791—ten years after the end of the Revolution—did Great Britain send a minister to the United States, and then only because Madison and the Republicans were threatening to place special trade restrictions on British ships. That was one of many symbols of the difficulty the new government had in establishing its legitimacy in the eyes of the British. Another crisis in Anglo-American relations emerged in 1793 when the new French government, created by the revolution of 1789, went to war with

Great Britain and its allies. Both the president and Congress took steps to establish American neutrality in that conflict. But the neutrality quickly encountered severe tests.

The first challenge to American neutrality came from revolutionary France and its first diplomatic representative to America, the brash and youthful Edmond Genet. Instead of landing at Philadelphia and presenting himself immediately to the president, Genet disembarked at Charleston. There he made plans to use American ports to outfit French warships, encouraged American shipowners to serve as French privateers, and commissioned the aging George Rogers Clark to lead a military expedition against Spanish lands to the south. (Spain was at the time an ally of Great Britain and an enemy of France.) In all of this, Genet was brazenly ignoring Washington's policies and flagrantly violating the Neutrality Act. His conduct infuriated Washington (who provided "Citizen Genet," as he was known, with an icy reception in Philadelphia) and the Federalists; it also embarrassed all but the most ardent admirers of the French Revolution among the Republicans. Washington eventually demanded that the French government recall him, but by then Genet's party was out of power in France. (The president granted him political asylum in the United States, and he settled with his American wife on a Long Island farm.) The neutrality policy had survived its first serious test.

A second and even greater challenge came from Great Britain. Early in 1794, the Royal Navy began seizing hundreds of American ships engaged in trade in the French West Indies, outraging public opinion in the United States. Anti-British feeling rose still higher at the report that the governor general of Canada had delivered a warlike speech to the Indians on the northwestern frontier. Hamilton was deeply concerned. War would mean an end to imports from England, and most of the revenue for maintaining his financial system came from duties on those imports.

Jay's Treaty and Pinckney's Treaty

This was, Hamilton believed, no time for ordinary diplomacy. He did not trust the State Department to reach a settlement with Britain. Jefferson had resigned as secretary of state in 1793 to devote more time to his political activities, but his successor, Edmund Randolph, was even more ardently pro-French than Jefferson had been. So Hamilton persuaded Washington to name a special commissioner to England: John Jay, chief justice of the United States Supreme Court and a staunch New York Federalist. Jay was instructed to secure compensation for the recent British assaults on American shipping, to demand withdrawal of British forces from the frontier posts, and to negotiate a new commercial treaty.

The long and complex treaty Jay negotiated in 1794 failed to achieve these goals. But it was not without merit. It settled the conflict with Britain and helped prevent what had seemed likely to become a war between the two nations. It established undisputed American sovereignty over the entire Northwest. And it produced a reasonably satisfactory commercial relationship with Britain, whose trade was important to the United States. Nevertheless, when the terms became public in America, there were bitter public denunciations of it for having failed to extract enough promises from the British. Jay himself was burned in effigy in various parts of the country. Opponents of the treaty—nearly all the Republicans and even some Federalists, encouraged by agents of France—went to extraordinary lengths to defeat it in the Senate. The American minister to France, James Monroe, and even the secretary of state, Edmund Randolph, joined the desperate attempt to prevent ratification. But in the end the Senate ratified what was by then known as Jay's Treaty.

Among other things, the treaty made possible a settlement of America's conflict with the Spanish, because it raised fears in Spain that the British and the Americans might now join together to challenge Spanish possessions in North America. When Thomas Pinckney arrived in Spain as a special negotiator, he had no difficulty in gaining nearly everything the United States had sought from the Spaniards for more than a decade. Under Pinckney's Treaty (signed in 1795), Spain recognized the right of Americans to navigate the Mississippi to its mouth and to deposit goods at New Orleans for reloading on oceangoing ships; agreed to fix the northern boundary of Florida where Americans always had insisted it should be, along the 31st parallel; and required Spanish authorities to prevent the Indians in Florida from launching raids across the border.

■ MOUNT VERNON
George and Martha Washington lavished enormous attention to their home at Mount Vernon, importing materials and workmen from Europe to create a house that they hoped would rival some of the elegant country homes of England. This detail from a mantle suggests the degree to which they—like many wealthy planters and merchants of their time—strove to bring refinement and gentility to their lives. *(Photograph Paul Rocheleau/Rebus, Inc.)*

THE DOWNFALL OF THE FEDERALISTS

The Federalists' impressive triumphs did not ensure their continued dominance in the national government. On the contrary, success seemed to produce problems of its own—problems that eventually led to their downfall.

Since almost all Americans in the 1790s agreed that there was no place in a stable republic for an organized opposition, the emergence of the Republicans as powerful contenders for popular favor seemed to the Federalists a grave threat to national stability. Beginning in the late 1790s, when major international perils confronted the government as well, the Federalists could not resist the temptation to move forcefully against the opposition. Facing what they believed was a stark choice between respecting individual liberties and preserving stability, the Federalists chose stability. The result was political disaster. After 1796, the Federalists never won another election. The popular respect for the institutions of the federal government, which they had worked so hard to produce among the people, survived. But the Federalists themselves gradually vanished as an effective political force.

The Election of 1796

Despite strong pressure from his many admirers to run for a third term as president, George Washington insisted on retiring from office in 1797. In a "Farewell Address" to the American people (actually a long letter, composed in part by Hamilton and published in a Philadelphia newsletter), he reacted sharply to the Republicans. His reference to the "insidious wiles of foreign influence" was not just an abstract warning against international entanglements; it was also a specific denunciation of those Republicans who had been conspiring with the French to frustrate the Federalist diplomatic program.

With Washington out of the running, no obstacle remained to an open expression of the partisan rivalries that had been building over the previous eight years. Jefferson was the uncontested candidate of the Republicans in 1796. The Federalists faced a more difficult choice. Hamilton, the personification of Federalism, had created too many enemies to be a credible candidate. So Vice President John Adams, who had been directly associated with none of the unpopular Federalist measures, became his party's nominee for president.

The Federalists were still clearly the dominant party, and there was little doubt of their ability to win a majority of the presidential electors. But without Washington to mediate, they fell victim to fierce factional rivalries that almost led to their undoing. Hamilton and many other Federalists (especially in the South) were not reconciled to Adams's candidacy and favored his running mate Thomas Pinckney instead. And when, as expected, the Federalists elected a majority of the presidential electors, some of these Pinckney supporters declined to vote for Adams; he

■ **JOHN ADAMS**
Adams's illustrious career as Revolutionary leader, diplomat, and president marked the beginning of four generations of public distinction among members of his family. His son, John Quincy Adams, served as secretary of state and president. His grandson, Charles Francis Adams, was one of the great diplomats of the Civil War era. His great-grandson, Henry Adams, was one of America's most distinguished historians and writers. *(Adams National Historic Site, Quincy, Massachusetts)*

managed to defeat Jefferson by only three electoral votes. Because a still larger number of Adams's supporters declined to vote for Pinckney, Jefferson finished second in the balloting and became vice president. (The Constitution provided for the candidate receiving the second highest number of electoral votes to become vice president—hence the awkward result of men from different parties serving in the nation's two highest elected offices. The Twelfth Amendment, adopted in 1804, reformed the electoral system to prevent such situations.)

Adams thus assumed the presidency under inauspicious circumstances. He presided over a divided party, which faced a strong and resourceful Republi-

can opposition committed to its extinction. Adams himself was not even the dominant figure in his own party; Hamilton remained the most influential Federalist, and Adams was never able to challenge him effectively. The new president was one of the country's most accomplished and talented statesmen, but he had few skills as a politician. Austere, rigid, aloof, he had little talent at conciliating differences, soliciting support, or inspiring enthusiasm. He was a man of enormous, indeed intimidating rectitude, and he seemed to assume that his own virtue and the correctness of his positions would alone be enough to sustain him. He was usually wrong.

The Quasi War with France

American relations with Great Britain and Spain improved as a result of Jay's and Pinckney's Treaties. But the nation's relations with revolutionary France quickly deteriorated. French vessels captured American ships on the high seas and at times imprisoned the crews. When the South Carolina Federalist Charles Cotesworth Pinckney, brother of Thomas Pinckney, arrived in France, the government refused to receive him as the official representative of the United States.

Some of President Adams's advisers favored war, most notably Secretary of State Thomas Pickering, a stern New Englander who detested France. But Hamilton recommended conciliation, and Adams agreed. In an effort to stabilize relations, Adams appointed a bipartisan commission—consisting of Charles Cotesworth Pinckney, the recently rejected minister; John Marshall, a Virginia Federalist, later chief justice of the Supreme Court; and Elbridge Gerry, a Massachusetts Republican but a personal friend of the president—to negotiate with France. When the Americans arrived in Paris in 1797, three agents of the French foreign minister, Prince Talleyrand, demanded a loan for France and a bribe for French officials before any negotiations could begin. Pinckney responded succinctly and angrily: "No! No! Not a sixpence!"

When Adams heard of the incident, he sent a message to Congress denouncing the French insults and urging preparations for war. He then turned the report of the American commissioners over to Congress, after deleting the names of the three French

■ PROTECTING AMERICAN SHIPPING
An American ship under the command of Gamaliel Bradford
engages four French privateers in the strait of Gibraltar in July
1800—part of an effort by the United States to protect its maritime
commerce. Bradford beat off the privateers after a short battle, but
lost his leg in the fighting. *(Naval Historical Center)*

agents and designating them only as "Messrs. X, Y,
and Z." When the report was published, it created
widespread popular outrage at France's actions and
strong support for the Federalists' response. For
nearly two years after the "XYZ Affair," as it became
known, the United States found itself engaged in an
undeclared war with France.

Adams persuaded Congress to cut off all trade
with France, to repudiate the treaties of 1778, and
to authorize American vessels to capture French
armed ships on the high seas. In 1798, Congress
created a Department of the Navy and appropriated
money for the construction of new warships. The
navy soon won a number of duels with French
vessels and captured a total of eighty-five ships, including armed merchantmen. The United States
also began cooperating closely with the British and
became virtually an ally of Britain in the war with
France.

In the end, France chose to conciliate the United
States before the conflict grew. Adams sent another
commission to Paris in 1800, and the new French
government (headed now by "first consul" Napoleon
Bonaparte) agreed to a treaty with the United States
that canceled the old agreement of 1778 and established new commercial arrangements. As a result, the
"quasi war" came to a reasonably peaceful end. In

the process, the United States had at last freed itself
from the entanglements and embarrassments of the
"perpetual" alliance with France it had forged during
the Revolution.

Repression and Protest

The conflict with France helped the Federalists increase their majorities in Congress in 1798. Armed
with this new strength, they began to consider ways
to silence the Republican opposition. The result was
some of the most controversial legislation in American history: the Alien and Sedition Acts.

The Alien Act placed new obstacles in the way of
foreigners who wished to become American citizens,
and it strengthened the president's hand in dealing
with aliens. The Sedition Act allowed the government to prosecute those who engaged in "sedition"
against the government. In theory only libelous or
treasonous activities were subject to prosecution;
but since such activities were subject to widely varying definitions, the law made it possible for the
federal government to stifle virtually any opposition.
The Republicans interpreted the new laws as part
of a Federalist campaign to destroy them and
fought back.

President Adams signed the new laws but was cautious in implementing them. He did not deport any
aliens, and he prevented the government from
launching a major crusade against the Republicans.
But the legislation had a significant repressive effect
nevertheless. The Alien Act helped discourage immigration and encouraged some foreigners already in
the country to leave. And the administration made
use of the Sedition Act to arrest and convict ten men,
most of them Republican newspaper editors whose
only crime had been to criticize the Federalists in
government.

Republican leaders pinned their hopes for a rever-
sal of the Alien and Sedition Acts on the state legislatures. (The Supreme Court had not yet established its
sole right to nullify congressional legislation, and
there were many who believed that the states had
that power too.) The Republicans laid out a theory
for state action in two sets of resolutions in
1798–1799, one written (anonymously) by Jefferson
and adopted by the Kentucky legislature and the
other drafted by Madison and approved by the Virginia

legislature. The Virginia and Kentucky Resolutions, as they were known, used the ideas of John Locke to argue that the federal government had been formed by a "compact" or contract among the states and possessed only certain delegated powers. Whenever it exercised any undelegated powers, its acts were "unauthoritative, void, and of no force." If the parties to the contract, the states, decided that the central government had exceeded those powers, the Kentucky Resolution claimed, they had the right to "nullify" the appropriate laws.

The Republicans did not win wide support for nullification; only Virginia and Kentucky declared the congressional statutes void. The Republicans did, however, succeed in elevating their dispute with the Federalists to the level of a national crisis. By the late 1790s, the entire nation was as deeply and bitterly divided politically as it would ever be in its history. State legislatures at times resembled battlegrounds. Even the United States Congress was plagued with violent disagreements. In one celebrated incident in the chamber of the House of Representatives, Matthew Lyon, a Republican from Vermont, responded to an insult from Roger Griswold, a Federalist from Connecticut, by spitting in Griswold's eye. Griswold attacked Lyon with his cane. Lyon fought back with a pair of fire tongs, and the two men ended up wrestling on the floor.

The "Revolution" of 1800

These bitter controversies shaped the 1800 presidential election. The presidential candidates were the same as four years earlier: Adams for the Federalists, Jefferson for the Republicans. But the campaign of 1800 was very different from the one preceding it. Indeed, it may have been the ugliest in American history. Adams and Jefferson themselves displayed reasonable dignity, but their supporters showed no such restraint. The Federalists accused Jefferson of being a dangerous radical and his followers of being wild men who, if they should come to power, would bring on a reign of terror comparable to that of the French Revolution. The Republicans portrayed Adams as a tyrant conspiring to become king, and they accused the Federalists of plotting to subvert human liberty and impose slavery on the people. There was considerable personal invective as well. For example, it was during this campaign that the story of Jefferson's alleged romantic involvement with a slave woman on his plantation was first widely aired.

The election was close, and the crucial contest was in New York. There, Aaron Burr had mobilized an organization of Revolutionary War veterans, the Tammany Society, to serve as a Republican political machine. And through Tammany's efforts, the Republicans carried the city by a large majority, and with it the state. Jefferson was, apparently, elected.

But an unexpected complication soon jeopardized the Republican victory. The Constitution called for each elector to "vote by ballot for two persons." The normal practice was for an elector to cast one vote for his party's presidential candidate and another for the vice presidential candidate. (The difficulties in sustaining this delicate practice in a highly partisan environment had led in 1796 to the election of Jefferson as vice president under his opponent, Adams.) To avoid a tie between Jefferson and Aaron Burr (the Republican vice presidential candidate in 1800), the Republicans had intended for one elector to refrain from voting for Burr. But the plan went awry. When the votes were counted, Jefferson and Burr each had 73. No candidate had a majority. According to the Constitution the House of Representatives had to choose between the two leading candidates when no one had a majority; in this case, that meant deciding between Jefferson and Burr. Each state delegation would cast a single vote.

The new Congress, elected in 1800 with a Republican majority, was not to convene until after the inauguration of the president, so it was the Federalist Congress that had to decide the question. Some Federalists hoped to use the situation to salvage the election for their party; others wanted to strike a bargain with Burr and elect him. But after a long deadlock, several leading Federalists, most prominent among them Alexander Hamilton, concluded that Burr (whom many suspected of having engineered the deadlock in the first place) was too unreliable to trust with the presidency. On the thirty-sixth ballot, Jefferson was elected.

After the election of 1800, the only branch of the federal government left in Federalist hands was the judiciary. The Adams administration spent its last months in office taking steps to make the party's hold on the courts secure. By the Judiciary Act of 1801, passed by the lame duck Congress, the Federalists reduced the number of Supreme Court justiceships by one but greatly increased the number of federal judgeships as a whole. Adams quickly appointed Federalists to the

■ CONGRESSIONAL BRAWLERS
This cartoon lampoons a celebrated fight on the floor of the House of Representatives in 1798 between Matthew Lyon, a Republican from Vermont, and Roger Griswold, a Federalist from Connecticut. The conflict began when Griswold insulted Lyon by attacking his military record in the Revolutionary War. Lyon replied by spitting in Griswold's face. Two weeks later, Griswold attacked Lyon with his cane, and Lyon seized a pair of fire tongs and fought back. That later scene is depicted (and ridiculed) here. Other members of Congress are portrayed as enjoying the spectacle. On the wall is a picture entitled "Royal Sport," showing animals fighting.
(New York Public Library)

newly created positions. Indeed, there were charges that he stayed up until midnight on his last day in office to finish signing the new judges' commissions. These officeholders became known as the "midnight appointments."

Even so, the Republicans viewed their victory as almost complete. The nation, they believed, had been saved from tyranny. A new era could now begin, one in which the true principles on which America had been founded would once again govern the land. The exuberance with which the victors viewed the future—and the importance they attributed to the Federalists' defeat—was evident in the phrase Jefferson himself later used to describe his election. He called it the "Revolution of 1800." It remained to be seen how revolutionary it would really be.

CONCLUSION

The writing of the Constitution of 1787 was the single most important political event in the history of the United States, and a notable event in the political history of the modern world. In creating a "federal" system of dispersed and divided authority—authority divided among national and state governments, authority divided among an executive, a legislature, and a judiciary—the young nation sought to balance its need for an effective central government against its fear of concentrated and despotic power. The ability of the delegates to the Constitutional Convention to compromise again and again to produce the ultimate structure gave evidence of the deep yearning among them for a stable political system. The same willingness to compromise allowed the greatest challenge to the ideals of the new democracy—slavery—to survive intact.

The writing and ratifying of the Constitution settled some questions about the shape of the new nation. The first twelve years under the government created by the Constitution solved others. And yet by the year 1800, a basic disagreement about the future of the nation—a disagreement personified by the differences between committed nationalist Alexander Hamilton and the self-proclaimed champion of democracy Thomas Jefferson—remained unresolved and was creating bitter divisions and conflicts within the political world. The election of Thomas Jefferson to the presidency that year opened a new chapter in the nation's public history. It also brought to a close, at least temporarily, savage political conflicts that had seemed to threaten the nation's future.

Significant Events

1783	Confederation Congress leaves Philadelphia
1785	Confederation Congress settles in New York
1786	Annapolis Conference meets
1787	Constitutional Convention in Philadelphia meets
	Constitution adopted (September 17)
1787–1788	States ratify Constitution
1789	First elections held under Constitution
	New government assembles in New York
	Washington becomes first president
	Bill of Rights adopted by Congress
	Judiciary Act of 1789 is passed
	French Revolution begins
1791	Hamilton issues "Report on Manufactures"
	First Bank of the United States chartered
	Vermont becomes fourteenth state
1792	Washington reelected without opposition
	Kentucky becomes fifteenth state
1793	Citizen Genet affair challenges American neutrality
1794	Whiskey Rebellion quelled in Pennsylvania
	Jay's Treaty signed
1795	Pinckney's Treaty signed
1796	John Adams elected president
	Tennessee becomes sixteenth state
1798	XYZ Affair precipitates state of quasi war with France
	Alien and Sedition Acts passed
	Virginia and Kentucky Resolutions passed
1800	Jefferson and Burr tie vote in electoral college
1801	Jefferson becomes president after Congress confirms election
	Judiciary Act of 1801 passed

FOR FURTHER REFERENCE

Suggested Readings   Charles Beard, *An Economic Interpretation of the Constitution of the United States* (1913) is one of the seminal works of modern American historical inquiry. Gordon Wood, *The Creation of the American Republic,* (1969) is still the leading analysis of the intellectual path from the Declaration of Independence to the American Constitution. Jack Rakove, *Original Meanings: Politics and Ideas in the Making of the Constitution* (1996) connects the politics of the 1780s with the political ideas embedded in the Constitution. Stanley Elkins and Eric McKitrick, *The Age of Federalism* (1993) provides a lengthy overview of political and economic development in the 1790s. Joyce Appleby, *Capital-*

ism and a New Social Order: The Republican Vision of the 1790s (1984) highlights liberal and capitalist impulses unleashed after the ratification of the Constitution. Dumas Malone, *Jefferson and His Time,* 6 vols. (1948–1981) is a magisterial biography of one of the greatest of the nation's founders.

Films   (The best source for information on how to find these and other films is *Bowker's Complete Video Directory*—3 volumes.) *The American Story: No. 3, Creating a Republic; No. 4, Experiment in Government; No. 5, The Federalist Era* (1985) cover the years from the American Revolution to 1800. *The Constitution: An American Ad-*

venture explores the development of the Constitution from colonial dissent in the 1760s through the Articles of Confederation. *The Background of the United States Constitution* (1982) explains the Constitutional Convention as well as the compromises hammered out to produce the Constitution and get it ratified. *The Constitution of the United States* (1982) is a dramatized version of the Constitutional Convention, seen through the eyes of James Madison. *George Washington—The Man Who Wouldn't Be King* (1992) explores the life of America's first President. *George Washington & the Whiskey Rebellion* (1975) illustrates an important episode in Washington's presidency,

one of the first challenges to the authority of the federal government.

Internet Resources   (For up-to-date URL addresses and links to these and other websites, consult the McGraw-Hill history site at *http://www.mhhe.com/socscience/history/usa/link/linktop.htm*) *The Papers of George Washington* is a comprehensive collection of Washington's public and private papers. *The Avalon Project at the Yale Law School: 18th Century documents* includes the Federalist Papers, the Articles of Confederation, Madison's record of the Constitutional Convention, and the Constitution.

BIBLIOGRAPHY

The Constitution   Douglas Adair, *Fame and the Founding Fathers* (1974). Lance Banning, *The Sacred Fire of Liberty: James Madison and the Founding of the Federal Republic* (1995). Robert E. Brown, *Charles Beard and the Constitution* (1956). Christopher Collier and James Lincoln Collier, *Decision: Philadelphia: The Constitutional Convention of 1787* (1986). Thomas Curry, *The First Freedom: Church and State in America to the Passage of the First Amendment* (1986). Linda G. DePauw, *The Eleventh Pillar: New York State and the Federal Constitution* (1966). Max Farrand, ed., *Records of the Federal Convention of 1787*, 4 vols. (1911-1937); *The Framing of the Constitution of the United States* (1913). Michael Kammen, *A Machine that Would Go of Itself: The Constitution in American Culture* (1986). Leonard Levy, *Constitutional Opinions: Aspects of the Bill of Rights* (1986); *Original Intent and the Framers' Constitution* (1988). Michael Lienesch, *New Order of the Ages: Time, the Constitution, and the Making of Modern American Political Thought* (1988). Donald S. Lutz, *Origins of American Constitutionalism* (1988). Jackson Turner Main, *The Anti-Federalists* (1961). Forrest McDonald, *E. Pluribus Unum: The Formation of the American Republic, 1776-1790* (1965); *Novus Ordo Seclorum: The Intellectual Origins of the Constitution* (1985). William L. Miller, *The First Liberty: Religion and the American Republic* (1986). Edmund S. Morgan, *Inventing the People: The Rise of Popular Sovereignty in England and America* (1988). Richard B. Morris, *The Forging of the Union, 1781-1789* (1987). Clinton Rossiter, *1787: The Grand Convention* (1965). Robert A. Rutland, *The Ordeal of the Constitution* (1966). Gerald Stourzh, *Alexander Hamilton and the Idea of Republican Government* (1970). Garry Wills, *Explaining America* (1981). John R. Wunder, *"Retained by the People": A History of American Indians and the Bill of Rights* (1994).

The Federalist Era   Richard Beeman, *The Old Dominion and the New Nation, 1788-1801* (1972). Irving Brant, *The Bill of Rights* (1965). Richard Brookhiser, *Founding Father: Rediscovering George Washington* (1996). Ralph Adams Brown, *The Presidency of John Adams* (1975). Jerald A. Combs, *The Jay Treaty* (1970). John F. Hoadley, *Origins of American Political Parties, 1789-1803* (1986). John R. Howe, *The Changing Political Thought of John Adams* (1966). Ralph Ketchum, *Presidents Above Party: The First American Presidency, 1789-1829* (1984). Richard Kohn, *Eagle and Sword: The Federalists and the Creation of the Military Establishment in America, 1783-1802* (1975). Daniel G. Lang, *Foreign Policy in the Early Republic* (1985). Leonard Levy, *Legacy of Suppression: Freedom of Speech and Press in Early American History*, rev. ed. (1985). Forrest McDonald, *The Presidency of George Washington* (1974). Carl E. Prince, *The Federalists and the Origins of the U.S. Civil Service* (1978). Thomas P. Slaughter, *The Whiskey Rebellion: Frontier Epilogue to the American Revolution* (1986). Wiley Sword, *President Washington's Indian War: The Struggle for the Old Northwest, 1790-1795* (1985). Mary K. B. Tachau, *Federal Courts in the Early Republic: Kentucky, 1789-1816* (1978). Leonard D. White, *The Federalists* (1948). Ann Fairfax Withington, *Toward More Perfect Union: Virtue and the Formation of American Republics* (1991).

The Jeffersonian Republicans   Lance Banning, *The Jeffersonian Persuasion* (1978). Charles A. Beard, *The Economic Origins of the Jeffersonian Opposition* (1915). Richard W. Buel, Jr., *Securing the Revolution: Ideology in American Politics, 1789-1815* (1972). Richard Hofstadter, *The Idea of a Party System* (1970). Drew McCoy, *The Elusive Republic: Political Economy in Jeffersonian America* (1980); *The Last of the Fathers: James Madison and* *the Republican Legacy* (1989). Thomas L. Pangle, *The Spirit of Modern Republicanism: The Moral Vision of the American Founders and the Followers of Locke* (1988). Merrill D. Peterson, *Thomas Jefferson and the New Nation* (1970). Norman K. Risjord, *Chesapeake Politics, 1781–1800* (1978). Patricia Watlington, *The Partisan Spirit* (1972). Alfred F. Young, *The Democratic-Republicans of New York (1967).* John Zvesper, *Political Philosophy and Rhetoric: A Study of the Origins of American Party Politics* (1977).

Federalist Diplomacy   Harry Ammon, *The Genet Mission* (1973). Felix Gilbert, *To the Farewell Address* (1961). Lawrence S. Kaplan, *Jefferson and France* (1967). Bradford Perkins, *The Cambridge History of American Foreign Relations, Vol 1: The Creation of a Republican Empire, 1776–1865* (1993); *The First Rapprochement: England and the United States* (1967). Charles Ritcheson, *Aftermath of Revolution: British Policy Toward the United States, 1783–1795* (1969). Louis M. Sears, *George Washington and the French Revolution* (1960). Paul A. Varg, *Foreign Policies of the Founding Fathers* (1963).

The Founders   Irving Brant, *James Madison* (1950). James T. Flexner, *George Washington,* 4 vols. (1965–1972). Douglas Southall Freeman, *George Washington,* 7 vols. (1948–1957). Milton Lomask, *Aaron Burr,* 2 vols. (1979, 1982). John C. Miller, *Alexander Hamilton* (1959). Richard B. Morris, *Witnesses at the Creation: Hamilton, Madison, Jay, and the Constitution* (1985). Merrill Peterson, *Thomas Jefferson and the New Nation* (1970). Barry Schwartz, *George Washington: The Making of a Symbol* (1987). Page Smith, *John Adams* (1962). William Stinchecombe, *The XYZ Affair* (1980). Garry Wills, *Cincinnatus: George Washington and the Enlightenment* (1984). Esmond Wright, *Franklin of Philadelphia* (1986).

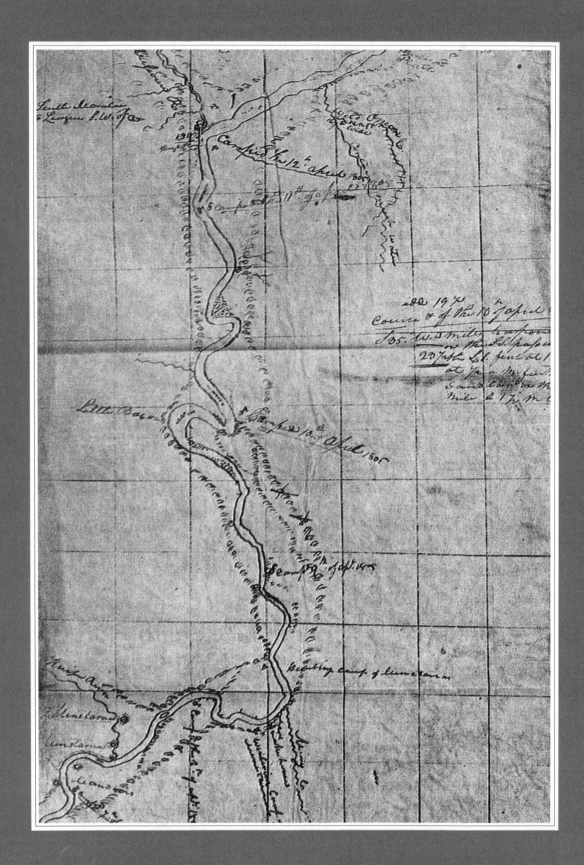

Chapter Seven

THE JEFFERSONIAN ERA

Thomas Jefferson and his followers assumed control of the national government in 1801 as the champions of a distinctive vision of America. They envisioned a society of sturdy, independent farmers, happily free from the workshops, the industrial towns, and the city mobs of Europe. They favored a system of universal education that would introduce all Americans to the scientific rationalism of the Enlightenment. They promoted a cultural outlook that emphasized localism and republican simplicity. And they proposed a federal government of sharply limited power, with most authority remaining at the level of the states.

Almost nothing worked out as they planned, for during their years in power the young republic was developing in ways that made much of their vision obsolete. The American economy in the period of Republican ascendancy became steadily more diversified and complex. Growing cities, surging commerce, and expanding industrialism made the ideal of a simple, agrarian society impossible to maintain. The quest for universal education floundered, and the nation's institutions of learning remained largely the preserve of privileged elites. American cultural life, far from reflecting localism and simplicity, reflected a vigorous and ambitious nationalism reminiscent of (and often encouraged by) the Federalists. And although American religion began, as the Jeffersonians had hoped, to confront and adjust to the spread of Enlightenment rationalism, the new skepticism did not survive unchallenged. A great wave of revivalism, beginning early in the century, ultimately almost submerged the new rational philosophy.

The Republicans did manage to translate some of their political ideals into reality. Jefferson dismantled much of the bureaucratic power structure that the Federalists had erected in the 1790s, and he helped ensure that in many respects the federal government would remain a relatively unimportant force in American life. Yet he also frequently encountered situations that required him to exercise strong national authority. On occasion, he used his power more forcefully and arbitrarily than his Federalist predecessors had used theirs.

The Republicans did not always like these nationalizing and modernizing trends, and on occasion they resisted them. For the most part, however, they had the sense to recognize what they could not change. In adjusting to the new realities, they began to become agents of the very transformation of American life they had once resisted.

■ **THE JOURNAL OF LEWIS
AND CLARK**
This page is from the journal the explorers Meriwether Lewis and William Clark kept on their famous journey through the territory the United States had acquired in the Louisiana Purchase—and beyond. Shown here is one of the rough maps they drew to describe the lands they had seen.
(British Museum)

THE RISE OF CULTURAL NATIONALISM

In many respects, American cultural life in the early nineteenth century seemed to reflect the Republican vision of the nation's future. Opportunities for education increased; the nation's literary and artistic life began to free itself from European influences; and American religion began to confront and adjust to the spread of Enlightenment rationalism. In other respects, however, the new culture was posing a serious challenge to Republican ideals.

Patterns of Education

Central to the Republican vision of America was the concept of a virtuous and enlightened citizenry. Jefferson himself called emphatically for a national "crusade against ignorance." Republicans believed, therefore, in the creation of a nationwide system of public schools to create the educated electorate they believed a republic required. All male citizens (the nation's prospective voters) should, they argued, receive free education. They were unable to realize that dream, although their efforts to do so sustained a vision that in later years would produce much more substantial results.

Some states endorsed the principle of public education for all in the early years of the republic, but none actually created a working system of free schools. A Massachusetts law of 1789 reaffirmed the colonial laws by which each town was obligated to support a school, but there was little enforcement. In Virginia, the state legislature ignored Jefferson's call for universal elementary education and for advanced education for the gifted. As late as 1815, not a single state had a comprehensive public school system.

Instead, schooling became primarily the responsibility of private institutions, most of which were open only to those who could afford to pay for them. In the South and in the mid-Atlantic states, religious groups ran most of the schools. In New England and elsewhere, private academies were usually more secular, many of them modeled on schools founded by the Phillips family at Andover, Massachusetts, in 1778, and at Exeter, New Hampshire, three years later. By 1815, there were thirty such private secondary schools in Massachusetts, thirty-seven in New York, and several dozen more scattered throughout

■ **SCHOOLMARMS AND SCHOOLMASTERS**
In this 1806 painting, Thomas Birch expresses his view of the relative merits of male and female teachers. The "schoolmarm," on the left, is dealing with rowdy and disorderly children. The elderly "schoolmaster" at the right watches over an exemplary student. As women began to move into teaching in the early nineteenth century, many men expressed similarly contemptuous views of their abilities. *(Private collection)*

the country. Many were frankly aristocratic in outlook, training their students to become members of the nation's elite. There were a few schools open to the poor, but not nearly enough to accommodate everyone, and the education they offered was usually clearly inferior to that provided at more exclusive schools.

Private secondary schools such as those in New England, and even many public schools, accepted only male students. The Republicans, like most of their contemporaries, clung to a paternal vision of society, in which virtuous white men presided benevolently over a world in which all other groups—including women—were dependents. Yet the early nineteenth century did see some important advances in female education.

In the eighteenth century, women had received very little education of any kind, and the female illiteracy rate at the time of the Revolution was very high—at least 50 percent. At the same time, however, Americans had begun to place a new value on the contribution of the "republican mother" to the training of the new generation. That raised an important question: If mothers remained ignorant, how could they raise their children to be enlightened? Beginning as early as the 1770s and accelerating thereafter, such concerns led to the creation of a network of female academies throughout the nation (usually for the daughters of affluent families). In 1789, Massachusetts required that its public schools serve females as well as males. Other states, although not all, soon followed.

But there were strict limits to this new belief in education for women. Most men, at least, assumed that female education should serve only to make women better wives and mothers. Women therefore had no need for advanced or professional training; there was no reason for colleges and universities to make space for female students. Some women, however, aspired to more. In 1784, Judith Sargent Murray published an essay defending women's right to education, a defense set in terms very different from those used by most men. Men and women were equal in intellect and potential, Murray argued. Women, therefore, should have precisely the same educational opportunities as men. What was more, they should have opportunities to earn their own living, to establish a role for themselves in society apart from their husbands and families. Murray's ideas became an inspiration to later generations of women, but during most of her own lifetime (1751–1820) they attracted relatively little support.

Reformers who believed in the power of education to reform and redeem ignorant and "backward" people spurred a growing interest in Indian education. Because Jefferson and his followers liked to think of Native Americans as "noble savages" (uncivilized, but unlike their view of African Americans, not necessarily innately inferior), they hoped that schooling the Indians in white culture would tame and "uplift" the tribes. Although white governments did little to promote Indian education, missionaries and mission schools proliferated among the tribes.

Almost no white people in the early nineteenth century believed that there was a need to educate African Americans, almost all of whom were still slaves. In a few northern states, some free black children attended segregated schools. In the South, slaveowners generally tried to prevent their black workers from learning to read or write, fearful that knowledge would make them unhappy with their condition. Some African Americans managed to acquire some education despite these obstacles, by teaching themselves and their own children. But the numbers of literate slaves remained very small.

Higher education was even less widely available than education at lower levels, despite republican hopes for a wide dispersion of advanced knowledge. (Jefferson himself founded the University of Virginia to promote that ideal.) The number of colleges and universities in America grew from nine at the start of the Revolution to twenty-two by 1800 and continued to increase thereafter. None of the new schools, however, was truly public. Even those established by state legislatures (in Georgia, North Carolina, Vermont, Ohio, and South Carolina, for example) relied on private contributions and on tuition fees. Scarcely more than one white man in a thousand (and no women, blacks, or Indians at all) had access to any college education, and those few who did attend universities were almost without exception members of prosperous, propertied families.

The education that the colleges provided was, moreover, exceedingly limited—narrow training in the classics and a few other areas and intensive work in theology. Indeed, the clergy was the only profession for which college training was generally a prerequisite. A few institutions attempted to provide their students advanced training in other fields. The College of William and Mary in Virginia, the University of Pennsylvania, and Columbia College in New York all created law schools before 1800, but most lawyers continued to train for their profession simply by apprenticing themselves to practicing attorneys.

The Practice of Medicine

The University of Pennsylvania created the first American medical school early in the nineteenth century, under the leadership of Benjamin Rush. Most doctors, however, studied medicine by working with an established practitioner. Some American physicians believed in applying new scientific methods to medicine and struggled against age-old prejudices and superstitions. Efforts to teach anatomy, for example, encountered strong public hostility because of the dissection of cadavers that the study required. Municipal authorities had virtually no understanding

■ **THE PENNSYLVANIA HOSPITAL**
As the ideas of the Enlightenment spread through American culture in the eighteenth and nineteenth centuries, encouraging the belief that every individual was a divine being and could be redeemed from even the most miserable condition, hospitals and asylums—such as this institution in Pennsylvania—began to emerge to provide settings for the redemption of the poor, the ill, and the deviant.
(Library Company of Philadelphia)

of medical science and almost no idea of what to do in the face of the severe epidemics that so often swept their populations; only slowly did they respond to the warnings of Rush and others that lack of adequate sanitation programs was to blame for disease.

Individual patients often had more to fear from their doctors than from their illnesses. Even the leading advocates of scientific medicine often embraced useless and dangerous treatments. Benjamin Rush, for example, was an advocate of the new and supposedly scientific techniques of bleeding and purging, and many of his patients died. George Washington's death in 1799 was probably less a result of the minor throat infection that had afflicted him than of his physicians' efforts to cure him by bleeding and purging.

The medical profession also used its newfound commitment to the "scientific" method to justify expanding its own control to kinds of care that had traditionally been outside its domain. Most childbirths, for example, had been attended by female midwives. In the early nineteenth century, physicians began to handle deliveries themselves and to demand restrictions on the role of midwives. Among the results of that change was a narrowing of opportunities for women (midwifery was an important female occupation) and a restriction of access to childbirth care for poor mothers (who could have afforded midwives, but who could not pay the higher physicians' fees).

Education and professional training in the early republic—in medicine and in many other fields—thus fell far short of the Jeffersonian vision. Indeed, efforts to promote education and increase professionalism often had the effect of strengthening existing elites rather than eroding them. Nevertheless, the ideal of equal educational opportunity survived, and in later decades it would become a vital force behind universal public education.

Cultural Aspirations in the New Nation

Many Americans in the Jeffersonian era may have repudiated the Federalist belief in political and economic centralization, but most embraced another form of nationalism with great fervor. Having won political independence from Europe, they aspired now to a form of cultural independence. In the process, they dreamed of an American literary and artistic life that would rival the greatest achievements of Europe. As a popular "Poem on the Rising Glory of America" had predicted as early as 1772, Americans believed that their "happy land" was destined to become the "seat of empire" and the "final stage" of civilization, with "glorious works of high invention and of wond'rous art." The United States, another eighteenth-century writer had proclaimed, would serve as "the last and greatest theatre for the improvement of mankind."

Such nationalism found expression, among other places, in early American schoolbooks. The Massachusetts geographer Jedidiah Morse, author of *Geography Made Easy* (1784), said the country must have its own textbooks to prevent the aristocratic ideas of England from infecting the people. The Connecticut schoolmaster and lawyer Noah Webster argued similarly that the American students should be educated as patriots, their minds filled with nationalistic, American thoughts. "As soon as he opens his lips," Webster wrote, "he should rehearse the history of his own country; he should lisp the praise of liberty, and of those illustrious heroes and statesmen who have wrought a revolution in her favor."

Further to encourage a distinctive American culture and help unify the new nation, Webster insisted on a simplified and Americanized system of spelling—"honor" instead of "honour," for example. His *American Spelling Book,* first published in 1783 and commonly known as the "blue-backed speller," eventually sold over 100 million copies, to become the best-selling book (except for the Bible) in the entire history of American publishing. Webster also wrote grammars and other schoolbooks. His school dictionary, issued in 1806, was republished in many editions and was eventually enlarged to become (in 1828) *An American Dictionary of the English Language.* His speller and his dictionary established a national standard of words and usages. Although Webster's Federalist political views fell into disfavor in the early nineteenth century, his cultural nationalism remained popular and influential.

Those Americans who aspired to create a more elevated national literary life faced a number of obstacles. There was, to be sure, a large potential audience for a national literature—a substantial reading public, created in part by the wide circulation of newspapers and political pamphlets during the Revolution. But there were few opportunities for would-be American authors to get their work before the public. Printers preferred to publish popular works by English writers (for which they had to pay no royalties); magazine publishers filled their pages largely with items clipped from British periodicals. Only those American writers willing to pay the cost and bear the risk of publishing their own works could compete for public attention.

Even so, a growing number of American authors struggled to create a strong native literature so that, as the poet Joel Barlow wrote, "true ideas of glory may be implanted in the minds of men here, to take the place of the false and destructive ones that have degraded the species in other countries." Barlow himself, one of a group of Connecticut writers known as the "Hartford Wits," published an epic poem, *The Columbiad,* in 1807, in an effort to convey the special character of American civilization. The acclaim it received helped to encourage other native writers.

Among the most ambitious was the Philadelphian Charles Brockden Brown. Like many Americans, he was attracted to the relatively new literary form of the novel, which had become popular in England in the late eighteenth century and had been successfully imported to America. But Brown sought to do more than simply imitate the English forms; he tried to use his novels to give voice to distinctively American themes, to convey the "soaring passions and intellectual energy" of the new nation. His obsession with originality led him to produce a body of work characterized by a fascination with horror and deviant behavior. Perhaps as a result, his novels failed to develop a large popular following.

Much more successful was Washington Irving, a resident of New York State who won wide acclaim for his satirical histories of early American life and his powerful fables of society in the New World. His popular folk tales, recounting the adventures of such American rustics as Ichabod Crane and Rip Van Winkle, made him the widely acknowledged leader of American literary life in the early nineteenth century and one of the few writers of that era whose works would continue to be read by later generations.

Perhaps the most influential works by American authors in the early republic were not poems, novels, or stories, but works of history that glorified the nation's past. Mercy Otis Warren, who had been an influential playwright and agitator during the 1770s, continued her literary efforts with a three-volume *History of the Revolution,* published in 1805 and emphasizing the heroism of the American struggle. Mason Weems, an Anglican clergyman, published a eulogistic *Life of Washington* in 1806, which became one of the best-selling books of the era. Weems had little interest in historical accuracy. He portrayed the aristocratic former president as a homespun man possessing simple republican virtues. (He also invented the famous story of the young Washington cutting down a cherry tree.) History, like literature, was serving as a vehicle for instilling a sense of nationalism in the American people.

Religious Skepticism

The American Revolution weakened traditional forms of religious practice by detaching churches from government and by elevating ideas of individual liberty and reason that challenged many ecclesiastical traditions. By the 1790s, only a small proportion of white Americans (perhaps as few as 10 percent) were members of formal churches, and ministers were complaining often about the "decay of vital piety." Religious traditionalists were particularly alarmed about the emergence of new, "rational" theologies that reflected modern, scientific attitudes and deemphasized the role of God in the world.

Some Americans, including Jefferson and Franklin, embraced "deism," which had originated among Enlightenment philosophers in France. Deists accepted the existence of God, but considered Him a remote being who, after having created the universe, had withdrawn from direct involvement with the human race and its sins. Books and articles attacking religious "superstitions" attracted wide readerships and provoked much discussion, among them Thomas Paine's *The Age of Reason,* published in parts between 1794 and 1796. Paine once declared that Christianity was the "strangest religion ever set up," for "it committed a murder upon Jesus in order to redeem mankind from the sin of eating an apple."

Religious skepticism also produced the philosophies of "universalism" and "unitarianism," which emerged at first as dissenting views within the New England Congregational Church. Disciples of these new ideas rejected the Calvinist belief in predestination, arguing that salvation was available to all. They rejected, too, the idea of the Trinity. Jesus was only a great religious teacher, they claimed, not the Son of God. So wide was the gulf between these dissenters and the Congregationalist establishment that it finally became a permanent schism. James Murray (who later married Judith Sargent Murray) founded the Universalist Church as a separate denomination in Gloucester, Massachusetts, in 1779; the Unitarian Church was established in Boston three years later.

Some Americans believed that the spread of rationalism marked the end of traditional, evangelistic religion in the new nation. But quite the contrary was true. In fact, most Americans continued to hold strong religious beliefs (even if the widespread popular fervor of the Great Awakening of the 1730s had largely faded). What had declined was their commitment to organized churches and denominations.

Deism, Universalism, Unitarianism, and other "rational" religions seemed more powerful than they actually were because for a time traditional evangelicals were confused and disorganized. But beginning in 1801, traditional religion staged a dramatic comeback in the form of a wave of revivalism known as the Second Great Awakening.

The Second Great Awakening

The origins of the Second Awakening lay in the efforts of conservative theologians of the 1790s to fight the spread of religious rationalism, and in the efforts of church establishments to revitalize their organizations.

Leaders of several different denominations participated in the evangelizing efforts that drove the revival. Presbyterians tried to arouse the faithful on the western fringe of white settlement, and conservatives in the church became increasingly militant in response to so-called New Light dissenters (people who had altered their religious views to make them more compatible with the world of scientific rationalism). Methodism, which John Wesley had founded in England, spread to America in the 1770s and became a formal denomination in 1784 under the leadership of Francis Asbury. Authoritarian and hierarchical in structure, the Methodist Church sent itinerant preachers throughout the nation to win recruits; it soon became the fastest-growing denomination in America. Almost as successful were the Baptists, who were themselves relatively new to America; they found an especially fervent following in the South.

By 1800, the revivalist energies of all these denominations were combining to create the greatest surge of evangelical fervor since the first Great Awakening sixty years before. Beginning among Presbyterians in several eastern colleges (most notably at Yale, under the leadership of President Timothy Dwight), the new awakening soon spread rapidly throughout the country, reaching its greatest heights in the western regions. In only a few years, a large proportion of the American people were mobilized by the movement, and membership in those churches embracing the revival—most prominently the Methodists, the Baptists, and the Presbyterians—was mushrooming. At Cane Ridge, Kentucky, in the summer of 1801, a group of evangelical ministers presided over the nation's first "camp meeting"—an extraordinary revival that lasted several days and impressed all who saw it with its size (some estimated that 25,000 people attended) and its fervor. Such events became common in subsequent years, as the Methodists in particular came to rely on them as a way to "harvest" new members. The Methodist circuit-riding preacher Peter Cartwright won national fame as he traveled from region to region exhorting his listeners to embrace the church. Even Cartwright, however, was often unprepared for the results of his efforts—a religious frenzy that at times produced convulsions, fits, rolling in the dirt, and the twitching "holy jerks."

The message of the Second Great Awakening was not entirely consistent, but its basic thrust was clear. Individuals must readmit God and Christ into their daily lives, must embrace a fervent, active piety, and must reject the skeptical rationalism that threatened traditional beliefs. Even so, the wave of revivalism did not serve to restore the religious ideas of the past. Few of the revivalist denominations any longer

accepted the idea of predestination; and the belief that a person could affect his or her own destiny, rather than encouraging irreligion as many had feared, added intensity to the individual's search for salvation. The Awakening, in short, combined a more active piety with a belief in God as an active force in the world whose grace could be attained through faith and good works.

The Second Awakening did not revive the strength of the old religious institutions any more than it revived old religious ideas. Instead, it accelerated the growth of different sects and denominations and helped create a broad popular acceptance of the idea that men and women could belong to different Protestant churches and still be committed to essentially the same Christian faith. Finally, the new evangelicalism—by spreading religious fervor into virtually every area of the nation, including remote regions where no formal church had ever existed—provided a vehicle for establishing a sense of order

■ **METHODIST CAMP MEETING, 1837**
Camp (or revival) meetings were popular among some evangelical Christians in America as early as 1800. By the 1820s, there were approximately 1,000 meetings a year, most of them in the South and the West. After one such meeting in 1806, a participant wrote: "Will I ever see anything more like the day of Judgement on this side of eternity—to see the people running, yes, running from every direction to the stand, weeping, shouting, and shouting for joy. . . . O! Glorious day they went home singing shouting." This lithograph, dated 1837, suggests the degree to which women predominated at many revivals. *(The Granger Collection)*

and social stability in communities still searching for an identity.

One of the most striking features of the Second Great Awakening was the preponderance of women within it. Young women, in particular, were drawn to the revivalism, and female converts far outnumbered males. In some areas, church membership became overwhelmingly female as a result. One reason for this was that women were more numerous in certain regions than men. Adventurous young men often struck out on their own and moved west; women, for the most part, had no such options. Their marriage prospects thus diminished and their futures plagued with uncertainty, some women discovered in religion a foundation on which to build their lives. But even where there was no shortage of men, women flocked to the revivals in enormous numbers, which suggests that they were responding to their changing economic roles as well. The movement of industrial work out of the home (where women had often contributed to the family economy through spinning and weaving) and into the factory—a process making rapid strides in the early nineteenth century (see pp. 343–344)—robbed older women, in particular, of one of their most important social roles. Younger, unmarried women with more mobility could follow the work out of the home and into the factory with less difficulty, but that movement, too, created personal and social strains. Religious enthusiasm helped compensate for the losses and adjustments these transitions produced; it also provided access to a new range of activities associated with the churches—charitable societies ministering to orphans and the poor, missionary organizations, and others—in which women came to play important roles.

Although revivalism was most widespread within white society, it penetrated other cultures as well. In some areas of the country, revivals were open to people of all races, and many blacks not only attended but eagerly embraced the new religious fervor. Out of these revivals, in fact, emerged a substantial group of black preachers, who became important figures within the slave community. Some of them translated the apparently egalitarian religious message of the Second Awakening—that salvation was available to all—into a similarly egalitarian message for blacks in the present world. For example, out of black revival meetings in Virginia arose an elaborate plan in 1800 (devised by Gabriel Prosser, the brother of a black preacher) for a slave rebellion and attack on Richmond. The plan was discovered and the rebellion forestalled by whites, but revivalism continued to stir racial unrest in the South.

The spirit of revivalism was particularly strong in these years among Native Americans, although very different in its origins and expression from revivalism in white or black society. It drew heavily from earlier tribal experiences. In the 1760s, the Delaware prophet Neolin had sparked a widespread revival in the Old Northwest with a message combining Christian and Indian imagery and bringing to Native American religion a vision of a personal God, intimately involved in the affairs of man. Neolin had also called for Indians to rise up in defense of their lands and had denounced the growth of trade and other relationships with white civilization. His vehement statements had helped stimulate the Indian military efforts of 1763 and beyond.

The dislocations and military defeats Indians suffered in the aftermath of the American Revolution created a sense of crisis among many of the eastern tribes in particular; as a result, the 1790s and early 1800s became another era of Indian religious fervor and prophecy. Presbyterian and Baptist missionaries were active among the southern tribes and sparked a great wave of conversions. But the most important revivalism came from the efforts of another great prophet: Handsome Lake, a Seneca whose seemingly miraculous "rebirth" after years of alcoholism helped give him a special stature within his tribe. Handsome Lake, like Neolin before him, called for a revival of traditional Indian ways. That meant repudiating the individualism of white society, which Handsome Lake argued had penetrated tribal life with alarming results, and restoring the communal quality of the Indian world. (He claimed to have met Jesus, who instructed him to "tell your people they will become lost when they follow the ways of the white man.") Handsome Lake's message spread through the scattered Iroquois communities that had survived the military and political setbacks of previous decades and inspired many Indians to give up whiskey, gambling, and other destructive customs derived from white society.

But the revival did not, in fact, lead to a true restoration of traditional Iroquois culture. Instead, Handsome Lake encouraged Christian missionaries to become active within the tribes, and he urged Iroquois men to abandon their roles as hunters (partly because so much of their hunting land had been seized by whites) and become sedentary farmers instead. Iroquois women, who had traditionally done the farming, were to move into more domestic roles. When some women resisted the change, Handsome Lake denounced them as witches.

The Second Great Awakening also had important effects on those Americans who did not accept its teachings. The rational "freethinkers," whose skeptical philosophies had done so much to produce the revivals, were in many ways victims of the new religious fervor. They did not disappear after 1800, but their influence rapidly declined, and for many years they remained a small and defensive minority within American Christianity. Instead, the dominant religious characteristic of the new nation became a fervent evangelicalism, which would survive into the mid-nineteenth century and beyond.

STIRRINGS OF INDUSTRIALISM

Despite the hopes of Jefferson and his followers that the United States would remain a simple agrarian republic, the nation took its first, tentative steps in these years toward its transformation into exactly the sort of urban, industrial society the early Republicans had warned against.

The Industrial Revolution in England

While Americans were engaged in a revolution to win their independence, an even more important revolution was in progress in England: the emergence of modern industrialism. Historians differ over precisely when the industrial revolution began, but it is clear that by the end of the eighteenth century it was well under way. Its essence was relatively simple: power-driven machines were taking the place of hand-operated tools and were permitting manufacturing to become more rapid and extensive. But however simple the causes, the social and economic consequences of the transformation were complex and profound.

The factory system in England took root first in the manufacture of cotton thread and cloth. There, one invention followed another in quick succession. Improvements in weaving drove improvements in spinning, and these changes created a demand for new devices for carding (combing and straightening the fibers for the spinner). Water, wind, and animal power continued to be important in the textile industry; but more important was the emergence of steam power—which began to proliferate after the appearance of James Watt's advanced steam engine (patented in 1769). Cumbersome and inefficient by modern standards, Watt's engine was nevertheless a major improvement over the earlier "atmospheric" engine of Thomas Newcomen. England's textile industry quickly became the most profitable in the world, and it helped encourage comparable advances in other fields of manufacturing as well.

At the same time, England's social system was undergoing a wrenching change. Hundreds of thousands of men and women were moving from rural areas into cities to work in factories, and there they experienced both the benefits and the costs of industrialization. The standard of living of the new working class, when objectively quantified, was significantly higher than that of the rural poor. Most of those who moved from farm to factory, in other words, experienced some improvement in their material circumstances. But the psychological costs of being suddenly uprooted from one way of life and thrust into another, fundamentally different one could outweigh the economic gains. There was little in most workers' prior experience to prepare them for the nature of industrial labor. It was disciplined, routinized work with a fixed and rigid schedule, a sharp contrast to the varying, seasonal work pattern of the rural economy. Nor were many factory workers prepared for life in the new industrial towns and expanding cities. Industrial workers experienced, too, a fundamental change in their relationship with their employers. Unlike the landlords and local aristocrats of rural England, factory owners and managers—the new class of industrial capitalists, many of them accumulating unprecedented wealth—were usually remote and inaccessible figures. They dealt with their workers impersonally, and the result was a growing schism between the two classes—each lacking access to or understanding of the other.

As a result, English life was changing at every level. The middle class was expanding and coming to dominate the economy (although not yet the culture or the nation's politics). Working men and women were beginning to think of themselves as a distinct class, with common goals and interests. And their efforts simultaneously to adjust to their new way of life and to resist its most damaging aspects made the late eighteenth and early nineteenth centuries a time of continuing social turbulence.

Not since the agrarian revolution thousands of years earlier, when many humans had turned from hunting to farming for sustenance, had there been an economic change of a magnitude comparable to the industrial revolution. Centuries of traditions, of social patterns, of cultural and religious assumptions were challenged and, often, shattered.

Technology in America

Nothing even remotely comparable to the English industrial revolution occurred in America in the first two decades of the nineteenth century. Indeed, it was opposition to the kind of economic growth occurring in England that had helped the Republicans defeat the Federalists in 1800; and many Americans continued to view British industrialization with deep ambivalence. Yet even while they warned of the dangers of rapid economic change, Americans of the Jeffersonian era were welcoming a series of technological advances that would ultimately help ensure that the United States too would be transformed.

Americans imported some of these technological advances from England. The British government attempted to protect the nation's manufacturing preeminence by preventing the export of textile machinery or the emigration of skilled mechanics. Despite such efforts, immigrants arrived in the United States with advanced knowledge of English technology, eager to introduce the new machines to America. Samuel Slater, for example, used the knowledge he had acquired before leaving England to build a spinning mill for the Quaker merchant Moses Brown in Pawtucket, Rhode Island, in 1790. It was the first modern factory in America.

America in the early nineteenth century also produced several important inventors of its own. Among them was Oliver Evans, of Delaware, who devised a number of ingenious new machines: an automated flour mill, a card-making machine, and others. He made several important improvements in the steam engine, and in 1795 he published America's first textbook of mechanical engineering: *The*

Young Mill-Wright's and Miller's Guide. His own flour mill, which began operations in 1787, required only two men to operate: one of them emptying a bag of wheat into the machinery, another putting the lid on the barrels of flour and rolling them away.

Even more influential for the future of the nation were the inventions of the Massachusetts-born, Yale-educated Eli Whitney, who revolutionized both cotton production and weapons manufacturing. The growth of the textile industry in England had created an enormous demand for cotton, a demand that planters in the American South were finding impossible to meet. Their greatest obstacle was separating the seeds from cotton fiber—a difficult and time-consuming process that was essential before cotton could be sold. Long-staple, or Sea Island, cotton, with its smooth black seeds and long fibers, was easy to clean, but it grew successfully only along the Atlantic coast or on the offshore islands of Georgia and South Carolina. There was not nearly enough of it to satisfy the demand. Short-staple cotton, by contrast, could grow inland through vast areas of the South. But its sticky green seeds were extremely difficult to remove. A skilled worker could clean no more than a few pounds a day by hand. Then, in 1793, Whitney, who was working at the time as a tutor on the Georgia plantation of General Nathanael Greene's widow, invented a machine that performed the arduous task quickly and efficiently. It was dubbed the cotton gin ("gin" was an abbreviation for "engine"), and it transformed the life of the South.

Mechanically, the gin was very simple. A toothed roller caught the fibers of the cotton boll and pulled them between the wires of a grating. The grating caught the seeds while a revolving brush removed the lint from the roller's teeth. With the device, a single operator could clean as much cotton in a few hours as a group of workers had once needed a whole day to do. The results were profound. Soon cotton growing spread into the upland South, and within a decade the total crop increased eightfold. African-American slavery, which with the decline of tobacco production some had considered a dwindling institution, regained its importance, expanded, and became more firmly fixed upon the South.

■ **PAWTUCKET BRIDGE AND FALLS**
One reason for the growth of the textile industry in New England in the early nineteenth century was that there were many sources of water power in the region to run the machinery in the factories. That was certainly the case with Slater's Mill, one of the first American textile factories, which was located in Pawtucket, Rhode Island, alongside a powerful waterfall. This view was painted by an anonymous artist in the 1810s. *(Rhode Island Historical Society)*

The cotton gin not only changed the economy of the South, it also helped transform the North. The large supply of domestically produced fiber was a strong incentive to entrepreneurs in New England and elsewhere to develop an American textile industry. Few northern states could hope to thrive on the basis of agriculture alone; by learning to turn cotton into yarn and thread, they could become industrially prosperous instead. The manufacturing preeminence of the North, which emerged with the development of the textile industry in the 1820s and 1830s, helped drive a wedge between the nation's two most populous regions—one becoming increasingly industrial, the other more firmly wedded to agriculture—and ultimately contributed to the coming of the Civil War. It also helped ensure the eventual Union victory.

Whitney also made a major contribution to the development of modern warfare and in the process made a contribution to other industrial techniques. During the two years of undeclared war with France (1798 and 1799), Americans were deeply troubled by their lack of sufficient armaments for the expected hostilities. Production of muskets—each carefully handcrafted by a skilled gunsmith—was discouragingly slow. Whitney devised a machine to make each part of a gun according to an exact pattern. Tasks could thus be divided among several workers, and one laborer could assemble a weapon out of parts made by several others. Before long, manufacturers of sewing machines, clocks, and many other complicated products were using the same system.

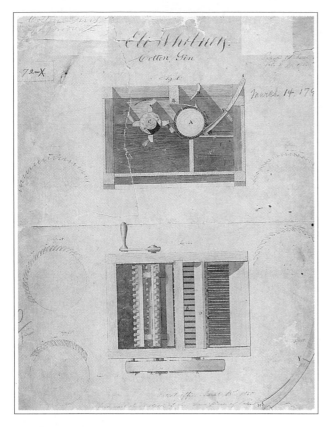

The new technological advances were relatively
isolated phenomena during the early years of the
nineteenth century. Not until at least the 1840s did
the nation begin to develop a true manufacturing
economy. But the inventions of this period were crucial in making the eventual transformation possible.

Trade and Transportation

One of the prerequisites for industrialization is an efficient system for transporting raw materials to factories and finished goods to markets. The United States
had no such system in the early years of the republic.
Without such a system, there could be no domestic
market extensive enough to justify large-scale production. But work was under way that would ultimately remove the transportation obstacle.

There were several ways to solve the problem of
the small American market. One was to look for customers overseas, and American merchants continued
their efforts to do that. Among the first acts of the new
Congress when it met in 1789 were two tariff bills giving preference to American ships in American ports,
helping to stimulate an expansion of domestic shipping. More important—indeed the principal reason
for the growth of American trade in this period—was
the outbreak of war in Europe in the 1790s, allowing
Yankee merchant vessels to take over most of the carrying trade between Europe and the Western Hemisphere. As early as 1793, the young republic had a
merchant marine and a foreign trade larger than those
of any country except England. In proportion to its
population, the United States had more ships and international commerce than any country in the world.
And the shipping business was growing fast. Between
1789 and 1810, the total tonnage of American vessels
engaged in overseas traffic rose from less than 125,000
to nearly 1 million. American ships had carried only 30
percent of the country's exports in 1789; they were
carrying over 90 percent in 1810. The figures for imports increased even more dramatically, from 17.5
percent to 90 percent in the same period.

Another solution to the problem of limited markets was to develop new markets at home, by improving transportation between the states and into
the interior of the continent. Progress was slower
here than in international shipping, but some improvements were occurring nevertheless. In river
transportation, a new era began with the development of the steamboat. A number of inventors began
experimenting with steam-powered craft in the late
eighteenth century; John Fitch exhibited a forty-five-
foot vessel with paddles operated by steam to some
of the delegates at the Constitutional Convention in
1787. But the real breakthrough was Oliver Evans's
development of a high-pressure engine, lighter and
more efficient than James Watt's, which made steam
more feasible for powering boats (and, eventually,
the locomotive) as well as mill machinery.

The inventor Robert Fulton and the promoter
Robert R. Livingston were principally responsible
for perfecting the steamboat and bringing it to the
attention of the nation. Their *Clermont*, equipped
with paddle wheels and an English-built engine,
sailed up the Hudson in the summer of 1807,
demonstrating the practicability of steam navigation
(even though it took the ship thirty hours to go

■ "A SCENE OF THE ROAD"
The watercolorist George Tattersall painted this image of a stagecoach negotiating the rough roads and bridges that were beginning to link together the disparate regions of early nineteenth-century America. *(Highways and Byeways of the Forest, A Scene of "The Road." Sketch by George Tattersall. M. and M. Karolik Collection of American Paintings, 1815–1865. Courtesy, Museum of Fine Arts, Boston)*

150 miles). In 1811, a partner of Livingston's, Nicholas J. Roosevelt (a remote ancestor of Theodore Roosevelt), introduced the steamboat to the West by sending the *New Orleans* from Pittsburgh down the Ohio and Mississippi. The next year, this vessel began a profitable career of service between New Orleans and Natchez.

Meanwhile, what was to become known as the "turnpike era" had begun. In 1792, a corporation constructed a toll road running the sixty miles from Philadelphia to Lancaster, with a hard-packed surface of crushed rock. This venture proved so successful that several other companies laid out similar turnpikes (so named from the kind of tollgate frequently used) from other cities to neighboring towns. Since the turnpikes had to produce profits for the companies that built them, construction costs had to be low

enough and the prospective traffic heavy enough to ensure an early and ample return. As a result these roads, radiating from eastern cities, ran comparatively short distances and through thickly settled areas. No private operators were willing to build similar highways over the mountains and into the less populated interior. State governments and the federal government eventually had to finance them.

Country and City

Despite all the changes and all the advances, America in the early nineteenth century remained an overwhelmingly rural and agrarian nation. Only 3 percent of the non-Indian population lived in towns of more than 8,000 at the time of the second census in 1800. Ten percent lived west of the Appalachian Mountains, far from what urban centers there were. Much of the country remained a wilderness. Even the nation's largest cities could not begin to compare, either in size or in cultural sophistication, with such European capitals as London and Paris.

Yet here too there were signs of change. The leading American cities might not yet have become world capitals, but they were large and complex enough to rival the important secondary cities of Europe. Philadelphia, with 70,000 residents, and New York, with 60,000, were becoming major centers of commerce and learning. They were developing a distinctively urban culture. So too were the next largest cities of the new nation: Baltimore (26,000 in 1800), Boston (24,000), and Charleston (20,000).

People living in towns and cities lived differently from the vast majority of Americans who continued to

work as farmers. Among other things, urban life produced affluence, and affluent people sought amenities that would not have entered the imaginings of all but the wealthiest farmers. They sought increasing elegance and refinement in their homes, their grounds, and their dress. They also looked for diversions—music, theater, dancing, and, for many people, one of the most popular entertainments of all, horse racing.

Much remained to be done before this small and still half-formed nation would become a complex modern society. It was still possible in the early nineteenth century to believe that those changes might not ever occur. But forces were already at work that, in time, would lastingly transform the United States. And Thomas Jefferson, for all his commitment to the agrarian ideal, found himself obliged as president to confront and accommodate them.

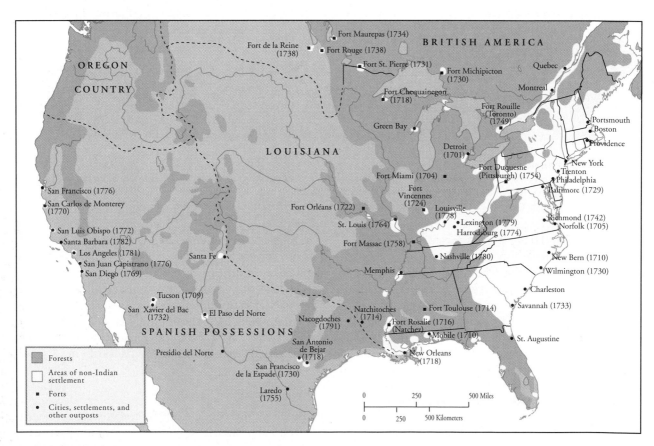

■ **AMERICA IN 1800**

By 1800, American settlement had moved farther west, particularly into the Ohio River valley and the southern backcountry. Still, only 10 percent of the non-Indian population in the United States lived west of the Appalachian Mountains in 1800. The United States remained a mostly rural and agricultural country with a population concentrated on the eastern seaboard. Much of the country was still a forested wilderness.

HORSE RACING

There were few respites from the daily struggle for survival for the first European settlers in North America. Men and women attended church and celebrated major religious holidays, but there was little in most of their lives that twentieth-century Americans would recognize as leisure or popular culture. For relatively affluent colonists, however, one sport emerged very early as an enduringly popular form of entertainment: horse racing.

It was natural, perhaps, that horse racing would become so appealing in the seventeenth and eighteenth centuries, when horses were, for most people, the only source of transportation over land other than walking. Those who could afford to own horses considered them part of the essential equipment of life. But people also formed attachments to their horses and prided themselves on their beauty and speed. Eventually, such attachments led to the creation of a spectator sport in which that beauty and speed were the central attractions.

Informal horse racing began almost as soon as Europeans settled the English colonies. Formal

■ **OAKLAND HOUSE AND RACE COURSE**
This 1840 painting by Robert Brammer and August A. Von Smith portrays an early race course in Louisville, Kentucky, which provided entertainment to affluent white southerners. *(Oakland House and Race Course, Louisville, 1840. By Robert Brammer and August A. Von Smith. Collection of The Speed Art Museum, Louisville, Kentucky. Purchase, Museum Art fund, 56.19)*

(continued)

■ **THE ECLIPSE-HENRY MATCH RACE**
"Match races" between famous horses were a popular feature of early nineteenth-century horse racing. This famous 1823 race on Long Island, New York, pitted prize-winning horses from the North and the South against one another. American Eclipse, the northern entry, won. *(Private collection)*

racing followed quickly. The first race track in North America—New Market (named for a popular race course in England)—was established in 1665 near the site of present-day Garden City, on Long Island in New York. It was, from the beginning, a showcase for horses bred in America by Americans, and in 1751 the track's authorities decreed that no imported horses could race there. For a time, New Market (and other horse racing sites) were dominated by English military officers stationed in the colonies. But tracks quickly developed a much wider appeal, and soon horse racing had spread up and down the Atlantic coast. By the time of the American Revolution, it was popular in almost every colony. It had a particularly avid following in Maryland, Virginia, and South Carolina;

and it was moving as well into the newly settled areas of the Southwest. Andrew Jackson was a founder of the first racing track in Nashville, Tennessee, in the early nineteenth century. Kentucky—whose native bluegrass was early recognized as ideal for grazing horses—had eight tracks by 1800.

Like almost everything else in the life of early America, the world of horse racing was bounded by lines of class and race. For many years, it was considered the exclusive preserve of "gentlemen," so much so that in 1674 a court in Virginia fined James Bullocke, a tailor, for proposing a race, "it being contrary to Law for a Labourer to make a race, being a sport only for Gentlemen." But while white aristocrats retained control of

JEFFERSON THE PRESIDENT

Privately, Thomas Jefferson may well have considered his victory over John Adams in 1800 to be what he later termed it: a revolution "as real . . . as that of 1776." Publicly, however, he was restrained and conciliatory at the time, attempting to minimize the dif-

ferences between the two parties and to calm the passions that the bitter campaign had aroused. "We are all republicans, we are all federalists," he said in his inaugural address. And during his eight years in office, he did much to prove those words correct. There was no complete repudiation of Federalist policies, no true "revolution." Indeed, at times Jefferson seemed to outdo the Federalists at their own

racing, they were not the only people who participated in it. Southern aristocrats often trained young male slaves as jockeys for their horses, just as northern horse owners employed the services of free blacks as riders. In the North and the South, African Americans eventually emerged as some of the most talented and experienced trainers of racing horses. And despite social and legal pressures, free blacks and poor whites often staged their own, informal races, which proved highly popular among lower-class men and women and which helped give racing a slightly disreputable image among more conservative white aristocrats.

Racing also began early to reflect the growing sectional rivalry between the North and the South. In 1824, the Union Race Course on Long Island established an astounding $24,000 purse for a race between two famous thoroughbreds: American Eclipse (from the North) and Sir Henry (from the South). American Eclipse won two of the three heats, but a southern racehorse prevailed in another such celebrated contest in 1836. These intersectional races, which drew enormous crowds and created tremendous publicity, continued into the 1850s, until the North-South rivalry began to take a more deadly form.

Horse racing remained popular after the Civil War, but two developments changed its character considerably. One was the successful effort to drive African Americans out of the sport. At least until the 1890s, black jockeys and trainers remained central to racing. At the first Kentucky Derby in 1875, fourteen of the fifteen horses had African-American riders. One black man, Isaac Murphy, became one of the greatest jockeys of all time, the winner of three Kentucky Derbys and a remarkable 44 percent of all races in which he rode. Gradually, however, the same social dynamics that enforced racial segregation on so many other areas of American life in this era penetrated racing as well. By the beginning of the twentieth century, through a combination of harassment, intimidation, and formal discrimination, white jockeys and the organized jockey clubs had driven almost all black riders, and many black trainers, out of the sport.

The second change was the introduction of formalized betting to the sport. Informal wages had been part of racing almost from the beginning, but in the late nineteenth century race tracks themselves began creating betting systems as a way to lure customers to the races. At the same time that the breeding of racehorses was moving into the hands of enormously wealthy families (many of them the beneficiaries of new industrial fortunes), the audience for racing was becoming increasingly working class and lower middle class. The people who now came to tracks were mostly white men, and some white women, lured to the races not by a love of horses—which were coming now to play a less central role in their everyday lives—but by the usually futile hope of quick and easy riches through gambling.

work—most notably in overseeing a remarkable expansion of the territory of the United States.

In some respects, however, the Jefferson presidency did indeed represent a fundamental, if temporary, change in the direction of the federal government. The new administration oversaw a drastic reduction in the powers of some national institutions, and it forestalled the development of new powers in areas where the Federalists would certainly have attempted to expand them. Neither the executive nor the legislative branch of government was willing or able to exercise decisive authority in most areas of national life by the end of the Jeffersonian era. Only the courts continued trying to assert federal power in the ways the Federalists had envisioned.

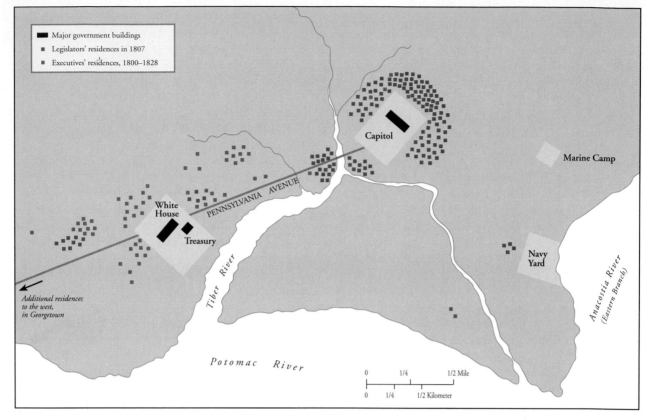

Major government buildings
Legislators' residences in 1807
Executives' residences, 1800–1828

Capitol

Marine Camp

White House

PENNSYLVANIA AVENUE

Treasury

Navy Yard

Tiber River

Additional residences to the west, in Georgetown

Anacostia River (Eastern Branch)

Potomac River

| 0 | 1/4 | 1/2 Mile |

| 0 | 1/4 | 1/2 Kilometer |

■ **WASHINGTON, D.C., IN THE EARLY NINETEENTH CENTURY**
The seat of the federal government was moved to the new city of Washington in 1800, for the last year of the presidency of John Adams. Although Pierre L'Enfant had designed the capital on a grand scale and many people expected Washington to grow quickly into a great capital city, it remained a straggling, provincial village for most of the nineteenth century. An inhospitable climate made the federal district unpopular, while the Republican administrations of the early nineteenth century did little to further the city's growth.

The Federal City

Symbolic of the relative unimportance of the federal government during the Jeffersonian era was the character of the newly founded national capital, the city of Washington. John Adams had moved to the new seat of government during the last year of his administration. There were many at that time who expected the raw, uncompleted town to emerge soon as a great and majestic city, a focus for the growing nationalism that the Federalists were promoting. The French architect Pierre L'Enfant had designed the capital on a grand scale, with broad avenues radiating out from the uncompleted Capitol building, set on one of the area's highest hills. Washington was, many Americans believed, to become the Paris of the United States.

In reality, however, throughout Jefferson's presidency—and indeed through most of the nineteenth century—Washington remained little more than a straggling, provincial village. Although the population increased steadily from the 3,200 counted in the 1800 census, it never rivaled that of New York, Philadelphia, or the other major cities of the nation. One problem was the climate: wet and cold in winter, hot and almost unbearably humid in summer, reflecting the marshy character of the site. Another problem, however, was that those in the federal government responsible for the development of the city did little to further its growth. The Republican administrations of the early nineteenth century oversaw the completion of several sections of the present-day Capitol build-

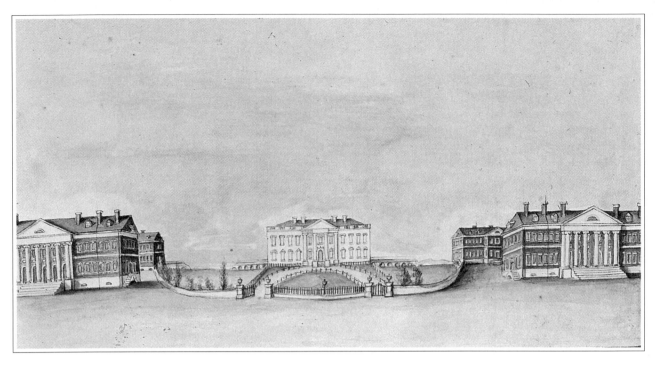

■ **"WASHINGTON CITY, 1821"**
This 1821 painting by a French artist shows one of Washington's most significant vistas: looking across Lafayette Park at the North Facade of the White House. The painting suggests both the grandeur to which the new capital aspired and the relative crudeness and simplicity of the city as it then existed. *(I.N. Phelps Stokes Collection, Miriam and Ira D. Wallach Division of Art, Prints and Photographs, The New York Public Library, Astor, Lenox and Tilden Foundations)*

ing, of the White House, and of a few other government buildings. Otherwise, they allowed the city to remain a raw, inhospitable community. Its muddy streets were at times almost impassable. The Capitol and the White House were often cut off from each other by rising creeks and washed-away bridges.

Members of Congress viewed the city not as a home but as a place to visit briefly during sessions of the legislature and leave as quickly as possible. Few owned houses in Washington. Most lived in a cluster of simple boardinghouses in the vicinity of the Capitol. It was not unusual for a member of Congress to resign his seat in the midst of a session to return home if he had an opportunity to accept the more prestigious post of member of his state legislature. During the summers, the entire government in effect packed up and left town. The president, the cabinet, the Congress, and most other federal employees spent the hot summer months far from the uncomfortable capital.

President and Party Leader

Jefferson set out as president to act in a spirit of democratic simplicity in keeping with the frontier-like character of the unfinished federal city. He was a wealthy and aristocratic planter by background, the owner of more than 100 slaves, and a man of rare cultivation and sophistication; but he conveyed to the public an image of plain, almost crude disdain for pretension. He walked like an ordinary citizen to and from his inauguration at the Capitol, instead of riding in a coach at the head of a procession. In the presidential mansion, which had not yet acquired the name "White House," he disregarded the courtly etiquette of his predecessors (in part, no doubt, because as a widower he had no first lady to take charge of social affairs). At state dinners, he let his guests scramble pell-mell for places at the table. He did not always bother to dress up, on one occasion prompting the fastidious British ambassador to complain of being received by the president in coat and pantaloons that were "indicative of utter slovenliness and indifference to appearances." Even when carefully dressed, the tall, freckle-faced, sandy-haired Jefferson was shy and awkward. He walked with a shambling gait. He was an ineffective public speaker.

Yet Jefferson managed nevertheless to impress most of those who knew him. He was a brilliant and charming conversationalist, a writer of great literary skills, and one of the nation's most intelligent and creative men, with perhaps a wider range of interests and accomplishments than any public figure in American history. In addition to politics and diplomacy, he was an active architect, educator, inventor, scientific farmer, and philosopher-scientist. He diverted himself with such pastimes as sorting the bones of prehistoric animals and collecting volumes for one of the nation's greatest private libraries (which later became the basis of the original Library of Congress).

Jefferson was, above all, a shrewd and practical politician. On the one hand, he went to great lengths to eliminate the aura of majesty surrounding the presidency that he believed his predecessors had created. He decided, for example, to submit his messages to Congress not by delivering them in person, as Washington and Adams had done, but by sending them in writing, thus avoiding even the semblance of attempting to dictate to the legislature. (The precedent he established survived for more than a century, until the administration of Woodrow Wilson.) At the same time, however, Jefferson worked hard to exert influence as the leader of his party, giving direction to Republicans in Congress by quiet and sometimes even devious means.

To his cabinet he appointed members of his own party who shared his philosophy. His secretary of state was James Madison, his friend and neighbor; their collaboration was so close that it was often difficult to tell which of the two men was more responsible for government policy. His secretary of the treasury was Albert Gallatin, a Swiss-born politician with a French accent, whose financial expertise rivaled that of Hamilton but who was a staunch opponent of Hamilton's policies.

Although the Republicans had objected strenuously to the efforts of their Federalist predecessors to build a network of influence through patronage, Jefferson, too, used his powers of appointment as an effective political weapon. Like Washington before him, he believed that federal offices should be filled with men loyal to the principles and policies of the administration. He did not attempt a sudden and

■ **THOMAS JEFFERSON**
This 1805 portrait by the noted American painter Rembrandt Peale shows Jefferson at the beginning of his second term as president. It also conveys (through the simplicity of dress and the slightly unkempt hair) the image of democratic simplicity that Jefferson liked to project. *(New-York Historical Society)*

drastic removal of Federalist officeholders, but at every convenient opportunity he replaced the holdovers from the Adams administration with his own trusted followers. By the end of his first term about half the government jobs, and by the end of his second term practically all of them, were in the hands of loyal Republicans.

When Jefferson ran for reelection in 1804, he won overwhelmingly. The Federalist presidential nominee, Charles C. Pinckney, could not even carry most of the party's New England strongholds. Jefferson won 162 electoral votes to Pinckney's 14, and the Republican majorities in both houses of Congress increased.

Dollars and Ships

Under the Federalists, the Republicans believed, the government had been needlessly extravagant. Yearly federal expenditures had nearly tripled between

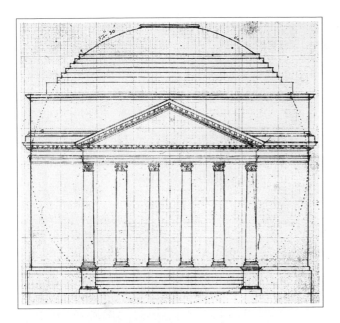

■ **JEFFERSON THE ARCHITECT**
Among his many other accomplishments, Thomas Jefferson was one of the most gifted architects in early America. This rotunda is the centerpiece of the central campus of the University of Virginia, which Jefferson designed near the end of his life. Earlier, he designed his own home near Charlottesville, Monticello; and his proposal for a president's mansion in Washington placed second in a blind competition. *(University of Virginia Library)*

1793 and 1800. Hamilton had, as he had intended, increased the public debt and created an extensive system of internal taxation, including the hated whiskey excise tax.

The Jefferson administration moved deliberately to reverse the trend. In 1802, it persuaded Congress to abolish all internal taxes, leaving customs duties and the sale of western lands as the only source of revenue for the government. Meanwhile, Secretary of the Treasury Gallatin drastically reduced government spending, cutting the already small staffs of the executive departments to minuscule levels. Although Jefferson was unable to retire the entire national debt as he had hoped, he did cut it almost in half (from $83 million to $45 million) during his presidency.

Jefferson also scaled down the armed forces. He reduced the tiny army of 4,000 men to 2,500. He cut the navy from twenty-five ships to seven and reduced the number of officers and sailors accordingly. Anything but the smallest of standing armies,

he argued, might menace civil liberties and civilian control of government. And a large navy, he feared, might promote overseas commerce, which Jefferson believed should remain secondary to agriculture. Yet despite his claims that "Peace is our passion," Jefferson was not a pacifist. At the same time that he was reducing the size of the army and navy, he was helping to establish the United States Military Academy at West Point, founded in 1802. And when trouble began brewing overseas, he began again to build up the fleet.

Such trouble appeared first in the Mediterranean, off the coast of northern Africa. For years the Barbary states of North Africa—Morocco, Algiers, Tunis, and Tripoli (now part of Libya)—had been demanding protection money from all nations whose ships sailed the Mediterranean. Even Great Britain gave regular contributions to the pirates. During the 1780s and 1790s the United States agreed to treaties providing for annual tribute to the Barbary states, but Jefferson was reluctant to continue this policy of appeasement. "Tribute or war is the usual alternative of these Barbary pirates," he said. "Why not build a navy and decide on war?"

In 1801, the pasha of Tripoli forced Jefferson's hand. Unsatisfied by the American response to his extortionate demands, he ordered the flagpole of the American consulate chopped down—a symbolic declaration of war. Jefferson responded cautiously, building up the American fleet in the region over the next several years. Finally, in 1805, the United States reached an agreement with the pasha that ended American payments of tribute to Tripoli but required the United States to pay a substantial (and humiliating) ransom of $60,000 for the release of American prisoners seized by Barbary pirates.

Conflict with the Courts

Having won control of the executive and legislative branches of government, the Republicans looked with suspicion on the judiciary, which remained largely in the hands of Federalist judges. Soon after Jefferson's first inauguration, his followers in Congress launched an attack on this last preserve of the opposition. Their first step was the repeal of the Judiciary Act of 1801, thus eliminating the judgeships to which Adams had made his "midnight appointments."

The debate over the courts led to one of the most important judicial decisions in the history of the

■ **WEST POINT**
Creating a professional military was an important task for the leaders of the early republic. Without an army, they realized, it would be difficult for the United States to win respect in the world. The establishment of the United States Military Academy at West Point (whose parade ground is pictured here) was, therefore, an important event in the early history of the republic. *(U.S. Military Academy, West Point)*

nation. Federalists had long maintained that the Supreme Court had the authority to nullify acts of Congress (although the Constitution said nothing specifically to support the claim), and the Court itself had actually exercised the power of judicial review in 1796 when it upheld the validity of a law passed by the legislature. But the Court's authority in this area would not be secure, it was clear, until it actually declared a congressional act unconstitutional.

In 1803, in the case of *Marbury* v. *Madison* it did so. William Marbury, one of Adams's "midnight appointments," had been named a justice of the peace in the District of Columbia. But his commission, although signed and sealed, had not been delivered to him before Adams left office. Once Jefferson became president, the new secretary of state, James Madison, was responsible for transmitting appointments. He had refused to hand over the commission. Marbury applied to the Supreme Court for an order directing

Madison to perform his official duty. In its historic ruling, the Court found that Marbury had a right to his commission but that the Court had no authority to order Madison to deliver it. On the surface, therefore, the decision was a victory for the administration. But of much greater importance than the relatively insignificant matter of Marbury's commission was the Court's reasoning in the decision.

The original Judiciary Act of 1789 had given the Court the power to compel executive officials to act in such matters as the delivery of commissions, and it was on that basis that Marbury had filed his suit. But the Court ruled that Congress had exceeded its authority in creating that statute: that the Constitution had defined the powers of the judiciary, and that the legislature had no right to expand them. The relevant section of the 1789 act was therefore void. In seeming to deny its own authority, the Court was in fact radically enlarging it. The justices had repudiated a relatively minor power (the power to force the delivery of a commission) by asserting a vastly greater one (the power to nullify an act of Congress).

The chief justice of the United States at the time of the ruling (and until 1835) was John Marshall, one of the towering figures in the history of American law. A leading Federalist and prominent Virginia lawyer, he had served John Adams as secretary of state. (It had been Marshall, ironically, who had neglected to deliver Marbury's commission in the closing hours of the administration.) In 1801, just before leaving office, Adams had appointed him chief justice, and almost immediately Marshall established himself as the dominant figure on the Court, shaping virtually all its most important rulings—including, of course, *Marbury* v. *Madison.* Through a succession of Republican administrations, he battled to give the federal government unity and strength. In so doing, he established the judiciary as a branch of government coequal with the executive and the legislature—a position that the founders of the republic had never clearly indicated it should occupy.

Jefferson recognized the threat that an assertive judiciary could pose to his policies. Even while the *Marbury* case was still pending, he was preparing for a renewed assault on this last Federalist stronghold. He urged Congress to impeach obstructive judges, and Congress attempted to oblige him. After successfully removing from office a district judge, John Pickering of New Hampshire (on the perhaps specious grounds that he was insane and thus unfit for office), the Republicans targeted a justice of the Supreme Court itself: Justice Samuel Chase, a highly partisan Federalist. Chase had certainly been injudicious; he had, for example, delivered stridently partisan speeches from the bench. But he had committed no crime. Some Republicans argued, however, that impeachment was not merely a criminal proceeding. Congress could properly impeach a judge for political reasons—for obstructing the other branches of the government and disregarding the will of the people.

At Jefferson's urging, the House impeached Chase and sent him to trial before the Senate early in 1805. But Republican leaders were unable to get the necessary two-thirds' vote for conviction in the Senate. Chase's acquittal set an important precedent. It helped establish that impeachment would not become a purely political weapon, that something more than partisan disagreement would have to underlie the process. Marshall remained secure in his position as chief justice. And the judiciary survived as a powerful force within the government—more often than not ruling on behalf of the centralizing, expansionary policies that the Republicans had been trying to reverse.

DOUBLING THE NATIONAL DOMAIN

In the same year that Jefferson became president of the United States, Napoleon Bonaparte made himself ruler of France with the title of first consul. In the year that Jefferson was reelected, Napoleon named himself emperor. The two men had little in common. Yet for a time they were of great help to each other in international politics—until Napoleon's ambitions moved from Europe to America and created conflict and estrangement.

Jefferson and Napoleon

Having failed in a grandiose plan to seize India from the British Empire, Napoleon began turning his imperial ambitions in a new direction: he began to dream of restoring French power in the New World. The territory east of the Mississippi, which France had ceded to Great Britain in 1763, was now mostly part of the United States and lost to France forever. But Napoleon wanted to regain the lands west of the Mississippi, which now belonged to Spain, over which Napoleon now exercised heavy influence. Under the secret Treaty of San Ildefonso of 1800 between the French and the Spanish, France regained title to Louisiana, which included almost the whole of the Mississippi Valley to the west of the river, plus New Orleans near its mouth. The Louisiana Territory would, Napoleon hoped, become the heart of a great French empire in America.

Also part of Napoleon's empire in the New World were the sugar-rich and strategically valuable West Indian islands that still belonged to France—Guadeloupe, Martinique, and above all Santo Domingo. But unrest among the Caribbean slaves posed a threat to Napoleon's hopes for the islands. Africans in Santo Domingo (inspired by the French Revolution as some American slaves had been inspired by the American Revolution) revolted and created a republic of their own, under the remarkable black leader Toussaint

L'Ouverture. Taking advantage of a truce in his war with England, Napoleon sent an army to the West Indies. It crushed the insurrection and restored French authority; but the incident was an early sign of the problems Napoleon would have in realizing his ambitions in America.

Jefferson was unaware at first of Napoleon's imperial ambitions in America, and for a time he pursued a foreign policy that reflected his well-known admiration for France. He appointed as American minister to Paris the ardently pro-French Robert R. Livingston. He worked to secure ratification of the Franco-American settlement of 1800 and began observing the terms of the treaty even before it was ratified. The Adams administration had joined with the British in recognizing and supporting the rebel regime of Toussaint L'Ouverture in Santo Domingo; Jefferson assured the French minister in Washington that the American people, especially those of the slaveholding states, did not approve of the black revolutionary, who was setting a bad example for their own slaves. He even implied that the United States might join with France in putting down the rebellion (although nothing ever came of the suggestion).

Jefferson began to reconsider his position toward France when he heard rumors of the secret transfer of Louisiana. "It completely reverses all the political relations of the U.S.," he wrote to Livingston in April 1802. Always before, America had looked to France as its "natural friend." But there was on the earth "one single spot" whose possessor was "our natural and habitual enemy." That spot was New Orleans, the outlet through which the produce of the fast-growing western regions of the United States traveled to the markets of the world. If France should actually seize New Orleans, Jefferson said, then "we must marry ourselves to the British fleet and nation."

Jefferson was even more alarmed when, in the fall of 1802, he learned that the Spanish intendant at New Orleans (who still governed the city, since the French had not yet taken formal possession of the region) had announced a disturbing new regulation. American ships sailing the Mississippi River had for many years been accustomed to depositing their cargoes in New Orleans for transfer to oceangoing vessels. The intendant now forbade the practice—even though Spain had guaranteed Americans that right in the Pinckney Treaty of 1795—thus effectively closing the lower Mississippi to American shippers.

Westerners demanded that the federal government do something to reopen the river. The president faced a dilemma. If he yielded to the frontier clamor and tried to change the policy by force, he would run the risk of a major war with France. If he ignored the westerners' demands, he might lose political support. But Jefferson saw another solution. He instructed Robert Livingston, the American ambassador in Paris, to negotiate the purchase of New Orleans. Livingston on his own authority proposed that the French sell the United States the vast western part of Louisiana as well.

In the meantime, Jefferson persuaded Congress to appropriate funds for an expansion of the army and the construction of a river fleet, and he deliberately gave the impression that American forces might soon descend on New Orleans and that the United States might form an alliance with Great Britain if the problems with France were not resolved. Perhaps that was why Napoleon suddenly decided to accept Livingston's proposal and offer the United States the entire Louisiana Territory.

Napoleon had good reasons for the decision. His plans for an American empire had already gone seriously awry, partly because a yellow fever epidemic had wiped out much of the French army in the New World and partly because the expeditionary force Napoleon wished to send to reinforce them and take possession of Louisiana had been frozen into a Dutch harbor through the winter of 1802–1803. By the time the harbor thawed in the spring of 1803, Napoleon was preparing for a renewed war in Europe. He would not, he realized, have the resources now to secure an American empire.

The Louisiana Purchase

Faced with Napoleon's startling proposal, Livingston and James Monroe, whom Jefferson had sent to Paris to assist in the negotiations, had to decide first whether they should even consider making a treaty for the purchase of the entire Louisiana Territory, since they had not been authorized by their government to do so. But fearful that Napoleon might withdraw the offer, they decided to proceed without further instructions from home. After some haggling over the price—Napoleon's negotiator Barbe-Marbois asked for and got somewhat more than the minimum

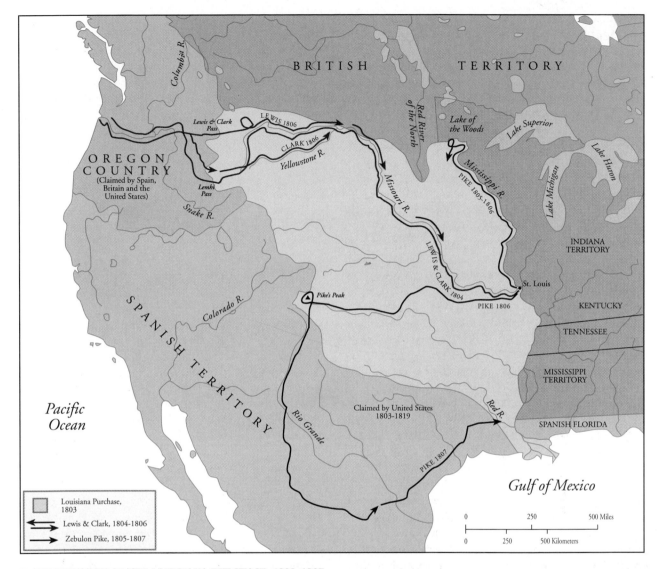

■ **EXPLORATION OF THE LOUISIANA PURCHASE, 1803–1807**
The Louisiana Purchase doubled the size of the United States, but Americans did not really know what they had bought. In 1804, Thomas Jefferson sent an expedition led by Meriwether Lewis and William Clark to investigate the new territories. Lewis and Clark's party, with their Shoshone guide Sacajawea, traveled up the Missouri River from St. Louis, reached the Pacific coast and returned with a wealth of information. In 1806, Lieutenant Zebulon Pike led a similar expedition into the southwest.

amount Napoleon had set—Livingston and Monroe signed the agreement on April 30, 1803.

By the terms of the treaty, the United States was to pay a total of 80 million francs ($15 million) to the French government. The United States was also to grant certain exclusive commercial privileges to France in the port of New Orleans and was to incorporate the residents of Louisiana into the Union with the same rights and privileges as other citizens. The boundaries of the purchase were not clearly defined; the treaty simply specified that Louisiana would occupy the "same extent" as it had when France and Spain had owned it.

In Washington, the president was both pleased and embarrassed when he received the treaty. He was pleased with the terms of the bargain but uncertain

UNDER MY WINGS EVERY THING PROSPERS

■ **NEW ORLEANS IN 1803**
Because of its location near the mouth of the Mississippi River, New Orleans was the principal port of western North America in the early nineteenth century. Through it, western farmers shipped their produce to markets in the east and Europe. This 1803 painting celebrates the American acquisition of the city from France as part of the Louisiana Purchase. *(Chicago Historical Society)*

whether the United States had authority to accept it, since he had always insisted that the federal government could rightfully exercise only those powers explicitly assigned to it. Nowhere did the Constitution say anything about the acquisition of new territory. But Jefferson's advisers persuaded him that his treaty-making power under the Constitution would justify the purchase of Louisiana. The president finally agreed, trusting, as he said, "that the good sense of our country will correct the evil of loose construction when it shall produce ill effects." The Republican Congress promptly approved the treaty and appropriated money to implement its provisions. Finally, late in 1803, the French assumed formal control of Louisiana from Spain just long enough to turn the territory over to General James Wilkinson, the commissioner of the United States and the commander of a

small occupation force. In New Orleans, beneath a bright December sun, United States soldiers lowered the recently raised French tricolor and raised the American flag in its place.

The government organized the Louisiana Territory much as it had organized the Northwest Territory, with the assumption that its various territories would eventually become states. The first of these was admitted to the Union as the state of Louisiana in 1812.

Lewis and Clark Explore the West

Meanwhile, several ambitious explorations were revealing the geography of the far-flung new territory to white Americans, few of whom had ever ventured much beyond the Mississippi River. In 1803, even before Napoleon's offer to sell Louisiana, Jefferson helped plan an expedition that was to cross the continent to the Pacific Ocean, gather geographical facts, and investigate prospects for trade with the Indians. He named as its leader his private secretary and Virginia neighbor, the thirty-two-year-old Meriwether Lewis, a veteran of Indian wars skilled in the ways of the wilderness. Lewis chose as a colleague the twenty-eight-year-old William Clark, who—like George Rogers Clark, his older brother—was an experienced frontiersman and Indian fighter. In the spring of 1804, Lewis and Clark, with a company of four dozen men, started up the Missouri River from St. Louis. With the Shoshone woman Sacajawea as their guide, they eventually crossed the Rocky Mountains, descended the Snake and Columbia Rivers, and in the late autumn of 1805 camped on the Pacific coast. In September 1806, they were back in St. Louis with elaborate records of the geography and the Indian civilizations they had observed along the way, and a lengthy diary recounting their experiences.

While Lewis and Clark were still on their journey, Jefferson dispatched other explorers to other parts of the Louisiana Territory. Lieutenant Zebulon Montgomery Pike, twenty-six years old, led an expedition in the fall of 1805 from St. Louis into the upper Mississippi Valley. In the summer of 1806, he set out again up the valley of the Arkansas River and into what later became Colorado, where he encountered, but failed in his attempt to climb, the peak that now bears his name. His account of his western travels created an enduring (and inaccurate) impression among many Americans in the East that the land between the Missouri River and the Rockies was an uncultivable desert. Pike believed it ought to be left forever to the nomadic Indian tribes.

The Burr Conspiracy

Jefferson's triumphant reelection in 1804 suggested that most of the nation approved the new territorial acquisition. But some New England Federalists raged against it. They realized that the more the West grew and the more new states joined the Union, the less power the Federalists and their region would retain. In Massachusetts, a group of the most extreme Federalists, known as the Essex Junto, concluded that the only recourse for New England was to secede from the Union and form a separate "Northern Confederacy." If a northern confederacy was to have any hope

for lasting success as a separate nation, the Federalists believed, it would have to include New York and New Jersey as well as New England. But the leading Federalist in New York, Alexander Hamilton, refused to support the secessionist scheme. "Dismemberment of our empire," he wrote, "will be a clear sacrifice of great positive advantages without any counterbalancing good, administering no relief to our real disease, which is democracy."

Federalists in New York then turned to Hamilton's greatest political rival: Vice President Aaron Burr, a politician without prospects in his own party, because Jefferson had never forgiven him for the 1800 election deadlock. Burr accepted a Federalist proposal that he become their candidate for governor of New York in 1804, and there were rumors (unsupported by any evidence) that he had also agreed to support the Federalist plans for secession. Hamilton accused Burr of plotting treason and made numerous private remarks, widely reported in the press, about Burr's "despicable" character. When Burr lost the election, he blamed his defeat on Hamilton's malevolence. "These things must have an end," Burr wrote. He challenged Hamilton to a duel.

Dueling had by then already fallen into some disrepute in America, but many people still considered it a legitimate institution for settling matters of "honor." Hamilton feared that refusing Burr's challenge would brand him a coward. And so, on a July morning in 1804, the two men met at Weehawken, New Jersey. Hamilton was mortally wounded; he died the next day.

The resourceful and charismatic Burr was now a political outcast who had to flee New York to avoid an indictment for murder. He found new outlets for his ambitions in the West. Even before the duel, he had begun corresponding with prominent white settlers in the Southwest, especially with General James Wilkinson, now governor of the Louisiana Territory. Burr and Wilkinson, it seems clear, hoped to lead an expedition that would capture Mexico from the Spanish. "Mexico glitters in all our eyes," Burr wrote; "the word is all we wait for." But there were also rumors that they wanted to separate the Southwest from the United States and create a western empire that Burr would rule. There is little evidence that these rumors were true.

Whether the rumors were true or not, many of Burr's opponents—including, ultimately, Jefferson himself—chose to believe them. When Burr led a group of armed followers down the Ohio River by boat in 1806, disturbing reports flowed into Washington (the most alarming from Wilkinson, who had suddenly turned against Burr and who now informed the president that treason was afoot) that an attack on New Orleans was imminent. Jefferson ordered Burr and his men arrested as traitors. Burr was brought to Richmond for trial. Determined to win a conviction, Jefferson carefully managed the government's case from Washington. But Chief Justice Marshall, presiding over the trial on circuit duty, limited the evidence the government could present and defined the charge in such a way that the jury had little choice but to acquit. Burr was free, but his political reputation was permanently destroyed. For several years, he lived in self-imposed exile in Europe. In 1812, he returned to America and established a successful legal practice in New York. He lived long enough to hail the Texas revolution of 1836 as the fruition of the movement to "liberate" Mexico that he had tried to launch.

The Burr "conspiracy" was in part the story of a single man's soaring ambitions and flamboyant personality. But it was also a symbol of the larger perils still facing the new nation. With a central government that remained deliberately weak, with vast tracts of land only nominally controlled by the United States, with ambitious political leaders willing, if necessary, to circumvent normal channels in their search for power, the legitimacy of the federal government, and indeed the existence of the United States as a stable and united nation, remained to be fully established.

EXPANSION AND WAR

Two very different conflicts were taking shape in the later years of Thomas Jefferson's presidency that would, together, draw the United States into a difficult and frustrating war. One was the continuing tension in Europe, which in 1803 escalated once again into a full-scale conflict (the Napoleonic Wars). As the fighting escalated, both the British and the French took steps to prevent the United States from trading with (and thus assisting) the other.

The other conflict was in North America itself, a result of the ceaseless westward expansion of white settlement, which was now stretching to the Mississippi River and beyond, colliding again with Native American populations committed to protecting their lands and their trade from intruders. In both the North and the South, the threatened tribes mobilized to resist white encroachments. They began as well to forge connections with British forces in Canada and Spanish forces in Florida. The Indian conflict on land therefore became intertwined with the European conflict on the seas, and ultimately helped cause the War of 1812, an unpopular conflict with ambiguous results.

Conflict on the Seas

The early nineteenth century saw a dramatic expansion of American shipping in the Atlantic. Britain retained significant naval superiority, but the British merchant marine was preoccupied with commerce in Europe and Asia and devoted little energy to trade with America. Thus the United States stepped effectively into the void and developed one of the most important merchant marines in the world, which soon controlled a large proportion of the trade between Europe and the West Indies.

In 1805, at the Battle of Trafalgar, a British fleet virtually destroyed what was left of the French navy. Because France could no longer challenge the British at sea, Napoleon now chose to pressure England through economic rather than naval means. The result was what he called the Continental System, designed to close the European continent to British trade. Napoleon issued a series of decrees (one in Berlin in 1806 and another in Milan in 1807) barring British ships and neutral ships that had called at British ports from landing their cargoes at any European port controlled by France or its allies. The British government replied to Napoleon's decrees by establishing—through a series of "orders in council"—a blockade of the European coast. The blockade required that any goods being shipped to Napoleon's Europe be carried either in British vessels or in neutral vessels stopping at British ports— precisely what Napoleon's policies forbade.

American ships were caught between Napoleon's Berlin and Milan decrees and Britain's orders in council. If they sailed directly for the European continent, they risked being captured by the British navy; if they sailed by way of a British port, they risked seizure by the French. Both of the warring powers were violating America's rights as a neutral nation. But most Americans considered the British, with their greater sea power, the worse offender. British ships pounced on Yankee merchantmen all over the ocean; the French could do so only in European ports. Particularly infuriating to Americans, British vessels stopped United States ships on the high seas and seized sailors off the decks, making them victims of "impressment."

Impressment

The British navy—with its floggings, low pay, and terrible shipboard conditions—was known as a "floating hell" to its sailors. Few volunteered. Most had to be "impressed" (forced) into the service. At every opportunity they deserted. By 1807, many of these deserters had joined the American merchant marine or the American navy. To check this loss of vital manpower, the British claimed the right to stop and search American merchant ships (although at first not naval vessels) and reimpress deserters. They did not claim the right to take native-born Americans, but they did claim the right to seize naturalized Americans born on British soil. In practice, the British navy often made no such distinctions, impressing British deserters and native-born Americans alike into service.

In the summer of 1807, the British went to more provocative extremes in an incident involving a vessel of the American navy. Sailing from Norfolk, with several alleged deserters from the British navy among the crew, the American naval frigate *Chesapeake* encountered the British ship *Leopard.* When the American commander, James Barron, refused to allow the British to search the *Chesapeake,* the *Leopard* opened fire. Barron had no choice but to surrender, and a boarding party from the *Leopard* dragged four men off the American frigate.

When news of the *Chesapeake-Leopard* incident reached the United States, there was great popular clamor for revenge. If Congress had been in session, it might have declared war. But Jefferson and Madison tried to maintain the peace. Jefferson expelled all British warships from American waters, to lessen the likelihood of future incidents. Then he sent instructions to his minister in England, James Monroe, to demand that the British government renounce impressment. The British government disavowed the action of the officer responsible for the *Chesapeake-Leopard* affair and recalled him; it offered compensation for those killed and wounded in the incident;

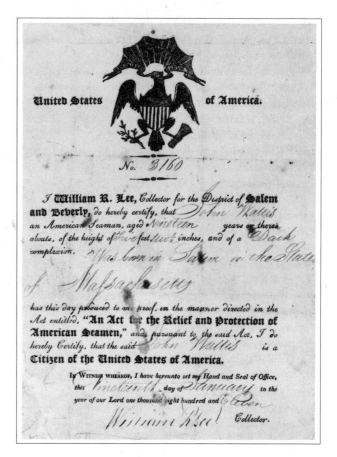

■ PROTECTION FROM IMPRESSMENT
To protect American sailors from British impressment, the federal government issued official certificates of United States citizenship—known as "protection papers." But British naval officers, aware that such documents were often forged, frequently ignored them. *(Essex Institute, Salem, Massachusetts)*

and it promised to return three of the captured sailors (one of the original four had been hanged). But the British refused to renounce impressment.

"Peaceable Coercion"

In an effort to prevent future incidents that might bring the nation again to the brink of war, Jefferson presented a drastic measure to Congress when it reconvened late in 1807. The Republican legislators promptly enacted it into law. It was known as the Embargo, and it became one of the most controversial political issues of its time. The Embargo prohibited American ships from leaving the United States for any foreign port anywhere in the world. (If it had specified only British and French ports, Jefferson reasoned, it could have been evaded by means of false clearance papers.) Congress also passed a "force act" to give the government power to enforce the Embargo.

The law was widely evaded, but it was effective enough to create a serious depression through most of the nation. Hardest hit were the merchants and shipowners of the Northeast, most of them Federalists. Their once lucrative shipping business was at a virtual standstill, and they were losing money every day. They became convinced that Jefferson had acted unconstitutionally.

The election of 1808 came in the midst of the Embargo-induced depression. James Madison, Jefferson's secretary of state and political ally, won the presidency. But the Federalists ran much more strongly than they had in 1804. The Embargo was clearly a growing political liability, and Jefferson decided to back down. A few days before leaving office, he approved a bill ending his experiment with what he called "peaceable coercion."

To replace the Embargo, Congress passed the Non-Intercourse Act just before Madison took office. The new law reopened trade with all nations but Great Britain and France. A year later, in 1810, Congress allowed the Non-Intercourse Act to expire and replaced it with Macon's Bill No. 2, which reopened free commercial relations with Britain and France, but authorized the president to prohibit commerce with either belligerent if one should continue violating neutral shipping after the other had stopped. Napoleon, in an effort to induce the United States to reimpose the Embargo against Britain, announced that France would no longer interfere with American shipping. Madison announced that an embargo against Great Britain alone would automatically go into effect early in 1811 unless Britain renounced its restrictions on American shipping.

In time, the new, limited embargo, although less well enforced than the earlier one had been, hurt the economy of England enough that the government repealed its blockade of Europe. But the repeal came too late to prevent war. In any case, naval policies were only part of the reason for tensions between Britain and the United States.

Conflicts in the West

Given the ruthlessness with which white settlers in North America had dislodged Indian tribes to make room for expanding settlement, it was hardly surprising that ever since the Revolution many Native Americans had continued to look to England—which had historically attempted to limit western expansion—for protection. The British in Canada, for their part, had relied on the tribes as partners in the lucrative fur trade and as potential military allies.

There had been relative peace in the Northwest for over a decade after Jay's Treaty and Anthony Wayne's victory over the tribes at Fallen Timbers in 1794. But the 1807 war crisis following the *Chesapeake-Leopard* incident revived the conflict between Indians and white settlers. Two important (and very different) leaders emerged to oppose one another in the conflict: William Henry Harrison and Tecumseh.

The Virginia-born Harrison, already a veteran Indian fighter at age twenty-six, went to Washington as the congressional delegate from the Northwest Territory in 1799. He was a committed advocate of growth and development in the western lands, and he was largely responsible for the passage in 1800 of the so-called Harrison Land Law, which enabled white settlers to acquire farms from the public domain on much easier terms than before.

In 1801, Jefferson appointed Harrison governor of the Indiana Territory to administer the president's proposed solution to the "Indian problem." Jefferson offered the Native Americans a choice: they could convert themselves into settled farmers and assimilate—become a part of white society; or they could migrate to the west of the Mississippi. In either case, they would have to give up their claims to their tribal lands in the Northwest.

Jefferson considered the assimilation policy a benign alternative to continuing conflict between Indians and white settlers, conflict he assumed the tribes were destined to lose. But to the tribes, the new policy seemed far from benign, especially given the bludgeonlike efficiency with which Harrison set out to implement it. He played off one tribe against another and used threats, bribes, trickery, and whatever other tactics he felt would help him conclude treaties. By 1807, the United States had extracted from reluctant tribal leaders treaty rights to eastern Michigan, southern Indiana, and most of Illinois. Meanwhile, in the Southwest, white Americans were taking millions of acres from other tribes in Georgia, Tennessee, and Mississippi. The Indians wanted desperately to resist, but the separate tribes were helpless by themselves against the power of the United

States. They might have accepted their fate passively but for the emergence of two new factors.

One factor was the policy of the British authorities in Canada. After the *Chesapeake* incident and the surge of anti-British feeling throughout the United States, the British colonial authorities began to expect an American invasion of Canada and took desperate measures for their own defense. Among those measures were efforts to renew friendship with the Indians—friendship badly frayed by the Battle of Fallen Timbers, in which the British had refused to provide assistance to the tribes—and efforts to provide them with increased supplies. "Are the Indians to be employed in case of a rupture with the United States?" the lieutenant governor of upper Canada asked Sir James Craig, governor general of the province, in 1807. The governor replied: "If we do not employ them, there cannot exist a moment's doubt that they will be employed against us."

Tecumseh and the Prophet

The second, and more important, factor intensifying the border conflict was the rise of two remarkable Native American leaders. One was Tenskwatawa, a charismatic religious leader and orator known as the Prophet. He had experienced a mystical awakening in the process of recovering from alcoholism. Having freed himself from what he considered the evil effects of white culture, he began to speak to his people of the superior virtues of Indian civilization and the sinfulness and corruption of the white world. In the process, he inspired a religious revival that spread through numerous tribes and helped unite them. Like Neolin before him, and like his contemporary to the east, Handsome Lake, Tenskwatawa demonstrated the power of religious leaders to mobilize Indians behind political and military objectives. The Prophet's headquarters at the confluence of

■ **THE TREATY OF GREENVILLE**
An unknown member of General Anthony Wayne's staff painted this scene of Indians and U.S. officers signing a treaty in Greenville, Ohio in 1795, by which twelve tribes agreed to surrender the southern half of the territory to the United States in exchange for payment of about 1/8 cent per acre. *(Chicago Historical Society)*

■ **TECUMSEH**

Tecumseh's efforts to unite the tribes of the Mississippi Valley against further white encroachments on their lands led him ultimately into an alliance with the British after the Battle of Tippecanoe in 1811. In the War of 1812, he was commissioned a brigadier general by the British and fought against the United States in the Battle of the Thames. He is shown in this painting (by the daughter of an English officer stationed near Detroit) wearing British military trousers.

(Fort Malden National Historical Park)

Tippecanoe Creek and the Wabash River (known as Prophetstown) became a sacred place for people of many tribes and attracted thousands of Indians from throughout the Midwest. Out of their common religious experiences, they began to consider joint political and military efforts as well.

The Prophet's brother Tecumseh—"the Shooting Star," chief of the Shawnees—emerged as the leader of these more secular efforts. Tecumseh understood, as few other Indian leaders had, that only through united action could the tribes hope to resist the advance of white civilization. Beginning in 1809, after tribes in Indiana had ceded vast lands to the United States, he set out to unite all the Indians of the Mississippi Valley, north and south. Together, he promised, they would halt white expansion, recover the whole Northwest, and make the Ohio River the boundary between the United States and the Indian country. He maintained that Harrison and others, by negotiating treaties with individual tribes, had obtained no real title to land. The land belonged to all the tribes; none of them could rightfully cede any of it without the consent of the others. "The Great Spirit gave this great island to his red children. He placed the whites on the other side of the big water," Tecumseh told Harrison. "They were not contented with their own, but came to take ours from us. They have driven us from the sea to the lakes—we can go no farther."

In 1811, Tecumseh left Prophetstown and traveled down the Mississippi to visit the tribes of the South and persuade them to join the alliance. During his absence, Governor Harrison saw a chance to destroy the growing influence of the two Native American leaders. He camped near Prophetstown with 1,000 soldiers, and on November 7, 1811, he provoked a fight. Although the white forces suffered losses as heavy as those of the natives, Harrison drove off the Indians and burned the town. The Battle of Tippecanoe (named for the creek near the fighting) disillusioned many of the Prophet's followers, who had believed that his magic would protect them. Tecumseh returned to find the confederacy in disarray. But there were still many warriors eager for combat, and by the spring of 1812 they were active along the frontier, from Michigan to Mississippi, raiding white settlements and terrifying white settlers.

The bloodshed along the western borders was largely a result of the Indians' own initiative, but Britain's agents in Canada had encouraged and helped supply the uprising. To Harrison and most white residents of the regions, there seemed only one way to make the West safe for Americans. That was to drive the British out of Canada and annex that province to the United States—a goal that many westerners had long cherished for other reasons as well.

A Fever for War

While white "frontiersmen" in the North demanded the conquest of Canada, those in the South wanted

■ **JAMES AND DOLLEY MADISON**

James Madison may have been the most brilliant of the early leaders of the republic, but he was also one of the most serious and humorless, as this grim portrait suggests. His wife (born Dolley Payne in North Carolina and raised a Quaker in Virginia) was twenty-six when she married the forty-three-year-old Madison in 1794. Her charm and social grace made her one of her husband's greatest political assets. She acted as hostess for Thomas Jefferson, a widower, while her husband was secretary of state. And she presided over a lively social life during her eight years in the White House as first lady. *(New-York Historical Society)*

the United States to acquire Spanish Florida, a territory that included the present state of Florida and the southern areas of what are now Alabama, Mississippi, and Louisiana. The territory was a continuing threat to whites in the southern United States. Slaves escaped across the Florida border; Indians in Florida launched frequent raids north into white settlements along the border. But white southerners also coveted Florida because through it ran rivers that could provide residents of the Southwest with access to valuable ports on the Gulf of Mexico.

In 1810, American settlers in West Florida (an area that is part of Mississippi and Louisiana today) seized the Spanish fort at Baton Rouge and asked the federal government to annex the territory to the United States. President Madison happily agreed and then began planning to get the rest of Florida, too. The de-

sire for Florida became yet another motivation for war with Britain. Spain was Britain's ally, and a war with Britain might provide a pretext for taking Spanish territory.

But sentiment for war with Britain was growing for other reasons as well, reasons closely tied to the Republican vision of America and what Jefferson and many others believed were the potential threats to that vision. Great Britain's growing restrictions on American commerce, of which the impressment of sailors was only the most obnoxious example, were threatening to cut off American farmers from access to world markets. Farmers in the United States were already growing much more food than the domestic market could absorb. If they could not sell their surplus abroad, the Jeffersonians feared, one of two dangerous things would happen. One unhappy alternative was for farm prices to plummet and for many farmers to leave the land and flock to the towns and cities in search of work. The vision of a republic of sturdy agrarian landowners would be in jeopardy, and America would instead face a future much like that of Europe—a rising urban population, increasing poverty and vagrancy, and a dwindling agrarian world. Another equally unhappy possibility was that America would expand its own domestic market for agricultural goods. That would keep the farmers on the land, but it would require the development of the kind of large-scale urban industrial life that the Jeffersonians disdained. Only continued access to world markets, in other words, could sustain the republican vision of a sturdy, agrarian nation.

By 1812, therefore, war fever was growing in many areas of the United States, spurred by territorial appetites in the North and the South and by Republican fears of the threats to their vision of their nation. In the congressional elections of 1810, voters elected a large number of representatives of both parties eager for war with Britain. They became known as the "war hawks." Some of them were ardent nationalists fired by passion for territorial expansion—among them two men, both recently elected to the House of Representatives, who would play a great role in national politics for much of the next four decades: Henry Clay of Kentucky and John C. Calhoun of South Carolina. Others were men impassioned in their defense of Republican values. Together, they formed a powerful coalition in favor of war.

Clay became Speaker of the House in 1811, and he filled committees with those who shared his eagerness for war. He appointed Calhoun to the crucial Committee on Foreign Affairs, and both men began agitating for the conquest of Canada. Madison still hoped for peace. But he shared the concerns of other Republicans about the dangers to American trade, and he was losing control of Congress. On June 18, 1812, he gave in to the pressure and approved a declaration of war against Britain.

THE WAR OF 1812

Preoccupied with their struggle against Napoleon in Europe, the British were not eager for an open conflict with the United States. Even after the Americans declared war, Britain largely ignored them for a time. But in the fall of 1812, Napoleon launched a catastrophic campaign against Russia that left his army in disarray and his power in Europe diminished. By late 1813, with the French Empire on its way to final defeat, Britain was able to turn its military attention to America.

Battles with the Tribes

Americans entered the War of 1812 with great enthusiasm, but events on the battlefield soon cooled their ardor. In the summer of 1812, American forces invaded Canada through Detroit. They soon had to retreat back to Detroit and in August surrendered the fort there. Other invasion efforts also failed. In the meantime, Fort Dearborn (Chicago) fell before an Indian attack.

Things went only slightly better for the United States on the seas. At first, American frigates won some spectacular victories over British warships, and American privateers destroyed or captured many British merchant ships, occasionally braving the coastal waters of the British Isles themselves and burning vessels within sight of the shore. But by 1813, the British navy—now less preoccupied with Napoleon—was counterattacking effectively, driving the American frigates to cover and imposing a blockade on the United States.

The United States did, however, achieve significant early military successes on the Great Lakes. First, the Americans took command of Lake Ontario, which permitted them to raid and burn York (now Toronto), the capital of Canada. American forces then seized control of Lake Erie, mainly through the work of the youthful Oliver Hazard Perry, who engaged and dispersed a British fleet at Put-In Bay on September 10, 1813. This made possible, at last, another invasion of Canada by way of Detroit, which Americans could now reach easily by water. William Henry Harrison, the American commander in the West, pushed up the river Thames into upper Canada and on October 5, 1813, won a victory notable for the death of Tecumseh, who was serving as a brigadier general in the British army. The Battle of the Thames weakened and disheartened the Native Americans of the Northwest and greatly diminished their ability to defend their claims to the region.

In the meantime, another white military leader was striking an even harder blow at the tribes of the

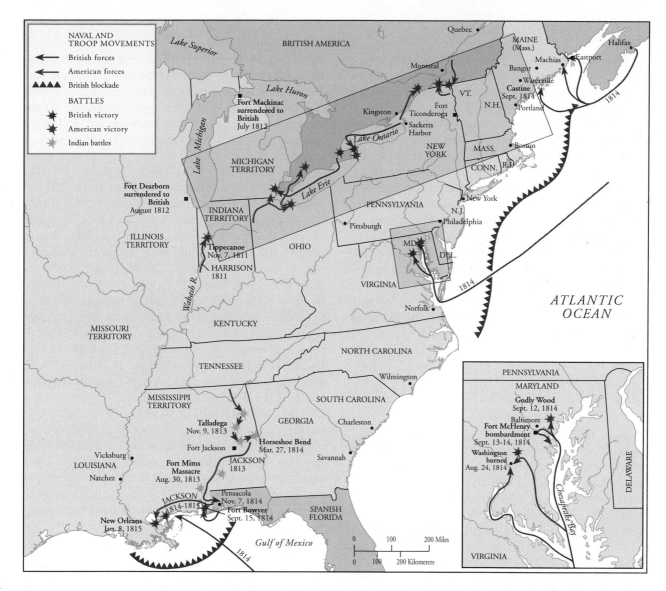

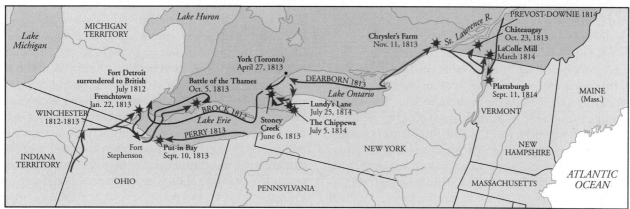

■ THE WAR OF 1812

The War of 1812 spanned the North American continent. While the British blockaded the Atlantic coast, the American navy won acclaim on the Great Lakes. In the Chesapeake, a British expeditionary force embarrassed the United States by burning Washington. In the southwest, Andrew Jackson crushed the Creek Nation in the Mississippi Territory and then repelled a British assault against New Orleans. News of Jackson's victory at New Orleans helped crystallize northern opinion against the Federalists.

Southwest. The Creeks, whom Tecumseh had aroused on a visit to the South and whom the Spanish had supplied with weapons, had been attacking white settlers near the Florida border. Andrew Jackson, a wealthy Tennessee planter and a general in the state militia, temporarily abandoned plans for an invasion of Florida and set off in pursuit of them. On March 27, 1814, in the Battle of Horseshoe Bend, Jackson's men took terrible revenge on the Indians—slaughtering women and children along with warriors—and broke the resistance of the Creeks. The tribe agreed to cede most of its lands to the United States and retreated westward, farther into the interior. The battle also won Jackson a commission as major general in the United States Army, and in that capacity he led his men farther south into Florida and, on November 7, 1814, seized the Spanish fort at Pensacola.

Battles with the British

The victories over the tribes were not enough to win the war. After the surrender of Napoleon in 1814, England prepared to invade the United States. A British armada sailed up the Patuxent River from Chesapeake Bay and landed an army that marched a short distance overland to Bladensburg, on the outskirts of Washington, where it dispersed a poorly trained force of American militiamen. On August 24, 1814, the British troops entered Washington and put the government to flight. Then they set fire to several public buildings, including the White House, in retaliation for the earlier American burning of the Canadian capital at York. This was the low point of American fortunes in the war.

Leaving Washington in partial ruins, the invading army proceeded up the bay toward Baltimore. But Baltimore harbor, guarded by Fort McHenry, was prepared. To block the approaching fleet, the American garrison had sunk several ships to clog the entry to the harbor, thus forcing the British to bombard the fort from a distance. Through the night of September 13, Francis Scott Key, a Washington lawyer who was on board one of the British ships trying to secure the release of an American prisoner, watched the bombardment. The next morning, "by the dawn's early light," he could see the flag on the fort still flying; he recorded his pride in the moment by scribbling a poem—"The Star-Spangled Banner"—on the back of an envelope. The British withdrew from Baltimore, and Key's words were soon set to the tune of an old English drinking song. In 1931, "The Star-Spangled Banner" became the official national anthem.

Meanwhile, American forces repelled another British invasion in northern New York at the Battle of Plattsburgh, on September 11, 1814, which turned back a much larger British naval and land force and secured the northern border of the United States. In the South, a formidable array of battle-hardened British veterans, fresh from the campaign against the French in Spain, landed below New Orleans and prepared to advance north up the Mississippi. Awaiting the British was Andrew Jackson with a motley collection of Tennesseans, Kentuckians, Creoles, blacks, pirates, and regular army troops behind earthen fortifications. On January 8, 1815, the British advanced, but their exposed forces were no match for Jackson's well-protected men. After the Americans had repulsed several waves of attackers, the British finally retreated, leaving behind 700 dead (including their commander, Sir Edward Pakenham), 1,400 wounded, and 500 prisoners. Jackson's losses were eight killed and thirteen wounded. Only later did news reach North America that the United States and Britain had signed a peace treaty several weeks before the Battle of New Orleans.

The Revolt of New England

With a few notable exceptions, such as the Battles of Put-In Bay and New Orleans, the military operations of the United States between 1812 and 1815 consisted of a series of humiliating failures. As a result, the American government faced increasing popular opposition as the contest dragged on. In New England, opposition both to the war and to the Republican government that was waging it was so extreme that some Federalists celebrated British victories. In Congress, in the meantime, the Republicans had continual trouble with the Federalist opposition, led by a young congressman from New Hampshire, Daniel Webster, who missed no opportunity to embarrass the administration.

■ **THE BURNING OF WASHINGTON**

This dramatic engraving somewhat exaggerates the extent of the blazes in Washington when the British occupied the city in August 1814. But the invaders did set fire to the Capitol, the White House, and other public buildings in retaliation for the American burning of the Canadian capital at York. *(Bettmann)*

■ **THE BOMBARDMENT OF FORT MCHENRY**

The British bombardment of Fort McHenry in Baltimore harbor in September 1814 was of modest importance to the outcome of the War of 1812. It is remembered as the occasion for Francis Scott Key to write his poem "The Star-Spangled Banner," which recorded his sentiments at seeing an American flag still flying over the fort "by the dawn's early light."

(I. N. Phelps Stokes Collection of American Historical Prints, The New York Public Library)

By now the Federalists were a minority in the country as a whole, but they were still the majority party in New England. Some of them began to dream again of creating a separate nation in that region, which they could dominate and in which they could escape what they saw as the tyranny of slaveholders and backwoodsmen. Talk of secession revived and reached a climax in the winter of 1814–1815.

On December 15, 1814, delegates from the New England states met in Hartford, Connecticut, to discuss their grievances. Those who favored secession at the Hartford Convention were outnumbered by a comparatively moderate majority. But while the convention's report only hinted at secession, it reasserted the right of nullification and proposed seven amendments to the Constitution (presumably as the condition of New England's remaining in the Union)—amendments designed to protect New England from the growing influence of the South and the West.

Because the war was going badly and the government was becoming desperate, the New Englanders assumed that the Republicans would have to agree to their demands. Soon after the convention adjourned, however, the news of Jackson's smashing victory at New Orleans reached the cities of the Northeast. A day or two later, reports arrived from abroad of a negotiated peace. In the euphoria of this apparent triumph, the Hartford Convention and the Federalist party came to seem futile, irrelevant, even treasonable. The failure of the secession effort was a virtual death blow to the Federalist Party.

The Peace Settlement

Peace talks between the United States and Britain had begun even before fighting in the War of 1812 began. But serious negotiations did not begin until August 1814, when American and British diplomats met in Ghent, Belgium. John Quincy Adams, Henry Clay, and Albert Gallatin led the American delegation.

Although both sides began with extravagant demands, the final treaty did little except end the fighting itself. The Americans gave up their demand for a British renunciation of impressment and for the cession of Canada to the United States. The British abandoned their call for the creation of an Indian buffer state in the Northwest and made other, minor territorial concessions. The negotiators referred other disputes to arbitration. Hastily drawn up, the treaty was signed on Christmas Eve 1814.

Both sides had reason to accept this skimpy agreement. The British were exhausted and in debt from their prolonged conflict with Napoleon and eager to settle the lesser dispute in North America. The Americans realized that with the defeat of Napoleon in Europe, the British would no longer have much incentive to interfere with American commerce. Indeed, by the end of 1815, impressment had all but ceased.

Other settlements followed the Treaty of Ghent and contributed to a long-term improvement in Anglo-American relations. A commercial treaty in 1815 gave Americans the right to trade freely with England and much of the British Empire. The Rush-Bagot agreement of 1817 provided for mutual disarmament on the Great Lakes; eventually (although not until 1872) the Canadian-American boundary became the longest "unguarded frontier" in the world.

For the other parties to the War of 1812, the Indian tribes east of the Mississippi, the Treaty of Ghent was of no lasting value. It required the United States to restore to the tribes lands seized by white Americans in the fighting, but those provisions were never enforced. Ultimately, the war was another disastrous blow to the capacity of Native Americans to resist white expansion. Tecumseh, their most important leader, was dead. The British, their most important allies, were gone from the Northwest. The alliance that Tecumseh and the Prophet had forged was in disarray. And the end of the war spurred a great new drive by white settlers deeper into the West, into land the Indians were less than ever able to defend.

■ ATTACKING THE FEDERALISTS
A Republican cartoonist derided the secession efforts of New England Federalists at the Hartford Convention in this cartoon. It portrays timid men representing Massachusetts, Connecticut, and Rhode Island preparing to leap into the arms of George III. *(Library of Congress)*

CONCLUSION

Thomas Jefferson called his election to the presidency the "Revolution of 1800," and his supporters believed that his victory would bring a dramatic change in the character of the nation—a retreat from Hamilton's dreams of a powerful, developing nation with great stature in the world; a return to an ideal of a simple agrarian republic happily isolated from the corruption and intrigue of Europe.

But American society was changing rapidly in the early nineteenth century, making it virtually impossible for the Jeffersonian dream to prevail. The nation's population was expanding and diversifying. Its cities were growing, and its commercial life was becoming ever more important. In 1803, Jefferson himself made one of the most important contributions to the growth of the United States: the Louisiana Purchase,

Significant Events

1769	James Watt patents steam engine
1778	Phillips Academy founded in Andover, Massachusetts
1779	Universalist Church founded in Gloucester, Massachusetts 1781
	Phillips Exeter Academy founded in New Hampshire
1782	Unitarian Church founded in Boston
1784	Judith Sargent Murray publishes essay on rights of women
	Methodist Church formally established
1789	Massachusetts law requires public schools to admit female students
1790	Samuel Slater builds textile mill, first modern factory in America, in Pawtucket, Rhode Island
1792	Toll road constructed from Philadelphia to Lancaster, beginning the turnpike era
1793	Eli Whitney invents cotton gin
1794–1796	Thomas Paine's *The Age of Reason* attacks traditional religion
1800	United States capital moves to Washington, D.C.
	Gabriel Prosser's plans for slave rebellion in Virginia foiled
1801	Second Great Awakening begins
	John Marshall appointed chief justice of the Supreme Court
1801–1805	Conflict with Tripoli
1802	Jefferson administration abolishes all internal federal taxes
	United States Military Academy founded at West Point
1803	Napoleonic Wars escalate in Europe
	Louisiana Territory purchased from French
	Supreme Court establishes power of judicial review in *Marbury* v. *Madison*
1804	Aaron Burr kills Alexander Hamilton in duel
	Thomas Jefferson reelected president
1804–1806	Lewis and Clark, and Zebulon Pike, explore Louisiana Territory
1805	British defeat French at Trafalgar
1806	Burr conspiracy uncovered

which dramatically expanded the physical boundaries of the nation—and which began extending white settlement deeper into the continent. In the process, it greatly widened the battles between Europeans and Native Americans.

The growing national pride and commercial ambitions of the United States gradually created another serious conflict with Great Britain: the War of 1812, a war that went badly for the Americans on the whole, but that was settled finally in 1814 on terms at least mildly favorable to the United States. By then, the bitter party rivalries that had characterized the first years of the republic had to some degree subsided, and the nation was poised to enter what became known as the "Era of Good Feelings." It was to be an era in which good feelings did not last for very long.

FOR FURTHER REFERENCE

Suggested Readings Henry Adams, *History of the United States During the Administration of Jefferson and Adams,* 9 vols. (1889–1891) is one of the great literary achievements of early American historiography. Thomas C. Cochran, *Frontiers of Change: Early Industrialization in America* (1981) summarizes economic development in the early republic. Jeanne Boydston, *Home and Work: Housework, Wages, and the Ideology of Labor in the Early Republic* (1990) argues that the cultural status of women declined as the market revolution began to transform the American economy. Drew McCoy, *The Elusive Republic: Political Economy in Jeffersonian America* (1980) traces the Jeffersonian struggle to keep the United States free from European-style corruption and

1806–1807	Napoleon issues Berlin and Milan decrees
1807	Fulton and Livingston launch the first steamboat, *Clermont.*
	Burr tried for conspiracy
	Chesapeake-Leopard incident nearly precipitates war with Great Britain
	Embargo begins
1808	Economy plunges into depression
	Madison elected president
1809	Embargo Act repealed
	Non-Intercourse Act passed
	Tecumseh establishes tribal confederacy to resist white expansion
1810	Macon's Bill No. 2 reopens trade with Britain and France
	United States annexes West Florida
1811	Harrison is victorious in Battle of Tippecanoe, destroys Tecumseh's Indian confederacy
1812	United States declares war on Great Britain (June 18)
	Madison reelected president
	Louisiana admitted to Union as a state
1813	British erect naval blockade
	American forces burn York (Toronto), Canadian capital
	Perry defeats British fleet at Put-In Bay on Lake Erie
	Harrison defeats British and Tecumseh at Battle of the Thames
1814	Jackson, at Battle of Horseshoe Bend, slaughters Creek Indians
	British troops capture and burn Washington
	Francis Scott Key writes "The Star-Spangled Banner"
	Americans win Battle of Plattsburgh
	Hartford Convention meets
	Treaty of Ghent signed
1815	Jackson wins Battle of New Orleans
	Naval war fought with Algiers
1828	Webster's *American Dictionary of the English Language* published

decay. Paul Finkleman, *Slavery and the Founders: Race and Liberty in the Age of Jefferson* (1996) considers the problem of slavery in the early Republic. J. C. A. Stagg, *Mr. Madison's War: Politics, Diplomacy, and Warfare in the Early American Republic, 1783–1830* (1983) argues that James Madison led the United States to war against Great Britain in order to preserve vital American commercial interests, but that he underestimated New England opposition to the war.

Films   (The best source for information on how to find these and other films is *Bowker's Complete Video Directory*—3 volumes.) *An Age of Revolutions* (1978) traces early American diplomacy from the Revolution through the early federal period, including the Louisiana Purchase and the War of 1812. *The Louisiana Purchase: Moving West of the Mississippi* (1990) highlights the political events that led to the Louisiana Purchase and links the settlement of the region with the era of "Manifest Destiny." *The War of 1812* (1982) introduces students to an impor-

tant but poorly understood event in American history. *The American Story, No. 6: Nationalism;* and *No. 7: The Emerging Nation* (1985) detail American political and economic development after the War of 1812, through the Era of Good Feelings. *Sea of Honor: The U.S. Navy Story, Vol. 3: The War of 1812,* explores one of the formative moments for the American military.

Internet Resources   (For up-to-date URL addresses and links to these and other websites, consult the McGraw-Hill history site at *http://www.mhhe.com/socscience/ history/usa/link/linktop.htm*) *The Avalon Project at the Yale Law School: The Papers of Thomas Jefferson* makes available Thomas Jefferson's most important writings, including Notes on the State of Virginia. *Thomas Jefferson Online* offers Jefferson's major writings, transcripts of interviews with historians, and a free Declaration of Independence screensaver. *The Avalon Project at the Yale Law School: The Louisiana Purchase* provides documents pertaining to the Louisiana Purchase.

❧

BIBLIOGRAPHY

General Histories Marcus Cunliffe, *The Nation Takes Shape, 1789–1832* (1959). Charles Mayfield, *The New Nation* (1981). Marshall Smelser, *The Democratic Republicans, 1801–1815* (1968).

Society and Culture Sydney Ahlstrom, *A Religious History of the American People* (1972). Terry D. Bilhartz, *Urban Religion and the Second Great Awakening* (1986). John Boles, *The Great Revival in the South* (1972). Priscilla F. Clement, *Welfare and the Poor in the Nineteenth-Century City* (1985). Lawrence A. Cremin, *American Education: The National Experience* (1981). Cathy Davidson, *The Revolution and the Word* (1986). Joseph J. Ellis, *After the Revolution: Profiles of Early American Culture* (1979). Carl F. Kaestle, *The Evolution of an Urban School System* (1973). Jan Lewis, *The Pursuit of Happiness: Family and Values in Jefferson's Virginia* (1983). William G. McLoughlin, *Revivals, Awakenings, and Reform* (1978). Russel B. Nye, *The Cultural Life of the New Nation* (1960). Kenneth Silverman, *A Cultural History of the American Revolution* (1976). Richard Slotkin, *Regeneration Through Violence* (1973). Alan Taylor, *William Cooper's Town* (1995).

Economic Growth W. Elliot Brownlee, *Dynamics of Ascent* (1979). Stuart Bruchey, *The Roots of American Economic Growth* (1965). James Henretta and Gregory Nobles, *The Evolution of American Society, 1700–1815*, rev. ed. (1987). Douglas C. North, *The Economic Growth of the United States, 1780–1860* (1961). W. J. Rorabaugh, *The Craft Apprentice: From Franklin to the Machine Age in America* (1986). Nathan Rosenberg, *Technology and American Economic Growth* (1972). Merritt Roe Smith, *Harpers Ferry Armory and the New Technology* (1977). George R. Taylor, *The Transportation Revolution* (1951). Barbara M. Tucker, *Samuel Slater and the Origins of the American Textile Industry, 1790–1860* (1984). Anthony F. C. Wallace, *Rockdale* (1978). Caroline F. Ware, *Early New England Cotton Manufacture* (1931).

Politics and Government Leonard Baker, *John Marshall: A Life in Law* (1974). James M. Banner, *To the Hartford Convention* (1967). Morton Borden, *Parties and Politics in the Early Republic* (1967). Noble E. Cunningham, *The Jeffersonian Republicans in Power* (1963); *The Process of Government Under Jefferson* (1978). Robert Dawidoff, *The Education of John Randolph* (1979). Richard Ellis, *The Jeffersonian Crisis: Courts and Politics in the Young Republic* (1971). David Hackett Fischer, *The Revolution of American Conservatism* (1965). Ronald P. Formisano, *The Transformation of Political Culture: Massachusetts Parties, 1790s–1840s* (1983). Robert M. Johnstone, Jr., *Jefferson and the Presidency* (1978). David P. Jordan, *Political Leadership in Jefferson's Virginia* (1983). Linda Kerber, *Federalists in Dissent* (1970). Shaw Livermore, *The Twilight of Federalism* (1962). Dumas Malone, *Jefferson the President: First Term* (1970); *Jefferson the President: Second Term* (1974). Forrest McDonald, *The Presidency of Thomas Jefferson* (1976). Merrill Peterson, *Thomas Jefferson and the New Nation* (1970). Robert W. Tucker and David C. Hendrickson, *Empire of Liberty: The Statecraft of Thomas Jefferson* (1990). James S. Young, *The Washington Community* (1966).

Jeffersonian and Madisonian Thought Joyce Appleby, *Capitalism and a New Social Order: The Republican Vision of the 1890s* (1984). Lance Banning, *The Jeffersonian Persuasion: Evolution of a Party Ideology* (1978). Leonard W. Levy, *Jefferson and Civil Liberties: The Darker Side* (1963). Drew McCoy, *The Last of the Fathers: James Madison and the Republican Legacy* (1989). Merrill Peterson, *The Jeffersonian Image in the American Mind* (1960).

Foreign Policy Harry Ammon, *James Monroe and the Quest for National Identity* (1971). Irving Brant, *James Madison*, 6 vols. (1953–1961). Alexander DeConde, *The Affair of Louisiana* (1976). Bernard De Voto, *Course of Empire* (1952); *The Journals of Lewis and Clark* (1953). Milton Lomask, *Aaron Burr*, 2 vols. (1979, 1982). Raymond O'Connor, *Origins of the American Navy* (1994). Bradford Perkins, *Prologue to War: England and the United States, 1805–1812* (1961).

Indians and the West Ray Allen Billington, *Westward Expansion* (1967). Gregory Evans Dowd, *A Spirited Resistance: The North American Indian Struggle for Unity, 1745–1815* (1992). R. David Edmunds, *The Shawnee Prophet* (1983); *Tecumseh and the Quest for Indian Leadership* (1984). Reginald Horsman, *Expansion and American Indian Policy, 1783–1812* (1962); Matthew Elliott, *British Indian Agent* (1964). Francis S. Philbrick, *The Rise of the New West* (1965). Francis P. Prucha, *American Indian Policy in the Formative Years* (1962). James P. Ronda, *Lewis and Clark Among the Indians* (1984). B. W. Sheehan, *Seeds of Extinction* (1973). Richard White, *The Roots of Dependency* (1983). Charles Wilkinson, *American Indians, Time, and the Law*, rev. ed. (1982).

The War of 1812   Samuel F. Bemis, *John Quincy Adams and the Foundations of American Foreign Policy* (1949). Roger H. Brown, *The Republic in Peril: 1812* (1964). Harry L. Coles, *The War of 1812* (1965). R. David Edmunds, *The Shawnee Prophet* (1983); *Tecumseh and the Quest for Indian Leadership* (1984). Donald R. Hickey, *The War of 1812* (1989). Reginald Horsman, *The Causes of the War of 1812* (1962); *The War of 1812* (1969). John Mahon, *The War of 1812* (1975). Bradford Perkins, *Prologue to War: England and the United States, 1805–1812* (1961); *Castlereagh and Adams* (1964). Robert V. Remini, *Andrew Jackson and the Course of American Empire* (1977). Robert Allen Rutland, *The Presidency of James Madison* (1990). Burton Spivak, *Jefferson's English Crisis: Commerce, Embargo, and the Republican Revolution* (1979). J. C. A. Stagg, *Mr. Madison's War: Politics, Diplomacy, and Warfare in the Early American Republic, 1783–1830* (1983).

Chapter Eight

VARIETIES OF AMERICAN NATIONALISM

Like a "fire bell in the night," as Thomas Jefferson put it, the issue of slavery arose after the War of 1812 to threaten the unity of the nation. The debate began when the territory of Missouri applied for admission to the Union, raising the question of whether it would be a free or a slaveholding state. But the larger issue, one that would arise again and again to plague the republic, was whether the vast new western regions of the United States would ultimately move into the orbit of the North or the South.

The Missouri crisis, which Congress settled by compromise in 1820, was significant at the time not only because it was a sign of the sectional crises to come but because it stood in such sharp contrast to the rising American nationalism of the years following the war. Whatever forces might be working to pull the nation apart, stronger ones were acting for the moment to draw it together. The American econ-

omy was experiencing remarkable growth. The federal government was acting in both domestic and foreign policy to assert a vigorous nationalism. Above all, perhaps, a set of widely (although never universally) shared sentiments and ideals worked to bind the nation together: the memory of the Revolution, the veneration of the Constitution and its framers, the belief that America had a special destiny in the world. These beliefs combined to produce among many Americans a vibrant, even romantic, patriotism.

Every year, Fourth of July celebrations reminded Americans of their common struggle for independence, as fife-and-drum corps and flamboyant orators appealed to patriotism and nationalism. When the Marquis de Lafayette, the French general who had aided the United States during the Revolution, traveled through the country in 1824, crowds in every region and of every party cheered him in frenzied celebration.

And on July 4, 1826—the fiftieth anniversary of the adoption of the Declaration of Independence—an event occurred which to many seemed to confirm that the United States was a nation specially chosen by God. On that remarkable day, Americans were to learn, two of the greatest of the country's founders and former presidents—Thomas Jefferson, author of the Declaration, and John Adams, whom Jefferson had called "its ablest advocate and defender"—died within hours of each other. Jefferson's last words, those at his bedside reported, were "Is it the Fourth?" And Adams comforted those around him moments before his death by saying, "Thomas Jefferson still survives."

■ **FOURTH OF JULY PICNIC AT WEYMOUTH LANDING (C. 1845), BY SUSAN MERRETT** Celebrations of Independence Day, like this one in eastern Massachusetts, became major festive events throughout the United States in the early nineteenth century, a sign of rising American nationalism. *(Art Institute of Chicago)*

For a time, it was possible for many Americans to overlook the very different forms their nationalism took—and to ignore the large elements of their population who were excluded from the national self-definition altogether. But the vigorous economic and territorial expansion this exuberant nationalism produced ultimately brought those differences to the fore.

A GROWING ECONOMY

The end of the War of 1812 allowed the United States to resume the economic growth and territorial expansion that, despite the Republicans' hopes for a simple agrarian society, had characterized the first decade of the nineteenth century. A vigorous postwar boom led to a disastrous bust in 1819. Brief though it was, the collapse was evidence that the United States continued to lack some of the basic institutions necessary to sustain long-term growth. In the years to follow, there were strenuous efforts to introduce stability to the expanding economy.

Banking, Currency, and Protection

The War of 1812 may have stimulated the growth of manufacturing, but it also produced chaos in shipping and banking, and it exposed dramatically the inadequacy of the existing transportation and financial systems. The aftermath of the war, therefore, saw the emergence of a series of political issues connected with national economic development: reestablishing the Bank of the United States (the first Bank's charter had expired in 1811, and Congress had declined to renew it), protecting the new industries, and providing a nationwide network of roads and waterways.

The wartime experience underlined the need for another national bank. After the expiration of the first Bank's charter, a large number of state banks had begun operations. They issued vast quantities of bank notes but did not always bother to retain a large enough reserve of gold or silver to redeem the notes on demand. The notes passed from hand to hand more or less as money, but their actual value depended on the reputation of the bank that issued them. Thus there was a wide variety of notes, of widely differing value, in circulation at the same time. The result was a confusion that made honest business difficult and counterfeiting easy.

Congress dealt with the currency problem by chartering a second Bank of the United States in 1816. It was essentially the same institution Hamilton had founded in 1791 except that it had more capital than its predecessor. The national bank could not forbid state banks from issuing currency, but its size and power enabled it to dominate the state banks. It could compel them to issue only sound notes or risk being forced out of business.

Congress also acted to promote the already burgeoning manufacturing sector of the nation's economy, which the war (by cutting off imports) had greatly stimulated. Manufactured goods had been so scarce during the conflict that, even with comparatively unskilled labor and inexperienced management, new factories could start operations virtually assured of quick profits.

The American textile industry had experienced a particularly dramatic growth. The first census of manufacturing, in 1810, listed 269 cotton and 24 woolen mills in the country. But the Embargo of 1807 and the War of 1812 had spurred a tremendous expansion. Between 1807 and 1815, the total number of cotton spindles increased more than fifteenfold, from 8,000 to 130,000. Until 1814, the textile factories—most of them in New England—produced only yarn and thread; families operating handlooms at home did the actual weaving of cloth. Then the Boston merchant Francis Cabot Lowell, after examining textile machinery in England, developed a power loom that was better than its English counterpart. In 1813, Lowell organized the Boston Manufacturing Company and, at Waltham, Massachusetts, founded the first mill in America to carry on the processes of spinning and weaving under a single roof. Lowell's company was an important step in revolutionizing American manufacturing and in shaping the character of the early industrial work force. (See pp. 345–348.)

But the end of the war suddenly dimmed the prospects for American industry. British ships—determined to recapture their lost markets—swarmed into American ports and unloaded cargoes of manufactured goods, many priced below cost. As one English leader explained to Parliament, it was "well worth while to incur a loss upon the first exportation, in order, by the glut, to stifle in the cradle those rising manufactures in the United States, which war had forced into existence, contrary to the

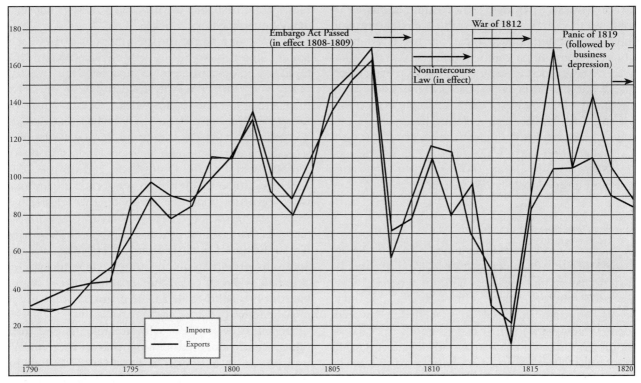

Embargo Act Passed
(in effect 1808-1809)

War of 1812

Panic of 1819
(followed by
business
depression)

Nonintercourse
Law (in effect)

Imports

Exports

■ **BALANCE OF TRADE: EXPORTS AND IMPORTS OF GOODS AND SERVICES TO AND FROM ALL COUNTRIES, 1790-1820**
American foreign trade generally increased from 1790 to 1807, but declined dramatically from 1807 until the end of the War of 1812, partly as a result of the Jeffersonian Embargo and Non-Intercourse Acts, and of the war itself. A boost in imports after the end of the war threatened some of the "infant industries" that had recently emerged. Fearing a glut of low-priced manufactured goods from England, protectionists won passage of a tariff law in 1816, limiting competition on a wide range of items including cotton cloth.

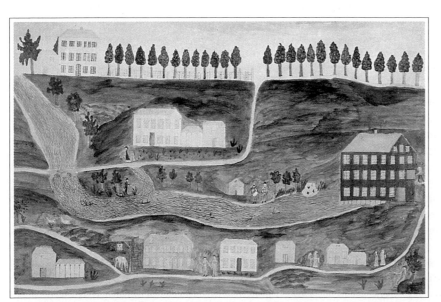

■ **AN EARLY MILL IN NEW ENGLAND**
This early folk painting of about 1814 shows the small town of East Chelmsford, Massachusetts—still primarily agrarian, with its rural houses, open fields, and grazing livestock, but with a small textile mill already operating along the stream, at right. A little more than a decade later, the town had been transformed into a major manufacturing center and renamed for the family that owned the mills: Lowell.
(Part of the Town of Chelmsford. *By Miss Warren. Abby Aldrich Rockefeller Folk Art Center, Williamsburg, Virginia*)

natural course of things." The "infant industries" cried out for protection against these tactics, arguing that they needed time to grow strong enough to withstand the foreign competition.

In 1816, protectionists in Congress won passage of a tariff law that effectively limited competition from abroad on a wide range of items, among the most important of which was cotton cloth. There were objections from agricultural interests, who would have to pay higher prices for manufactured goods as a result. But the nationalist dream of creating an important American industrial economy prevailed.

Transportation

The nation's most pressing economic need in the aftermath of the war, however, was for improvements in its transportation system. Without a better transportation network, manufacturers would not have access to the raw materials they needed and would not be able to send their finished goods to markets within the United States. So an old debate resumed: Should the federal government help to finance roads and other "internal improvements"?

The idea of using government funds to finance road building was not a new one. When Ohio entered the Union in 1803, the federal government agreed that part of the proceeds from the government's sale of public lands there should finance road construction. In 1807, Jefferson's secretary of the treasury, Albert Gallatin, proposed that revenues from the Ohio land sales should help finance a National Road from the Potomac River to the Ohio River. Both Congress and the president approved. After many delays, construction of the National Road finally began in 1811 at Cumberland, Maryland, on the Potomac; and by 1818, this highway—with a crushed stone surface and massive stone bridges—ran as far as Wheeling, Virginia, on the Ohio River. Meanwhile the state of Pennsylvania gave $100,000 to a private company to extend the Lancaster pike westward to Pittsburgh. Over both of these roads a heavy traffic soon moved: stagecoaches, Conestoga wagons, private carriages, and other vehicles, as well as droves of cattle. Despite high tolls, the roads made transportation costs across the mountains lower than ever before—still too high to permit the long-distance hauling of such bulky loads as wheat or flour, but low enough to justify transporting commodities with a high value in proportion to their weight, such as textiles. Manufactures moved from the Atlantic seaboard to the Ohio Valley in unprecedented quantities.

At the same time, on the rivers and the Great Lakes, steam-powered shipping was expanding rapidly. The development of steamboat lines was already well under way before the War of 1812, thanks to the technological advances introduced by Robert Fulton and others. The war had retarded expansion of the system for a time, but by 1816, river steamers were beginning to journey up and down the Mississippi to the Ohio River, and up the Ohio as far as Pittsburgh. Within a few years, steamboats were carrying far more cargo on the Mississippi than all the earlier forms of river transport—flatboats, barges, and others—combined. They stimulated the agricultural economy of the West and the South, by providing much readier access to markets at greatly reduced cost. They enabled eastern manufacturers to send their finished goods west much more readily.

Despite the progress with steamboats and turnpikes, there remained serious gaps in the nation's transportation network, as experience during the War of 1812 had shown. Once the British blockade cut off Atlantic shipping, the coastal roads became choked by the unaccustomed volume of north-south traffic. Long lines of wagons waited for a chance to use the ferries that were still the only means of crossing most rivers. Oxcarts, pressed into emergency service, took six or seven weeks to go from Philadelphia to Charleston. In some areas there were serious shortages of goods that normally traveled by sea, and prices rose to new heights. Rice cost three times as much in New York as in Charleston, flour three times as much in Boston as in Richmond—all because of the difficulty of transportation. There were military consequences, too. On the northern and western frontiers, the absence of good roads had frustrated American campaigns.

In 1815, with this wartime experience in mind, President Madison called the attention of Congress to the "great importance of establishing throughout our country the roads and canals which can be best executed under the national authority," and suggested that a constitutional amendment would resolve any doubts about Congress's authority to provide for their construction. Representative John C. Calhoun promptly introduced a bill that would have used the funds owed the government by the Bank of the United States to finance internal improvements. "Let

■ **DECK LIFE ON THE *PARAGON*, 1811–1812**
The *North River Steamboat Clermont,* launched in 1806 by the inventor Robert Fulton and propelled by an engine he had developed, traveled from Manhattan to Albany (about 150 miles) in thirty-two hours. That was neither the longest nor the fastest steam voyage to date, but the *Clermont* proved to be the first steam-powered vessel large enough and reliable enough to be commercially valuable. Within a few years Fulton and his partner Robert R. Livingston had several steamboats operating profitably around New York. The third vessel in their fleet, the *Paragon,* shown here in a painting by the Russian diplomat and artist Pavel Petrovich Svinin, could carry 150 people and contained an elegant dining salon fitted with bronze, mahogany, and mirrors. Svinin called it "a whole floating town," and Fulton told a friend that the *Paragon* "beats everything on the globe, for made as you and I are we cannot tell what is in the moon." *(Metropolitan Museum of Art)*

us, then, bind the republic together with a perfect system of roads and canals," Calhoun urged. "Let us conquer space."

Congress passed Calhoun's internal improvements bill, but President Madison, on his last day in office (March 3, 1817), vetoed it. He supported the purpose of the bill, he explained, but he still believed that Congress lacked authority to fund the improvements without a constitutional amendment. And so on the issue of internal improvements, at least, the nationalists fell short of their goals. It remained for state governments and private enterprise to undertake the tremendous task of building the transportation network necessary for the growing American economy.

EXPANDING WESTWARD

One reason for the growing interest in internal improvements was the sudden and dramatic surge in westward expansion in the years following the War of 1812. "Old America seems to be breaking up and moving westward," wrote an English observer at the time. By the time of the census of 1820, white settlers had pushed well beyond the Mississippi River, and the population of the western regions was increasing more rapidly than that of the nation as a whole. Almost one of every four white Americans lived west of the Appalachians in 1820; ten years before, only one in seven had resided there.

The Great Migrations

The westward movement of the white American population was one of the most important developments of the nineteenth century. It had a profound effect on the nation's economy, bringing vast new regions into the emerging capitalist system. It had great political ramifications, which ultimately became a major factor in the coming of the Civil War. And like earlier movements west, it thrust peoples of different cultures and traditions into intimate association with one another—with effects that were ultimately disastrous for some, but important on all sides. There were several important reasons for this expansion. Population pressures and economic pressures pushed many Americans from the East; the availability of new lands and the decline of Indian resistance drew them to the West.

The pressures driving white Americans out of the East came in part from the continued growth of the nation's population—both through natural increase and through immigration. Between 1800 and 1820, the population nearly doubled—from 5.3 million to 9.6 million. The growth of cities absorbed some of that increase, but most Americans were still farmers. The agricultural lands of the East were by now largely occupied, and some of them were exhausted. In the South, the spread of the plantation system, and of a slave labor force, limited opportunities for new settlers.

Meanwhile, the West itself was becoming increasingly attractive to white settlers. The War of 1812 had helped diminish (although it did not wholly eliminate) one of the traditional deterrents to western expansion: Native American opposition. And in the aftermath of the war, the federal government continued its policy of pushing the remaining tribes farther and farther west. A series of treaties in 1815 wrested more land from the Indians. In the meantime, the government was erecting a chain of stockaded forts along the Great Lakes and the upper Mississippi to protect the frontier. It also created a "factor" system, by which government factors (or agents) supplied the tribes with goods at cost. This not only worked to drive Canadian traders out of the region, it also helped create a situation of dependency that made Native Americans themselves easier to control.

Now that fertile lands were secure for white settlement, migrants from throughout the East flocked to what was then known as the Old Northwest

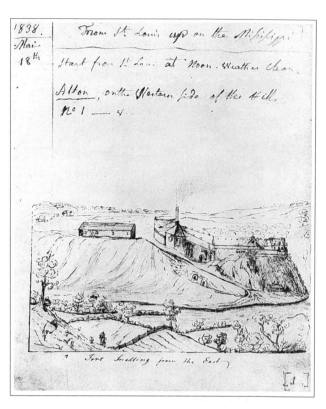

■ **FORT SNELLING**
This is an 1838 sketch of Fort Snelling (at the juncture of the Minnesota and Mississippi Rivers), containing instructions for reaching it from St. Louis. It was one of a string of fortifications built along the western edge of European settlement along the Great Lakes and the upper Mississippi in the first three decades of the nineteenth century. The forts were designed to protect the new white communities from hostile Indians. Fort Snelling stands today in Minnesota as a "living history" site. *(Minnesota Historical Society)*

(now part of the Midwest). The Ohio and Monongahela Rivers were the main routes westward, until the completion of the Erie Canal in 1825. The pioneers reached the river by traveling along the turnpike to Pittsburgh or along the National Road to Wheeling, or by sailing down one of its tributaries—such as the Kanawha, the Cumberland, or the Tennessee. Once on the Ohio, they floated downstream on flatboats bearing all their possessions, then left the river (often at Cincinnati, which was becoming one of the region's—and the nation's—principal cities) and pressed on overland with wagons, handcarts, packhorses, cattle, and hogs.

White Settlers in the Old Northwest

Having arrived at their destination, preferably in the spring or early summer, most settlers built lean-tos or cabins, then hewed clearings out of the forest and put in crops of corn to supplement the wild game they caught and the domestic animals they had brought with them. It was a rough existence, plagued by loneliness, poverty, dirt, and disease. Men, women, and children worked side by side in the fields—and at times had virtually no contact for weeks or months at a time with anyone outside their own families.

Life in the western territories was not, however, as solitary and individualistic as later myth suggested. Migrants often journeyed westward in groups, and sometimes stayed together, formed new communities, and built schools, churches, stores, and other institutions. The labor shortage in the interior led neighbors to develop systems of mutual aid, gathering periodically to raise a barn, clear land, harvest crops, or make quilts. Gradually, the settlers built a thriving farm economy based largely on family units of modest size and committed to the cultivation of grain and the raising of livestock.

Another common feature of life in the Northwest (and indeed in much of early-nineteenth-century America) was mobility. Individuals and families were constantly on the move, settling for a few years in one place, then selling their land (often at a significant profit, given the rapidly rising price of farm properties in the region) and settling again somewhere else. When new areas for settlement opened farther to the west, it was often the people already on the western edges of white settlement—rather than those who remained in the East—who flocked to them first.

The Plantation System in the Southwest

In the Southwest, the new agricultural economy emerged along different lines—just as the economy of the Old South had long been different from that of the Northeast. The principal attraction there was cotton. The cotton lands in the uplands of the Old South had lost much of their fertility through overplanting and erosion. But the market for cotton continued to grow, so there was no lack of ambitious farmers seeking fresh soil in a climate suitable for the crop. In the Southwest, around the end of the Appalachian

range, stretched a broad zone within which cotton could thrive. That zone included what was to become known as the Black Belt of central Alabama and Mississippi, a vast prairie with a dark, productive soil of rotted limestone.

The advance of southern settlement meant the spread of cotton, plantations, and slavery. The first arrivals in an uncultivated region were usually ordinary people like the settlers farther north, small farmers who made rough clearings in the forest. But wealthier planters soon followed. They bought up the cleared or partially cleared land, while the original settlers moved farther west and started over again.

The large planters made the westward journey in a style quite different from that of the first pioneers. Over the alternately dusty and muddy roads came great caravans consisting of herds of livestock, wagonloads of household goods, long lines of slaves, and—bringing up the rear—the planter's family riding in carriages. Success in the wilderness was by no means assured, even for the wealthiest settlers. But many planters soon expanded small clearings into vast cotton fields. They replaced the cabins of the early pioneers with more sumptuous log dwellings and ultimately with imposing mansions that symbolized the emergence of a newly rich class. In later years, these western planters would assume the airs of a longstanding aristocracy. But by the time of the Civil War, few planter families in the Southwest had been there for more than one or two generations.

The rapid growth of the Northwest and Southwest resulted in the admission of four new states to the Union in the immediate aftermath of the War of 1812: Indiana in 1816, Mississippi in 1817, Illinois in 1818, and Alabama in 1819.

Trade and Trapping in the Far West

Not many Anglo-Americans yet knew much about or were much interested in the far western areas of the continent. But a significant trade nevertheless began to develop between these western regions and the United States early in the nineteenth century, and it grew steadily for decades.

Mexico, which continued to control Texas, California, and much of the rest of the Southwest, won its independence from Spain in 1821. Almost immediately, it opened its northern territories to trade with the United States, hoping to revive an economy that had grown stagnant during its war with Spain. American traders poured into the region—overland into Texas and New Mexico, by sea into California. Merchants from the United States quickly displaced Indian traders who had dominated trade with Mexico in some areas of the Southwest. They also displaced some of the same Mexicans who had hoped this new commerce would improve their fortunes. In New Mexico, for example, the Missouri trader William Becknell began in 1821 to offer American manufactured goods for sale, priced considerably below the inferior Mexican goods that had dominated the market in the past. Mexico effectively lost its markets in its own colony, and a steady traffic of commercial wagon trains was moving back and forth along the Santa Fe Trail between Missouri and New Mexico.

Becknell and those who followed him diverted an established trade from Mexico to the United States. Fur traders created a wholly new commerce with the West. Before the War of 1812, John Jacob Astor's American Fur Company had established Astoria as a trading post at the mouth of the Columbia River in Oregon. But when the war came, Astor sold his suddenly imperiled interests to the Northwestern Fur Company, a British concern operating out of Canada. After the war Astor centered his own operations in the Great Lakes area, from which he eventually extended them westward to the Rockies. Other companies carried on operations up the Missouri and its tributaries and into the Rocky Mountains.

At first, fur traders did most of their business by purchasing pelts from the Indians. But increasingly, white trappers entered the region and began to hunt beaver on their own. Substantial numbers of Anglo-Americans and French Canadians moved deep into the Great Lakes region and beyond to join the Iroquois and other Indians in pursuit of furs.

The trappers, or "mountain men," who began trading in and exploring the Far West were, without knowing it, the first wedge of a white movement into those lands that would ultimately dominate the region and transform it. Even in small numbers, they were developing important relationships with the existing residents of the West—Indian and Mexican—

■ **THE RENDEZVOUS**
The annual rendezvous of fur trappers and traders was a major event in the lives of the lonely men who made their livelihoods gathering furs. It was also a gathering of representatives of the many cultures that mingled in the Far West, among them Anglo-Americans, French Canadians, Indians, and Hispanics. *(Denver Public Library)*

and altering the character of society there. White trappers were almost without exception relatively young single men. Not surprisingly, many of them entered into sexual relationships with Indian and Mexican women. They also recruited them as helpers in the difficult work of preparing furs and skins for trading. Perhaps two-thirds of the white trappers married Indian or Hispanic women while living in the West, and their marriages (according to one study) lasted an average of fifteen years and produced an average of three children.

As the trappers moved west from the Great Lakes region, they began to establish themselves in what is now Utah and in parts of New Mexico. In 1822, Andrew and William Ashley founded the Rocky Mountain Fur Company and recruited white trappers to move permanently into the Rockies in search of furs, which were becoming increasingly scarce farther east. The Ashleys dispatched supplies annually to their trappers in exchange for furs and skins. The arrival of the supply train became the occasion for a gathering of scores of mountain men, some of whom lived much of the year in considerable isolation.

But however isolated their daily lives, these mountain men were closely bound up with the expanding market economy of the United States. Some were employees of the Rocky Mountain Fur Company (or some other, similar enterprise), earning a salary in return for providing a steady supply of furs. Others were nominally independent but relied on the companies for credit; they were almost always in debt and hence economically bound to the companies. Some trapped entirely on their own and simply sold their furs for cash, but they too depended on merchants from the East for their livelihoods. And it was to those merchants that the bulk of the profits from the trade flowed.

Many trappers and mountain men lived peacefully and successfully with the Native Americans and Mexicans whose lands they came to share. But some did not. Jedediah S. Smith, a trapper who became an Ashley partner, founded his own fur company to profit from trade in the northern Rockies in 1826. He also led a series of forays deep into Mexican territory that ended in disastrous battles with the Mojaves and other tribes. When an 1827 expedition to Oregon he had organized was attacked by Indians he managed to escape. Sixteen other members of his party of twenty died. Four years later, he set out for New Mexico and was killed by Co-

manches, who took the weapons he was carrying and sold them to Mexican settlers.

Eastern Images of the West

Americans in the East were only dimly aware of the world the trappers were entering and helping to reshape. Smith and others became the source of dramatic (and often exaggerated) popular stories. But the trappers themselves did not often write of their lives or draw maps of the lands they explored.

More important in increasing eastern awareness of the West were explorers, many of them dispatched by the United States government with instructions to chart the territories they visited. In 1819 and 1820, with instructions from the War Department to find the sources of the Red River, Stephen H. Long led nineteen soldiers on a journey up the Platte and South Platte Rivers through what is now Nebraska and eastern Colorado (where he discovered a peak that would be named for him), and then returned eastward along the Arkansas River through what is now Kansas. He failed to find the headwaters of the Red River. But he wrote an influential report on his trip, including an assessment of the region's potential for future settlement and development that echoed the dismissive conclusions of Zebulon Pike fifteen years before. "In regard to this extensive section of country between the Missouri River and the Rocky Mountains," Long wrote, "we do not hesitate in giving the opinion that it is almost wholly unfit for cultivation, and of course uninhabitable by a people depending upon agriculture for their subsistence." On the published map of his expedition, he labeled the Great Plains the "Great American Desert."

THE "ERA OF GOOD FEELINGS"

The expansion of the economy, the growth of white settlement and trade in the West, the creation of new states—all reflected the rising spirit of nationalism that was permeating the United States in the years following the War of 1812. That spirit found reflection, for a time, in the course of American politics. Whatever divisions and disagreements existed within American society found little expression in the nation's political life in these years. Party competition virtually disappeared; James Monroe, who became

■ **PLATTE RIVER CROSSING**
The trails to the West, along which hundreds of thousands of white, English-speaking people migrated in the antebellum period, were filled with hardships: steep hills, rugged mountains with narrow passes through them, broad deserts, and rivers—some broad, some rapid—that had to be crossed, in the absence of bridges, with makeshift rafts and barges. Joseph Goldsborough Bruff, who traveled to California along the Overland trail, sketched this crossing on the Platte River, which runs from Nebraska into the Missouri River. *(This item is reproduced by permission of* The Huntington Library, *San Marino, California)*

president in 1817, was elected twice almost by acclamation. Many Americans celebrated the arrival of an "era of good feelings."

But beneath this surface calm, serious social and political divisions remained that, inevitably, intruded into the nation's public life. Indeed, the years of Monroe's presidency became in the end a time of very bad feelings—a time in which the dream of a harmonious republic unsullied by party and faction was shattered forever.

The End of the First Party System

Ever since 1800, the presidency seemed to have been the special possession of Virginians, passing from one to another in unvarying sequence. After two terms in office Jefferson named his secretary of state, James Madison, to succeed him; and after two more terms, Madison secured the presidential nomination for his secretary of state, James Monroe. Many in the North were expressing impatience with the so-called Virginia Dynasty, but the Republicans had no difficulty electing their candidate in the listless campaign of 1816. Monroe received 183 ballots in the electoral college; his Federalist opponent, Rufus

King of New York, only 34—from Massachusetts, Connecticut, and Delaware.

Monroe was sixty-one years old when he became president, and he seemed in many respects a relic of an earlier age. Tall and dignified, he wore such old-fashioned garb as knee-length pantaloons and white-topped boots. In the course of his long and varied career, he had served as a soldier in the Revolution, as a diplomat, and most recently as a cabinet officer. He had once seemed an impulsive man, but he was now widely admired for his caution and patience.

Monroe entered office under what seemed to be remarkably favorable circumstances. With the decline of the Federalists, his party faced no serious opposition. With the conclusion of the War of 1812, the nation faced no important international threats. American politicians had dreamed since the first days of the republic of a time when partisan divisions and factional disputes might come to an end, a time when the nation might learn to exhibit the harmony and virtue that the founders had envisioned. The prosperity of the postwar years seemed to make that harmony possible. Monroe attempted to use his office to realize that dream.

He made that desire clear, above all, in the selection of his cabinet. For secretary of state, he chose the New Englander and former Federalist John Quincy Adams. Jefferson, Madison, and Monroe had all served as secretary of state before becoming president; Adams therefore immediately became the heir apparent, suggesting that the "Virginia Dynasty" would soon come to an end. He named John C. Calhoun of South Carolina his secretary of war. And in his other appointments, Monroe seemed to go out of his way to include both northerners and southerners, Federalists and Republicans, to harmonize the various interests and sections of the country in a government of national unity.

Soon after his inauguration, Monroe did what no other president since Washington had done: he made a goodwill tour through the country, eastward to New England, westward as far as Detroit. In New England, so recently the scene of rabid Federalist discontent, he was greeted everywhere with enthusiastic demonstrations. The *Columbian Centinel,* a Federalist newspaper in Boston, commenting on the "Presidential Jubilee" in that city, observed that an "era of good feelings" had arrived. This phrase soon spread throughout the country and became a popular label for Monroe's presidency.

On the surface, at least, it was indeed an "era of good feelings," of happy national unity. In 1820, when Monroe ran for reelection, only one elector voted against him, and he did so to ensure that Washington would remain the only unanimously elected president. For all practical purposes, the Federalist Party, which did not even offer a candidate that year, had ceased to exist. The first party system had come to an end.

John Quincy Adams and Florida

Monroe's secretary of state, John Quincy Adams, was the most important member of the cabinet. Like his father, the second president of the United States, Adams had spent much of his life in diplomatic service. He had represented the United States in Britain, Russia, the Netherlands, and Prussia. He had helped negotiate the Treaty of Ghent. And he had demonstrated in all his assignments a calmness and firmness that made him one of the great diplomats in American history.

He was also a committed nationalist, and when he assumed the office of secretary of state, he considered his most important task to be the promotion of American expansion. His first major challenge was Florida. The United States had already annexed West Florida, but most Americans still believed the nation should gain possession of the entire peninsula. Even the claim to West Florida was under dispute. Spain

still claimed the whole of the province, east and west, and actually occupied most of it. In 1817, Adams began negotiations with the Spanish minister, Luis de Onís, in hopes of resolving the dispute and gaining the entire colony for the United States.

In the meantime, however, events were taking their own course in Florida itself. Andrew Jackson, now in command of American troops along the Florida frontier, had orders from Secretary of War Calhoun to "adopt the necessary measures" to put a stop to the continuing raids on American territory by the Seminole Indians south of the Florida border. Jackson (with, he later claimed, tacit encouragement from Washington) used those orders as an excuse to invade Florida in 1818, seize the Spanish forts at St. Marks and Pensacola, and order the hanging of two British subjects on the charge of supplying the Indians and inciting them to hostilities.

Instead of condemning or disavowing Jackson's raid, Adams urged the government to assume complete responsibility for it, because he saw it as a chance to win an important advantage in his negotiations with Spain. The United States, he told the Spanish, had the right under international law to defend itself against threats from across its borders. Since Spain was unwilling or unable to curb those threats, America had simply done what was necessary. And he implied that the nation might consider even more drastic action in the future. Jackson's raid had demonstrated to the Spanish that the United States

■ **SEMINOLE DANCE**
This 1838 drawing by a U.S. military officer portrays a dance by Seminole Indians near Fort Butler in Florida. It was made in the midst of the prolonged Second Seminole War, which ended in 1842 with the removal of most of the tribe from Florida to reservations west of the Mississippi. *(This item is reproduced by permission of* The Huntington Library, *San Marino, California)*

could easily take Florida by force. Onís realized, therefore, that he had little choice but to come to terms with the Americans. Under the terms of the Adams-Onís Treaty of 1819, the United States gave up its claims to Texas, but Spain gave up much more in return: all of Florida, and all of its possessions in the Pacific Northwest. Adams and Onís had concluded something more than a Florida agreement; it was a "transcontinental treaty."

The Panic of 1819

The Monroe administration had little time to revel in its diplomatic successes. At the same time that Adams was completing his negotiations with Onís, the nation was falling victim to a serious economic crisis that helped revive many of the political disputes that the "era of good feelings" had presumably settled.

The Panic of 1819 followed a period of high foreign demand for American farm goods (a result of the disruption of European agriculture by the Napoleonic Wars) and thus of exceptionally high prices for American farmers. The rising prices for farm goods had stimulated a land boom in the western United States. Fueled by speculative investments, land prices soared well above the government-established minimum of $2 an acre; some land in the Black Belt of Alabama and Mississippi went for $100 an acre and more.

The availability of easy credit to settlers and speculators—from the government (under the land acts of 1800 and 1804), from state banks and wildcat banks, even for a time from the rechartered Bank of the United States—fueled the land boom. Beginning in 1819, however, new management at the national bank began tightening credit, calling in loans, and foreclosing mortgages. The new governors of the Bank also collected state bank notes and demanded payment in cash from the banks, many of which could not meet the demand, and hence failed. These bank failures launched a financial panic, which many Americans, particularly those in the West, blamed on the Bank of the United States. Thus began a process that would eventually make the Bank's existence one of the nation's most burning political issues.

Six years of depression followed. Prices for both manufactured goods and agricultural produce fell rapidly. Manufacturers secured passage of a new tariff in 1824 to protect them from foreign competition. Indebted farmers won some relief through the land law of 1820 and the relief act of 1821, which lowered the price of land and reduced existing debts while extending their payment schedules.

Some Americans saw the Panic of 1819 and the widespread distress that followed as a warning that rapid economic growth and territorial expansion would destabilize the nation and threaten its survival. But by 1820 most Americans were irrevocably committed to such growth and expansion. And public debate in the future would revolve less around whether such growth was good or bad than how to encourage and control it. That debate, which the Panic of 1819 did much to encourage, created new factional divisions within the Republican party and ultimately brought the era of nonpartisanship—the "era of good feelings"—to an acrimonious end.

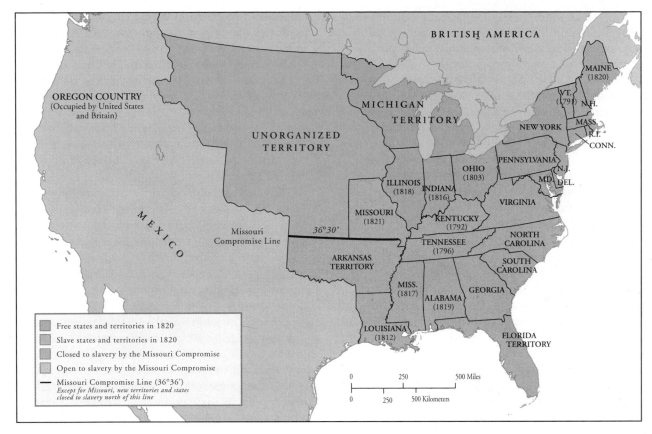

■ THE MISSOURI COMPROMISE, 1820
The Missouri crisis of 1819–1820 exposed a political rift between the slaveholding and nonslaveholding states of the Union. The Missouri Compromise allowed Missouri to enter the Union as a slave state, admitted Maine as a free state, and prohibited slavery in the rest of the Louisiana Purchase territory north of 36° 30´ latitude (the southern boundary of Missouri). Thomas Jefferson called the Missouri issue a "fire bell in the night," and warned against growing northern opposition to slavery.

SECTIONALISM AND NATIONALISM

For a brief but alarming moment in 1819—1820, the increasing differences between the nation's two leading sections threatened the unity of the United States. But the Missouri Compromise averted a sectional crisis for a time. The forces of nationalism continued to assert themselves, and the federal government began to assume the role of promoter of economic growth.

The Missouri Compromise

When Missouri applied for admission to the Union as a state in 1819, slavery was already well established there. The French and Spanish inhabitants of the Louisiana Territory (including what became Missouri) had owned slaves, and in the Louisiana Purchase treaty of 1803 the American government promised to protect the human property of the inhabitants. By 1819, approximately 60,000 people resided in Missouri Territory, of whom about 10,000 were slaves.

Even so, Representative James Tallmadge, Jr., of New York, proposed an amendment to the Missouri statehood bill to prohibit the further introduction of slaves into Missouri and to provide for the gradual emancipation of those already there. The Tallmadge Amendment provoked a controversy that was to rage for the next two years.

Since the beginning of the republic, partly by chance and partly by design, new states had entered the Union more or less in pairs, one from the North, another from the South. In 1819, there were eleven free states and eleven slave states; the admission of Missouri would upset that balance and establish a precedent that in the future might increase the political power of one section over another. Hence the interest of both the North and the South in the question of slavery and freedom in Missouri.

To some degree, the battle over Missouri reflected concern about slavery itself. In both the North and the South, there were groups opposed to slavery on moral grounds and committed to its destruction. On the eve of the dispute over Missouri, for example, the Manumission Society of New York was busy with attempts to rescue runaway slaves; and Quakers were conducting a campaign to strengthen the laws against the African slave trade and to protect free blacks from kidnappers who sold them into slavery.

Northern opposition to slavery also reflected political interests. Most northern critics of slavery were affluent philanthropists and reformers associated with the Federalist Party, and for many of them, the Missouri controversy seemed to provide the opportunity some Federalist leaders had long awaited: the opportunity to revive and reinvigorate their party. In New York, the De Witt Clinton faction of the Republicans, who had joined with the Federalists in opposition to the War of 1812 and were outspoken in their hostility to "Virginia influence" and "Southern rule," were more than willing to cooperate with the Federalists again. The cry against slavery in Missouri, Thomas Jefferson wrote, was "a mere party trick." He explained: "[Rufus] King [a leading Federalist] is ready to risk the union for any chance of restoring his party to power and wriggling himself to the head of it, nor is Clinton without his hopes nor scrupulous as to the means of fulfilling them."

On the whole, though, concern about slavery itself—whether driven by moral or political concerns—was secondary to concerns about the economic competition between North and South for the western territories. The plantation system of the South and the free-labor system of the North had already taken very different forms; the futures of those systems seemed to depend in part on which of them prevailed in the West.

Complicating the Missouri question was the application of Maine (previously the northern part of Massachusetts) for admission as a new state. Speaker of the House Henry Clay informed northern members that if they blocked Missouri from entering the union as a slave state, southerners would block the admission of Maine. But Maine ultimately offered a way out of the impasse, when the Senate agreed to combine the Maine and Missouri proposals into a single bill. Maine would be admitted as a free state, Missouri as a slave state. Then Senator Jesse B. Thomas of Illinois proposed an amendment prohibiting slavery in the rest of the Louisiana Purchase territory north of the southern boundary of Missouri. The Senate adopted the Thomas Amendment, and Speaker Clay, although with great difficulty, guided the amended Maine-Missouri bill through the House.

Nationalists in both North and South hailed the Missouri Compromise as a happy resolution of a danger to the Union. Others were less optimistic. Thomas Jefferson, for example, saw in the controversy a "speck on our horizon" which might ultimately "burst on us as a tornado." And he added, "The line of division lately marked out between the different portions of our confederacy is such as will never, I fear, be obliterated." (That was one reason why Jefferson, who for all his reservations about slavery was a defender of the South's social and economic systems, devoted so much attention in his last years to the construction of the University of Virginia. It was an institution that would, he hoped, confirm southern students in the values of their own region and protect them against the taint of "anti-Missourianism" that he believed pervaded the northern universities.) The debate over Missouri had, in short, revealed a strong undercurrent of sectionalism that was competing with—although at the moment failing to derail—the powerful tides of nationalism.

Marshall and the Court

John Marshall served as chief justice of the United States for almost thirty-five years, from 1801 to 1835, and he dominated the Court as no one else before or since. Republican presidents filled vacancies with one Republican justice after another. But so influential was Marshall, a Federalist, with his colleagues that he continued to carry a majority with him in most of the Court's decisions. More than anyone but the framers themselves, he molded the development of the Constitution: strengthening the judicial branch at the expense of the executive and legislative branches; increasing the power of the federal government at the expense of the states; and advancing the interests of the propertied and commercial classes.

■ **JOHN MARSHALL**
Marshall became Chief Justice of the United States Supreme Court in 1801 after establishing himself as one of the leaders of the Federalist Party. He served as Chief Justice for thirty-five years, longer than anyone else in American history. And despite the frequent opposition of a series of Republican presidents, he used his position to make the judiciary a vigorous instrument for asserting and strengthening American nationalism. *(Boston Athenaeum)*

Committed to promoting commerce, the Marshall Court firmly strengthened the inviolability of contracts as a cornerstone of American law. In *Fletcher* v. *Peck* (1810), which arose out of a series of notorious land frauds in Georgia, the Court had to decide whether the Georgia legislature of 1796 could rightfully repeal the act of the previous legislature granting lands under shady circumstances to the Yazoo Land Companies. In a unanimous decision, Marshall held that a land grant was a valid contract and could not be repealed even if corruption was involved.

Dartmouth College v. *Woodward* (1819) further expanded the meaning of the contract clause of the Constitution. Having gained control of the New Hampshire state government, Republicans tried to revise Dartmouth's charter (granted by King George III in 1769) to convert the private college into a state university. The trustees were represented before the Court by Daniel Webster, a Dartmouth graduate. The Court, he reminded the judges, had decided in *Fletcher* v. *Peck* that "a grant is a contract." The Dartmouth charter, he went on, "is embraced within the very terms of that decision," since "a grant of corporate powers and privileges is as much a contract as a grant of land." Then, according to legend, he brought the justices to tears with an irrelevant passage that concluded: "It is, sir, . . . a small college. And yet there are those who love it." The Court ruled for Dartmouth, stating that the legislature had unconstitutionally violated the college's contract. By proclaiming that corporation charters were contracts and that contracts were inviolable, the decision also placed important restrictions on the ability of state governments to control corporations.

In overturning not only the act of the legislature but the decisions of New Hampshire courts, the Dartmouth College case also claimed for the Supreme Court the right to override the decisions of state courts. But some advocates of states' rights, notably in the South, continued to challenge its right to do so. In *Cohens* v. *Virginia* (1821), Marshall explicitly affirmed the constitutionality of federal review of state court decisions. The states had given up part of their sovereignty in ratifying the Constitution, he explained, and their courts must submit to federal jurisdiction; otherwise the federal government would be prostrated "at the feet of every state in the Union."

Meanwhile, in *McCulloch* v. *Maryland* (1819), Marshall confirmed the "implied powers" of Congress by upholding the constitutionality of the Bank of the United States. The Bank had become so unpopular in the South and the West that several of the states tried to drive branches out of business by outright prohibition or by confiscatory taxes. This case presented two constitutional questions to the Supreme Court: Could Congress charter a bank? And if so, could individual states ban it or tax it? Daniel Webster, one of the Bank's attorneys, argued that establishing such an institution came within the "necessary and proper" clause of the Constitution and added that the power to tax involved a "power to destroy." If the states could tax the Bank at all, they could tax it to death. Marshall adopted Webster's words in deciding for the Bank.

In the case of *Gibbons* v. *Ogden* (1824), the Court strengthened Congress's power to regulate interstate commerce. The state of New York had granted Robert Fulton and Robert Livingston's steamboat company the exclusive right to carry passengers on the Hudson River to New York City. Fulton and Livingston then gave Aaron Ogden the business of carrying passengers across the river between New York and New Jersey. But Thomas Gibbons, with a license granted under an act of Congress, began competing with Ogden for the ferry traffic. Ogden brought suit against him and won in the New York courts. When Gibbons appealed to the Supreme Court, the justices faced two questions: Did "commerce," as defined by the Constitution's commerce clause, include navigation? And did Congress alone or Congress and the states together have the authority to regulate interstate commerce? Marshall replied that "commerce" was a broad term embracing navigation as well as the buying and selling of goods, and he claimed that the power of Congress to regulate such commerce was "complete in itself" and might be "exercised to its utmost extent." Ogden's state-granted monopoly, therefore, was void.

The lasting significance of *Gibbons* v. *Ogden* was that it freed transportation systems from restraints by the states and helped pave the way for unfettered capitalist growth. But its more immediate effect was to head off a movement to weaken the Supreme Court. Influential Republicans, mostly from the South and the West, were arguing that the Marshall Court was not merely interpreting the Constitution but illegitimately changing it. In Congress, they proposed measures to curb the Court's power. One Kentucky senator suggested making the Senate, not the Court, the agency to decide the constitutionality of state laws and to settle interstate disputes. Other members introduced bills to increase the size of the Court (from seven to ten justices) and to require more than a simple majority to declare a state law unconstitutional. Still others argued for "codification": for making legislative statutes the basis of the law, rather than the accumulation of precedent that judges used. Such a reform, codifiers argued, would limit the power of the judiciary and prevent "judge-made" law. The Court reformers failed to pass any of their measures, and after *Gibbons* v. *Ogden,* with its popular stand against monopoly power, hostility to the judicial branch of the government gradually died down.

The decisions of the Marshall Court established the primacy of the federal government over the states in regulating the economy and opened the way for an increased federal role in promoting economic growth. They protected corporations and other private economic institutions from local government interference. They were, in short, highly nationalistic decisions, designed to promote the growth of a strong, unified, and economically developed United States.

The Court and the Tribes

The nationalist inclinations of the Marshall Court were visible as well in a series of decisions concerning the legal status of Indian tribes within the United States. But these decisions did not just affirm the supremacy of the United States; they also carved out a distinctive position for Native Americans within the constitutional structure.

The first of the crucial Indian decisions was in the case of *Johnson* v. *McIntosh* (1823). Leaders of the Illinois and Pinakeshaw tribes had sold parcels of their land to a group of white settlers (including Johnson), but had later signed a treaty with the federal government ceding to the United States territory that included those same parcels. The government proceeded to grant homestead rights to new white settlers (among them McIntosh) on the land claimed by Johnson. The Court was asked to decide which claim had precedence. Marshall's ruling, not surprisingly, favored the United States. But in explaining it, he offered a preliminary definition of the place of Indians within the nation. The tribes had a basic right to their tribal lands, he said, that preceded all other American laws. Individual American citizens could not buy or take land from the tribes; only the federal government could do that.

Eight years later, in *Cherokee Nation* v. *Georgia,* the Marshall Court refused to hear a case filed by the Cherokees against a Georgia law abolishing their tribal legislature and courts. The Cherokees argued that because the tribe was a "foreign nation," the Supreme Court (which had constitutional responsibility for mediating disputes between the states and foreign nations) had jurisdiction. Marshall's earlier and later rulings suggested considerable sympathy

■ CHEROKEE LEADERS
Sequoyah (who also used the name George Guess) was a mixed-blood Cherokee who translated his tribe's language into writing through an elaborate alphabet of his own invention, pictured here. He opposed Indian assimilation into white society and saw the preservation of the Cherokee language as a way to protect the culture of his tribe. He moved to Arkansas in the 1820s and became a chief of the western Cherokee tribes. Major George Lowery, shown on the right, was also a mixed-blood Cherokee and served as assistant principal chief of the Cherokee from 1828 to 1838. He supported acculturation but remained a Cherokee nationalist. He wears a U.S. presidential medal around his neck. *(Left, National Anthropological Archives, Smithsonian; Right, Gilcrease Institute)*

for tribal claims that states could not regulate them, but he could not accept the Cherokee argument in this case. The tribes were not foreign nations, he said. Rather, they had a special status within the nation. "The conditions of the Indians in relation to the United States is perhaps unlike that of any two people in existence," he wrote. "Their relation to the United States resembles that of a ward to his guardian." This was the origin of what became known as the "trust relationship," by which the United States claimed broad powers over the tribes but accepted substantial responsibility for protecting their welfare.

Most important was the Court's 1832 decision in *Worcester* v. *Georgia.* The Georgia state government had passed a law requiring any U.S. citizen desiring to enter Cherokee territory to obtain permission from the governor. Two missionaries (one of them named Worcester) sued, claiming the state was encroaching on the federal government's constitutionally mandated role to regulate trade with the tribes. Marshall invalidated the Georgia law, another important step in consolidating federal authority over the states (and over the tribes). In doing so, he further defined the nature of the Indian nations. The tribes, he explained, were sovereign entities in much the same way Georgia was a sovereign entity, "distinct political communities, having territorial boundaries within which their authority is exclusive." In defending the power of the federal government, he was also affirming, indeed expanding, tribal authority.

The Marshall decisions, therefore, did what the Constitution itself had not done: they defined a place for Indian tribes within the American political system. The tribes had basic property rights. They were sovereign entities not subject to the authority of state governments. But the federal government, like a "guardian" governing its "ward," had ultimate authority over tribal affairs—even if that authority was, according to the Court, limited by the government's obligation to protect Indian welfare. These provisions were seldom enough to defend Indians from the steady westward march of white civilization. But they formed the basis of what legal protections they had.

The Latin American Revolution and the Monroe Doctrine

Just as the Supreme Court was asserting American nationalism in the shaping of the country's economic life, so the Monroe administration was asserting nationalism in foreign policy. As always, American diplomacy was principally concerned with Europe. But in the 1820s, dealing with Europe forced Americans to develop a policy toward Latin America, which was suddenly winning its independence.

Americans looking southward in the years following the War of 1812 beheld a gigantic spectacle: the Spanish Empire in its death throes, a whole continent in revolt, new nations in the making. Already the United States had developed a profitable trade with Latin America and was rivaling Great Britain as the principal trading nation there. Many believed the success of the anti-Spanish revolutions would further strengthen America's position in the region.

In 1815, the United States proclaimed neutrality in the wars between Spain and its rebellious colonies, implying a partial recognition of the rebels' status as nations. Moreover, the United States sold ships and supplies to the revolutionaries, a clear indication that it was not genuinely neutral but was trying to help the insurgents. Finally, in 1822, President Monroe established diplomatic relations with five new nations—La Plata (later Argentina), Chile, Peru, Colombia, and Mexico—making the United States the first country to recognize them. In 1823, Monroe went further and announced a policy that would ultimately be known (beginning some thirty years later) as the "Monroe Doctrine," even though it was primarily the work of John Quincy Adams. "The American continents," Monroe declared, ". . . are henceforth not to be considered as subjects for future colonization by any European powers." The United States would consider any foreign challenge to the sovereignty of existing American nations an unfriendly act. At the same time, he proclaimed, "Our policy in regard to Europe . . . is not to interfere in the internal concerns of any of its powers."

The Monroe Doctrine emerged directly out of America's relations with Europe in the 1820s. After Napoleon's defeat, the major nations of Europe combined in a "concert" to prevent future challenges to the "legitimacy" of established governments. Great Britain soon withdrew from the concert, leaving Russia and France the strongest of its four remaining members. In 1823, the four allies authorized France to intervene in Spain to restore the Bourbon dynasty, which a revolution had toppled. Some in England and the Americas feared the allies might next support a French effort to retake the lost Spanish Empire in America.

To most Americans, and certainly to the secretary of state, an even greater threat was Great Britain itself. Adams suspected that the English had designs on Cuba. He thought Cuba eventually should belong to the United States and wanted to keep it in Spanish hands until it fell to the Americans. For a time, Monroe and Adams considered making their pronouncements about Latin America part of a joint statement with Great Britain. But Adams soon came to believe that the American government should act alone instead of following along like a "cock-boat in the wake of a British man-of-war." When the British lost interest in a joint statement, they only strengthened an already growing inclination within the administration to make its own pronouncement.

Monroe and Adams hoped the message would rally the people of Latin America to resist foreign intervention. They also hoped that by appealing to national pride, the message would help arouse the United States from a business depression, divert the nation from sectional politics, and increase popular interest in the otherwise lackluster administration of Monroe. It did neither. But the Monroe Doctrine was important nevertheless for several reasons. It was an expression of the growing spirit of nationalism in the United States in the 1820s. It was an expression of concern about the forces that were already gathering to threaten that spirit. And it established the idea of American hegemony in the Western Hemisphere that later U.S. governments would invoke at will to justify policies in Latin America.

THE REVIVAL OF OPPOSITION

After 1816, the Federalist Party offered no presidential candidate and soon ceased to exist as a national political force. The Republican Party (which considered itself not a party at all but an organization representing the whole of the population) was the only organized force in national politics.

Yet the policies of the federal government continued to spark opposition. At first, criticism remained contained within the existing one-party structure. But by the late 1820s partisan divisions were emerging once again.

In some respects, the division mirrored the schism that had produced the first party system in the 1790s. The Republicans had in many ways come to resemble the early Federalist regimes in their promotion of economic growth and centralization. (That was one of the principal reasons for the Federalists' demise: the Republicans had adopted much of their program.) And the opposition, like the opposition in the 1790s, opposed the federal government's expanding role in the economy. There was, however, a crucial difference. At the beginning of the century, the opponents of centralization had also often been opponents of economic growth. Now, in the 1820s, the controversy involved not whether but how the nation should continue to expand.

The "Corrupt Bargain"

Until 1820, when the Federalist Party effectively ceased operations and James Monroe ran for reelection unopposed, presidential candidates were nominated by caucuses of the two parties in Congress. In 1824, had the caucus system prevailed, Republicans in Congress would have again produced a candidate who would have run unopposed. But "King Caucus" did not prevail in 1824. The Republican caucus did nominate a candidate: William H. Crawford of Georgia, the secretary of the treasury and the favorite of the extreme states' rights faction of the party. But other candidates received nominations from state legislatures and endorsements from irregular mass meetings throughout the country.

One of them was Secretary of State John Quincy Adams, who held the office that was the traditional stepping-stone to the presidency. But as he himself ruefully understood, he was a man of cold and forbidding manners, with little popular appeal. Another contender was Henry Clay, the Speaker of the House. He had a devoted personal following and a definite and coherent program: the "American System," which proposed creating a great home market for factory and farm producers by raising the protective tariff, strengthening the national bank, and financing internal improvements. Andrew Jackson, the fourth major candidate, had no significant political record—even though he had served briefly as a representative in Congress and was now a new member of the United States Senate. But he was a military hero and had the help of shrewd political allies from his home state of Tennessee.

Jackson received a plurality, although not a majority, of both the popular and the electoral vote. In the electoral college, he had 99 votes to Adams's 84, Crawford's 41, and Clay's 37. The Twelfth Amendment to the Constitution (passed in the aftermath of the contested 1800 election) required the House of Representatives to choose between the three candidates with the largest numbers of electoral votes. Clay was out of the running, but he was in a strong position to influence the result, both because he was Speaker of the House and because thirty-seven electors were committed to him and presumably open to his advice on where to turn now.

Supporters of Jackson, Crawford, and Adams all wooed Clay as the congressional vote approached. But Clay's course was already set. Crawford was no longer a serious candidate, since he was suffering from a paralyzing disease. And Jackson was Clay's most dangerous political rival in the West and had not supported Clay's legislative program. Adams was no friend of Clay's either; but alone among the candidates, he was an ardent nationalist and a likely supporter of the American System. Clay gave his support to Adams, and the House elected him.

The Jacksonians—who believed their large popular and electoral pluralities entitled their candidate to the presidency—were enraged enough at this. But they became much angrier when the new president announced that Clay was to be his secretary of state. The State Department was the well-established route to the presidency, and Adams thus appeared to be naming Clay as his own successor. The Jacksonians expressed outrage at this "corrupt bargain." Very likely there had been some sort of understanding between Clay and Adams, and although there

was nothing corrupt, or even unusual, about it, it proved to be politically costly for both men.

The Second President Adams

Throughout Adams's term in the White House, the political bitterness arising from the "corrupt bargain" thoroughly frustrated his policies. In his inaugural address and in his first message to Congress, Adams recommended "laws promoting the improvement of agriculture, commerce, and manufactures, the cultivation of the mechanic and of the elegant arts, the advancement of literature, and the progress of the sciences, ornamental and profound": a nationalist program reminiscent of Clay's American System. But Jacksonians in Congress prevented him from securing appropriations for most of these goals. He did win several million dollars to improve rivers and harbors and to extend the National Road westward from Wheeling—more than Congress had appropriated for internal improvements under all his predecessors together, but far less than he and Clay had envisioned.

Adams also experienced diplomatic frustrations. He appointed delegates to an international conference that the Venezuelan liberator, Simín Bolívar, had called in Panama in 1826. But southerners in Congress opposed the idea of white Americans mingling with black delegates from Haiti, which would be represented in Panama. And supporters of Jackson charged that Adams intended to sacrifice American interests and involve the nation in an entangling alliance. Congress delayed approving the Panama mission so long that the American delegation did not arrive until after the conference was over.

Adams also lost a contest with the state of Georgia, which wished to remove the remaining Creek and Cherokee Indians from the state to gain additional soil for cotton planters. The United States government, in a 1791 treaty, had guaranteed that land to the Creeks; but in 1825, white Georgians had extracted a new treaty from William McIntosh, the leader of one faction in the tribe and a longtime advocate of Indian cooperation with the United States. Adams believed the new treaty had no legal force, since McIntosh clearly did not represent the wishes of the tribe; and he refused to enforce the treaty, setting up a direct conflict between the president and the state. The governor of Georgia defied the president and proceeded with plans for Indian removal. In 1827, the Creeks succumbed to pressure from Georgia and agreed to still another treaty, in which

■ **JOHN QUINCY ADAMS**
This photograph of the former president was taken shortly before his death in 1848—almost twenty years after he had left the White House—when he was serving as a congressman from Massachusetts. During his years as president, he was—as he had been throughout his life—an intensely disciplined and hard-working man. He rose at four in the morning and made a long entry in his diary for the previous day. He wrote so much that his right hand at times became paralyzed with writer's cramp, so he taught himself to write with his left hand as well. *(Brown Brothers)*

they again yielded their land, thus undercutting Adams's position further.

Even more damaging to the administration was its support for a new tariff on imported goods in 1828. This measure originated in the demands of Massachusetts and Rhode Island woolen manufacturers, who complained that the British were dumping textiles on the American market at prices with which the domestic mill owners could not compete. They won support from middle and western states, but at the cost of provisions that antagonized the original New England supporters of the bill. The western provi-

sions placed high duties not only on woolens, as the New Englanders had wanted, but also on items the West produced. That distressed New England manufacturers; the benefits of protecting their manufactured goods from foreign competition now had to be weighed against the prospects of having to pay more for raw materials. The bill presented Adams with a dilemma, for he would lose support whether he signed or vetoed it. Adams signed it, earning the animosity of southerners, who cursed it as the "tariff of abominations."

Jackson Triumphant

By the time of the 1828 presidential election, a new two-party system had begun to emerge out of the divisions among the Republicans. On one side stood the supporters of John Quincy Adams, who called themselves the National Republicans and who supported the economic nationalism of the preceding years. Opposing them were the followers of Andrew Jackson, who took the name Democratic Republicans and who called for an assault on privilege and a widening of opportunity. Adams attracted the support of most of the remaining Federalists; Jackson appealed to a broad coalition that opposed the "economic aristocracy." But issues seemed to count for little in the end, as the campaign degenerated into a war of personal invective. The Jacksonians charged that Adams as president had been guilty of gross waste and extravagance and had used public funds to buy gambling devices (a chess set and a billiard table) for the White House. They also claimed, falsely, that when Adams had served as minister to Russia he had tried to procure a beautiful American girl for the sinful pleasures of the czar. Adams's supporters hurled even worse accusations at Jackson. They called him a murderer and distributed a "coffin handbill," which listed, within coffin-shaped outlines, the names of militiamen whom Jackson was said to have shot in cold blood during the War of 1812. (The men had been deserters who were legally executed after sentence by a court-martial.) And they called him an adulterer, fanning rumors that Jackson had knowingly lived in sin with the wife of another man. Actually, he had married the woman, his beloved Rachel, at a time when the pair apparently believed her first husband had divorced her. (When Jackson's wife first read of the accusations against her shortly after the election, she collapsed and, a few weeks later, died; with

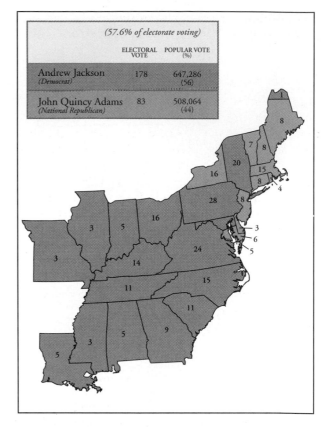

(57.6% of electorate voting)		
	ELECTORAL VOTE	POPULAR VOTE (%)
Andrew Jackson *(Democrat)*	178	647,286 (56)
John Quincy Adams *(National Republican)*	83	508,064 (44)

■ **THE ELECTION OF 1828**
Andrew Jackson won a decisive victory over John Quincy Adams in the presidential election of 1828. For the first time in American history, over one million votes were cast, and Jackson won large majorities of both the popular vote and the electoral college, sweeping the South and West and running strongly in the mid-Atlantic states. Some Jacksonians claimed that the election of 1828 ushered in a new era of democracy in the United States, an "era of the common man."

considerable reason, Jackson blamed his opponents for her death.)

Jackson's victory was decisive, if sectional. He won 56 percent of the popular vote and an electoral majority of 178 votes to 83. Adams swept virtually all of New England, and he showed significant strength in the mid-Atlantic region. Nevertheless, the Jacksonians considered their victory as complete and as important as Jefferson's in 1800. Once again, the forces of privilege had been driven from Washington. Once again, a champion of democracy would occupy the White House and restore liberty to the people and to the economy. America had entered, some Jacksonians claimed, a new era of democracy, the "era of the common man."

Significant Events

1813	Francis Lowell establishes textile factories in Waltham, Massachusetts
1815	U.S. signs treaties with tribes taking western lands from Indians
1816	Second Bank of the United States chartered
	Monroe elected president
	Tariff protects textile industry from foreign competition
	Indiana enters Union
1817	Madison vetoes internal improvements bill
	Mississippi enters Union
1818	Jackson invades Florida, ends first Seminole War
	Illinois enters Union
1819	Commercial panic destabilizes economy
	Spain cedes Florida to United States in Adams-Onís Treaty
	Supreme Court hears *Dartmouth College* v. *Woodward* and *McCulloch* v. *Maryland*
	Alabama enters Union
1819-1820	Stephen H. Long explores Kansas, Nebraska, and Colorado
1820	Missouri Compromise enacted
	Monroe reelected president without opposition
1821	Mexico wins independence from Spain
	William Becknell opens trade between U.S. territories and New Mexico
1822	Rocky Mountain Fur Company established
1823	Monroe Doctrine proclaimed
1824	John Quincy Adams wins disputed presidential election
	Supreme Court rules in *Gibbons* v. *Ogden*
1826	Thomas Jefferson and John Adams die on July 4
1827	Creek Indians cede lands to Georgia
1828	"Tariff of abominations" passed
	Andrew Jackson elected president

CONCLUSION

In the aftermath of the War of 1812, a vigorous nationalism came increasingly to characterize the political and popular culture of the United States. In all regions of the country, white men and women celebrated the achievements of the early leaders of the republic, the genius of the Constitution, and the success of the nation in withstanding serious challenges both from without and within. Party divisions faded to the point that James Monroe, the fifth president, won reelection in 1820 without opposition.

But the broad nationalism of the so-called era of good feelings disguised some deep divisions within the United States. Indeed, the character of American nationalism differed substantially from one region, and one group, to another. Battles continued between those who favored a strong central government committed to advancing the economic development of the nation and those who wanted a decentralization of power to open opportunity to more people. Battles continued as well over the role of slavery in American life—and in particular over the place of slavery in the new western territories that the United States was rapidly populating (and wresting from the tribes). The Missouri Compromise of 1820 postponed the day of reckoning on that issue—but only for a time, as Andrew Jackson would discover soon after becoming president in 1829.

FOR FURTHER REFERENCE

Suggested Readings   Frederick Jackson Turner, *The Frontier in American History* (1920) is the classic statement of American exceptionalism. Turner argued that the western frontier endowed the United States with a distinctive, individualist, and democratic national character. John Mack Faragher, *Women and Men on the Overland Trail* (1979) was an early and influential book in the "new western history" that challenged Turner. Robert V. Remini, *Andrew Jackson and the Course of American Empire: 1767–1821* (1977) emphasizes Andrew Jackson's importance in American territorial expansion in the South prior to 1821 and in the development of American nationalism. Morton J. Horwitz, *The Transformation of American Law, 1780–1865* (1977), an important work in American legal history, connects changes in the law to changes in the American economy. Ernest R. May, *The Making of the Monroe Doctrine* (1975) presents the history of a leading principle of American foreign policy.

Films   (The best source for information on how to find these and other films is *Bowker's Complete Video Directory*—3 volumes.) *Expansionism,* Vol. 6 (1996) discusses American expansion from the Louisiana Purchase to the California gold rush. *Expansion & Growth: Nineteenth Century America* explores similar themes. *Lewis & Clark,* an A&E Biography, traces the historic expedition that mapped the Louisiana Purchase. *Daniel Boone's Final Frontier* (1995) reenacts Daniel Boone's last years in the Louisiana territory, based on the journals of Nathan and Jemima Boone. *Marbury v. Madison* (1977) dramatizes the 1803 Supreme Court case that established the legitimacy of judicial review. *John Marshall* (1983) focuses on the 1807 treason trial of Aaron Burr. *McCulloch v. Maryland* (1977) discusses the case that helped to establish federal supremacy over the states.

Internet Resources   (For up-to-date URL addresses and links to these and other websites, consult the McGraw-Hill history site at *http://www.mhhe.com/socscience/history/usa/link/linktop.htm*) The Avalon Project at the Yale Law School: British-American Diplomacy contains documents pertaining to British-American relations from the American Revolution through the 1840s. *A History of the NW Coast* provides historical descriptions of the Indians of the Pacific Northwest. *Mountain Men and the Fur Trade* is an extensive collection of documents from the fur trade in the Rocky Mountains, mainly dating from 1810 to 1840. *Rare Map Collection—Union and Expansion* includes contemporary maps of the Louisiana Purchase and other newly acquired territory of the United States.

BIBLIOGRAPHY

Economic Growth   George Dangerfield, *The Awakening of American Nationalism* (1965); *The Era of Good Feelings* (1952). Bray Hammond, *Banks and Politics in America from the Revolution to the Civil War* (1957). Shaw Livermore, Jr., *The Twilight of Federalism* (1962). Murray N. Rothbard, *The Panic of 1819* (1962).

Expanding Westward   Thomas P. Abernethy, *The South in the New Nation* (1961). Ray Allen Billington, *The Far Western Frontier* (1965); *Westward Expansion* (1974). Colin Calloway, *Crown and Calumet* (1987). John Mack Faragher, *Daniel Boone: The Life of and Legend of an American Pioneer* (1992). John A. Hawgood, *America's Western Frontier* (1967). Julie Roy Jeffrey, *Frontier Women: The Trans-Mississippi West* (1979). Frederick Merk, *History of the Westward Movement* (1978). Francis S. Philbrick, *The Rise of the West, 1745–1830* (1965). Glenda Riley, *The Female Frontier* (1988). Malcolm J. Rohrbough, *The Land Office Business: The Settlement and Administration of American Public Lands, 1789–1837* (1968). Frederick Jackson Turner, *The Rise of the New West* (1906).

The "Era of Good Feelings"   Harry Ammon, *James Monroe: The Quest for National Identity* (1971). Samuel F. Bemis, *John Quincy Adams and the Union* (1956). George Dangerfield, *The Awakening of American Nationalism* (1965); *The Era of Good Feelings* (1952). Don E. Fehrenbacher, *The South and Three Sectional Crises* (1980). Shaw Livermore, *The Twilight of Federalism* (1962). Paul C. Nagle, *One Nation Indivisible: The Union in American Thought, 1815–1828* (1965). Robert V. Remini, *The Election of Andrew Jackson* (1963). Norman K. Risjord, *The Old Republicans: Southern Conservatism in the Age of Jefferson* (1965). Charles M. Wiltse, *John C. Calhoun: American Nationalist* (1944).

The Courts Leonard Baker, *John Marshall: A Life in Law* (1974). Alexander M. Bickel, *Justice Joseph Story and the Rise of the Supreme Court* (1971). D. O. Dewey, *Marshall Versus Jefferson: The Political Background of Marbury v. Madison* (1970). Richard E. Ellis, *The Jeffersonian Crisis: Courts and Politics in the Young Republic* (1971). Charles G. Haines, *The Role of the Supreme Court in American Government and Politics, 1789-1835* (1970). James McClellan, *Joseph Story and the American Constitution* (1971). R. Kent Newmyer, *The Supreme Court Under Marshall and Taney* (1968). Thomas Shevory, *John Marshall's Law* (1994). Francis N. Stites, *John Marshall: Defender of the Constitution* (1981).

The Monroe Doctrine Samuel F. Bemis, *John Quincy Adams and the Foundations of American Foreign Policy* (1940). Walter LaFeber, ed., *John Quincy Adams and the Continental Empire* (1965). Bradford Perkins, *Castlereagh and Adams: England and the United States, 1812-1823* (1964). Frank Thistlethwaite, *The Anglo-American Connection in the Early Nineteenth Century* (1959). Arthur P. Whitaker, *The United States and the Independence of Latin America* (1941).

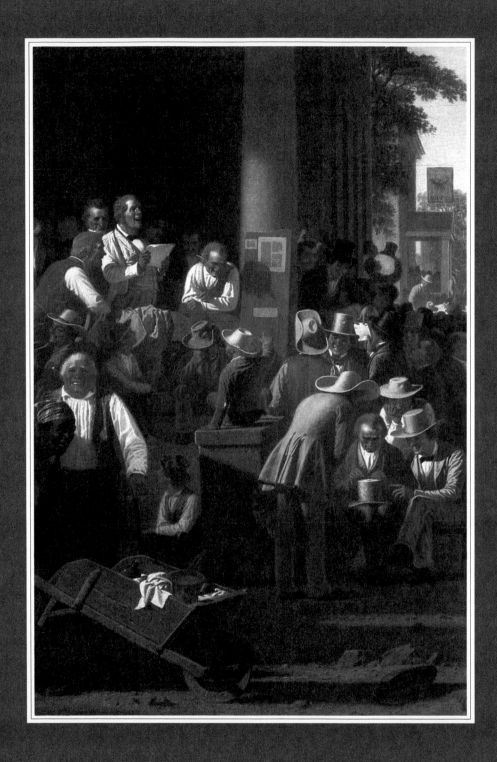

Chapter Nine

JACKSONIAN AMERICA

When the French aristocrat Alexis de Tocqueville visited the United States in 1831, one feature of American society struck him as "fundamental": the "general equality of condition among the people." Unlike older societies, in which privilege and wealth passed from generation to generation within an entrenched upper class, America had no rigid distinctions of rank. "The government of democracy," he wrote in his classic study *Democracy in America* (1835–1840), "brings the notion of political rights to the level of the humblest citizens, just as the dissemination of wealth brings the notion of property within the reach of all the members of the community."

Yet Tocqueville also wondered how long the fluidity of American society could survive in the face of the growth of manufacturing and the rise of the factory system. Industrialism, he feared, would create a large class of dependent workers and a small

■ **DETAIL FROM *THE VERDICT OF THE PEOPLE* (1855), BY GEORGE CALEB BINGHAM**
This scene of an election-day gathering is peopled almost entirely by white men. Women and blacks were barred from voting, but among white males political rights expanded substantially in the 1830s and 1840s.
(Boatmen's National Bank, St. Louis)

group of new aristocrats. For, as he explained it, "at the very moment at which the science of manufactures lowers the class of workmen, it raises the class of masters."

Americans, too, pondered the future of their democracy in these years of economic and territorial expansion. Some feared that the nation's rapid growth would produce social chaos and insisted that the country's first priority must be to establish order and a clear system of authority. Others argued that the greatest danger facing the nation was privilege and that society's goal should be to eliminate the favored status of powerful elites and make opportunity more widely available. Advocates of this latter vision seized control of the federal government in 1829 with the inauguration of Andrew Jackson.

Jackson and his followers were not egalitarians. They did nothing to challenge the existence of slavery; they supervised one of the harshest assaults on American Indians in the nation's history; and they accepted the necessity of economic inequality and social gradation. Jackson himself was a frontier aristocrat, and most of those who served him were people of wealth and standing. They were not, however, usually aristocrats by birth. They had, they believed, risen to prominence on the basis of their own talents and energies, and their goal in public life was to ensure that others like themselves would have the opportunity to do the same.

The "democratization" of government over which Andrew Jackson presided was accompanied by a lofty rhetoric of equality and aroused the excitement of working people. To the national leaders who

■ **ANDREW JACKSON TRAVELS TO WASHINGTON**
President-elect Andrew Jackson attracted enormous crowds along his well-publicized route to Washington in 1829. Even larger crowds gathered in the capital for his inauguration, prompting some of his opponents to complain of the triumph of "King Mob." *(Library of Congress)*

promoted that democratization, however, its purpose was not to aid farmers and laborers, Jackson's greatest champions. Still less was it to assist the truly disenfranchised: African Americans (both slave and free), women, Native Americans. It was to challenge the power of eastern elites for the sake of the rising entrepreneurs of the South and the West.

❧ THE RISE OF MASS POLITICS

On March 4, 1829, an unprecedented throng—thousands of Americans from all regions of the country, including farmers, laborers, and others of modest social rank—crowded before the Capitol in Washington, D.C., to witness the inauguration of Andrew Jackson. After the ceremonies, the boisterous crowd poured down Pennsylvania Avenue, following their hero to the White House. There, at a public reception open to all, they filled the state rooms to over-

flowing, trampling one another, soiling the carpets, ruining elegantly upholstered sofas and chairs in their eagerness to shake the new president's hand. "It was a proud day for the people," wrote Amos Kendall, one of Jackson's closest political associates. "General Jackson is their own President." To other observers, however, the scene was less appealing. Justice of the Supreme Court Joseph Story, a friend and colleague of John Marshall, looked on the inaugural levee, as it was called, and remarked with disgust: "The reign of King 'Mob' seems triumphant."

The Expanding Electorate

What some have called the "age of Jackson" did not much advance the cause of economic equality. The distribution of wealth and property in America was little different at the end of the Jacksonian era than it was at the start. But it did mark a transformation of American politics that extended the right to vote widely to new groups.

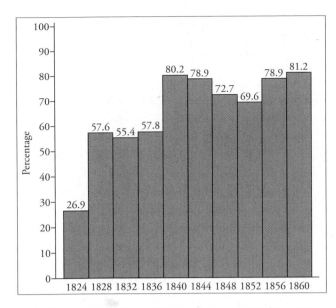

■ PARTICIPATION BY ELIGIBLE VOTERS IN PRESIDENTIAL ELECTIONS, 1824-1860
Political participation expanded during the age of Jackson. Every state reduced or eliminated property qualifications for voting, and intense two-party competition consistently produced high levels of turnout in presidential elections throughout the antebellum period. The process of democratization did not enfranchise women and slaves, and free blacks were stripped of the right to vote throughout the northern states during the antebellum era.

Until the 1820s, relatively few Americans had been permitted to vote. Most states restricted the franchise to white males who were property owners or taxpayers or both, effectively barring an enormous number of the less affluent from the voting rolls. But beginning even before Jackson's election, the rules governing voting began to expand. Changes came first in Ohio and other new states of the West, which, on joining the Union, adopted constitutions that guaranteed all adult white males the right to vote and gave all voters the right to hold public office. Older states, concerned about the loss of their population to the West and thinking that extending the franchise might encourage some residents to stay, began to grant similar political rights to their citizens, dropping or reducing their property ownership or taxpaying requirements. Eventually, every state democratized its electorate to some degree, although some much later and less fully than others.

Change provoked resistance, and at times the democratic trend fell short of the aims of the more radical reformers, as when Massachusetts held its constitutional convention in 1820. Reform-minded delegates complained that in the Massachusetts government the rich were better represented than the poor, both because of restrictions on voting and officeholding and because of a peculiar system by which members of the state senate represented property rather than simply people. But Daniel Webster, one of the conservative delegates, opposed democratic changes on the grounds that "power naturally and necessarily follows property" and that "property as such should have its weight and influence in political arrangement." Webster and the rest of the conservatives could not prevent the reform of the rules for representation in the state senate; nor could they prevent elimination of the property requirement for voting. But, to the dismay of the radicals, the new constitution required that every voter be a taxpayer and that the governor be the owner of considerable real estate.

More often, however, the forces of democratization prevailed in the states. In the New York convention of 1821, for example, conservatives led by James Kent insisted that a taxpaying requirement for suffrage was not enough and that, at least in the election of state senators, the property qualification should survive. Kent argued that society "is an association for the protection of property as well as of life" and that "the individual who contributes only one cent to the common stock ought not to have the same power and influence in directing the property concerns of the partnership as he who contributes his thousands." But reformers, citing the Declaration of Independence, maintained that life, liberty, and the pursuit of happiness, not property, were the main concerns of society and government. The property qualification was abolished.

The wave of state reforms was generally peaceful, but in Rhode Island democratization efforts created considerable instability. The Rhode Island constitution (which was still basically the old colonial charter) barred more than half the adult males of the state from voting. The conservative legislature, chosen by this restricted electorate, consistently blocked all efforts at reform. In 1840, the lawyer and activist Thomas L. Dorr and a group of his followers formed a "People's party," held a convention, drafted a new constitution, and submitted it to a popular vote. It was overwhelmingly approved. The existing legislature, however, refused to accept the Dorr document and submitted a new constitution of its own to the voters. It was narrowly defeated. The Dorrites, in the meantime, had begun to set up a new government,

■ **THE DORR REBELLION**
The battle over the extension of the
franchise in Rhode Island grew so bitter
that in 1842, two competing state
governments were battling for authority.
On May 18, Thomas Dorr, one of two men
claiming to be the elected governor of the
state, led armed followers in an
unsuccessful attempt to capture the Rhode
Island state arsenal. He is shown here
brandishing a sword before his troops in
the midst of the assault. In the aftermath of
his failure, Dorr was captured and
imprisoned. Three years later, he was
pardoned and released.
*(Courtesy The Rhode Island Historical Society.
RHi(X3))*

under their own constitution, with Dorr as governor;
and so, in 1842, two governments were claiming legitimacy in Rhode Island. The old state government
proclaimed that Dorr and his followers were rebels
and began to imprison them. Meanwhile, the Dorrites made a brief and ineffectual effort to capture
the state arsenal. The Dorr Rebellion, as it was
known, quickly failed. Dorr himself surrendered and
was briefly imprisoned. But the episode helped pressure the old guard to draft a new constitution, which
greatly expanded the suffrage.

The democratization process was far from complete. In much of the South, election laws continued
to favor the planters and politicians of the older
counties and to limit the influence of more newly settled western areas. Slaves, of course, were disenfranchised by definition; they were not considered citizens and were believed to have no legal or political
rights. Free blacks could not vote anywhere in the
South and hardly anywhere in the North. Pennsylvania, in fact, amended its state constitution in 1838 to
strip blacks of the right to vote they had previously
enjoyed. In no state could women vote. Nowhere
was the ballot secret, and often voters had to cast a
spoken vote rather than a written one, which meant
that political bosses could, and often did, bribe and
intimidate them.

Despite the persisting limitations, however, the
number of voters increased far more rapidly than did
the population as a whole. Indeed, one of the most
striking political trends of the early nineteenth cen-

tury was the change in the method of choosing presidential electors and the dramatic increase in popular
participation in the process. In 1800, the legislature
had chosen the presidential electors in ten of the
states, and the people in only six. By 1828, electors
were chosen by popular vote in every state but South
Carolina. In the presidential election of 1824, fewer
than 27 percent of adult white males had voted. In
the election of 1828, the figure rose to 58 percent
and in 1840 to 80 percent.

The Legitimization of Party

The high level of voter participation was only partly
the result of an expanded electorate. It was also the
result of a growing interest in politics and a strengthening of party organization and, perhaps equally important, party loyalty. Although party competition
was part of American politics almost from the beginning of the republic, acceptance of the idea of party
was not. For more than thirty years, most Americans
who had opinions about the nature of government
considered parties evils to be avoided and thought
the nation should seek a broad consensus in which
permanent factional lines would not exist. But in the
1820s and 1830s, those assumptions gave way to a
new view: that permanent, institutionalized parties
were a desirable part of the political process, that indeed they were essential to democracy.

The elevation of the idea of party occurred first at
the state level, most prominently in New York. There

Martin Van Buren led a dissident political faction (known as the "Bucktails" or the "Albany Regency"). In the years after the War of 1812, this group began to challenge the established political leadership—led by the aristocratic governor, De Witt Clinton—that had dominated the state for years. Factional rivalries were not new, of course. But the way Van Buren and his followers posed their challenge was new. Refuting the traditional view of a political party as undemocratic, they argued that only an institutionalized party, based in the populace at large, could ensure genuine democracy. The alternative was the sort of closed elite that Clinton had created. In the new kind of party the Bucktails proposed, ideological commitments would be less important than loyalty to the party itself. Preservation of the party as an institution—through the use of favors, rewards, and patronage—would be the principal goal of the leadership. Above all, for a party to survive, it must have a permanent opposition. Competing parties would give each political faction a sense of purpose; they would force politicians to remain continually attuned to the will of the people; and they would check and balance each other in much the same way that the different branches of government checked and balanced one another.

By the late 1820s, this new idea of party was spreading beyond New York. The election of Jackson in 1828, the result of a popular movement that seemed to stand apart from the usual political elites, seemed further to legitimize the idea of party as a popular, democratic institution. "Parties of some sort must exist," said a New York newspaper. " 'Tis in the nature and genius of our government." Finally, in the 1830s, a fully formed two-party system began to operate at the national level, with each party committed to its own existence as an institution and willing to accept the legitimacy of its opposition. The anti-Jackson forces began to call themselves Whigs. Jackson's followers called themselves Democrats (no longer Democratic Republicans), thus giving a permanent name to what is now the nation's oldest political party.

"President of the Common Man"

Unlike Thomas Jefferson, Jackson was no democratic philosopher. The Democratic Party, much less than Jefferson's Republicans, embraced no clear or uniform ideological position. But Jackson himself did embrace a distinct, if simple, theory of democracy. It should offer "equal protection and equal benefits" to all its white male citizens and favor no region or class over another. In practice, that meant an assault on what Jackson and his associates considered the citadels of the eastern aristocracy and an effort to extend opportunities to the rising classes of the West and the South. It also meant a firm commitment to the continuing subjugation of African Americans and Indians (and, although for different reasons, women), for the Jacksonians believed that only by keeping these "dangerous" elements from the body politic could the white-male democracy they valued be preserved.

Jackson's first targets were the entrenched officeholders in the federal government, many of whom had been in place for a generation or more. "Office is considered as a species of property," Jackson told Congress in a bitter denunciation of the "class" of permanent officeholders, "and government rather as a means of promoting individual interests than as an instrument created solely for the service of the people." Official duties, he believed, could be made "so plain and simple that men of intelligence may readily qualify themselves for their performance." Offices belonged to the people, he argued, not to the entrenched officeholders. Or, as one of his henchmen, William L. Marcy of New York, more cynically put it, "To the victors belong the spoils."

In the end, Jackson removed a total of no more than one-fifth of the federal officeholders during his eight years in office, many of them less for partisan reasons than because they had misused government funds or engaged in other corruption. Proportionally, Jackson dismissed no more jobholders than Jefferson had dismissed during his presidency. But by embracing the philosophy of the "spoils system," a system already well entrenched in a number of state governments, the Jackson administration helped make the right of elected officials to appoint their own followers to public office an established feature of American politics.

Jackson's supporters also worked to transform the process by which presidential candidates won their party's nominations. They had long resented the congressional caucus, a process they believed worked to restrict access to the office to those favored by entrenched elites and a process Jackson

THE "AGE OF JACKSON"

To many Americans in the 1820s and 1830s, Andrew Jackson was a champion of democracy, a symbol of a spirit of anti-elitism and egalitarianism that was sweeping American life. In the twentieth century, however, historians have disagreed sharply not only in their assessments of Jackson himself, but in their portrayal of American society in his era.

The "progressive" historians of the early twentieth century tended to see the politics of Jackson and his supporters as a forerunner of their own generation's battles against economic privilege and political corruption. Frederick Jackson Turner encouraged scholars to see Jacksonianism as the product of the democratic West: a protest by the people of the frontier against the conservative aristocracy of the East, which they believed restricted their own freedom and opportunity. Jackson represented those who wanted to make government responsive to the will of the people rather than to the power of special interests. The culmination of this progressive interpretation of Jacksonianism was the publication in 1945 of Arthur M. Schlesinger, Jr.'s *The Age of Jackson.* Schlesinger was less interested in the regional basis of Jacksonianism than Turner's disciples had been. Jacksonian democracy, he argued, was the effort "to control the power of the capitalist groups, mainly Eastern, for the benefit of non-capitalist groups, farmers and laboring men, East, West, and South." He portrayed Jacksonianism as an early version of modern reform efforts (in the progressive era and the New Deal) to "restrain the power of the business community."

Richard Hofstadter, in an influential 1948 essay in *The American Political Tradition,* sharply disagreed. He argued that Jackson was the spokesman of rising entrepreneurs—aspiring businessmen who saw the road to opportunity blocked by the monopolistic power of eastern aristocrats. The Jacksonians opposed special privileges only to the extent those privileges blocked their own road to success. They were less sympathetic to the aspirations of those below them. Similarly, Bray Hammond, writing in 1957, argued that the Jacksonian cause was "one of enterpriser against capitalist," of rising elites against entrenched ones. Other historians, exploring the ideological origins of the movement saw Jacksonianism less as a democratic reform movement than as a nostalgic effort to restore a lost (and largely imagined) past. Marvin Meyer's *The Jacksonian Persuasion* (1957) argued that Jackson and his followers looked with misgivings on the new industrial society emerging around them and yearned instead for a restoration of the agrarian, republican virtues of an earlier time.

Historians of the 1960s began examining Jacksonianism in entirely new ways: looking less at Jackson himself, less at the rhetoric and ideas of his supporters, and more at the nature of American society in the early nineteenth century. Lee Benson's *The Concept of Jacksonian Democracy* (1961)—a pathbreaking work of quantitative history—emphasized the role of religion and ethnicity in determining political divisions in the 1830s. If there was an egalitarian spirit alive in America in those years, it extended well beyond the Democratic

(Courtesy The Rhode Island Historical Society. RHi(X3))

Party and the followers of Jackson. Edward Pessen's *Jacksonian America* (1969) revealed that the democratic rhetoric of the age disguised the reality of an increasingly stratified society, in which inequality was growing more, not less, severe. Richard McCormick (1963) and Glyndon Van Deusen (1963) similarly emphasized the pragmatism of Jackson and the Democrats and de-emphasized clear ideological and partisan divisions.

Scholars in more recent years have also paid relatively little attention to Jackson and the Democratic Party and instead have focused on a series of broad social changes occurring in the early and mid-nineteenth century which some have called a "market revolution." Those changes had profound effects on class relations, and the political battles of the era reflected only a part of their impact. Sean Wilentz, in *Chants Democratic* (1984), identified the rise in the 1820s of a powerful class identity among workers in New York, who were attracted less to Jackson himself than to the idea that power in a republic should be widely dispersed.

John Ashworth, in *"Agrarians" and "Aristocrats"* (1983), and Harry Watson, in *Liberty and Power* (1990), have also seen party politics as a reflection of much larger social changes. The party system was an imperfect reflection of a struggle between people committed to unrestricted opportunities for all white men and those committed to advancing the goals of capitalists, in part through government action.

Recent scholarship may have turned the focus of discussion away from Jackson and the Democratic Party and toward the larger society. But its success in revealing inequality and oppression in antebellum America has produced some withering reassessments of Jackson himself. In *Fathers and Children: Andrew Jackson and the Subjugation of the American Indian* (1975), Michael Rogin portrays Jackson as a man obsessed with escaping from the imposing shadow of the revolutionary generation. He would lead a new American revolution, not against British tyranny but against those who challenged the ability of white men to control the continent. He displayed special savagery toward American Indians, whom he pursued, Rogin argued, with an almost pathological violence and intensity. Alexander Saxton, in *The Rise and Fall of the White Republic* (1990), likewise points to the contradiction between the image of the age of Jackson as a time of expanding democracy and the reality of constricted rights for women, blacks, and Indians. The Democratic Party, he argues, was committed above all to defending slavery and white supremacy.

But the portrayal of Jackson as a champion of the common man has not vanished from scholarly life. The leading Jackson biographer of the postwar era, Robert V. Remini, has noted the flaws in Jackson's concept of democracy; but within the context of his time, Remini claims, Jackson was a genuine "man of the people."

Election Scene at Catonsville

■ **ELECTION SCENE**
Frequent and often boisterous campaign rallies were characteristic of electoral politics in the 1840s, when party loyalties were high and political passions intense—as this 1845 drawing by Alfred Jacob Miller of a rally in Catonsville, Maryland suggests. *(M. and M. Karolik Collection of American Watercolors and Drawings, 1800-1875. Courtesy, Museum of Fine Arts, Boston. ©1998. Museum of Fine Arts Boston. All rights reserved)*

himself had avoided in 1828. In 1832, the president's followers staged a national party convention to renominate him for the presidency—one year after the Anti-Masons (see p. 313) became the first party to hold such a meeting. In later generations, some would see the party convention as a source of corruption and political exclusivity. But those who created it in the 1830s considered it a great triumph for democracy. Through the convention, they believed, power would arise directly from the people, not from aristocratic political institutions such as the caucus.

The spoils system and the political convention did serve to limit the power of two entrenched elites—permanent officeholders and the exclusive party caucus. Yet neither really transferred power to the people. Appointments to office almost always went to prominent political allies of the president and his associates. Delegates to national conventions were less often common men than members of local party organizations. Political opportunity within the party was expanding, but much less so than Jacksonian rhetoric suggested.

⟡ "OUR FEDERAL UNION"

Jackson's commitment to assaulting privileged elites led him to try to reduce the functions of the federal government (as Jefferson had done a generation before). A concentration of power in Washington would, he believed, restrict opportunity to the favored few with political connections. But Jackson believed, too, in forceful presidential leadership. And although he spoke frequently of the importance of states' rights, he was strongly committed to the preservation of the Union. Thus at the same time that he was promoting an economic program to reduce the power of the national government, he was asserting the supremacy of the Union in the face of a potent challenge. For no sooner had he entered office than his own vice president, John C. Calhoun, began to assert a dangerous constitutional theory: nullification.

Calhoun and Nullification

Calhoun was forty-six years old in 1828, with a distinguished past and an apparently promising future. He had been a congressional leader during the War of 1812; he had served for eight years as a widely-admired Secretary of War; he had been vice president in John Quincy Adams's administration. And now, he was running for another term as vice president, this time with Andrew Jackson. Presumably he could look forward to the presidency itself.

But the smoldering issue of the tariff created a dilemma for Calhoun. Once he had been an outspoken protectionist, strongly supporting the tariff of 1816. But since that time many South Carolinians had changed their minds on the subject. Carolina cotton planters were disturbed because their state's economy appeared to be stagnating. One reason was the exhaustion of the South Carolina soil, which could not compete effectively with the fertile, newly opened lands of the Southwest. But most Carolinians blamed their problems on the "tariff of abominations" of 1828, which they claimed had raised the prices they had to pay for the manufactured goods they could not produce for themselves. Some Carolinians had become so angry about the tariff, so certain that it was the source of all their

■ **JOHN C. CALHOUN**
This photograph, by Matthew Brady, captured Calhoun toward the end of his life, when he was torn between his real commitment to the ideals of the Union and his equally fervent commitment to the interests of the South. The younger generation of southern leaders, who would dominate the politics of the region in the 1850s, were less idealistic and more purely sectional in their views. *(Library of Congress)*

problems, that they were ready to consider a drastic remedy: secession.

Calhoun knew that the tariff was not as important a cause of South Carolina's distress as many of his constituents believed. But he also knew that his future political hopes rested on how he met this challenge in his home state. He did so by developing the theory of nullification, which he believed offered a more moderate alternative to secession. Drawing from the ideas of Madison and Jefferson and their Virginia and Kentucky Resolutions of 1798–1799, Calhoun argued that since the federal government was a creation of the states, the states themselves—not the courts or the Congress—were the final arbiters of the constitutionality of federal laws. If a state concluded that Congress had passed an unconstitutional law, it could hold a special convention and declare that law null and void within the state. The law would remain void until three-fourths of the states ratified it as an amendment to the Constitution. The nullifying state would then have to choose between submitting to the law and seceding from the Union. The South Carolina legislature published Calhoun's first statement of his theory in 1828, anonymously, in a document entitled *The South Carolina Exposition and Protest,* which attacked the "tariff of abominations" as unconstitutional and unfair—a fit target for nullification. The nullification doctrine—and the idea of using it to kill the 1828 tariff—quickly attracted broad support in South Carolina.

What Calhoun really hoped, however, was that the nullification theory would never be put to the test, that it would simply pressure the federal government to reduce tariff rates. But he soon discovered that he did not have as much influence in the Jackson administration as he had expected, for he had a powerful rival in Martin Van Buren.

The Rise of Van Buren

Van Buren was about the same age as Calhoun and equally ambitious. As leader of the Democratic Party organization of New York, he had helped carry the state for Jackson in 1828 while getting himself elected governor. By this time he had a reputation as a political wizard. Short and slight, with reddish-gold sideburns and a quiet manner, he was known by such nicknames as "the Sage of Kinderhook," "the Little Magician," and "the Red Fox." He resigned the governorship and went to Washington in 1829 when Jackson appointed him secretary of state.

Van Buren's influence with the president was unmatched. Jackson relied for advice on an unofficial circle of allies who came to be known as the "Kitchen Cabinet." It included such Democratic newspaper editors as Isaac Hill of New Hampshire and Amos Kendall and Francis P. Blair of Kentucky. Van Buren alone was a member of both the official cabinet and this unofficial circle. He and the president grew closer still through a curious quarrel over etiquette that helped drive a wedge between the president and Calhoun.

The quarrel centered on Peggy O'Neale, the attractive and vivacious daughter of a Washington tav-

■ **MARTIN VAN BUREN**
As leader of the so-called Albany Regency in New York in the 1820s, Van Buren helped create one of the first modern party organizations in the United States. Later, as Andrew Jackson's secretary of state and (after 1832) vice president, he helped bring party politics to the national level. So it was ironic that in 1840, when he ran for reelection to the presidency, he lost to William Henry Harrison, whose Whig Party made effective use of many of the techniques of mass politics that Van Buren himself had pioneered. *(Library of Congress)*

ern keeper with whom both Andrew Jackson and his friend John H. Eaton had taken lodgings while serving as senators from Tennessee. O'Neale was married and the mother of two children, but rumors began to circulate in Washington in the mid-1820s that she and Senator Eaton were romantically involved. O'Neale's husband died in 1828, and she and Eaton were soon married. A few weeks later, Jackson named his friend Eaton secretary of war and thus made the new Mrs. Eaton a cabinet wife. The rest of the administration wives, led by Mrs. Calhoun, citing the rumors of a premarital affair between the Eatons, refused to receive her as a member of Washington society. A furious Jackson remembered the public slander that he believed had killed his own wife. He was also convinced, probably correctly, that it was Mrs. Eaton's relatively modest social background at least as much as the rumors about her behavior that offended the cabinet wives. He demanded that the members of his cabinet accept Mrs. Eaton into their social world. Calhoun, however, bowed to his wife's adamant demands and refused, thus taking sides against the president. Van Buren, a widower, befriended the Eatons and thus ingratiated himself with Jackson.

By 1831, partly as a result of the Peggy Eaton affair, Jackson had settled on Van Buren as his choice to succeed him in the White House. Calhoun's dreams of the presidency had all but vanished. His diminished political hopes in the nation only reinforced Calhoun's commitment to the passions of his own state.

The Webster-Hayne Debate

In January 1830, a great debate in the United States Senate dramatically revealed the degree to which sectional issues were intruding into national politics. The controversy grew out of a seemingly routine Senate discussion of federal policy toward the public lands in the West. In the midst of the debate, a senator from Connecticut suggested that all land sales and surveys be temporarily discontinued. Another senator, Thomas Hart Benton of Missouri, the Jacksonian leader in the Senate, charged that the proposal to suspend the sales served the economic needs of the Northeast at the expense of the West.

Robert Y. Hayne, a young senator from South Carolina, took up Benton's argument. He had no direct interest in the western lands, but he and other southerners saw the issue as a way to win western support for their drive to lower the tariff. Hayne argued in a memorable speech that the South and the West were both victims of the tyranny of the Northeast and hinted that the two regions might combine to defend themselves against that tyranny. He gave implicit support to Calhoun's theory of nullification.

Daniel Webster, now a senator from Massachusetts, took the floor the day after Hayne's speech. Although once an advocate of states' rights and an op-

■ **THE WEBSTER-HAYNE DEBATE**
This painting by G. P. A. Healy portrays Daniel Webster's famous reply to Senator Robert Y. Hayne of South Carolina during their dramatic 1830 debate. Until 1860, it hung in the Senate chamber where the debate took place. Today it is in Faneuil Hall in Boston. Webster challenged Hayne's contention that the Union was simply a voluntary association of independent states. The people, not the states, had made the Constitution, he argued, and no state could reject the Union. Rejecting the South's position, which he described as "Liberty first and Union afterwards," Webster called dramatically for "Liberty and Union, now and forever, one and inseparable." Webster's speech was widely distributed throughout the North, and schoolchildren memorized its most famous passages for generations. *(Courtesy Boston Art Commission 1998)*

ponent of the tariff, he had changed his position as the interests of his region had changed. Now he attacked Hayne, and through him Calhoun, for what he considered their challenge to the integrity of the Union. He was, in effect, challenging Hayne to a debate not on public lands and the tariff, but on the issue of states' rights versus national power. Hayne, now coached by Calhoun, responded with an open defense of the theory of nullification. Webster then spent two full afternoons delivering what became known as his "Second Reply to Hayne," a speech that northerners quoted and revered for years to come. He concluded with the ringing appeal: "Liberty and Union, now and for ever, one and inseparable!"

Calhoun's followers believed Hayne had the better of the argument, but their main concern was what President Jackson thought. The answer became clear at the annual Democratic Party banquet in honor of Thomas Jefferson. After dinner, guests delivered a series of toasts. The president arrived with a written

■ **CHARLESTON, 1831**

The little-known South Carolina artist S. Bernard painted this view of Charleston's East Battery in 1831. Then, as now, residents and vistors liked to stroll along the battery and watch the activity in the city's busy harbor. But Charleston in the 1830s was a less important commercial center than it had been a few decades earlier. By then, overseas traders were increasingly avoiding southern ports and doing more and more business in New York. *(Yale University Art Gallery)*

text in which he had underscored certain words: "Our Federal Union—It must be preserved." While he spoke he looked directly at Calhoun. The diminutive Van Buren, who stood on his chair to see better, thought he saw Calhoun's hand shake and a trickle of wine run down his glass as he responded to the president's toast with the words: "The Union—next to our liberty most dear." Sharp and dangerous lines were being drawn.

The Nullification Crisis

In 1832, the controversy over nullification finally produced a genuine crisis when South Carolina responded angrily to a congressional tariff bill that offered them no relief from the 1828 "tariff of abominations." Some militant South Carolinians were ready to secede from the Union, but Calhoun persuaded them to try nullification instead. The supporters of nullification won a substantial victory in the state elections of 1832. And almost immediately, the newly elected legislature summoned a state convention, which

voted to nullify the tariffs of 1828 and 1832 and to forbid the collection of duties within the state. At the same time, South Carolina elected Hayne governor and Calhoun (who had resigned as vice president) to replace Hayne as senator.

Jackson insisted that nullification was treason and that its adherents were traitors. (Privately, he threatened to hang Calhoun.) He strengthened the federal forts in the state and ordered a warship and several revenue ships to Charleston. When Congress convened early in 1833, Jackson's followers won approval of a "force bill" authorizing the president to use the military to enforce acts of Congress. Violence seemed a real possibility early in 1833.

Calhoun faced a predicament as he took his place in the Senate. Not a single state had come to South Carolina's support. Even South Carolina itself was divided, since most realized the state could not hope to prevail in a showdown with the federal government. In the end, the timely intervention of Henry Clay, newly elected to the Senate, saved Calhoun. Clay devised a compromise that lowered the tariff gradually so that by 1842 it would reach approximately the same level as in 1816. The compromise and the force bill were passed on the same day, March 1, 1833. Jackson signed them both.

In South Carolina, the convention reassembled and repealed its nullification of the tariffs. But unwilling to allow Congress to have the last word, the convention nullified the force bill—a largely symbolic action, since the force bill had no meaning once the tariff toward which it was directed had been repealed. Jackson chose to ignore this last statement of defiance and to focus instead on the repeal of the tariff nullification. Calhoun and his followers, however, claimed a victory for nullification, which had, they insisted, forced the revision of the tariff. Their claim had some justification. But the episode taught Calhoun and his allies an important lesson: No state could defy the federal government alone.

THE REMOVAL OF THE INDIANS

There had never been any doubt about Andrew Jackson's attitude toward the Indian tribes that continued to live in the eastern states and territories of the United States. He wanted them to move west, beyond the Mississippi, out of the way of expanding white settlement. Jackson's antipathy toward the Native Americans had a special intensity because of his own earlier experiences leading military campaigns against tribes along the Southern border. But in most respects, his views were little different from those of most other white Americans.

White Attitudes Toward the Tribes

In the eighteenth century, many white Americans had considered the Indians "noble savages," peoples without real civilization but with an inherent dignity that made civilization possible among them. By the first decades of the nineteenth century, this vaguely paternalistic attitude (the attitude of Thomas Jefferson, among others) was giving way to a new and more hostile one, particularly among the whites in the western states and territories whom Jackson came to represent. Such whites were coming to view Native Americans simply as "savages," not only uncivilized but uncivilizable. That was one reason for the commitment to Indian removal: the belief that whites should not be expected to live in close proximity to the "savage" Indians, that Indian cultures and societies were unworthy of respect.

White westerners favored removal as well because they feared that continued contact between the expanding white settlements and the Indians would produce endless conflict and violence. Most of all, however, they favored Indian removal because of their own insatiable desire for territory. The tribes possessed valuable land in the path of expanding white settlement. Whites wanted it.

Legally, only the federal government had authority to negotiate with the Indians over land, a result of Supreme Court decisions that established the tribes as, in effect, "nations within the nation." The tribal nations that the Court identified were not, however, securely rooted in Native American history. The large tribal aggregations with which white Americans dealt were, in fact, relatively new entities. Most Indians were accustomed to thinking in much more local terms. They created these larger tribes when they realized they would need some collective strength to deal with whites; but as new and untested political entities, the tribes were often weak and divided. The Marshall Court had seemed to acknowledge this in declaring the tribes not only sovereign nations, but also dependent ones, for whom the federal government must take considerable responsibility. Through most of the nineteenth century, the government interpreted that responsibility as finding ways to move the Native Americans out of the way of expanding white settlement.

The Black Hawk War

The federal government had already taken substantial strides toward removing Native Americans from the East by the time Jackson entered the White House. But substantial tribal enclaves remained. In the Old Northwest, the long process of expelling the woodland Indians culminated in a last battle in 1831–1832, between white settlers in Illinois and an alliance of Sauk (or Sac) and Fox Indians under the fabled and now aged warrior Black Hawk. An earlier treaty had ceded tribal lands in Illinois to the United States; but Black Hawk and his followers refused to recognize the legality of the agreement, which a rival tribal faction had signed. Hungry and resentful, a thousand of them crossed the river and reoccupied vacant lands in Illinois. White settlers in the region feared that the

■ **BLACK HAWK AND WHIRLING THUNDER**
After his defeat by white settlers in Illinois in 1832, the famed Sauk warrior Black Hawk and his son, Whirling Thunder, were captured and sent on a tour by Andrew Jackson, displayed to the public as trophies of war. They showed such dignity through the ordeal that much of the white public quickly began to sympathize with them. This portrait, by John Wesley Jarvis, was painted on the tour's final stop, in New York City. Black Hawk wears the European-style suit, while Whirling Thunder wears native costume to emphasize his commitment to his tribal roots. Soon thereafter, Black Hawk returned to his tribe, wrote a celebrated autobiography, and died in 1838. *(Bettmann)*

resettlement was the beginning of a substantial invasion, and they assembled the Illinois state militia and federal troops to repel the "invaders."

The Black Hawk War, as it became known, was notable chiefly for the viciousness of the white military efforts. White leaders in western Illinois vowed to exterminate the "bandit collection of Indians" and attacked them even when Black Hawk attempted to surrender. The Sauks and Foxes, defeated and starving, retreated across the Mississippi into Iowa. White troops (and some bands of Sioux whom they encouraged to join the chase) pursued them as they fled and slaughtered most of them. United States troops captured Black Hawk himself and sent him on a tour of the East, where Andrew Jackson was one of many curious whites who arranged to meet him. (Abraham Lincoln served as a captain of the militia, but saw no action, in the Black Hawk War; Jefferson Davis was a lieutenant in the regular army.)

The "Five Civilized Tribes"

More troubling to the government in the 1830s were the tribes remaining in the South. In western Geor-

gia, Alabama, Mississippi, and Florida lived what were known as the "Five Civilized Tribes"—the Cherokee, Creek, Seminole, Chickasaw, and Choctaw—most of whom had established settled agricultural societies with successful economies. The Cherokees in Georgia had formed a particularly stable and sophisticated culture, with their own written language and a formal constitution (adopted in 1827) that created an independent Cherokee Nation. They were more closely tied to their lands than many of the more nomadic tribes to the north.

Even some whites argued that the Cherokees, unlike other tribes, should be allowed to retain their eastern lands, since they had become such a "civilized" society and had, under pressure from missionaries and government agents, given up many of their traditional ways. Cherokee men had once been chiefly hunters and had left farming mainly to women. By now the men had given up most of their hunting and (like most white men) took over the farming themselves; Cherokee women, also like their white counterparts, restricted themselves largely to domestic tasks.

The federal government, to which the Constitution had delegated the power to negotiate with the tribes, had worked steadily through the first decades of the nineteenth century to negotiate treaties with the southern Indians that would remove them to the West and open their lands for white settlement. But the negotiating process often did not proceed fast enough to satisfy the region's whites. The State of Georgia's independent effort to dislodge the Creeks, over the objection of President Adams, was one example of this impatience. That same impatience became evident early in Jackson's administration, when the legislatures in Georgia, Alabama, and Mississippi began passing laws to regulate the tribes remaining in their states. They received assistance in these efforts from Congress, which in 1830 passed the Removal Act (with Jackson's approval), which appropriated money to finance federal negotiations with the southern tribes aimed at relocating them to the West. The president quickly dispatched federal officials to negotiate nearly a hundred new treaties with the remaining tribes. Thus, the southern tribes faced a combination of pressures from both the state and federal governments. Most tribes were too weak to resist, and they ceded their lands in return for only token payments. Some, however, balked.

In Georgia, the Cherokees tried to stop the white encroachments by appealing to the Supreme Court. The Court's decisions in *Cherokee Nation* v. *Georgia,* and *Worcester* v. *Georgia* in 1831 and 1832 (see pp. 280–281) seemed at least partially to vindicate the tribe. But Jackson's longtime hostility toward Native Americans and his longtime commitment to their removal left him with little sympathy for the Cherokees and little patience with the Court. He was eager to retain the support of white southerners and westerners in the increasingly bitter partisan battles in which his administration was becoming engaged. That was one reason why the president had vigorously supported (and even actively encouraged) Georgia's efforts to remove the Cherokees before the Court decision. His reaction to Marshall's rulings reflected his belief that the justices were using the issue to express their hostility to the larger aims of his presidency. When the chief justice announced the decision in *Worcester* v. *Georgia,* Jackson reportedly responded with contempt. "John Marshall has made his decision," he was reported to have said. "Now let him enforce it." The decision was not enforced.

In 1835, the federal government extracted a treaty from a minority faction of the Cherokees, none of them a chosen representative of the Cherokee Nation. The treaty ceded the tribe's land to Georgia in return for $5 million and a reservation west of the Mississippi. The great majority of the 17,000 Cherokees did not recognize the treaty as legitimate and refused to leave their homes. But Jackson would not be thwarted. He sent an army of 7,000 under General Winfield Scott to round them up and drive them westward at bayonet point.

Trails of Tears

About 1,000 Cherokee fled across the state line to North Carolina, where the federal government eventually provided a small reservation for them in the Smoky Mountains, which survives today. But most of the rest made the long, forced trek to "Indian Territory" (which later became Oklahoma) beginning in the winter of 1838. Along the way, a Kentuckian observed: "Even aged females, apparently nearly ready to drop in the grave, were travelling with heavy burdens attached to their backs, sometimes on frozen ground and sometimes on muddy streets, with no covering for their feet."

Thousands, perhaps an eighth or more of the emigrés, perished before or soon after reaching their unwanted destination. In the harsh new reservations in which they were now forced to live, the survivors never forgot the hard journey. They called their route "The Trail Where They Cried," the Trail of Tears. Jackson claimed that the "remnant of that ill-fated race" was now "beyond the reach of injury or oppression," apparently trying to convince himself or others that he had supported removal as a way to protect the tribes.

The Cherokees were not alone in experiencing the hardships of the Trail of Tears. Between 1830 and 1838, virtually all the "Five Civilized Tribes" were expelled from the southern states and forced to relocate in the new Indian Territory, which Congress had officially created by the Indian Intercourse Act of 1834. The Choctaws of Mississippi and western Alabama were the first to make the trek, beginning in 1830. The army moved out the Creeks of eastern Alabama and western Georgia in 1836. The Chickasaw in northern Mississippi began the long march westward a year later, and the Cherokees, finally, a year after that. The government thought the Indian Territory was safely distant from existing white settlements and consisted of land that most whites considered undesirable. It had the additional advantage, the government believed, of being on the eastern edge of what earlier white explorers had christened the "Great American Desert," land unfit for habitation. It seemed unlikely that whites would ever seek to settle along the western borders of the Indian Territory; and thus the prospect of whites surrounding the reservation and producing further conflict seemed remote.

Only the Seminoles in Florida managed to resist the pressures to relocate, and even their success was limited. Like other tribes, the Seminoles had agreed under pressure to a settlement (the 1832–1833 treaties of Payne's Landing), by which they ceded their lands to the government and agreed to move to Indian Territory within three years. Most did move west, but a substantial minority, under the leadership of the chieftain Osceola, refused to leave and staged an uprising beginning in 1835 to defend their lands. (Joining the Indians in their struggle was a group of runaway black slaves who had been living with the tribe.) The Seminole War dragged on for years. Jackson sent troops to Florida, but the Seminoles with their African-American associates were masters of

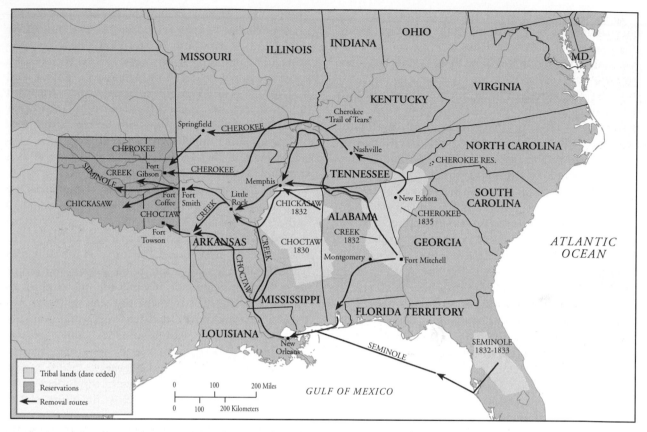

■ THE EXPULSION OF INDIANS FROM THE SOUTH, 1830-1835

Andrew Jackson was famous in his time for his military exploits against the tribes. As president, he helped ensure that few Indians would remain in the southern states, where white settlement was expanding, by supporting the forced removal of the tribes from their traditional lands. Despite the Supreme Court's decision vindicating Cherokee rights in *Worcester* v. *Georgia,* the Cherokee, Choctaw, Creek, Chickasaw, and Seminole Indian nations were resettled in the area that later became Oklahoma. This map shows the major routes along which Indians traveled to the new territory, routes they remembered as "Trails of Tears."

guerrilla warfare in the jungly Everglades. Even after Osceola had been treacherously captured by white troops while under a flag of truce and had died in prison; even after white troops had engaged in a systematic campaign of extermination against the resisting Indians and their black allies; even after 1,500 white soldiers had died and the federal government had spent $20 million on the struggle—even then, followers of Osceola remained in Florida. Finally, in 1842, the government abandoned the war. By then, many of the Seminoles had been either killed or forced westward. But the relocation of the Seminoles, unlike the relocation of most of the other tribes, was never complete.

The Meaning of Removal

By the end of the 1830s, virtually all the important Indian societies east of the Mississippi (with such exceptions as the Seminoles and a few Cherokee in the South and some tribal enclaves in northern Michigan and Wisconsin) had been removed to the West. The tribes had ceded over 100 million acres of eastern land to the federal government; they had received in return about $68 million and 32 million acres in the far less hospitable lands west of the Mississippi between the Missouri and Red Rivers. There they lived, divided by tribe into a series of carefully defined reservations, in a territory surrounded by a string of United States forts to keep them in (and to keep most

OCEOLA'S MODE OF SIGNING THE TREATY.

■ **OSCEOLA DEFIANT**
This contemporary drawing portrays the Seminole chieftain Osceola plunging his knife through a treaty that would have paid the tribe for their land and required them to move out of Florida. The gesture was only the beginning of Osceola's defiance. In 1835, he led his people in a war against the U.S. government's efforts to remove them from the territory. *(Florida State Archives)*

whites out), in a region whose climate and topography bore little relation to anything they had known before. Eventually, even this forlorn enclave would face incursions from white civilization.

What were the alternatives to the removal of the eastern Indians? There was probably never any realistic possibility that the government could stop white expansion westward. White people had already been penetrating the West for nearly two centuries, and such penetrations were certain to continue. But did that expansion really require removal?

There were, in theory at least, several alternatives to the brutal removal policy. There were many examples in the West of white settlers and native tribes living side by side and creating a shared (if not necessarily equal) world. In the pueblos of New Mexico, in the fur trading posts of the Pacific Northwest, in parts of Texas and California, settlers from Mexico, Canada, and the United States had created societies

in which Indians and whites were in intimate contact with each other. Even during the famous Lewis and Clark expedition, white explorers had lived with western Indians on terms of such intimacy that many of them contracted venereal disease from Indian sexual partners. Sometimes these close contacts between whites and Indians were beneficial to both sides, even reasonably equal. Sometimes they were cruel and exploitive. But the early multiracial societies of the West did not separate whites and Indians. They demonstrated ways in which the two cultures could interact, each shaping the other.

By the mid-nineteenth century, however, white Americans had adopted a different model as they contemplated westward expansion. Much as the early British settlers along the Atlantic coast had established "plantations," from which natives were, in theory, to be excluded, so the westward-moving whites of later years came to imagine the territories they were entering as virgin land, with no preexisting civilization. Native Americans, they believed, could not be partners—either equal or subordinate—in the creation of new societies in the West. They were obstacles, to be removed and, as far as possible, isolated. Indians, Andrew Jackson once said, had "neither the intelligence, the industry, the moral habits, nor the desire of improvement" to be fit partners in the project of extending white civilization westward. By dismissing Native American cultures in that way, white Americans justified to themselves a series of harsh policies that they believed (incorrectly) would make the West theirs alone.

JACKSON AND THE BANK WAR

Jackson was quite willing to use federal power against rebellious states and against the tribes. On economic issues, however, he was consistently opposed to concentrating power either in the federal government or in powerful and, in his view, aristocratic institutions associated with it. An early example of his skeptical view of federal power was his 1830 veto of a congressional measure providing a subsidy to the proposed Maysville Road in Kentucky. The bill was unconstitutional, Jackson argued, because the road in question lay entirely within Kentucky and was not, therefore, a part of "interstate commerce." But the bill was also unwise, he believed, because it committed the government to what Jackson considered extravagant expenditures.

Jackson's opposition to federal power and aristocratic privilege lay behind the most celebrated episode of Jackson's presidency: the war against the Bank of the United States.

Biddle's Institution

The Bank of the United States in the 1830s was a mighty institution indeed, and it is not surprising that it would attract Jackson's wrath. Its stately headquarters in Philadelphia seemed to symbolize its haughty image of itself. It had branches in twenty-nine other cities, making it the most powerful and far-flung financial institution in the nation. By law, the Bank was the only place that the federal government could deposit its own funds; the government, in turn, owned one-fifth of the bank's stock. The

Bank did a tremendous business in general banking. It provided credit to growing enterprises; it issued bank notes, which served as a dependable medium of exchange throughout the country; and it exercised a restraining effect on the less well-managed state banks. Nicholas Biddle, who served as president of the Bank from 1823 on, had done much to put the institution on a sound and prosperous basis. Nevertheless, Andrew Jackson was determined to destroy it.

Opposition to the Bank came from two very different groups: the "soft-money" faction and the "hard-money" faction. Advocates of soft money—people who wanted more currency in circulation and believed that issuing bank notes unsupported by gold and silver was the best way to circulate more currency—consisted largely of state bankers and their allies. They objected to the Bank of the United States because it restrained the state banks from issuing notes freely. The hard-money people believed that gold and silver were the only basis for money. They condemned all banks that issued bank notes, including the Bank of the United States. The soft-money advocates were believers in rapid economic growth and speculation; the hard-money forces embraced older ideas of "public virtue" and looked with suspicion on expansion and speculation.

Jackson himself supported the hard-money position. Many years before, he had been involved in some grandiose land and commercial speculations based on paper credit. His business had failed, and he had fallen deeply into debt as a result of the Panic of 1797. After that, he was suspicious of all banks and all paper currency. But as president he was also sensitive to the complaints of his many soft-money supporters in the West and the South. He made it clear that he would not favor renewing the charter of the Bank of the United States, which was due to expire in 1836.

Biddle was a Philadelphia aristocrat, unaccustomed to politics. But in his efforts to save the Bank, he began granting financial favors to influential men who he thought might help him preserve the bank. In particular, he turned to Daniel Webster and cultivated a close personal friendship with him. He named Webster the Bank's legal counsel and director of its Boston branch; Webster was also a frequent, heavy borrower from the Bank. Perhaps unsurprisingly, he helped Biddle win the support of other important figures, among them Henry Clay.

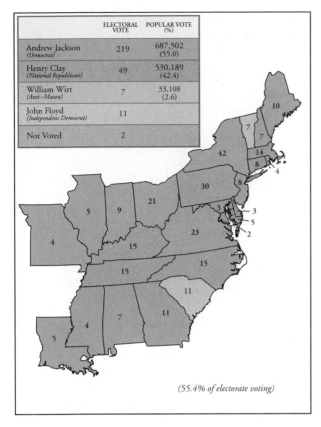

	ELECTORAL VOTE	POPULAR VOTE (%)
Andrew Jackson *(Democrat)*	219	687,502 (55.0)
Henry Clay *(National Republican)*	49	530,189 (42.4)
William Wirt *(Anti--Mason)*	7	33,108 (2.6)
John Floyd *(Independent Democrat)*	11	
Not Voted	2	

(55.4% of electorate voting)

■ **ELECTION OF 1832**
In the Presidential election of 1832, Andrew Jackson again won a resounding victory. In the South, Jackson lost only South Carolina, the nullifier state, and Kentucky, the home of favorite son Henry Clay. Jackson even made inroads into New England, winning New Hampshire and Maine. The Democratic victory of 1832 was an even more resounding national triumph than Jackson's victory four years earlier, and it vindicated the president's war against the Bank of the United States. The inability of Jackson's opposition to unite around an opposition candidate (representatives of three different parties divided the few electoral votes Jackson failed to win) helped spur the formation of the Whig party several years later.

Clay, Webster, and other advisers persuaded Biddle to apply to Congress in 1832 for a bill to renew the Bank's charter. That was four years ahead of the date the original charter was scheduled to expire. But forcing a vote now would allow the Bank to become a major issue in the 1832 national elections. Congress passed the recharter bill; Jackson, predictably, vetoed it; and the Bank's supporters in Congress failed to override the veto. Just as Clay had hoped, the 1832 campaign now centered on the future of the Bank.

Clay himself ran for president that year as the unanimous choice of the National Republicans, who held a nominating convention in Baltimore late in 1831. But the bank war failed to provide him with the winning issue for which he had hoped. Jackson, with Van Buren as his running mate, overwhelmingly defeated Clay (and several minor party candidates) with 55 percent of the popular vote and 219 electoral votes (more than four times as many as Clay received). These results were a defeat not only for Clay, but also for Biddle.

The "Monster" Destroyed

Jackson was now more determined than ever to destroy the "monster" Bank as quickly as possible. He could not legally abolish the institution before the expiration of its charter. Instead, he tried to weaken it. He decided to remove the government's deposits from the Bank. His secretary of the treasury believed that such an action would destabilize the financial system and refused to give the order. Jackson fired him and appointed a new one. When the new secretary similarly balked, Jackson fired him too and named a third, more compliant secretary: Attorney General Roger B. Taney, his close friend and loyal ally. Taney began placing the government's deposits not in the Bank of the United States, as it had in the past, but in a number of state banks (which Jackson's enemies called "pet banks").

The arrogant Nicholas Biddle, whom Jacksonians derisively called "Czar Nicholas," did not give in without a fight. "This worthy President," he wrote sarcastically, "thinks that because he has scalped Indians and imprisoned Judges, he is to have his way with the Bank. He is mistaken." When the administration began to transfer funds directly from the Bank of the United States to the pet banks (as opposed to the initial practice of simply depositing new funds in those banks), Biddle called in loans and raised interest rates, explaining that without the government deposits the Bank's resources were stretched too thin. He realized his actions were likely to cause financial distress. He hoped a short recession would persuade Congress to recharter the Bank. "Nothing but the evidence of suffering," he told a colleague, would "produce any effect in Congress." By now, the struggle had become not just a conflict over policy and principle, but a bitter and even petulant personal battle

■ **"THE DOWNFALL OF MOTHER BANK"**
This 1832 Democratic cartoon celebrates Andrew Jackson's destruction of the Bank of the United States. The president is shown here driving away the Bank's corrupt supporters by ordering the withdrawal of government deposits. *(New-York Historical Society)*

between two proud men—both of them acting reck-lessly in an effort to humiliate and defeat the other.

As financial conditions worsened in the winter of 1833–1834, supporters of the Bank blamed Jackson's policies for the recession. They organized meetings around the country and sent petitions to Washington urging a rechartering of the Bank. But the Jacksoni-ans blamed the recession on Biddle and refused to budge. When distressed citizens appealed to the president for help, he dismissively answered, "Go to Biddle."

Finally, Biddle contracted credit too far even for his own allies in the business community, who began to fear that in his effort to save his own bank he was threatening their interests. Some of them did "go to Biddle." A group of New York and Boston merchants protested (as one of them reported) that the business community "ought not and would not sustain him in

further pressure, which he very well knew was not necessary for the safety of the bank, and in which his whole object was to coerce a charter." To appease the business community, Biddle at last reversed himself and began to grant credit in abundance and on reason-able terms. His vacillating and unpopular tactics ended his chances of winning a recharter of the Bank.

Jackson had won a considerable political victory. But when the Bank of the United States died in 1836, the country lost a valuable financial institution and was left with a fragmented and chronically unstable banking system that would plague the economy for more than a century.

The Taney Court

In the aftermath of the Bank War, Jackson moved against the most powerful institution of economic nationalism of all: the Supreme Court. In 1835, when John Marshall died, the president appointed as the new chief justice his trusted ally Roger B. Taney. Taney did not bring a sharp break in constitutional interpretation, but he gradually helped modify Marshall's vigorous nationalism.

Perhaps the clearest indication of the new judicial mood was the celebrated case of *Charles River Bridge* v. *Warren Bridge* of 1837. The case involved a dispute between two Massachusetts companies over the right to build a bridge across the Charles River between Boston and Cambridge. One company had a longstanding charter from the state to operate a toll bridge and claimed that this charter guaranteed it a monopoly of the bridge traffic. Another company had applied to the legislature for authorization to construct a second, competing bridge that would—since it would be toll free—greatly reduce the value of the first company's charter.

The first company contended that in granting the second charter the legislature was engaging in a breach of contract and noted that the Marshall Court, in the *Dartmouth College* case and other decisions, had ruled that states had no right to abrogate contracts. But now Taney, speaking for the Democratic majority on the Court, supported the right of Massachusetts to award the second charter. The object of government, Taney maintained, was to promote the general happiness, an object that took precedence over the rights of contract and property. A state, therefore, had the right to amend or abrogate a contract if such action was necessary to advance the well-being of the community. Such an abrogation was clearly necessary in the case of the Charles River Bridge, he argued, because the original bridge company, by exercising a monopoly, was benefiting from unjustifiable privilege. (It did not help the first company that its members were largely Boston aristocrats and that it was closely associated with elite Harvard College; the challenging company, by contrast, consisted largely of newer, aspiring entrepreneurs—the sort of people with whom Jackson and his allies instinctively identified.) The decision reflected one of the cornerstones of the Jacksonian ideal: that the key to democracy was an expansion of economic opportunity, which would not occur if older corporations could maintain monopolies and choke off competition from newer companies.

THE CHANGING FACE OF AMERICAN POLITICS

Jackson's forceful—some claimed tyrannical—tactics in crushing first the nullification movement and then the Bank of the United States helped galvanize a growing opposition coalition that by the mid-1830s was ready to assert itself in national politics. It began as a gathering of national political leaders opposed to Jackson's use of power. Denouncing the president as "King Andrew I," they began to refer to themselves as Whigs, after the party in England that had traditionally worked to limit the power of the king. With the emergence of the Whigs, the nation once again had two competing political parties. What scholars now call the "second party system" had begun what turned out to be its relatively brief life.

Democrats and Whigs

The two parties were different from one another in their philosophies, in their constituencies, and in the character of their leaders. But they became increasingly alike in the way they approached the process of electing their followers to office.

Democrats in the 1830s envisioned a future of steadily expanding economic and political opportunities for white males. The role of government should be limited, they believed, but it should include efforts to remove obstacles to opportunity and to avoid creating new ones. That meant defending the Union, which Jacksonians believed was essential to the dynamic economic growth they favored. It also meant attacking centers of corrupt privilege. As Jackson himself said in his farewell address, the society of America should be one in which "the planter, the farmer, the mechanic, and the laborer, all know that their success depends on their own industry and economy," in which artificial privilege would stifle no one's opportunity. Among the most radical members of the party—the so-called Locofocos, mainly workingmen and small businessmen and professionals in the Northeast—sentiment was strong for a vigorous, perhaps even violent assault on monopoly and privilege far in advance of anything Jackson himself ever contemplated.

The political philosophy that became known as Whiggery was very different. It favored expanding the power of the federal government, encouraging

A BEAUTIFUL GOBLET OF
WHITE-HOUSE CHAMPAGNE

AN UGLY *MUG* OF
LOG-CABIN HARD CIDER

■ **AN ATTACK ON VAN BUREN**
This "pull card," made during the 1840 presidential campaign, which Van Buren lost to William Henry Harrison, satirizes the president as an aristocratic dandy. The card displays Van Buren grinning while he drinks champagne in the White House. Pulling a tab on the card changes his champagne glass to a mug of hard cider (with Harrison's initials on it) and changes his expression from delight to revulsion. *(Division of Political History, American History Museum, Smithsonian Institution, Washington, D.C.)*

industrial and commercial development, and knitting the country together into a consolidated economic system. Whigs embraced material progress enthusiastically; but unlike the Democrats, they were cautious about westward expansion, fearful that rapid territorial growth would produce instability. Their vision of America was of a nation embracing the industrial future and rising to world greatness as a commercial and manufacturing power. Thus while Democrats were inclined to oppose legislation establishing banks, corporations, and other modernizing institutions, Whigs generally favored such measures.

To some extent, the constituencies of the two major parties reflected these diffuse philosophies. The Whigs were strongest among the more substantial merchants and manufacturers of the Northeast; the wealthier planters of the South (those who fa-

vored commercial development and the strengthening of ties with the North); and the ambitious farmers and rising commercial class of the West—usually migrants from the Northeast—who advocated internal improvements, expanding trade, and rapid economic progress. The Democrats drew more support from smaller merchants and the workingmen of the Northeast; from southern planters suspicious of industrial growth; and from westerners—usually with southern roots—who favored a predominantly agrarian economy and opposed the development of powerful economic institutions in their region. Whigs tended to be wealthier than Democrats, to have more aristocratic backgrounds, and to be more commercially ambitious.

But Whigs and Democrats alike were more interested in winning elections than in maintaining philosophical purity. And both parties made frequent adjustments in their public postures to attract the largest possible number of voters. In New York, for example, the Whigs worked to develop a popular following by making a connection to a movement known as Anti-Masonry. The Anti-Mason movement had emerged in the 1820s in response to widespread resentment against the secret, exclusive, and hence supposedly undemocratic, Society of Freemasons. Such resentments greatly increased in 1826 when a former Mason, William Morgan, mysteriously disappeared (and was assumed to have been murdered) from his home in Batavia, New York, shortly before he was scheduled to publish a book purporting to expose the secrets of Freemasonry. Whigs seized on the Anti-Mason frenzy to launch harsh attacks on Jackson and Van Buren (both Freemasons), implying that the Democrats were part of the antidemocratic conspiracy. In the process, the Whigs presented themselves as opponents of aristocracy and exclusivity. They were, in other words, attacking the Democrats with the Democrats' own issues.

Religious and ethnic divisions also played an important role in determining the constituencies of the two parties. Irish and German Catholics, among the largest of the recent immigrant groups, tended to support the Democrats, who appeared to share their own vague aversion to commercial development and entrepreneurial progress and who seemed to respect their family- and community-centered values and habits. Evangelical Protestants gravitated toward the Whigs because they associated the party with constant development and improvement, goals their own faith embraced. These and other ethnic, religious, and cultural tensions were often more influential in determining party alignments than any concrete political or economic proposals.

The Whig Party was more successful at defining its positions and attracting a constituency than it was in uniting behind a national leader. No single person was ever able to command the loyalties of the party in the way Andrew Jackson commanded the loyalties of the Democrats. Instead, Whigs tended to divide their loyalties among three figures, each of whom was so substantial a figure that together they became known as the "Great Triumvirate": Henry Clay, Daniel Webster, and John Calhoun.

Clay won support from many of those who favored his program for internal improvements and economic development, what he called the American System; but his image as a devious operator and his identification with the West proved serious liabilities. He ran for president three times and never won. Daniel Webster, the greatest orator of his era, won broad support with his passionate speeches in defense of the Constitution and the Union; but his close connection with the Bank of the United States and the protective tariff, his reliance on rich men for financial support, and his excessive and often embarrassing fondness for brandy prevented him from developing enough of a national constituency to win him the office he so desperately wanted. John C. Calhoun, the third member of what became known as the Great Triumvirate, never considered himself a true Whig, and his identification with the nullification controversy in effect disqualified him from national leadership in any case. But he had tremendous strength in the South, supported a national bank, and shared with Clay and Webster a strong animosity toward Andrew Jackson.

The problems that emerged from this divided leadership became particularly clear in 1836. The Democrats were united behind Andrew Jackson's personal choice for president, Martin Van Buren. The Whigs could not even agree on a single candidate. Instead, they ran several candidates, hoping to profit from the regional strength of each. Webster represented the party in New England; Hugh Lawson White of Tennessee ran in the South; and the former Indian fighter and hero of the War of 1812 from Ohio, William Henry Harrison, was the candidate in the middle states and the West. Party leaders hoped the three candidates together might draw enough votes from Van Buren to prevent his getting a majority and throw the election to the House of Representatives, where the Whigs might be able to elect one of their own leadres. In the end, however, Van Buren won easily, with 170 electoral votes to 124 for all his opponents.

Van Buren and the Panic of 1837

Andrew Jackson retired from public life in 1837, the most beloved political figure of his age. Martin Van Buren was very different from his predecessor and far less fortunate. He was never able to match Jackson's personal popularity, and his administration encountered economic difficulties that devastated the Democrats and helped the Whigs.

■ **"THE TIMES," 1837**
This savage caricature of the economic troubles besetting the United States in 1837 illustrates, among other things, popular resentment of the hard-money orthodoxies of the time. A sign on the Custom House reads: "All bonds must be paid in Specie." Next door, the bank announces: "No specie payments made here." Women and children are shown begging in the street, while unemployed workers stand shoeless in front of signs advertising loans and "grand schemes." *(New-York Historical Society)*

Van Buren's success in the 1836 election was a result in part of a nationwide economic boom that was reaching its height in that year. Canal and railroad builders were at a peak of activity. Prices were rising, money was plentiful, and credit was easy as banks increased their loans and notes with little regard to their reserves of cash. The land business, in particular, was booming. Between 1835 and 1837, the government sold nearly 40 million acres of public land, nearly three-fourths of it to speculators, who purchased large tracts in hopes of reselling them at a profit. These land sales, along with revenues the government received from the tariff of 1833, created a series of substantial federal budget surpluses and made possible a steady reduction of the national debt (something Jackson had always advocated). From 1835 to 1837, the government for the first and only time in its history was out of debt, with a substantial surplus in the Treasury.

Congress and the administration now faced the question of what to do with the Treasury surplus. Reducing the tariff was not an option, since no one wanted to raise that thorny issue again. Instead, support grew for returning the federal surplus to the states. In 1836, Congress passed a "distribution" act requiring the federal government to pay its surplus funds to the states each year in four quarterly installments as interest-free, unsecured loans. No one expected the "loans" to be repaid. The states spent the money quickly, mainly to encourage construction of highways, railroads, and canals. The distribution of the surplus thus gave further stimulus to the economic boom. At the same time, the withdrawal of federal funds strained the state (or "pet") banks in which they had been deposited by the government; they had to call in their own loans to make the transfer of funds to the state governments.

Congress did nothing to check the speculative fever, with which many congressmen themselves were badly infected. Webster, for one, was buying up thousands of acres in the West. But Jackson, always suspicious of paper currency, was unhappy that the government was selling good land and receiving in return various state bank notes worth no more than the credit of the issuing bank.

In 1836, not long before leaving office, he issued a presidential order, the "specie circular." It provided that in payment for public lands the government would only accept gold or silver coins or currency securely backed by gold or silver. Jackson was right to fear the speculative fever but wrong in thinking the specie circular would cure it. On the contrary, it produced a financial panic that began in the first months of Van Buren's presidency. Hundreds of banks and businesses failed. Unemployment grew. Bread riots broke out in some of the larger cities. Prices fell, especially the price of land. Many railroad and canal projects failed. Several of the debt-burdened state governments ceased to pay interest on their bonds, and a few repudiated their debts, at least temporarily. It was the worst depression in American history to that point, and it lasted for five years. It was a political catastrophe for Van Buren and the Democrats.

Both parties bore some responsibility for the panic. The distribution of the Treasury surplus, which had weakened the state banks and helped cause the crash, had been a Whig measure. Jackson's specie circular, which had started a run on the banks as land buyers rushed to trade in their bank notes for specie, was also to blame. But the depression was only partly a result of federal policies. England and western Europe were facing panics of their own, which caused European (and especially English) investors to withdraw funds from America, putting an added strain on American banks. A succession of crop failures on American farms reduced the purchasing power of farmers and required increased imports of food, which sent more money out of the country. But whatever its actual causes, the Panic of 1837 occurred during a Democratic administration, and the Democrats paid the political price for it. The Van Buren administration, which strongly opposed government intervention in the economy, did little to fight the depression. Some of the steps it took—borrowing money to pay government debts and accepting only specie for payment of taxes—may have made things worse. Other efforts failed in Congress: a "preemption" bill that would have given settlers the right to buy government land near them before it was opened for public sale, and another bill lowering the price of land. Van Buren did succeed in establishing a ten-hour workday on all federal projects, by presidential order, but he had only a few legislative achievements.

The most important and controversial of them was the creation of a new financial system to replace the Bank of the United States. Under Van Buren's plan, known as the "independent treasury" or "subtreasury" system, the government would place its funds in an independent treasury at Washington and in subtreasuries in other cities. No private banks would have the government's money or name to use as a basis for speculation; the government and the banks would be "divorced."

Van Buren called a special session of Congress in 1837 to consider the proposal, which failed in the House. In 1840, the last year of Van Buren's presidency, the administration finally succeeded in driving the measure through both houses of Congress.

The Log Cabin Campaign

As the campaign of 1840 approached, the Whigs realized that they would have to settle on one candidate for president this time if they were to have any hope of winning. As a result, they held their first national nominating convention in Harrisburg, Pennsylvania, in December 1839. Passing over the controversial Henry Clay, who had expected the nomination, the convention chose William Henry Harrison and, for vice president, John Tyler of Virginia. Harrison was a descendant of the Virginia aristocracy but had spent his adult life in the Northwest. He was a renowned soldier, a famous Indian fighter, and a popular national figure. The Democrats nominated Van Buren. But because they were not much more united than the Whigs, they failed to nominate a vice presidential candidate, leaving the choice of that office to the electors.

THE PENNY PRESS

On September 3, 1833, a small newspaper appeared in New York City for the first time: the *New York Sun*, published by a young former apprentice from Massachusetts named Benjamin Day. It was four pages long; it contained mostly trivial local news, with particular emphasis on sex, crime, and violence; and it sold for a penny. It launched a new age in the history of American journalism, the age of the "penny press."

Before the advent of the penny press, newspapers in America were produced almost entirely by and for the upper classes. Some published mainly business news, others worked to advance the aims of a political party. All were far too expensive for most ordinary citizens to buy. But several important changes in the business of journalism and the character of American society paved the way for Benjamin Day and others to challenge the established press. New technologies—the steam-powered cylinder printing press, new machines for making paper, railroads and canals for distributing issues to a larger market—made it possible to publish newspapers inexpensively and to sell them widely. A rising popular literacy rate, a result in part of the spread of public education, created a bigger reading public.

The penny press was also a response to the changing culture of the 1820s and 1830s. The spread of an urban, market economy contributed to the growth of the penny press by drawing a large population of workers, artisans, and clerks—the genesis of an industrial working class and a modern middle class—into large cities, where they became an important market for the new papers. The spirit of democracy—symbolized by the popularity of Andrew Jackson and the rising numbers of white male voters across the country—helped create an appetite for journalism that spoke to and for "the people," rather than the parties or the upper classes. Hence Benjamin Day's slogan for his new paper: "It Shines for ALL." The *Sun*, and other papers like it, were self-

■ **THE NEW YORK SUN**
This 1834 front page of the *Sun*, which had begun publication a year earlier, contains advertisements, light stories, a description of a slave auction in Charleston, S.C., and homespun advice: "Life is short. The poor pittance of several years is not worth being a villain for." *(Collection of the New York Historical Society)*

consciously egalitarian. They were eager to tweak and embarrass the rich and powerful (through their popular gossip columns). They were also committed to feeding the appetites of the people of modest means, who constituted most of their readership. "Human interest stories" helped solidify their hold on the working public. Condescending stories about poor black men and women—ridiculing their subjects' illiteracy and their accents—were also popular among their virtually all-white readership.

Within six months of its first issue, the *Sun* had the largest circulation in New York—8,000 readers, more than twice its nearest competitors. Its success encouraged others to begin publishing penny papers of their own. James Gordon Bennett's *New York Herald,* which began publication in 1835, soon surpassed the *Sun* in popularity with its lively combination of sensationalism and local gossip and with its aggressive pursuit of national and international stories. The *Herald* pioneered a "letters to the editor" column. It was the first paper to have regular reviews of books and the arts. It even launched the first daily sports section. By 1860, it had the largest circulation of any daily newspaper in the world: more than 77,000.

Not all the new penny papers were as sensationalist as the *Sun* and the *Herald.* Both the *Philadelphia Public Ledger* and the *Baltimore Sun,* founded in 1836 and 1837 respectively, strove to provide more serious coverage of the news. The *Baltimore Sun* even developed a Washington bureau, the first of the penny papers to do so. The *New York Tribune,* founded in 1841 by Horace Greeley (later a major antislavery leader and a Republican presidential candidate), hired some of the most important writers of the day—among them Charles A. Dana, Margaret Fuller, Henry James, and William Dean Howells—and prided itself on serious reporting and commentary. All of it was tinged with a conspicuous sympathy for socialism (Greeley once hired Karl Marx as a London correspondent) and for the aspirations of working people. As serious as the *Tribune,* but more sober and self-consciously "objective" in its reportage, was the *New York Times,* which Henry Raymond founded in 1851. "We do not mean to write as if we were in a passion—unless that shall really be the case," the *Times* huffily proclaimed in its first issue, in an obvious reference to Greeley and his impassioned reportage; "and we shall make it a point to get into a passion as rarely as possible."

But the *Times's* dutiful restraint and self-conscious respectability was rare in the penny press. More typical was the front page of the June 4, 1836 *Herald,* devoted in its entirety to the sensational murder of a prostitute by a frequent patron of broth-

els. "Why is not the militia called?" Bennett's paper asked breathlessly at the beginning of the main story. "We give . . . testimony up to the latest hour. . . . The mystery of the bloody drama increases—increases—increases."

No papers in the 1830s had yet begun to use the large banner headlines of modern tabloids. None had photographs, and only a few—Bennett's *Herald* notable among them—ran drawings to accompany their stories with any regularity. But within their columns of unbroken newsprint lay the origins of the press we know today. They were the first papers to pay their reporters and thus began the process of turning journalism into a profession. They were the first to rely heavily on advertisements and often devoted up to half their space to paid advertising. They reached beyond the business world and the political clubs and communicated with a genuinely mass market. They were often sensationalist and usually opinionated. But they were often also aggressive in uncovering serious and important news—in police stations, courts, jails, streets, and private homes as well as in city halls, state capitals, Washington, and the world.

■ **WHIG HEADQUARTERS, 1840**
The Whig Party in 1840 managed to disguise its relatively elite
character by portraying its presidential candidate, the patrician
General William Henry Harrison, as a man of the people—a man
born in a log cabin who enjoyed drinking hard cider from a jug.
Pictures of log cabins abounded during the Whig campaign. One
of them is visible in this drawing of a party rally in Philadelphia.
(Stock Montage)

The 1840 campaign was the first in which the
new popular "penny press" carried news of the candidates to a large audience of workers and tradespeople. It also illustrated how fully the concept of party
competition, the subordination of ideology to immediate political needs, had established itself in America. The Whigs—who had emerged as a party largely
because of their opposition to Andrew Jackson's
common-man democracy, who in most regions represented the more affluent elements of the population, and who favored government policies that
would aid business—presented themselves in 1840
as the party of the common people. So, of course,
did the Democrats. Both parties used the same techniques of mass voter appeal, the same evocation of
simple, rustic values. What mattered now was not

the philosophical purity of the party but its ability to
win votes. The Whig campaign was particularly effective in portraying William Henry Harrison, a
wealthy member of the frontier elite with a considerable estate, as a simple man of the people who loved
log cabins and hard cider. They accused Van Buren
of being an aloof aristocrat who used cologne, drank
champagne, and ate from gold plates. The Democrats
had no defense against the combination of these
campaign techniques and the effects of the depression. Harrison won the election with 234 electoral
votes to 60 for Van Buren and with a popular vote
majority of 53 percent.

The Frustration of the Whigs

Despite their decisive victory, the Whigs found their
four years in power frustrating and divisive ones. In
large part, that was because their popular new president, "Old Tippecanoe," William Henry Harrison,
died of pneumonia one month after taking office.
Vice President Tyler succeeded him. Control of the
administration thus fell to a man with whom the
Whig party leadership had relatively weak ties. Harrison had generally deferred to Henry Clay and Daniel
Webster, whom he named secretary of state. Under
Tyler, things soon changed.

Tyler was a former Democrat who had left the
party in reaction to what he considered Jackson's excessively egalitarian program and imperious methods. But there were still signs of his Democratic past
in his approach to public policy. The president did
agree to bills abolishing Van Buren's independent
treasury system and raising tariff rates. But he refused
to support Clay's attempt to recharter a Bank of the
United States. And he vetoed several internal improvement bills that Clay and other congressional
Whigs sponsored. Finally, a conference of congressional Whigs read Tyler out of the party. Every cabinet member but Webster resigned; five former Democrats took their places. When Webster, too, left the
cabinet, Tyler appointed Calhoun, who had rejoined
the Democratic Party, to replace him.

A new political alignment was emerging. Tyler
and a small band of conservative southern Whigs
were preparing to rejoin the Democrats. Joining the
"common man's party" of Jackson and Van Buren
was a faction with decidedly aristocratic political
ideas, who thought that government had an obligation to protect and even expand the institution of

slavery, and who believed in states' rights with almost fanatical devotion.

Whig Diplomacy

In the midst of these domestic controversies, a series of incidents in the late 1830s brought Great Britain and the United States once again to the brink of war.

Residents of the eastern provinces of Canada launched a rebellion against the British colonial government in 1837, and some of the rebels chartered an American steamship, the *Caroline,* to ship supplies across the Niagara River to them from New York. British authorities in Canada seized the *Caroline* and burned it, killing one American in the process. The British government refused either to disavow the attack or to provide compensation for it, and resentment in the United States ran high. But the British soon had reasons for anger as well. Authorities in New York, attempting to exploit the *Caroline* affair, arrested a Canadian named Alexander McLeod and charged him with the murder of the American who had died in the incident. The British government, expressing majestic rage, insisted that McLeod could not be accused of murder because he had acted under official orders. The foreign secretary, the bellicose Lord Palmerston, demanded McLeod's release and threatened that his execution would bring "immediate and frightful" war.

Webster as secretary of state did not think McLeod was worth a war, but he was powerless to release him. The prisoner was under New York jurisdiction and had to be tried in the state courts, a peculiarity of American jurisprudence that the British did not seem to understand. A New York jury did what Webster could not: it defused the crisis by acquitting McLeod.

At the same time, tensions flared over the boundary between Canada and Maine, which had been in dispute since the Treaty of 1783. In 1838, groups of Americans and Canadians, mostly lumberjacks, began moving into the Aroostook River region in the disputed area, precipitating a violent brawl between the two groups that became known as the "Aroostook War."

Several years later, there were yet more Anglo-American problems. In 1841, an American ship, the *Creole,* sailed from Virginia for New Orleans with more than 100 slaves aboard. En route the slaves mutinied, took possession of the ship, and took it to the Bahamas. British officials there declared the slaves free, and the English government refused to overrule them. Many Americans, especially southerners, were furious.

At this critical juncture, a new government eager to reduce the tensions with the United States came to power in Great Britain. In the spring of 1842, it sent Lord Ashburton, an admirer of America, to negotiate an agreement on the Maine boundary and other matters. The result of his negotiations with Secretary of State Webster and representatives from Maine and Massachusetts was the Webster-Ashburton Treaty of 1842. Its terms established a firm northern boundary between the United States and Canada along the Maine-New Brunswick border that survives to this day; the new border gave the United States a bit more than half of the previously disputed territory. Other, smaller provisions placated Maine and Massachusetts and protected critical trade routes in both the northern United States and southern Canada. In a separate exchange of notes, Ashburton eased the memory of the *Caroline* and *Creole* affairs by expressing regret and promising no future "officious interference" with American ships. The Webster-Ashburton treaty was generally popular in America, and in its aftermath Anglo-American relations substantially improved.

During the Tyler administration, the United States established its first diplomatic relations with China. In 1842, Britain forced China to open certain ports to foreign trade. Eager to share the new privileges, American mercantile interests persuaded Tyler and Congress to send a commissioner—Caleb Cushing—to China to negotiate a treaty giving the United States some part in the China trade. In the Treaty of Wang Hya, concluded in 1844, Cushing secured most-favored-nation provisions giving Americans the same privileges as the English. He also won for Americans the right of "extraterritoriality"—the right of Americans accused of crimes in China to be tried by American, not Chinese, officials. In the next ten years, American trade with China steadily increased.

In their diplomatic efforts, at least, the Whigs were able to secure some important successes. But by the end of the Tyler administration, the party could look back on few other victories. In the election of 1844, the Whigs lost the White House. They were to win only one more national election in their history before a great sectional crisis arose that would shatter their party and, for a time, the Union.

Significant Events

1820–1840	State constitutions revised
1823	Nicholas Biddle becomes president of Bank of the United States
1826	William Morgan's disappearance inflames Anti-Masonry
1828	Calhoun's *South Carolina Exposition and Protest* outlines nullification doctrine
1829	Andrew Jackson inaugurated
1830	Webster and Hayne debate
	Jackson vetoes Maysville Road Bill
	Indian Removal Act passed
1830–1838	Indians expelled from Southeast
1831	Anti-Mason party established
	Supreme Court rules in *Cherokee Nation* v. *Georgia*
1832	Democrats hold first national party convention
	Jackson vetoes bill to recharter Bank of the United States
	Jackson reelected president
1832–1833	Nullification crisis erupts
1833	Jackson and Taney remove federal deposits from Bank of the United States
	Commercial panic disrupts economy
1834	Indian Trade and Intercourse Act renewed
1835	Roger Taney succeeds Marshall as chief justice of the Supreme Court
	Federal debt retired
1835–1840	Tocqueville publishes *Democracy in America*
1835–1842	Seminole War
1836	Jackson issues "specie circular"
	Martin Van Buren elected president
1837	Supreme Court rules in *Charles River Bridge* case
1837–1842	Commercial panic and depression
1838	"Aroostook War" fought in Maine and Canada
1839	Whigs hold their first national convention
1840	William Henry Harrison elected president
	Independent Treasury Act passed
1841	Harrison dies
	John Tyler becomes president
1842	Dorr Rebellion hastens reform in Rhode Island
	Webster-Ashburton Treaty signed

CONCLUSION

The election of Andrew Jackson to the presidency in 1828 marked not only the triumph of a particular vision of government and democracy. It represented as well the emergence of a new political world. Throughout the American nation, the laws governing political participation were loosening and the number of people permitted to vote (which eventu-ally included most white males, but almost no one else) was increasing. Along with this expansion of the electorate was emerging a new spirit of party politics. Parties had once been reviled by American leaders as contributing to the spirit of faction. Now a new set of ideas was emerging that saw in institu-tionalized parties not a challenge, but a contribution to democracy. Party competition would be a way of containing and muting disagreements that might otherwise run amok. It would be another of the healthy restraints—another part of the system of checks and balances—that made American government work.

Andrew Jackson was a party man, and he set out as president to entrench his party, the Democrats, in power. He was also a fierce defender of his region, the West, and a sharp critic of what he considered the stranglehold of the aristocratic East on the nation's economic life. He sought to limit the role of the federal government in economic affairs, fearful that it would serve to entrench existing patterns of wealth and power. He worked to destroy the Bank of the United States, which he considered a corrupt vehicle of aristocratic influence. Jackson was, finally, a nationalist. And he confronted the greatest challenge to American unity yet to have emerged in the young nation—the nullification crisis of 1832-1833—with a strong assertion of the power and importance of the Union. These positions won him broad popularity and ensured his reelection in 1832 and the election of his designated successor, Martin Van Buren, in 1836.

But the Democrats were not the only ones to have learned the lessons of the age of parties. A new coalition of anti-Jacksonians, who called themselves the Whigs, launched a powerful new party that used much of the same anti-elitist rhetoric the Democrats had used to win support for their own much more nationalist program. Their emergence culminated in the campaign of 1840 with the election of the first Whig president.

FOR FURTHER REFERENCE

Suggested Readings   Arthur M. Schlesinger, Jr., *The Age of Jackson* (1945) represents Jacksonian politics as an eastern, urban democratic movement of working men and upper-class intellectuals. Bray Hammond, *Banks and Politics in America from the Revolution to the Civil War* (1957) challenged Schlesinger by arguing that the Bank War was essentially a struggle between different groups of capitalist elites. Harry L. Watson, *Liberty and Power: The Politics of Jacksonian America* (1990) provides an important newer synthesis of Jacksonian politics. Daniel Walker Howe, *The Political Culture of the American Whigs* (1979) analyzes the careers of several leading Whig politicians including the Whig triumvirate of Calhoun, Clay, and Webster. William V. Freehling, *Prelude to Civil War: The Nullification Controversy in South Carolina* (1966) argues that South Carolina planters' anxiety over the fate of slavery was at the heart of the nullification crisis. Francis P. Prucha, *American Indian Policy in the Formative Years* (1962) is an overview of early Indian policy by the leading scholar of the subject. Michael Rogin, *Fathers and Children: Andrew Jackson and the Destruction of American Indians* (1975) offers a more radical and idiosyncratic perspective on Jackson's career as an Indian fighter using the methods of psychoanalysis. Sean Wilentz, *Chants Democratic: New York City and the Rise of the American Working Class, 1788-1850* (1984) is an important study of working-class ideology during the Jacksonian period.

Films   (The best source for information on how to find these and other films is *Bowker's Complete Video Directory*—3 volumes.) *Andrew Jackson: A Man for the People* is part of the Arts & Entertainment Network biography series. *The Jackson Years: The New Americans* (1971) dramatizes episodes in Jackson's life. *The Jackson Years: Toward Civil War* (1971) focuses on Jackson's dominant personality in an analysis of the major events of Jackson's presidential administration. *The Jacksonian Persuasion* uses a country store in the West and in Charleston, South Carolina to illustrate themes in Jacksonian politics from Indian removal to nullification. *The American Story, No. 8: Expansion and Removal* (1985) examines the removal of Indians from their lands east of the Mississippi and the expansion of United States settlement to the west. *Trail of Tears* (1973) follows the forced removal of the Cherokee Indians to the West, and the subsequent Cherokee struggle to retain a sense of identity and heritage. See also *The Seminole* (1993).

Internet Resources   (For up-to-date URL addresses and links to these and other websites, consult the McGraw-Hill history site at *http://www.mhhe.com/socscience/history/usa/link/linktop.htm*) *Democracy in America* provides the complete text of Tocqueville's classic, as well as copious information on religion, women, and everyday life in Jacksonian America. *American Notes, by Charles Dickens* contains the novelist's observations of America in 1842. *The Trail of Tears* gathers material on the expulsion of the Cherokee Indians from Georgia.

☙

BIBLIOGRAPHY

General Histories   James C. Curtis, *Andrew Jackson and the Search for Vindication* (1976). Daniel Feller, *The Jacksonian Promise: America, 1815-1840* (1995). John Mayfield, *The New Nation, 1800-1845* (1981). Edward Pessen, *Jacksonian America,* rev. ed. (1979). Robert V. Remini, *The Jacksonian Era* (1989). Charles Sellers, *The Market Revolution: Jacksonian America, 1815-1846* (1991). Glyndon Van Deusen, *The Jacksonian Era* (1959).

Democracy   Patrick T. Conley, *Democracy in Decline* (1977). Marvin E. Gettleman, *The Dorr Rebellion* (1973). Louis Hartz, *The Liberal Tradition in America* (1955). Michael Kammen, *Spheres of Liberty: Changing Perceptions of Liberty in American Culture* (1986). Fred Somkin, *Unquiet Eagle: Memory and Desire in the Idea of American Freedom, 1815-1860* (1967). Alexis de Tocqueville, *Democracy in America,* 2 vols. (1835). Chilton Williamson, *American Suffrage from Property to Democracy, 1760-1860* (1960).

Jacksonian Society   Kenneth Cmiel, *Democratic Eloquence: The Fight over Popular Speech in Nineteenth-Century America* (1990). Nancy Hewitt, *Women's Activism and Social Change: Rochester, New York, 1822-1872* (1984). Douglas T. Miller, *Jacksonian Aristocracy* (1967). Edward Pessen, *Riches, Class, and Power Before the Civil War* (1973). Mary Ryan, *Cradle of the Middle Class: The Family in Oneida County, New York, 1790-1865* (1981). Carroll Smith-Rosenberg, *Religion and the Rise of the City* (1971). Christine Stansell, *City of Women: Sex and Class in New York, 1789-1860* (1986).

Jacksonian Politics   Lee Benson, *The Concept of Jacksonian Democracy* (1961). Ronald P. Formisano, *The Birth of Mass Political Parties: Michigan, 1828-1861* (1971). Tony Freyer, *Producers Versus Capitalists: Constitutional Conflict in Antebellum America* (1994). Paul Goodman, *Towards a Christian Republic: Antimasonry and the Great Tradition in New England, 1826-1836* (1988). Richard Hofstadter, *The American Political Tradition* (1948). Morton Horwitz, *The Transformation of American Law, 1780-1860* (1977). Richard B. Latner, *The Presidency of Andrew Jackson: White House Politics, 1829-1837* (1979). Richard B. McCormick, *The Second American Party System: Party Formation in the Jacksonian Era* (1966). Marvin Meyers, *The Jacksonian Persuasion* (1960). Robert V. Remini, *The Age of Jackson* (1972); *Andrew Jackson and the Bank War* (1967). John William Ward, *Andrew Jackson: Symbol for an Age* (1955). Harry L. Watson, *Jacksonian Politics and Community Conflict: The Emergence of the Second Party System in Cumber-*

land County, North Carolina (1981). Leonard White, *The Jacksonians: A Study in Administrative History* (1954).

Andrew Jackson   Robert V. Remini, *Andrew Jackson and the Course of American Empire: 1767-1821* (1977); *Andrew Jackson and the Course of American Freedom: 1822-1832* (1981); *Andrew Jackson and the Course of American Democracy* (1984); *The Life of Andrew Jackson* (1988).

Nullification   Irving H. Bartlett, *John C. Calhoun: A Biography* (1993). Merrill D. Peterson, *Olive Branch and Sword: The Compromise of 1833* (1983). Charles S. Sydnor, *The Development of Southern Sectionalism 1819-1848* (1948). Charles M. Wiltse, *John C. Calhoun: Nullifier* (1949).

Indian Policies   William Brandon, *The Last Americans* (1974). Duane Champagne, *Social Order and Political Change: Constitutional Governments Among the Cherokee, the Choctaw, the Chickasaw, and the Creek* (1992). Angie Debo, *A History of the Indians of the United States* (1970); *The Road to Disappearance: A History of the Creek Indians* (1941); *And Still the Waters Run: The Betrayal of the Five Civilized Tribes* (1973). Arthur H. DeRosier, Jr., *The Removal of the Choctaw Indians* (1970). Cecil Elby, *"That Disgraceful Affair"* (1973). Patricia Galloway, *Choctaw Genesis, 1500-1700* (1995). Michael D. Green, *The Politics of Indian Removal: Cherokee Government and Society in Crisis* (1982). Clara Sue Kidwell, *Choctaws and Missionaries in Mississippi, 1818-1918* (1995). Daniel F. Littlefield, Jr., *Africans and Seminoles: From Removal to Emancipation* (1976); *Africans and Creeks: From the Colonial Period to the Civil War* (1979). William McLoughlin, *After the Trail of Tears* (1993). Theda Perdue, *Slavery and the Evolution of Cherokee Society, 1540-1866* (1979). Ronald N. Satz, *American Indian Policy in the Jacksonian Era* (1975). B. W. Sheehan, *Seeds of Extinction: Jeffersonian Philanthropy and the American Indian* (1973). Anthony Wallace, *The Long Bitter Trail: Andrew Jackson and the Indians* (1993). Wilcomb E. Washburn, *The Indian in America* (1975). Richard White, *The Roots of Dependency* (1983). Thurman Wilkins, *Cherokee Tragedy* (1970).

The Bank War   John M. McFaul, *The Politics of Jacksonian Finance* (1972). Robert V. Remini, *Andrew Jackson and the Bank War* (1967). William G. Shade, *Banks or No Banks: The Money Issue in Western Politics, 1832-1865* (1972). James R. Sharp, *The Jacksonians Ver-*

sus the Banks (1970). Peter Temin, *The Jacksonian Economy* (1969). J. A. Wilburn, *Biddle's Bank* (1967).

Post-Jacksonian Politics   John Ashworth, *"Agrarians" and "Aristocrats": Party Political Ideology in the United States, 1837–1846* (1983). Irving Bartlett, *Daniel Webster* (1978). Maurice Baxter, *One and Inseparable: Daniel Webster and the Union* (1984); *Henry Clay and the American System* (1995). Norman D. Brown, *Daniel Webster and the Politics of Availability* (1969). Thomas Brown, *Politics and Statesmanship: Essays on the American Whig Party* (1985). Donald B. Cole, *Martin Van Buren and the American Political System* (1984). Richard N. Current, *Daniel Webster and the Rise of National Conservatism* (1955). James C. Curtis, *The Fox at Bay: Martin Van Buren and the Presidency* (1970). Robert Dalzell, *Daniel Webster and the Trial of American Nationalism* (1973). Paul Goodman, *Toward a Christian Republic: Anti-Masonry and the Great Transition in New England, 1826–1836* (1988). Howard Jones, *To the Webster-Ashburton Treaty* (1977). Sydney Nathans, *Daniel Webster and Jacksonian Democracy* (1973). John Niven, *Martin Van Buren: The Romantic Age of American Politics* (1983). Thomas H. O'Connor, *Lords of the Loom: The Cotton Whigs and the Coming of the Civil War* (1968). Merrill D. Peterson, *The Great Triumvirate: Webster, Clay, and Calhoun* (1987). Robert V. Remini, *Martin Van Buren and the Making of the Democratic Party* (1959); *Henry Clay: Statesman for the Union* (1991). Alexander Saxton, *The Rise and Fall of the White Republic: Class Politics and Mass Culture in Nineteenth-Century America* (1990). William Preston Vaughn, *The Anti-Masonic Party in the United States, 1826–1843* (1983). Major L. Wilson, *The Presidency of Martin Van Buren* (1984).

Chapter Ten

AMERICA'S ECONOMIC REVOLUTION

When the United States entered the War of 1812, it was still an essentially agrarian nation. There were, to be sure, cities in America, several of substantial size. In some of them there was a flourishing mercantile economy, based largely on overseas trade. There was also modest but growing manufacturing activity, concentrated mainly in the Northeast. But the overwhelming majority of Americans were farmers and tradespeople, working within an economy that was still mainly local.

By the time the Civil War began in 1861, the United States had transformed itself. Most Americans were still rural people, to be sure. But even most American farmers were now part of a national, and increasingly international, market economy. Above all, perhaps, the United States had developed a major manufacturing sector and was beginning to challenge the industrial nations of Europe for supremacy. The nation had experienced the first stage of its industrial revolution; and while the changes that revolution produced were far from complete, most Americans understood that their world had changed irrevocably.

These dramatic changes—changes that affected not just the economy, but society, culture, and politics—did not have the same impact everywhere. The Northeast, and its new economic ally the Northwest, were rapidly developing a complex, modern economy and society, increasingly dominated by large cities, important manufacturing, and profitable commercial farming. It was in many ways an unequal society, but it was also a fluid one, firmly committed to the ideal of free labor. Relatively few white Americans yet lived west of the Mississippi River, but parts of those western lands, too, were becoming part of large-scale commercial agriculture and other enterprises and were creating links to the capitalist economy of the Northeast.

In the South and Southwest, there were changes, too. Southern agriculture, particularly cotton farming, flourished as never before in response to the growing demand from textile mills in New England and elsewhere. But while the southern states were becoming increasingly a part of the national and international capitalist world, they also

■ **THE LOWELL MILLS**
Fifteen years earlier, Lowell, Massachusetts had been a small farming village known as East Chelmsford. By the 1840s, when Fitzhugh Lane painted "The Middlesex Company Woolen Mills," the town had become one of the most famous manufacturing centers in America and a magnet for visitors from around the world. Lane's painting shows female workers, who dominated the labor force in Lowell, entering the factory. *(American Textile History Museum, Lowell, Massachusetts)*

remained much less economically developed than their northern counterparts. And as the North became ever more committed to the fluidity and mobility of its free-labor system, the South was becoming more and more resolute in its defense of slavery.

The industrial revolution, which was doing so much to draw the nation into a single, integrated economy, was also working to isolate—and, increasingly, to alarm—the residents of one of its regions. The economic revolution was transforming the nation. It was also dividing it.

THE CHANGING AMERICAN POPULATION

The American industrial revolution was a result of many factors. Before it could occur, the United States needed a population large enough both to grow its own food and to provide a work force for the industrial economy. It needed a transportation and communications system capable of sustaining commerce over a large geographical area. It needed the technology to permit manufacturing on a large scale. And it needed systems of business organization capable of managing large industrial enterprises. By 1860, the northern regions of the nation had acquired at least the beginnings of all those things.

The American Population, 1820–1840

Between 1820 and 1840, not only did the population of the United States dramatically increase, but much of it became concentrated in the industrial centers of the Northeast and Northwest, where it provided a labor force for the growing factory system. Three trends characterized the American population in these years, all of them contributing in various ways to economic growth. The population was increasing rapidly. Much of it was migrating westward. And much of it was moving to towns and cities.

The American population had stood at only 4 million in 1790. By 1820, it had reached 10 million;

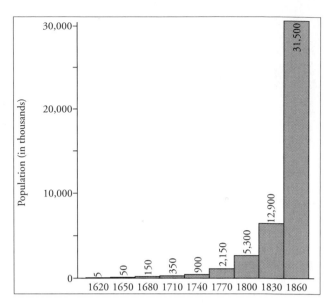

■ POPULATION GROWTH, 1620–1860
Between 1620 and 1860, the population of the United States more than doubled every thirty years. This growth far surpassed that of Europe, and by 1860, the United States had become one of the most populous countries in the world. This growth stemmed from both natural increase and European immigration.

by 1830, nearly 13 million; and by 1840, 17 million. The United States was growing much more rapidly in population than Britain or Europe. One reason for this substantial population growth was improvements in public health. The number and ferocity of epidemics (such as the great cholera plague of 1832)—which had periodically decimated urban and even rural populations in America—slowly declined, as did the nation's mortality rate as a whole. The population increase was also a result of a high birth rate. In 1840, white women bore an average of 6.14 children each, a decline from the very high rates of the eighteenth century but still substantial enough to produce rapid population increases, particularly since a larger proportion of children could expect to grow to adulthood than had been the case a generation or two earlier.

Immigration, choked off by wars in Europe and economic crises in America, contributed little to the American population in the first three decades

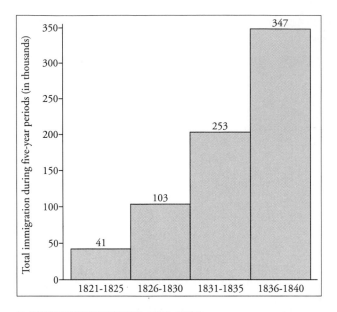

■ TOTAL IMMIGRATION, 1820-1840

The immigration boom of the 1820s and 1830s was stimulated by declining transportation costs for transatlantic travel, growing economic opportunity in the United States, and deteriorating social and economic conditions in Europe. Although the rate of increase in immigration slowed briefly after the Panic of 1837, more immigrants (84,000) arrived in the United States in 1840 than in any previous year. This number would pale, however, in comparison to the massive immigration of the following two decades.

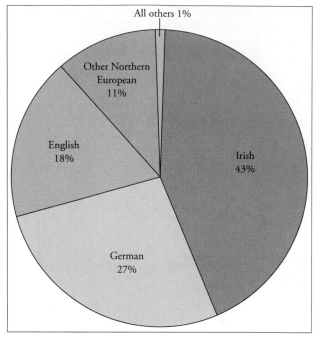

■ SOURCES OF IMMIGRATION, 1820-1840

Beginning in the 1830s, European immigration to the United States began to grow considerably. During the 1820s and 1830s, more immigrants came from Ireland than from any other country in Europe, marking the beginning of a tremendous influx of Irish immigrants in the three decades prior to the Civil War. Most of the new immigrants flowed into the rapidly growing cities of the Northeast.

of the nineteenth century but rapidly revived beginning in the 1830s. Of the total 1830 population of nearly 13 million, the foreign-born numbered fewer than 500,000. But the number of immigrants climbed to 60,000 in 1832 and nearly 80,000 in 1837. Reduced transportation costs and increasing economic opportunities in America helped stimulate the immigration boom, as did deteriorating economic conditions in some areas of Europe. The migrations introduced new groups to the United States. In particular, the number of immigrants arriving from the southern (Catholic) counties of Ireland began to grow, marking the beginning of a tremendous influx of Irish Catholics that was to continue through the three decades before the Civil War.

Much of this new European immigration flowed into the rapidly growing cities of the Northeast. But urban growth was a result of substantial internal migration as well. As the agricultural regions of New England and other areas grew less profitable, more and more people picked up stakes and moved—some to more promising agricultural regions in the West, but many to eastern cities. In 1790, one person in thirty had lived in a city (defined as a community of 8,000 or more); in 1820, one in twenty; and in 1840, one in twelve. The largest such cities were in the Northeast.

The rise of New York City was particularly dramatic. By 1810 it was the largest city in the United States. That was partly a result of its superior natural harbor. It was also a result of the Erie Canal (completed in 1825), which gave the city unrivaled access to the interior. New York's growth was a result, too, of liberal state laws that made the city attractive for both foreign and domestic commerce.

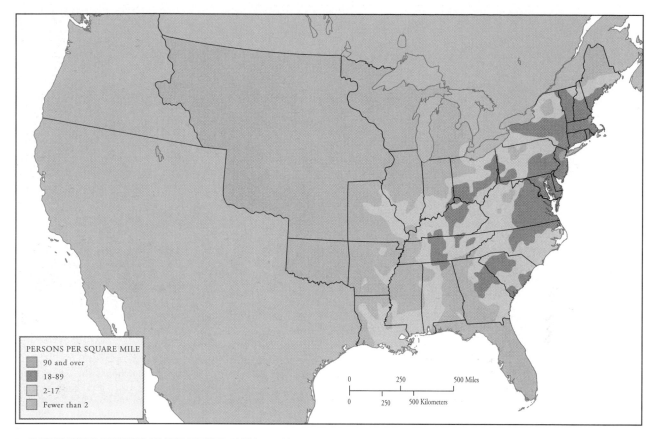

■ **POPULATION DENSITY OF THE UNITED STATES, 1820**
In 1820, the population of the United States was still overwhelmingly rural, and concentrated in the thirteen original states, although settlement in the Ohio River valley and southern upcountry was growing. Only one person in twenty lived in a city (defined as a community of 8,000 or more), and most of the cities were located in the northeast.

Immigration and Urban Growth, 1840–1860

The growth of cities accelerated dramatically between 1840 and 1860. The population of New York, for example, rose from 312,000 to 805,000. (New York's population would have numbered 1.2 million in 1860 if Brooklyn, which was then a separate municipality, had been included in the total.) Philadelphia's population grew over the same twenty-year period from 220,000 to 565,000; Boston's from 93,000 to 177,000. By 1860, 26 percent of the population of the free states was living in towns (places of 2,500 people or more) or cities (8,000 people or more), up from 14 percent in 1840. That percentage was even higher for the industrializing states of the Northeast. (In the South, by contrast, the increase of urban residents was only from 6 percent in 1840 to 10 percent in 1860.)

The booming agricultural economy of the western regions of the nation produced significant urban growth as well. Between 1820 and 1840, communities that had once been small western villages or trading posts became major cities: St. Louis, Pittsburgh, Cincinnati, Louisville. All of them benefited from strategic positions on the Mississippi River or one of its major tributaries. All of them became centers of the growing carrying trade that connected the farmers of the Midwest with New Orleans and, through it, the cities of the Northeast. After 1830, however, substantial shipping began from the Mississippi River to the Great Lakes, creating major new urban centers that gradually superseded the river ports. Among them were Buffalo, Detroit, Milwaukee, Cleveland, and—most important in the end—Chicago.

The enlarged urban population was in part simply a reflection of the growth of the national population

■ **THE PORT OF NEW YORK, 1828**
This view of South Street in Manhattan shows the East River lined with docks. Other docks, similarly busy, lined the Hudson River on the opposite side of the island, a sign of the city's emergence as the preeminent commercial center in the nation. The population of New York City was approaching 150,000 by 1828. *(New York Public Library)*

as a whole, which rose by more than a third—from 23 million to over 31 million—in the decade of the 1850s alone. By 1860, the American population was larger than Britain's and quickly approaching that of France and Germany. Urban growth was also a result of the continuing, indeed increasing, flow of people into cities from the farms of the Northeast, which continued to decline because of competition from Europe and the American West (and because of the relative disadvantages of their own soil). Immigration from abroad continued to increase as well. The number of foreigners arriving in the United States in 1840—84,000—was the highest for any one year to that point in the nineteenth century. But in later years, even that number would come to seem insignificant. Between 1840 and 1850, more than 1.5 million Europeans moved to America, three times the number of arrivals in the 1830s; in the last years of that decade, average annual immigration was almost

300,000. Of the 23 million people in the United States in 1850, 2.2 million (almost 10 percent) were foreign-born. Still greater numbers arrived in the 1850s—over 2.5 million. Almost half the residents of New York City in the 1850s were recent immigrants. In St. Louis, Chicago, and Milwaukee, the foreign-born outnumbered those of native birth. Few immigrants settled in the South. Only 500,000 lived in the slave states in 1860, and a third of these were concentrated in Missouri, mostly in St. Louis.

The newcomers came from many different countries and regions: England, France, Italy, Scandinavia, Poland, and Holland. But the overwhelming majority came from Ireland and Germany. In 1850, the Irish constituted approximately 45 percent and the Germans over 20 percent of the foreign-born in America. By 1860, there were more than 1.5 million Irish-born and approximately 1 million German-born people in the United States. There were several reasons for this

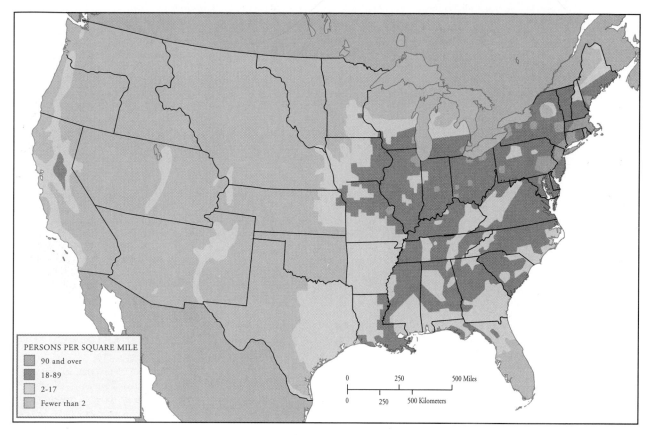

■ POPULATION DENSITY OF THE UNITED STATES, 1860

By 1860, the population of the United States had spread much more evenly across the entire country. Communities that had been small trading posts along the western rivers became major cities, including St. Louis, Pittsburgh, Cincinnati, and Louisville, while the Erie Canal opened up a large and prosperous hinterland in western New York. This map also indicates the emergence of a new southern "black belt" devoted to cotton production stretching from South Carolina to Louisiana.

flood of immigration. In Germany, the economic dislocations of the industrial revolution had caused widespread poverty, and the collapse of the liberal revolution there in 1848 also persuaded many Germans to emigrate. In Ireland, the oppressiveness and unpopularity of English rule drove many people to emigrate. But these political factors were dwarfed in the mid-nineteenth century by the greatest disaster in Ireland's history: a catastrophic failure of the potato crop (and other food crops) that caused the devastating "potato famine" of 1845–1849. Nearly a million people died of starvation and disease. Well over a million more emigrated to the United States.

The Irish and German patterns of settlement in America were very different. The great majority of the Irish settled in the eastern cities, where they swelled the ranks of unskilled labor. Most Germans moved on to the Northwest, where they became farmers or went into business in the western towns. One reason for the difference was wealth: German immigrants generally arrived with at least some money; the Irish had practically none. Another important reason was gender. Most German immigrants were members of family groups or were single men, for whom movement to the agricultural frontier was both possible and attractive. Many Irish immigrants were young, single women, for whom movement west was much less plausible. They were more likely to stay in the eastern cities, where factory and domestic work was available.

The Rise of Nativism

Needless to say, the vast new foreign-born population had a profound effect on the character of American society. Some native-born Americans saw in the new immigration a source of great opportunity. In-

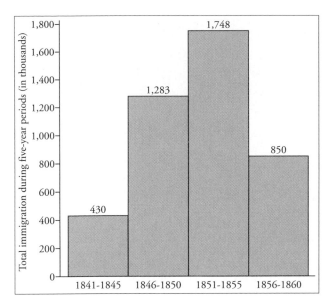

■ TOTAL IMMIGRATION, 1840–1860

Over four million immigrants arrived in the United States between 1841 and 1860. The numbers of immigrants increased sharply between 1845 and 1855, due to an agricultural crisis in Ireland and the collapse of the liberal revolution in Germany in 1848. The flood of immigrants in the 1840s and 1850s sparked nativist movements throughout the northern states, culminating in the rise of the Know-Nothing Party in the late 1840s and early 1850s.

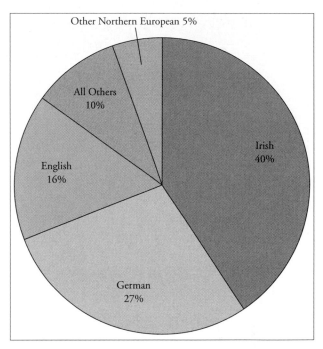

■ SOURCES OF IMMIGRATION, 1840–1860

In the two decades prior to the Civil War, immigration into the United States reached record levels, led by Irish and German immigrants. Many of the Irish immigrants settled in the eastern cities where they swelled the ranks of the unskilled poor. German immigrants were more likely than the Irish to arrive with money and family; they tended to move to the Northwest, where they became farmers or businessmen.

dustrialists and other employers welcomed the arrival of a large supply of cheap labor, which they believed would help them keep wage rates low. Land speculators and others with investments in the sparsely populated West hoped that many of the immigrants would move into the region and help expand the population, and thus the market for land and goods, there. Political leaders in western states and territories hoped the immigrants would, by swelling their population, also increase the political influence of the region. Wisconsin, for example, permitted foreign-born residents to become voters as soon as they had declared their intention of seeking citizenship and had resided in the state for a year; other western states soon followed their lead. In eastern cities, too, urban political organizations eagerly courted immigrant voters, hoping to enhance their own political strength.

Other Americans, however, viewed the growing foreign-born population with alarm. Their fears led to the rise of what is known as "nativism," a defense of native-born people and a hostility to the foreign-born, usually combined with a desire to stop or slow immi-

gration. The emerging nativism took many forms. Some of it was a result of simple racism. Many nativists (conveniently overlooking their own immigrant heritage) argued that the new immigrants were inherently inferior to older-stock Americans. Some viewed them with the same contempt and prejudice—and the same low estimate of their potential abilities—with which they viewed African Americans. Many nativists avoided racist arguments but argued nevertheless that the newcomers were socially unfit to live alongside people of older stock, that they did not bring with them sufficient standards of civilization. Evidence for that, they claimed, was the wretched urban and sometimes rural slums in which they lived. (Many nativists seemed to assume that such wretchedness was something immigrants chose, rather than the result of their extreme poverty.) Others—especially workers— complained that because foreigners were willing to work for low wages, they were stealing jobs from the native labor force. Protestants, observing the success

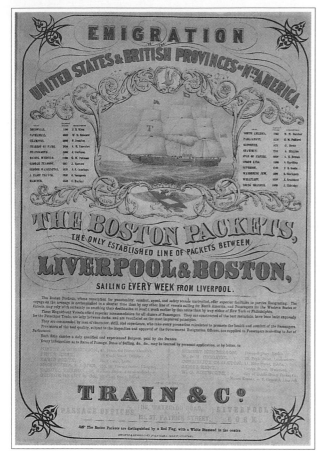

■ AN APPEAL TO EMIGRANTS
This widely-distributed advertising card was one of many such appeals to potential English and Irish travelers to America in the 1830s and 1840s. Like many such companies, it tried to appeal both to affluent passengers (by boasting of "superior accommodations") and working-class people of modest means. *(Courtesy of The Bostonian Society/Old State House)*

■ A "KNOW NOTHING" FLAG
The American Party, which began as a secret organization with the popular nickname "Know Nothings" (from their refusal to divulge any information about their activities), was in the forefront of antebellum campaigns against immigration—as this flag (which refers to the older-stock white members of the party as "Native Americans") suggests. The Know Nothings were particularly alarmed about the rising number of Catholic immigrants to the United States and warned that this "monster" (Catholicism) was "only waiting for the hour to approach to plant its flag of tyranny, persecution, and oppression among us." *(Photo Courtesy of Milwaukee County Historical Society)*

of Irish Catholics in establishing footholds in urban politics, warned that the church of Rome was gaining a foothold in American government. Whig politicians were outraged because so many of the newcomers voted Democratic. Others complained that the immigrants corrupted politics by selling their votes. Many older-stock Americans of both parties feared that immigrants would bring new, radical ideas into national life.

Out of these tensions and prejudices emerged a number of new secret societies created to combat what nativists had come to call the "alien menace." Most of them originated in the Northeast. Some later spread to the West and even to the South. The first of these, the Native American Association, began agitating against immigration in 1837. In 1845, nativists held

a convention in Philadelphia and formed the Native American Party (unaware that the term they used to describe themselves would one day become a common label for American Indians). Anti-immigrant sentiment crested in the 1850s. Many of the nativist groups combined in 1850 to form the Supreme Order of the Star-Spangled Banner. It endorsed a list of demands that included banning Catholics or the foreign-born from holding public office, more restrictive naturalization laws, and literacy tests for voting. The order adopted a strict code of secrecy, which included the secret password, used in lodges across the country, "I know nothing." Ultimately, members of the movement became known as the "Know-Nothings."

Gradually, the Know-Nothings turned their attention to party politics, and after the election of 1852 they created a new political organization that they called the American Party. In the East, the new organization scored an immediate and astonishing success in the elections of 1854: the Know-Nothings cast a large vote in Pennsylvania and New York and won control of the state government in Massachusetts. Elsewhere, the progress of the Know-Nothings was more modest. Western members of the party, because of the presence of many German voters in the area, found it expedient not to oppose natural-

ized Protestants. After 1854, the strength of the Know-Nothings declined. The Know-Nothing Party's most lasting impact was its contribution to the collapse of the existing party system (organized around the Whig and Democratic parties) and the creation of new national political alignments.

TRANSPORTATION, COMMUNICATIONS, AND TECHNOLOGY

Just as the industrial revolution required an expanding population, it also required an efficient and effective system of transportation and communications. Without such a system, merchants and manufacturers would be unable to ship their goods to distant markets or communicate effectively with trading partners in other regions. Without such a system, the industrial work force would not have access to the food supplies it needed to sustain itself. The first half of the nineteenth century saw dramatic changes in transportation communications in the United States.

Both transportation and communications required, in turn, significant advances in technological knowledge—as did many other areas of the econ-

omy. The antebellum era was notable as well for remarkable technological advances.

The Canal Age

From 1790 until the 1820s, the so-called turnpike era, Americans had relied largely on roads for internal transportation. But in a country as large as the United States was becoming, roads alone (and the mostly horse-drawn vehicles that used them) were not adequate for the nation's expanding needs. And so, in the 1820s and 1830s, Americans began to turn to other means of transportation as well.

The larger rivers, especially the Mississippi and the Ohio, had been important transportation routes for years, but most of the traffic on them consisted of flat barges—little more than rafts—that floated downstream laden with cargo and were broken up at the end of their journeys because they could not navigate back upstream. To return north, shippers had to send goods by land or by agonizingly slow upstream vessels that sometimes took up to four months to travel the length of the Mississippi.

These rivers had become vastly more important by the 1820s, as steamboats grew in number and improved in design. The new riverboats carried the corn and wheat of northwestern farmers and the cotton and tobacco of southwestern planters to New Orleans in a fraction of the time of the old barges. From New Orleans, oceangoing ships took the cargoes on to eastern ports. Steamboats also developed a significant passenger traffic, and companies built increasingly lavish vessels to compete for this lucrative trade (even though most passengers could not afford the luxurious amenities and slept in the hold or on the deck).

But neither the farmers of the West nor the merchants of the East were wholly satisfied with this pattern of trade. Farmers would pay less to transport their goods (and eastern consumers would pay less to consume them) if they could ship them directly eastward to market, rather than by the roundabout river-sea route; and northeastern merchants, too, could sell larger quantities of their manufactured goods if they could transport their merchandise more directly and economically to the West. New highways across the

mountains provided a partial solution to the problem. But the costs of hauling goods overland, although lower than before, were still too high for anything except the most compact and valuable merchandise. The thoughts of some merchants and entrepreneurs began, therefore, to turn to an alternative: canals.

A team of four horses could haul one and a half tons of goods eighteen miles a day on the turnpikes. But the same four horses, walking along the "towpaths" next to canals while yoked to barges, could draw a boatload of a hundred tons twenty-four miles a day. By the 1820s, the economic advantages of canals had generated a booming interest in expanding the water routes to the West. Canal building was too expensive for private enterprise, and the job of digging canals fell largely to the states. The ambitious state governments of the Northeast took the lead in constructing them. New York was the first to act. It had

■ **"BUILDING THE ERIE CANAL"**
This lithograph by Anthony Imbert suggests something of the enormous engineering challenges that the builders of the Erie Canal faced. This picture shows excavations at Lockport, New York, where a horse-powered crane and a large crew of Irish immigrant workers clear boulders from the channel. Imbert created these and other images to illustrate a book published in 1825 to celebrate the completion of the canal. *(Building the Erie Canal. Lithograph by Anthony Imbert. From Cadwallader Colden's* Memoir on the Celebration of the Completion of the New York Canals. *The Metropolitan Museum of Art, Harris Brisbane Dick Fund, 1941. (41.51))*

The American Environment

THE FLOW OF WATER

No element of the North American landscape was more basic to the development of the young republic than water. The earliest settlements on the eastern seaboard were all at the ocean's edge, where they had ready access to transatlantic trade. Each major city in the new nation— Boston, New York, Philadelphia, Baltimore, Charleston, New Orleans—began life as a port. The interior trade of the continent was concentrated almost entirely along natural watercourses. Water was the catalyst that made trade and settlement possible.

Thus it is not surprising that some of the earliest large-scale manipulations of the American landscape had to do with redirecting the flow of water. Until the 1820s, most crops raised west of the Appalachians traveled to market by floating downstream toward New Orleans on the Ohio, the Mississippi, or the Missouri River. The great wave of canal building that swept the nation in the 1820s and 1830s was designed to divert that southward flow of commerce north toward the Great Lakes and east to the port towns on the Atlantic coast. The most dramatic success was, of course, the Erie Canal, which enabled New York City to capture the trade of the Great Lakes and the Ohio Valley. The emergence of New York as the greatest metropolis on the continent occurred at the same time that settlement exploded on the shores of the Great Lakes, and both were encouraged by the canal. The canal also contributed to the decline of agriculture in New England, as farmers on marginal land found themselves unable to compete with abundant grain crops from the western prairies.

In addition to rearranging the American agricultural landscape, canals had unexpected eco-logical consequences. The Erie Canal introduced to Lake Ontario the sea lamprey, a parasitic fish that attaches itself to other fish and weakens or kills them by sucking their blood. It had never before inhabited the Great Lakes, but it began to put pressure on the lake's native whitefish, trout, and salmon. A complex redistribution of the lake's fish population was the long-term result, with many species declining and even disappearing.

If canals created an artificial system of waterways, dams created an equally artificial system of power that altered traditional ways of consuming energy in the American economy. The industrial revolution came to the United States not with the steam engine but with the water-wheel. Falling water had been used since the earliest colonial times to grind flour and saw lumber. But large-scale exploitation of water power did not occur until New England capitalists used British technology to mechanize the production of textiles. The best known of the New England textile towns is probably Lowell, Massachusetts, which is justly renowned in American history for the new labor system it introduced in its factories. But Lowell's success would have been impossible had the city not harnessed the potential energy of the Merrimack River to drive its factories.

The implications of this new use of water were dramatic. Formerly, the energy that had driven the American economy had been biologically limited by the strength of horses and human workers. Now an even larger share of the energy came from inanimate rivers (until they were supplanted by coal-powered steam). The harnessing of water power had disastrous results for certain fish species, like the salmon, which formerly had swum upstream to spawn. As dams

(*continued*)

blocked major rivers of the east coast to create power sources, salmon disappeared from most of their former homes.

The typical industrial town of the water power era had certain features that are evident even today. It was always located beside a natural waterfall or rapids where a river dropped quickly from a higher to a lower elevation. A dam upstream from the town diverted water into a complicated network of canals and underground conduits. These diverted water to the factories, which straddled the natural drop in elevation. As the water flowed beneath the buildings, it turned large waterwheels and turbines. Long leather belts transmitted the resulting energy to driveshafts running the length of the factory.

Water power towns lived and died with water. In winter, when rivers froze with ice, factories sometimes had to shut down for lack of power. (The same was true of canals: the canal economy regularly went into hibernation during the winter months, with trade coming nearly to a standstill between December and April.) Worse, water power towns were regularly subject to flooding during storms and spring runoffs, and could suffer devastating destruction from the very source that ordinarily sustained them. This was one reason why the housing in such towns was often arranged so that the workers lived nearest the factories, in flimsy structures erected on the floodplain, while managers and owners lived on the hillsides in more expensive houses that were less exposed to flooding.

The final elements of the new water landscape of nineteenth-century America were in the cities. To increase their supply of drinking water and to protect themselves from frequent fires, the great port cities of the east coast constructed great reservoir systems like New York's Croton Aqueduct, completed in 1842, which brought water from dozens of miles away. A little later, they introduced sewers to dispose of dangerous urban wastes downstream from drinking supplies. As a result, the water-borne epidemics of cholera that had devastated the United States in 1832, 1849, and 1866 had nearly vanished by the end of the century.

Ports, canals, dams, factories, reservoirs, sewers: today these are familiar features of the American landscape. At the time they were constructed, however, they constituted a revolution in the way Americans traveled, worked, drank, bathed, and protected themselves from disease. Controlling the flow of water was among the greatest environmental and technological changes of the nineteenth century.

■ **WATER-POWERED FACTORY ON THE GREEN RIVER, MASSACHUSETTS**
American factories in the early nineteenth century depended much more on water than on steam. They were typically located near major falls or rapids on large rivers, so that canals could divert water through wheels and turbines beneath the factory, supplying power to the machinery within.
(Bettmann)

■ THE GREAT NEW YORK FIRE OF DECEMBER 16, 1835

One of the most devastating fires in New York City's history destroyed hundreds of buildings on December 16, 1835. Without an effective municipal water supply, firefighters had to bring water to the scene in tank carts and hand-pump it onto the flames. The fire encouraged New York citizens to support construction of the Croton Aqueduct. *(Bettmann)*

■ THE CROTON AQUEDUCT BRINGS WATER TO NEW YORK CITY, 1842

When the Croton Aqueduct was completed, bringing water from the upper Hudson Valley to the southern tip of Manhattan, the residents of New York City staged an immense celebration. A new fountain was built in honor of the event. The aqueduct continues to supply the city with water today.

(The Research Library, The New York Public Library)

the natural advantage of a good land route between the Hudson River and Lake Erie through the only real break in the Appalachian chain. But the engineering tasks were still imposing. The distance was more than 350 miles, several times as long as any of the existing canals in America. The route was interrupted by high ridges and a wilderness of woods. After a long public debate over whether the scheme was practical, canal advocates prevailed when De Witt Clinton, a late but ardent convert to the cause, became governor in 1817. Digging began on July 4, 1817.

The building of the Erie Canal was the greatest construction project Americans had ever undertaken. The canal itself was simple: basically a ditch forty feet wide and four feet deep, with towpaths along the banks for the horses or mules that were to draw the canal boats. But hundreds of difficult cuts and fills, some of them enormous, were required to enable the canal to pass through hills and over valleys; stone aqueducts were necessary to carry it across streams; and eighty-eight locks, of heavy masonry with great wooden gates, were needed to permit ascents and descents. The Erie Canal was not just an engineering triumph, but an immediate financial success. It opened in October 1825, amid elaborate ceremonies and celebrations, and traffic was soon so heavy that within about seven years tolls had repaid the entire cost of construction. By providing a route to the Great Lakes, the canal gave New York direct access to Chicago and the growing markets of the West. New York could now compete with (and increasingly replace) New Orleans as a destination for agricultural goods (particularly wheat) and other products of the West, and as a source for manufactured goods to be sold in the region.

The system of water transportation—and the primacy of New York—extended farther when the states of Ohio and Indiana, inspired by the success of the Erie Canal, provided water connections between Lake Erie and the Ohio River. These canals helped connect them by an inland water route all the way to New York, although it was still necessary to transfer cargoes several times between canal, lake, and river craft. One of the immediate results of these new transportation routes was increased white settlement in the Northwest, because canals made it easier for migrants to make the westward journey and to ship their goods back to eastern markets.

Rival cities along the Atlantic seaboard took alarm at the prospect of New York's acquiring so vast a hinterland (the area supplying goods to and buying products from a port). These other cities believed that New York's phenomenal growth would come at their expense. But they had limited success in catching up. Boston, its way to the Hudson River blocked by the Berkshire Mountains, did not even try to connect itself to the West by canal; its hinterland would remain confined largely to New England. Philadelphia and Baltimore had the still more formidable Allegheny Mountains to contend with. They made a serious effort at canal building, nevertheless, but with discouraging results. Pennsylvania's effort ended in an expensive failure. Maryland constructed part of the Chesapeake and Ohio Canal beginning in 1828, but completed only the stretch between Washington, D.C., and Cumberland, Maryland, and thus never crossed the mountains. In the South, Richmond and Charleston also aspired to build water routes to the Ohio Valley, but never completed them.

In the end, canals did not provide a satisfactory route to the West for any of New York's rivals. Some cities, however, saw their opportunity in a different and newer means of transportation. Even before the canal age had reached its height, the era of the railroad was already beginning.

The Early Railroads

Railroads played no more than a secondary role in the nation's transportation system in the 1820s and 1830s, but railroad pioneers laid the groundwork in those years for the great surge of railroad building in midcentury that would link the nation together as never before. Eventually, railroads became the primary transportation system for the United States, and they remained so until the construction of the interstate highway system in the mid-twentieth century.

Railroads emerged from a combination of technological and entrepreneurial innovations. The technological breakthroughs included the invention of tracks, the creation of steam-powered locomotives, and the development of railroad cars that could serve as public carriers of passengers and freight. By 1804, both English and American inventors had experimented with steam engines for propelling land vehicles. In 1820, John Stevens ran a locomotive and cars around a circular track on his New Jersey estate. And in 1825, the Stockton and Darlington Railroad in England opened a short length of track and became the first line to carry general traffic.

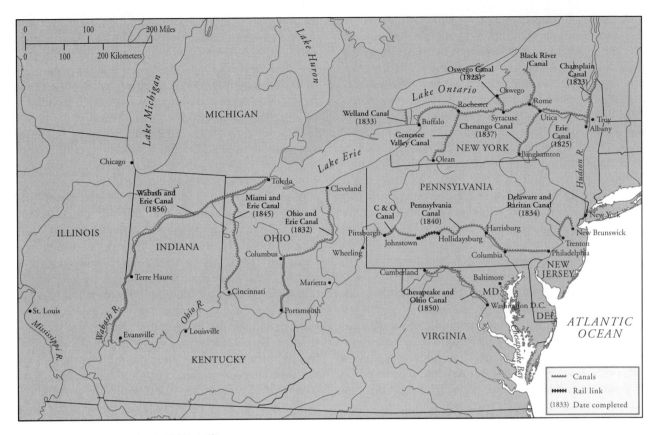

■ CANALS IN THE NORTHEAST, TO 1860

Following the stunning success of the Erie Canal, completed in 1825, a wave of canal building swept the northern states, in an effort to compete with New York in access to western trade. Although Maryland, Pennsylvania, and Massachusetts all tried to reach markets in the Northwest, the canal systems that developed in these states were unable to displace the dominance of New York.

■ RACING ON THE RAILROAD

Peter Cooper, who in later years was best known as a philanthropist and as the founder of the Cooper Union in New York City, was also a successful iron manufacturer. Cooper designed and built the first steam-powered locomotive in America in 1830 for the Baltimore and Ohio railroad. On August 28 of that year, he raced his locomotive (the "Tom Thumb") against a horse-drawn railroad car. This sketch depicts the moment when Cooper's engine overtook the horse-car. *(Museum of the City of New York)*

American entrepreneurs, especially in those northeastern cities that sought better communication with the West, quickly grew interested in the English experiment. The first company to begin actual operations was the Baltimore and Ohio, which opened a thirteen-mile stretch of track in 1830. In New York, the Mohawk and Hudson began running trains along the sixteen miles between Schenectady and Albany in 1831. By 1836, more than a thousand miles of track had been laid in eleven states.

But there was not yet a true railroad system. Even the longest of the lines was comparatively short in the 1830s, and most of them served simply to connect water routes, not to link one railroad to another. Even when two lines did connect, the tracks often differed in gauge (width), so that cars from one line often could not fit onto the tracks of another. Schedules were erratic, and wrecks were frequent. But railroads made some important advances in the 1830s and 1840s. The introduction of heavier iron rails improved the roadbeds. Steam locomotives became more flexible and powerful. Redesigned passenger cars became stabler, more comfortable, and larger.

Railroads and canals were soon competing bitterly. For a time, the Chesapeake and Ohio Canal Company blocked the advance of the Baltimore and Ohio Railroad through the narrow gorge of the upper Potomac, which it controlled; and the state of New York prohibited railroads from hauling freight in competition with the Erie Canal and its branches. But railroads had so many advantages that when they were able to compete freely with other forms of transportation they almost always prevailed.

The Triumph of the Rails

After 1840, railroads gradually supplanted canals and all other modes of transport. In 1840, there were 2,818 miles of railroad tracks in the United States; by 1850, there were 9,021. An unparalleled burst of railroad construction followed in the 1850s, tripling the amount of trackage in just ten years. The most comprehensive and efficient system was in the Northeast, which had twice as much trackage per square mile as the Northwest and four times as much as the South. But the expansion of the rails left no region untouched. Railroads were even reaching west of the Mississippi, which was spanned at several points by great iron bridges. One line ran from Hannibal to St. Joseph on the Missouri River, and another was under construction between St. Louis and Kansas City.

An important change in railroad development—one that would profoundly affect the nature of sectional alignments—was the trend toward the consolidation of short lines into longer lines (known as "trunk lines"). By 1853, four major railroad trunk lines had crossed the Appalachian barrier to connect the Northeast with the Northwest. Two, the New York Central and the New York and Erie, gave New York City access to the Lake Erie ports. The Pennsylvania railroad linked Philadelphia and Pittsburgh, and the Baltimore and Ohio connected Baltimore with the Ohio River at Wheeling. From the terminals of these lines, other railroads into the interior touched the Mississippi River at eight points. Chicago became the rail center of the West, served by fifteen lines and more than a hundred daily trains. The appearance of the great trunk lines tended to divert traffic from the main water routes—the Erie Canal and the Mississippi River. By lessening the dependence of the West on the Mississippi, the railroads helped weaken further the connection between the Northwest and the South.

Capital to finance the railroad boom came from many sources. Private American investors provided part of the necessary funding, and railroad companies borrowed large sums from abroad. But local governments—states, counties, cities, towns—also often contributed capital, because they were eager to have railroads serve them. This support came in the form of loans, stock subscriptions, subsidies, and donations of land for rights-of-way. The railroads obtained substantial additional assistance from the federal government in the form of public land grants. In 1850, Senator Stephen A. Douglas of Illinois and other railroad-minded politicians persuaded Congress to grant federal lands to aid the Illinois Central, which was building from Chicago toward the Gulf of Mexico. Other states and their railroad promoters demanded the same privileges, and by 1860, Congress had allotted over 30 million acres to eleven states to assist railroad construction.

Innovations in Communications and Journalism

Facilitating the operation of the railroads was an important innovation in communications: the magnetic

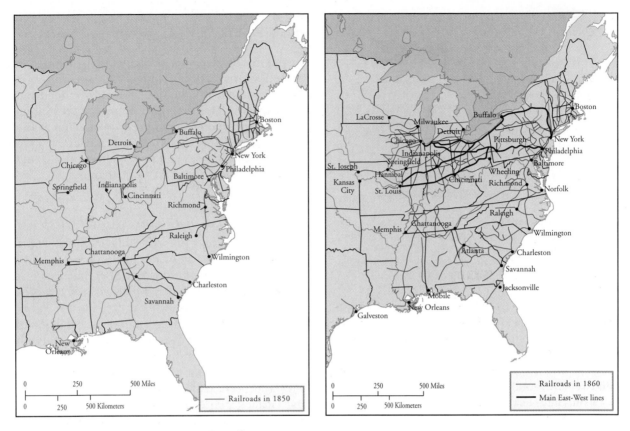

■ THE GROWTH OF THE RAILROADS, 1850-1860

The amount of railroad trackage in the United States tripled between 1850 and 1860. The Northeast developed the most comprehensive and efficient system, with twice as much trackage per square mile as the Northwest and four times as much as the South. Over time, the main "trunk lines" (shown in black) tended to displace traffic from the Erie Canal and the Mississippi River. By lessening the dependence of the West on the Mississippi, the railroads helped to weaken the link between the Northwest and the South.

telegraph. Telegraph lines extended along the tracks, connecting one station with another and aiding the scheduling and routing of trains. But the telegraph had an importance to the nation's economic development beyond its contribution to the railroads. On the one hand, it permitted instant communication between distant cities, tying the nation together as never before. On the other hand, it helped reinforce the schism between the North and South. Like railroads, telegraph lines were far more extensive in the North than in the South, and they helped similarly to link the North to the Northwest (and thus to separate the Northwest further from the South).

The telegraph had burst into American life in 1844, when Samuel F. B. Morse, after several years of experimentation, succeeded in transmitting from Baltimore to Washington the news of James K. Polk's nomination for the presidency. The relatively low cost of constructing wire systems made the Morse telegraph system seem the ideal answer to the problems of long-distance communication. By 1860, more than 50,000 miles of wire connected most parts of the country; and a year later, the Pacific telegraph, with 3,595 miles of wire, opened between New York and San Francisco. By then, nearly all the independent lines had joined in one organization, the Western Union Telegraph Company.

New forms of journalism also drew communities together into a common communications system. In 1846, Richard Hoe invented the steam cylinder rotary press, making it possible to print newspapers rapidly and cheaply. The development of the telegraph, together with the introduction of the rotary press, made possible much speedier collection and

■ THE CYLINDRICAL PRESS
The revolving cylindrical press revolutionized newspaper (and other) publishing in the decades before the Civil War by making possible the printing of large numbers of papers relatively quickly. This ten-cylinder model dates from about 1850. *(Bettmann)*

distribution of news than ever before. In 1846, newspaper publishers from around the nation formed the Associated Press to promote cooperative news gathering by wire; no longer did they have to depend on the cumbersome exchange of newspapers for out-of-town reports.

Major metropolitan newspapers began to appear in the larger cities of the Northeast. In New York alone, there were Horace Greeley's *Tribune,* James Gordon Bennett's *Herald,* and Henry J. Raymond's *Times.* All gave serious attention to national and even international events and had substantial circulations beyond the city.

In the long run, journalism would become an important unifying factor in American life. In the 1840s and 1850s, however, the rise of the new journalism helped to feed sectional discord. Most of the major magazines and newspapers were in the North, reinforcing the South's sense of subjugation. Southern newspapers tended to have smaller budgets and reported largely local news. Few had any impact outside their immediate communities. The combined circulation of the *Tribune* and the *Herald* exceeded that of all the daily newspapers published in the South put together. Above all, the news revolution—along with the revolutions in transportation and communications that accompanied it—contributed to a growing awareness within each section of how the other sections lived and of the deep differences that had grown up between the North and the South—differences that would ultimately seem irreconcilable.

COMMERCE AND INDUSTRY

By the middle years of the nineteenth century, the United States had developed the beginnings of a modern capitalist economy and an advanced industrial capacity. This emerging economy created enormous wealth and changed the face of all areas of the nation. But it did not, of course, affect everyone equally. Some classes and regions benefited from the economic development far more than others.

The Expansion of Business, 1820–1840

American business grew rapidly in the 1820s and 1830s, partly because of population growth and the transportation revolution, but also because of the daring, imagination, and ruthlessness of a new generation of entrepreneurs.

One important change came in the retail distribution of goods, which was becoming increasingly systematic and efficient. In the larger cities, stores specializing in groceries, dry goods, hardware, and other lines appeared, although residents of smaller towns and villages still depended on general stores (stores that did not specialize and carried small selections of a great many different kinds of merchandise). In these less populous areas, many people did much of their business by barter.

The organization of business was also changing. Individuals or limited partnerships continued to operate most businesses, and the dominating figures were still the great merchant capitalists, who generally had sole ownership of their enterprises. In some larger businesses, however, the individual merchant capitalist was giving way to the corporation. Corporations had the advantage of combining the resources of a large number of shareholders, and they began to develop particularly rapidly in the 1830s, when some legal obstacles to their formation were removed. Previously, a corporation could obtain a charter only by a special act of the state legislature—a cumbersome process that stifled corporate growth. By the 1830s, however, states were beginning to pass general incorporation laws, under which a group could secure a charter merely by paying a fee.

The new laws also permitted a system of limited liability, which meant that individual stockholders risked losing only the value of their own investment if a corporation should fail, and that they were not li-

■ **CHICAGO, 1858**
This photograph of the busy freight depot and grain elevators of the Illinois Central Railroad suggests the dramatic growth of Chicago in the 1850s as the great trading center of the central part of the United States.
(Chicago Historical Society)

able (as they had been in the past) for the corporation's larger losses. The rise of these new corporations made possible the accumulation of much greater amounts of capital and hence made possible much larger manufacturing and business enterprises.

Investment alone, however, still provided too little capital to meet the demands of the most ambitious businesses. Such businesses relied heavily on credit, and their borrowing often created dangerous instability. Credit mechanisms remained very crude in the early nineteenth century. The government alone could issue official currency, but the official currency consisted only of gold and silver (or paper certificates backed literally by gold and silver), and there was thus too little of it to support the growing demand for credit. Under pressure from corporate promoters, many banks issued large quantities of bank notes—unofficial currency that circulated in much the same way that government currency did but was of much less stable value. Banks issued these notes to meet the growing demand for capital for expanding business ventures. But the notes had value only to the degree that the bank could sustain public confidence in their value; and some banks issued so many notes that their own reserves could not cover

them. As a result, bank failures were frequent, and bank deposits were often insecure. The difficulty of obtaining credit for business investment remained, therefore, an impediment to economic growth.

The Emergence of the Factory

The most profound economic development in mid-nineteenth-century America was the rise of the factory. Before the War of 1812, most of what manufacturing there was in the United States took place within private households or in small, individually operated workshops. Men and women built or made products by hand, or with simple machines such as hand-operated looms. Gradually, however, improved technology and increasing demand produced a fundamental change. It came first in the New England textile industry. There, beginning early in the nineteenth century, entrepreneurs were beginning to make use of new and larger machines driven by water power that allowed them to bring textile operations together under a single roof. This factory system, as it came to be known, spread rapidly in the 1820s and began to make serious inroads into the old home-based system of spinning thread and weaving cloth.

Factories also penetrated the shoe industry, concentrated in eastern Massachusetts. Shoes were still largely handmade, but manufacturers were beginning to employ workers who specialized in one or another of the various tasks involved in production. Some factories began producing large numbers of identical shoes in ungraded sizes and without distinction as to rights and lefts. By the 1830s, factory production was spreading from textiles and shoes into other industries and from New England to other areas of the Northeast.

Machine technology advanced more rapidly in the United States in the mid-nineteenth century than in any other country in the world—partly because Americans were still catching up with the more advanced technologies of Europe and had to move quickly in order to compete; and partly because the American economy was growing so rapidly that the rewards of technological innovation were very great. Change was so rapid, in fact, that some manufacturers built their new machinery out of wood; by the time the wood wore out, they reasoned, improved technology would have made the machine obsolete. By the end of the 1830s, American technology had become so advanced—particularly in textile manufacturing—that industrialists in Britain and Europe were beginning to travel to the United States to learn new techniques, instead of the other way around.

The Expansion of Industry and Technology, 1840–1860

Between 1840 and 1860, American industry experienced even more dramatic growth as the factory system spread rapidly. In 1840, the total value of manufactured goods produced in the United States stood at $483 million; ten years later the figure had climbed to over $1 billion; and in 1860 it reached close to $2 billion. For the first time, the value of manufactured goods was approximately equal to that of agricultural products.

Of the approximately 140,000 manufacturing establishments in the country in 1860, 74,000 were located in the Northeast. Moreover, they included most of the larger enterprises. The Northeast had only a little more than half the mills and factories in the United States; but the plants there were so large

that the region produced more than two-thirds of the nation's manufactured goods. Of the 1,311,000 workers in manufacturing in the United States, about 938,000 were employed in the mills and factories of New England and the mid-Atlantic states.

Even the most highly developed industries were still relatively immature and were able to produce only a fraction of the goods that they would later be able to make. Cotton manufacturers, for example, could produce only goods of coarse grade; fine items continued to come from England. The woolens industry suffered from a limited supply of domestic raw wool and could not even produce enough coarse goods to satisfy the home market. American industry exported little. It was not even able to meet the demands of American consumers. But technology and industrial ingenuity were helping to prepare the way for a much more productive future.

By the 1840s, the machine tools used in the factories of the Northeast—such as the turret lathe, the grinding machine, and the universal milling machine—were already better than those in European factories. At the same time, the principle of interchangeable parts, first applied decades earlier in gun factories by Eli Whitney and Simeon North, was being introduced into many other industries. Coal was replacing wood as an industrial fuel, particularly in the smelting of iron. Coal was also generating power in steam engines, which were replacing the water power that had in the past driven most of the factory machinery in the Northeast. The production of coal, most of it mined around Pittsburgh in western Pennsylvania, leaped from 50,000 tons in 1820 to 14 million tons in 1860. The new power source made it possible to locate mills away from running streams and thus permitted industry to expand still more widely.

The great technological advances in American industry owed much to American inventors, as the patent records of the time make clear. In 1830, the number of inventions patented was 544; by 1850, the figure had risen to 993; and in 1860, it stood at 4,778. Several industries provide particularly vivid examples of how a technological innovation can produce a major economic change. In 1839, Charles Goodyear, a New England hardware merchant, discovered a method of vulcanizing rubber (treating it to give it greater strength and elasticity); by 1860, his process had found over 500 uses and had helped create a major American rubber industry. In 1846, Elias

Howe of Massachusetts constructed a sewing machine; Isaac Singer made improvements on it, and the Howe-Singer machine was soon being used in the manufacture of ready-to-wear clothing. A few years later, during the Civil War, it would supply the Northern troops with uniforms.

The merchant capitalists—entrepreneurs who were engaged primarily in foreign and domestic trade and who at times invested some of their profits in small-scale manufacturing ventures—remained figures of importance in the 1840s. In such cities as New York, Philadelphia, and Boston, important and influential mercantile groups operated shipping lines to southern ports—carrying off cotton, rice, and sugar—or dispatched fleets of trading vessels to the ports of Europe and Asia. Many of these vessels were the famous clippers, the fastest (and most beautiful) sailing ships afloat. In their heyday in the late 1840s and early 1850s, the clippers could average 300 miles a day, which compared favorably with the best time of the steamships of the day.

But merchant capitalism was declining in the middle years of the century. This was partly because of the declining profitability of the export trade. The value of American exports, still largely agricultural, increased quite substantially—from $124 million in 1840 to $334 million in 1860; but much of the transport and marketing of these exports was falling into the hands of British competitors, who enjoyed the advantages of steam-driven iron ships and government subsidies. The more important reason for the decline of merchant capitalism, however, was the discovery by the merchants themselves that there were greater opportunities for profit in manufacturing than in trade. They reduced their mercantile investments and invested instead in factories, at times becoming owners and operators of them. Indeed, one reason why industries developed first in the Northeast was that an affluent merchant class already existed there and had the money and the will to finance them.

As in the past, many business firms continued to be owned by individuals, families, or small groups of partners. But by the 1840s, particularly in the textile industry, the corporate form of organization was spreading rapidly. In their overseas ventures, merchants had been accustomed to diversifying their risks by buying shares in a number of vessels and voyages. They employed the same device when they moved their capital from trade to manufacturing, often purchasing shares in several textile companies. Ownership of American enterprise, in other words, was moving away from individuals and families and toward its highly dispersed modern form: many stockholders, each owning a relatively small proportion of the total. The discovery of new and more flexible forms of financing was, along with the technological innovations of the era, a crucial factor in the advancement of industrialization.

Whatever the form of business organization—and there continued to be many different forms—industrial capitalists soon became the new ruling class, the aristocrats of the Northeast. And just as they sought and secured economic dominance, they reached for and often achieved political influence. In local or national politics, the capitalists liked to be represented by highly literate lawyers who could articulate their interests, their prejudices, and their philosophies. Their ideal of a representative was Daniel Webster of Massachusetts, whom the business leaders of the Northeast, at considerable financial cost to themselves, supported for years in the United States Senate.

&

MEN AND WOMEN AT WORK

However sophisticated industrial firms became technologically and administratively, manufacturers still relied above all on a supply of labor. In the 1820s and 1830s, factory labor came primarily from the native-born population. After 1840, the growing immigrant population became the most important new source of workers.

Recruiting a Native Work Force

Recruiting a labor force was not an easy task in the early years of the factory system. Ninety percent of the American people in the 1820s still lived and worked on farms. City residents, although increasing in number, were still relatively few, and the potential workers among them even fewer. Many urban residents were skilled artisans—independent craft workers who owned and managed their own shops as small businessmen; they were not likely to flock to factory jobs. The available unskilled workers were not numerous enough to form a reservoir from which the new industries could draw.

■ **WOMEN AT WORK, 1834**
This engraving shows women at work in a
New England textile mill, processing cotton
into cloth. It illustrates the growing
importance of heavy machinery in the
textile industry, which made factory labor
increasingly noisy, hot, and dangerous.
(The Granger Collection)

The beginnings of an industrial labor supply
came instead from the transformation of American
agriculture in the nineteenth century. The opening
of vast, fertile new farmlands in the Midwest, the
improvement of transportation systems, the development of new farm machinery—all combined to
increase food production dramatically. New farming
methods were also less labor intensive than the old
ones; the number of workers required to produce
large crops in the West was much smaller than the
number required to produce smaller crops in the
Northeast. No longer did each region have to feed
itself entirely from its own farms; it could import
food from other regions. As as result, farmers and
their families began to abandon some of the relatively unprofitable farming areas of the East. In the
Northeast, and especially in New England, where
poor land had always placed harsh limits on farm
productivity, rural people began leaving the land to
work in the factories.

Two systems of recruitment emerged to bring
this new labor supply to the expanding textile mills.
One, common in the mid-Atlantic states (especially
in such major manufacturing centers as New York
and Philadelphia), brought whole families from the
farm to the mill. Parents tended looms alongside
their children, some of whom were no more than
four or five years old. The second system, common
in Massachusetts, enlisted young women, mostly
farmers' daughters in their late teens and early
twenties. It was known as the Lowell or Waltham
system, after the factory towns in which it first
emerged. Many of these women worked for several
years in the factories, saved their wages, and returned home to marry and raise children. Others
married men they met in the factories or in town
and remained part of the industrial world. But they
often stopped working in the mills and took up domestic roles instead.

Labor conditions in these early years of the factory
system were significantly better than those in English
industry, better too than they would ultimately become in much of the United States. The employment
of young children created undeniable hardships. But
the misery was not as great as in European factories,
since working children in America usually remained
under the supervision of their parents. In England, by
contrast, asylum authorities often hired out orphans
to factory owners who showed little concern for
their welfare and kept them in something close to
slavery.

Even more different from the European labor system was a second labor system, common in Lowell
and factory towns like it. This was a system that relied heavily, indeed almost exclusively, on young unmarried women. In England and other areas of industrial Europe, the conditions of work for women
were often horrifyingly bad. A British parliamentary
investigation revealed, for example, that women
workers in the coal mines endured unimaginably

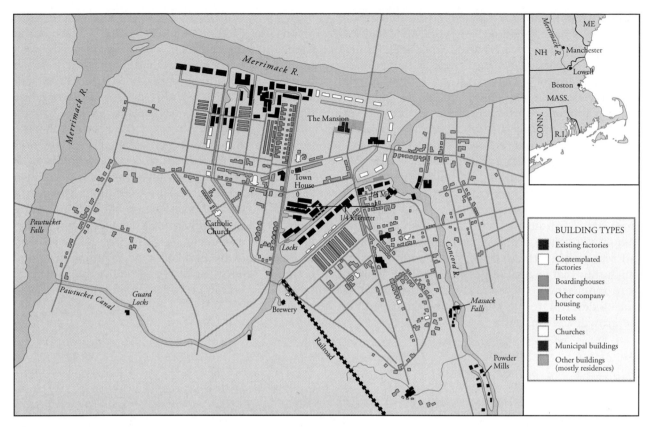

■ SPECIALIZED MANUFACTURING TOWNS: LOWELL, MASSACHUSETTS, 1832
The textile industry in Massachusetts relied heavily on women workers, mostly farmers' daughters in their teens and twenties. Because many New Englanders regarded the employment of women to be vaguely immoral, the factory owners established a system of paternalistic supervision for their workers. The factory owners maintained clean and well-supervised boardinghouses and dormitories (shown on the map in blue and green) for their workers, enforced strict curfews, and required regular church attendance.

wretched conditions. Some had to crawl on their hands and knees, naked and filthy, through cramped, narrow tunnels, pulling heavy coal carts behind them. It was little wonder that English visitors to America considered the Lowell mills a female paradise by contrast. The Lowell workers lived in clean boardinghouses and dormitories, which the factory owners maintained for them. They were well fed and carefully supervised. Because many New Englanders considered the employment of women to be vaguely immoral, the factory owners placed great emphasis on maintaining a proper environment for their employees, enforcing strict curfews and requiring regular church attendance. Employers quickly dismissed women suspected of immoral conduct. Wages for the Lowell workers were low, but generous by the standards of the time. The women

even found time to write and publish a monthly magazine, the *Lowell Offering*.

Yet even these relatively well treated workers often found the transition from farm life to factory work difficult, even traumatic. Uprooted from everything familiar, forced to live among strangers in a regimented environment, many women suffered from severe loneliness and disorientation. Still more had difficulty adjusting to the nature of factory work—the repetition of fixed tasks hour after hour, day after day. That the women had to labor from sunrise to sunset was not in itself a new experience; many of them had worked similarly long days on the farm. But that they now had to spend those days performing tedious, unvarying chores, and that their schedules did not change from week to week or season to season, made the adjustment to factory work especially painful. But however uncomfortable women may have found factory work, they had few other options. They were barred from such manual labor as construction or from work as sailors or on the docks. Most of society considered it unthinkable for women to travel the country alone, as many men did, in search of opportunities. Work in the mills was in many cases virtually the only alternative to returning to farms that could no longer support them.

The paternalistic factory system of Lowell did not, in any case, survive for long. In the competitive textile market as it developed in the 1830s and 1840s—a market prey to the booms and busts that afflicted the American economy as a whole—manufacturers found it difficult to maintain the high living standards and reasonably attractive working conditions with which they had begun. Wages declined; the hours of work lengthened; the conditions of the boardinghouses deteriorated as the buildings decayed and overcrowding increased.

In 1834, mill workers in Lowell organized a union—the Factory Girls Association—which staged a strike to protest a 25 percent wage cut. Two years later, the association struck again—against a rent increase in the boardinghouses. Both strikes failed, and a recession in 1837 virtually destroyed the organization. Eight years later the Lowell women, led by the militant Sarah Bagley, created the Female Labor Reform Association and began agitating for a ten-hour day and for improvements in conditions in the mills. The new association not only made demands of management; it also turned to state government and asked for legislative investigation of conditions in the mills. By then, however, the character of the factory work force was changing again. The mill girls were gradually moving into other occupations: teaching, domestic service, or marriage. And textile manufacturers were turning to a less contentious labor supply: immigrants.

▨ **FOUR WOMEN WEAVERS**
This tintype shows four young women employed in the textile factories of Lowell, Massachusetts. Neatly dressed in matching uniforms, they conveyed the image the factory managers wanted the public to absorb: that women could work in the mills and still be protected from the rough and tumble world of industrialization.
(American Textile History Museum. Lowell, Massachusetts)

The Immigrant Work Force

The rapidly increasing supply of immigrant workers after 1840 was a boon to manufacturers and other entrepreneurs. At last they had access to a source of labor that was both large and inexpensive. These new workers, because of their vast numbers and their unfamiliarity with their new country, had even less leverage than the women they at times displaced. As a result, they often encountered far worse working conditions. Construction gangs, made up increasingly of Irish immigrants, performed the heavy, unskilled work on turnpikes, canals, and railroads under often intolerable conditions. Because most of these workers had no marketable skills and because of native prejudice against them, they received wages so low—and received them so intermittently, since the work was seasonal and uncertain—that they generally did not earn enough to support their families in even minimal comfort. Many of them lived in flimsy shanties, in grim conditions that endangered the health of their families (and reinforced native prejudices toward the "shanty Irish").

Irish workers began to predominate in the New England textile mills as well in the 1840s, and their arrival accelerated the deterioration of working conditions there. There was far less social pressure on owners to provide a decent environment for Irish workers than there had been to provide the same for native women. Employers began paying piece rates (wages tied to how much a worker produced) rather than a daily wage and employed other devices to speed up production and use the labor force more profitably and efficiently. By the mid-1840s, Lowell—once a model for foreign visitors of enlightened industrial development—had become a squalid slum. Similarly miserable working-class neighborhoods were emerging in other northeastern cities.

In almost all industrial areas, factories themselves were becoming large, noisy, unsanitary, and often dangerous places to work. The average workday was extending to twelve, often fourteen hours. Wages were declining, so that even skilled male workers could hope to earn only from $4 to $10 per week, while unskilled laborers were likely to earn only about $1 to $6 per week. Women and children, whatever their skills, also earned less than most men. Conditions were still not as bad as in most factory towns in England and Europe, but neither were American factories the models of cleanliness, efficiency, and human concern that many people had once believed them to be.

The Factory System and the Artisan Tradition

It was not only the mill workers who suffered from the transition to the modern factory system. It was also the skilled artisans whose trades the factories were displacing. The artisan tradition was as much a part of the older, republican vision of America as the tradition of sturdy, independent, yeoman farmers. Independent craftsmen considered themselves embodiments of the American ideal; they clung to a vision of economic life that was in some ways very different from that the new capitalist class was promoting. It was a vision based not just on the idea of individual, acquisitive success (although they were not, of course, averse to profits) but also on a sense of a "moral community." Skilled artisans valued their independence; they also valued the stability and relative equality within their economic world.

The factory system threatened that world with obsolescence. Some artisans made successful transitions into small-scale industry. But others found themselves unable to compete with the new factory-made goods that sold for a fraction of the artisans' prices. In the face of this competition from industrial capitalists, craftsmen began early in the nineteenth century to form organizations—workingmen's political parties and the first American labor unions—to protect their endangered positions and to resist the new economic order in which they sensed they would have no role. As early as the 1790s, printers and cordwainers took the lead. The cordwainers—makers of high-quality boots and shoes—suffered from the competition of the new shoe factories capitalists were building in New England and elsewhere. The development of mass-production methods threatened their livelihoods; it also threatened their independence and their status in their communities. Members of other skilled trades—carpenters, joiners, masons, plasterers, hatters, and shipbuilders—felt similarly vulnerable.

In such cities as Philadelphia, Baltimore, Boston, and New York, the skilled workers of each craft formed societies for mutual aid. During the 1820s and 1830s, the craft societies began to combine on a citywide basis and set up central organizations

■ **"THE SHOP AND WAREHOUSE OF DUNCAN PHYFE"**
Duncan Phyfe was a celebrated and (as this watercolor by John Rubens Smith suggests) prosperous furniture maker in New York for many decades, serving the growing population of affluent households in search of elegance and display. The elegant Georgian details on Phyfe's shop on Fulton Street suggest how even places of business were adapting to the new conception of refinement.
(The Metropolitan Museum of Art, Rogers Fund, 1922(22.28.1) Photograph © 1982 The Metropolitan Museum of Art)

known as trade unions. With the widening of markets, the economies of cities were interconnected, so workers soon realized there were advantages in joining forces and established national unions or federations of local ones. In 1834, delegates from six cities founded the National Trades' Union; and in 1836, the printers and the cordwainers set up their own national craft unions.

This early craft union movement fared poorly. Labor leaders struggled against the handicap of hostile laws and hostile courts. The common law, as interpreted by the courts in the industrial states, viewed a combination among workers as, in itself, an illegal conspiracy. Adverse court decisions, however, were not the only things obstructing the rising unions. The Panic of 1837, a dramatic financial collaspe that produced a severe recession, weakened the movement further. Still, the failure of these first organizations did not end the efforts by workers—artisans and factory operatives alike—to gain some control over their productive lives.

Fighting for Control

Workers at all levels of the emerging industrial economy made continuous efforts to improve their lots.

They tried, with little success, to persuade state legislatures to pass laws setting a maximum workday. Two states—New Hampshire in 1847 and Pennsylvania in 1848—actually passed ten-hour laws, limiting the workday unless the workers agreed to an "express contract" calling for more time on the job. Such measures were virtually without impact, however, because employers could simply require prospective employees to sign the "express contract" as a condition of hiring. Three states—Massachusetts, New Hampshire, and Pennsylvania—passed laws regulating child labor. But again, the results were minimal. The laws simply limited the workday to ten hours for children unless their parents agreed to something longer; employers had little difficulty persuading parents to consent to additional hours.

Perhaps the greatest legal victory of industrial workers came in Massachusetts in 1842, when the supreme court of the state, in *Commonwealth* v. *Hunt,* declared that unions were lawful organizations and that the strike was a lawful weapon. Other state courts gradually accepted the principles of the Massachusetts decision. On the whole, however, the union movement of the 1840s and 1850s remained generally ineffective. Some workers were reluctant to think of themselves as members of a permanent laboring force and resisted joining unions. But even those unions that did manage to recruit significant numbers of industrial workers were usually not large enough or strong enough to stage strikes, and even less frequently strong enough to win them.

Artisans and skilled workers, despite their setbacks in the 1830s, had somewhat greater success than did factory workers. But their unions often had more in common with preindustrial guilds than with modern labor organizations. In most cases, their primary purpose was to protect the favored position of their members in the labor force by restricting admission to the skilled trades. The organizing effort that had floundered in the 1830s revived impressively in the 1850s. Among the new organizations skilled workers created were the National Typographical Union, founded in 1852, the Stone Cutters in 1853, the Hat Finishers in 1854, and the Molders and the Machinists, both in 1859.

Virtually all the early craft unions excluded women, even though female workers were numerous in almost every industry and craft. As a result, women began establishing their own protective unions by the 1850s, often with the support of middle-class female reformers. Like the male craft unions, the female protective unions had little power in dealing with employers. They did, however, serve an important role as mutual aid societies for women workers.

Despite these persistent efforts at organization and protest, the American working class in the 1840s and 1850s was notable for its relatively modest power. In England, workers were becoming a powerful, united, and often violent economic and political force. They were creating widespread social turmoil and helping to transform the nation's political structure. In America, nothing of the sort happened. Many factors combined to inhibit the growth of effective labor resistance. Among the most important was the flood of immigrant laborers into the country. The newcomers were usually willing to work for lower wages than native workers. Because they were so numerous, manufacturers had little difficulty replacing disgruntled or striking workers with eager immigrants. Ethnic divisions and tensions—both between natives and immigrants and among the various immigrant groups themselves—often led workers to channel their resentments into internal bickering rather than into their shared grievances against employers. There was, too, the sheer strength of the industrial capitalists, who had not only economic but also political and social power and could usually triumph over even the most militant challenges.

PATTERNS OF SOCIETY

The industrial revolution was making the United States—and particularly its more economically developed regions—dramatically wealthier by the year. It was also making society more unequal, and it was transforming social relationships and everyday life at almost every level—from the workplace to the family.

The Rich and the Poor

The commercial and industrial growth of the United States greatly elevated the average income of the American people. But what evidence there is—and it is admittedly sketchy—suggests that this increasing wealth was being distributed highly unequally. Substantial groups of the population, of course, shared hardly at all in the economic growth: slaves, Indians, landless farmers, and many of the unskilled workers on the fringes of the manufacturing system. But even among the rest of the population, disparities of income were marked. Wealth had always been unequally distributed in the United States, to be sure. Even in the era of the Revolution, according to some estimates, 45 percent of the wealth was concentrated in the hands of about 10 percent of the population. But by the mid-nineteenth century, that concentration had become far more pronounced. In Boston in 1845, for example, 4 percent of the citizens are estimated to have owned more than 65 percent of the wealth; in Philadelphia in 1860, 1 percent of the population possessed more than half the wealth. Among the American people overall in 1860, according to scholarly estimates, 5 percent of the families possessed more than 50 percent of the wealth.

There had been wealthy classes in America almost from the beginning of European settlement. But the extent and character of wealth was changing in response to the commercial revolution of the mid-nineteenth century. Merchants and industrialists were accumulating enormous fortunes; and because there was now a significant number of rich people living in

■ **CENTRAL PARK**
To affluent New Yorkers, the construction of the city's great Central Park was important because it provided them with an elegant setting for their daily carriage rides—an activity ostensibly designed to expose the riders to fresh air but that was really an occasion for them to display their finery to their neighbors. *(Museum of the City of New York)*

cities, a distinctive culture of wealth began to emerge. In large cities, people of great wealth gathered together in neighborhoods of astonishing opulence. They founded clubs and developed elaborate social rituals. They looked increasingly for ways to display their wealth—in the great mansions they built, the showy carriages in which they rode, the lavish household goods they accumulated, the clothes they wore, the elegant social establishments they patronized. New York, which had more wealthy families than anywhere else, developed a particularly elaborate high society. The construction of the city's great Central Park, which began in the 1850s, was in part a result of pressure from the members of high society, who wanted an elegant setting for their daily carriage rides.

There was also a significant population of genuinely destitute people emerging in the growing urban centers of the nation. These were people who were not merely poor, in the sense of having

to struggle to sustain themselves—most Americans were poor in that sense. They were almost entirely without resources, often homeless, dependent on charity or crime or both for survival. Substantial numbers of people actually starved to death or died of exposure.

Some of these "paupers," as contemporaries called them, were recent immigrants who had failed to find work or to adjust to life in the New World. Some were widows and orphans, stripped of the family structures that allowed most working-class Americans to survive. Some were people suffering from alcoholism or mental illness, unable to work. Others were victims of native prejudice—barred from all but the most menial employment because of race or ethnicity. The Irish were particular victims of such prejudice.

Among the worst victims were free blacks. African-American communities in antebellum northern cities were small by later standards, but most major urban areas had significant black populations. Some of these African Americans were descendants of families that had lived in the North for generations. Others were former slaves who had escaped from the South or been released by their masters or had bought their freedom; some former slaves, once free, then worked to buy the freedom of relatives left behind. In material terms, at least, life was not always much better for them in the North than it had been in slavery. Most had access only to very menial jobs, which usually paid too little to allow workers to support their families or educate their children; in bad times many had access to no jobs at all. In most parts of the North, blacks could not vote, could not attend public schools, indeed could not use any of the public services available to white residents. Most blacks preferred life in the North, however arduous, to life in the South because it permitted them at least some level of freedom. But that freedom did not bring anything approaching equality.

Social Mobility

One might expect the contrasts between conspicuous wealth and conspicuous poverty in antebellum America to have encouraged more class conflict than actually occurred. But a number of factors operated to quell resentments. For one thing, however much the relative economic position of American workers may have been declining, the absolute living standard of most laborers was improving. Life, in material terms at least, was usually better for factory workers than it had been on the farms or in the European societies from which they had migrated. They ate better, they were often better clothed and housed, and they had greater access to consumer goods.

There was also a significant amount of mobility within the working class, which helped to limit discontent. Opportunities for social mobility, for working one's way up the economic ladder, were limited, but the opportunities did exist. A few workers did manage to move from poverty to riches by dint of work, ingenuity, and luck—a very small number, but enough to support the dreams of those who watched them. And a much larger number of workers managed to move at least one notch up the ladder—for example, becoming in the course of a lifetime a skilled, rather than an unskilled, laborer. Such people

could envision their children and grandchildren moving up even further.

More common than social mobility was geographical mobility, which was even more extensive in the United States than in Europe, where it was considerable. America had a huge expanse of uncultivated land in the West, much of it open for settlement for the first time in the 1840s and 1850s. Some workers saved money, bought land, and moved west to farm it. The historian Frederick Jackson Turner later referred to the availability of western lands as a "safety valve" for discontent, a basic explanation for the relative lack of social conflict in the antebellum United States. But few urban workers, and even fewer poor ones, could afford to make such a move or had the expertise to know how to work land even if they could have bought it. Much more common was the movement of laborers from one industrial town to another. Restless, questing, sometimes hopeful, sometimes despairing, these frequently-moving people were often the victims of layoffs, looking for better opportunities elsewhere. Their search may seldom have led to a marked improvement in their circumstances, but the rootlessness of this large segment of the work force—one of the most distressed segments—made effective organization and protest far more difficult.

There was, finally, another "safety valve" for working-class discontent: politics. Economic opportunity may not have greatly expanded in the nineteenth century, but opportunities to participate in politics did. And to many white, male working people, access to the ballot seemed to offer a way to help guide their society and to feel like a significant part of their communities.

Middle-Class Life

For all the visibility of the very rich and the very poor in antebellum society, the fastest-growing group in America was the middle class. The expansion of the middle class was in part a result of the growth of the industrial economy and the increasing commercial life that accompanied it. Economic development opened many more opportunities for people to own or work in businesses, to own shops, to engage in trade, to enter professions, and to administer organizations. In earlier times, when ownership of land had been the only real basis of wealth, society had been divided between people with little or no land (people Europeans generally called peasants) and a landed gentry (which in Europe usually became an inherited aristocracy). Once commerce and industry became a source of wealth, these rigid distinctions broke down; and many people could become prosperous without owning land, but by providing valuable services to the new economy.

Middle-class life in the years before the Civil War rapidly established itself as the most influential cultural form of urban America. Middle-class families lived in solid and often substantial homes. Their rowhouses lined city streets, larger in size and more elaborate in design than the cramped, functional rowhouses in working-class neighborhoods—but also far less lavish than the great houses of the very rich. Like the wealthy, middle-class people tended to own their homes. Workers and artisans were increasingly becoming renters—a relatively new phenomenon in American cities that spread widely in the early nineteenth century.

Middle-class women tended to remain in the home and care for the children and the household, although increasingly they were also able to hire servants—usually young, unmarried immigrant women who put in long hours of arduous work for very little money. One of the aspirations of middle-class women in an age when doing the family's laundry could take an entire day was to escape from some of the drudgery of housework.

New household inventions altered, and greatly improved, the character of life in middle-class homes. Perhaps the most important was the invention of the cast-iron stove, which began to replace fireplaces as the principal vehicle for cooking and also as an important source of heat. These wood- or coal-burning devices were hot, clumsy, and dirty by the standards of the twentieth century; but compared to the inconvenience and danger of cooking on an open hearth, they seemed a great luxury to nineteenth-century families. Stoves gave cooks more control over the preparation of food and allowed them to cook several things at once.

Middle-class diets were changing rapidly in the antebellum years, and not just because of the wider range of cooking the stove made possible. The expansion and diversification of American agriculture, and the ability of farmers to ship goods to urban markets by rail from distant regions greatly increased the variety of food available in cities. Fruits and vegetables were difficult to ship over long distances in an

age with little refrigeration, but families had access to a greater variety of meats, grains, and dairy products than they had had in the past. A few households acquired iceboxes in the years before the Civil War, and the sight of wagons delivering large chunks of ice to wealthy and middle-class homes began to become a familiar part of urban life. Iceboxes allowed their owners to keep fresh meat and dairy products for as long as several days without spoilage. Most families, however, did not yet have any kind of refrigeration. Preserving food for them meant curing meat with salt and preserving fruits in sugar. Diets were generally much heavier and starchier than they are today, and middle-class people tended to be considerably stouter than would be fashionable in the twentieth century.

Middle-class homes came to differentiate themselves from those of workers and artisans in other ways as well. They were more elaborately decorated and furnished, with goods made available for the first time through factory production of household goods. Houses that had once had bare walls and floors now had carpeting, wallpaper, and curtains. The spare, simple styles of eighteenth-century homes gave way to the much more elaborate, even baroque household styles of the early Victorian era—styles increasingly characterized by crowded, even cluttered rooms, dark colors, lush fabrics, and heavy furniture and draperies. Middle-class homes also became larger. It became less common for children to share beds and for all family members to sleep in the same room. Parlors and dining rooms separate from the kitchen—once a luxury reserved largely for the wealthy—became the norm for the middle class as well. Some urban middle-class homes had indoor plumbing and indoor toilets by the 1850s—a significant advance over the outdoor wells and privies that had been virtually universal only a few years earlier (and that remained common among working-class people).

The Changing Family

The new industrializing society of the northern regions of the United States produced profound changes in the nature and function of the family. At the heart of the transformation was the movement of families from farms to urban areas, where jobs, not land, were the most valued commodities. The patriarchal system of the countryside, where fathers con-

■ **PASTORAL AMERICA, 1848**
This painting by the American artist Edward Hicks suggests the degree to which Americans continued to admire the "Peaceable Kingdom" (the name of another, more famous Hicks work) of the agrarian world. Hicks entitled this work *An Indian Summer view of the Farm w. Stock of James C. Cornell of Northampton Bucks county Pennsylvania. That took the Premium in the Agricultural Society, October the 12, 1848.* It portrays the diversified farming of a prosperous Pennsylvania family, shown here in the foreground with their cattle, sheep, and workhorses. In the background stretches a field ready for plowing and another ready for harvesting. *(National Gallery of Art, Washington)*

trolled their children's futures by controlling the distribution of land to them, could not survive the move to a city or town. Sons and daughters were much more likely to leave the family in search of work than they had been in the rural world.

Another important change was the shift of income-earning work out of the home and into the shop, mill, or factory. In the early decades of the nineteenth century (and for many years before that), the family itself had been the principal unit of economic activity. Family farms, family shops, and family industries were the norm throughout most of the United States. Men, women, and children worked together, sharing tasks and jointly earning the income that sustained the family. But in the middle years of the nineteenth century, there were important changes.

Those changes occurred even among the farming population, which continued to constitute the majority of the American people. As farming spread to the fertile lands of the Northwest and as the size and profitability of farms expanded, agricultural work became more commercialized. Farm owners in need of labor began to rely less on their families (which often were not large enough to satisfy the demand) and more on hired male workers. These farmhands performed many of the tasks that on smaller farms had once been the jobs of the women and children of the family. As a result, farm women tended to work increasingly at domestic tasks—cooking, sewing, gardening, and dairying—a development that spared them from some heavy labor but that also removed them from the principal income-producing activities of the farm. Farm women in the new agricultural

■ **"NATHAN HAWLEY AND FAMILY"**
Nathan Hawley, seated at center in this 1801 painting, was typical of many early-nineteenth-century fathers in having a very large family. Nine members are visible here. Hawley at the time was the warden of the Albany County jail in New York, and the painting was by William Wilkie, one of the inmates there. The painting suggests that Hawley was a man of modest but not great means. His family is fashionably dressed, and there are paintings on the walls—signs of style and affluence. But the house is very simply furnished, without drapes for the windows, with a simple painted floor cloth in the front room, and a bare floor in the back. *(Collection of the Albany Institute of History and Art)*

regions of the Northwest tended, therefore, to have a lower economic status within the family (and within the community) than their earlier counterparts in the East, who had been more crucial to the family economy. (See Chapter 11 for a discussion of family relations in the agrarian South.)

In the industrial economy of the rapidly growing cities, there was an even more significant decline in the traditional economic function of the family. The urban household itself became less important as a center of production. Instead, most income earners left home each day to work elsewhere. A sharp distinction began to emerge between the public world of the workplace—the world of commerce and industry—and the private world of the family. The world of the family was now dominated not by pro-

duction, but by housekeeping, child rearing, and other primarily domestic concerns. It was also a world dominated by women.

Accompanying (and perhaps in part caused by) the changing economic function of the family was a decline in the birth rate. In 1800, the average American woman could be expected to give birth to approximately seven children during her childbearing years. By 1860, the average woman bore five children. The birth rate fell most quickly in urban areas and among middle-class women. Mid-nineteenth-century Americans had access to some birth control devices, which undoubtedly contributed in part to the change. There was also a significant rise in abortions, which remained legal in some states until after the Civil War and which, according to some estimates, may have terminated as many as 20 percent of all pregnancies in the 1850s. But the most important cause of the declining birth rate was almost certainly changes in sexual behavior—including increased abstinence.

The deliberate effort among middle-class men and women, in particular, to limit family size was a reflection of a much larger shift in the nature of society in the mid-nineteenth-century North. In a world in which the economy was becoming increasingly organized, in which production was moving out of the home, in which individuals were coming to expect more from the world, in which people placed more emphasis on calculations about the future, making careful decisions about bearing children seemed important. It expressed the increasingly secular, rationalized, and progressive orientation of the rapidly developing American North.

Women and the "Cult of Domesticity"

The emerging distinction between the public and private worlds, between the workplace and the home, accompanied (and helped cause) increasingly sharp distinctions between the social roles of men and women. Those distinctions affected not only factory workers and farmers, but members of the growing middle class as well. There had, of course, always been important differences between the male and female spheres in American society. Women had long been denied many legal and political rights enjoyed by men; within the family, the husband and father had traditionally ruled, and the wife and mother had generally bowed to his demands and desires. It had long been practically impossible for most women to obtain divorces, although divorces initiated by men were often easier to arrange. (Men were also far more likely than women to win custody of children in case of a divorce.) In most states, husbands retained almost absolute authority over both the property and persons of their wives. Wife beating was illegal in only a few areas, and the law did not acknowledge that rape could occur within marriage. Women traditionally had very little access to the worlds of business or politics. Indeed, custom in most communities dictated that women never speak in public before mixed audiences.

Most women also had much less access to education than men, a situation that survived into the mid-nineteenth century. Although they were encouraged to attend school at the elementary level, they were strongly discouraged—and in most cases effectively barred—from pursuing higher education. Oberlin in Ohio became the first college in America to accept female students; it permitted four to enroll in 1837, despite criticism that coeducation was a rash experiment approximating free love. Oberlin authorities were confident that "the mutual influence of the sexes upon each other is decidedly happy in the cultivation of both mind & manners." But few other institutions shared their views. Coeducation remained extraordinarily rare until long after the Civil War; and only a very few women's colleges—such as Mount Holyoke, founded in Massachusetts by Mary Lyon in 1837—emerged.

However unequal the positions of men and women were in the preindustrial era, those positions were generally defined within the context of a household in which all members played crucial roles in generating family income. In the middle-class family of the new industrial society, however, the husband was assumed to be the principal, usually the only, income producer. The wife was now expected to remain in the home and to engage in largely domestic activities.

The result was an important shift in the middle-class concept of the woman's place within the family and of the family's place within the larger society. The proper role of women became a subject of broad discussion in middle-class society in the mid-nineteenth century; and out of this discussion came a widespread view of women as guardians of the "domestic virtues." Their role as mothers, entrusted with the nurturing of the young, seemed more central to the family than it had in the past. And their role as wives—as companions and helpers to their husbands—grew more important as well. Middle-class women, no longer producers, now became more important as consumers. They learned to place a high value on keeping a clean, comfortable, and well-appointed home, on entertaining, and on dressing elegantly and stylishly.

Occupying their own "separate sphere," some women began to develop a distinctive female culture. Friendships among women became increasingly intense; women began to form their own social networks (and, ultimately, to form female clubs and associations that were of great importance to the advancement of various reforms). A distinctive feminine literature began to emerge to meet the demands of middle-class women. There were romantic novels (many of them by female writers), which focused on the private sphere that women now inhabited. There were women's magazines, of which the most prominent was *Godey's Lady's Book,* edited after 1837 by Sarah Hale, who had earlier founded a women's magazine of her own. The magazine scrupulously avoided dealing with public controversies or political issues and focused instead on fashions, shopping and homemaking advice, and other purely domestic concerns. Politics and religion were inappropriate for the magazine, Hale explained in 1841, because "other subjects are more important for our sex and more proper for our sphere."

By the standards of a later era, the increasing isolation of women from the public world seems to be a form of oppression and discrimination. And it is true that few men considered women fit for business, politics, or the professions. On the other hand, most middle-class men—and many middle-class women as well—considered the new female sphere a vehicle for expressing special qualities that made women in some ways superior to men. Women were to be the custodians of morality and benevolence, just as the home—shaped by the influence of women—was to be a refuge from the harsh, competitive world of the marketplace. It was women's responsibility to provide religious and moral instruction to their children and to counterbalance the acquisitive, secular impulses of their husbands. Thus the "cult of domesticity," as some scholars have called it, brought both benefits and costs to middle-class women. It allowed them to live lives of greater material comfort than in the past, and it placed a higher value on their "female virtues" and on their roles as wife and mother. At the same time, it left women increasingly detached from the public world, with fewer outlets for their interests and energies.

The costs of that detachment were particularly clear among unmarried women of the middle class. By the 1840s, the ideology of domesticity had grown so powerful that few genteel women would any longer consider working (as many had in the past) in shops or mills, and few employers would consider hiring them. But unmarried women nevertheless required some income-producing activity. They had few choices. Some could become teachers or nurses, professions that seemed to call for the same female

qualities that made women important within the home; and both those professions began in the 1840s and 1850s to attract significant numbers of women, although not until the Civil War did females begin to dominate them. Otherwise, unmarried females were largely dependent on the generosity of relatives.

Middle-class people gradually came to consider work by women outside the household to be unseemly, something characteristic of the lower classes—as indeed it was. Working-class women could not afford to stay home and cultivate the "domestic virtues." They had to produce income for their families. They continued to work in factories and mills, but under conditions far worse than those that the original, more "respectable" woman workers had enjoyed. They also frequently found employment in middle-class homes. Domestic service became one of the most frequent sources of female employment. In other words, now that production had moved outside the household, women who needed to earn money had to move outside their own households to do so.

Leisure Activities

Leisure time was scarce for all but the wealthiest Americans in the mid-nineteenth century. Most people worked long hours. Saturday was a normal working day. Vacations—paid or unpaid—were rare. For most people, Sunday was the only respite from work; and Sundays were generally reserved for religion and rest. Almost no commercial establishments did any business at all on Sunday, and even within the home most families frowned upon playing games or engaging in other kinds of entertainment on the Sabbath. For many working-class and middle-class people, therefore, holidays took on a special importance. That was one reason for the strikingly elaborate Fourth of July celebrations throughout the country in the nineteenth century. The celebrations were not just expressions of patriotism. They were a way of enjoying one of the few holidays from work available to most Americans.

In rural America, where most people still lived, the erratic pattern of farmwork gave many people some relief from the relentless working schedules of city residents. For urban people, however, leisure was something to be seized in what few free moments they had. Men gravitated to taverns for drinking, talking, and game-playing. Women gathered in one another's homes for conversation, card games, or to share work on such household tasks as sewing. For educated people, whose numbers were rapidly expanding, reading became one of the principal leisure activities. Newspapers and magazines proliferated rapidly, and books—novels, histories, autobiographies, biographies, travelogues, and others—became staples of affluent homes. Women were particularly avid readers, and women writers created a new genre of fiction specifically for females—the "sentimental novel," which often offered idealized visions of women's lives and romances (see pp. 422–423).

There was also a vigorous culture of public leisure, even if many families had to struggle to find time or means to participate in it. In larger cities, theaters were becoming increasingly popular; and while some of them catered to particular social groups, others attracted audiences that crossed class lines. Wealthy people, middle-class people, workers and their families: all could sometimes be found watching a performance of Shakespeare or a melodrama based on a popular novel or an American myth. Minstrel shows—in which white actors mimicked (and ridiculed) African-American culture—became increasingly popular (see pp. 536–537). Public sporting events—boxing, horse racing, cockfighting (already becoming controversial), and others—often attracted considerable crowds. Baseball—not yet organized into professional leagues—was beginning to attract large crowds when played in city parks or fields on the edges of towns (see pp. 486–487). A particularly exciting event in many communities was the arrival of the circus—a traveling entertainment with roots in the middle ages that continued to entertain, delight, and bamboozle children and adults alike.

Popular tastes in public spectacle tended toward the bizarre and the fantastic. Most men and women lived in a constricted world of familiar things. Relatively few people traveled; and in the absence of film, radio, television, or even much photography, they hungered for visions of unusual phenomena that contrasted with their normal experiences. People going to the theater or the circus or the museum wanted to see things that amazed and even frightened them. Perhaps the most celebrated provider of such experiences was the famous and unscrupulous showman P. T. Barnum, who opened the American Museum in New York in 1842—not a showcase for art or nature, but a great freak show populated by midgets (the most famous named Tom Thumb), Siamese twins, magicians, and ventriloquists. Barnum was a genius in publicizing his ventures with garish posters and elaborate newspaper announcements. Only later, in the 1870s, did he launch the famous circus for which he is still best remembered. But he was always a pioneer in exploiting public tastes for the wild and exotic.

One of the ways Barnum tried to draw visitors to his museum was by engaging lecturers. He did so because he understood that the lecture was one of the most popular forms of entertainment in nineteenth-century America. Men and women flocked in enormous numbers to lyceums (see pp. 454–455), churches, schools, and auditoriums to hear lecturers explain the latest advances in science, or describe their visits to exotic places, or to provide vivid historical narratives, or to rail against the evils of alcohol or slavery. Messages of social uplift and reform attracted rapt audiences, particularly among women eager for guidance as they adjusted to the often jarring changes in the character of family life in the industrializing world.

THE AGRICULTURAL NORTH

Even in the rapidly urbanizing and industrializing Northeast, and more so in what nineteenth-century Americans called the Northwest (and what Americans today call the Midwest), most people remained tied to the agricultural world. But agriculture, like industry and commerce, was becoming increasingly a part of the new capitalist economy, linked to the national and international market. Where agriculture could not compete in this new commercial world—as in much of the Northeast—it declined. Where it could compete—as in most of the Northwest—it simultaneously flourished and changed.

Northeastern Agriculture

The story of agriculture in the Northeast after 1840 is one of decline and transformation. The reason

SHAKESPEARE IN AMERICA

One of the characters Huckleberry Finn encountered in his journey down the Mississippi in Mark Twain's famous novel was a roguish traveling actor who called himself "the Duke of Bridgewater." The duke improvised performances almost anywhere there was anyone willing to pay. One of his favorite encores, he claimed, was "Hamlet's soliloquy . . . the most celebrated thing in Shakespeare." He recited it with bravado, and with very little fidelity to the original text:

To be, or not to be; that is the bare bodkin
That makes calamity of so long life.

The events of Twain's novel were set in the years before the Civil War, when Shakespeare's work was familiar to Americans of all ages, classes, and regions. From elegant theaters in the great eastern cities, to makeshift stages and rickety "opera houses" in farming villages and mining towns in the West, Americans gathered to watch productions of Shakespeare's plays just as they gathered to watch now-forgotten comedies and melodramas written in their own time. Whether performed by famous actors or by hand-to-mouth hustlers like Twain's "duke," Shakespeare was entertainment for the masses.

Performances of Shakespeare had begun in America as early as 1750, but public interest in his plays reached its peak in the 1830s, 1840s, and 1850s, when theater was the single most popular performing art throughout the United States, and Shakespeare the single most popular playwright. Many, perhaps most, performances of Shakespearean plays were irreverent, inaccurate, and romanticized. Tragedies had happy endings. Comedies were interlaced with contemporary, regional humor. Texts were reworked with American dialect, and plays were abbreviated and

■ **THE ASTOR PLACE RIOT**

This later watercolor of the Astor Place riot in 1849 conveys something of the violence and bedlam that the great rivalry between Edwin Forrest and William Macready produced. Here, anti-English mobs demonstrate outside the theater in which the English actor Macready was performing. During the rioting, they set the theater on fire, and the turmoil only subsided when the Seventh Regiment guard was called out.

(The Great Riot at the Astor Place Opera House, New York, Thursday Evening, May 10, 1849. Published by N. Currier, 1849. Museum of the City of New York, The Harry T. Peters Collection)

sandwiched into programs containing other popular work of the time. So familiar were many Shakespearean plots that audiences took delight in seeing them parodied in productions such as "Julius Sneezer," "Hamlet and Egglet," and "Much Ado About a Merchant of Venice."

People from all walks of life went regularly to the theater and mingled with one another in ways that would become unusual in later eras. Seating was often divided by class—a tier of boxes for the wealthiest patrons, orchestra seats for the middle class, and balconies for those too poor to sit anywhere else (and for virtually all nonwhite members of the audience). But despite these distinctions, going to the theater was a vibrantly democratic experience of a kind seldom visible in twentieth-century America except occasionally at sports events.

One result was that American audiences were often noisy, rambunctious, and—at least in the eyes of many actors—obnoxious. Men and women did not sit quietly in theaters as most do today. They shouted out reactions to the plays, taunted actors, and occasionally—as in an 1832 performance of *Richard III* in New York—climbed onto the stage and joined the performance, mingling with the actors during a battle scene and charging across the stage as if they were soldiers.

The leading Shakespearean actors of the antebellum era became figures of enormous public interest, and at times could spur great popular passion. Evidence of that came from events in New York City in 1849. The celebrated American actor Edwin Forrest—beloved by working-class audiences as a great patriot and a common man who had risen to greatness—gave a performance of *Macbeth* on the same evening that a renowned English actor, William Macready, was performing the same play elsewhere in the city. Many New Yorkers believed that the aloof, aristocratic Macready, and through him the city's wealthy elites, were attempting to humiliate Forrest. Forrest supporters crowded into Macready's performance and hooted him off the stage. Three days later, Macready tried again at the Astor Place Opera House. Ten thousand people, most of them Forrest enthusiasts, gathered outside and tried to force their way into the theater. Militia, called out for the occasion, fired into the crowd killing at least 22 and wounding more than 150. It was one of the bloodiest civil conflicts of the first half of the nineteenth century.

Shakespeare remained popular throughout the Civil War. In 1864 enthusiastic crowds greeted

■ **THE PARK THEATER**
This 1821 watercolor by John Searle shows the interior of the Park Theater in New York, which had recently been rebuilt after a fire. The play is a farce by the English playwright William T. Moncrieffe. The faces in the audience are all portraits of real New Yorkers at the time. (© *Collection of the New-York Historical Society*)

(continued)

361

a performance in New York of *Julius Caesar,* featuring three members of America's most celebrated theatrical family: William Junius Booth, an aging giant who had been the foremost tragic actor of his generation, and his two sons Edwin and John Wilkes. "No playgoer has seen Shakespere [sic] presented with attraction more likely to draw and charm the true lover of the drama since the days when Shakespere himself appeared in his own plays," the New York *Herald* editorialized in a fit of civic pride. "Only English cities could hope to rival us in this."

Edwin Booth went on to become America's most revered actor of the last half of the nineteenth century, renowned in particular for his performances of *Hamlet* and other great Shakespearean roles at the Booth Theater he founded in New York. His brother, John Wilkes, is best remembered leaping to the stage of Ford's Theater in Washington on April 14, 1865 after having fatally shot Abraham Lincoln. His famous exclamation at the time, *"Sic semper tyrannis,"* was the motto of the state of Virginia. But it was better known as the phrase Brutus supposedly uttered after killing Julius Caesar, an event most familiar to nineteenth-century audiences—and to Booth himself—from performances of Shakespeare's play.

Huckleberry Finn was published in 1884, when the broad popularity of Shakespeare that Twain described was already beginning to fade. By the end of the nineteenth century, Shakespeare's work was beginning to be treated with much more gravity and was starting to be associated with the educated upper classes. The great Shakespearean actors of these later years had no large followings among workers and ordinary people. They were favorites of the aristocracy, who sought to protect them and the

■ **THE BOOTHS IN *JULIUS CAESAR***

The Booths were America's leading acting family in the 1860s, and this photograph by Matthew Brady captures a rare event: the appearance together in a play of Edwin Booth, the most famous and talented member of the family, and two of his acting brothers, John Wilkes (left, remembered today as Lincoln's assassin but well know at the time as a popular actor) and Junius Brutus Booth, Jr. (right). They are performing Shakespeare's *Julius Caesar* in New York. *(Library of Congress)*

plays they performed from being debased by common audiences they considered incapable of understanding them. A clear distinction had grown up between "high culture," of which Shakespeare was now a part, and "lowbrow culture," from which Shakespeare was gradually excluded. That distinction has survived into our own time.

for the decline was simple: the farmers of the section could no longer compete with the new and richer soil of the Northwest. Centers of production were gradually shifting westward for many of the farm goods that had in the past been most important to northeastern agriculture: wheat, corn, grapes, cattle, sheep, and hogs. In 1840, the leading wheat-growing states were New York, Pennsylvania, Ohio, and Virginia; in 1860 they were Illinois, Indiana, Wisconsin, Ohio, and Michigan. In raising corn, Illinois, Ohio, and Missouri supplanted New York, Pennsylvania, and Virginia. In 1840 the most important cattle-raising areas in the country were New York, Pennsylvania, and New England; but by the 1850s the leading cattle states were Illinois, Indiana, Ohio, and Iowa in the West, and Texas in the South.

Some eastern farmers responded to these changes by moving west themselves and establishing new farms. Still others moved to mill towns and became laborers. Some farmers, however, remained on the land and managed to hold their own against the Northwest, and at times even surpass it, in certain areas of agriculture. As the eastern urban centers increased in population, many farmers turned to the task of supplying food to the cities; they raised vegetables (truck farming) or fruit and sold it in nearby towns. New York, for example, led all other states in apple production.

The rise of cities also stimulated the rise of profitable dairy farming. Supplying milk, butter, and cheese to local markets attracted many farmers in central New York, southeastern Pennsylvania, and various parts of New England. Approximately half the dairy products of the country were produced in the East; most of the rest came from the West, where Ohio was the leading dairy state. Partly because of the expansion of the dairy industry, the Northeast led other sections in the production of hay. New York was the leading hay state in the nation; Pennsylvania and New England grew large crops as well. The Northeast also exceeded other areas in producing potatoes.

But while agriculture in the region remained an important part of the economy, it was steadily becoming less important relative both to the agriculture of the Northwest and to the industrial growth of the Northeast itself. As a result, the rural population in many parts of the Northeast continued to decline.

The Old Northwest

Life was different in the states of the Northwest in the mid-nineteenth century. There was some industry in this region, more than in the South; and in the two decades before the Civil War, the section experienced steady industrial growth. By 1860, it had 36,785 manufacturing establishments employing 209,909 workers. There was a flourishing industrial and commercial area along the shore of Lake Erie, with Cleveland at its center. Another manufacturing region was in the Ohio River valley; the meatpacking city of Cincinnati was its nucleus. Farther west, the rising city of Chicago, destined to become the great metropolis of the section, was emerging as the national center of the agricultural machinery and meatpacking industries.

Most of the major industrial activities of the West either served agriculture (as in the case of farm machinery), or relied on agricultural products (as in flour milling, meatpacking, whiskey distilling, and the making of leather goods). As this suggests, industry was, on the whole, much less important in the Northwest than farming.

Some areas of the Northwest were not yet dominated by whites. Indians remained the most numerous inhabitants of large portions of most of the upper third of the Great Lakes states until after the Civil War. In those areas, hunting and fishing, along with some sedentary agriculture, remained the principal economic activities of both whites and Native Americans. But the tribes did not become integrated into the new commercialized economy that was emerging elsewhere in the Northwest.

For the white (and occasionally black) settlers who populated the lands farther south that they had by now largely wrested from the natives, the Northwest was primarily an agricultural region. Its rich and plentiful lands made farming a lucrative and expanding activity there, in contrast to the declining agrarian Northeast. Thus the typical citizen of the Northwest was not an industrial worker or poor, marginal farmer, but the owner of a reasonably prosperous family farm. The average size of western farms was 200 acres, the great majority of them owned by the people who worked them.

Rising farm prices around the world provided a strong incentive for these western farmers to engage in commercial agriculture: to concentrate on growing a single crop for market (corn, wheat, cattle, sheep, hogs, and others). In the early years of white settlement in the Northwest, farm prices rose because of the debilitation of European agriculture in the aftermath of the Napoleonic Wars and the growing urban population (and hence the growing demand for food) of industrializing areas of Europe. Europe found it necessary to import American products to feed its people. The Northwest, with good water routes on the Mississippi for getting its crops to oceangoing vessels, profited from this international trade.

But industrialization, in both the United States and Europe, provided the greatest boost to agriculture. With the growth of factories and cities in the Northeast, the domestic market for farm goods increased dramatically. The growing national and worldwide demand for farm products resulted in steadily rising farm prices. For most farmers, the 1840s and early 1850s were years of increasing prosperity.

The expansion of agricultural markets had profound effects on sectional alignments in the United States. The Northwest sold most of its products to the residents of the Northeast and was thus dependent on eastern purchasing power. Eastern industry, in turn, found an important market for its products in the prospering West. Between the two sections a strong economic relationship was emerging that was profitable to both—and that was increasing the isolation of the South within the Union.

To meet the increasing demand for its farm products, residents of the Northwest worked strenuously, and often frantically, to increase their productive capacities. Many tried to take advantage of the large areas of still uncultivated land and to enlarge the area of white settlement during the 1840s. By 1850, the growing western population was moving into the prairie regions both east and west of the Mississippi: into areas of Indiana, Michigan, Illinois, Missouri, Iowa, and Minnesota. They cleared forest lands or made use of fields the Indians had cleared many years earlier. And they began to develop a timber industry to make use of the forests that remained. Wheat was the staple crop of the region, but other crops—corn, potatoes, and oats—and livestock were also important.

The Northwest increased production not only by expanding the area of settlement, but also by adopting new agricultural techniques that greatly reduced the labor necessary for producing a crop. The new methods were also less destructive than earlier ones and slowed the exhaustion of the region's rich soil. Farmers began to cultivate new varieties of seed, notably Mediterranean wheat, which was hardier than the native type; and they imported better breeds of animals, such as hogs and sheep from England and Spain, to take the place of native stock. Most important were improved tools and farm machines, which American inventors and manufacturers produced in rapidly increasing numbers. During the 1840s, more efficient grain drills, harrows, mowers, and hay rakes came into wide use. The cast-iron plow, an earlier innovation, remained popular because its parts could be replaced when broken. An even better tool appeared in 1847, when John Deere established at Moline, Illinois, a factory to manufacture steel plows, which were more durable than those made of iron.

Two new machines heralded a coming revolution in grain production. The most important was the automatic reaper, the invention of Cyrus H. McCormick of Virginia. The reaper enabled a crew of six or seven men to harvest in a day as much wheat (or any other small grain) as fifteen men could harvest using a sickle or other older methods. McCormick, who had patented his device in 1834, established a factory at Chicago, in the heart of the grain belt, in 1847. By 1860, more than 100,000 reapers were in use on western farms. Almost as important to the grain grower was the thresher—a machine that separated the grain from the wheat stalks. Threshers appeared in large numbers after 1840. Before that, farmers generally flailed grain by hand (seven bushels a day was a good average for a farm) or used farm animals to tread it (twenty bushels a day on the average). A threshing machine could thresh twenty-five bushels or more in an hour. The Jerome I. Case factory in Racine, Wisconsin manufactured most of the threshers.

The Northwest considered itself the most democratic section of the country. But its democracy was based on a defense of economic freedom and the rights of property—a white, middle-class vision of democracy that was becoming common in many other parts of the country as well. Abraham Lincoln, an Illinois Whig, voiced the economic opinions of many of the people of his section. "I take it that it is best for all to leave each man free to acquire property as fast as he can," said Lincoln. "Some will get wealthy. I don't believe in a law to prevent a man from getting rich; it would do more harm than good. . . . When one starts poor, as most do in the race of life, free society is such that he knows he can better his condition; he knows that there is no fixed condition of labor for his whole life."

Rural Life

Life for farming people was very different from life in towns and cities. It also varied greatly from one farming region to another. In the more densely populated farm areas east of the Appalachians and in the easternmost areas of the Northwest, farmers were usually part of relatively vibrant communities and made extensive use of the institutions of those communities—the churches, schools, stores, and taverns. As white settlement moved further west, farmers became more isolated and had to struggle to find any occasions for contact with people outside their own families.

Although the extent of social interaction differed from one area to another, the forms of interaction—outside the South at least—were usually very similar. Religion drew farm communities together perhaps more than any other force, particularly since so many farm areas were populated by people of common ethnic (and therefore religious) backgrounds. Town or village churches were popular meeting places, both for services and for social events—most of them dominated by women. Even in areas with no organized churches, farm families—and, again, women in particular—gathered in one another's homes for prayer meetings, Bible readings, and other religious activities. Weddings, baptisms, and funerals also brought communities together in celebration or mourning.

But religion was only one of many reasons for interaction. Farm people joined together frequently to share tasks that a single family would have difficulty performing on its own; barn raisings were among the most frequent. And on those occasions, families would gather and create a festive atmosphere of celebration. Women prepared large suppers while the men worked on the barn and the children played. Large numbers of families also gathered together at harvest time to help bring in crops, husk corn, or thresh wheat. Women came together to share domestic tasks as well, holding "bees" in which groups of women joined together to make quilts, baked goods, preserves, and other products.

Rural life was not always as isolating as it was sometimes portrayed. But despite the many social gatherings farm families managed to create, they lived in a world with much less contact with popular culture and public social life than people who lived in towns and cities. Rural people, often even more than urban ones, treasured their links to the outside world—letters from relatives and friends in distant places, newspapers and magazines from cities they had never seen, catalogs advertising merchandise that their local stores never had. Yet many also valued their separation from urban culture and cherished the relative autonomy that farm life gave them. One reason many rural Americans looked back nostalgically on country life once they moved to the city was that they sensed that in the urban world they did not have as much control over the patterns of their daily lives as they had once known.

CONCLUSION

Between the 1820s and the 1850s, the American economy experienced the beginnings of an industrial revolution—a change so profound that in the United States, as in Europe, it transformed almost every area of life in fundamental ways.

The American industrial revolution was a result of many things: population growth (through both natural increase and immigration), advances in transportation and communication, new technologies that spurred the development of factories capable of mass producing goods, the recruiting of a large industrial labor force, and the creation of corporate bodies capable of managing large enterprises. The new economy created great wealth, expanding the ranks of the wealthy and helping to create a large new middle class. It also created high levels of inequality, which was particularly visible in the growth of a large industrial working class.

Culture in the industrializing areas of the North changed too, and there were important changes in the structure and behavior of the family, in the role of women, and in the way people used their leisure time and encountered popular culture. The changes were often alluring, often disorienting, and often both. They helped widen the gap in experience and understanding between the generation of the Revolution and the generation of the mid-nineteenth century. They also helped widen the gap between North and South.

Significant Events

1813	Lowell establishes textile mill at Waltham, Massachusetts
1817–1825	Erie Canal constructed
1830	Baltimore and Ohio becomes first American railroad to begin operations
1830s	Major immigration from southern (Catholic) Ireland begins
	Factory system spreads in textile and shoe industries
	First national craft unions founded
1832	Cholera plague
1834	Women workers at Lowell mills stage strike
	Cyrus McCormick patents mechanical reaper
1837	Native American Association begins efforts to restrict immigration
	Oberlin becomes first American coeducational college
	Mt. Holyoke College for women opens
1842	Massachusetts Supreme Court, in *Commonwealth* v. *Hunt,* declares unions and strikes legal
	P. T. Barnum opens American Museum in New York
1844	Samuel F. B. Morse sends first telegraph message
1845	Irish potato famine begins, spurring major emigration to America
	Native American Party formed to combat immigration
	Female Labor Reform Association established at Lowell
1846	Rotary press invented, making possible rapid printing of newspapers
	Associated Press organized
1847	John Deere begins manufacturing steel plows
1848	Failed revolution in Germany spurs emigration to America
	Wisconsin enters Union
1850	Nativists form Supreme Order of the Star-Spangled Banner to oppose immigration
1852	American Party (Know-Nothings) formed

FOR FURTHER REFERENCE

Suggested Readings   George R. Taylor, *The Transportation Revolution* (1951) remains the authoritative account of economic development in the antebellum period. Charles G. Sellers, *The Market Revolution: Jacksonian America, 1815–1846* (1991) demonstrates the overwhelming impact of the market revolution on American social and political development, but from a pessimistic perspective. Daniel Feller, *The Jacksonian Promise: America, 1815–1840* (1995) challenges Sellers with a more optimistic portrait of the impact of economic change. Sean Wilentz, *Chants Democratic: New York City and the Rise of the American Working Class, 1788–1850* (1984) is an influential account of the impact of early industrialization on mostly male artisans in the most industrialized city of the era. Alice Kessler-Harris, *Out to Work: A History of Wage-Earning Women in the United States* (1982), in contrast, reminds readers that women were a substantial part of the early wage labor force. Mary Ryan, *Cradle of the Middle Class: The Family in Oneida County, New York, 1790–1865* (1981) demonstrates the relationship between the market revolution and the changing character of middle-class family structure. John Bodnar, *The Transplanted: A History of Immigrants in America* (1985) is an excellent survey.

Films   (The best source for information on how to find these and other films is *Bowker's Complete Video Directory*—3 volumes.) *The Industrial Revolution: Beginnings in the United States* (1968) traces the explosive growth of American industry beginning in the 1790s. *Samuel Slater & the Industrial Revolution* (1981) is the biography of a pioneer in early American textile manufacturing. *Irish Americans* (1993) celebrates the history and culture of Irish Americans. *Her Own Words: Pioneer Women's*

Diaries (1986) brings to life the observations of pioneer women in the upper Midwest in the 1830s, 1840s, and 1850s. *In Search of the Oregon Trail* (1996) focuses on the role of women in the epic migration on the Oregon Trail. *California Gold: Stories of Two Women* (1985) traces the lives of two women who lived through the gold rush.

Internet Resources   (For up-to-date URL addresses and links to these and other websites, consult the McGraw-Hill

history site at *http://www.mhhe.com/socscience/history/ usa/link/linktop.htm*) *Five Points Home Page* presents archaeological discoveries about New York's infamous slum. *Mary Anne Sadlier Archive* provides material by and about the novelist who described the experience of Irish immigration in the mid-19th century. *Quilts, Counterpanes, and Throws* contains images of textiles, primarily from the nineteenth century.

BIBLIOGRAPHY

The Market Revolution   W. Elliot Brownlee, *Dynamics of Ascent* (1974). Stuart Bruchey, *The Growth of the Modern American Economy* (1975). Christopher Clark, *The Roots of Rural Capitalism: Western Massachusetts, 1780–1860* (1990). Thomas C. Cochran, *Frontiers of Change: Early Industrialization in America* (1981). Daniel Feller, *The Jacksonian Promise: America, 1815–1840* (1995). Paul W. Gates, *The Farmer's Age* (1960). Douglass North, *The Economic Growth of the United States, 1790–1860* (1961). Donald Parkerson, *The Agricultural Transition in New York State* (1995). Peter Temin, *The Jacksonian Economy* (1969).

Immigration   Rowland T. Berthoff, *British Immigrants in Industrial America, 1790–1950* (1953). Kathleen N. Conzen, *Immigrant Milwaukee: 1836–1860* (1976). Thomas J. Curran, *Xenophobia and Immigration, 1820–1930* (1975). Hasia Diner, *Erin's Daughters in America* (1983). Jay P. Dolan, *The Immigrant Church: New York's Irish and German Catholics* (1975). Charlotte Erickson, *Invisible Immigrants* (1972). Oscar Handlin, *The Uprooted* (1951, rev. 1973); *Boston's Immigrants* (1941). Noel Ignatiev, *How the Irish Became White* (1995). Maldwyn A. Jones, *American Immigration* (1960). I. M. Leonard and R. D. Parmet, *American Nativism, 1830–1860* (1971). Stuart C. Miller, *The Unwelcome Immigrant* (1969). Harold Runblom and Hans Norman, *From Sweden to America* (1976). Philip Taylor, *The Distant Magnet: European Emigration to the United States of America* (1971).

Transportation and Communications   Colleen A. Dunlavy, *Politics and Industrialization: Early Railroads in the United States and Prussia* (1994). Albert Fishlow, *American Railroads and the Transformation of the Ante-Bellum Economy* (1965). Robert W. Fogel, *Railroads and American Economic Growth* (1964). Carter Goodrich, *Government Promotion of American Canals and Railroads, 1800–1890* (1960). Eric K. Haites, James

Mak, and Gary M. Walton, *Western River Transportation: The Era of Early Internal Development, 1800–1860* (1975). Nathan Miller, *The Enterprise of a Free People* (1962). Frank Luther Mott, *American Journalism* (1950). Robert J. Parks, *Democracy's Railroads: Public Enterprise in Michigan* (1972). Harry N. Scheiber, *Ohio Canal Era* (1969). Ronald E. Shaw, *Erie Water West: A History of the Erie Canal* (1966). Carol Sheriff, *The Artificial River: The Erie Canal and the Paradox of Progress, 1817–1862* (1996). John F. Stover, *American Railroads* (1961); *The Life and Decline of the American Railroad* (1970); *Iron Road to the West: American Railroads in the 1850s* (1978).

Business and Technology   Menahem Blondheim, *News Over the Wires: The Telegraph and the Flow of Public Information in America, 1844–1897* (1994). Richard D. Brown, *Modernization: The Transformation of American Life, 1600–1865* (1976). Alfred D. Chandler, Jr., *The Visible Hand: The Managerial Revolution in American Business* (1977). Thomas C. Cochran, *Business in American Life* (1972). Thomas C. Cochran and William Miller, *The Age of Enterprise* (1942). E. P. Douglas, *The Coming of Age of American Business* (1971). H. J. Habbakuk, *American and British Technology in the Nineteenth Century* (1962). David J. Jeremy, *Transatlantic Industrial Revolution: The Diffusion of Textile Technologies Between Britain and America, 1780–1830* (1981). John F. Kasson, *Civilizing the Machine: Technology and Republican Values in America, 1776–1900* (1976). Diane Lindstrom, *Economic Development in the Philadelphia Region, 1810–1850* (1978). Otto Mayr and Robert C. Post, eds., *Yankee Enterprise: The Rise of the American System of Manufacturers* (1981). Judith A. McGaw, *Most Wonderful Machine: Mechanization and Social Change in Berkshire Paper Making, 1815–1885* (1987). James Norris, *R. G. Dun & Co., 1841–1900* (1978). Nathan Rosenberg, *Technology and American Economic Growth* (1972). Merritt Roe Smith, *Harpers Ferry Armory and the New*

Technology (1977). Peter Temin, *Iron and Steel in Nineteenth-Century America* (1964).

Factories and the Working Class   Mary H. Blewett, *Men, Women, and Work* (1988); *We Will Rise in Our Might: Workingwomen's Voices from Nineteenth-Century New England* (1991). Alan Dawley, *Class and Community: The Industrial Revolution in Lynn* (1976). Thomas Dublin, *Women at Work* (1979); *Transforming Women's Work: New England Lives in the Industrial Revolution* (1994). Susan E. Hirsch, *Roots of the American Working Class: The Industrialization of Crafts in Newark, 1800–1860* (1978). David A. Hounshell, *From the American System to Mass Production, 1800–1932: The Development of Manufacturing Technology in the United States* (1985). Neville Kirk, *Labour and Society in Britain and the USA.* 2 Vols. (1994). Bruce Laurie, *Working People of Philadelphia* (1980). Jama Lazerow, *Religion and the Working Class in Antebellum America* (1995). Bruce Levine, *The Spirit of 1848: German Immigrants, Labor Conflict, and the Coming of the Civil War* (1992). Walter Licht, *Getting Work: Philadelphia, 1840–1950* (1992). David Montgomery, *Citizen Worker* (1993). Henry Pelling, *American Labor* (1960). David R. Roediger, *The Wages of Whiteness: Race and the Making of the American Working Class* (1991). W. J. Rorabaugh, *The Craft Apprentice: From Franklin to the Machine Age* (1986). Steven J. Ross, *Workers on the Edge: Work, Leisure, and Politics in Industrializing Cincinnati, 1788–1890* (1985). Christine Stansell, *City of Women: Sex and Class in New York, 1789–1860* (1986). Christopher Tomlins, *Law, Labor and Ideology in the Early American Republic* (1993). Barbara M. Tucker, *Samuel Slater and the Origins of the American Textile Industry, 1790–1860* (1985). Joseph E. Walker, *Hopewell: A Social and Economic History of an Ironmaking Community* (1966). Caroline Ware, *The Early New England Cotton Manufacture* (1931). Norman Ware, *The Industrial Worker, 1840–1860* (1924). Peter Way, *Common Labor: Workers and the Digging of North American Canals, 1780–1860* (1993). David A. Zonderman, *Aspirations and Anxieties: New England Workers and the Mechanized Factory System, 1815–1850* (1992).

Society and Culture   Rowland T. Berthoff, *An Unsettled People: Social Order and Disorder in American History* (1971). Stuart Blumin, *The Urban Threshold: Growth and Change in a Nineteenth-Century Community* (1976). Daniel Boorstin, *The Americans: The National Experience* (1965). John L. Brooke, *The Heart of the Commonwealth: Society and Political Culture in Worcester County, Massachusetts, 1713–1861* (1989). Colin Campbell, *The Romantic Ethic* (1987). Leonard P. Curry, *The Free Black in Urban America, 1800–1850* (1981). Don Doyle, *The So-

cial Order of a Frontier Community: Jacksonville, Illinois, 1825–1870* (1978). Michael Frisch, *Town into City: Springfield, Massachusetts, and the Meaning of Community, 1840–1880* (1972). Timothy J. Gilfoyle, *City of Eros: New York City, Prostitution and the Commercialization of Sex, 1790–1920* (1992). Paul A. Gilje, *The Road to Mobocracy: Popular Disorder in New York City, 1763–1834* (1987). Jonathan A. Glickstein, *Concepts of Free Labor in Antebellum America* (1991). Clyde Griffen and Sally Griffen, *Natives and Newcomers: The Ordering of Opportunity in Mid-Nineteenth-Century Poughkeepsie* (1978). Karen Halttunen, *Confidence Men and Painted Women: A Study of Middle-Class Culture in America, 1830–1870* (1982). Paul Johnson, *A Shopkeeper's Millennium: Society and Revivals in Rochester, New York, 1815–1837* (1978). Peter Knights, *The Plain People of Boston, 1830–1860* (1971). Raymond A. Mohl, *Poverty in New York, 1783–1825* (1971). Scott C. Martin, *Killing Time: Leisure and Culture in Southwestern Pennsylvania, 1800–1850* (1995). Teresa Anne Murphy, *Ten Hours' Labor: Religion, Reform and Gender in Early New England* (1992). Edward Pessen, *Riches, Classes, and Power Before the Civil War* (1973). David Thelen, *Paths of Resistance: Tradition and Dignity in Industrializing Missouri* (1986). Stephan Thernstrom, *Poverty and Progress* (1964). Daniel Vickers, *Farmers & Fishermen: Two Centuries of Work in Essex County, Massachusetts, 1630–1850* (1994). Richard C. Wade, *The Urban Frontier, 1790–1830* (1957). Anthony F. C. Wallace, *Rockdale: The Growth of an American Village in the Early Industrial Revolution* (1977). Sam Bass Warner, Jr., *The Urban Wilderness* (1972).

Women and Family   Jeanne Boydston, *Home and Work* (1990). Nancy F. Cott, *The Bonds of Womanhood: "Woman's Sphere" in New England, 1780–1835* (1977). Ruth Schwartz Cowan, *More Work for Mother: The Ironies of Household Technology from the Open Hearth to the Microwave* (1983). Carl Degler, *At Odds: Women and the Family in America from the Revolution to the Present* (1980). Dolores Hayden, *The Grand Domestic Revolution: A History of Feminist Designs for American Homes, Neighborhoods, and Cities* (1981). Marilynn Wood Hill, *Their Sisters' Keepers: Prostitution in New York City, 1830–1870* (1993). Ellen K. Rothman, *Hands and Heart: A History of Courtship in America* (1987). Kathryn K. Sklar, *Catherine Beecher: A Study in American Domesticity* (1973). Carroll Smith-Rosenberg, *Disorderly Conduct: Visions of Gender in Victorian America* (1985). Christine Stansell, *City of Women: Sex and Class in New York, 1789–1860* (1986). Susan Strasser, *Never Done: A History of American Housework* (1983). Gwendolyn Wright, *Building the Dream: A Social History of Housing in America* (1981).

Chapter Eleven

COTTON, SLAVERY, AND THE OLD SOUTH

The South, like the North, experienced dramatic growth in the middle years of the nineteenth century. Southerners fanned out into the new territories of the Southwest and established new communities, new states, and new markets. The southern agricultural economy grew increasingly productive and increasingly prosperous. Trade in such staples as sugar, rice, tobacco, and above all cotton made the South a major force in international commerce and created substantial wealth within the region. It also tied the South securely to the emerging capitalist world of the United States and its European trading partners.

Southern society, southern culture, southern politics—all changed in response to these important demographic and economic changes. The South in the 1850s was a very different place from the South of the first years of the century.

Yet for all the expansion and all the changes, the South experienced a much less fundamental transformation in these years than did the North. It had begun the nineteenth century a primarily agricultural region; it remained overwhelmingly agrarian in 1860. It had begun the century with few important cities and little industry; so it remained sixty years later. In 1800, a plantation system dependent on slave labor had dominated the southern economy; by 1860, that system had only strengthened its grip on the region. One historian has written, "The South grew, but it did not develop." As a result, it became increasingly unlike the North and increasingly sensitive to what it considered to be threats to its distinctive way of life.

■ **THE NEW ORLEANS COTTON EXCHANGE**
Edgar Degas, the great French impressionist, painted this scene of cotton traders examining samples in the New Orleans cotton exchange in 1873. By this time the cotton trade was producing less impressive profits than those that had made it the driving force of the booming southern economy of the 1850s. Degas's mother came from a Creole family of cotton brokers in New Orleans, and two of the artist's brothers (depicted here reading a newspaper and leaning against a window) joined the business in America. *(Giraudon/Art Resource)*

THE COTTON ECONOMY

The most important economic development in the mid-nineteenth-century South was the shift of economic power from the "upper South" (the original southern states along the Atlantic coast) to the "lower South" (the expanding agricultural regions in the new states of the Southwest). That shift reflected above all the growing dominance of cotton in the southern economy.

The Rise of King Cotton

Much of the upper South continued in the nineteenth century to rely, as it always had, on the cultivation of tobacco. But the market for that crop was notoriously unstable. Tobacco prices were subject to frequent depressions, including a prolonged one that began in the 1820s and extended into the 1850s. Tobacco also rapidly exhausted the land on which it grew; it was difficult for most growers to remain in business in the same place for very long. By the 1830s, therefore, many farmers in the old tobacco-growing regions of Virginia, Maryland, and North Carolina were shifting to other crops—notably wheat—while the center of tobacco cultivation was moving westward, into the Piedmont area.

The southern regions of the coastal South—South Carolina, Georgia, and parts of Florida—continued to rely on the cultivation of rice, a more stable and lucrative crop. Rice, however, demanded substantial irrigation and needed an exceptionally long growing season (nine months), so cultivation of that staple remained restricted to a relatively small area. Sugar growers along the Gulf Coast, similarly, enjoyed a reasonably profitable market for their crop. But sugar cultivation required intensive (and debilitating) labor and a long growing time. Only relatively wealthy planters could afford to engage in it, and they faced major competition from the great sugar plantations of the Caribbean. Sugar cultivation, therefore, did not spread much beyond a small area in southern Louisiana and eastern Texas. Long-staple (Sea Island) cotton was another lucrative crop, but like rice and sugar, it could grow only in a limited area—the coastal regions of the Southeast.

The decline of the tobacco economy in the upper South, and the inherent limits of the sugar, rice, and long-staple cotton economies farther south, might have forced the region to shift its attention in the nineteenth century to other, nonagricultural pursuits, had it not been for the growing importance of a new product which soon overshadowed all else: short-staple cotton. This was a hardier and coarser strain of cotton that could grow successfully in a variety of climates and in a variety of soils. It was harder to process than the long-staple variety; its seeds were more difficult to remove from the fiber. But the invention of the cotton gin (see p. 230) had largely solved that problem.

Demand for cotton was growing rapidly. The growth of the textile industry in Britain in the 1820s and 1830s, and in New England in the 1840s and 1850s, created an enormous new demand for the crop. Existing cotton lands could not satisfy the demand, and ambitious men and women rapidly moved into previously uncultivated lands—many of them newly open to planter settlement after the relocation of the tribes in the 1820s and 1830s—to establish new cotton-growing regions.

Beginning in the 1820s, therefore, cotton production spread rapidly. From the western areas of South Carolina and Georgia, production moved steadily westward—first into Alabama and Mississippi, then into northern Louisiana, Texas, and Arkansas. By the 1850s, cotton had become the linchpin of the southern economy. In 1820, the South had produced about 500,000 bales of cotton. By 1850 it was producing nearly 3 million bales a year, and by 1860 nearly 5 million. There were periodic fluctuations in cotton prices, resulting generally from overproduction; periods of boom frequently gave way to abrupt busts. But the cotton economy continued to grow, even if in fits and starts. By the time of the Civil War, cotton constituted nearly two-thirds of the total export trade of the United States and was bringing in nearly $200 million a year. The annual value of the rice crop, in contrast, was $2 million. It was little wonder that southern politicians now proclaimed: "Cotton is king!"

Cotton production dominated the more recently settled areas of what came to be known as the "lower South" (or, in a later era, the "Deep South"). Some began to call this region the "Cotton Kingdom." Settlement of the area resembled in some ways the rush of gold seekers to a new strike. The prospect of tremendous profits from growing cotton drew white settlers to the lower South by the thousands. Some were wealthy planters from the older states who transferred their assets and slaves to a cotton plantation. Most were small slaveholders or slaveless farmers who hoped to move into the planter class.

■ **SLAVERY AND COTTON: THE SOUTH IN 1820 AND 1860**
In 1820, cotton production had begun to move into the Carolina and Georgia upcountry, as well as central Alabama and the Mississippi River valley. The slave population was still concentrated in the Chesapeake and the low country of South Carolina and Georgia. By 1860, the "Black Belt" had taken shape, marking the expansion of cotton production from the Carolinas all the way to Texas. The internal slave trade also shifted the slave population from the eastern seaboard to new cotton producing regions.

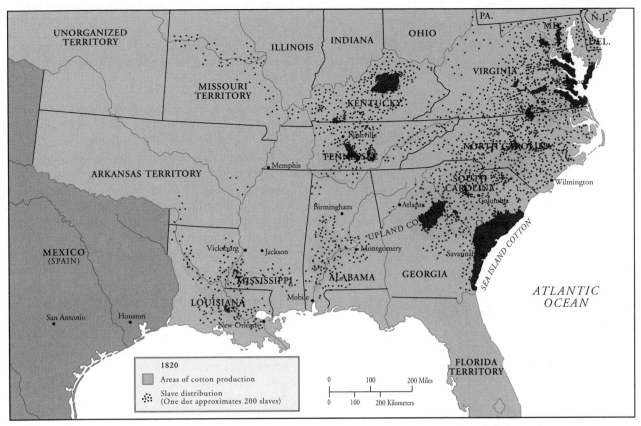

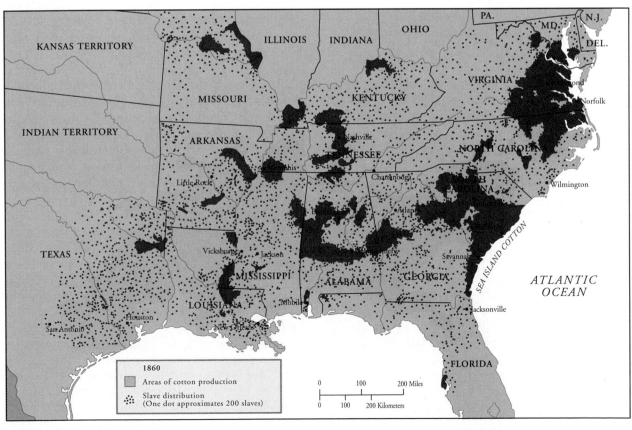

A similar shift, if an involuntary one, occurred in the slave population. Between 1820 and 1860, the number of slaves in Alabama leaped from 41,000 to 435,000, and in Mississippi from 32,000 to 436,000. In the same period, the increase in Virginia was only from 425,000 to 490,000. Between 1840 and 1860, according to some estimates, 410,000 slaves moved from the upper South to the cotton states—either accompanying masters who were themselves migrating to the Southwest, or (more often) sold to planters already there. Indeed, the sale of slaves to the Southwest became an important economic activity in the upper South and helped the troubled planters of that region compensate for the declining value of their crops.

Southern Trade and Industry

In the face of this booming agricultural expansion, other forms of economic activity developed slowly in the South. The business classes of the region—the manufacturers and merchants—were not unimportant. There was growing activity in flour milling and in textile and iron manufacturing, particularly in the upper South. The Tredegar Iron Works in Richmond, for example, compared favorably with the best iron mills in the Northeast. But industry remained an insignificant force in comparison with the agricultural economy. The total value of southern textile manufactures in 1860 was $4.5 million—a threefold increase over the value of those goods twenty years before, but only about 2 percent of the value of the raw cotton exported that year.

To the degree that the South developed a non-farm commercial sector, it was largely to serve the needs of the plantation economy. Particularly important were the brokers, or "factors," who marketed the planters' crops. These merchants tended to live in such towns as New Orleans, Charleston, Mobile, and Savannah, where they worked to find buyers for cotton and other crops and where they purchased goods for the planters they served. The South had only a very rudimentary financial system, and the factors often also served the planters as bankers, providing them with credit. Planters frequently accumulated substantial debts, particularly during periods when cotton prices were in decline; and the southern merchant-bankers thus became figures of considerable influence and importance in the region. There were also substantial groups of profes-

sional people in the South—lawyers, editors, doctors, and others. In most parts of the region, however, they too were closely tied to and dependent on the plantation economy. However important manufacturers, merchants, and professionals might have been to southern society, they were relatively unimportant in comparison with the manufacturers, merchants, and professionals of the North, on whom southerners were coming more and more (and increasingly unhappily) to depend.

The primitive character of the region's banking system matched a lack of development in other basic services and structures necessary for industrial development. Perhaps most notable was the South's inadequate transportation system. In the North in the antebellum period, enormous sums were invested in roads, canals, and above all railroads to knit the region together into an integrated market. In the South there were no such investments. Canals were almost nonexistent; most roads were crude and unsuitable for heavy transport; and railroads, although they expanded substantially in the 1840s and 1850s, failed to tie the region together effectively. Such towns as Charleston, Atlanta, Savannah, and Norfolk had direct connections with Memphis, and thus with the Northwest; and Richmond was connected, via the Virginia Central, with the Memphis and Charleston Railroad. In addition, several independent lines furnished a continuous connection between the Ohio River and New Orleans. Most of the South, however, remained unconnected to the national railroad system. Most lines in the region were short and local. The principal means of transportation was water. Planters generally shipped their crops to market along rivers or by sea; most manufacturing was in or near port towns.

Perceptive southerners recognized the economic subordination of their region to the North. "From the rattle with which the nurse tickles the ear of the child born in the South to the shroud that covers the cold form of the dead, everything comes to us from the North," the Arkansas journalist Albert Pike lamented. Perhaps the most prominent advocate of southern economic independence was James B. D. De Bow, a resident of New Orleans. He published a magazine advocating southern commercial and agricultural expansion, *De Bow's Review,* which survived from its founding in 1846 until 1880. De Bow made his journal into a tireless advocate of southern economic independence from the North, warning constantly of the dangers of the "colonial" relationship between the sections. One writer noted in the pages of his magazine: "I think it would be safe to estimate the amount which is lost to us annually by our vassalage to the North at $100,000,000. Great God!" Yet *De Bow's Review* was itself evidence of the dependency of the South on the North. It was printed in New York, because no New Orleans printer had facilities adequate for the task; it was filled with advertisements from northern manufacturing firms; and its circulation was always modest in comparison with those of northern publications. In Charleston, for example, it sold an average of 173 copies per issue; *Harper's Magazine* of New York, in contrast, regularly sold 1,500 copies to South Carolinians.

Sources of Southern Difference

Despite this growing concern about the region's "colonial dependency," the South made few serious efforts to build an economy that might challenge that dependency. An important question about antebellum southern history, therefore, is why the region did so little to develop a larger industrial and commercial economy of its own. Why did it remain so different from the North?

Part of the reason was the great profitability of the region's agricultural system, and particularly of cotton production. In the Northeast, many people had turned to manufacturing as the agricultural economy of the region declined. In the South, the agricultural economy was booming, and ambitious people eager to profit from the emerging capitalist economy had

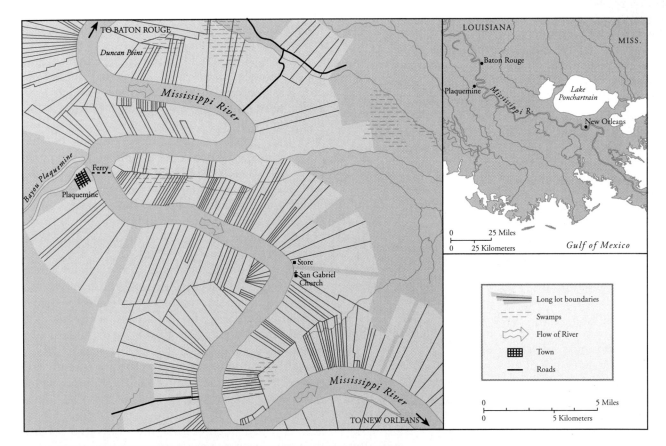

■ **FRENCH LONG LOT LANDSCAPE IN IBERVILLE PARISH, LOUISIANA, 1858**

In Louisiana, French social, cultural, and legal patterns persisted into the antebellum period. In contrast to the grid system of land distribution in western federal lands, the parishes of Louisiana along the Mississippi retained the French cadastral system. By extending land holdings out from the banks of the Mississippi, planters along the Mississippi took advantage of the rich soils deposited by the river's periodic floods.

little incentive to look beyond it. Another reason was that wealthy southerners had so much capital invested in their land and, particularly, their slaves that they had little left for other investments. Some historians have suggested that the southern climate—with its long, hot, steamy summers—was less suitable for industrial development than the climate of the North. Still others have gone so far as to claim that southern work habits (perhaps a reflection of the debilitating effects of the climate) impeded industrialization; some white southerners appeared—at least to many northern observers—not to work very hard, to lack the strong work ethic that fueled northern economic development.

But the southern failure to create a flourishing commercial or industrial economy was also in part the result of a set of values distinctive to the South that discouraged the growth of cities and industry. Many white southerners liked to think of themselves as representatives of a special way of life: one based on traditional values of chivalry, leisure, and elegance. White southerners were, they argued, "cavaliers"—people happily free from the base, acquisitive instincts of the "yankees" to their north. Southern white people were, they believed, more concerned with a refined and gracious way of life than with rapid growth and development. But appealing as the "cavalier" image was to southern whites, it conformed to the reality of southern society in very limited ways.

WHITE SOCIETY IN THE SOUTH

Only a small minority of southern whites owned slaves. In 1850, when the total white population of the South was over 6 million, the number of slaveholders was only 347,525. In 1860, when the white population was just above 8 million, the number of slaveholders had risen to only 383,637. These figures are somewhat misleading, since each slaveholder was normally the head of a family averaging five members. But even with all members of slaveowning families included in the figures, those owning slaves still amounted to perhaps no more than one quarter of the white population. And of the minority of whites holding slaves, only a small proportion owned them in substantial numbers.

The Planter Class

How, then, did the South come to be seen—both by the outside world and by many southerners themselves—as a society dominated by great plantations and wealthy landowning planters? In large part, it was because the planter aristocracy—the cotton magnates, the sugar, rice, and tobacco nabobs, the whites who owned at least forty or fifty slaves and 800 or more acres—exercised power and influence far in excess of their numbers. They stood at the apex of society, determining the political, economic, and even social life of their region. Enriched by vast annual incomes, dwelling in palatial homes, surrounded by broad acres and many black servants, they became a class to which all others deferred. The wealthiest of them maintained homes in towns or cities and spent several months of the year there, engaged in a glittering social life. Others traveled widely, especially to Europe, as an antidote to the isolation of plantation life. And many used their plantations to host opulent social events.

White southerners liked to compare their planter class to the old upper classes of England and Europe: true aristocracies, long entrenched. In fact, however, the southern upper class was in most cases not at all similar to the landed aristocracies of the Old World. In some areas of the upper South—the Tidewater region of Virginia, for example—some of the great aristocrats were indeed people whose families had occupied positions of wealth and power for generations. In most of the South, however, a longstanding landed aristocracy, although central to the "cavalier" image, was largely a myth. Even the most important planters in the cotton-growing areas of the South were, typically, new to their wealth and power. As late as the 1850s, many of the great landowners in the lower South were still first-generation settlers, who had arrived with only modest resources, struggled for many years to clear land and develop a plantation in what was at first a rugged wilderness, and only relatively recently had started to live in the comfort and luxury for which they became famous. Large areas of the "Old South" (as Americans later called the South of the pre-Civil War era) had been settled and cultivated for less than two decades at the time of the Civil War.

Nor was the world of the planter nearly as leisured and genteel as the "cavalier" myth would suggest. Growing staple crops was a business—

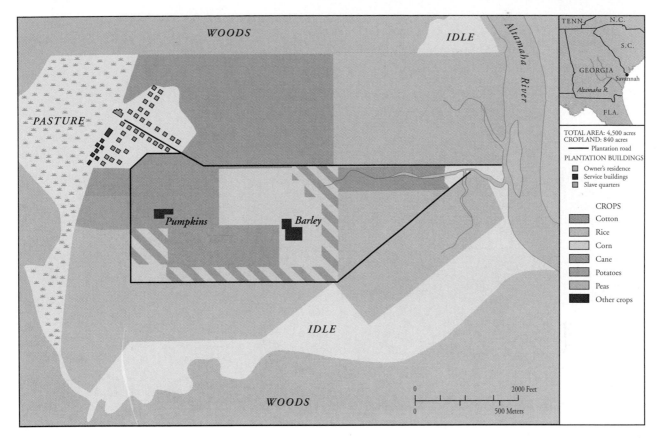

TENN. N.C.
S.C.
GEORGIA Savannah
Altamaha R.
FLA.

TOTAL AREA: 4,500 acres
CROPLAND: 840 acres
——— Plantation road
PLANTATION BUILDINGS
■ Owner's residence
■ Service buildings
□ Slave quarters

CROPS
Cotton
Rice
Corn
Cane
Potatoes
Peas
Other crops

0   2000 Feet
0   500 Meters

■ **HOPETON PLANTATION, GEORGIA**
Hopeton Plantation was a well-coordinated and highly organized business. Agricultural production was diversified for the sake both of maximizing profits and maintaining the self-sufficiency of farm households. The slave quarters were built in orderly rows in close proximity to the master's house, allowing for maximum supervision and control over slave life.

often a big and highly profitable business—that was in its own way just as competitive and just as risky as the industrial enterprises of the North. Planters had to supervise their operations carefully if they hoped to make a profit. They were, in many respects, just as much competitive capitalists as the industrialists of the North whose lifestyles they claimed to hold in contempt. Even many affluent planters lived rather modestly, their wealth so heavily invested in land and slaves that there was little left for personal comfort. And white planters, even some substantial ones, tended to move frequently as new and presumably more productive areas opened up to cultivation.

Indeed, it may have been the very newness and precariousness of the plantation way of life, and the differences between the reality of that life and the image of it, that made many southern planters determined to portray themselves as genteel aristocrats. Having struggled so hard to reach and maintain their positions, they were all the more determined to defend them. Perhaps that was why the defense of slavery and of the South's "rights" was stronger in the new, booming regions of the lower South and weaker in the more established and less flourishing areas of the Tidewater.

Wealthy southern whites sustained their image of themselves as aristocrats in many ways. They avoided such "coarse" occupations as trade and commerce; those who did not become planters often gravitated toward the military, a "suitable" career for men raised in a culture in which medieval knights (as

■ **ST. JOHN PLANTATION, LOUISIANA**
This Greek Revival "big house" of the St. John Plantation in St. Martin Parish, Louisiana, still stands today. In 1861, when the artist Adrien Persac painted this view of it, it occupied the center of a 5,000-acre sugar plantation and was the setting of the self-consciously elegant life of the planter and his family. To the right is a brick sugar factory and the cabins of the plantation's slaves, who performed the arduous work of sugar harvesting and production. *(Louisiana State University Museum of Art)*

portrayed in the novels of Walter Scott) were a powerful and popular image. The aristocratic ideal also found reflection in the definition of a special role for southern white women.

"Honor"

Above all perhaps white males adopted an elaborate code of chivalry, which obligated them to defend their "honor," often through dueling—which survived in the South long after it had largely vanished in the North. Southern white males placed enormous stock in conventional forms of courtesy and respect in their dealings with one another—perhaps as a way of distancing themselves from the cruelty and disrespect that were so fundamental to the slave system they controlled. Violations of such forms often

brought what seemed to outsiders a disproportionately heated and even violent response.

The idea of honor in the South was only partly connected to the idea of ethical behavior and bravery. It was also tied to the importance among white males of the public appearance of dignity and authority—of saving face in the presence of others. Anything that seemed to challenge the dignity, social station, or "manhood" of a white southern male might be the occasion for a challenge to duel, or at least for a stern public rebuke. When the South Carolina congressman Preston Brooks strode into the chamber of the United States Senate and savagely beat Senator Charles Sumner of Massachusetts with a cane to retaliate for what he considered an insult to a relative, he was acting wholly in accord with the idea of southern honor. In the North, he was reviled as a

■ **"CLEAR STARCHING IN LOUISIANA"**
This 1837 etching by August Hervieu offers a strikingly unromanticized view of plantation women in the South. The white plantation mistress, soberly dressed, speaks harshly to two black household servants, presumably criticizing the way they are doing the laundry. The slaves cower, carefully hiding whatever resentment they might feel behind a submissive pose. Nothing in this picture suggests anything like the kind of ease and luxury often associated with plantation life in popular mythology at the time and since.
(General Research Division, New York Public Library, Astor, Lenox and Tilden Foundations)

savage. In the South, he became a popular hero. But Brooks was only the most public example of a code of behavior that many white southern men followed. Avenging insults was a social necessity in many parts of southern society, and avenging insults to white southern women was perhaps the most important obligation of a white southern "gentleman."

The "Southern Lady"

In some respects, affluent white women in the South occupied roles very similar to those of middle-class white women in the North. Their lives generally centered in the home, where (according to the South's social ideal) they served as companions to and hostesses for their husbands and as nurturing mothers for their children. Even less frequently than in the North did "genteel" southern white women engage in public activities or find income-producing employment.

But the life of the "southern lady" was also in many ways very different from that of her northern counterpart. For one thing, the cult of honor in the region meant in theory that southern white men gave particular importance to the "defense" of women. In practice, this generally meant that white men were even more dominant and white women even more subordinate in southern culture than they were in the North. George Fitzhugh, one of the South's most important social theorists, wrote in the 1850s: "Women, like children, have but one right, and that

is the right to protection. The right to protection involves the obligation to obey."

More important in determining the role of southern white women, however, were the social and economic realities in which they lived. The vast majority of females in the region lived on farms, relatively isolated from people outside their own families, with virtually no access to the "public world" and thus few opportunities to look beyond their roles as wives and mothers. Because the family was the principal economic unit on most farms, the dominance of husbands and fathers over wives and children was even greater than in those northern families in which income-producing activities had moved out of the home and into the factory or office. For many white women, living on farms of modest size meant a fuller engagement in the economic life of the family than was becoming typical for middle-class women in the North. These women engaged in spinning, weaving, and other production; they participated in agricultural tasks; they helped supervise the slave work force. On some of the larger plantations, however, even these limited roles were sometimes considered unsuitable for white women; and the "plantation mistress" became, in some cases, more an ornament for her husband than an active part of the economy or the society.

Southern white women also had less access to education than their northern counterparts. Nearly a quarter of all white women over twenty were completely illiterate; relatively few women had more than a rudimentary exposure to schooling. Even wealthy planters were not much interested in extensive schooling for their daughters. The few female "academies" in the South trained women primarily to be suitable wives.

Southern white women had other special burdens as well. The southern white birth rate remained nearly 20 percent higher than that of the nation as a whole, and infant mortality in the region remained higher than elsewhere; nearly half the children born in the South in 1860 died before they reached five years of age. The slave labor system had a mixed impact on white women. It helped spare many of them from certain kinds of arduous labor, but it also threatened their relationships with their husbands. Male slaveowners had frequent sexual relationships with the female slaves on their plantations; the children of those unions became part of the plantation labor force and served as a constant reminder to white women of their husbands' infidelity. Black women (and men) were obviously the most important victims of such practices. But white women suffered too.

A few southern white women rebelled against their roles and against the prevailing assumptions of their region. Some became outspoken abolitionists and joined northerners in the crusade to abolish slavery. Some agitated for other reforms within the South itself. Most white women, however, found few outlets for whatever discontent they may have felt with their lives. Instead, they generally convinced themselves of the benefits of their position and—often even more fervently than southern white men— defended the special virtues of the southern way of life. Upper-class white women in the South were particularly energetic in defending the class lines that separated them from poorer whites.

The Plain Folk

The typical white southerner was not a great planter and slaveholder, but a modest yeoman farmer. Some of these "plain folk," as they have become known, owned a few slaves, with whom they worked and lived far more closely than did the larger planters. Most (in fact, three-quarters of all white families) owned no slaves at all. Some plain folk, most of whom owned their own land, devoted themselves largely to subsistence farming; others grew cotton or other crops for the market, but usually could not pro-

duce enough to allow them to expand their operations or even get out of debt. During the 1850s, the number of nonslaveholding landowners increased much faster than the number of slaveholding landowners. While there were occasional examples of poor farmers moving into the ranks of the planter class, such cases were rare. Most yeomen knew that they had little prospect of substantially bettering their lot.

One reason was the southern educational system, which provided poor whites with few opportunities to learn and thus limited their chances of advancement. For the sons of wealthy planters, the region provided ample opportunities to gain an education. In 1860 there were 260 southern colleges and universities, public and private, with 25,000 students enrolled in them, or more than half the total number of students in the United States. But universities were only within the reach of the upper class. The elementary and secondary schools of the South were not only fewer but also inferior to those of the Northeast (although not much worse than the crude schools of the Northwest). The South had more than 500,000 illiterate whites, or over half the country's total.

That a majority of the South's white population consisted of modest farmers largely excluded from the dominant plantation society raises another important question about the antebellum South. Why did the plain folk have so little power in the public world of the Old South? Why did they not oppose the aristocratic social system in which they shared so little? Why did they not resent the system of slavery, from which they generally did not benefit?

Some nonslaveowning whites did oppose the planter elite, but for the most part in limited ways and in a relatively few, isolated areas. These were southern highlanders, the "hill people," who lived in the Appalachian ranges east of the Mississippi, in the Ozarks to the west of the river, and in other "hill country" or "backcountry" areas cut off from the more commercial world of the plantation system. Of all southern whites, they were the most isolated from the mainstream of the region's life. They practiced a simple form of subsistence agriculture, owned practically no slaves, and had a proud sense of seclusion. They were, in most respects, unconnected to the new commercial economy that dominated the great cotton-planting region of the South. They produced almost no surplus for the market, had little access to money, and often bartered for the goods they could not grow themselves.

To such men and women, slavery was unattractive for many of the same reasons it was unappealing to workers and small farmers in the North: because it threatened their sense of their own independence. Upcountry farmers lived in a society of unusual individual personal freedom and unusual isolation from modern notions of property. They also held to older political ideals, which for many included the ideal of fervent loyalty to the nation as a whole.

Such whites frequently expressed animosity toward the planter aristocracy of the other regions of the South. The mountain region was the only part of the South to defy the trend toward sectional conformity, and it was the only part to resist the movement toward secession when it finally developed. Even during the Civil War itself, many refused to support the Confederacy; some went so far as to fight for the Union.

Far greater in number, however, were the non-slaveowning whites who lived in the midst of the plantation system. Many, perhaps most of them, accepted that system because they were tied to it in important ways. Small farmers depended on the local plantation aristocracy for many things: access to cotton gins, markets for their modest crops and their livestock, credit or other financial assistance in time of need. In many areas, there were also extensive kinship networks linking lower- and upper-class whites. The poorest resident of a county might easily be a cousin of the richest aristocrat. Taken together, these mutual ties helped mute what might otherwise have been pronounced class tensions.

Small farmers felt tied to the plantation society in other ways as well. For white men, at least, the South was an unusually democratic society, in the sense that participation in politics—both through voting and through attending campaign meetings and barbecues—was even more widespread than in the North, where participation was also high. Just as political participation gave workers in the North a sense of connection to the social order, so it did for farmers in the South—even though officeholders in the South, even more than in the North, were almost always members of the region's elites. In the 1850s, moreover, the boom in the cotton economy allowed many small farmers to improve their economic fortunes. Some bought more land, became slaveowners, and moved into at least the fringes of plantation soci-

ety. Others simply felt more secure now in their positions as independent yeomen and hence more likely to embrace the fierce regional loyalty that was spreading throughout the white South in these years.

Small farmers, even more than great planters, were also committed to a traditional, male-dominated family structure. Their household-centered economies required the participation of all family members and, they believed, a stable system of gender relations to ensure order and stability. Men were the unquestioned masters of their homes; women and children, who were both family and work force, were firmly under the master's control. As the northern attack on slavery increased in the 1840s and 1850s, it was easy for such farmers to believe—and easy for ministers, politicians, and other propagandists for slavery to persuade them—that an assault on one hierarchical system (slavery) would open the way to an assault on another such system (patriarchy).

There were other white southerners, however, who did not share in the plantation economy in even limited ways and yet continued to accept its premises. These were the members of a particularly degraded class—numbering perhaps a half-million in 1850—known variously as "crackers," "sand hillers," or "poor white trash." Occupying the infertile lands of the pine barrens, the red hills, and the swamps, they lived in miserable cabins amid genuine squalor. Many owned no land (or owned land on which virtually nothing could be grown) and supported themselves by foraging or hunting. Others worked at times as common laborers for their neighbors, although the slave system limited their opportunities. Their degradation resulted partly from dietary deficiencies and disease. They resorted at times to eating clay (hence the tendency of more affluent whites to refer to them disparagingly as "clay eaters"); and they suffered from pellagra, hookworm, and malaria. Planters and small farmers alike held them in contempt. They formed a true underclass. In some material respects, their plight was worse than that of the African-American slaves (who themselves often looked down on the poor whites).

Even among these southerners—the true outcasts of white society in the region—there was no real opposition to the plantation system or slavery. In part, undoubtedly, this was because these men and women were so benumbed by poverty that they had little strength to protest. But their relative passivity resulted also from perhaps the single greatest unifying factor among the southern white population, the one force that was most responsible for reducing tensions among the various classes. That force was their perception of race. However poor and miserable these white southerners might have been, they could still consider themselves members of a ruling race; they could still look down on the black population of the region and feel a bond with their fellow whites born of a determination to maintain their racial supremacy. As Frederick Law Olmsted, a northerner who visited the South and chronicled southern society in the 1850s, wrote: "From childhood, the one thing in their condition which has made life valuable to the mass of whites has been that the niggers are yet their inferiors."

THE "PECULIAR INSTITUTION"

White southerners often referred to slavery as the "peculiar institution." By that they meant not that the institution was odd, but that it was distinctive, special. The description was apt, for American slavery was indeed distinctive. The South in the mid-nineteenth century was the only area in the Western world—except for Brazil, Cuba, and Puerto Rico—where slavery still existed. Slavery, more than any other single factor, isolated the South from the rest of American society. And as that isolation increased, so did the commitment of southerners to defend the institution. William Harper, a prominent South Carolina politician in the 1840s, wrote: "The judgment is made up. We can have no hearing before the tribunal of the civilized world. Yet, on this very account, it is more important that we, the inhabitants of the slave-holding States, insulated as we are by this institution, and cut off, in some degree, from the communion and sympathies of the world by which we are surrounded, . . . and exposed continually to their animadversions and attacks, should thoroughly understand this subject, and our strength and weakness in relation to it."

Within the South itself, the institution of slavery had paradoxical results. On the one hand, it isolated blacks from whites, drawing a sharp and inviolable racial line dividing one group of southerners from another. As a result, African Americans under slavery began to develop a society and culture of their own, one in many ways unrelated to the white civilization around them. On the other hand, slavery created a unique bond between blacks and whites—masters and slaves—in the South. The two groups may have maintained separate spheres, but each sphere was deeply influenced by, indeed dependent on, the other.

Varieties of Slavery

Slavery was an institution established and regulated in detail by law. The slave codes of the southern states forbade slaves to hold property, to leave their masters' premises without permission, to be out after dark, to congregate with other slaves except at church, to carry firearms, or to strike a white person even in self-defense. The codes prohibited whites from teaching slaves to read or write and denied to slaves the right to testify in court against white people. The laws contained no provisions to legalize slave marriages or divorces. If an owner killed a slave while punishing him, the act was generally not considered a crime. Slaves, however, faced the death penalty for killing or even resisting a white person and for inciting revolt. The codes also contained extraordinarily rigid provisions for defining a person's race. Anyone with even a trace of African ancestry was defined as black. And anyone even rumored to possess any such trace was presumed to be black unless he or she could prove otherwise—which was, of course, difficult to do.

These and dozens of other restrictions might seem to suggest that slaves lived under a uniformly harsh and dismal regime. Had the laws been rigidly enforced, that might have been the case. In fact, however, enforcement was spotty and uneven. Some slaves did acquire property, did learn to read and write, and did assemble with other slaves, in spite of laws to the contrary. Although the major slave offenses generally fell under the jurisdiction of the courts (and thus of the slave codes), white owners handled most transgressions and inflicted widely varying punishments. In other words, despite the rigid provisions of law, there was in reality considerable variety within the slave system. Some blacks lived in almost prisonlike conditions, rigidly and harshly controlled by their masters. Many (probably most) others enjoyed some flexibility and (at least in comparison to the regimen prescribed by law) a striking degree of autonomy.

HAULING THE WHOLE WEEKS PICKING

■ *"HAULING THE WHOLE WEEK'S PICKING"*
This watercolor by William Henry Brown, painted in approximately 1842, portrays a slave family loading cotton onto a wagon, presumably after a hard day of picking. Even young children participate in the chores. Brown was an artist known for his silhouettes, a form popular in the nineteenth century. (One of his later subjects was Abraham Lincoln.) This picture, however, is part of a five-foot cutout he made as a gift to a family he was visiting. *(Historic New Orleans Collection)*

The nature of the relationship between masters and slaves depended in part on the size of the plantation. The typical master had a different image of slavery from that of the typical slave. Most masters possessed very few slaves, and their experience with (and image of) slavery was a reflection of the special nature of slavery on the small farm. White farmers with few slaves generally supervised their workers directly and often worked closely alongside them. On such farms, blacks and whites developed a form of intimacy unknown on larger plantations. The paternal relationship between such masters and their slaves could, like relationships between fathers and children, be warm and affectionate. It could also be tyrannical and cruel. In either case, it was a relationship based on the relative powerlessness of the slaves and the nearly absolute authority of their masters. In general, African Americans themselves preferred to live on larger plantations, where they had more privacy and a chance to build a cultural and social world of their own.

Although the majority of slaveowners were small farmers, the majority of slaves lived on plantations of medium or large size, with sizable slave work forces. Thus the relationship between master and slave was much less intimate for the typical slave than for the typical slaveowner. Substantial planters often hired overseers and even assistant overseers to represent them. "Head drivers," trusted and responsible slaves often assisted by several subdrivers, acted under the overseer as foremen.

Larger planters generally used one of two methods of assigning slave labor. One was the task system (most common in rice culture), under which slaves were assigned a particular task in the morning, for example, hoeing one acre; after completing the job, they were free for the rest of the day. The other, far more common, was the gang system (employed on the cotton, sugar, and tobacco plantations), under which slaves were simply divided into groups, each of them directed by a driver, and compelled to work for as many hours as the overseer considered a reasonable workday.

Life Under Slavery

Slaves generally received at least enough necessities to enable them to live and work. Their masters usually furnished them with an adequate diet, consisting mainly of cornmeal, salt pork, molasses, and on special occasions fresh meat or poultry. Many slaves cultivated gardens for their own use. They received cheap clothing and shoes. They lived in crude cabins, called slave quarters, usually clustered together

THE CHARACTER OF SLAVERY

No issue in American history has produced a richer literature or a more spirited debate than the nature of American slavery. The debate began even before the Civil War, when abolitionists strove to expose slavery to the world as a brutal, dehumanizing institution, while southern defenders of slavery tried to depict it as a benevolent, paternalistic system. That same debate continued for a time after the Civil War; but by the late nineteenth century, with white Americans eager for sectional conciliation, both northern and southern chroniclers of slavery began to accept a romanticized and unthreatening picture of the Old South and its "peculiar institution."

The first major scholarly examination of slavery was fully within this romantic tradition. Ulrich B. Phillips's *American Negro Slavery* (1918) portrayed slavery as an essentially benign institution in which kindly masters looked after submissive, childlike, and generally contented African Americans. Phillips's apologia for slavery remained the authoritative work on the subject for nearly thirty years.

In the 1940s, as concern about racial injustice increasingly engaged the attention of white Americans, challenges to Phillips began to emerge. In 1941, Melville J. Herskovits challenged Phillips's contention that black Americans retained little of their African cultural inheritance. In 1943, Herbert Aptheker published a chronicle of slave revolts as a way of challenging Phillips's claim that blacks were submissive and content.

A somewhat different challenge to Phillips emerged in the 1950s from historians who emphasized the brutality of the institution. Kenneth Stampp's *The Peculiar Institution* (1956) and, even more damningly, Stanley Elkins's *Slavery* (1959) described a labor system that did serious

(General Research Division, New York Public Library, Astor, Lenox and Tilden Foundations)

physical and psychological damage to its victims. Stampp and Elkins portrayed slavery as something like a prison, in which men and women had virtually no space in which to develop their own social and cultural lives. Elkins compared the system to Nazi concentration camps during World War II and likened the childlike "Sambo" personality of slavery to the distortions of character that many scholars believed the Holocaust had produced.

In the early 1970s, an explosion of new scholarship on slavery shifted the emphasis away from the damage the system inflicted on African Americans and toward the striking success of the slaves in building a culture of their own despite their enslavement. John Blassingame in 1973, echoing Herskovitz's claims of thirty years earlier, argued that "the most remarkable aspect of the whole process of enslavement is the extent to which the American-born slaves were able to retain their ancestors' culture." Herbert Gutman, in *The Black Family in Slavery and Freedom* (1976) challenged the prevailing belief that slavery had weakened and even destroyed the African-American family. On the contrary, he argued, the black family survived slavery with impressive strength, although with some significant differences from the prevailing form of the white family. Eugene Genovese's *Roll, Jordan, Roll* (1974) and other works revealed how African Americans manipulated the paternalist assumptions at the heart of slavery to build a large cultural space of their own within the system where they could develop their own family life, social traditions, and religious patterns. That same year, Robert Fogel and Stanley Engerman published

their controversial *Time on the Cross,* a highly quantitative study that supported some of the claims of Gutman and Genovese about black achievement, but that went much further in portraying slavery as a successful and reasonably humane (if ultimately immoral) system. Slave workers, they argued, were better treated and lived in greater comfort than most northern industrial workers of the same era. Their conclusions produced a storm of criticism.

Some of the most important recent scholarship on slavery has focused on the role of women within it. Elizabeth Fox-Genovese's *Within the Plantation Household* (1988) examined the lives of both white and black women on the plantation. Rejecting the claims of some feminist historians that black and white women shared a common female identity born of their shared subordination to men, she portrayed slave women as defined by their dual roles as members of the plantation work force and anchors of the black family. Slave women, she argued, professed loyalty to their mistresses when forced to serve them as domestics; but their real loyalty remained to their own communities and families.

in a complex near the master's house. The plantation mistress or a doctor retained by the owner provided some medical care; but slave women themselves—as "healers" and midwives, or simply as mothers—were the more important source.

Slaves worked hard, beginning with light tasks as children; and their workdays were longest at harvest time. Slave women worked particularly hard. They generally labored in the fields with the men, and they assumed as well the crucial chores traditionally reserved for women—cooking, cleaning, and child rearing. Because slave families were often divided, with husbands and fathers frequently living on neighboring plantations (or, at times, sold to plantation owners far away), black women often found themselves acting in effect as single parents. Within the slave family, therefore, women had special burdens but also a special authority.

Slaves were, as a group, much less healthy than southern whites. After 1808, when the importation of slaves became illegal, the proportion of blacks to whites in the nation as a whole steadily declined. In 1820, there was one African American to every four whites; in 1840, one to every five. The slower increase of the black population was a result of its comparatively high death rate. Slave mothers had large families, but the enforced poverty in which virtually all African Americans lived ensured that fewer of their children would survive to adulthood than the children of white parents. Even those who did survive typically died at a younger age than the average white person.

Even so, according to some scholars, the actual material conditions of slavery may, in fact, have been better than those of many northern factory workers and considerably better than those of both peasants and industrial workers in nineteenth-century Europe. The conditions of American slaves were certainly less severe than those of slaves in the Caribbean and South America. That was in part because plantations in other parts of the Americas tended to grow crops that required more arduous labor; sugar production in the Caribbean islands, in particular, involved extraordinarily backbreaking work. In addition, Caribbean and South American planters continued to use the African slave trade well into the nineteenth century to replenish their labor supply, so they had less incentive than American planters (who no longer had much access to that trade) to protect their existing laborers. Working and living conditions in these other slave societies were arduous, and masters at times literally worked their slaves to death. Growing cotton, the principal activity for most slaves in the United States, was much less debilitating than growing sugar; and planters had strong economic incentives to maintain a healthy slave population. One result of this was that America became the only country where a slave population actually increased through natural reproduction (although it grew much more slowly than the white population).

Most masters did make some effort to preserve the health—and thus the usefulness—of their slaves. One example was the frequent practice of protecting slave children from hard work until early adolescence. Masters believed that doing so would make young slaves more loyal and would also ensure better health as adults. Another example was the use of hired labor, when available, for the most unhealthy or dangerous tasks. A traveler in Louisiana noted, for example, that Irishmen were employed to clear malarial swamps and to handle cotton bales at the bottom of chutes extending from the river bluff down to a boat landing. If an Irish worker died of disease or in an accident, a master could hire another for a dollar a day or less. But a master would lose an investment of perhaps $1,000 or more if a prime field hand died. Still, cruel masters might forget their pocketbooks in the heat of anger. Slaves were often left to the discipline of overseers, who had less of an economic stake in their well-being; overseers were paid in proportion to the amount of work they could get out of the slaves they supervised.

Household servants had a somewhat easier life—physically at least—than did field hands. On a small plantation, the same slaves might do both field work and housework. But on a large estate, there would generally be a separate domestic staff: nursemaids, housemaids, cooks, butlers, coachmen. These people lived close to the master and his family, eating the leftovers from the family table and in some cases even sleeping in the "big house." Between the blacks and whites of such households affectionate, almost familial relationships might sometimes develop. More often, however, house servants resented their isolation from their fellow slaves and the lack of privacy that came with living in such close proximity to the master's family. Among other things, that proximity meant that their transgressions were more visible than those of field hands, and so they received punishments more often than did other slaves. When

■ **NURSING THE MASTER'S CHILD**
Louisa, a slave on a Missouri plantation owned by the Hayward
family in the 1850s, is photographed here holding the master's
infant son. Black women typically cared for white children on
plantations, sometimes with great affection and sometimes—as
this photograph may suggest—dutifully and without enthusiasm.
(Missouri Historical Society)

emancipation came after the Civil War, it was often
the house servants who were the first to leave the
plantations of their former owners.

Female household servants were especially vulnerable to sexual abuse by their masters and white overseers, who sometimes pressured them into supposedly consensual sexual relationships and sometimes
literally raped them. In addition to unwanted sexual
attention from white men, female slaves often received vindictive treatment from white women. Plantation mistresses naturally resented the sexual liaisons between their husbands and female slaves.
Punishing their husbands was not usually possible, so
they often punished the slaves instead—with arbitrary beatings, increased workloads, and various
forms of psychological torment.

Slavery in the Cities

The conditions of slavery in the cities differed significantly from those in the countryside. On the relatively isolated plantations, slaves had little contact
with free blacks and lower-class whites, and masters
maintained fairly direct and effective control; a deep
and seemingly unbridgeable chasm yawned between
slavery and freedom. In the city, however, a master
often could not supervise his slaves closely and at the
same time use them profitably. Even if they slept at
night in carefully watched backyard barracks, slaves
moved about during the day alone, performing er-
rands of various kinds.

There was a considerable market in the South for
common laborers, particularly since, unlike in the
North, there were few European immigrants to perform menial chores. Even the poorest whites tended
to prefer working on farms to doing ordinary labor,
and so masters often hired out slaves for such tasks.
Slaves on contract worked in mining and lumbering
(often far from cities); but others worked on the
docks and on construction sites, drove wagons, and
performed other unskilled jobs in cities and towns.
Slave women and children worked in the region's
few textile mills. Particularly skilled workers such as
blacksmiths or carpenters were also often hired out.
After regular working hours, many of them fended
for themselves; neither their owners nor their employers bothered to supervise them. Thus urban
slaves gained numerous opportunities to mingle with
free blacks and with whites. In the cities, the line
between slavery and freedom became increasingly
indistinct.

Indeed, white southerners generally considered
slavery to be incompatible with city life, and as
southern cities grew the number of slaves in them
declined, relatively if not absolutely. The reasons
were social rather than economic. Fearing conspiracies and insurrections, urban slaveowners sold off
much of their male property to the countryside. Remaining behind in the cities was a slave population
in which black women outnumbered black men. The
same cities also had more white men than women—
a situation that helped account for the birth of many
mulattoes. Even while slavery in the cities was declining, forced segregation of urban blacks, both free
and slave, from white society increased. Segregation
was a means of social control intended to make up
for the loosening of the discipline of slavery itself in
urban areas.

Free African Americans

There were about 250,000 free African Americans in the slaveholding states by the start of the Civil War, more than half of them in Virginia and Maryland. In some cases, they were slaves who had somehow earned money with which they managed to buy their own and their families' freedom, usually by developing a skill they could market independently of their masters. It was usually urban blacks, with their greater freedom of movement and activity, who could take that route. One example was Elizabeth Keckley, a slave woman who bought freedom for herself and her son with proceeds from sewing. She later became a seamstress, personal servant, and companion to Mary Todd Lincoln in the White House. But few masters had any incentive, or inclination, to give up their slaves, so this route was open to relatively few people.

Some slaves were set free by a master who had moral qualms about slavery, or by a master's will after his death—for example, the more than 400 slaves belonging to John Randolph of Roanoke, freed in 1833. From the 1830s on, however, state laws governing slavery became more rigid. That was in part a response to the fears Nat Turner's revolt (see p. 390) created among white southerners: free blacks, removed from close supervision by whites, might generate more violence and rebellion than slaves. It was also in part because the community of free blacks in southern cities was becoming larger and, to whites, more threatening—a dangerous example to blacks still in slavery. The rise of abolitionist agitation in the North—and the fear that it would inspire slaves to rebel—also persuaded southern whites to tighten their system. The new laws made it more and more difficult, and in some cases practically impossible, for owners to set free (or "manumit") their slaves; all southern states forbade free African Americans from entering. Arkansas even forced the freed slaves living there to leave.

A few free blacks (generally those on the northern fringes of the slaveholding regions) attained wealth and prominence. Some owned slaves themselves, usually relatives whom they had bought in order to ensure their ultimate emancipation. In a few cities—New Orleans, Natchez, Charleston—free black communities managed to flourish relatively unmolested by whites and with some economic stability. Most free blacks, however, lived in abject poverty, under conditions worse than those of blacks in the North. Law or custom closed many occupations to them, forbade them to assemble without white supervision, and placed numerous other restraints on them. They were only quasi-free, and yet they had all the burdens of freedom: the necessity to support themselves, to find housing, to pay taxes. Yet great as were the hardships of freedom, blacks usually preferred them to slavery.

The Slave Trade

The transfer of slaves from one part of the South to another was one of the most important consequences of the development of the Southwest. Sometimes slaves moved to the new cotton lands in the company of their original owners, who were migrating themselves. More often, however, the transfer occurred through the medium of professional slave traders. Traders transported slaves over long distances on trains or on river or ocean steamers. On shorter journeys, the slaves moved on foot, trudging in coffles of hundreds along dusty highways—just as their ancestors had marched to the ports in Africa from which they had embarked to America. Eventually they arrived at some central market such as Natchez, New Orleans, Mobile, or Galveston, where purchasers gathered to bid for them. At the auction, the bidders checked the slaves like livestock, watching them as they were made to walk or trot, inspecting their teeth, feeling their arms and legs, looking for signs of infirmity or age. Some traders tried to deceive buyers by blacking gray hair, oiling withered skin, and concealing physical defects in other ways. A sound young field hand would fetch a price that, during the 1840s and 1850s, varied from $500 to $1,700, depending mainly on fluctuations in the price of cotton. An attractive, sexually desirable woman might bring much more.

The domestic slave trade was essential to the growth and prosperity of the whole system. It was also one of its most horrible aspects. The trade dehumanized all who were involved in it. It separated children from parents, and parents from each other. Even families kept together by scrupulous masters might be broken up in the division of the estate after the master's death. Planters might deplore the trade,

■ THE BUSINESS OF SLAVERY

The offices of slave dealers were familiar sights on the streets of pre-Civil War southern cities and towns. They provide testimony to the way in which slavery was not just a social system, but a business, deeply woven into the fabric of southern economic life.

(Library of Congress)

but they eased their consciences by holding the traders in contempt and assigning them a low social position.

The foreign slave trade was as bad or worse. Although federal law had prohibited the importation of slaves from 1808 on, some continued to be smuggled into the United States as late as the 1850s. The numbers can only be estimated. There were not enough such imports to satisfy all planters, and the southern commercial conventions, which met annually to consider means of making the South economically independent, began to discuss the legal reopening of the trade. "If it is right to buy slaves in Virginia and carry them to New Orleans," William L. Yancey of Alabama asked his fellow delegates at the 1858 meeting, "why is it not right to buy them in Cuba, Brazil, or Africa and carry them there?" The convention that year voted to recommend the repeal of all laws against slave imports. Only the delegates from the states of the upper South, which profited from the domestic trade, opposed the foreign competition.

Slave Resistance

Few issues have sparked as much debate among historians as the effects of slavery on the blacks themselves. (See "Where Historians Disagree," pp. 384–385.) Slaveowners, and many white Americans after emancipation, liked to argue that the slaves were generally content, "happy with their lot." That may well have been true in some cases. But it is clear that the vast majority of southern blacks were not content with being slaves, that they yearned for freedom even though most realized there was little they could do to secure it. Evidence for that conclusion can be found, if nowhere else, from the reaction of slaves when emancipation finally came. Virtually all reacted to freedom with joy and celebration; relatively few chose to remain in the service of the whites who had owned them before the Civil War (although most blacks, of course, remained for many years subservient to whites in one way or another).

Rather than contented acceptance, the dominant response of blacks to slavery was a complex one: a combination of adaptation and resistance. At the extremes, slavery could produce two very different reactions, each of which served as the basis for a powerful stereotype in white society. One extreme was what became known as the "Sambo"— the shuffling, grinning, head-scratching, deferential slave who acted out the role that he recognized the white world expected of him. More often than not, the "Sambo" pattern of behavior was a charade, a facade assumed in the presence of whites. The other extreme was the slave rebel—the African American who could not bring himself or herself to either acceptance or accommodation but remained forever rebellious. Actual slave revolts were extremely rare, but the knowledge that they were possible struck terror into the hearts of white southerners everywhere. In 1800, Gabriel Prosser gathered 1,000 rebellious slaves outside Richmond; but two Africans gave the plot away, and the Virginia militia stymied the uprising before it could begin. Prosser and thirty-five others were executed. In 1822, the Charleston free black Denmark Vesey and his followers—rumored to total 9,000— made preparations for revolt; but again word leaked out, and suppression and retribution followed. In 1831, Nat Turner, a slave preacher, led a band of African Americans who armed themselves with guns and axes and, on a summer night, went from house to house in Southampton County, Virginia. They killed sixty white men, women, and children before being overpowered by state and federal troops. More than a hundred blacks were executed in the aftermath. Nat Turner's was the only actual slave insurrection in the nineteenth-century South, but fear of slave conspiracies and renewed violence pervaded the section as long as slavery lasted.

For the most part, however, resistance to slavery took other, less drastic forms. Some blacks attempted to resist by running away. A small number managed to escape to the North or to Canada, especially after sympathetic whites began organizing the so-called underground railroad to assist them in flight. But the odds against a successful escape, particularly from the Deep South, were impossibly high. The hazards

of distance and the slaves' ignorance of geography were serious obstacles. So were the white "slave patrols," which stopped wandering blacks on sight throughout the South demanding to see travel permits. Without such a permit, slaves were presumed to be runaways and were taken captive. Slave patrols often employed bloodhounds to track blacks who attempted to escape through the woods. Despite all the obstacles to success, however, blacks continued to run away from their masters in large numbers. Some did so repeatedly, undeterred by the whippings and other penalties inflicted on them when captured.

But perhaps the most important method of resistance was simply a pattern of everyday behavior by which blacks defied their masters. That whites so often considered blacks to be lazy and shiftless suggests one means of resistance: refusal to work hard.

■ **HARRIET TUBMAN WITH ESCAPED SLAVES**
Harriet Tubman (c. 1820–1913) was born into slavery in Maryland. In 1849, when her master died, she escaped to Philadelphia to avoid being sold out of state. Over the next ten years, she assisted first members of her own family and then up to 300 other slaves to escape from Maryland to freedom. During the Civil War, she served alternately as a nurse and as a spy for Union forces in South Carolina. She is shown here, on the left, with some of the slaves she had helped to free. *(Smith College)*

Some slaves stole from their masters or from neighboring whites. Some performed isolated acts of sabotage: losing or breaking tools (southern planters gradually began to buy unusually heavy hoes because so many of the lighter ones got broken) or performing tasks improperly. In extreme cases, blacks might make themselves useless by cutting off their fingers or even committing suicide. Or, despite the terrible consequences, a few turned on their masters and killed them. The extremes, however, were very rare. For the most part, blacks resisted by building into their normal patterns of behavior subtle methods of rebellion.

THE CULTURE OF SLAVERY

Resistance was only part of the slave response to slavery. Another was an elaborate process of adaptation—a process that did not imply contentment with bondage but a recognition that there was no realistic alternative. One of the ways blacks adapted was by developing their own, separate culture, one that enabled them to sustain a sense of racial pride and unity.

Language and Music

In many areas, slaves retained a language of their own, sometimes incorporating African speech patterns into English. Having arrived in America speaking many different African languages, the first generations of slaves had as much difficulty communicating with one another as they did with white people. To overcome these barriers, they learned a simple, common language (known to linguists as "pidgin"). It retained some African words, but it drew primarily, if selectively, from English. And while slave language grew more sophisticated as blacks spent more time in America—and as new generations grew up never having known African tongues—some features of this early pidgin survived in black speech for many generations.

Music was especially important in slave society. In some ways, it was as important to African Americans as language. Again, the African heritage was an important influence. African music relied heavily on rhythm, and so did black music in America. Africans thought of music as an accompaniment to dance, and so did blacks in America. The banjo, an instrument original to Africa, became important to slave music. But most important were voices and song.

Field workers often used songs to pass the time in the fields; since they sang them in the presence of whites, they usually attached relatively innocuous words to them. But African Americans also created more emotionally rich and politically challenging music in the relative privacy of their religious services. It was there that the tradition of the spiritual emerged in the early nineteenth century. And through the spiritual, Africans in America not only expressed their religious faith, but also lamented their bondage and expressed continuing hope for freedom. Similar sentiments surfaced throughout slave religion.

African-American Religion

A separate slave religion was not supposed to exist. Almost all African Americans were Christians by the early nineteenth century. Some had converted voluntarily and some after coercion by their masters and Protestant missionaries who evangelized among them. Masters expected their slaves to worship under the supervision of white ministers. Indeed, autonomous black churches were banned by law; and many slaves became members of the same denominations as their owners—usually Baptist or Methodist. In the 1840s and 1850s, as slavery expanded in the South, missionary efforts increased. Vast numbers of blacks became members of Protestant churches in those years.

Nevertheless, blacks throughout the South developed their own version of Christianity, at times incorporating into it such practices as voodoo or other polytheistic religious traditions of Africa. Or they simply bent religion to the special circumstances of bondage. Natural leaders emerging within the slave community rose to the rank of preacher.

African-American religion was more emotional than its white counterparts and reflected the influence of African customs and practices. Slave prayer meetings routinely involved fervent chanting, spontaneous exclamations from the congregation, and ecstatic conversion experiences. Black religion was also more joyful and affirming than that of many white denominations. And above all, black religion emphasized the dream of freedom and deliverance. In their prayers and songs and sermons,

THE SLAVES' MUSIC

For African Americans living as slaves on southern plantations, there was little leisure time—and little opportunity for the kinds of cultural activities that were beginning to appeal to other groups of Americans. But slaves managed nevertheless to create a culture of their own. And among its most distinctive and pervasive features was music.

Indeed to white observers at least, nothing was more striking about slave life than the role music played within it. African Americans sang frequently, sometimes alone, even more often in groups. They sang while they worked together in the fields, as they shucked corn, slaughtered hogs, or repaired fences. They sang whenever they had social gatherings—on Sundays or on the rare other holidays from work. They sang when they gathered for chores in the evenings. They sang during their religious services. And they sang with a passion, at times even an ecstasy, that was completely unfamiliar to whites—and sometimes troubling to them.

Their songs were rarely written down and often seemed entirely spontaneous; but much slave music was really derived from African and Caribbean traditions passed on through generations and from snatches of other songs the performers had heard before and from which they improvised variations. In its emotionalism, its pulsing rhythms, and its lack of conventional formal structure, it resembled nothing its white listeners had ever heard before.

Slaves sang whether or not there were any musical instruments to accompany them, but they often created instruments for themselves out of whatever materials were at hand. "Us take pieces of sheep's rib or cow's jaw or a piece of iron, with an old kettle or a hollow gourd and some horsehair to make the drum," one former slave recalled years later. "They'd take the buffalo horn and scrape it out to make the flute." When they could, they would build banjos, an instrument that had originated in Africa. Their masters sometimes gave them violins and guitars. When the setting permitted it, African Americans danced to their music— dances very different from and much more spontaneous than the formal steps that nineteenth century whites generally learned. They also used music to accompany one of their other important cultural traditions: storytelling.

Black music on the plantations took a number of forms. The most common was religious songs, the precursors of modern gospel music, which expressed—in terms that their white masters, who usually did not listen to the words very carefully, usually found acceptable—a faith in their eventual freedom and salvation and often spoke of Africans as a chosen people waiting for redemption. At other times, the songs would express a bitterness toward white slaveholders. The great black abolitionist Frederick Douglass remembered one:

> We raise de wheat,
> Dey gib us de corn;
> We bake de bread,
> Dey gib us de crust;
> We sif the meal,
> Dey gib us de huss;
> We peel de meat,
> Dey gib us de skin;
> And dat's de way
> Dey take us in;
> We skim de pot,
> Dey gib us de liquor,
> And say dat's good enough for nigger.
> Your butter and the fat;
> Poor nigger, you can't ever get that.

■ **"THE OLD PLANTATION"**
This painting, by an unidentified folk artist of the early nineteenth century, suggests the importance of music in the lives of plantation slaves in America. The banjo, which the black musician at right is playing, was originally an African instrument. *(Abby Aldrich Rockefeller Folk Art Center)*

To African Americans, in other words, music was a treasured avenue of escape from the hardships of slavery. It was also a vehicle through which they could express anger, resentment, and hope. Their masters generally tolerated their slaves' music—and even valued it, both because they often enjoyed listening to it and because the more intelligent understood that without this means of emotional and spiritual release, active resistance to slavery might be more frequent.

The powerful music that emerged from slavery helped shape the lives of African Americans on the plantations. It also helped lay the foundations for music that almost all Americans later embraced: gospel, blues, jazz, rhythm and blues, rock, and rap.

■ **PLANTATION RELIGION**
A black preacher leads his fellow slaves, as well as the family of
the master, in a Sunday service in the modest plantation chapel.
African-American religious services were considerably less
restrained when white people were not present—one reason why
blacks withdrew so quickly from white churches after the Civil
War and formed their own. *(Bettmann)*

black Christians talked and sang of the day when
the Lord would "call us home," "deliver us to freedom," "take us to the Promised Land." And while
their white masters generally chose to interpret
such language merely as the expression of hopes
for life after death, many blacks themselves used
the images of Christian salvation to express their
own dream of freedom in the present world. Christian images, and biblical injunctions, were central
to Gabriel Prosser, Denmark Vesey, Nat Turner,
and others who planned or engaged in open resistance to slavery.

In cities and towns in the South, some African
Americans had their own churches, where free
blacks occasionally worshiped alongside slaves. In
the countryside, however, slaves usually attended the
same churches as their masters—sometimes a chapel
on the plantation itself, sometimes a church serving a
larger farm community. Seating in such churches was
usually segregated. Blacks sat in the rear or in balconies. They held their own services later, often in
secret, usually at night.

The Slave Family

The slave family was the other crucial institution of
black culture in the South. Like religion, it suffered
from certain legal restrictions—most notably the lack
of legal marriage. Nevertheless, what we now call
the "nuclear family" consistently emerged as the
dominant kinship model among African Americans.

Such families did not always operate according to
white customs. Black women generally began bearing children at younger ages than most whites, often
as early as age fourteen or fifteen. Slave communities
did not condemn premarital pregnancy in the way
white society did, and black couples would often
begin living together before marrying. It was customary, however, for couples to marry—in a ceremony
involving formal vows—soon after conceiving a
child. Often, marriages occurred between slaves living on neighboring plantations. Husbands and wives
sometimes visited each other with the permission of
their masters, but often such visits had to be in secret, at night. Family ties were no less strong than
those of whites, and many slave marriages lasted
throughout the course of long lifetimes.

When marriages did not survive, it was often because of circumstances over which blacks had no
control. Up to a third of all black families were broken apart by the slave trade; an average slave might
expect during a lifetime to see ten or more relatives
sold. And that accounted for some of the other distinctive characteristics of the black family, which
adapted itself to the cruel realities of its own uncertain future. Extended kinship networks—which grew
to include not only spouses and their children, but
also aunts, uncles, grandparents, even distant
cousins—were strong and important and often
helped compensate for the breakup of nuclear families. A slave forced suddenly to move to a new area,
far from his or her family, might create fictional kinship ties and become "adopted" by a family in the
new community. Even so, the impulse to maintain
contact with a spouse and children remained strong
long after the breakup of a family. One of the most
frequent causes of flight from the plantation was a
slave's desire to find a husband, wife, or child who
had been sent elsewhere.

It was not only by breaking up families through
sale that whites intruded on black family life. Black

Significant Events

1800	Gabriel Prosser organizes unsuccessful slave revolt in Virginia
1808	Importation of slaves to United States banned
1820s	Prolonged depression in tobacco prices begins
	English market for cotton textiles boosts prices and causes explosion in cotton production in the Southwest
1822	Denmark Vesey thwarted in plans for slave rebellion in Charleston
1831	Nat Turner slave rebellion breaks out in Virginia
1833	John Randolph of Roanoke frees 400 slaves
1837	Cotton prices plummet
1846	*De Bow's Review* founded in New Orleans
1849	Rise in cotton prices spurs production boom

women, usually powerless to resist the sexual advances of their masters, often bore the children of whites—children whom the whites almost never recognized as their own and who were consigned to slavery from birth.

In addition to establishing social and cultural institutions of their own, slaves adapted themselves to slavery by forming complex relationships with their masters. However much blacks resented their lack of freedom, they often found it difficult to maintain an entirely hostile attitude toward their owners. Not only were they dependent on whites for the material means of existence—food, clothing, and shelter; they also often derived from their masters a sense of security and protection. There was, in short, a paternal relationship between slave and master—sometimes harsh, sometimes kindly, but almost invariably important. That paternalism, in fact, became (even if not always consciously) a vital instrument of white control. By creating a sense of mutual dependence, whites helped reduce resistance to an institution that, in essence, served only the interests of the ruling race.

CONCLUSION

While the North was creating a complex and rapidly developing commercial-industrial economy, the South was expanding its agrarian economy without making many fundamental changes in its character. Great migrations took many southern whites, and even more African-American slaves, into new agricultural areas in the Deep South, where they created a booming "cotton kingdom" that raised crops for export around the world. The cotton economy created many great fortunes, and some modest ones. It also entrenched the planter class as the dominant force within southern society—both as owners of vast numbers of slaves, and as patrons, creditors, landlords, and marketers for the large number of poor whites who lived on the edge of the planter world.

The differences between the North and the South were a result of differences in natural resources, differences in social structure, differences in climate, and differences in culture. Above all, they were the result of the existence within the South of an unfree labor system that prevented the kind of social fluidity that an industrializing society usually requires and that kept a large proportion of the southern population in debilitating bondage.

FOR FURTHER REFERENCE

Suggested Readings   Frederick Douglass's *Narrative of the Life of Frederick Douglass,* first published in 1845, is an American classic. Peter Kolchin, *American Slavery, 1619-1877* (1993) is an excellent recent synthesis of the history of slavery in the United States from the settlement of Virginia through Reconstruction. James Oakes, *Slavery and Freedom* (1990) provides an overview of southern politics and society in the antebellum period. Eugene Genovese, *Roll, Jordan, Roll: The World the Slaves Made* (1974) argues that masters and slaves forged a system of mutual obligations within a fundamentally coercive social system. Genovese's *The Political Economy of Slavery* (1965) argues that slavery blocked southern economic development. Elizabeth Fox-Genovese, *Within the Plantation Household* (1988) argues against the idea that black and white women shared a community of interests on southern plantations. Charles Joyner, *Down by the Riverside: A South Carolina Slave Community* (1984) may be the best study of slavery in a single community. Bertram Wyatt-Brown, *Southern Honor: Ethics and Behavior in the Old South* (1982) argues that concepts of honor lay at the core of southern white identity in the antebellum period. Steven Hahn, *The Roots of Southern Populism: Yeomen Farmers and the Transformation of the Georgia Upcountry, 1850-1890* (1983) argues that white farmers in upcountry regions of the antebellum South maintained economically self-sufficient communities on the periphery of the market.

Films   (The best source for information on how to find these and other films is *Bowker's Complete Video Directory*—3 volumes.) *The Antebellum South* (1987) is a brief introduction to the economic and political consequences of the rise of the cotton economy. *The Plantation South* portrays the development of the plantation system in antebellum southern society. *The African American Experience: 1500-1864* covers the role and contributions of black Americans from the earliest presence of Africans on American soil. See also *Black Americans of Achievement, No. 24: A History of Slavery in America* (1994). *African American Gender Roles* (1994) examines the gender patterns established in the slave community. *A Slave's Story: Running a Thousand Miles to Freedom* (1972) is based on the story of fugitive slaves William and Ellen Craft. *Virginia Plantations: Mount Vernon, Monticello & Other Great Houses of Old Virginia* (1986) is an introduction to the planter class through their architecture.

Internet Resources   (For up-to-date URL addresses and links to these and other websites, consult the McGraw-Hill history site at *http://www.mhhe.com/socscience/history/usa/link/linktop.htm*) *Documenting the South* presents narratives of fugitive and former slaves written before the Civil War. *Third Person, First Person* contains life experiences of American slaves from the late eighteenth century through the nineteenth century. *American Slave Narratives* offers transcripts of interviews with former slaves made by the Works Progress Administration in the 1930s. *The Jesuit Plantation Project: Maryland's Jesuit Plantations, 1650-1838* presents text and images of documents describing the Jesuit plantations in the 1820s and 1830s; includes a Jesuit's defense of slavery. *African American Perspectives: Pamphlets from the Daniel A. P. Murray Collection, 1818-1907* has searchable text of 351 pamphlets; recurrent themes include the desire for uplift and improvement, the fight for civil rights, and the future of freed slaves. *Rare Map Collection-19th Century Georgia—from Frontier to New South* contains contemporary maps chronicling the transformation of nineteenth-century Georgia.

BIBLIOGRAPHY

Slavery: General Works   Ira Berlin, *Slaves Without Masters* (1974). John Blassingame, *The Slave Community* (1973). John B. Boles, *Black Southerners, 1619-1869* (1983). Shearer Davis Bowman, *Masters & Lords: Mid-19th-Century U.S. Planters and Prussian Junkers* (1993). David Brion Davis, *Slavery and Human Progress* (1984). Carl Degler, *Neither Black nor White* (1971). Robert Fogel, *Without Consent or Contract: The Rise and Fall of American Slavery* (1989). Claudia D. Goldin, *Urban Slavery in the American South, 1820-1860* (1976). Peter Kolchin, *Unfree Labor: American Slavery and Russian Serfdom* (1987). James Oakes, *The Ruling Race: A History of American Slaveholders* (1982); *Slavery and Freedom: An Interpretation of the Old South* (1990). Stephen B. Oates, *The Fires of Jubilee* (1974). Leslie Howard Owens, *This Species of Property: Slave Life and Slave Culture in the Old South* (1976). Orlando Patterson, *Slavery and Social Death: A Comparative Study* (1982). Kenneth Stampp, *The Peculiar Institution* (1955). Richard C. Wade, *Slavery in the Cities* (1964).

Politics and Ideology in the Antebellum South

Edward L. Ayers, *Vengeance and Justice: Crime and Punishment in the Nineteenth-Century American South* (1984). Drew Gilpin Faust, *A Sacred Circle: The Dilemma of the Intellectual in the Old South* (1977); *James Henry Hammond and the Old South: A Design for Mastery* (1982). John Hope Franklin, *The Militant South* (1956). Eugene Genovese, *The Slaveholder's Dilemma: Freedom and Progress in Southern Conservative Thought* (1992); *The World the Slaveholders Made* (1969). Kenneth S. Greenberg, *Masters and Statesmen: The Political Culture of American Slavery* (1985). J. William Harris, *Plain Folk and Gentry in a Slave Society* (1985). John McCardell, *The Idea of a Southern Nation* (1979). Stephanie McCurry, *Masters of Small Worlds: Yeoman Households, Gender Relations, and the Political Culture of the Antebellum South Carolina Low Country* (1995). Thomas D. Morris, *Southern Slavery and the Law, 1619-1860* (1996). Charles S. Sydnor, *The Development of Southern Sectionalism, 1819-1848* (1948). Ralph A. Wooster, *Politicians, Planters, and Plain Folk* (1975).

The Antebellum Southern Economy

Fred Bateman, *A Deplorable Scarcity: The Failure of Industrialism in the Slave Economy* (1981). P. A. David et al., *Reckoning with Slavery* (1976). Charles Dew, *Bond of Iron* (1994). Wilma A. Dunaway, *The First American Frontier: Transition to Capitalism in Southern Appalachia, 1700-1860* (1996). Robert Fogel and Stanley Engerman, *Time on the Cross*, 2 vols. (1974). Herbert Gutman, *Slavery and the Numbers Game* (1975). Steven Hahn, *The Roots of Southern Populism: Yeomen Farmers and the Transformation of the Georgia Upcountry, 1850-1890* (1983). Roderick McDonald, *The Economy and Material Culture of Slaves* (1993). Frank L. Owsley, *Plain Folk of the Old South* (1949). Robert Starobin, *Industrial Slavery in the Old South* (1970). Gavin Wright, *The Political Economy of the Cotton South: Households, Markets, and Wealth in the Nineteenth Century* (1978).

Regional, State, and Local Studies

Charles Bolton, *Poor Whites in the Antebellum South* (1994). Orville Vernon Burton, *Class, Conflict, and Consensus: Antebellum Southern Community Studies* (1982); *In My Father's House Are Many Mansions: Family and Community in Edgefield, South Carolina* (1985). Leonard P. Curry, *The Free Black in Urban America: The Shadow of the Dream* (1981). William Dusinberre, *Them Dark Days: Slavery in the American Rice Swamps* (1996). Stanley Elkins, *Slavery* (1959). Barbara Jean Fields, *Slavery and Freedom on the Middle Ground* (1985). Donald Grant, *The Way It Was in the South: The Black Experience in Georgia* (1993). Michael P. Johnson and James L. Roark, *Black Masters* (1984). Leon Litwack, *North of Slavery* (1961). Marion Lucas, *A History of Blacks in Kentucky*, 2 vols. (1992). William S. McFeely, *Sapelo's People: A Long Walk to Freedom* (1994). Christopher Morris, *Becoming Southern: The Evolution of a Way of Life, Warren County and Vicksburg, Mississippi, 1770-1860* (1995). Bernard Powers, Jr., *Black Charlestonians* (1994). Joseph P. Reidy, *From Slavery to Agrarian Capitalism in the Cotton Plantation of the South: Central Georgia, 1800-1880* (1992).

Culture and Religion

Roger D. Abrahams, *Singing the Master: The Emergence of African American Culture in the Plantation South* (1992). David T. Bailey, *Shadow on the Church: Southwestern Evangelical Religion and the Issue of Slavery, 1783-1860* (1985). Dickson D. Bruce, *Violence and Culture in the Antebellum South* (1979). W. J. Cash, *The Mind of the South* (1941). Judith Chase, *Afro-American Art and Craft* (1971). Bruce Collins, *White Society in the Antebellum South* (1985). Dena J. Epstein, *Sinful Tunes and Spirituals: Black Folk Music to the Civil War* (1977). Lawrence W. Levine, *Black Culture and Black Consciousness: Afro-American Folk Thought from Slavery to Freedom* (1977). Ann C. Loveland, *Southern Evangelicals and the Social Order, 1800-1860* (1980). Donald G. Mathews, *Religion in the Old South* (1977). Albert J. Raboteau, *Slave Religion* (1978). George P. Rawick, *From Sundown to Sunup: The Making of the Black Community* (1973). Mitchell Snay, *Gospel of Disunion: Religion and Separation in the Antebellum South* (1993). Randy Sparks, *On Jordan's Story Banks: Evangelicalism in Mississippi, 1773-1876* (1994). William R. Taylor, *Cavalier and Yankee: The Old South and American National Character* (1961). Thomas L. Weber, *Deep Like Rivers: Education in the Slave Quarters, 1831-1865* (1978).

Family

Peter W. Bardaglio, *Reconstructing the Household: Families, Sex, and the Law in the Nineteenth-Century South* (1996). Carol Blesser, *The Hammonds of Redcliffe* (1981). Victoria E. Bynum, *Unruly Women: The Politics of Social and Sexual Control in the Old South* (1992). Jane Turner Censer, *North Carolina Planters and Their Children, 1800-1860* (1984). Mary Boykin Chesnut, *A Dairy from Dixie* (1981, C. Vann Woodward, ed.). Catherine Clinton, *The Plantation Mistress: Woman's World in the Old South* (1982). Herbert Gutman, *The Black Family in Slavery and Freedom* (1976). Jacqueline Jones, *Labor of Love, Labor of Sorrow: Black Women, Work and the Family from Slavery to the Present* (1985). Suzanne Lebsock, *The Free Women of Petersburg: Status and Culture in a Southern Town* (1984). Robert Manson Myers, ed., *The Children of Pride* (1972). Mary D. Robertson, ed., *Lucy Breckinridge of Grove Hill* (1979). Anne Firor Scott, *The Southern Lady* (1970). Deborah G. White, *Ar'n't I a Woman?* (1985). Joel Williamson, *New People: Miscegenation and Mulattoes in the United States* (1980). Margaret Ripley Wolfe, *Daughters of Canaan: A Saga of Southern Women* (1995).

Chapter Twelve

ANTEBELLUM CULTURE AND REFORM

The United States in the mid-nineteenth century was a rapidly changing society. The nation was growing in geographical extent, in the size and diversity of its population, and in the dimensions and complexity of its economy. Like any people faced with such rapid and fundamental alterations in their surroundings, most Americans reacted with ambiguity. On the one hand, many were excited by the new possibilities that economic growth was providing. On the other hand, many were painfully aware of the dislocations that it was creating: the challenges to traditional values and institutions, the social instability, the increasing inequality, the uncertainty about the future.

One result of these conflicting attitudes was the emergence of a broad array of movements intended to adapt society to its new conditions, to "reform" the nation. These reform efforts took many different shapes, but in general they reflected one of two basic impulses, and at times elements of both. Many of these movements rested on an optimistic faith in human nature, a belief that within every individual resided a spirit that was basically good and that society should attempt to unleash.

This assumption—which spawned in both Europe and America a movement known, in its artistic aspects at least, as romanticism—stood in marked contrast to traditional Protestant assumptions of original sin, which humans needed to overcome through a disciplined, virtuous life. Instead, reformers now argued, individuals should strive to give full expression to the inner spirit, should work to unleash their innate capacity to experience joy and to do good.

A second impulse, which appeared directly to contradict the first but in practice often existed alongside it, was a desire for order and control. With society changing so rapidly, with traditional values and institutions under assault and often eroding, many Americans yearned above all for a restoration of stability and discipline to their nation. Often, this impulse embodied a conservative nostalgia for better, simpler times. But it also inspired forward-looking efforts to create new institutions of social control, suited to the realities of the new age.

The reforms that flowed from these two impulses came in many guises and mobilized many different groups. Reformers were far more numerous and influential in the North and Northwest than in the South, but reform activity could be found in all areas of the nation. In the course of the 1840s, however, one issue—slavery—came to overshadow all others.

■ **GIRLS' EVENING SCHOOL (C. 1840), ANONYMOUS**
Schooling for women, which expanded significantly in the mid-nineteenth century, included training in domestic arts (as indicated by the sewing table at right), as well as in reading, writing, and other basic skills. *(Museum of Fine Arts, Boston)*

And one group of reformers—the abolitionists—became the most visible of all. At that point, the reform impulse, which at first had been a force that tended to unify the sections, became another wedge between the North and the South.

THE ROMANTIC IMPULSE

"In the four quarters of the globe," wrote the English wit Sydney Smith in 1820, "who reads an American book? or goes to an American play? or looks at an American picture or statue?" The answer, he assumed, was obvious: no one. American intellectuals were painfully aware of the low regard in which Europeans held their artistic and intellectual life, and in the middle decades of the nineteenth century they continued to work for both an elevation and a liberation of their nation's culture—for the creation of an American artistic world independent of Europe, one that would express their nation's special virtues.

At the same time, however, some of the nation's cultural leaders were beginning to strive for another kind of liberation, one that would gradually come almost to overshadow their self-conscious nationalism. That impulse—which was, ironically, largely an import from Europe—was the spirit of romanticism. In literature, in philosophy, in art, even in politics and economics, American intellectuals were committing themselves to the liberation of the human spirit.

Nationalism and Romanticism in American Painting

When Sidney Smith asked in 1820 who looked at an American painting, he was expressing the almost universal belief among European artists that they—and they alone—stood at the center of the world of art. But in the United States, a great many people were, in fact, looking at American paintings in the antebellum era—and they were doing so not because the paintings introduced them to the great traditions of Europe, but because they believed Americans were creating important new artistic traditions of their own.

The most important and popular American paintings of the first half of the nineteenth century set out to evoke the wonder of the nation's landscape. Unlike their European counterparts, American painters did not favor gentle scenes of carefully cultivated countrysides. They sought instead to capture the undiluted power of nature by portraying some of the nation's wildest and most spectacular areas. The first great school of American painters emerged in New York. Frederic Church, Thomas Cole, Thomas Doughty, and Asher Durand—who were, along with others, known as the Hudson River School—painted the spectacular vistas of the rugged and still largely unsettled Hudson Valley. Like Emerson and Thoreau, whom many of the painters read and admired, they considered nature—more than civilization—the best source of wisdom and spiritual fulfillment. In portraying the Hudson Valley, they seemed to announce that in America, unlike in Europe, "wild nature" still existed; and that America, therefore, was a nation of greater promise than the played-out lands of the Old World. Yet there was also a sense of nostalgia in many of the Hudson River paintings, an effort to preserve and cherish a kind of nature that many Americans feared was fast disappearing.

In later years, some of the Hudson River painters traveled further west, in search of even more profound spiritual experiences in an even more rugged and spectacular natural world. Their enormous canvases of great natural wonders—the Yosemite Valley, Yellowstone, the Rocky Mountains—touched a passionate chord among the public. Some of the most famous of their paintings—particularly the works of Albert Bierstadt and Thomas Moran—traveled around the country attracting enormous crowds.

Literature and the Quest for Liberation

American readers in the first decades of the nineteenth century were relatively indifferent to the work of their nation's own writers. The most popular novelist in America in these years was the British writer Sir Walter Scott, whose swashbuckling historical novels set in eighteenth-century England and Scotland won him an impassioned readership in both Britain and America.

But even during the heyday of Scott in the 1820s, the effort to create a distinctively American literature—which Washington Irving and others had advanced in the first decades of the century—made considerable progress with the emergence of the first great American novelist: James Fenimore Cooper. The author of over thirty novels in the space of three decades, Cooper was known to his contemporaries as a master of adventure and suspense. What most distinguished his work, however, was its evocation of the American wilderness. Cooper had grown up in central New York, at a time when the edge of white settlement was not far away; and he retained throughout his life a fascination with man's relationship to nature and with the challenges (and dangers) of America's expansion westward. His most important novels were known as the "Leatherstocking Tales." Among them were *The Last of the Mohicans* (1826) and *The Deerslayer* (1841). They explored the American frontiersman's experience with Indians, pioneers, violence, and the law.

Cooper's novels were a continuation, in many ways a culmination, of the early-nineteenth-century effort to produce a truly American literature. But they also served as a link to the concerns of later intellectuals. For in the "Leatherstocking Tales" could be seen not only a celebration of the American spirit and landscape but an evocation, through the central character of Natty Bumppo, of the ideal of the independent individual with a natural inner goodness. There was also evidence of another impulse that would motivate American reform: the fear of disorder. Many of Cooper's less savory characters illustrated the vicious, grasping nature of some of the nation's western settlers and suggested a need for social discipline even in the wilderness.

Another group of important American writers emerged on the heels of Cooper. They displayed even more clearly the grip of romanticism on the nation's intellectual life. Walt Whitman, the self-proclaimed poet of American democracy, was the son of a Long Island carpenter and lived for many years roaming from place to place, doing odd jobs. Finally, in 1855, he hired a printer and published a first volume of work: *Leaves of Grass*. His poems were an unrestrained celebration of democracy, of the liberation of the individual, and of the pleasures of the flesh as well as of the spirit. They also expressed Whitman's personal yearning for emotional and physical release and personal fulfillment—a yearning perhaps rooted in part in his own experience as a homosexual living in a society profoundly intolerant of unconventional sexuality. In these poems, as well as in a large body of other work spanning nearly forty more years until his death in 1892, Whitman not only helped liberate verse from traditional, restrictive conventions but also helped ex-

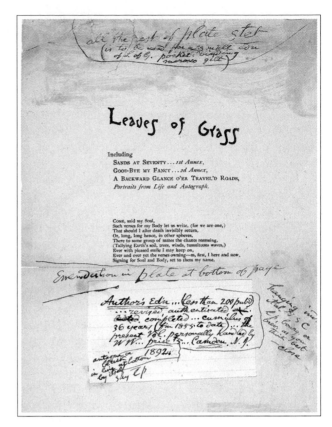

■ **TITLE PAGE FOR WHITMAN'S *LEAVES OF GRASS***
For more than thirty years after the publication of the original *Lavs of Grass* in 1855, Walt Whitman constantly revised and expanded the collection of poems and issued numerous subsequent editions. This sample title page, with notations by Whitman indicating changes and additions he wanted made, is for the final such edition, published in 1892, the year of Whitman's death. In a public announcement he prepared to announce publication, he said that "the book *Leaves of Grass,* which he has been working on at great intervals and partially issued for the past thirty-five or forty years, is now completed . . . Faulty as it is, he decides it is by far his special and entire self-chosen poetic utterance." *(Rare Book and Special Collections Division, Library of Congress)*

press the soaring spirit of individualism that characterized his age.

The new literary concern with the unleashing of human emotions did not always produce such optimistic works, as the work of Herman Melville suggests. Born in New York in 1819, Melville ran away to sea as a youth and spent years sailing the world (including the South Seas) before returning home to become the greatest American novelist of his era. The most important of his novels was *Moby Dick,* published in 1851. His portrayal of Ahab, the powerful, driven captain of a whaling vessel, was a story of courage and of the strength of individual will; but it was also a tragedy of pride and revenge. Ahab's maniacal search for Moby Dick, a great white whale that had maimed him, suggested how the search for personal fulfillment and triumph could not only liberate but destroy. The result of Ahab's great quest was the annihilation of Ahab himself, reflecting Melville's conviction that the human spirit was a troubled, often self-destructive force.

Similarly bleak were the works of one of the few southern writers of the time to embrace the search for the essence of the human spirit: Edgar Allan Poe. In the course of his short and unhappy life (he died in 1849 at the age of forty), Poe produced stories and poems that were primarily sad and macabre. His first book, *Tamerlane and Other Poems* (1827), received little recognition. But later works, including his most famous poem, "The Raven" (1845), established him as a major, if controversial, literary figure. Poe evoked images of individuals rising above the narrow confines of intellect and exploring the deeper world of the spirit and the emotions. Yet that world, he seemed to say, contained much pain and horror. Other American writers were contemptuous of Poe's work and his message, but he was ultimately to have a profound effect on European poets such as Baudelaire.

Literature in the Antebellum South

Poe, however, was something of an exception in the world of southern literature. The South experienced a literary flowering of its own in the mid-nineteenth century, and it produced writers and artists who were, like their northern counterparts, concerned with defining the nature of American society and of the American nation. But white southerners tended to produce very different images of what that society was and should be.

Southern novelists of the 1830s (among them Beverly Tucker, William Alexander Caruthers, and John Pendleton Kennedy), some of them writers of great talent, many of them residents of Richmond, produced historical romances or romantic eulogies of the plantation system of the upper South. In the 1840s, the southern literary capital moved to Charleston, home of the most distinguished of the region's men of letters: William Gilmore Simms. For a time, his work expressed a broad nationalism that

transcended his regional background; but by the 1840s he too had become a strong defender of southern institutions—especially slavery—against the encroachments of the North. There was, he believed, a unique quality to southern life that it was the duty of intellectuals to defend.

One group of southern writers, however, produced works that were more broadly American and less committed to a glorification of the peculiarities of southern life. These were writers from the fringes of plantation society, who depicted the world of the backwoods rural areas. Augustus B. Longstreet, Joseph G. Baldwin, Johnson J. Hooper, and others focused not on aristocratic "cavaliers," but on ordinary people and poor whites. Instead of romanticizing their subjects, they were deliberately and sometimes painfully realistic. And they seasoned their sketches with a robust, vulgar humor that was new to American literature. These southern realists established a tradition of American regional humor that was ultimately to find its most powerful voice in Mark Twain.

The Transcendentalists

One of the outstanding expressions of the romantic impulse in America came from a group of New England writers and philosophers known as the transcendentalists. Borrowing heavily from German philosophers such as Kant, Hegel, and Schelling, and from the English writers Coleridge and Carlyle, the transcendentalists embraced a theory of the individual that rested on a distinction (first suggested by Kant) between what they called "reason" and "understanding"—words they used in ways that seem unfamiliar, even strange, to modern ears. Reason, as they defined it, had little to do with rationality. It was, rather, the individual's innate capacity to grasp beauty and truth through giving full expression to the instincts and emotions; and as such, it was the highest human faculty. Understanding, the transcendentalists argued, was the use of intellect in the narrow, artificial ways imposed by society; it involved the repression of instinct and the victory of externally imposed learning. Every person's goal, therefore, should be liberation from the confines of "understanding" and the cultivation of "reason." Each individual should strive to "transcend" the limits of the intellect and allow the emotions, the "soul," to create an "original relation to the Universe."

Transcendentalist philosophy emerged first among a small group of intellectuals centered in Concord, Massachusetts. Their leader and most eloquent voice was Ralph Waldo Emerson. A Unitarian minister in his youth, Emerson left the church in 1832 to devote himself entirely to writing and teaching the elements of transcendentalism. He was a dazzling figure to his contemporaries—a lecturer whose public appearances drew rapturous crowds; a conversationalist who drew rapt intellectuals to his Concord home almost daily. He was the most important intellectual of his age.

Emerson produced a significant body of poetry, but he was most renowned for his essays and lectures. In "Nature" (1836), one of his best-known essays, Emerson wrote that in the quest for self-fulfillment, individuals should work for a communion with the natural world: "in the woods, we return to reason and faith. . . . Standing on the bare ground—my head bathed by the blithe air, and uplifted into infinite space,—all mean egotism vanishes. . . . I am part and particle of God." In other essays, he was even more explicit in advocating a commitment of the individual to the full exploration of inner capacities. "Nothing is at last sacred," he wrote in "Self-Reliance" (1841), perhaps his most famous essay, "but the integrity of your own mind." The quest for self-reliance, he explained, was really a search for communion with the unity of the universe, the wholeness of God, the great spiritual force that he described as the "Oversoul." Each person's innate capacity to become, through his or her private efforts, a part of this essence was perhaps the classic expression of the romantic belief in the "divinity" of the individual.

Emerson was also a committed nationalist, an ardent proponent of American cultural independence. In a famous 1837 lecture, "The American Scholar," he boasted that "Our day of dependence, our long apprenticeship to the learning of other lands, draws to a close." His belief that truth and beauty could be derived as much from instinct as from learning suggested that Americans, lacking the rich cultural heritage of European nations, could still aspire to artistic and literary greatness. Artistic and intellectual achievement need not rely on tradition and history; it could come from the instinctive creative genius of individuals. "Let the single man plant himself indomitably on his instincts and there abide," Emerson once said, "and the huge world will come round to him."

Almost as influential as Emerson was another leading Concord transcendentalist, Henry David Thoreau. Thoreau went even further than his friend Emerson in repudiating the repressive forces of society, which produced, he said, "lives of quiet desperation." Individuals should work for self-realization by resisting pressures to conform to society's expectations and responding instead to their own instincts. Thoreau's own effort to free himself—immortalized in his most famous book, *Walden* (1854)—led him to build a small cabin in the Concord woods on the edge of Walden Pond, where he lived alone for two years as simply as he could. "I went to the woods," he explained, "because I wished to live deliberately, to front only the essential facts of life, and see if I could not learn what it had to teach, and not, when I came to die, discover that I had not lived." Living simply, he believed, was a desirable alternative to the rapidly modernizing world around him—a world, he believed, that the disruptive and intrusive railroad unhappily symbolized.

Thoreau's rejection of what he considered the artificial constraints of society extended as well to his relationship with government. In 1846, he went to jail (briefly) rather than agree to pay a poll tax. He would not, he insisted, give financial support to a government that permitted the existence of slavery. In his 1849 essay "Resistance to Civil Government," he explained his refusal by claiming that the individual's personal morality had the first claim on his or her actions, that a government which required violation of that morality had no legitimate authority. The proper response was "civil disobedience," or "passive resistance"—a public refusal to obey unjust laws.

Visions of Utopia

Although transcendentalism was above all an individualistic philosophy, it helped spawn the most famous of all nineteenth-century experiments in communal living: Brook Farm, which the Boston transcendentalist George Ripley established as an experimental community in West Roxbury, Massachusetts, in 1841. There, according to Ripley, individuals would gather to create a new form of social organization, one that would permit every member of the community full opportunity for self-realization. All residents would share equally in the labor of the community so that all could share too in the leisure, for it was

■ **PLAN FOR THE COLONY AT NEW HARMONY**
The English reformer Robert Owen came to America in the 1820s to create an experimental community in which to test his own theories of cooperative living. This architect's drawing reveals the grandiose plans Owen and his followers had for the colony, which was in Indiana on the banks of the Wabash River on the site of an earlier social experiment by German idealists. In this plan, which was never constructed, the architecture reflects the sense of order and rationality Owen hoped to bring to the community. The plan was designed "to form a new combination of circumstances, capable of producing permanently greater physical, moral, and intellectual advantages . . . than have ever yet been realized in any age or country." *(Library of Congress)*

leisure that was the first necessity for cultivation of the self. (Ripley was one of the first Americans to attribute positive connotations to the idea of leisure; most of his contemporaries equated it with laziness and sloth.) Participation in manual labor served another purpose as well: it helped individuals bridge the gap between the world of the intellect and learning, and the world of instinct and nature. The obvious tension between the ideal of individual freedom and the demands of a communal society took their toll on Brook Farm. Increasingly, individualism gave way to a form of socialism. Many residents became disenchanted and left; when a fire destroyed the central building of the community in 1847, the experiment dissolved.

Among the original residents of Brook Farm was the writer Nathaniel Hawthorne, who expressed his disillusionment with the experiment and, to some extent, with transcendentalism in a series of notable novels. In *The Blithedale Romance* (1852), he wrote scathingly of Brook Farm itself, portraying the disastrous consequences of the experiment on the individuals who submitted to it and describing the great fire that destroyed the community as

a kind of liberation from oppression. In other novels—most notably *The Scarlet Letter* (1850) and *The House of Seven Gables* (1851)—he wrote equally passionately about the price individuals pay for cutting themselves off from society. Egotism, he claimed (in an indirect challenge to the transcendentalist faith in the self), was the "serpent" that lay at the heart of human misery.

The failure of Brook Farm did not, however, prevent the formation of other experimental communities. Some borrowed, as Ripley had done, from the ideas of the French philosopher Charles Fourier, whose ideas of socialist communities organized as cooperative "phalanxes" received wide attention in America. Others drew from the ideas of the Scottish industrialist and philanthropist Robert Owen. Owen himself founded an experimental community in Indiana in 1825, which he named New Harmony. It was to be a "Village of Cooperation," in which every resident worked and lived in total equality. The community was an economic failure, but the vision that had inspired it continued to enchant Americans. Dozens of other "Owenite" experiments began in other locations in the following years.

Redefining Gender Roles

One of the principal concerns of many of the new utopian communities (and of the new social philosophies on which they rested) was the relationship between men and women. Transcendentalism and other movements of this period fostered expressions of a kind of feminism that would not gain a secure foothold in American society until the late twentieth century.

One of those most responsible for drawing issues of gender into the larger discussion of individual liberation was Margaret Fuller. A leading transcendentalist and a close associate of Emerson, she suggested the important relationship between the discovery of the "self" that was so central to antebellum reform and the questioning of gender roles: "Many women are considering within themselves what they need and what they have not," she wrote in a famous feminist work, *Woman in the Nineteenth Century* (1844). "I would have Woman lay aside all thought, such as she habitually cherishes, of being taught and led by men." Fuller herself, before her premature death in a shipwreck in 1850, lived a life far different from the domestic ideal of her time. She had intimate relationships with many men; became a great admirer of European socialists and a great champion of the Italian revolution of 1848, which she witnessed during travels there; and established herself as an intellectual leader whose power came in part from her perspective as a woman.

A redefinition of gender roles was crucial to one of the most enduring of the utopian colonies of the nineteenth century: the Oneida Community, established in 1848 in upstate New York by John Humphrey Noyes. The Oneida "Perfectionists," as residents of the community called themselves, rejected traditional notions of family and marriage. All residents, Noyes declared, were "married" to all other residents; there were to be no permanent conjugal ties. But Oneida was not, as its horrified critics often claimed, an experiment in unrestrained "free love." It was a place where the community carefully monitored sexual behavior; where women were to be protected from unwanted childbearing; in which children were raised communally, often seeing little of their own parents. The Oneidans took special pride in what they considered the liberation of their women from the demands of male "lust" and from the traditional bonds of family.

The Shakers, even more than the Oneidans, made a redefinition of traditional sexuality and gender roles central to their society. Founded by "Mother" Ann Lee in the 1770s, the society of the Shakers survived throughout the nineteenth century and into the twentieth. (A tiny remnant survives today.) But the Shakers attracted a particularly large following in the antebellum period and established more than twenty communities throughout the Northeast and Northwest in the 1840s. They derived their name from a unique religious ritual, a sort of ecstatic dance, in which members of a congregation would "shake" themselves free of sin while performing a loud chant.

The most distinctive feature of Shakerism, however, was its commitment to complete celibacy—which meant, of course, that no one could be born to Shakerism; all Shakers had to choose the faith voluntarily. Shaker communities attracted about 6,000 members in the 1840s, more women than men; and members lived in conditions in which contact between men and women was very limited. Shakers openly endorsed the idea of sexual equality; they even embraced the idea of a God who was not clearly male or female. Indeed, within the Shaker society as a whole, it was women who exercised the most power. Mother Ann Lee was succeeded as leader of the movement by Mother Lucy Wright. Shakerism, one observer wrote in the 1840s, was a refuge from the "perversions of marriage" and "the gross abuses which drag it down."

The Shakers were not, however, motivated only by a desire to escape the burdens of traditional gender roles. They were trying as well to create a society separated and protected from the chaos and disorder that they believed had come to characterize American life as a whole. They were less interested in personal freedom than in social discipline. And in that, they were like some other dissenting religious sects and utopian communities of their time. Another example was the Amana Community, founded by German immigrants in 1843; its members settled in Iowa in 1855. The Amanas attempted to realize Christian ideals by creating an ordered, socialist society.

The Mormons

Among the most important efforts to create a new and more ordered society within the old was that of the Church of Jesus Christ of Latter Day Saints—the

Mormons. Mormonism began in upstate New York as a result of the efforts of Joseph Smith, a young, energetic, but economically unsuccessful man, who had spent most of his twenty-four years moving restlessly through New England and the Northeast. Then, in 1830, he published a remarkable document—the Book of Mormon, named for the ancient prophet who he claimed had written it. It was, he said, a translation of a set of golden tablets he had found in the hills of New York, revealed to him by an angel of God. The Book of Mormon told the story of an ancient and successful civilization in America, peopled by one of the lost tribes of Israel who had found their way to the New World centuries before Columbus. Its members waited patiently for the appearance of the Messiah, and they were rewarded when Jesus actually came to America after his resurrection. Subsequent generations, however, had strayed from the path of righteousness that Jesus had laid out for them. Ultimately, their civilization collapsed, and God punished the sinful by making their skin dark. These darkened people, Smith believed, were the descendants of the American Indians, although the modern tribes had no memory of their origins. But while the ancient Hebrew kingdom in America had ultimately vanished, Smith believed, its history as a righteous society could serve as a model for a new holy community in the United States.

In 1831, gathering a small group of believers around him, Smith began searching for a sanctuary for his new community of "saints," an effort that would continue unhappily for more than twenty years. Time and again, the Mormons attempted to establish their "New Jerusalem." Time and again, they met with persecution from surrounding communities suspicious of their radical religious doctrines—which included polygamy (the right of men to take several wives), a rigid form of social organization, and particularly damaging to their image, an intense secrecy, which gave rise to wild rumors among their critics of conspiracy and depravity.

Driven from their original settlements in Independence, Missouri, and Kirtland, Ohio, the Mormons moved on to the new town of Nauvoo, Illinois, which in the early 1840s became an imposing and economically successful community. In 1844, however, Joseph Smith was arrested, charged with treason (for allegedly conspiring against the government to win foreign support for a new Mormon colony in the Southwest), and imprisoned in Carthage, Illinois.

There an angry mob attacked the jail, forced Smith from his cell, and shot and killed him. The Mormons now abandoned Nauvoo and, under the leadership of Smith's successor, Brigham Young, traveled across the desert—a society of 12,000 people, in one of the largest single group migrations in American history—and established a new community in Utah, the present Salt Lake City. There, at last, the Mormons were able to create a permanent settlement. And although they were not long to remain as isolated from the rest of American society as they were at the beginning, never again were they to be dislodged.

Like other experiments in social organization of the era, Mormonism reflected a belief in human perfectibility. God had once been a man, the church taught, and thus every man or woman could aspire to become—as Joseph Smith had become—a god. But unlike other new communities, the Mormons did not embrace the doctrine of individual liberty. Instead, they created a highly organized, centrally directed, almost militarized social structure, a refuge against the disorder and uncertainty of the secular world. They placed particular emphasis on the structure of the family. Mormon religious rituals even included a process by which men and women went through a baptism ceremony in the name of a deceased ancestor; as a result, they believed, they would be reunited with those ancestors in heaven. The intense Mormon interest in genealogy, which continues today, is a reflection of this belief in the possibility of reuniting present generations with those of the past.

The original Mormons were, for the most part, men and women who felt displaced in their rapidly changing society—economically marginal people left behind by the material growth and social progress of their era. In the new religion, they found genuine faith. In the society it created, they found security and order.

REMAKING SOCIETY

The simultaneous efforts to liberate the individual and impose order on a changing world also helped create a wide range of new movements to remake society—movements in which, to a striking degree, women formed the real rank and file and often the leadership as well. By the 1830s, such movements

"WINTER QUARTERS"
The artist C. C. A. Christensen, who chronicled the great Mormon migration westward to Utah, suggested the scale of the enterprise in this large painting of a winter encampment on the banks of the Missouri River in 1847. Christensen, a Danish immigrant and Mormon convert, painted this and other events of the journey about a decade after they occurred, with the avowed aim of showing later generations something of their heritage. *(Brigham Young University)*

had taken the form of organized reform societies. "In no country in the world," Tocqueville had observed, "has the principle of association been more successfully used, or more unsparingly applied to a multitude of different objects, than in America. . . . for there is no end which the human will, seconded by the collective exertions of individuals, despairs of attaining."

The new organizations did indeed work on behalf of a wide range of goals: temperance; education; peace; the care of the poor, the handicapped, and the mentally ill; the treatment of criminals; the rights of women; and many more. Few eras in American history have witnessed as wide a range of reform efforts. And few eras have exposed more clearly the simultaneous attraction of Americans to the ideas of personal liberty and social order.

Revivalism, Morality, and Order

The philosophy of reform arose from two distinct sources. One was the optimistic vision of those who, like the transcendentalists, rejected Calvinist doctrines and preached the divinity of the individual. These included not only Emerson, Thoreau, and their followers, but a much larger group of Americans who embraced the doctrines of Unitarianism and Universalism and absorbed European romanticism.

The second, and in many respects more important, source was Protestant revivalism—the movement that had begun with the Second Great Awakening early in the century and had, by the 1820s, evolved into a powerful force for social reform. Although the New Light revivalists were theologically far removed from the transcendentalists and

Unitarians, they had come to share the optimistic belief that every individual was capable of salvation. According to Charles Grandison Finney, an evangelistic Presbyterian minister who became the most influential revival leader of the 1820s and 1830s, traditional Calvinist doctrines of predestination and individual human helplessness were both obsolete and destructive. Each person, he preached, contained within himself or herself the capacity to experience spiritual rebirth and achieve salvation. A revival of faith need not depend on a miracle from God; it could be created by individual effort.

Finney enjoyed particular success in upstate New York, where he helped launch a series of passionate revivals in towns along the Erie Canal—a region so prone to religious awakenings that it was known as the "burned-over district." It was no coincidence that the new revivalism should prove so powerful there, for this region of New York was experiencing—largely as a result of the construction of the canal—a major economic transformation. And with that transformation had come changes in the social fabric so profound that many men and women felt baffled and disoriented. (It was in roughly this same area of New York that Joseph Smith first organized the Mormon church.)

Finney's doctrine of personal regeneration appealed strongly to those who felt threatened by change. In Rochester, New York, the site of his greatest success, he staged a series of emotionally wrenching religious meetings that aroused a large segment of the community. He had particular success in mobilizing women, on whom he tended to concentrate his efforts—both because women found the liberating message of revivalism particularly appealing and because, Finney discovered, they provided him with access to their male relatives. Gradually, he developed a large following among the relatively prosperous citizens of the region, who were enjoying the economic benefits of the new commercial growth but who were also uneasy about some of the social changes accompanying it (among them the introduction into their community of a new, undisciplined pool of transient laborers). For them, revivalism became not only a means of personal salvation but a mandate for the reform (and control) of the larger society. Finney's revivalism became a call for a crusade against personal immorality. "The church," he maintained, "must take right ground on the subject of Temperance, the Moral Reform, and all the subjects of practical morality which come up for decision from time to time."

The Temperance Crusade

Evangelical Protestantism added major strength to one of the most influential reform movements of the era: the crusade against drunkenness. No social vice, argued some reformers (including, for example, many of Finney's converts in cities such as Rochester), was more responsible for crime, disorder, and poverty than the excessive use of alcohol. Women, who were particularly active in the temperance movement, claimed that alcoholism placed a special burden on wives: men spent money on alcohol that their families needed for basic necessities, and drunken husbands often abused their wives and children.

In fact, alcoholism was an even more serious problem in antebellum America than it has been in the twentieth century. The supply of alcohol was growing rapidly, particularly in the West; farmers there grew more grain than they could sell in the still-limited markets in this prerailroad era, so they distilled much of it into whiskey. But in the East, too, commercial distilleries and private stills were widespread. The appetite for alcohol was growing as well: in isolated western areas, where drinking provided a social pastime in small towns and helped ease the loneliness and isolation on farms; in pubs and saloons in eastern cities, where drinking was the principal leisure activity for many workers. The average male in the 1830s drank nearly three times as much alcohol as the average person does today. And as that figure suggests, many people drank habitually and excessively, with bitter consequences for themselves and others. Among the many supporters of the temperance movement were people who saw it as a way to overcome their own problems with alcoholism.

Although advocates of temperance had been active since the late eighteenth century, the new reformers gave the movement an energy and influence it had never previously known. In 1826, the American Society for the Promotion of Temperance emerged as a coordinating agency among various groups; it attempted to use many of the techniques of revivalism in preaching abstinence. Then, in 1840, six reformed alcoholics in Baltimore organized the Washington Temperance Society and began to draw

■ THE DRUNKARD'S PROGRESS
This 1846 lithograph by Nathaniel Currier shows what temperance advocates argued was the inevitable consequence of alcohol consumption. Beginning with an apparently innocent "glass with a friend," the young man rises step by step to the summit of drunken revelry, then declines to desperation and suicide while his abandoned wife and child grieve. *(Library of Congress)*

large crowds—in which workers (many of them attempting to overcome their own alcoholism) were heavily represented—to hear their impassioned and intriguing confessions of past sins. By then, temperance advocates had grown dramatically in numbers; more than a million people had signed a formal pledge to forgo hard liquor.

As the movement gained in strength, it also became divided in purpose. Some temperance advocates now urged that abstinence include not only liquor but beer and wine; not everyone agreed. Some began to demand state legislation to restrict the sale and consumption of alcohol (Maine passed such a law in 1851); others insisted that temperance must rely on the conscience of the individual. Whatever their disagreements, however, most temperance advocates shared similar motives. By promoting abstinence, reformers were attempting to promote the moral self-improvement of individuals. They were also trying to impose discipline on society.

The latter impulse was particularly clear in the battle over prohibition laws, which pitted established Protestants against new Catholic immigrants, to many of whom drinking was an important social ritual and an integral part of the life of their community. The arrival of the immigrants was profoundly disturbing to established residents of many communities, and the restriction of alcohol seemed to them a way to curb the disorder they believed the new population was creating.

Health, Science, and Phrenology

For some Americans, the search for individual and social perfection led to an interest in new theories of health and knowledge. Threats to public health were critical to the sense of insecurity that underlay many reform movements, especially after the terrible cholera epidemics of the 1830s and 1840s. Cholera is a severe bacterial infection of the intestines, usually a

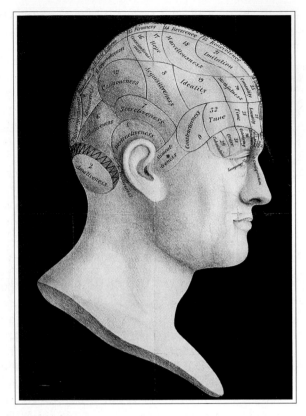

■ **PHRENOLOGY**
This lithograph illustrates some of the ideas of the popular "science" of phrenology in the 1830s. Drawing from the ideas of the German writer Johann Gaspar Spurzheim, American phrenologists promoted the belief that a person's character and talents could be understood by the formation of his or her skull; that the brain was, in fact, a cluster of autonomous organs, each controlling some aspect of human thought or behavior. In this diagram, the areas of the brain that supposedly control "identity," "acquisitiveness," "secretiveness," "marvelousness," and "hope" are clearly identified. The theory has no scientific basis. *(Library of Congress)*

result of consuming contaminated food or water. In the nineteenth century, long before the discovery of antibiotics, fewer than half of those who contracted the disease normally survived. Thousands of people died of cholera during its occasional outbreaks, and in certain cities—New Orleans in 1833 and St. Louis in 1849—the effects were truly catastrophic. Nearly a quarter of the population of New Orleans died in the 1833 epidemic. Many municipalities, pressured by reformers, established city health boards to try to find solutions to the problems of epidemics. But the medical profession of the time, unaware of the na-

ture of bacterial infections, had no answers; and the boards therefore found little to do.

Instead, many Americans turned to nonscientific theories for improving health. Affluent men and, especially, women flocked to health spas for the celebrated "water cure" (known to modern scientists as hydrotherapy), which purported to improve health through immersing people in hot or cold baths or wrapping them in wet sheets. Although the water cure in fact delivered few of the benefits its promoters promised, it did have some therapeutic value; some forms of hydrotherapy are still in use today. Other people adopted new dietary theories. Sylvester Graham, a Connecticut-born Presbyterian minister and committed reformer, won many followers with his prescriptions for eating fruits, vegetables, and bread made from coarsely ground flour—a prescription not unlike some dietary theories today—instead of meat. (The "Graham cracker" is made from a kind of flour named for him.) Graham accompanied his dietary prescriptions with moral warnings about the evils of excess and luxury.

Perhaps strangest of all to modern sensibilities was the widespread belief in the new "science" of phrenology, which appeared first in Germany and became popular in the United States beginning in the 1830s through the efforts of Orson and Lorenzo Fowler, publishers of the *Phrenology Almanac.* Phrenologists argued that the shape of an individual's skull was an important indicator of his or her character and intelligence. They made elaborate measurements of bumps and indentations to calculate the size (and, they claimed, the strength) of different parts of the brain, each of which, they argued, controlled a specific kind of intelligence or behavior. For a time, phrenology seemed to many Americans an important vehicle for improving society. It provided a way of measuring an individual's fitness for various positions in life and seemed to promise an end to the arbitrary process by which people matched their talents to occupations and responsibilities. The theory is now universally believed to have no scientific value at all.

Reforming Education

One of the outstanding reform movements of the mid-nineteenth century was the effort to produce a system of universal public education. As of 1830, no state yet had such a system, although some states—

■ **"SPOUT BATH AT WARM SPRINGS"**
Among the many fads and theories about human health to gain
currency in the 1830s and 1840s, one of the most popular was the
idea that bathing in warm, sulphurous water was restorative.
Visitors to "warm springs" all over the United States and Europe
"took the baths," drank the foul-smelling water, sometimes staying
for weeks as part of a combination vacation and "cure." This 1837
drawing is by Sophie Dupont, a visitor to a popular spa. She wrote
to a friend that the water, "notwithstanding its odour of half
spoiled eggs and its warmth, is not very nauseous to the taste."
(Courtesy of Hagley Museum and Library)

the salaries of male and female teachers), enriched
the curriculum, and introduced new methods of professional training for teachers.

Other states experienced similar expansion and
development. They built new schools, created teachers' colleges, and offered vast new groups of children
access to education. Henry Barnard helped produce a
new educational system in Connecticut and Rhode
Island. Pennsylvania passed a law in 1835 appropriat-
ing state funds for the support of universal education. Governor William Seward of New York extended public support of schools throughout the
state in the early 1840s. By the 1850s, the principle
of tax-supported elementary schools had been accepted in all the states; and all, despite continuing
opposition from certain groups, were making at least
a start toward putting the principle into practice.

Yet the quality of the new education continued to
vary widely. In some places—Massachusetts, for example, where Mann established the first American
state-supported teachers' college in 1839 and where
the first professional association of teachers was created in 1845—educators were usually capable men
and women, often highly trained, and with an emerging sense of themselves as career professionals. In
other areas, however, teachers were often barely literate, and limited funding for education restricted
opportunities severely. In the newly settled regions
of the West, where the white population was highly
dispersed, many children had no access to schools at
all. In the South, the entire black population was
barred from formal education (although approximately 10 percent of the slaves managed to achieve
literacy anyway), and only about a third of all white
children of school age actually enrolled in schools in
1860. In the North the percentage was 72 percent,
but even there, many students attended classes only
briefly and casually.

The interest in education (and, implicitly, in the
unleashing of individual talents that could result from
it) was visible too in the growing movement to educate American Indians in the antebellum period.
Some reformers held racist assumptions about the
unredeemability of nonwhite peoples; but even
many who accepted that idea about African Americans continued to believe that Indians could be "civilized" if only they could be taught the ways of the
white world. Efforts by missionaries and others to educate Native Americans and encourage them to assimilate were particularly prominent in such areas of

such as Massachusetts—had supported a limited version for many years. In the 1830s, however, interest
in public education grew rapidly. It was a reflection
of the new belief in the innate capacity of every person and of society's obligation to tap that capacity;
but it was a reflection, too, of the desire to expose
students to stable social values as a way to resist
instability.

The greatest of the educational reformers was
Horace Mann, the first secretary of the Massachusetts
Board of Education, which was established in 1837.
To Mann and his followers, education was the only
way to "counterwork this tendency to the domination of capital and the servility of labor." It was also
the only way to protect democracy, for an educated
electorate was essential to the workings of a free political system. Mann reorganized the Massachusetts
school system, lengthened the academic year (to six
months), doubled teachers' salaries (although he did
nothing to eliminate the large disparities between

the Far West as Oregon, where substantial numbers of whites were beginning to settle in the 1840s but where conflicts with the natives had not yet become acute. Nevertheless, the great majority of Native Americans remained outside the reach of educational reform, either by choice or by circumstance or both.

Despite limitations and inequities, the achievements of the school reformers were impressive by any standard. By the beginning of the Civil War, the United States had one of the highest literacy rates of any nation of the world: 94 percent of the population of the North and 83 percent of the white population of the South (58 percent of the total southern population).

The conflicting impulses that underlay the movement for school reform were visible in some of the different educational institutions that emerged. In New England, for example, the transcendentalist Bronson Alcott established a controversial experimental school in Concord that reflected his strong belief in the importance of complete self-realization. He urged children to learn from their own inner wisdom, not from the imposition of values by the larger society. Children were to teach themselves, rather than rely on teachers.

A similar emphasis on the potential of the individual sparked the creation of new institutions to help the handicapped, institutions that formed part of a great network of charitable activities known as the Benevolent Empire. Among them was the Perkins School for the Blind in Boston, the first such school in America. Nothing better exemplified the romantic impulse of the era than the belief of those who founded Perkins that even society's supposedly least-favored members—the blind and otherwise handicapped—could be helped to discover inner strength and wisdom. One teacher at the school expressed such attitudes when he described to the visiting English writer Charles Dickens the case of a blind, deaf, and speechless young woman who had been taught to communicate with the world. Although the "darkness and the silence of the tomb were around her," the teacher explained, "the immortal spirit which had been implanted within her could not die, nor be maimed nor mutilated." Gradually, she had learned to deal with the world around her, even to sew and knit, and most importantly, to speak through sign language. No longer was she a "dog or parrot." She was "an immortal spirit, eagerly seizing upon a new link of union with other spirits!"

More typical of educational reform, however, were efforts to use schools to impose a set of social values on children—the values that reformers believed were appropriate for their new, industrializing society. These values included thrift, order, discipline, punctuality, and respect for authority. Horace Mann, for example, spoke frequently of the role of public schools in extending democracy and expanding individual opportunity. But he spoke, too, of their role in creating social order. "The unrestrained passions of men are not only homicidal, but suicidal," he said, suggesting a philosophy very different from that of Alcott and other transcendentalists, who emphasized instinct and emotion. "Train up a child in the way he should go, and when he is old he will not depart from it."

Rehabilitation

Similar impulses helped create another powerful movement of reform: the creation of "asylums" (as they now began to be called) for criminals and for the mentally ill. On the one hand, in advocating prison and hospital reform, Americans were reacting to one of society's most glaring ills. Criminals of all kinds, debtors unable to pay their debts, the mentally ill, even senile paupers—all were crowded together indiscriminately into prisons and jails, which in some cases were literally holes in the ground; one jail in Connecticut was an abandoned mine shaft. Beginning in the 1820s, numerous states replaced these antiquated facilities with new "penitentiaries" and mental institutions designed to provide a proper environment for inmates. New York built the first penitentiary at Auburn in 1821. In Massachusetts, the reformer Dorothea Dix began a national movement for new methods of treating the mentally ill. Imprisonment of debtors and paupers gradually disappeared, as did such traditional practices as legal public hangings.

But the creation of "asylums" for social deviants was not simply an effort to curb the abuses of the old system. It was also an attempt to reform and rehabilitate the inmates. New forms of rigid prison discipline were designed to rid criminals of the "laxness" that had presumably led them astray. Solitary confinement and the imposition of silence on work crews (both adopted in Pennsylvania and New York in the 1820s) were meant to give prisoners opportunities to meditate on their wrongdoings. (Hence the term

■ **A PENNSYLVANIA ASYLUM**
In 1843 the United States had only thirteen mental hospitals. Most communities locked the mentally ill in jails with common criminals and often confined them to the worst quarters. By the 1880s, largely as a result of the work of the Massachusetts reformer Dorothea Dix, who worked tirelessly prodding states to build new facilities, there were more than 120 asylums for the insane—including this one in Berks County, Pennsylvania, which also served as an almshouse for the poor. *(Historical Society of Berks County, Reading, Pennsylvania)*

"penitentiary": a place for individuals to cultivate penitence.) Some reformers argued that the discipline of the asylum could serve as a model for other potentially disordered environments—for example, factories and schools. But penitentiaries and many mental hospitals soon fell victim to overcrowding, and the original reform ideal gradually faded. Many prisons ultimately degenerated into little more than warehouses for criminals, with scant emphasis on re-

habilitation. The idea, in its early stages, had been more optimistic.

The "asylum" movement was not, however, restricted only to criminals and people otherwise considered "unfit." The idea that a properly structured institution could prevent moral failure or rescue individuals from failure and despair helped spawn the creation of new orphanages designed as educational institutions. Such institutions, reformers believed, would provide an environment in which children who might otherwise be drawn into criminality could be trained to become useful citizens. Similar institutions emerged to provide homes for "friendless" women—women without families or homes, but otherwise respectable, for whom the institutions might provide an opportunity to build a new life. (Such homes were in part an effort to prevent such women from turning to prostitution.) There were also new facilities for the poor: almshouses and workhouses, which created closely supervised environments for those who had failed to work their way up in society. Such an environment, reformers believed, would train them to live more productive lives.

The Indian Reservation

Some of these same beliefs underlay the emergence in the 1840s and 1850s of a new "reform" approach to the problems of Native Americans: the idea of the reservation. For several decades, the dominant thrust of U.S. policy toward the Indians in areas of white settlement had been relocation. The principal motive behind relocation had always been a simple one: getting the tribes out of the way of white civilization. But among some whites there had also been another, if secondary, intent: to move the Indians to a place where they would be protected from whites and allowed to develop to a point where assimilation might be possible. Even Andrew Jackson, whose animus toward Indians was legendary, once described the removals as part of the nation's "moral duty . . . to protect and if possible to preserve and perpetuate the scattered remnants of the Indian race."

It was a small step from the idea of relocation to the idea of the reservation: the idea of creating an enclosed region in which Indians would live in isolation from white society. Again, the reservations served white economic purposes above all—moving Native Americans out of good lands that white settlers wanted. But they were also supposed to serve a reform purpose. Just as prisons, asylums, and orphanages would provide society with an opportunity to train and uplift misfits and unfortunates within white society, so the reservations might provide a way to undertake what one official called "the great work of regenerating the Indian race." Native Americans on reservations, reformers argued, would learn the ways of civilization in a protected setting and would

progress toward (in the words of an Indian commissioner of the time) "a point at which they will be able to compete with a white population, and to sustain themselves under any probable circumstances of contact or connexion with it."

The Rise of Feminism

The reform ferment of the antebellum period had a particular meaning for American women. They played central roles in a wide range of reform movements and a particularly important role in the movements on behalf of temperance and the abolition of slavery. In the process, they expressed their awareness of the problems that women themselves faced in a male-dominated society. The result was the creation of the first important American feminist movement, one that laid the groundwork for more than a century of agitation for women's rights.

Women in the 1830s and 1840s suffered not only all the traditional restrictions imposed on members of their sex by society, but a new set of barriers that had emerged from the transformation of the family into a unit in which women were expected to focus their energies on the home and the raising of children and leave the income-producing activities to their husbands. Many women who began to involve themselves in reform movements in the 1820s and 1830s came to look on such restrictions with rising resentment. Some began to defy them. Sarah and Angelina Grimké, sisters born in South Carolina who had become active and outspoken abolitionists, ignored attacks by men who claimed that their activities were inappropriate for their sex. "Men and women were CREATED EQUAL," they argued. "They are both moral and accountable beings, and whatever is right for man to do, is right for women to do." Other reformers—Catharine Beecher, Harriet Beecher Stowe (her sister), Lucretia Mott, Elizabeth Cady Stanton, and Dorothea Dix—also chafing at the restrictions placed on them by men, similarly pressed at the boundaries of "acceptable" female behavior.

Finally, in 1840, the patience of several women snapped. A group of American female delegates arrived at a world antislavery convention in London, only to be turned away by the men who controlled the proceedings. Angered at the rejection, several of the delegates—notably Lucretia Mott and Elizabeth Cady Stanton—became convinced that their first

7

FREDERICK DOUGLASS, AMY POST, CATHARINE STEBBINS, and ELIZABETH C. STANTON, and was unanimously adopted, as follows :

DECLARATION OF SENTIMENTS.

When, in the course of human events, it becomes necessary for one portion of the family of man to assume among the people of the earth a position different from that which they have hitherto occupied, but one to which the laws of nature and of nature's God entitle them, a decent respect to the opinions of mankind requires that they should declare the causes that impel them to such a course.

■ **THE DECLARATION OF SENTIMENTS**
Frederick Douglass joined female abolitionists in signing the famous "Declaration of Sentiments" that emerged out of the Women's Rights Convention at Seneca Falls, New York in 1848—one of the founding documents of American feminism. This introduction to the declaration makes clear how closely it was modeled on the 1776 Declaration of Independence. (*National Park Service, U.S. Department of the Interior*)

duty as reformers should now be to elevate the status of women. Over the next several years, Mott, Stanton, Susan B. Anthony, and others began drawing pointed parallels between the plight of women and the plight of slaves; and in 1848, they organized a convention in Seneca Falls, New York, to discuss the question of women's rights. Out of the meeting emerged a "Declaration of Sentiments and Resolutions" (patterned on the Declaration of Independence), which stated that "all men and women are created equal," that women no less than men have certain inalienable rights. Their most prominent demand was for the right to vote, thus launching a movement for woman suffrage that would continue until 1920. But the document was in many ways more important for its rejection of the whole notion that men and women should be assigned separate "spheres" in society.

It should not be surprising, perhaps, that many of the women involved in these feminist efforts were Quakers. Quakerism had long embraced the ideal of sexual equality and had tolerated, indeed encouraged, the emergence of women as preachers and community leaders. Women taught to expect the ab-

sence of gender-based restrictions in their own communities naturally resented the restrictions they encountered when they moved outside them. Quakers had also been among the leaders of the antislavery movement, and Quaker women played a leading role within those efforts.

Not all Quakers went so far as to advocate full sexual equality in American society; but enough Quaker women coalesced around such demands to cause a schism in the yearly meeting of the Society of Friends in Genesee, New York, in 1848. That dissident faction formed the core of the group that organized the Seneca Falls convention. Of the women who drafted the Declaration of Sentiments there, all but Elizabeth Cady Stanton were Quakers.

Progress toward feminist goals was limited in the antebellum years, but certain individual women did manage to break the social barriers to advancement. Elizabeth Blackwell, born in England, gained acceptance and fame as a physician. Her sister-in-law Antoinette Brown Blackwell became the first ordained woman minister in the United States; and another sister-in-law, Lucy Stone, took the revolutionary step of retaining her maiden name after marriage (as did the abolitionist Angelina Grimké). Stone became a successful and influential lecturer on women's rights. Emma Willard, founder of the Troy Female Seminary in 1821, and Catharine Beecher, who founded the Hartford Female Seminary in 1823, worked on behalf of women's education. Some women expressed their feminist sentiments even in their choice of costume—by wearing a distinctive style of dress (introduced in the 1850s) that combined a short skirt with full length pantalettes—an outfit that allowed freedom of movement without loss of modesty. Introduced by the famous actress Fanny Kemble, it came to be called the "bloomer" costume, after one of its advocates, Amelia Bloomer. (It provoked so much controversy that feminists finally abandoned it, convinced that the furor was drawing attention away from their more important demands.) Yet there was an irony in this rise of interest in the rights of women. Feminists benefited greatly from their association with other reform movements, most notably abolitionism; but they also suffered from them. For the demands of women were usually assigned—even by some women themselves—a secondary position to what many considered the far greater issue of the rights of slaves.

THE CRUSADE AGAINST SLAVERY

The antislavery movement was not new to the mid-nineteenth century. There had been efforts even before the Revolution to limit, and even eliminate, the institution. Those efforts had helped remove slavery from most of the North by the end of the eighteenth century. There were powerful antislavery movements in England and Europe that cried out forcefully against human bondage. But American antislavery sentiment remained relatively muted in the first decades after independence. Not until 1830 did it begin to gather the force that would ultimately enable it to overshadow virtually all other efforts at social reform.

Early Opposition to Slavery

In the early years of the nineteenth century, those who opposed slavery were, for the most part, a calm and genteel lot, expressing moral disapproval but engaging in few overt activities. To the extent that there was an organized antislavery movement, it centered on the concept of colonization—the effort to encourage the resettlement of African Americans in Africa or the Caribbean. In 1817, a group of prominent white Virginians organized the American Colonization Society (ACS), which worked carefully to challenge slavery without challenging property rights or southern sensibilities. The ACS proposed a gradual manumission (or freeing) of slaves, with masters receiving compensation through funds raised by private charity or appropriated by state legislatures. The Society would then transport liberated slaves out of the country and help them to establish a new society of their own elsewhere.

The ACS was not without impact. It received some funding from private donors, some from Congress, some from the legislatures of Virginia and Maryland. And it arranged the shipment of several groups of African Americans out of the country, some of them to the west coast of Africa where in 1830 they established the nation of Liberia (which became an independent republic in 1846—its capital, Monrovia, was named for the American president who had presided over the initial settlement).

But the ACS was in the end a negligible force. Neither private nor public funding was nearly enough to carry out the vast projects its supporters envisioned. In the space of a decade, they managed to "colonize" fewer slaves than were born in the United States in a month. No amount of funding, in fact, would have been enough; there were far too many black men and women in America in the nineteenth century to

■ **FUGITIVE SLAVE LAW CONVENTION** Abolitionists gathered in Cazenovia, New York in August 1850 to consider how to respond to the law recently passed by Congress requiring northern states to return fugitive slaves to their owners. Frederick Douglass is seated just to the left of the table in this photograph of some of the participants. The gathering was unusual among abolitionist gatherings in including substantial numbers of African Americans.
(Madison County Historical Society, Oneida, NY)

be transported to Africa by any conceivable program. And in any case, the ACS met resistance from African Americans themselves, many of whom were now three or more generations removed from Africa and had no wish to move to a land of which they knew almost nothing. (The Massachusetts free black Paul Cuffe had met similar resistance from members of his race in the early 1800s when he proposed a colonization scheme of his own.)

By 1830, in other words, the early antislavery movement was rapidly losing strength. Colonization was proving not to be a viable method of attacking the institution, particularly since the cotton boom in the Deep South was increasing the commitment of planters to their "peculiar" labor system. Those opposed to slavery had reached what appeared to be a dead end.

Garrison and Abolitionism

It was at this crucial juncture, with the antislavery movement seemingly on the verge of collapse, that a new figure emerged to transform it into a dramatically different phenomenon. He was William Lloyd Garrison. Born in Massachusetts in 1805, Garrison was an assistant in the 1820s to the New Jersey Quaker Benjamin Lundy, who published the leading antislavery newspaper of the time—the *Genius of Universal Emancipation*—in Baltimore. Garrison shared Lundy's abhorrence of slavery, but he soon grew impatient with his employer's moderate tone and mild proposals for reform. In 1831, therefore, he returned to Boston to found his own weekly newspaper, the *Liberator.*

Garrison's simple philosophy was genuinely revolutionary. Opponents of slavery, he said, should view the institution from the point of view of the black man, not the white slaveowner. They should not, as earlier reformers had done, talk about the evil influence of slavery on white society; they should talk about the damage the system did to blacks. And they should, therefore, reject "gradualism" and demand the immediate, unconditional, universal abolition of slavery. Garrison spoke with particular scorn about the advocates of colonization. They were not emancipationists, he argued; on the contrary, their real aim was to strengthen slavery by ridding the country of those African Americans who were already free. The true aim of foes of slavery, he insisted, must be to extend to African Americans all the rights of American citizenship. As startling as the drastic nature of his proposals was the relentless, uncompromising tone with which he promoted them. "I am aware," he wrote in the very first issue of the *Liberator,* "that many object to the severity of my language; but is there not cause for severity? I will be as harsh as truth, and as uncompromising as justice. . . . I am in earnest—I will not equivocate—I will not excuse—I will not retreat a single inch—AND I WILL BE HEARD."

Garrison soon attracted a large group of followers throughout the North, enough to enable him to found the New England Antislavery Society in 1832 and a year later, after a convention in Philadelphia, the American Antislavery Society. Membership in the new organizations mushroomed. By 1835, there were more than 400 chapters of the societies; by 1838, there were 1,350 chapters, with more than 250,000 members. Antislavery sentiment was developing a strength and assertiveness greater than at any point in the nation's history.

This success was in part a result of the similarity between abolitionism and other reform movements of the era. Like reformers committed to other causes, abolitionists were calling for an unleashing of the individual human spirit, the elimination of artificial social barriers to fulfillment. Who, after all, was more in need of assistance in realizing individual potential than enslaved men and women? Theodore Dwight Weld, a prominent New England abolitionist (and husband of Angelina Grimké), expressed this belief in an 1833 letter to Garrison. Slavery was a sin, Weld wrote, because "no condition of birth, no shade of color, no mere misfortune of circumstances can annul the birthright charter, which God has bequeathed to every being upon whom he has stamped his own image, by making him a free moral agent."

Black Abolitionists

Abolitionism had a particular appeal to the free blacks of the North, who in 1850 numbered about 250,000, mostly concentrated in cities. They lived in conditions of poverty and oppression often worse than those of their slave counterparts in the South. An English traveler who had visited both sections of the country wrote in 1854 that he was "utterly at a loss to imagine the source of that prejudice which subsists against [African Americans] in the Northern states, a prejudice unknown in the South, where the relations between the Africans and the European [white American] are so much more intimate." This confirmed an earlier observation by Tocqueville that "the prejudice which repels the Negroes seems to increase in proportion as they are emancipated." Northern blacks were often victimized by mob violence; they had virtually no access to education; they could vote in only a few states; and they were barred from all but the most menial of occupations. Most worked either as domestic servants or as sailors in the American merchant marine, and their wages were such that they lived, for the most part, in squalor. Some were kidnapped by whites and forced back into slavery.

For all their problems, however, northern blacks were aware of, and fiercely proud of, their freedom. And they remained acutely sensitive to the plight of those members of their race who remained in bondage, aware that their own position in society would remain precarious as long as slavery existed. Many in the 1830s came to support Garrison, to sub-

scribe to his newspaper, and to sell subscriptions to it in their own communities. Indeed, the majority of the *Liberator's* early subscribers were free blacks.

There were also important African American leaders who expressed the aspirations of their race. One of the most militant was David Walker, a free black from Boston, who in 1829 published a harsh pamphlet: *Walker's Appeal . . . to the Colored Citizens.* In it he declared: "America is more our country than it is the whites'—we have enriched it with our blood and tears." He warned: "The whites want slaves, and want us for their slaves, but some of them will curse the day they ever saw us." Slaves should, he declared, cut their masters' throats, should "kill, or be killed!"

Most black critics of slavery, however, were less violent in their rhetoric. One of them was Sojourner Truth, a freed black who after spending several years involved in a strange religious cult in upstate New York, emerged as a powerful and eloquent spokeswoman for the abolition of slavery. The greatest

■ **FREDERICK DOUGLASS**
Frederick Douglass, an escaped slave and active abolitionist, was one of the great orators of his age, widely admired among antislavery groups in the United States and Great Britain. So central did he become in the imaginations of antislavery men and women that he inspired tributes such as this "Fugitive's Song," published in Boston in 1845. *(Bettmann)*

African-American abolitionist of all—and one of the most electrifying orators of his time, black or white—was Frederick Douglass. Born a slave in Maryland, Douglass escaped to Massachusetts in 1838, became an outspoken leader of antislavery sentiment, and spent two years lecturing in England, where members of that country's vigorous antislavery movement lionized him. On his return to the United States in 1847, Douglass purchased his freedom from his Maryland owner and founded an antislavery newspaper, the *North Star,* in Rochester, New York. He achieved wide renown as well for his autobiography, *Narrative of the Life of Frederick Douglass* (1845), in which he presented a damning picture of slavery. Douglass demanded for African Americans not only freedom but full social and economic equality. Black abolitionists had been active for years before Douglass emerged as a leader of their cause; they had held their first national convention in 1830. But with Douglass's leadership, they became a more influential force; and they began, too, to forge alliances with white antislavery leaders such as Garrison.

Anti-Abolitionism

The rise of abolitionism was a powerful force, but it provoked a powerful opposition as well. Almost all white southerners, of course, looked on the movement with fear and contempt. But so too did many northern whites. Indeed, even in the North, abolitionists were never more than a small, dissenting minority.

To its critics, the abolitionist crusade was a dangerous and frightening threat to the existing social system. Some whites (including many substantial businessmen) warned that it would produce a destructive war between the sections. Others feared that it might lead to a great influx of free blacks into the North. The strident, outspoken movement seemed to many northern whites a sign of the disorienting social changes their society was experiencing, yet another threat to stability and order.

The result was an escalating wave of violence directed against abolitionists in the 1830s. When Prudence Crandall attempted to admit several African-American girls to her private school in Connecticut, local citizens had her arrested, threw filth into her well, and forced her to close down the school. A mob in Philadelphia attacked the abolitionist headquarters, the "Temple of Liberty," in 1834, burned it

to the ground, and began a bloody race riot. Another mob seized Garrison on the streets of Boston in 1835 and threatened to hang him. Authorities saved him from death only by locking him in jail. Elijah Lovejoy, the editor of an abolitionist newspaper in Alton, Illinois, was a repeated victim of mob violence. Three times angry whites invaded his offices and smashed his presses. Three times Lovejoy installed new machines and began publishing again. When a mob attacked his office a fourth time, late in 1837, he tried to defend his press. The attackers set fire to the building and, as Lovejoy fled, shot and killed him.

That so many men and women continued to embrace abolitionism in the face of such vicious opposition from within their own communities suggests much about the nature of the movement. Abolitionists were not people who made their political commitments lightly or casually. They were strong-willed, passionate crusaders, displaying enormous courage and moral strength, and displaying, too, at times a level of fervency that many of their contemporaries (and some later historians) found disturbing. Abolitionists were widely denounced, even by some who shared their aversion to slavery, as wild-eyed fanatics bent on social revolution. The anti-abolitionist mobs, in other words, were only the most violent expression of a sentiment that many other white Americans shared.

Abolitionism Divided

By the mid-1830s, the abolitionist crusade had become impossible to ignore. It had also begun to experience serious internal strains and divisions. One reason was the violence of the anti-abolitionists, which persuaded some members of the movement that a more moderate approach was necessary. Another reason was the growing radicalism of William Lloyd Garrison, who shocked even many of his own allies (including Frederick Douglass) by attacking not only slavery but the government itself. The Constitution, he said, was "a covenant with death and an agreement with hell." The nation's churches, he claimed, were bulwarks of slavery. In 1840, finally, Garrison precipitated a formal division within the American Antislavery Society by insisting that women, who had always been central to the organization's work, be permitted to participate in the movement on terms of full equality. He continued after 1840 to arouse controversy with new and even more radical stands: an extreme pacifism that rejected even defensive wars; opposition to all forms of coercion—not just slavery but prisons and asylums; and finally, in 1843, a call for northern disunion from the South. The nation could, he suggested, purge itself of the sin of slavery by expelling the slave states from the Union.

From 1840 on, therefore, abolitionism moved in many channels and spoke with many different voices. The Garrisonians remained influential, with their uncompromising moral stance. Others operated in more moderate ways, arguing that abolition could be accomplished only as the result of a long, patient, peaceful struggle—"immediate abolition gradually accomplished," as they called it. At first, such moderates depended on "moral suasion." They would appeal to the conscience of the slaveholders and convince them that their institution was sinful. When that produced no results, they turned to political action, seeking to induce the northern states and the federal government to aid the cause wherever possible. They joined the Garrisonians in helping runaway slaves find refuge in the North or in Canada through the so-called underground railroad (although their efforts were never as highly organized as the term suggests). They helped fund the legal battle over the Spanish slave vessel, *Amistad.* Africans destined for slavery in Cuba had seized the ship from its crew in 1839 and tried to return it to Africa. But the U.S. navy had seized the ship and held the Africans as pirates. But with abolitionist support, legal efforts to declare the Africans free (because the slave trade was by then illegal) finally reached the Supreme Court, where the antislavery position was argued by former president John Quincy Adams. The court declared the Africans free in 1841 and antislavery groups funded their passage back to Africa. Later, after the Supreme Court (in *Prigg* v. *Pennsylvania,* 1842) ruled that states need not aid in enforcing the 1793 law requiring the return of fugitive slaves to their owners, abolitionists secured the passage of "personal liberty laws" in several northern states. These laws forbade state officials to assist in the capture and return of runaways. Above all, the antislavery societies petitioned Congress to abolish slavery in places where the federal government had jurisdiction—in the territories and in the District of Columbia—and to prohibit the interstate slave trade. But political abolitionism had severe limits. Few members of the movement believed that Congress could constitutionally interfere with a "domestic" institution such as slavery within the individual states themselves.

Although the abolitionists engaged in pressure politics, they never actually formed a political party. Antislavery sentiment underlay the formation in 1840 of the Liberty Party, which offered the Kentucky antislavery leader James G. Birney as its presidential candidate. But this party, and its successors, never campaigned for outright abolition (an illustration of the important fact that "antislavery" and "abolitionism" were not always the same thing). They stood instead for "free soil," for keeping slavery out of the territories. Some free-soilers were concerned about the welfare of African Americans; others cared nothing about the slaves but simply wanted to keep the West a country for whites. Garrison dismissed free-soilism as "white-manism." But the free-soil position would ultimately do what abolitionism never could accomplish: attract the support of large numbers, even a majority, of the white population of the North.

The frustrations of political abolitionism drove some critics of slavery to embrace more drastic measures. A few began to advocate violence; it was a group of prominent abolitionists in New England, for example, who funneled money and arms to John Brown for his bloody uprisings in Kansas and Virginia (see pp. 451–452). Others attempted to arouse widespread public anger through propaganda. Abolitionist descriptions of slavery—for example, Theodore Dwight Weld and Angelina Grimké's *American Slavery as It Is: Testimony of a Thousand Witnesses* (1839)—presented what the authors claimed were careful, factual pictures of slavery, but what were in fact highly polemical, often wildly distorted images.

The most powerful document of abolitionist propaganda, however, was a work of fiction: Harriet Beecher Stowe's *Uncle Tom's Cabin.* It appeared first, in 1851–1852, as a serial in an antislavery weekly. Then, in 1852, it was published as a book. It rocked the nation. It sold more than 300,000 copies within a year of publication and was later issued again and again to become one of the most remarkable best-sellers in American history.

Stowe's novel emerged not just out of abolitionist politics, but also out of a popular tradition of sentimental novels written by, and largely for, women (see "Patterns of Popular Culture," pp. 422–423). Most such novels had no political message at all. But Stowe combined the emotional conventions of the sentimental novel with the political ideas of the abolition movement, and to sensational effect. Her novel, by embedding the antislavery message within a familiar and popular literary form, succeeded in

Significant Events

1817	American Colonization Society founded
1821	New York constructs first penitentiary
1823	Catharine Beecher founds Hartford Female Seminary
1825	Robert Owen founds New Harmony community in Indiana
1826	James Fenimore Cooper publishes *The Last of the Mohicans*
	American Society for the Promotion of Temperance founded
1829	David Walker publishes *Appeal . . . to the Colored Citizens*
1830	Joseph Smith publishes the Book of Mormon
	American Colonization Society helps create Liberia for emigrating American slaves
1831	William Lloyd Garrison begins publishing the *Liberator*
1833	American Antislavery Society founded
1834	Anti-abolitionist mob burns abolitionist headquarters in Philadelphia
1837	Horace Mann becomes first secretary of Massachusetts Board of Education
	Elijah Lovejoy killed by anti-abolitionist mob in Illinois
1840	Garrison demands admission of women into American Antislavery Society, precipitating schism
	Liberty Party formed
1841	Brook Farm founded in Roxbury, Massachusetts
1842	Supreme Court, in *Prigg* v. *Pennsylvania* rules states do not have to enforce return of fugitive slaves
1843	Amana Community founded
1844	Joseph Smith killed
1845	Frederick Douglass publishes autobiography
	Edgar Allan Poe publishes "The Raven"
	First professional teachers' association formed in Massachusetts
1847	Brook Farm dissolved
	Mormons found Salt Lake City
1848	Women's rights convention held at Seneca Falls, New York
	Oneida Community founded in New York
	Debate over women's rights causes schism in Society of Friends (Quakers)
1850	Nathaniel Hawthorne publishes *The Scarlet Letter*
1851	Herman Melville publishes *Moby Dick*
1852	Harriet Beecher Stowe publishes *Uncle Tom's Cabin*
1854	Henry David Thoreau publishes *Walden*
1855	Walt Whitman publishes *Leaves of Grass*

bringing the message of abolitionism to an enormous new audience—not only those who read the book but also those who watched dramatizations of its story by countless theater companies throughout the nation. The novel's emotional portrayal of good, kindly blacks victimized by a cruel system; of the loyal, trusting Uncle Tom; of the vicious overseer Simon Legree (described as a New Englander so as to prevent the book from seeming to be an attack on southern whites); of the escape of the beautiful Eliza; of the heart-rending death of Little Eva—all became a part of American popular legend. Reviled throughout the South, Stowe became a hero to many in the North. And in both regions, her novel helped to inflame sectional tensions to a new level of passion. Few books in American history have had so great an impact on the course of public events.

Even divided, therefore, abolitionism remained a powerful influence on the life of the nation. Only a relatively small number of people before the Civil War ever accepted the abolitionist position that slavery must be entirely eliminated in a single stroke. But the crusade that Garrison had launched, and that thousands of committed men and women kept alive for three decades, was a constant, visible reminder of how deeply the institution of slavery was dividing America.

SENTIMENTAL NOVELS

"America is now wholly given over to a damned mob of scribbling women," Nathaniel Hawthorne complained in 1855, "and I should have no chance of success while the public taste is occupied with their trash." Hawthorne was one of the leading novelists of his time; and what he was complaining about was the most popular form of fiction in mid-nineteenth-century America—not his own dark and serious works, but the "sentimental novel," a genre of literature written and read mostly by middle-class women.

In an age when affluent women occupied primarily domestic roles, and in which finding a favorable marriage was the most important thing many women could do to secure or improve their lots in life, the sentimental novel gave voice to both female hopes and female anxieties. The heroines in such books were almost always beautiful, and often vaguely helpless—requiring special attention from and protection by men, and using their looks and charms to get it. The plots of sentimental novels were usually filled with character-improving problems and domestic trials, but most of them ended with the heroine securely and happily married. They were phenomenally successful, as Hawthorne lamented. Many of them sold over 100,000 copies each—far more than almost any other books of the time—and the more celebrated of such novels were the subject of rapt discussion among middle-class women when they gathered for social occasions.

Sentimental heroines were not only beautiful. They were also endowed with specifically female qualities—"all the virtues," one novelist wrote, "that are founded in the sensibility of the heart: Pity, the attribute of angels, and friendship, the balm of life, delight to dwell in the female breast." Women were highly sensitive creatures, the sentimental writers believed, incapable of disguising their feelings, and subject to such emotional expressions as fainting, mysterious illnesses, trances, and, of course, tears—

■ **"A SAD STORY"**
This nineteenth-century engraving shows a reader gazing sadly and wistfully away from a popular sentimental novel of the time. The magazine that published this picture wrote a disapproving story to accompany it, which began: "The young girl whose tender heart is so powerfully stirred with imaginative sorrow by the reading of some fictitious tale of distress might in our judgment have been provided by wise parents with a more wholesome form of entertainment." *(Culver Pictures)*

things rarely expected of men. But they were also capable of a kind of nurturing love and natural sincerity that was hard to find in the predominantly male public world. In Susan Warner's *The Wide, Wide World* (1850), for example, the heroine, a young girl named Ellen Montgomery, finds herself suddenly thrust into the "wide, wide world" of male competition after her father loses his fortune. She is unable to adapt to it, but she is saved in the end when she is taken in by wealthy relatives, who will undoubtedly prepare her for a successful marriage. They restore to her the security and comfort to which she had been born and without which she seemed unable to thrive.

Sentimental novels created idealized images of conventional female success. In doing so, they performed something of the same function that romance novels of the twentieth century perform today (although without the overt sexuality that is so central to modern romances). They accepted uncritically the popular assumptions about women's special needs and desires, and they offered stirring tales of how women satisfied them.

But sentimental novels did not stop with romanticized images of female fulfillment through protection and marriage. They hinted as well at the increasing role of women in movements of social and moral reform. Many such books portrayed women dealing with problems of drunkenness, poverty, irreligion, and prostitution—and using their highly developed female sensibilities to help other women escape from their troubles. Women were particularly suitable for such reform work, the writers implied, because they were specially gifted at helping and nurturing others.

The most famous sentimental novelist of her day was Harriet Beecher Stowe. Most of her books— *The Minister's Wooing, My Wife and I, We and Our Neighbors,* and others—portrayed the travails and ultimate triumphs of women as they became wives, mothers, and hostesses. But Stowe was and remains best known for her 1852 antislavery novel *Uncle Tom's Cabin,* one of the most influential books ever published in America. As a story about slavery, and about an aging black man—Uncle Tom—who is unfailingly submissive to his white masters, it is in many ways very different from her other novels. But *Uncle Tom's Cabin* is a sentimental novel, too. Stowe's critique of slavery is based on her belief in the importance of domestic values and family security. Slavery's violation of those values, and its denial of that security, is what made it so abhorrent to her. The simple, decent Uncle Tom faces many of the same dilemmas that the simple, decent female heroines of other sentimental novels encounter in their struggles to find security and tranquility in their lives.

■ **UNCLE TOM'S CABIN**
Uncle Tom's Cabin did much to inflame public opinion in both the North and the South in the last years before the Civil War. When Abraham Lincoln was introduced to Stowe once in the White House, he reportedly said to her: "So you are the little lady that has brought this great war." At the time, however, Stowe was equally well known as one of the most successful American writers of sentimental novels. *(Bettmann)*

Women were emerging from their domestic sphere in at least one other important way in the mid-nineteenth century. They were becoming consumers of the expanding products of America's industrializing economy. The female characters in sentimental novels, therefore, searched not just for love, security, and social justice. They also searched for luxury, and for the pleasure of buying some favored item. Susan Warner illustrated this aspect of the culture of the sentimental novel—and the desires of the women who read them—in *The Wide, Wide World,* in her description of the young Ellen Montgomery in an elegant bookstore, buying a Bible: "Such beautiful Bibles she had never seen; she pored in ecstasy over their varieties of type and binding, and was very evidently in love with them all."

⌒

CONCLUSION

The rapidly changing society of antebellum America produced a remarkable upsurge of cultural nationalism and reform. Writers, artists, intellectuals, and others drew heavily from new European notions of personal liberation—a set of ideas often known as romanticism. But they also strove to create a truly American culture, unbeholden to European models. The literary and artistic life of the nation expressed the rising interest in personal liberation—in giving individuals the freedom to explore their own souls and to find in nature a full expression of their divinity. It also called attention to some of the nation's glaring social problems.

Reformers, too, made use of the romantic belief in the divinity of the individual. They flocked to religious revivals, worked on behalf of such "moral" reforms as temperance, supported education, and stirred the beginnings of feminism. Above all, in the North, they rallied against slavery. Out of this growing antislavery movement emerged a new and powerful phenomenon: abolitionism, which rejected moderate reform and insisted on nothing less than immediate emancipation of the slaves. The abolitionist crusade galvanized much of the North. It also contributed greatly to the growing schism between North and South.

⌒

FOR FURTHER REFERENCE

Suggested Readings   David Reynolds, *Walt Whitman's America* (1995) is both a cultural biography of Whitman and an evocation of the society Whitman celebrated. Leo Marx, *The Machine in the Garden* (1964) is an influential study of the tension between technological progress and the veneration of nature in the era of early industrialization. Paul Johnson, *A Shopkeeper's Millennium: Society and Revivals in Rochester, New York, 1815-1837* (1978) links revivalism in the "Burnt-Over District" to changing patterns of work and social control. Nancy F. Cott, *The Bonds of Womanhood: "Woman's Sphere" in New England, 1780-1835* (1977) argues that nineteenth-century feminism emerged from the separation of home and work in the early nineteenth century. James Brewer Stewart, *Holy Warriors* (1976) is a good summary of the trajectory of abolitionism from the American Revolution through the emancipation. Ronald G. Walters, *The Antislavery Appeal: American Abolitionists After 1830* (1976) emphasizes the religious motivations of antebellum abolitionism.

Films   (The best source for information on how to find these and other films is *Bowker's Complete Video Directory*—3 volumes.) *The American Story, No. 9: Social Reform* (1985)documents attempts by reformers to eliminate the disruptive effects of industrialization and to abolish slavery. *Walt Whitman: Poet for a New Age* (1971) reveals Whitman's faith in democracy, as well as his mystical ideas about life and death, personality, and love. *Thoreau's Walden* re-creates the two-year period

when Henry David Thoreau lived alone at Walden Pond. *The Second Great Awakening* (1994) illuminates the resurgence of religious reform in the early nineteenth century. *Reforming the Republic* weaves together the urges for religious revivalism and reform in antebellum America. *The Abolitionists* (1987) discusses abolitionists such as Frederick Douglass and William Garrison. *Frederick Douglass—An American Life* (1985) explores the life and times of one of the most famous fugitive slaves and black abolitionists. *Rebel Hearts* (1995) is a lively portrait of Sarah and Angelina Grimké, two important white women abolitionists. *Black Americans of Achievement, No. 8: Sojourner Truth,* and *Black Americans of Achievement, No. 9: Harriet Tubman* explore the lives of two very important black women abolitionists.

Internet Resources   (For up-to-date URL addresses and links to these and other websites, consult the McGraw-Hill history site at http://www.mhhe.com/socscience/history/am-hist.mhtml.) *Poems by Ralph Waldo Emerson* and *Nathaniel Hawthorne* provide texts and criticism of the work of these two major writers. *19th Century American Women Writers Web* includes an electronic library of poems and fiction by women writers. *America's First Look into the Camera: Daguerreotype Portraits and Views, 1842-1862* contains 600 photographs dating from 1842 to 1862, many of them portraits by Mathew Brady and his assistants. *A Good Day's Sport* provides Currier & Ives images of fishing, hunting, and horse racing in antebellum America. *Women's Studies: Manuscript Diaries* contains scanned images of American women's diaries from the 1850s to the 1940s. *Votes for Women: Selections from the National American Woman Suffrage Association Collection, 1848–1921* provides searchable books and pamphlets, primarily concerning women's suffrage but also touching on other reform movements. *Taking the Train to Freedom* is a National Park Service study of the underground railroad.

BIBLIOGRAPHY

Antebellum Literature and Popular Culture   Nina Baym, *Woman's Fiction: A Guide to Novels by and About Women in America, 1820–1870* (1978). Carl Bode, *The American Lyceum: Town Meeting of the Mind* (1968). Van Wyck Brooks, *The Flowering of New England, 1815–1865* (1936). Lawrence Buell, *The Environmental Imagination: Thoreau, Nature Writing, and the Formation of American Culture* (1995). Vincent Buranelli, *Edgar Allan Poe* (1977). Mary Kupiec Cayton, *Emerson's Emergence: Self and Society in the Transformation of New England, 1800–1845* (1989). Ann Douglas, *The Feminization of American Culture* (1977). David Grimsted, *Melodrama Unveiled: American Theater and Culture, 1800–1850* (1968). Neil Harris, *Humbug: The Art of P. T. Barnum* (1973). Mary Kelley, *The Limits of Sisterhood* (1988). David Levin, *History as Romantic Art: Bancroft, Prescott, Motley, and Parkman* (1963). Eric Lott, *Love and Theft: Blackface Minstrelsy and the American Working Class* (1993). Kenneth S. Lynn, *Mark Twain and Southwestern Humor* (1972). F. O. Matthiessen, *American Renaissance* (1941). Henry F. May, *The Enlightenment in America* (1976). James Mellow, *Nathaniel Hawthorne in His Time* (1980). Vernon L. Parrington, *The Romantic Revolution in America, 1800–1860* (1927). David Reynolds, *Beneath the American Renaissance: The Subversive Imagination in the Age of Emerson and Melville* (1988). Henry Nash Smith, *Democracy and the Novel: Popular Resistance to Classic American Writers* (1978). Robert C. Toll, *Blacking Up: The Minstrel Show in Nineteenth-Century America* (1974). Larzer Ziff, *Literary Democracy: The Declaration of Cultural Independence in America* (1981).

Social Philosophies and Utopias   Robert H. Abzug, *Cosmos Crumbling: American Reform and the Religious Imagination* (1994). Gay Wilson Allen, *Waldo Emerson* (1981). P. F. Boller, Jr., *American Transcendentalism, 1830–1860: An Intellectual Inquiry* (1974). Priscilla Brewer, *Shaker Communities and Shaker Lives* (1986). John L. Brooke, *The Refiner's Fire: The Making of Mormon Cosmology, 1644–1844* (1994). Maren L. Carden, *Oneida: Utopian Community to Modern Corporation* (1971). Henry Steele Commager, *Theodore Parker* (1936). Paul Conkin, *The Uneasy Center: Reformed Christianity in Antebellum America* (1995). Walter Conser, Jr., *God and the Natural World: Religion and Science in Antebellum America* (1993). Michael Fellman, *The Unbounded Frame: Freedom and Community in Nineteenth-Century America* (1973). Lawrence Foster, *Religion and Sexuality: The Shakers, the Mormons, and the Oneida Community* (1984); *Women, Family, and Utopia: Communal Experiments of the Shakers, the Oneida Community, and the Mormons* (1991). J. F. C. Harrison, *Quest for the New Moral World: Robert Owen and the Owenites in Britain and America* (1969). Carol Kolmerten, *Women in Utopia* (1990). Richard Lebeaux, *Young Man Thoreau* (1977). Perry Miller, *The Transcendentalists* (1950); *The Life of the Mind in America: From the Revolution to the Civil War* (1966). Raymond Muncy, *Sex and Marriage in Utopian Communities* (1973). Robert Richardson, Jr., *Emerson* (1995). Ann Rose, *Transcendentalism as a Social Movement* (1981). Arthur M. Schlesinger, Jr., *Orestes A. Brownson: A Pilgrim's Progress* (1939). Wallace Stegner, *The Gathering of Zion* (1964). R. D. Thomas, *The Man Who Would Be Perfect: John Humphrey Noyes and the Utopian Impulse* (1977).

Antebellum Religion and Reform   Jon Butler, *Awash in a Sea of Faith: Christianizing the American People* (1990). Estelle Freedman, *Their Sister's Keepers: Women's Prison Reform in America, 1830–1930* (1981). Gerald W. Grob, *Mental Institutions in America: Social Policy to 1875* (1973). Nathan O. Hatch, *The Democratization of American Christianity* (1989). W. David Lewis, *From Newgate to Dannemora: The Rise of the Penitentiary* (1965). Robert Mennel, *Thorns and Thistles* (1973). William G. McLoughlin, *Revivals, Awakenings, and Reform* (1978). Stephen L. Nissenbaum, *Sex, Diet, and Debility in Jacksonian America: Sylvester Graham and Health Reform* (1980). Richard Rabinowitz, *The Spiritual Self in Everyday Life* (1989). W. J. Rorabaugh, *The Alcoholic Republic* (1979). Charles Rosenberg, *The Cholera Years: The United States in 1832, 1849, and 1866* (1962). David Rothman, *The Discovery of the Asylum* (1971). Alice Felt Tyler, *Freedom's Ferment* (1944). Ian R. Tyrrell, *Sobering Up: From Temperance to Prohibition in Antebellum America, 1800–1860* (1979). Ronald G. Walters, *American Reformers, 1815–1860* (1978).

Education   Carl Bode, *The American Lyceum* (1956). Lawrence A. Cremin, *American Education: The National Experience* (1980). Michael Katz, *The Irony of Early School Reform* (1968). Jonathan Messerli, *Horace Mann* (1972). Stanley K. Schultz, *The Culture Factory: Boston's Public Schools, 1789–1860* (1973). Robert Trennert, *Alternatives to Extinction: Federal Indian Policy and the Beginning of the Reservation System* (1975).

Feminism   Margaret H. Bacon, *Mothers of Feminism: The Story of Quaker Women in America* (1986). Lois Banner, *Elizabeth Cady Stanton* (1980). Kathleen Barry, *Susan B. Anthony* (1988). Elizabeth Ann Bartlett, *Liberty, Equality, Sorority* (1994). Barbara J. Berg, *The Remembered Gate: Origins of American Feminism, The Woman and the City, 1800–1860* (1977). Janet Farrell Brodie, *Contraception and Abortion in Nineteenth-Century America* (1994). Carl Degler, *At Odds, Women and the Family in America from the Revolution to the Present* (1980). Ellen C. Du Bois, *Feminism and Suffrage: The Emergence of an Independent Woman's Movement in America, 1848–1860* (1978). Barbara Leslie Epstein, *The Politics of Domesticity: Women, Evangelism, and Temperance in Nineteenth-Century America* (1981). Eleanor Flexner, *Century of Struggle,* rev. ed. (1975). Lori D. Ginzberg, *Women and the Work of Benevolence: Morality, Politics, and Class in the Nineteenth-Century United States* (1990). Elisabeth Griffith, *In Her Own Right: The Life of Elizabeth Cady Stanton* (1984). Nancy A. Hewitt, *Women's Activism and Social Change: Rochester, New York, 1822–1872* (1988). Carolyn Karcher, *The First Woman in the Republic: A Cultural Biography of Lydia Maria Child* (1994). William L. O'Neill, *Everyone Was Brave: The Rise and Fall of Feminism in the United States* (1970). Anne Firor Scott, *Natural Allies: Women's Associations in American History* (1991). Kathryn K. Sklar, *Catharine Beecher: A Study in American Domesticity* (1973). Jean Fagan Yellin, ed., *The Abolitionist Sisterhood: Women's Political Culture in Antebellum America* (1994).

Antislavery and Abolitionism   Richard H. Abbott, *Cotton and Capital: Boston Businessmen and Antislavery Reform, 1854–1868* (1991). Robert Abzug, *Theodore Dwight Weld* (1980). Irving Bartlett, *Wendell Phillips* (1962). Arna Bontemps, *Free at Last: The Life of Frederick Douglass* (1971). David Brion Davis, *The Problem of Slavery in the Age of Revolution, 1770–1823* (1975). M. L. Dillon, *The Abolitionists* (1974). Martin Duberman, ed., *The Anti-Slavery Vanguard* (1965). Louis Filler, *The Crusade Against Slavery* (1960). George Frederickson, *The Black Image in the White Mind: The Debate on Afro-American Character and Destiny, 1817–1914* (1971). Lawrence J. Friedman, *Gregarious Saints: Self and Community in American Abolitionism* (1982). Stanley Harrold, *The Abolitionists and the South, 1831–1861* (1995). Blanche G. Hersh, *Slavery of Sex: Feminist Abolitionists in America* (1978). Nathan Huggins, *Slave and Citizen* (1980). Aileen Kraditor, *Means and Ends in American Abolitionism: Garrison and His Critics on Strategy and Tactics, 1834–1850* (1967). Alan Kraut, ed., *Crusaders and Compromisers* (1983). Gerda Lerner, *The Grimké Sisters of South Carolina: Rebels Against Slavery* (1967). William S. McFeely, *Frederick Douglass* (1991). John McKivigan, *The War Against Proslavery Religion* (1984). William Lee Miller, *Arguing About Slavery: The Great Battle in the United States Congress* (1996). William H. Pease and Jane H. Pease, *They Would Be Free* (1974). Lewis Perry, *Radical Abolitionism: Anarchy and the Government of God in Antislavery Thought* (1973). Lewis Perry and Michael Fellman, eds., *Antislavery Reconsidered: New Perspectives on the Abolitionists* (1979). Benjamin Quarles, *Black Abolitionists* (1969). Leonard L. Richards, *"Gentlemen of Property and Standing": Anti-Abolition Mobs in Jacksonian America* (1970). Gerald Sorin, *Abolitionism* (1972); *Wendell Phillips* (1987). John L. Thomas, *The Liberator* (1963). Peter F. Walker, *Moral Choices: Memory, Desire, and Imagination in Nineteenth Century Abolition* (1978). Bertram Wyatt-Brown, *Lewis Tappan and the Evangelical War Against Slavery* (1969). Jean Fagan Yellin, *The Antislavery Feminists in American Culture* (1989).

KANSAS A FREE STATE.

Squatter Sovereignty
VINDICATED!

NO WHITE
SLAVERY!

The Squatters of Kansas who are favora-ble to FREEDOM OF SPEECH on all subjects which interest them, and an un-muzzled PRESS: who are determined to do their own THINKING and VOTING independent of FOREIGN DICTATION, are requested to assemble in

MASS MEETING

at the time and places following to wit:

The following speakers will be in attendance, who will address you on the important questions now before the people of Kansas.

At Fish's Store	Monday	September 24th		Lane	Saturday Oct	6th
Fort Scott	Friday	28th		Scott's Town	September 29th	
Stockton's Store, Little Sugar Creek	Sat	29th		Hampden	Monday Oct	1st
Elijah Tucker's, Big	Monday Oct	1st		Neosho, at R. Smith's Store	Tuesday	2d
Osawatomie,	Thursday	2d		Columbia	Wednesday	3d
Mr. Partridge's Pottawatomie Creek	Wed	3d		Palmyra	Friday	5th
Baptist Posta	Thursday	4th		Bloomer	Saturday	6th
Springfield	Friday	5th				

DR. CHAS. ROBINSON,

J. A. Wakefield, C. K. Holliday, M. F. Conway,

W. K. Vail, J. L. Speer, W. A. Ela, Josiah Miller, O. C. Brown, J. K. Goodin, Doct. Gilpatrick, Revs. Mr. Tuton and J. E. Stewart, C. A. Foster, J. P. Fox, H. Bronson, G. W. Brown, A. H. Malley and others.

TURN OUT AND HEAR THEM!

Plakat aus den Parteikämpfen im Kansasgebiete

Chapter Thirteen

THE IMPENDING CRISIS

Until the 1840s, the tensions between the North and the South remained relatively contained. Had no new sectional controversies arisen, the United States might have avoided a civil war and the two sections might have resolved their differences peaceably over time. But new controversies did arise, all of them centered on slavery. From the North came the strident and increasingly powerful abolitionist movement, which kept the issue alive in the public mind and increased sectional animosities. From the South came an increasingly belligerent defense of slavery and a rising insistence on its expansion.

But it was the West that brought these differences to a head most forcefully. Ironically, the vigorous nationalism that was in some ways helping to keep the United States together was also producing a desire for territorial expansion that would tear the nation apart. As the nation annexed extensive new lands—Texas, the Southwest territories, California, Oregon country, and others—the question began to arise: What would be the status of slavery in the territories? By the late 1840s, differences over this question had created a dangerous and persistent crisis. And by the end of the 1850s, that crisis had produced such bitterness, such anger, and such despair on both sides that it could no longer be contained.

LOOKING WESTWARD

The United States acquired more than a million square miles of new territory in the 1840s—the greatest wave of expansion since the Louisiana Purchase nearly forty years before. By the end of the decade, the nation possessed all the territory of the present-day United States except Alaska, Hawaii, and a few relatively small areas acquired later through border adjustments. Many factors accounted for this great new wave of expansion, the most important of which were the hopes and ambitions of the many thousands of Americans who moved into or invested in these new territories. Advocates of expansion justified their goals with a carefully articulated set of ideas—an ideology known as "Manifest Destiny,"

■ **"BLEEDING KANSAS"**
The battle over the fate of slavery in Kansas was one of the most turbulent events of the 1850s. This 1855 poster invites antislavery forces to a meeting to protest the actions of the "bogus" pro-slavery territorial legislature, which had passed laws that, among other things, made it illegal to speak or write against slavery. "Squatter sovereignty" was another term for "popular sovereignty," the doctrine that gave residents of a prospective state the power to decide the fate of slavery there.
(Bettmann)

which itself became one of the factors driving white Americans to look to the West.

Manifest Destiny

Manifest Destiny reflected both the burgeoning pride that characterized American nationalism in the mid-nineteenth century and the idealistic vision of social perfection that fueled so much of the reform energy of the time. It rested on the idea that America was destined—by God and by history—to expand its boundaries over a vast area, an area that included, but was not necessarily restricted to, the continent of North America. American expansion was not selfish, its advocates insisted; it was an altruistic attempt to extend American liberty to new realms. John L. O'Sullivan, the influential Democratic editor who gave the movement its name, wrote in 1845 that the American claim to new territory

> . . . is by the right of our manifest destiny to overspread and to possess the whole of the continent which Providence has given us for the development of the great experiment of liberty and federative self government entrusted to us. It is a right such as that of the tree to the space of air and earth suitable for the full expansion of its principle and destiny of growth.

Manifest Destiny represented more than pride in the nation's political system. Running throughout many of the arguments for expansion was an explicitly racial justification. Throughout the 1840s, many Americans defended the idea of westward expansion by citing the superiority of the "American race"—white people of northern European origins. The peoples of the territories into which American civilization was destined to spread, these advocates of Manifest Destiny argued, could not be absorbed into the republican system. The Indians, the Mexicans, and others in the western regions were racially unfit to be part of an "American" community. Westward expansion was, therefore, a movement to spread both a political system and a racially-defined society.

By the 1840s, the idea of Manifest Destiny had spread throughout the nation, publicized by the new "penny press" (inexpensive newspapers aimed at a mass audience), and fanned by the rhetoric of nationalist politicians. Advocates of Manifest Destiny disagreed, however, about how far and by what means the nation should expand. Some had relatively limited territorial goals; others envisioned a vast new "empire of liberty" that would include Canada, Mexico, Caribbean and Pacific islands, and ultimately, a few dreamed, much of the rest of the world. Some believed America should use force to achieve its expansionist goals, while others felt that the nation should expand peacefully or not at all.

Not everyone embraced the idea of Manifest Destiny. Henry Clay and other prominent politicians feared, correctly as it turned out, that territorial expansion would reopen the painful controversy over slavery and threaten the stability of the Union. But their voices were barely audible over the clamor of enthusiasm for expansion in the 1840s, which began with the issues of Texas and Oregon.

Americans in Texas

The United States had once claimed Texas—which until the 1830s was part of the Republic of Mexico—as a part of the Louisiana Purchase, but it had renounced the claim in 1819. Twice thereafter the United States had offered to buy Texas, only to meet with indignant Mexican refusals.

But in the early 1820s, the Mexican government launched an ill-advised experiment that would eventually cause it to lose its great northern province: it encouraged American immigration into Texas. The Mexicans hoped to strengthen the economy of the territory and increase their own tax revenues. They also liked the idea of the Americans sitting between Mexican settlement and the large and sometimes militant Indian tribes to the north. They convinced themselves, too, that settlers in Texas would serve as an effective buffer against United States expansion into the region; the Americans, they thought, would soon become loyal to the Mexican government. An 1824 colonization law designed to attract American settlers promised the newcomers cheap land and a four-year exemption from taxes.

Thousands of Americans, attracted by the rich soil in Texas, took advantage of Mexico's welcome. Since much of the available land was suitable for growing cotton, the great majority of the immigrants were southerners, many of whom brought slaves with them. By 1830, there were about 7,000 Americans living in Texas, more than twice the number of Mexicans there.

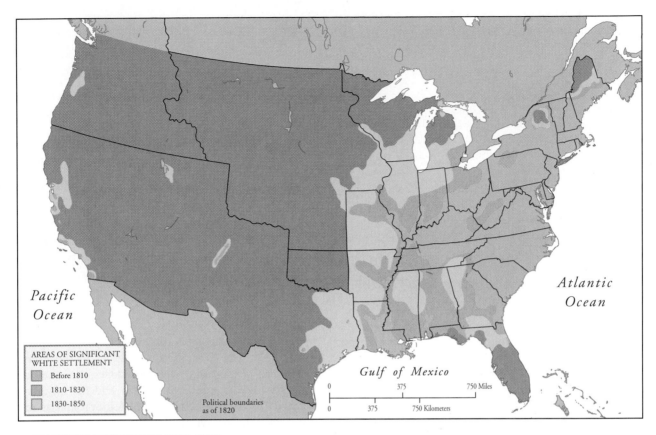

AREAS OF SIGNIFICANT
WHITE SETTLEMENT

Before 1810

1810–1830

1830–1850

*Pacific
Ocean*

*Atlantic
Ocean*

Gulf of Mexico

Political boundaries
as of 1820

0   375   750 Miles

0   375   750 Kilometers

■ **EXPANDING SETTLEMENT, 1810–1850**
In the 1840s, the United States acquired more than a million square miles of new territory, the greatest wave of expansion since the
Louisiana Purchase. White American settlers moved into the regions wrested from Indian nations in the removal battles of the 1830s and
poured into new territories west of the Mississippi, including Missouri and Texas. Advocates of expansion justified their goals with an
ideology known as "Manifest Destiny."

■ **THE LONE STAR FLAG**
Almost from the moment Texas won its independence from
Mexico in 1836, it sought admission to the United States as a
state. Controversies over the status of slavery in the
territories prevented its admission until 1845, and so for nine
years it was an independent republic. The tattered banner
pictured here was one of the republic's original flags.
*(Frank Lerner, from Showers-Brown Collection, Star of the Republic
Museum)*

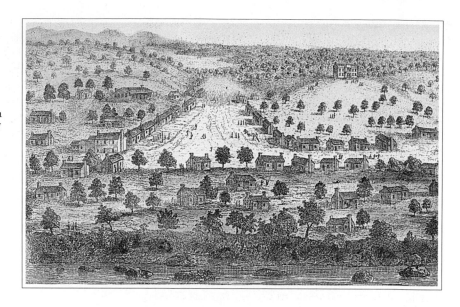

The Mexican government offered land directly to immigrants, but most of the settlers came to Texas through the efforts of American intermediaries, who received sizable land grants from Mexico in return for promising to bring settlers into the region. The most successful of them was Stephen F. Austin, a young immigrant from Missouri who had established the first legal American settlement in Texas in 1822. Austin and other intermediaries were effective in recruiting American immigrants to Texas, but they also created centers of power in the region that competed with the Mexican government. In 1826, one of these American intermediaries led a revolt to establish Texas as an independent nation (which he proposed calling Fredonia.) The Mexicans quickly crushed the revolt and, four years later, passed new laws barring any further American immigration into the region. They were too late. Americans kept flowing into the territory, and in 1833 Mexico dropped the futile immigration ban. By 1835 over 30,000 Americans, white and black, had settled in Texas.

Mexican-American Tensions

Friction between the American settlers and the Mexican government continued to grow. It arose, in part, from the continuing cultural and economic ties of the immigrants to the United States and their desire to create stronger bonds with their former home. It arose, too, from their desire to legalize slavery, which the Mexican government had made illegal in Texas (as it was in Mexico) in 1830. But the Americans were divided over how to address their unhappiness with Mexican rule. Austin and his followers wanted to reach a peaceful settlement that would give Texas more autonomy within the Mexican republic. Others wanted to fight for independence.

In the mid-1830s, instability in Mexico itself drove General Antonio Lopez de Santa Anna to seize power as a dictator and impose a new, more conservative and autocratic regime on the nation and its territories. A new law increased the powers of the national government of Mexico at the expense of the state governments, a measure that Texans from the United States assumed Santa Anna was aiming specifically at them. The Mexicans even imprisoned Stephen Austin in Mexico City for a time, claiming that he was encouraging revolts among his fellow Americans in Texas. Sporadic fighting between Americans and Mexicans in Texas began in 1835 and escalated as the Mexican government sent more troops into the territory. In 1836, the American settlers defiantly proclaimed their independence from Mexico.

Santa Anna led a large army into Texas, where the American settlers were having enormous difficulties organizing an effective defense of their new "nation." Several different factions claimed to be the legitimate government of Texas, and American soldiers could not even agree on who their commanders were. Mexican forces annihilated an American garrison at the Alamo mission in San Antonio after a famous, if futile, defense by a group of Texas "patriots," a group that included, among others, the renowned frontiersman and former Tennessee congressman Davy Crockett. Another garrison at Goliad suffered substantially the same fate when the Mexicans executed most of the force after it had surrendered. By the end of 1836, the rebellion appeared to have collapsed. Americans were fleeing east toward Louisiana to escape Santa Anna's army.

But General Sam Houston managed to keep a small force together. And on April 23, 1836, at the Battle of San Jacinto (near the present-day city of Houston), he defeated the Mexican army and took Santa Anna prisoner. American troops then killed many of the Mexican soldiers in retribution for the executions at Goliad. Santa Anna, under pressure from his captors, signed a treaty giving Texas independence. And while the Mexican government repudiated the treaty, there were no further military efforts to win Texas back.

A number of Mexican residents of Texas *(Tejanos)* had fought with the Americans in the revolution. But soon after Texas won its independence, their positions grew difficult. The Americans did not trust them, fearing that they were agents of the Mexican government, and in effect drove many of them out of the new republic. Most of those who stayed had to settle for a politically and economically subordinate status within the fledgling nation.

Above all, American Texans hoped for annexation by the United States. One of the first acts of the new president of Texas, Sam Houston, was to send a delegation to Washington with an offer to join the Union. There were supporters of expansion in the United States who welcomed these overtures; indeed, expansionists in the United States had been supporting and encouraging the revolt against Mexico for years. But there was also opposition. Many American northerners opposed acquiring a large new slave territory, and others opposed increasing the southern votes in Congress and in the electoral college. Unfortunately for the Texans, one of the opponents was President Jackson, who feared annexation might cause a dangerous sectional controversy and even a war with Mexico. He therefore did not support annexation and even delayed recognizing the new republic until 1837. Presidents Martin Van Buren and William Henry Harrison also refrained from pressing the issue during their terms of office.

Spurned by the United States, Texas cast out on its own. Its leaders sought money and support from Europe. Some of them dreamed of creating a vast southwestern nation, stretching to the Pacific, that would rival the United States—a dream that appealed to European nations eager to counter the growing power of America. England and France quickly recognized and concluded trade treaties with Texas. In response, President Tyler persuaded Texas to apply for statehood again in 1844. But when Secretary of State Calhoun presented an annexation treaty to Congress as if its only purpose were to extend slavery, northern senators rebelled and defeated it. Rejection of the treaty only spurred advocates of Manifest Destiny to greater efforts toward their goal. The Texas question quickly became the central issue in the election of 1844.

Oregon

Control of what was known as Oregon country, in the Pacific Northwest, was another major political issue in the 1840s. Its half-million square miles included the present states of Oregon, Washington, and Idaho, parts of Montana and Wyoming, and half of British Columbia. Both Britain and the United States claimed sovereignty in the region—the British on the basis of explorations in the 1790s by George Vancouver, a naval officer; the Americans on the basis of simultaneous claims by Robert Gray, a fur trader. Unable to resolve their conflicting claims diplomatically, they agreed in an 1818 treaty to allow citizens of each country equal access to the territory. This arrangement, known as "joint occupation," continued for twenty years.

In fact, by the time of the treaty neither Britain nor the United States had established much of a presence in Oregon country. White settlement in the region consisted largely of American and Canadian fur traders; and the most significant white settlements were the fur trading post established by John Jacob Astor's company at Astoria and other posts built by the British Hudson Bay Company north of the Columbia River—where residents combined fur trading with farming and recruited Indian labor to compensate for their small numbers.

But American interest in Oregon grew substantially in the 1820s and 1830s. Missionaries considered the territory an attractive target for evangelical efforts, especially after the strange appearance of

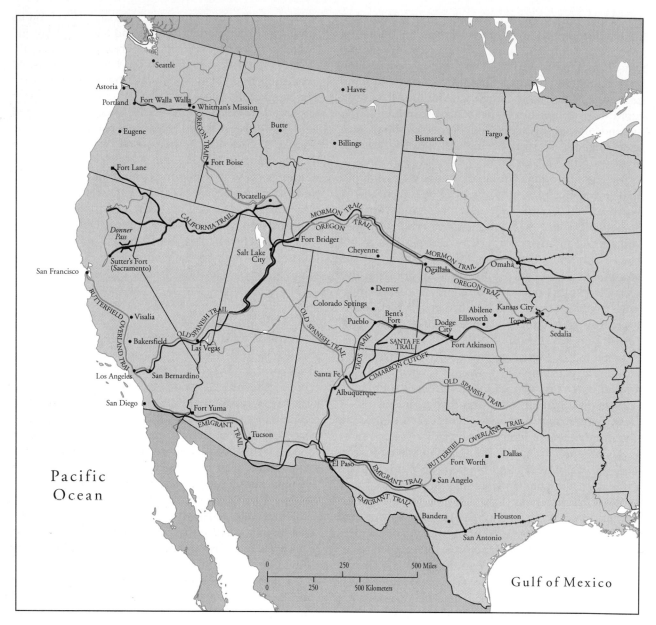

■ **WESTERN TRAILS IN 1860**

As American migrants moved west into Texas, California, and Oregon, they traveled along the great overland trails. Indians were generally more helpful than hostile to these migrants, but the harsh terrain, inhospitable weather and periodic disease epidemics took their toll. Although western migrants have often been portrayed as rugged individualists, they relied on the collective strength of friends and relatives to survive the passage.

four Nez Percé and Flathead Indians in St. Louis in 1831. White Americans never discovered what had brought the Indians (who spoke no English) from Oregon to Missouri, and all four died before they could find out. But some missionaries considered the visit a divinely inspired invitation to extend their efforts westward. They were also motivated by a desire

to counter the Catholic missionaries from Canada, whose presence in Oregon, many believed, threatened American hopes for annexation. The missionaries had little success with the tribes they attempted to convert, and some—embittered by Indian resistance to their efforts—began encouraging white immigration into the region, arguing that by repudiating

"WESTWARD THE COURSE OF EMPIRE TAKES ITS WAY" WITH McCORMICK REAPERS IN THE VAN.

■ **PROMOTING THE WEST**
Cyrus McCormick was one of many American businessmen with an interest in the peopling of the American West. The reaper he invented was crucial to the cultivation of the new agricultural regions, and the rapid settlement of those regions was, in turn, essential to the health of his company. In this poster, the McCormick Reaper Company presents a romantic, idealized image of vast, fertile lands awaiting settlement, an image that drew many settlers westward. *(Chicago Historical Society)*

Christianity the Indians had abdicated their right to the land. "When a people refuse or neglect to fill the designs of Providence, they ought not to complain of the results," said the missionary Marcus Whitman, who, with his wife Narcissa, had established an important, if largely unsuccessful, mission among the Cayuse Indians east of the Cascade Mountains.

Significant numbers of white Americans began emigrating to Oregon in the early 1840s, and they soon substantially outnumbered the British settlers there. They also devastated much of the Indian population, in part through a measles epidemic that spread through the Cayuse. The tribe blamed the Whitman mission for the plague, and in 1847 they attacked it and killed thirteen whites, including Marcus and Narcissa. But such resistance did little to stem the white immigration. By the mid-1840s, American settlements had spread up and down the Pacific coast; and the new settlers (along with advocates of Manifest Destiny in the East) were urging the United States government to take possession of the disputed Oregon territory.

The Westward Migration

The migrations into Texas and Oregon were part of a larger movement that took hundreds of thousands of white and black Americans into the far western regions of the continent between 1840 and 1860. Southerners flocked mainly to Texas. But the largest number of migrants came from the Old Northwest (today's Midwest)—white men and women, and a few blacks, who undertook arduous journeys in search of new opportunities. Most traveled in family groups, until the early 1850s, when the great gold rush attracted many single men (see pp. 443-446). Most were relatively young people. Most had undertaken earlier, if usually shorter, migrations in the past. Few were wealthy, but many were relatively prosperous. Poor people could not afford the expensive trip and the cost of new land. Those without money who wished to migrate usually had to do so by joining more established families or groups as laborers—men as farm or ranch hands, women as domestic servants, teachers, or, in some cases, prostitutes. The character of the migrations varied according to the destination of the migrants. Groups headed for areas where mining or lumbering was the principal economic activity consisted mostly of men. Those heading for farming regions traveled mainly as families.

All the migrants were in search of a new life, but they harbored many different visions of what the new life would bring. Some—particularly after the discovery of gold in California in 1848—hoped for quick riches. Others planned to take advantage of the vast public lands the federal government was selling at modest prices to acquire property for farming or speculation. Still others hoped to establish themselves as merchants and serve the new white communities developing in the West. Some (among them the Mormons) were on religious missions or were attempting to escape the epidemic diseases that were plaguing many cities in the East. But the vast majority of migrants were looking for economic opportunities. They formed a vanguard for the expanding capitalist economy of the United States. Perhaps not surprisingly, migrations were largest during boom times in the United States and dwindled during recessions.

Life on the Trail

Most migrants—about 300,000 between 1840 and 1860—traveled west along the great overland trails. They generally gathered in one of several major depots in Iowa and Missouri (Independence, St. Joseph, or Council Bluffs), joined a wagon train led by hired guides, and set off with their belongings piled in covered wagons, livestock trailing behind. The major route west was the 2,000-mile Oregon Trail, which stretched from Independence across the Great Plains and through the South Pass of the Rocky Mountains. From there, migrants moved north into Oregon or south (along the California trail) to the northern California coast. Other migrations moved along the Santa Fe Trail, southwest from Independence into New Mexico.

However they traveled, overland migrants faced considerable hardships—although the death rate for travelers was only slightly higher than the rate for the American population as a whole. The mountain and desert terrain in the later portions of the trip were particularly difficult. Most journeys lasted five or six months (from May to November), and there was always pressure to get through the Rockies before the snows began, not always an easy task given the very slow pace of most wagon trains (about fifteen miles a day). And although some migrants were moving west at least in part to escape the epidemic diseases of eastern cities, they were not immune from plagues. Thousands of people died on the trail of cholera during the great epidemic of the early 1850s.

Only a very small number of expeditions encountered Indian attacks. Indeed, in the twenty

■ **CROSSING THE PLAINS**
A long wagon train carries migrants across the Plains toward Montana in 1866. This photograph gives some indication of the rugged condition of even some of the most well-traveled trails. (© *Collection of the New York Historical Society*)

years before the Civil War, fewer than 400 migrants (about one-tenth of 1 percent) died in conflicts with the tribes. In fact, Indians were usually more helpful than dangerous to the white migrants. They often served as guides through difficult terrain or aided travelers in crossing streams or herding livestock. They maintained an extensive trade with the white travelers in horses, clothing, and fresh food. But stories of the occasional conflicts between migrants and Indians on the trail created widespread fear among white travelers, even though more Indians than white people (and relatively few of either) died in those conflicts.

Life on the trail was obviously very different from life on a farm or in a town. But the society of the trail re-created many of the patterns of conventional American society. Families divided tasks along gender lines: the men driving and, when necessary, repairing the wagons or hunting game; the women cooking, washing clothes, and caring for children. Almost everyone, male or female, walked the great majority of the time, to lighten the load for the horses drawing the wagons;

and so the women, many of whose chores came at the end of the day, generally worked much harder than the men, who usually rested when the caravan halted.

Despite the traditional image of westward migrants as rugged individualists, most travelers found the journey a highly collective experience. That was partly because many expeditions consisted of groups of friends, neighbors, or relatives who had decided to pull up stakes and move west together. And it was partly because of the intensity of the experience: many weeks of difficult travel with no other human contacts except, occasionally, with Indians. Indeed, one of the most frequent causes of disaster for travelers was the breakdown of the necessarily communal character of the migratory companies. Even so, it was a rare expedition in which there were not some internal conflicts before the trip was over.

EXPANSION AND WAR

The increasing numbers of white Americans in the lands west of the Mississippi put great pressure on the government in Washington. Advocates of Manifest Destiny were propagandizing on behalf of annexing Texas, Oregon, and other lands. The settlers themselves—and their friends, relatives, and business partners in the East—were lobbying for expansion as well. Others, however, feared annexation would cause sectional conflicts, and they sought to avoid or at least defer action. Their efforts were in vain, for in the 1840s the expansionists helped push the United States into a war that—however dubious its origins—became a triumph for Manifest Destiny.

The Democrats and Expansion

Most Americans had expected the election of 1844 to be a contest between two old foes: the Whig Henry Clay and the Democratic former president Martin Van Buren. In preparing for the race, both men tried to avoid taking a stand on the controversial issue of the annexation of Texas. Their separate statements on the question were so similar that many suspected they had collaborated in preparing them. Both favored annexation, but only with the consent

of Mexico. Since such consent was unlikely, the statements meant virtually nothing.

Because sentiment for expansion was mild within the Whig Party, Clay had no difficulty securing the nomination despite his noncommittal position. Among the Democrats, however, there were many supporters of annexation, particularly in the South, and they resented Van Buren's equivocal stand. The expansionists took control of the Democratic convention and nominated a strong supporter of annexation, James K. Polk—the first "dark horse" to win the presidential nomination of his party.

Polk was not as obscure as his Whig critics claimed, but neither was he a genuinely major figure within his party. For fourteen years, beginning in 1825, he had represented Tennessee in the U.S. House of Representatives, four of them as Speaker. Most recently, he had been governor of Tennessee. But in 1844 he had been out of public office—and for the most part out of the public mind—for three years. What made his victory possible was the belief, expressed in the Democratic platform, "that the re-occupation of Oregon and the re-annexation of Texas at the earliest practicable period are great American measures." By combining the Oregon and Texas questions, the Democrats hoped to appeal to both northern and southern expansionists. In a belated effort to catch up with public sentiment in mid-campaign, Clay announced support for annexing Texas. But his tardy and apparently cynical straddling probably cost him more votes than it gained. Polk carried the election by 170 electoral votes to 105, although his popular majority was less than 40,000. The Liberty Party, running James G. Birney a second time, polled 62,000 votes (as compared with 7,000 in 1840), mainly from antislavery Whigs who had turned against Clay.

Polk may have been obscure, but he was intelligent and energetic. He entered office with a clear set of goals and with plans for attaining them. John Tyler accomplished the first of Polk's goals for him in the last days of his presidency. Interpreting the election returns as a mandate for accepting Texas into the Union, the outgoing president persuaded Congress to approve an annexation treaty in February 1845. That December, Texas became a state.

Polk himself resolved the Oregon question, although not without difficulty and not without disappointing some expansionist Democrats. Publicly, Polk seemed to support American title to all of the

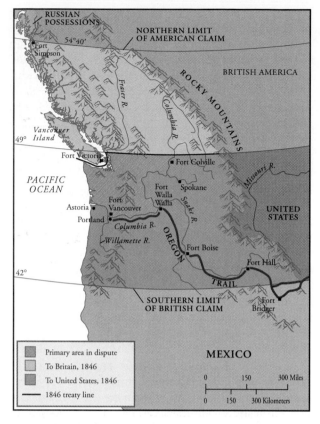

■ SETTLEMENT OF THE OREGON BOUNDARY DISPUTE, 1846
In 1844, James K. Polk won the presidential election on a platform that called for the annexation of Texas and Oregon. A boundary dispute with Britain over the Oregon issue spurred bellicose rhetoric in the United States, but neither country really wanted a war. Over the objections of the most ardent American expansionists, Polk and Britain agreed on a compromise boundary along the 49th parallel.

Oregon Territory, but privately he was willing to compromise—to set the boundary at the 49th parallel. When the British minister in Washington rejected Polk's offer without even referring it to London, Polk toughened his stance and reasserted the American claim to all of Oregon. There was loose talk of war on both sides of the Atlantic—talk that in the United States often took the form of the bellicose slogan "Fifty-four forty or fight!" (a reference to the latitude where some Americans hoped to draw the northern boundary of Oregon). But neither country really wanted to fight. Finally, the British government offered to accept Polk's original proposal and divide the territory at the 49th parallel. The president, reluctant to alienate nationalists

who wanted more, submitted the British proposal to the Senate without supporting it. No doubt to his relief, the Senate accepted the agreement; and on June 15, 1846, a treaty fixed the boundary between the United States and Canada at the 49th parallel, where it remains today.

The Southwest and California

Just as the United States was settling the Oregon question, new tensions were emerging in the Southwest—tensions that ultimately led to a war with Mexico. As soon as the United States admitted Texas to statehood in 1845, the Mexican government broke diplomatic relations with Washington. To make matters worse, a dispute then developed over the boundary between Texas and Mexico. Texans claimed the Rio Grande as both their western and southern border, a claim that would have added much of what is now New Mexico to Texas. Mexico still refused formally to concede the loss of Texas but argued nevertheless that the border had always been the Nueces River, to the north of the Rio Grande. Polk recognized the Texas claim, and in the summer of 1845 he sent a small army under General Zachary Taylor to the Nueces line—to protect Texas, he claimed, against a possible Mexican invasion.

Part of the area in dispute was New Mexico, which remained one of the northernmost outposts of Mexican civilization. Its trading center was the town of Santa Fe, 300 miles from the nearest settlements to the south and more than 1,000 miles from Mexico City and Vera Cruz; and its Spanish and Indian residents lived in a multiracial society that had by the 1840s lasted for nearly a century and a half.

In the 1820s, the Mexican government had invited American traders into the region (just as it was inviting American settlers into Texas), hoping to speed development of the province. And New Mexico, like Texas, soon began to become more American than Mexican. A flourishing commerce soon developed between Santa Fe and Independence, Missouri, with long caravans moving back and forth along the Santa Fe Trail, carrying manufactured goods west and bringing gold, silver, furs, and mules east in return. The Santa Fe trade, as it was called, further increased the American presence in New Mexico and signaled to advocates of expansion another direction for their efforts.

Americans were also increasing their interest in an even more distant province of Mexico: California. In

■ **SACRAMENTO IN THE 1850S**
The busy river port of Sacramento served the growing agricultural and mining economies of north central California in the 1850s—years in which the new state began the dramatic population growth that a century later would make it the nation's largest. *(California State Library, Sacramento)*

this vast region lived members of several western Indian tribes and perhaps 7,000 Mexicans, mostly descendants of Spanish colonists. Gradually, however, white Americans began to arrive: first maritime traders and captains of Pacific whaling ships, who stopped to barter goods or buy supplies; then merchants, who established stores, imported merchandise, and developed a profitable trade with the Mexicans and Indians; and finally pioneering farmers, who entered California from the east by land and settled in the Sacramento Valley. By 1845, there were 700 Americans in California, most of them concentrated in the valley of the Sacramento River, and their numbers were increasing rapidly. The overlord of this region was John A. Sutter, who had lived in Germany and Switzerland before moving to America and who had migrated to California in 1839 and become a Mexican citizen. His headquarters at Sutter's Fort was the center of a magnificent domain where he ranched thousands of cattle and horses and maintained a network of small manufacturing shops to supply his armed retainers.

Some of these new settlers began to dream of bringing California into the United States. Thomas O. Larkin, for example, set up a business in Monterey in 1832, established himself as a leading citizen of the region, and in 1844 accepted appointment as American consul, with quiet instructions from Washington to arouse sentiment among Californians for annexation.

Annexationists supported their demands for acquiring these western lands by citing the racial differences between white Americans and their Mexican rivals. Citing the visible physiological differences between the two peoples—skin color, facial characteristics, and others—they argued that Mexicans represented a different and inferior race. Their claims to the territories they occupied were, therefore, worthy of no more respect than the claims of other supposedly inferior peoples, such as

Indians, for members of these "lesser" races were, they believed, incapable of participating as equals in America's republican system.

President Polk soon came to share the annexationists' dream (although he did not publicly endorse its racial justifications), and he committed himself to acquiring both New Mexico and California for the United States. At the same time that he dispatched the troops under Taylor to the Nueces in Texas, he sent secret instructions to the commander of the Pacific naval squadron to seize the California ports if Mexico declared war on the United States. Representatives of the president quietly informed Americans in California that the United States would respond sympathetically to a revolt against Mexican authority there.

The Mexican War

Having appeared to prepare for war, Polk turned once more to diplomacy and dispatched a special minister, John Slidell, to try to buy off the Mexicans. But Mexican leaders rejected Slidell's offer to purchase the disputed territories. On January 13, 1846, as soon as he heard the news, Polk ordered Taylor's army in Texas to move across the Nueces to the Rio Grande. For months, the Mexicans refused to fight. But finally, according to the accounts of American commanders, some Mexican troops crossed the Rio Grande and attacked a unit of American soldiers. Polk, who had been planning to request a declaration of war even without a military encounter, now told Congress: "War exists by the act of Mexico herself." On May 13, 1846, Congress declared war by votes of 40 to 2 in the Senate and 174 to 14 in the House. The war had many opponents in the United States. Whig critics charged from the beginning (perhaps correctly) that the Polk administration had deliberately maneuvered the country into the conflict and had staged the border incident that had precipitated the declaration of war. Many argued that the hostilities with Mexico were draining resources and attention away from the more important issue of the Pacific Northwest; and when the United States finally reached its agreement with Britain on the Oregon question, opponents claimed that Polk had settled for less than he should have because he was preoccupied with Mexico. Opposition intensified as the war continued and as the public became aware of the casualties and expense.

Although American forces were generally successful in their campaigns against the Mexicans, final victory did not come nearly as quickly as Polk had hoped. Through most of the war, the president himself planned the military strategy. He ordered Taylor to cross the Rio Grande and seize parts of northeastern Mexico, beginning with the city of Monterrey, before marching south to Mexico City itself. Taylor attacked Monterrey in September 1846 and, after a hard fight, captured it. But he let the Mexican garrison evacuate without pursuit. Polk now began to doubt the feasibility of the advance on Mexico City. Among other things, he came to believe that Taylor lacked the tactical skill for the campaign, and he became convinced that an advance south through the mountains would involve impossible supply problems. He also feared that, if successful, Taylor would become a powerful political rival (as, in fact, he did).

In the meantime, Polk ordered other offensives against New Mexico and California. In the summer of 1846, a small army under Colonel Stephen W. Kearny made the long march to Santa Fe and occupied the town with no opposition. Kearny then proceeded with a few hundred soldiers to California, where he joined a conflict already in progress. Organizing the fighting were American settlers, a well-armed exploring party led by John C. Fremont, and the American navy. The conflict became known as the "Bear Flag Revolution." Kearny brought the disparate American forces together under his command, and by the autumn of 1846 he had completed the conquest of California.

The United States now controlled the two territories for which it had gone to war. But Mexico still refused to end the hostilities or cede the conquered land. At this point, Polk and General Winfield Scott, the commanding general of the army and its finest soldier, devised a plan to force peace on the Mexicans—and perhaps gain even more new territory for the United States. Scott would assemble an army at Tampico, and the navy would transport it down the Mexican coast to Vera Cruz, where the Americans would establish a base. From Vera Cruz Scott would move west along the National Highway to Mexico City. Scott conducted the campaign brilliantly. He took Vera Cruz and began moving inland. With an army that never numbered more than 14,000, he advanced 260 miles into enemy territory, keeping casualties low by making flanking movements instead of frontal assaults, and finally achieved

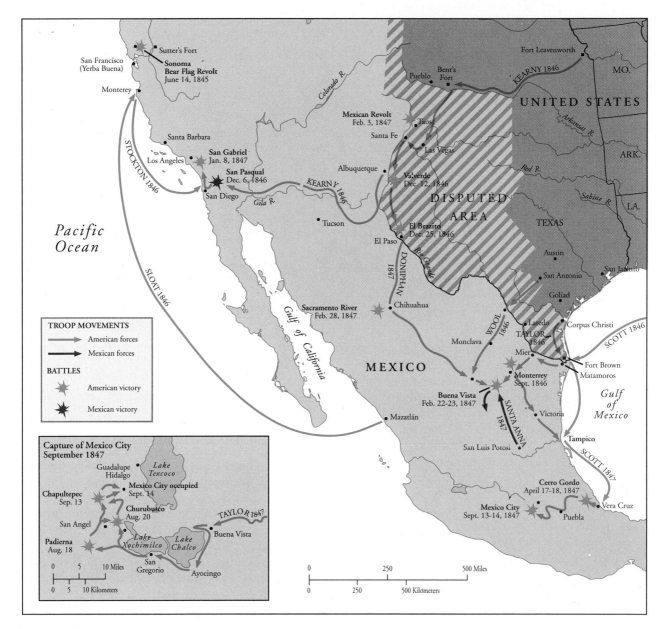

■ THE MEXICAN WAR, 1846–1848

On May 13, 1846, the United States declared war on Mexico after Mexican troops crossed the Rio Grande and entered disputed territory claimed by the United States. American victory did not come as quickly as President Polk hoped, and opposition to the war intensified as the war continued. The Treaty of Guadalupe Hidalgo ended the war on February 2, 1848. Mexico was forced to cede California and New Mexico to the United States and to recognize the Rio Grande as the boundary of Texas in return for $15 million.

his objective without losing a battle. He inflicted a crushing defeat on the much larger Mexican army in the mountains at Cerro Gordo and met no further resistance until he was within a few miles of Mexico City. After a hard fight on the outskirts of the capital, Americans occupied the city. A new Mexican government then took power and announced its willingness to negotiate a peace treaty.

President Polk was now growing thoroughly unclear about his objectives. He continued to encourage those who demanded that the United States annex much of Mexico itself. At the same

■ **STEPHEN KEARNY IN SANTA FE**
Colonel Stephen Kearny led a small U.S.
military party to Santa Fe in 1846 and
seized the town without opposition. In
this 1909 drawing (which the artist
Stephen Chapman acknowledged was
not entirely accurate), Kearny raises
the American flag over the "old palace"
in Santa Fe. The image appeared on a
U.S. postage stamp in 1946.
(Museum of New Mexico)

time, concerned about the approaching presidential election, he was eager to get the war finished quickly. Polk had sent a special presidential envoy to Mexico with the army, who was authorized to negotiate a settlement. The agent, Nicholas Trist, concluded an agreement with the new Mexican government on February 2, 1848: the Treaty of Guadalupe Hidalgo. In it, Mexico agreed to cede California and New Mexico to the United States and acknowledged the Rio Grande as the boundary of Texas. In return, the United States promised to take over Mexico's debts to the citizens of the new territories against Mexico and to pay the Mexicans $15 million. When the treaty reached Washington, Polk faced a dilemma. Trist had obtained most of Polk's original demands, but had not satisfied the new, more expansive dreams of acquiring more territory in Mexico itself. Polk angrily claimed that Trist had violated his instructions, but he soon realized that he had no choice but to accept the treaty.

Some ardent expansionists were demanding that he hold out for annexation of—in a phrase widely bandied about at the time—"All Mexico!" Antislavery leaders, in the meantime, were charging that the idea of acquiring Mexico was part of a southern scheme to extend slavery to new realms. To silence this bitter and potentially destructive debate, Polk submitted the Trist treaty to the Senate, which approved it by a vote of 38 to 14. The war was over, and America had gained a vast new territory in the West. But it had also acquired a new set of troubling and divisive issues.

THE SECTIONAL DEBATE

James Polk tried to be a president whose policies transcended sectional issues. But conciliating the sections was becoming an ever more difficult task, and Polk gradually earned the enmity of both northerners and westerners, many of whom believed his policies (and particularly his enthusiasm for territorial expansion in the Southwest) favored the South at their expense. In this tense political climate, an exceptionally dangerous issue emerged.

Slavery and the Territories

In August 1846, while the Mexican War was still in progress, Polk asked Congress to appropriate $2 million for purchasing peace with Mexico. Representative David Wilmot of Pennsylvania, an antislavery Democrat, introduced an amendment to the appropriation bill that would have prohibited slavery in any territory acquired from Mexico. The so-called Wilmot Proviso passed in the House but failed in the Senate. It would resurface in congressional debates for years.

Southern militants, in the meantime, had a plan of their own. They claimed that since the territories belonged to the entire nation, all Americans had equal rights in them, including the right to move their slaves (which they considered property) there. Neither Congress nor a territorial legislature (which was a creation of Congress) had the authority to prohibit or even regulate slavery in any territories. As the sectional debate intensified, moderates attempted to craft a new compromise. President Polk supported a proposal to extend the Missouri Compromise line through the new territories to the Pacific coast, banning slavery north of the line and permitting it south of the line. Others supported a plan, originally known as "squatter sovereignty" and later by the more dignified title of "popular sovereignty," which would allow the people of each territory (acting through their legislature) to decide the status of slavery there. The debates over these various proposals dragged on for many months, and they remained unresolved when Polk left office in 1849. There was still no territorial government for California or the New Mexico Territory (which included most of present New Mexico and Arizona, all of Utah and Nevada, and parts of Colorado and Wyoming).

The presidential campaign of 1848 dampened the controversy for a time as both Democrats and Whigs tried to avoid the slavery question. Polk, damaged politically by the sectional animosities his policies had helped arouse, and in declining health (he would die

in 1849), refused to run again. The Democrats nominated Lewis Cass of Michigan, a dull, aging party regular. The Whigs nominated a military hero of the Mexican War with no political record, General Zachary Taylor of Louisiana. Opponents of slavery found the choice of candidates unsatisfying, and out of their discontent emerged the Free-Soil Party, which drew from the existing Liberty Party and the antislavery wings of the Whig and Democratic Parties, and which endorsed the Wilmot Proviso. Its candidate was former president Martin Van Buren.

Taylor won a narrow victory. But while Van Buren failed to carry a single state, he polled an impressive 291,000 votes (10 percent of the total), and the Free-Soilers elected ten members to Congress. Van Buren probably drew enough Democratic votes away from Cass, particularly in New York, to throw the election to Taylor. The emergence of the Free-Soil Party as an important political force, like the emergence of the Know-Nothing and Liberty Parties before it, signaled the inability of the existing parties to contain the political passions slavery was creating, and was an important step toward the collapse of the second party system in the 1850s.

The California Gold Rush

By the time Taylor took office, the pressure to resolve the question of slavery in the far western territories had become more urgent as a result of

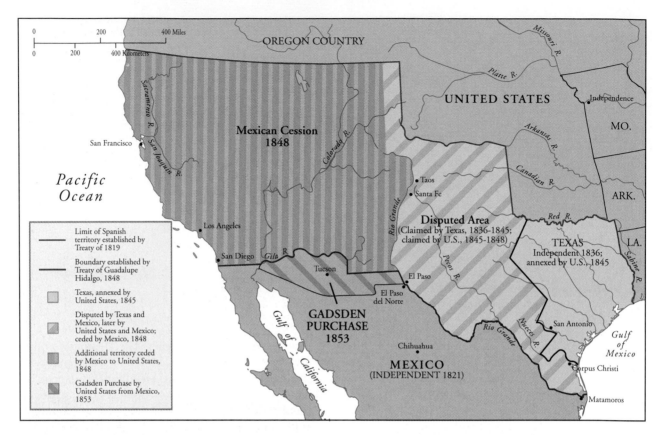

■ AMERICAN EXPANSION INTO THE SOUTHWEST, 1845–1853
The annexation of Texas, the Treaty of Guadalupe Hidalgo, and the Gadsden Purchase added a vast extent of territory to the United States from 1845 to 1853. Debates over the status of these new territories reintroduced the slavery issue into national politics, as proslavery southerners and antislavery northerners clashed over the expansion of slavery into the West.

dramatic events in California. In January 1848, James Marshall, a carpenter working on one of John Sutter's sawmills, found traces of gold in the foothills of the Sierra Nevadas. Sutter tried to suppress the news, fearing a gold rush would destroy his own substantial empire in the region. But by May, word of the discovery had reached San Francisco; by late summer, it had reached the east coast of the United States and much of the rest of the world. Almost immediately, hundreds of thousands of people from around the world began flocking to California in a frantic search for gold. The non-Indian population increased nearly twentyfold in four years: from 14,000 in 1848 to over 220,000 in 1852.

The atmosphere in California at the peak of the gold rush was one of almost crazed excitement and greed. For a short time San Francisco was almost completely depopulated as residents raced to the mountains to search for gold; the city's principal

newspaper (which had been criticizing the gold mania) had to stop publication because it could no longer find either staff or readers. "Nothing but the introduction of insane asylums can effect a cure," one visitor remarked of the gold mania.

Most migrants to the Far West prepared carefully before making the journey. But the California migrants (known as "Forty-niners") threw caution to the winds. They abandoned farms, jobs, homes, families; they piled onto ships and flooded the overland trails—many carrying only what they could pack on their backs. The overwhelming majority of the Forty-niners (perhaps 95 percent) were men, and the society they created on their arrival in California was unusually fluid and volatile because of the almost total absence of women, children, or families.

The gold rush also attracted some of the first Chinese migrants to the western United States. News of the discoveries created great excitement in China,

■ **"MINERS WITH ROCKERS AND BLUE SHIRTS"**
Despite its romantic image, mining for gold during the great California Gold Rush was for most people hard, discouraging, and ultimately profitless work—as this photograph of a grim band of miners with their equipment suggests. Most of those who came to California in search of gold eventually either returned home with nothing to show for their efforts or remained in California to make their way in some other occupation. *(Collection of W. Bruce Lundberg. Photograph courtesy Oakland Museum of California)*

particularly in impoverished areas, where letters from Chinese already in California and reports from Americans visiting in China spread the word. It was, of course, extremely difficult for a poor Chinese peasant to get to America; but many young, adventurous people (mostly men) decided to go anyway— believing that they could quickly become rich and then return to China. Emigration brokers loaned many migrants money for passage to California, which the migrants paid off out of their earnings there. The migration was almost entirely voluntary (unlike the forced movement of kidnapped "coolies" to such places as Peru and Cuba at about the same time). The Chinese in California were, therefore, free

laborers and merchants, looking for gold or, more often, hoping to profit from other economic opportunities the gold boom was creating.

The gold rush created a serious labor shortage in California, as many male workers left their jobs and flocked to the gold fields. This shortage created opportunities for many people who needed work (including Chinese immigrants). It also led to an overt exploitation of Indians that resembled slavery in all but name. At the same time that white vigilantes, who called themselves "Indian hunters," were hunting down and killing thousands of Indians (contributing to the process by which the Native American population of California declined from 150,000 to

30,000 between the 1850s and 1870), a state law permitted the arrest of "loitering" or orphaned Indians and their assignment to a term of "indentured" labor.

The gold rush was of critical importance to the growth of California, but not for the reasons most of the migrants hoped. There was substantial gold in the hills of the Sierra Nevada, and many people got rich from it. But only a tiny fraction of the Forty-niners ever found gold, or even managed to stake a claim to land on which they could look for gold. Some disappointed migrants returned home after a while. But many stayed in California and swelled both the agricultural and urban populations of the territory. By 1856, for example, San Francisco—whose population had been 1,000 before the gold rush (and at one point declined to about 100 as people left for the mines)—was the home of over 50,000 people. By the early 1850s, California, which had always had a diverse population, had become remarkably heterogeneous. The gold rush had attracted not just white Americans, but Europeans, Chinese, South Americans, Mexicans, free blacks, and slaves who accompanied southern migrants. Conflicts over gold intersected with racial and ethnic tensions to make the territory an unusually turbulent place. As a result, pressure grew to create a more stable and effective government. The gold rush, therefore, became another factor putting pressure on the United States to resolve the status of the territories—and of slavery within them.

Rising Sectional Tensions

Zachary Taylor was a southerner and a slaveholder, but from his long years in the army he had acquired a national outlook. He recognized at once the importance of dealing with the problems of the newly acquired territories, which—in the absence of territorial governments—were still under the control of the military. There was particular pressure to establish a new government in California, after the enormous boom following the gold rush that had begun in 1848. Taylor believed statehood could become the solution to the issue of slavery in the territories. As long as the new lands were territories, the federal government was responsible for deciding the fate of slavery within them. But once they became states, their own governments would be able to settle the slavery question. Taylor ordered military officials in California and New Mexico to speed up the state-

hood movements. California promptly adopted a constitution that prohibited slavery, and in December 1849 Taylor asked Congress to admit California as a free state. New Mexico, he added, should be granted statehood as soon as it was ready and should, like California, be permitted to decide for itself what it wanted to do about slavery.

Congress balked, in part because of several other controversies involving slavery that were complicating the debate over the territories. One was the effort of antislavery forces to abolish slavery in the District of Columbia, a movement white southerners bitterly resisted. Another was the emergence of the "personal liberty laws" in northern states, which barred courts and police officers from helping to return runaway slaves to their owners. In response, southerners in Congress demanded a stringent national law to require northern states to return fugitive slaves to their owners. Still another controversy involved a border dispute between Texas and New Mexico, and the Texans' resentment at the failure of the federal government to take over the debts they had accumulated during their brief independence. But the biggest obstacle to the president's program was the white South's fear that two new free states would tip the balance of national politics further against them. The number of free and slave states in 1849 was equal—fifteen of each. But the admission of California would upset the balance; and New Mexico, Oregon, and Utah—all of which seemed likely to become free states—might upset it further, leaving the South with a minority in the Senate as it already had in the House.

Tempers were now rising to dangerous levels. Even many otherwise moderate southern leaders were beginning to talk about secession from the Union, while all but one northern state legislature adopted a resolution demanding the prohibition of slavery in the territories.

The Compromise of 1850

Faced with this mounting crisis, moderates and Unionists spent the winter of 1849–1850 trying to frame a great compromise. The aging Henry Clay, who was spearheading the effort, believed that no compromise could work unless it settled all the issues in dispute between the sections. As a result, he took several originally separate measures and combined them into a single piece of legislation, which he presented to the Senate on January 29, 1850. The bill had five provisions: (1) that California be admitted as a free state; (2) that in the rest of the lands acquired from Mexico, territorial governments be formed without restrictions on slavery; (3) that Texas yield in its boundary dispute with New Mexico and that the federal government compensate it by taking over its public debt; (4) that the slave trade, but not slavery itself, be abolished in the District of Columbia; and (5) that a new and more effective fugitive slave law be passed. These resolutions launched a debate that raged for seven months—both in Congress and throughout the nation. The debate occurred in two phases, and the differences between them revealed much about how American politics was changing in the 1850s.

In the first phase of the debate, the dominant voices in Congress were those of older men— national leaders who still remembered Jefferson, Adams, and other founders—who argued for or against the compromise on the basis of broad ideals. Clay himself, seventy-three years old in 1850, was the most prominent of these spokesmen. He made a broad plea for sectional conciliation and appealed to shared sentiments of nationalism.

Early in March, another of the older leaders— John C. Calhoun, sixty-eight years old and so ill that he had to sit grimly in his seat while a colleague read his speech for him—joined the debate. Calhoun insisted that the North grant the South equal rights in the territories, that it agree to observe the laws concerning fugitive slaves, that it cease attacking slavery,

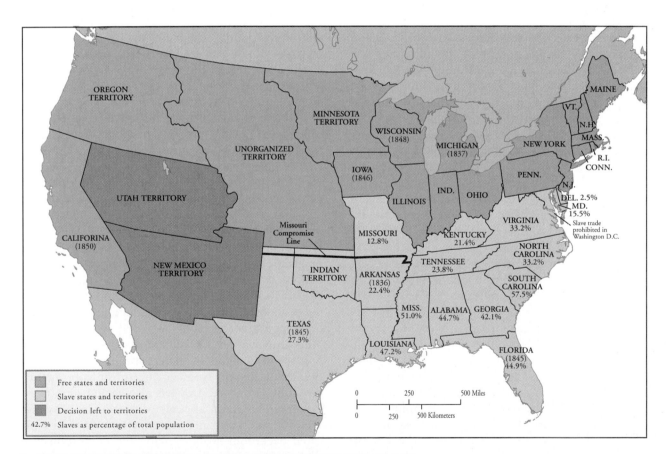

■ **SLAVE AND FREE TERRITORIES ACCORDING TO THE COMPROMISE OF 1850**
Conflicts over slavery led to a sectional crisis in 1849–1850. Congress temporarily defused the crisis by passing a series of measures known as the Compromise of 1850. It admitted California to the Union as a free state, allowed "popular sovereignty" on the slavery issue (that is, allowed the people of a territory to vote on the status of slavery within it) in the Utah and New Mexico Territories, settled the Texas boundary dispute, abolished the slave trade in the District of Columbia, and strengthened the fugitive slave law. After 1850, free states outnumbered slave states.

and that it accept an amendment to the Constitution guaranteeing a balance of power between the sections. The amendment would provide for the election of dual presidents, one from the North and one from the South, each possessing a veto power. Calhoun was making radical demands that had no chance of passage. But he was expressing his belief in the importance of saving the Union; and like Clay, he was offering what he considered a comprehensive, permanent solution to the sectional problem—admittedly, one that would have required an abject surrender by the North.

After Calhoun came the third of the elder statesmen, the sixty-eight-year-old Daniel Webster. His "Seventh of March Address" was probably the greatest oratorical effort of his long career. Still nourishing presidential ambitions, he sought to calm angry passions and to rally northern moderates to support Clay's compromise.

After six months of debate, however—a debate dominated by ringing appeals to the memory of the founders, to nationalism, to idealism—the effort to win approval of the compromise failed. In July, Congress defeated the Clay proposal; and with that the controversy moved into its second phase, in which a very different cast of characters predominated. Clay, ill and tired, left Washington to spend the summer resting in the mountains. He would return, but never with his old vigor; he died in 1852. Calhoun had died even before the vote in July. And Webster in the course of the summer accepted a new appointment as secretary of state, thus removing himself from the Senate and from the debate.

In place of these leaders, a new, younger group now emerged as the dominant voices. William H. Seward of New York, forty-nine years old and a wily political operator, staunchly opposed the proposed compromise. The ideals of Union were less important to him than the issue of eliminating slavery. The new voice of the South was Jefferson Davis of Mississippi, forty-two years old, a representative not of the old aristocratic South of Calhoun but of the new, cotton South—a hard, newly settled, and rapidly growing region. To him, the slavery issue was one not only of principles and ideals but also of economic self-interest.

Most important of all, there was Stephen A. Douglas, a thirty-seven-year-old Democratic senator from Illinois. A westerner from a rapidly growing state, he was an open spokesman for the economic needs of his section—and especially for the construction of railroads. His was a career devoted not to broad national goals, as Clay's, Webster's, and even Calhoun's had often been, but one frankly committed to sectional gain and personal self-promotion.

The new leaders of the Senate were able, where the old leaders were not, to produce a compromise in 1850. In part they benefited from the great prosperity of the early 1850s, which was a result of expanding foreign trade, the flow of gold from California, and a boom in railroad construction. Conservative economic interests everywhere wanted to end the sectional dispute and concentrate on economic growth. Progress toward the compromise was also helped by the disappearance of its most powerful opponent: the president. President Taylor had been adamant that only after the admission of California and possibly New Mexico as states could other measures be discussed. He had threatened not only to veto any measure that diverged from this proposal but also to use force against the southern states, even to lead the troops in person, if they attempted to secede. But on July 9, 1850, Taylor suddenly died. He had attended a Fourth of July celebration in a blazing sun, eaten too much, and succumbed to heat prostration and a violent stomach disorder. His successor was Millard Fillmore of New York—a handsome, dignified, lightly regarded man who understood the political importance of flexibility. He supported the compromise and used his powers of persuasion to swing northern Whigs into line.

The new leaders also benefited from their own pragmatic tactics. Douglas's first step, after Clay's departure, was to break up the "omnibus bill" that Clay had envisioned as a great comprehensive solution to the sectional crisis and to introduce instead a series of separate measures to be voted on individually. Thus representatives of different sections could support those elements of the compromise favorable to them and abstain from voting on or vote against those they opposed. Douglas also gained support by avoiding the grand appeals to patriotism Clay and Webster had made and resorting instead to complicated backroom deals—linking the compromise to such non-ideological matters as the sale of government bonds and the construction of railroads. As a result of his efforts, by mid-September Congress had passed all the components of the compromise and the president had signed them.

The outcome was a great but clouded victory for Douglas and the forces of conciliation. The Compromise of 1850, unlike the Missouri Compromise thirty years before, was not a product of widespread agreement on common national ideals. It was, rather, a triumph of self-interest that did not resolve the underlying problems. Still, members of Congress hailed the measure as a triumph of statesmanship; and Millard Fillmore, approving it, called it a just settlement of the sectional problem, "in its character final and irrevocable."

THE CRISES OF THE 1850s

For a few years after the Compromise of 1850, sectional conflict seemed to subside amid booming prosperity and growth. But tensions between North and South remained. And in 1854, they burst into the open once more.

The Uneasy Truce

Both major parties endorsed the Compromise of 1850 in their platforms in 1852, and both parties nominated presidential candidates unlikely to arouse passionate opposition in either North or South. The Democrats chose the obscure New Hampshire politician Franklin Pierce. The Whigs selected the military hero General Winfield Scott, a man whose political views were so undefined that no one knew what he thought about the Compromise.

The gingerly way in which party leaders dealt with the sectional question could not prevent its divisive influence from intruding on the election. The Whigs were the principal victims. Already plagued by the continuing defections of antislavery northerners into the Free-Soil Party (which had repudiated the Compromise of 1850), they alienated still more party members—the "Conscience" Whigs—by straddling the slavery issue and refusing openly to condemn it. The divisions among the Whigs helped produce a victory for the Democrats in 1852. Franklin Pierce, a charming, amiable man of no great distinction, attempted to maintain party—and national—harmony by avoiding divisive issues, and particularly by avoiding the issue of slavery. But those issues arose despite his efforts to skirt them. They arose, in particular, because of northern opposition to the Fugitive Slave Act, which had been part of the compromise of 1850. Under the law, blacks accused of having escaped from slavery had no right to a trial by jury and could not testify on their own behalf; a federal judge or commissioner could turn alleged runaways over to slaveowners simply on the basis of affidavits from slaveowners. Northern hostility to these provisions intensified after 1850 when southerners began appearing occasionally in northern states to pursue fugitives or to claim as slaves blacks who had been living in northern communities for years. Several northern states passed new personal liberty laws, which attempted to use state authority to interfere with the deportation of fugitive slaves. The supreme court of Wisconsin, in *Ableman* v. *Booth* (1857), even declared the federal Fugitive Slave Act void and ignored the U.S. Supreme Court when it overruled the Wisconsin ruling.

So fervent was the resentment of many opponents of slavery that mobs formed in several cities to prevent enforcement of the law. In 1854, for example, a Boston mob stormed a courthouse and killed a guard in an effort to rescue a fugitive slave who was about to be returned to the South. President Pierce sent troops to Boston to ensure enforcement of the law; tens of thousands of Bostonians lined the streets in protest as the soldiers marched the fugitive to the ship that would return him to slavery.

White southerners watched with growing anger and alarm as the one element of the Compromise of 1850 they had considered a victory became, as they saw it, virtually meaningless because of mob action and unconstitutional legalisms in the North.

"Young America"

One of the ways Franklin Pierce tried to dampen sectional controversy was through his support of a movement in the Democratic Party known as "Young America." Those who joined the movement hoped the expansion of American democracy throughout the world could become a diversion from what they considered the transitory issue of slavery. The great liberal and nationalist revolutions of 1848 in Europe stirred them to dream of a republican Europe with governments based on the model of the United States. They dreamed as well of expanding American commerce in the Pacific and acquiring new territories in the Western Hemisphere.

Few Americans in North or South objected to displays of nationalism. But efforts to extend the nation's domain could not avoid becoming entangled with the sectional crisis. Pierce had been unsuccessfully attempting through diplomacy to buy Cuba from the Spanish Empire (efforts begun in 1848 by Polk), when a group of his envoys sent him a private document from Ostend, Belgium, making the case for seizing Cuba by force. When the Ostend Manifesto, as it became known, leaked to the public, it enraged many antislavery northerners, who charged the administration with conspiring to bring a new slave state into the Union.

The South, for its part, opposed all efforts to acquire new territory that would not support a slave system. The kingdom of Hawaii—which had a substantial population of American planters—agreed to join the United States in 1854; but the treaty died in the Senate because it contained a clause prohibiting slavery in the islands. A powerful movement to annex Canada to the United States—a movement that had the support of many Canadians eager for access to American markets—similarly foundered, at least in part because of slavery.

Slavery, Railroads, and the West

What fully revived the sectional crisis, however, was the same issue that had produced it in the first place: slavery in the territories. By the 1850s, the line of white settlement had moved west to the great bend of the Missouri River. Beyond the boundaries of what is now Minnesota, Iowa, and Missouri stretched a great expanse of plains, which many white Americans had long believed was unfit for cultivation. (Some called it the Great American Desert.) The government had assigned much of this territory to the Indian tribes it had dislodged from the more fertile lands to the east. Now it was becoming apparent that large sections of this region were, in fact, suitable for farming. In the states of the Old Northwest, prospective settlers urged the government to open the area to them, provide territorial governments, and—despite its previous solemn assurances to the Indians of the sanctity of their lands—dislodge the tribes so as to make room for white settlers. There was relatively little opposition from any segment of white society to the violation of Indian rights proposed by these demands. But the interest in further settlement raised two issues that did prove highly divisive and that gradually became intertwined: railroads and slavery.

As the nation expanded westward and as the problem of communication between the older states and the so-called trans-Mississippi West (the areas west of the Mississippi River) became more and more critical, broad support began to emerge for building a transcontinental railroad. The problem was where to place it—and in particular, where to locate the railroad's eastern terminus. Northerners favored Chicago, the rapidly growing capital of the free states of the Northwest. Southerners supported St. Louis, Memphis, or New Orleans—all located in slave states.

Pierce's secretary of war, Jefferson Davis of Mississippi, tried to enhance the chances of a southern route, by removing a territorial obstacle. After surveys indicated that a railroad with a southern terminus would have to pass through an area in Mexican territory, Davis dispatched James Gadsden, a southern railroad builder, to buy the region in question from Mexico. In 1853 Gadsden persuaded the Mexican government to accept $10 million in exchange for a strip of land that today comprises part of Arizona and New Mexico, the so-called Gadsden Purchase. The acquisition intensified the sectional debate.

The Kansas-Nebraska Controversy

As a senator from Illinois, a resident of Chicago, and the acknowledged leader of northwestern Democrats, Stephen Douglas naturally wanted the transcontinental railroad for his own city and section. He also realized the strength of the principal argument against the northern route: that west of the Mississippi it would run largely through country with a substantial Indian population. Like Jefferson Davis, therefore, Douglas attempted to improve his region's chances by removing the obstacle. In the process, he made a fateful proposal that finally destroyed the Compromise of 1850. In 1854 he introduced a bill to organize (and thus open to white settlement) a huge new territory west of Iowa and Missouri. It would be known as Nebraska.

Douglas knew the South would oppose his bill because it would prepare the way for a new free state: the proposed territory was in the area of the Louisiana Purchase north of the Missouri Compromise line and hence closed to slavery. In an effort to make the measure acceptable to southerners,

Douglas inserted a provision that the status of slavery in the new territory would be determined by the territorial legislature—that is, according to popular sovereignty. In theory, the region could choose to open itself to slavery (although few believed it actually would). When southern Democrats demanded more, Douglas agreed to two changes in the bill: a clause specifically repealing the antislavery provision of the Missouri Compromise (which the popular sovereignty provision of his original bill had done implicitly); and the division of the area into two territories, Nebraska and Kansas, instead of one. The new second territory (Kansas) was more likely to become a slave state. In its final form the measure was known as the Kansas-Nebraska Act. President Pierce supported the bill; and after a strenuous debate, it became law in May 1854 with the unanimous support of the South and the partial support of northern Democrats.

No other piece of legislation in American history produced so many immediate, sweeping, and ominous changes as the Kansas-Nebraska Act. It destroyed the Whig Party, which virtually disappeared by 1856, and along with it a conservative, nationalistic influence in American politics. It divided the northern Democrats (many of whom were appalled at the repeal of the Missouri Compromise, which they considered an almost sacred part of the fabric of the Union) and drove many of them from the party.

Most important of all, it spurred the creation of a new party that was frankly sectional in composition and creed. In 1854, Whigs, Democrats, and Free-Soilers opposed to the Kansas-Nebraska Act formed the Republican Party. Instantly, it became a major force in American politics. In the elections of that year, the Republicans won enough seats in Congress to permit them, in combination with allies among the Know-Nothings, to organize the House of Representatives.

"Bleeding Kansas"

Events in Kansas itself in the next two years increased the popular excitement in the North. White settlers from both the North and the South began moving into the territory almost immediately after the passage of the Kansas-Nebraska Act. In the spring of 1855, there were elections for a territorial legislature. Only about 1,500 legal voters lived in Kansas by then, but more than 6,000 people actually voted.

That was because thousands of Missourians, some traveling in armed bands, crossed into Kansas to vote. As a result, pro-slavery forces elected a majority to the legislature, which proceeded immediately to enact a series of laws legalizing slavery. Outraged free-staters defied the legislature and in a separate election chose delegates to a constitutional convention, which met at Topeka and adopted a constitution excluding slavery. The free-staters then chose their own governor and legislature and petitioned Congress for statehood. President Pierce denounced the free-staters as traitors and threw the full support of the federal government behind the pro-slavery territorial legislature.

A few months later a pro-slavery federal marshal assembled a large posse, consisting mostly of Missourians, to arrest the free-state leaders, who had set up their headquarters in Lawrence. The posse sacked the town, burned the "governor's" house, and destroyed several printing presses. Retribution came quickly.

Among the most fervent opponents of slavery in Kansas was John Brown, a fiercely committed abolitionist originally from Ohio, who considered himself an instrument of God's will to destroy slavery. He had moved to Kansas with his sons so they could fight to make it a free state. After the events in Lawrence, he gathered six followers (including four of his sons) and in one night murdered five pro-slavery settlers, leaving their mutilated bodies to discourage other supporters of slavery from entering Kansas. The episode, known as the Pottawatomie Massacre, led to more civil strife in Kansas—irregular, guerrilla warfare conducted by armed bands, some of them more interested in land claims or loot than in ideologies. Northerners and southerners alike came to believe the events in Kansas illustrated (and were a result of) the aggressive designs of the other section. "Bleeding Kansas" became a powerful symbol of the sectional hostility.

Another symbol soon appeared, in the United States Senate. In May 1856, Charles Sumner of Massachusetts rose to give a speech entitled "The Crime Against Kansas." Handsome, eloquent, humorless, and passionately doctrinaire, Sumner was a militant opponent of slavery. And in his speech, he gave particular attention to his colleague, Senator Andrew P. Butler of South Carolina, an outspoken defender of slavery. The South Carolinian was, Sumner claimed, the "Don Quixote" of slavery, having "chosen a

■ **THE BATTLE FOR KANSAS**
The conflicts over Kansas eventually took on much of the character of a civil war, as this picture of a battle between free-soilers and proslavery forces at Hickory Point, Kansas makes clear. *(Anne S. K. Brown Military Collection, Brown University Library)*

mistress . . . who, though ugly to others, is always lovely to him, though polluted in the sight of the world, is chaste in his sight . . . the harlot slavery."

The pointedly sexual references and the general viciousness of the speech enraged Butler's nephew, Preston Brooks, a member of the U.S. House of Representatives from South Carolina, who decided to punish Sumner publicly. Several days after the speech, Brooks approached Sumner at his desk in the Senate chamber during a recess, raised a heavy cane, and began beating him repeatedly on the head and shoulders. Sumner, trapped behind his desk, rose in agony with such strength that he tore the desk from the bolts holding it to the floor; he then collapsed, bleeding and unconscious. So severe were his injuries that he was unable to return to the Senate for four years, during which time his state refused to replace him. He became a symbol throughout the North—a martyr to the barbarism of the South.

Preston Brooks became a symbol, too. Censured by the House, he resigned his seat, returned to South Carolina, and stood successfully for reelection. He had become a southern hero. Like Sumner, he served as evidence of how deep the antagonism between North and South had become.

The Free-Soil Ideology

What had happened to produce such deep hostility between the two sections? In part, the tensions were a reflection of the two sections' differing economic and territorial interests. But they were also a reflection of a hardening of ideas in both North and South. As the nation expanded and political power grew more dispersed, each section became concerned with ensuring that its vision of America's future would be the dominant one. And those visions were becoming—partly as a result of internal developments within the sections themselves, partly because of each region's conceptions (and misconceptions) of what was happening outside it—increasingly distinct and increasingly rigid.

In the North, assumptions about the proper structure of society came to center on the belief in "free soil" and "free labor"—ideas spreading widely through the public lectures of the new Lyceum Movement (see pp. 454–455). The abolitionists generated some support for their argument that slavery was a moral evil and must be eliminated. But theirs was never the dominant voice of the North. Instead, an increasing number of northerners, gradually becoming a majority, came to believe that the existence of slavery was dangerous not because of what it did to blacks but because of what it threatened to do to whites. At the heart of American democracy, they believed, was the right of all citizens to own property, to control their own labor, and to have access to opportunities for advancement. The ideal society, in other words, was one of small-scale capitalism, in which everyone could aspire to a stake and to upward mobility.

According to this vision, the South was the antithesis of democracy. It was a closed, static society, in which the slave system preserved an entrenched aristocracy and where common whites had no opportunity to improve themselves. More than that, the South was a backward society—decadent, lazy, dilapidated. While the North was growing and prospering, displaying thrift, industry, and a commitment to progress, the South was stagnating, rejecting the northern values of individualism and progress. The South was, northern free-laborites further maintained, engaged in a conspiracy to extend slavery throughout the nation and thus to destroy the openness of northern capitalism and replace it with the closed, aristocratic system of the South. This "slave power conspiracy," as it came to be known, threatened the future of every white laborer and property owner in the North. The only solution was to fight the spread of slavery and work for the day when the nation's democratic (i.e., free-labor) ideals extended to all sections of the country—the day of the victory of what northerners called "Freedom National."

This ideology lay at the heart of the new Republican Party. There were abolitionists and others in the party who sincerely believed in the rights of African Americans to freedom and citizenship. More predominant, however, were those who cared principally about the threat they believed slavery posed to white labor and to individual opportunity. This ideology also strengthened the commitment of Republicans to the Union. Since the idea of continued growth and progress was central to the free-labor vision, the prospect of dismemberment of the nation—a diminution of America's size and economic power—was unthinkable.

The Pro-Slavery Argument

In the South, in the meantime, a very different ideology was emerging—one that was entirely incompatible with the free-labor ideology developing in the North. It emerged out of a rapid hardening of position among southern whites on the issue of slavery. As late as the early 1830s, a substantial number of southern whites had harbored reservations about slavery. Between 1829 and 1832, for example, a Virginia constitutional convention, and then the state legislature—under pressure from non-slaveholders in the western part of the state—had seriously considered ending slavery through compensated emancipation. The effort failed in large part because of the tremendous expense it would have entailed. There had been many antislavery societies in the South—more there in 1827 than there were in the North, most of them in the border states. And there were prominent southern politicians who spoke openly in opposition to slavery—among them Cassius M. Clay of Kentucky, who edited an abolitionist newspaper for a time in Lexington.

By the mid-1830s, however, a militant defensiveness regarding the system was beginning to replace this ambivalence. In part, the change was a result of events in the South. The Nat Turner uprising in 1831 (see p. 420) terrified whites throughout the region, and reinforced their determination to make slavery secure. There was also an economic incentive to defend the system. With the expansion of the cotton economy into the Deep South, slavery—which had begun to seem unprofitable in many areas of the upper South—now became lucrative once again.

But the change was also a result of events in the North, and particularly of the growth of the Garrisonian abolitionist movement, with its strident attacks on southern society. The popularity of Harriet Beecher Stowe's *Uncle Tom's Cabin* (see p. 420) was perhaps the most glaring evidence of the success of those attacks; but other abolitionist writings

LYCEUMS

Two passions of the mid-nineteenth century—education and oratory—combined in the 1830s to create a movement that was both popular and, its creators believed, educational: the lyceum.

The lyceum was not a place, although some places were given its name (which came from a building in ancient Greece where Aristotle had taught). It was an idea. It was the brainchild of Josiah Holbrook, a Yale graduate and schoolteacher who dreamed of bringing knowledge to adults. Holbrook himself gave a series of lectures in Millbury, Massachusetts, in 1826 to an audience of "farmers and mechanics," offering "instruction in the sciences and other branches of useful knowledge." From that modest experiment, the "lyceum movement" quickly spread through Massachusetts, New England, and other parts of the American North and Northwest. (The movement had only a small impact in the South.)

Making use of public libraries, vacant schools, and other existing spaces, lyceum organizers recruited some of the leading scholars, politicians, and orators of their time to provide entertainment and instruction to adult audiences. The topics of lectures were as various as the speakers. The lyceum in Salem, Massachusetts, for example, sponsored lectures in 1838 on "Causes of the American Revolution," "The Sun," "The Legal Rights of Women," and "The Satanic School of Literature and Reform." At the Lowell Institute in Boston, founded in 1830 as "a perennial source of public good—a dispensation of sound science, of useful knowledge, of truth," there were lectures by the geologist Benjamin Silliman (who spoke there ninety-six times), the naturalist Louis Aggasiz, the Russian traveler George Kennan, and the writer Oliver Wendell Holmes (who appeared many times to give a popular lecture on "The Common Law"). Organizers estimated that 13,000 people attended the Lowell lectures in the 1837–1838 season alone. Lectures were open to all (for a small admission charge), but those who attended had to be "neatly dressed and of orderly behavior," and no one could leave the hall while a lecture was in progress. Lyceums may have entertained, but their purpose was to educate. Their founders considered them serious business and expected their audiences to do the same.

As the nation became increasingly preoccupied with sectional divisions and battles over slavery, the lyceums became important forums for discussion of public controversies. In Springfield, Illinois, in 1838, Abraham Lincoln spoke at the Young Men's Lyceum to denounce the lynchings of several slaves in Mississippi and an attack on a free black man in St. Louis—examples, he said, of the "mobocratic spirit" and a challenge to the "reverence for the laws" that should be the "political religion of the nation." In the years that followed, prominent abolitionists—William Lloyd Garrison, Wendell Phillips, Frederick Douglass, and others—became among the most popular

lyceum orators in the North. Douglass, a former slave turned antislavery orator, traveled widely speaking at lyceums as far-flung as central Ohio, the island of Nantucket, Massachusetts, and England (where he created a sensation within the British lyceum movement). Douglass mesmerized audiences with his scathing descriptions of life under slavery, and his lyceum lectures helped make him one of the best known and, in the North, most widely admired public figures of his time.

At their heart, lyceums always remained what they had been at the start: a place for men and women to educate and improve themselves by listening to knowledgeable speakers talk about what they knew. They both reflected, and helped strengthen, the growing interest in education in mid-nineteenth-century America. They helped drive the expansion and improvement of the public school system in many areas, and they marked the beginning of many decades of efforts to extend the benefits of education to adults. They helped popularize the lecture system of instruction, which remains a staple of university education even today. In the fevered years preceding the Civil War, however, lyceums also helped spread explosive ideas about slavery, freedom, and union that fanned the popular passions of the age.

had been antagonizing white southerners for years. Abolitionists were a minority in the North, mistrusted and even despised by many people who were much less opposed to slavery (and much more concerned about avoiding sectional conflict) than they were. But an increasing number of white southerners came to believe that the abolitionists represented the opinion of the North as a whole.

In response to these pressures, a growing number of white southerners began to elaborate an intellectual defense of slavery. It began as early as 1832, when Professor Thomas R. Dew of the College of William and Mary outlined the case for slavery. It matured in 1852, when apologists for slavery summarized their views in an anthology that gave their ideology its name: *The Pro-Slavery Argument.* John C. Calhoun stated the essence of the case in 1837: Southerners should stop apologizing for slavery as a necessary evil and defend it as "a good—a positive good." It was good for the slaves, pro-slavery southerners argued, because, blacks needed the guidance of white masters. Indeed, they claimed, the slaves were better off—better fed, better clothed, better housed, more secure—than northern factory workers. Slavery was also good for southern society as a whole because it was the only way the two races could live together in peace. It was good for the entire country because the southern economy, based on slavery, was the key to the prosperity of the nation.

Racist assumptions about the inferiority of blacks—sustained by elaborate philosophical and even "scientific" arguments—underlay the pro-slavery rationale. No group was more effective in using such assumptions to promote the argument than the southern Protestant clergy. Many southern ministers had opposed slavery as late as the 1820s; but by the end of the 1830s, the great majority of the clergy was defending the institution in simultaneously racist and Christian terms. Because African Americans were inferior, they argued, it was the responsibility of the white race to nurture them, to teach them morality and efficiency, and to protect them from the evils of the world; it was necessary, in other words, to maintain slavery, not just because of the economic needs of slaveowners, but also because of the physical and spiritual needs of the slaves themselves. Since many northern clergy were, at the same time, making powerful religious arguments against slavery, serious tensions arose within some denominations. Both the Baptist and Methodist churches divided into northern and southern branches in the 1840s.

The pro-slavery argument became an essential part of a larger project: a defense of the southern way of life. It was, many white southerners argued, a way of life superior to any other in the United States, perhaps in the world. White southerners believed northern society was abandoning traditional American values and replacing them with a spirit of greed, debauchery, and destructiveness. "The masses of the North are venal, corrupt, covetous, mean and selfish," wrote one southerner. Others wrote with horror of the factory system and the crowded, pestilen-

■ **ANTI-ABOLITIONIST VIOLENCE**
This 1838 woodcut depicts the anti-abolitionist riot in Alton, Illinois, in which Elijah P. Lovejoy, publisher of an abolitionist newspaper, was slain on November 7, 1837. The death of Lovejoy aroused the antislavery movement throughout the United States.
(Library of Congress)

tial cities filled with unruly immigrants. The South, in contrast, was a stable, orderly society, operating at a slow and human pace. Its labor system avoided the feuds between capital and labor plaguing the North, protected the welfare of its workers, and allowed the aristocracy to enjoy a refined and accomplished cultural life. It was, in short, as nearly perfect as any human civilization could become, an ideal social order in which all elements of the population were secure and content.

Some pro-slavery propagandists even argued that slavery was such a valuable institution that it should extend to the North and include white workers there. George Fitzhugh of Virginia—in *Sociology for the South, or the Failure of Free Society* (1854), *Cannibals All* (1857), and other writings—claimed that all societies lived on forced labor, that some of the greatest civilizations (ancient Greece, ancient Rome) had thrived because of it. In the South, he claimed, masters at least acknowledged responsibility for those whose labor they were exploiting. In the North, employers felt no obligation to care for their workers. Such arguments fueled the fears of those northern advocates of free labor who argued that the South was plotting to extend slavery everywhere, even into the factory system.

By the 1850s, some southern leaders had not only committed themselves to a militant pro-slavery ideology, they had also become convinced that they must silence their opponents. Some southern critics of slavery found it advisable to leave the region. Beginning in 1835 (when a Charleston mob destroyed sacks containing abolitionist literature in the city post office), southern postmasters generally refused to deliver antislavery mail. Southern state legislatures passed resolutions demanding that northern states suppress the "incendiary" agitation of the abolitionists. Southern representatives even managed for a time to impose a "gag rule" (adopted in 1836, repealed in 1844) on Congress, according to which all antislavery petitions would be tabled without being read. This growing intolerance of criticism further encouraged those northerners who warned of the "slave power conspiracy" against their liberties.

Buchanan and Depression

In this unpromising climate—with much of the nation passionately aroused by the Brooks assault on Sumner and the continuing violence in Kansas; with citizens of each section becoming increasingly militant in support of their own ideologies—the presidential campaign of 1856 began. Democratic Party leaders wanted a candidate who had not made many enemies and who was not closely associated with the explosive question of "Bleeding Kansas." They chose James Buchanan of Pennsylvania, a reliable party stalwart who as minister to England had been conveniently out of the country during the recent troubles. The Republicans, participating in their first presidential contest, denounced the Kansas-Nebraska Act and the expansion of slavery but also endorsed a program of internal improvements, thus combining the idealism of antislavery with the North's economic aspirations. They were as eager as the Democrats to present a safe candidate. They nominated John C. Fremont, who had made a national reputation as an explorer of the Far West and who had no political record.

In the meantime, the Native American, or Know-Nothing, Party was beginning to break apart. At its convention, many northern delegates withdrew because the platform was not sufficiently firm in opposing the expansion of slavery. The remaining delegates nominated former president Millard Fillmore. The remnant of the Whig Party, those who could not bring themselves to support either Buchanan or Fremont, endorsed Fillmore as well.

After a heated, even frenzied campaign, Buchanan won a narrow victory. He polled a plurality but not a majority of the popular votes: 1,833,000 to 1,340,000 for Fremont and 872,000 for Fillmore. A slight shift of votes in Pennsylvania and Illinois would have thrown those states into the Republican column and elected Fremont. More significant, perhaps, was that Fremont, who attracted virtually no votes at all in the South, received a third of all votes cast. In the North, he outpolled all other candidates.

At the time of his inauguration Buchanan had been in public life for more than forty years, and at age sixty-five he was the oldest president, except for William Henry Harrison, ever to have taken office. Whether because of his age and physical infirmities or because of a more fundamental weakness of character, he became a painfully timid and indecisive president at a time when the nation cried out for strong, effective leadership.

In the year Buchanan took over, a financial panic struck the country, followed by a depression that lasted several years. European demand for American agricultural products had risen during the Crimean War of 1854–1856. When the war ended and that demand fell off, prices declined. In the North, the depression strengthened the Republican Party. Distressed manufacturers and farmers came to believe that the hard times were the result of the unsound policies of southern-controlled Democratic administrations. They advocated a high protective tariff (Congress had lowered the tariff again in 1857), a homestead act, and internal improvements—all measures the South opposed. The frustrated economic interests of the North were moving into an alliance with antislavery elements, and thus into the Republican Party.

The Dred Scott *Decision*

The Supreme Court of the United States now thrust itself into the sectional disputes of the 1850s with one of the most controversial decisions in its history: its ruling in the case of *Dred Scott v. Sandford,* handed down two days after Buchanan was inaugurated. Dred Scott had been the property of an army surgeon in Missouri, and he travelled with his master into Illinois and Wisconsin, where slavery was forbidden. In 1846, after the death of the surgeon, Scott sued his master's widow for freedom on the grounds that his residence in free territory had made him a free man. The claim was well grounded in Missouri law, and in 1850, the circuit court in which Scott filed the suit declared him free. By now, John Sanford, the brother of the surgeon's widow, claimed ownership of Scott, and he appealed the ruling to the Missouri Supreme Court, which reversed the lower court decision. When Scott appealed to the federal courts, Sanford's attorneys claimed that Scott had no standing to sue because he was not a citizen, but private property. They also endorsed the extreme proslavery position that Congress had no authority to forbid slavery in the territories because such laws interfered with constitutionally protected rights of private property.

The Supreme Court (which misspelled Sanford's name in its ruling) was so divided that it was unable to issue a single ruling on the case and released separate decisions on each of several major issues. Each of the justices wrote a separate opinion. The thrust of the rulings, however, was a major defeat for the antislavery movement and an affirmation of the South's argument that the Constitution guaranteed the existence of slavery. Chief Justice Roger Taney, who wrote one of the majority opinions, declared that Scott was not a citizen of Missouri or of the United States and hence could not bring a suit in the federal courts. According to Taney, no person of African descent could be a citizen; indeed, blacks had virtually no rights at all under the Constitution. Scott's sojourn in the North, he claimed, had not affected his status as a slave. Slaves were property, said Taney, and the Fifth Amendment prohibited Congress from taking property without "due process of law." Consequently, Congress possessed no authority to pass a law depriving persons of their slave property in the territories. The Missouri Compromise, therefore, had always been unconstitutional.

The ruling did not challenge the right of an individual state to prohibit slavery within its borders, but the statement that the federal government was powerless to act on the issue was a drastic and startling one. Few judicial opinions have stirred as much popular anger and elation. Southern whites were ecstatic. The highest tribunal in the land had sanctioned parts of the most extreme southern argument. In the North, the decision produced widespread dismay. Republicans claimed that the decision deserved as much respect as a pronouncement by a group of political hacks "in any Washington bar room." When they secured control of the national government, they threatened, they would reverse the decision—by "packing" the Court with new members. Frederick Douglass, however, most accurately predicted the impact of *Dred Scott* when he said: "This very attempt to blot out forever the hopes of an enslaved people may be one necessary link in the chain of events preparatory to the complete overthrow of the whole slave system."

Deadlock over Kansas

President Buchanan endorsed the *Dred Scott* decision. At the same time, he sought to resolve the controversy over Kansas by supporting its admission to the Union as a slave state. In response, the proslavery territorial legislature called an election for delegates to a constitutional convention. The free-state residents refused to participate, claiming that the legislature had discriminated against them in drawing district lines. As a result, the pro-slavery forces won control of the convention in an election in which fewer than 10 percent of the eligible voters participated. The convention met in 1857 at Lecompton, framed a constitution legalizing slavery, and scheduled a referendum not on the constitution itself, but on the narrower question of whether to allow more slaves to enter Kansas. At the next election for the territorial legislature, antislavery groups turned out in force and won a majority. The new legislature promptly submitted the whole Lecompton constitution to the voters, who rejected it by more than 10,000 votes.

Both sides had resorted to fraud and violence, but it was clear nevertheless that a majority of the people of Kansas opposed slavery. Buchanan, however, ignored the evidence and urged Congress to admit Kansas under the Lecompton constitution. Stephen A. Douglas and other western Democrats refused to support the president's position, on the grounds that it violated the principle of popular sovereignty. "I care not whether [slavery] is voted down or voted up," Douglas explained. But in Kansas, he said, the "fair expression of the will of the people" had clearly opposed slavery; only through "trickery and jugglery" had pro-slavery forces prevailed. Buchanan's proposal passed the Senate, but western Democrats helped block it in the House.

Finally, in April 1858, Congress approved a compromise: The Lecompton constitution would be resubmitted to the voters of Kansas. If the document won approval, Kansas would be admitted to the Union; if it was rejected, statehood would be postponed until the population of the territory reached the 93,600 level required for a representative in Congress. Again, Kansas voters decisively rejected the Lecompton constitution. Not until the closing months of Buchanan's administration in 1861, when a number of southern states had withdrawn from the Union, did Kansas finally enter the Union—as a free state.

The Emergence of Lincoln

Given the gravity of the sectional crisis, the congressional elections of 1858 took on a special importance. Of particular note was the U.S. Senate election in Illinois, which pitted Stephen A. Douglas, the most prominent northern Democrat, against Abraham Lincoln, the most skillful politician in the Republican Party.

Lincoln had been the leading Whig and was now the leading Republican in Illinois. But since he was not a national figure comparable to Douglas, he sought to increase his visibility by engaging Douglas in a series of debates. The Lincoln-Douglas debates attracted enormous crowds and received wide national attention. By the time they ended, Lincoln had become nationally prominent.

The content of the debates revealed the deep disagreements between the two parties in the North. Douglas, defending popular sovereignty, accused the Republicans of promoting a war of sections, of wishing to interfere with slavery in the South, and of advocating social equality of the races. Lincoln denied these charges (properly, since neither he nor his party had ever advocated any of these things). He, in turn, accused the Democrats of conspiring to extend slavery into the territories and possibly into the free states as well (a charge that was equally unfounded).

At the heart of the debate, however, was a basic difference on the issue of slavery. Douglas appeared to have no moral position on the issue; as evidence for that, Lincoln cited Douglas's statement that he did not care whether slavery was "voted up, or voted down" in Kansas. Lincoln's opposition to slavery was more fundamental. If the nation could accept that African Americans were not entitled to basic human rights, he argued, then it could accept that other groups—immigrant laborers, for example—could be deprived of rights too. And if slavery were to extend into the western territories, he argued, opportunities for poor white laborers to better their lots there might be lost. The nation's future, he argued (reflecting the central idea of the Republican Party), rested on the spread of free labor.

Lincoln believed slavery was morally wrong, but he was not an abolitionist. That was in large part because he could not envision an alternative to slavery in the areas where it already existed. He shared the prevailing view among northern whites that the black race was not prepared (and perhaps never would be) to live on equal terms with whites. "We have a due regard to the actual presence of [slavery] amongst us and the difficulties of getting rid of it in any satisfactory way and all the constitutional obligations thrown about it," he once said. He and his party would "arrest the further spread" of slavery—that is, prevent its expansion into the territories—but they would not directly challenge it where it already existed.

Yet the implications of Lincoln's argument were more sweeping than this relatively moderate formula suggests, for both he and other Republicans believed that by restricting slavery to the South, they would be consigning the institution to its "ultimate extinction," that the institution would ultimately wither away. As he said in the most famous speech of the campaign:

> A house divided against itself cannot stand. I believe this government cannot endure permanently half slave and half free. I do not expect the Union to be dissolved—I do not expect the house to fall—but I do expect it will cease to be divided. It will become all one thing, or all the other.

In the debate at Freeport, Lincoln asked Douglas if the people of a territory could exclude slavery prior to the formation of a state constitution. Or, in other words, was popular sovereignty still workable despite the *Dred Scott* decision? Douglas replied that the people of a territory could legally exclude slavery before forming a state constitution simply by refusing to pass laws recognizing the right of slave ownership. Without such laws, he claimed, slavery could not exist. Douglas's reply became known as the Freeport Doctrine or, in the South, the Freeport Heresy. It satisfied his antislavery followers suffi-

ciently to win him reelection to the Senate, but it destroyed his hopes of attracting support in the South and damaged his national political ambitions.

Outside Illinois, the elections went heavily against the Democrats, who lost ground in almost every northern state. The party retained control of the Senate but lost its majority in the House, the results were bitterly deadlocked congressional sessions in 1858 and 1859.

John Brown's Raid

The battles in Congress, however, were almost entirely overshadowed by a spectacular event that enraged and horrified the entire South and greatly hastened the rush toward disunion. In the fall of 1859, John Brown, the antislavery zealot whose bloody actions in Kansas had inflamed the crisis there, staged an even more dramatic episode, this time in the South itself. With encouragement and financial aid from some eastern abolitionists (later known as the "Secret Six"), he had been making elaborate plans for over a year to seize a mountain fortress in Virginia to

■ **THE HARPERS FERRY ARSENAL**
John Brown's famous raid on Harpers Ferry in 1859 centered on this arsenal, from which he and his followers hoped, in vain, to foment a slave rebellion throughout the South. *(National Park Service, Harper's Ferry. U.S. Department of the Interior)*

which slaves and free blacks might flee. From there, he believed, he could foment a slave insurrection in the South. On October 16, he and a group of eighteen followers attacked and seized control of a United States arsenal in Harpers Ferry, Virginia. But the slave uprising Brown hoped to inspire did not occur, and he quickly found himself besieged in the arsenal by citizens, local militia companies, and before long United States troops under the command of Robert E. Lee. After ten of his men were killed, Brown surrendered. He was promptly tried in a Virginia court for treason against the state, found guilty, and sentenced to death. On December 2, 1859, he was hanged. Six of his followers met a similar fate.

Probably no other single event had as much influence as the Harpers Ferry raid in convincing white southerners that they could not live safely in the Union. Despite their militant defense of slavery, many were consumed with one great, if often secret, fear: the possibility of a general slave insurrection. And John Brown's raid suggested to them that the North was now committed to producing just such an insurrection. Southern whites were wrong in believing that the raid had the support of the North generally or of the Republican Party; most northerners and most Republicans condemned Brown's actions. But correspondence seized when Brown was arrested made clear the extent of his broad ties to northern abolitionists. The southern fear of a northern conspiracy against slavery grew stronger when abolitionists such as Wendell Phillips and Ralph Waldo Emerson began to glorify Brown as a new saint and when his execution made him a martyr to thousands of northerners.

The Election of Lincoln

The presidential election of 1860 had the most momentous consequences of any in American history. It was also among the most complicated.

Battles between southerners, who demanded a strong endorsement of slavery, and westerners, who supported popular sovereignty, had torn apart the Democratic Party. The party convention met in April in Charleston, South Carolina—an inopportune location, given that South Carolina was the center of proslavery extremism. When the convention endorsed popular sovereignty, delegates from eight states in the lower South walked out. The remaining delegates could not agree on a presidential candidate and fi-

nally adjourned the convention to meet again in Baltimore in June. The decimated convention at Baltimore nominated Stephen Douglas for president. Meanwhile, some disenchanted southern Democrats met in Richmond and nominated John C. Breckinridge of Kentucky.

The leaders of the Republican Party, in the meantime, were working to broaden the base of their party. No longer content to present themselves just as opponents of slavery, they now tried to appeal to every major interest group in the North that feared the South was blocking its economic aspirations. Their platform endorsed such traditional Whig positions as a high tariff, internal improvements, a homestead bill, and a railroad to the Pacific to be built with federal financial assistance. They supported the right of each state to decide the status of slavery within its borders. But they also insisted that neither Congress nor territorial legislatures could legalize slavery in the territories. Passing over better known candidates (among them William H. Seward of New York, the most prominent Republican in the country), the convention chose Abraham Lincoln as the

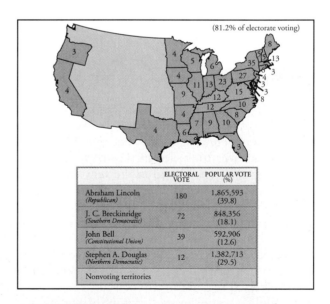

	ELECTORAL VOTE	POPULAR VOTE (%)
Abraham Lincoln *(Republican)*	180	1,865,593 (39.8)
J. C. Breckinridge *(Southern Democratic)*	72	848,356 (18.1)
John Bell *(Constitutional Union)*	39	592,906 (12.6)
Stephen A. Douglas *(Northern Democratic)*	12	1,382,713 (29.5)
Nonvoting territories		

(81.2% of electorate voting)

■ **ELECTION OF 1860**
The presidential election of 1860 had the most momentous consequences of any in American history. Abraham Lincoln won a majority of the electoral votes but only two-fifths of the popular vote. Moreover, although the Republican Lincoln won almost all the free states, he failed to win a single slave state. Thus, many southern slaveholders considered Lincoln's election to be a purely sectional and northern triumph that threatened slavery.

party's presidential nominee. Lincoln was eminent enough to be respectable but (unlike Seward) obscure enough to have made few enemies. He was radical enough to please the antislavery faction in the party but conservative enough to satisfy many ex-Whigs.

But the Republicans were not yet conservative enough to satisfy all the former Whigs. In May, a group of them—mostly moderates from the North and the South, many of them conservative elder statesmen—met in Baltimore and formed the Constitutional Union Party in an effort to transcend sectional passions and create a truly national political movement. They nominated John Bell of Tennessee for president and Edward Everett of Massachusetts for vice president. They endorsed the Constitution and the Union and avoided taking a clear stand on the issue of slavery.

In the November election, Lincoln won the presidency with a majority of the electoral votes but only about two-fifths of the fragmented popular vote. Moreover, the Republicans failed to win a majority in Congress; and, of course, they did not control the Supreme Court. Even so, the election of Lincoln became the final signal to many white southerners that their position in the Union was hopeless. And within a few weeks of Lincoln's victory, the process of disunion began—a process that would quickly lead to a prolonged and bloody war between two groups of Americans, each heir to more than a century of struggling toward nationhood, each now convinced that it shared no common ground with the other.

CONCLUSION

In the decades following the War of 1812, a vigorous sense of nationalism pervaded much of American life, helping to smooth over the growing differences among the very different societies emerging in the regions of the United States. During the 1850s, however, the forces that had worked to hold the nation together in the past fell victim to new and much more divisive pressures that were working to split the nation apart.

Driving the sectional tensions of the 1850s was a battle over national policy toward the western territories, which were clamoring to become states of the Union—and over the place of slavery within them. Should slavery be permitted in the new states? And who should decide whether to permit it or not? There were strenuous efforts to craft compromises and solutions to this dilemma: the Compromise of 1850, the Kansas-Nebraska Act of 1854, and others. But despite these efforts, positions on slavery continued to harden in both the North and the South until ultimately each region came to consider the other its enemy. Bitter battles in the territory of Kansas over whether to permit slavery there; growing agitation by abolitionists in the North and pro-slavery advocates in the South; the Supreme Court's controversial *Dred Scott* decision in 1857; the popularity of *Uncle Tom's Cabin* throughout the decade; and the emergence of a new political party—the Republican party—openly and centrally opposed to slavery: all worked to destroy the hopes for compromise and push the South toward secession.

In 1860, all pretense of common sentiment collapsed when no political party presented a presidential candidate capable of attracting national support. The Republicans nominated Abraham Lincoln of Illinois, a little-known politician recognized for his eloquent condemnations of slavery in a Senate race two years earlier. The Democratic party split apart, with its northern and southern wings each nominating different candidates. A third party, devoted to the Constitution and the Union, forlornly nominated a candidate of its own who found almost no constituency at all. Lincoln won the election easily, but with less than forty percent of the vote. And almost immediately after his victory, the states of the South began preparing to secede from the Union.

Significant Events

1818	United States and Great Britain sign treaty sharing rights to Oregon country
1822	Mexico wins independence from Spain
	Stephen F. Austin establishes first legal American settlement in Texas
1824	Mexico passes colonization law to attract American settlers to Texas
1826	American settlers in Texas revolt unsuccessfully against Mexican rule
1830	Mexican Government bars further American immigration into Texas
1833	Mexico drops Texas immigration ban
1836	Texas declares independence from Mexico
	Battle of San Jacinto in Texas revolution
1844	James K. Polk elected president
1845	Texas admitted to Union
1846	Oregon boundary dispute settled
	United States declares war on Mexico
	Wilmot Proviso introduced in Congress
1848	Treaty of Guadalupe Hidalgo settles Mexican War
	Antislavery Free-Soil Party formed
	Zachary Taylor elected president
	Gold discovered in Sacramento Valley, California, sparking gold rush
1850	Compromise of 1850 enacted
	Taylor dies
	Millard Fillmore succeeds Taylor as president
	California admitted to Union
1852	Franklin Pierce elected president
	The Pro-Slavery Argument published
	Harriet Beecher Stowe publishes *Uncle Tom's Cabin*
1853	Gadsden Purchase
1854	Kansas-Nebraska Act passed
	Republican Party formed
1855–1856	Violence breaks out in "Bleeding Kansas"
1856	Preston Brooks canes Charles Sumner
	James Buchanan elected president
1857	George Fitzhugh publishes *Cannibals All*
	Supreme Court hands down *Dred Scott* decision
1858	Pro-slavery Lecompton constitution defeated by popular referendum in Kansas
	Lincoln and Douglas debate
1859	John Brown raids Harpers Ferry
1860	Democratic Party splits
	Lincoln elected president
	Process of secession begins

FOR FURTHER REFERENCE

Suggested Readings   Anders Stephanson, *Manifest Destiny* (1995) briefly traces the origins of American expansion ideology. David M. Pletcher, *The Diplomacy of Annexation: Texas, Oregon, and the Mexican War* (1973) is the standard work on war and diplomacy in the 1840s. William W. Freehling, *The Road to Disunion, Vol. 1: Secessionists at Bay, 1776–1854* (1990) explores the successful containment of sectionalism prior to the 1850s. David Potter, *The Impending Crisis* (1976) is a thorough summary of the decisive decade. Eric Foner, *Free Soil, Free Labor, Free Men* (1970) traces the emergence of the Republican Party. Michael Holt, *The Political Crisis of the 1850s* (1978) challenges Foner by emphasizing ethnic and religious alignment in northern politics. Don E. Fehrenbacher, *The Dred Scott Case* (1978) explains the Supreme Court's most infamous decision.

Films   (The best source for information on how to find these and other films is *Bowker's Complete Video Directory*—3 volumes.) *The American Story, No. 10: Manifest Destiny* (1985) traces American industrial growth and commercial expansion through the Taylor, Fillmore, and Polk presidencies. *Manifest Destiny* examines the implications of this concept for war and diplomacy in the United States. *Texas & the Mexican Cession* (1990) brings to life the days of Davy Crockett and Sam Houston. *Uncle Tom's Cabin* (1987) is a recent adaptation of Harriet Beecher Stowe's influential and controversial novel. *The Back-*

ground of the Civil War (1981) introduces the differences between North and South that eventually led to war. *The Civil War: Union at Risk* (1989) presents the pre-Civil War differences between North and South and argues that the war was fought over constitutional interpretation. *Abraham Lincoln: A New Birth of Freedom* (1992) features commentators from Mario Cuomo to Ted Koppel. *The Lincoln-Douglas Debates: The House Divides* (1989) examines the two barnstorming politicians' pivotal debates over the status of slavery in the western territories.

Internet Resources   (For up-to-date URL addresses and links to these and other websites, consult the McGraw-Hill history site at http://www.mhhe.com/socscience/history/usa/link/linktop.htm) *The Avalon Project at the Yale Law School: Texas-American Relations 1838–1846* contains documents relating to the annexation of Texas by the United States. *The Road to Disunion Civil War Timeline* presents the events leading up to the Civil War from 1830 to 1860. *Nineteenth Century Documents Project* has the full text of dozens of political documents and newspaper stories, most of them relating the sectional crisis and the Civil War; many can be searched. *The Mexican-American War Memorial Page* presents both American and Mexican documents; particularly rich in paintings and lithographs. *Maps of the Pimería: Early Cartography of the Southwest* has original maps of the areas acquired by the United States in 1848.

BIBLIOGRAPHY

Westward Expansion   Ray Allen Billington, *Westward Expansion,* rev. ed. (1974); *The Far Western Frontier, 1830–1860* (1956). Robert R. Dystra, *Bright Radical Star: Black Freedom and White Supremacy on the Hawkeye Frontier* (1993). John M. Faragher, *Women and Men on the Overland Trail* (1979). T. R. Fehrenbach, *Lone Star: A History of Texas and the Texans* (1968). William H. Goetzmann, *Exploration and Empire* (1966). J. S. Holiday, *The World Rushed In* (1981). David Alan Johnson, *Founding the Far West: California, Oregon, and Nevada, 1840–1890* (1992). Donald D. Johnson with Gary Dean Best, *The United States in the Pacific: Private Interests and Public Policies, 1784–1899* (1995). Laura Maffly-Kipp, *Religion and Society in Frontier California* (1994). Frederick Merk, *History of the Westward Movement* (1978); *Manifest Destiny and Mission in American History* (1963); *Fruits of Propaganda in the Tyler Administration* (1971); *Slavery and the Annexation of Texas* (1972); *The Oregon Question* (1967); *The Monroe Doctrine and American Expansionism, 1843–1849* (1966). Francis Parkman, *The Oregon Trail* (1849). R. W. Paul, *California Gold* (1947). Henry Nash Smith, *Virgin Land* (1950). John D. Unruh, *The Plains Across: The Overland Emigrants and the Trans-Mississippi West, 1840–1860* (1979).

Expansion and the Mexican War   K. Jack Bauer, *The Mexican-American War, 1846–1848* (1974). G. M. Brack, *Mexico Views Manifest Destiny, 1821–1846* (1975). S. V. Conner and O. B. Faulk, *North America Divided* (1971). Robert W. Johnson, *To the Halls of Montezuma: The Mexican War in the American Imagination* (1985). Robert E.

May, *The Southern Dream of a Caribbean Empire, 1854-1861* (1973). John H. Schroeder, *Mr. Polk's War: American Opposition and Dissent* (1973). Charles G. Sellers, *James K. Polk: Continentalist, 1843-1846* (1966). Otis A. Singletary, *The Mexican War* (1960). David J. Weber, *The Mexican Frontier, 1821-1846: The American Southwest Under Mexico* (1982).

The Sectional Crisis: General Studies   William J. Cooper, *The South and the Politics of Slavery, 1828-1856* (1978); *Liberty and Slavery* (1983). Avery Craven, *The Coming of the Civil War* (1942). James M. McPherson, *Ordeal by Fire* (1981); *Battle Cry of Freedom* (1988). Allan Nevins, *The Ordeal of the Union*, 2 vols. (1947); *The Emergence of Lincoln*, 2 vols. (1950). James G. Randall and David Donald, *The Civil War and Reconstruction*, rev. ed. (1969). Richard H. Sewell, *A House Divided: Sectionalism and the Civil War, 1848-1865* (1988).

The Compromise of 1850   Kinley J. Bauer, *Cotton Versus Conscience: Massachusetts Whig Politics and Southern Expansion, 1843-1858* (1967). Richard N. Current, *Daniel Webster and the Rise of National Conservatism* (1955). Robert F. Dalzell, Jr., *Daniel Webster and the Trial of American Nationalism, 1843-1852* (1973). Thelma Jennings, *The Nashville Convention* (1980). Robert W. Johannsen, *Stephen A. Douglas* (1973). Chaplain W. Morrison, *Democratic Politics and Sectionalism: The Wilmot Proviso Controversy* (1973). Robert V. Remini, *Henry Clay: Statesman for the Union*

(1991). Charles M. Wiltse, *John C. Calhoun: Sectionalist, 1840-1850* (1951).

Sectional Crises in the 1850s   Tyler Anbinder, *Nativism and Slavery: The Northern Know Nothings and the Politics of the 1850s* (1992). Dale Baum, *The Civil War Party System: The Case of Massachusetts 1848-1876* (1984). Frederick Blue, *Charles Sumner and the Conscience of the North* (1994). R. O. Boyer, *The Legend of John Brown* (1973). David Donald, *Charles Sumner and the Coming of the Civil War* (1960). Eric Foner, *Politics and Ideology in the Age of the Civil War* (1980). William E. Gienapp, *The Origins of the Republican Party, 1852-1856* (1987). Truman Nelson, *The Old Man: John Brown at Harpers Ferry* (1973). Stephen Oates, *To Purge This Land with Blood: A Biography of John Brown* (1970). Benjamin Quarles, *Allies for Freedom* (1974). Gunja SenGupta, *For God and Mammon: Evangelicals and Entrepreneurs, Masters and Slaves in Territorial Kansas, 1854-1860* (1996). Mitchell Snay, *Gospel of Disunion: Religion and Separatism in the Antebellum South* (1993). Kenneth M. Stampp, *America in 1857: A Nation on the Brink* (1990). Gerald Wolff, *The Kansas-Nebraska Bill* (1977).

The Emergence of Lincoln   Richard N. Current, *The Lincoln Nobody Knows* (1958). David Donald, *Lincoln Reconsidered* (1956). Don E. Fehrenbacher, *Prelude to Greatness: Lincoln in the 1850's* (1962). George B. Forgie, *Patricide in the House Divided* (1979).

Chapter Fourteen

THE CIVIL WAR

By the end of 1860, the cords that had once bound the Union together seemed to have snapped. The almost mystical veneration of the Constitution and its framers was no longer working to unite the nation; most residents of the North and South—particularly after the controversial *Dred Scott* decision—now differed fundamentally on their interpretations of the Constitution and what the framers had meant. The romantic vision of America's great national destiny had ceased to be a unifying force; the two sections now defined that destiny in different and apparently irreconcilable terms. The stable two-party system could not dampen sectional conflict any longer; that system had collapsed in the 1850s, to be replaced by a new one that accentuated, rather than muted, regional controversy. Above all, the federal government was no longer the remote, unthreatening presence it once had been; the need to resolve the status of the territories had made it necessary for Washington to deal with sectional issues in a direct and forceful way. And thus, beginning in 1860, the divisive forces that had always existed within the United States were no longer counterbalanced by unifying forces. As a result, the Union began to dissolve.

THE SECESSION CRISIS

Almost as soon as the news of Abraham Lincoln's election reached the South, the militant leaders of the region—the champions of the new concept of "Southern nationalism," men known both to their contemporaries and to history as the "fire-eaters"—began to demand an end to the Union.

The Withdrawal of the South

South Carolina, long the hotbed of Southern separatism, seceded first. It called a special convention, which voted unanimously on December 20, 1860, to withdraw the state from the Union. By the time Lincoln took office, six other states—Mississippi (January 9, 1861), Florida (January 10), Alabama (January 11), Georgia (January 19), Louisiana (January 26), and Texas (February 1)—had seceded. In February 1861, representatives of the seven seceded states

■ **"YOUNG SOLDIER"**
This somber 1864 painting by Winslow Homer portrays a young Union soldier—perhaps a drummer boy. When they were not playing music, drummers and buglers performed other functions in camp, as barbers, valets, and members of burial teams. Boys as young as 12 and 13 sometimes joined the army and grew up quickly in the rough surroundings of the camps.
(Cooper-Hewitt Museum, Smithsonian Institution. Gift of Charles Savage Homer, 1912-12-110/Art Resource, NY)

met at Montgomery, Alabama, and formed a new nation: the Confederate States of America. The response from the North was confused and indecisive.
President James Buchanan told Congress in December 1860 that no state had the right to secede from
the Union but suggested that the federal government
had no authority to stop a state if it did.

The seceding states immediately seized the federal
property—forts, arsenals, government offices—
within their boundaries. But at first they did not have
sufficient military power to seize two fortified offshore military installations: Fort Sumter, on an island
in the harbor of Charleston, South Carolina, gar-
risoned by a small force under Major Robert Anderson; and Fort Pickens in the harbor of Pensacola,
Florida. South Carolina sent commissioners to Washington to ask for the surrender of Sumter; but
Buchanan, timid though he was, refused to yield it.
Indeed, in January 1861 he ordered an unarmed merchant ship to proceed to Fort Sumter with additional
troops and supplies. Confederate guns on shore fired
at the vessel—the first shots between North and
South—and turned it back. Still, neither section was
yet ready to concede that war had begun. And
in Washington, efforts began once more to forge a
compromise.

The Failure of Compromise

Gradually, the compromise forces gathered behind a
proposal first submitted by Senator John J. Crittenden of Kentucky and known as the Crittenden Compromise. It called for several constitutional amendments, which would guarantee the permanent
existence of slavery in the slave states and would satisfy Southern demands on such issues as fugitive
slaves and slavery in the District of Columbia. But
the heart of Crittenden's plan was a proposal to
reestablish the Missouri Compromise line in all present and future territory of the United States: Slavery
would be prohibited north of the line and permitted
south of it. The remaining southerners in the Senate
seemed willing to accept the plan, but the Republicans were not. The compromise would have required the Republicans to abandon their most fundamental position: that slavery not be allowed to
expand.

And so nothing had been resolved when Abraham
Lincoln arrived in Washington for his inauguration—
sneaking into the city in disguise on a night train to
avoid assassination as he passed through the slave
state of Maryland. In his inaugural address, which
dealt directly with the secession crisis, Lincoln laid
down several basic principles. Since the Union was
older than the Constitution, no state could leave it.
Acts of force or violence to support secession were
insurrectionary. And the government would "hold,
occupy, and possess" federal property in the seceded
states—a clear reference to Fort Sumter.

Fort Sumter

Conditions at Fort Sumter were deteriorating quickly.
Union forces were running short of supplies; unless
they received fresh provisions the fort would have to
be evacuated. Lincoln believed that if he surrendered
Sumter, his commitment to maintaining the Union
would no longer be credible. So he sent a relief expedition to the fort, carefully informing the South Carolina authorities that there would be no attempt to

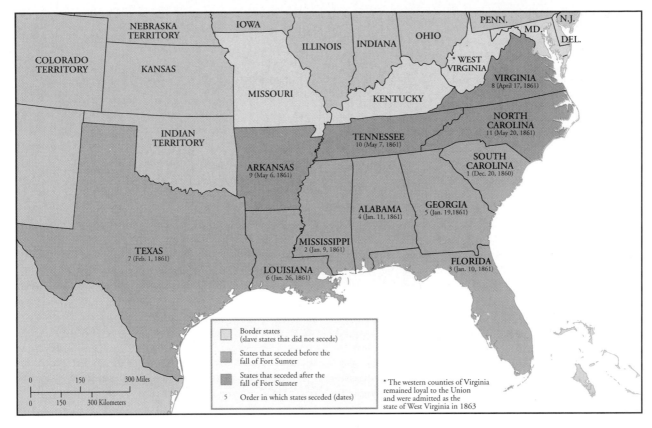

Map legend:
Border states (slave states that did not secede)
States that seceded before the fall of Fort Sumter
States that seceded after the fall of Fort Sumter
5 Order in which states seceded (dates)

* The western counties of Virginia remained loyal to the Union and were admitted as the state of West Virginia in 1863

■ THE PROCESS OF SECESSION

The slaveholding states did not secede from the United States in unison. Led by South Carolina, only the states of the Deep South seceded prior to the fall of Fort Sumter. After April 14, 1861, when the Confederacy captured Fort Sumter, Virginia led a wave of Upper South states out of the Union. The slaveholding border states of Delaware, Maryland, Kentucky and Missouri all remained in the Union. In 1863, loyal Unionist counties in Virginia were organized into a new state, West Virginia.

send troops or munitions unless the supply ships met with resistance.

The new Confederate government now faced a dilemma. Permitting the expedition to land would seem to be a tame submission to federal authority. Firing on the ships or the fort would seem (to the North at least) to be aggression. But Confederate leaders finally decided that to appear cowardly would be worse than to appear belligerent, and they ordered General P. G. T. Beauregard, commander of Confederate forces at Charleston, to take the island, by force if necessary. When Anderson refused to surrender the fort, the Confederates bombarded it for two days, April 12–13, 1861. On April 14, Anderson surrendered. The Civil War had begun.

Almost immediately, Lincoln began mobilizing the North for war. And equally promptly, four more slave states seceded from the Union and joined the Confederacy: Virginia (April 17, 1861), Arkansas (May 6), Tennessee (June 8), and North Carolina (May 20). The four remaining slave states—Maryland, Delaware, Kentucky, and Missouri—cast their lot with the Union (under heavy political and even military pressure from Washington).

Was there anything that Lincoln (or those before him) could have done to settle the sectional conflict peaceably? That question has preoccupied historians for more than a century without resolution (see "Where Historians Disagree," pp. 471–473). There were, of course, actions that might have prevented a war: if, for example, northern leaders had

■ **"THE FLAG OF SUMTER, 1863"**
Fort Sumter, the site of the first battle of
the Civil War, became a Confederate
fortress after the Union forces evacuated.
This 1863 painting by Conrad Wise
Champman shows a sentry standing guard
on the island beneath the Stars and Bars.
*(The Museum of the Confederacy, Richmond,
Virginia. Photography by Katherine Wetzel)*

decided to let the South withdraw in peace. The
real question, however, is not what hypothetical
situations might have reversed the trend toward
war but whether the preponderance of forces in
the nation were acting to hold the nation together
or to drive it apart. And by 1861, it seems clear that
in both the North and the South, sectional antagonisms—whether justified or not—had risen to such
a point that the existing terms of union had become untenable.

People in both regions had come to believe that
two distinct and incompatible civilizations had developed in the United States and that those civilizations were incapable of living together in peace.
Ralph Waldo Emerson, speaking for much of the
North, said at the time: "I do not see how a barbarous community and a civilized community can
constitute one state." And a slaveowner, expressing
the sentiments of much of the South, said shortly
after the election of Lincoln: "These [Northern]
people hate us, annoy us, and would have us assassinated by our slaves if they dared. They are a different people from us, whether better or worse,
and there is no love between us. Why then continue
together?"

That the North and the South had come to believe
these things helped lead to secession and war.
Whether these things were actually true—whether

the North and the South were really as different and
incompatible as they thought—is another question,
one that the preparations for and conduct of the war
help to answer.

The Opposing Sides

As the war began, only one thing was clear: all the
important material advantages lay with the North.
Its population was more than twice as large as that
of the South (and nearly four times as large as the
nonslave population of the South), so the Union had
a much greater manpower reserve both for its
armies and its work force. The North had an advanced industrial system and was able by 1862 to
manufacture almost all its own war materials. The
South had almost no industry at all and, despite impressive efforts to increase its manufacturing capacity, had to rely on imports from Europe throughout
the war.

In addition, the North had a much better transportation system than did the South, and in particular
more and better railroads: twice as much trackage
as the Confederacy, and a much better integrated
system of lines. During the war, moreover, the already inferior Confederate railroad system steadily
deteriorated and by the beginning of 1864 had almost collapsed.

THE CAUSES OF THE CIVIL WAR

In his second inaugural address in March 1865, Abraham Lincoln looked back at the beginning of the Civil War four years earlier. "All knew," he said, that slavery "was somehow the cause of the war." Few historians in the decades since Lincoln spoke have doubted the basic truth of Lincoln's statement; no credible explanation of the causes of the Civil War can ignore slavery. But historians have, nevertheless, disagreed sharply about many things. Was the Civil War inevitable, or could it have been avoided? Was slavery the only, or even the principal, cause of the war? Were other factors equally or more important?

This debate began even before the war itself. In 1858, Senator William H. Seward of New York took note of two competing explanations of the sectional tensions that were then inflaming the nation. On one side, he claimed, stood those who believed the sectional hostility to be "accidental, unnecessary, the work of interested or fanatical agitators." Opposing them stood those (like Seward himself) who believed there to be "an irrepressible conflict between opposing and enduring forces." For at least a century, the division Seward described remained at the heart of scholarly debate.

The "irrepressible conflict" argument was the first to dominate historical discussion. In the first decades after the fighting, histories of the Civil War generally reflected the views of Northerners who had themselves participated in the conflict. To them, the war appeared to be a stark moral conflict in which the South was clearly to blame, a conflict that arose inevitably as a result of the militant immorality of slave society. Henry Wilson's *History of the Rise and Fall of the Slave Power* (1872–1877) was a particularly

vivid version of this moral interpretation of the war, which argued that Northerners had fought to preserve the Union and a system of free labor against the aggressive designs of the South.

A more temperate interpretation, but one that reached generally the same conclusions, emerged in the 1890s, when the first serious histories of the war began to appear. Preeminent among them was the seven-volume *History of the United States from the Compromise of 1850 . . .* (1893–1900) by James Ford Rhodes. Like Wilson and others, Rhodes identified slavery as the central, indeed virtually the only, cause of the war. "If the Negro had not been brought to America," he wrote, "the Civil War could not have occurred." And because the North and South had reached positions on the issue of slavery that were both irreconcilable and unalterable, the conflict had become "inevitable."

Although Rhodes placed his greatest emphasis on the moral conflict over slavery, he suggested that the struggle also reflected fundamental differences between the Northern and Southern economic systems. In the 1920s, the idea of the war as an irrepressible economic, rather than moral, conflict received fuller expression from Charles and Mary Beard in *The Rise of American Civilization* (2 vols., 1927). Slavery, the Beards claimed, was not so much a social or cultural institution as an economic one, a labor system. There were, they insisted, "inherent antagonisms" between Northern industrialists and Southern planters. Each group sought to control the federal government so as to protect its own economic interests. Both groups used arguments over slavery and states' rights largely as smoke screens.

(continued)

The economic determinism of the Beards influenced a generation of historians in important ways, but ultimately most of those who believed the Civil War to have been "irrepressible" returned to an emphasis on social and cultural factors. Allan Nevins argued as much in his great work, *The Ordeal of the Union* (8 vols., 1947–1971). The North and the South, he wrote, "were rapidly becoming separate peoples." At the root of these cultural differences was the "problem of slavery," but the "fundamental assumptions, tastes, and cultural aims" of the two regions were diverging in other ways as well.

More recent proponents of the "irrepressible conflict" argument have taken different views of the Northern and Southern positions on the conflict but have been equally insistent on the role of culture and ideology in creating them. Eric Foner, in *Free Soil, Free Labor, Free Men* (1970) and other writings, emphasized the importance of the "free-labor ideology" to Northern opponents of slavery. The moral concerns of the abolitionists were not the dominant sentiments in the North, he claimed. Instead, most Northerners (including Abraham Lincoln) opposed slavery largely because they feared it might spread to the North and threaten the position of free white laborers. Convinced that Northern society was superior to that of the South, and increasingly persuaded of the South's intentions to extend the "slave power" beyond its existing borders, Northerners were embracing a viewpoint that made conflict almost inevitable. Eugene Genovese, writing of Southern slaveholders in *The Political Economy of Slavery* (1965), emphasized their conviction that the slave system provided a far more humane society than industrial labor, that the South had constructed "a special civilization built on the relation of master to slave." Just as Northerners were becoming convinced of a Southern threat to their economic system, so Southerners believed that the North had aggressive and hostile designs on the Southern way of life. Like Foner, therefore, Genovese saw in the cultural outlook of the section the source of an all but inevitable conflict.

Historians who argue that the conflict emerged naturally, even inevitably, out of a fundamental divergence between the sections have therefore disagreed markedly over whether moral, cultural, social, ideological, or economic issues were the primary causes of the Civil War. But they have been in general accord that the conflict between North and South was deeply embedded in the nature of the two societies, that the crisis that ultimately emerged was irrepressible. Other historians, however, have questioned that assumption and have argued that the Civil War might have been avoided, that the differences between North and South were not so fundamental as to have necessitated war. Like proponents of the "irrepressible conflict" school, advocates of the war as a "repressible conflict" emerged first in the nineteenth century. President James Buchanan, for example, believed that extremist agitators were to blame for the conflict, and many Southerners writing of the war in the late nineteenth century claimed that only the fanaticism of the Republican Party could account for the conflict.

The idea of the war as avoidable gained wide recognition among historians in the 1920s and 1930s, when a group known as the "revisionists" began to offer new accounts of the origins of the conflict. One of the leading revisionists was James G. Randall, who saw in the social and economic systems of the North and the South no differences so fundamental as to require a war. Slavery, he suggested, was an essentially benign institution; it was in any case already "crumbling in the presence of nineteenth century tendencies." Only the political ineptitude of a "blundering generation" of leaders could account for the Civil War, he claimed. Avery Craven, another leading revisionist, placed more emphasis on the issue of slavery than had Randall. But in *The Coming of the Civil War* (1942) he too argued that slave laborers were not much worse off than Northern industrial workers, that the institution was already on the road to "ultimate extinction," and that war could therefore have been averted had skillful and responsible leaders worked to produce compromise.

More recent students of the war have kept elements of the revisionist interpretation alive by emphasizing the role of political agitation and ethnocultural conflicts in the coming of the war. In 1960, for example, David Herbert Donald argued that the politicians of the 1850s were not unusually inept, but that they were operating in a society in which traditional restraints were being eroded in the face of the rapid extension of democracy. Thus the sober, statesmanlike solution of differences was particularly difficult. Michael Holt, in *The Political Crisis of the 1850s* (1978), emphasized the role of political parties and especially the collapse of the second party system, rather than the irreconcilable differences between sections, in explaining the conflict, although he avoided placing blame on any one group.

Holt, however, also helped introduce another element to the debate. He was, along with Paul Kleppner, Joel Silbey, and William Gienapp, one of the creators of an "ethnocultural" interpretation of the war. The Civil War began, the ethnoculturalists argue, in large part because the party system—the most effective instrument for containing and mediating sectional differences—collapsed in the 1850s and produced a new Republican party that aggravated, rather than calmed, the divisions in the nation. But unlike other scholars, who saw the debate over slavery as the central factor in the collapse of the party system, the ethnoculturalists argue for other factors. For example, William Gienapp, in *The Origins of the Republican Party, 1852-1856* (1987) argues that the disintegration of the party system in the early 1850s was less a result of the debate over slavery in the territories than of such ethnocultural issues as temperance and nativism. The Republican Party itself, he argues, was less a product of antislavery fervor than of a sustained competition with the Know-Nothing Party over ethnic and cultural issues. Gienapp and the other ethnoculturalists would not entirely dispute Lincoln's claim that slavery was "somehow the cause of the war." But they do challenge the arguments of Eric Foner and others that the "free labor ideal" of the North—and the challenge slavery, and its possible expansion into the territories, posed to that ideal—was the principal reason for the conflict.

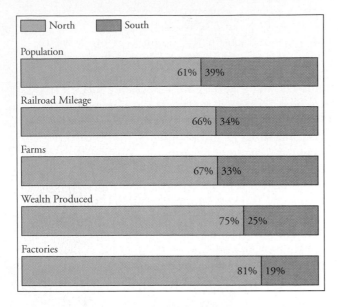

North   South

Population

61% | 39%

Railroad Mileage

66% | 34%

Farms

67% | 33%

Wealth Produced

75% | 25%

Factories

81% | 19%

■ **UNION VERSUS CONFEDERATE RESOURCES
IN THE CIVIL WAR**
The Union enjoyed substantial advantages over the Confederacy in almost every index of economic power, agricultural as well as industrial. While the North was able to manufacture most of its own war materials and to transport them anywhere in the country, the South had a poorly developed railroad system and almost no industry at all. On the other hand, white Southerners held the advantage of fighting a defensive war on familiar territory.

But in the beginning the North's material advantages were not as decisive as they appear in retrospect. The South was, for the most part, fighting a defensive war on its own land and thus had the advantage of local support and familiarity with the territory. The Northern armies, on the other hand, were fighting mostly within the South, with long lines of communications, amid hostile local populations, and with access only to the South's own inadequate transportation system. The commitment of the white population of the South to the war was, with limited exceptions, clear and firm. In the North, opinion about the war was more divided and support for it remained shaky until very near the end. A major Southern victory at any one of several crucial moments might have proved decisive by breaking the North's will to continue the struggle. Finally, many Southerners believed that the dependence of the English and French textile industries on American cotton would require them to intervene on the side of the Confederacy.

THE MOBILIZATION OF THE NORTH

In the North, the war produced considerable discord, frustration, and suffering. But it also produced prosperity and economic growth by giving a major stimulus to both industry and agriculture.

Economic Measures

With Southern forces now gone from Congress, the Republican Party could exercise virtually unchallenged authority. During the war, it enacted an aggressively nationalistic program to promote economic development, particularly in the West. The Homestead Act of 1862 permitted any citizen or prospective citizen to claim 160 acres of public land and to purchase it for a small fee after living on it for five years. The Morrill Land Grant Act of the same year transferred substantial public acreage to the state governments, which were to sell the land and use the proceeds to finance public education. This act led to the creation of many new state colleges and universities, the so-called land-grant institutions. Congress also passed a series of tariff bills that by the end of the war had raised duties to the highest level in the nation's history—a great boon to domestic industries eager for protection from foreign competition.

Congress also moved to complete the dream of a transcontinental railroad. It created two new federally chartered corporations: the Union Pacific Railroad Company, which was to build westward from Omaha, and the Central Pacific, which was to build eastward from California. The two projects were to meet in the middle and complete the link. The government provided free public lands and generous loans to the companies.

The National Bank Acts of 1863–1864 created a new national banking system. Existing or newly formed banks could join the system if they had enough capital and were willing to invest one-third of it in government securities. In return, they could issue U.S. Treasury notes as currency. The new system eliminated much of the chaos and uncertainty in the nation's currency and created a uniform system of national bank notes.

More difficult than promoting economic growth was financing the war itself. The government tried to

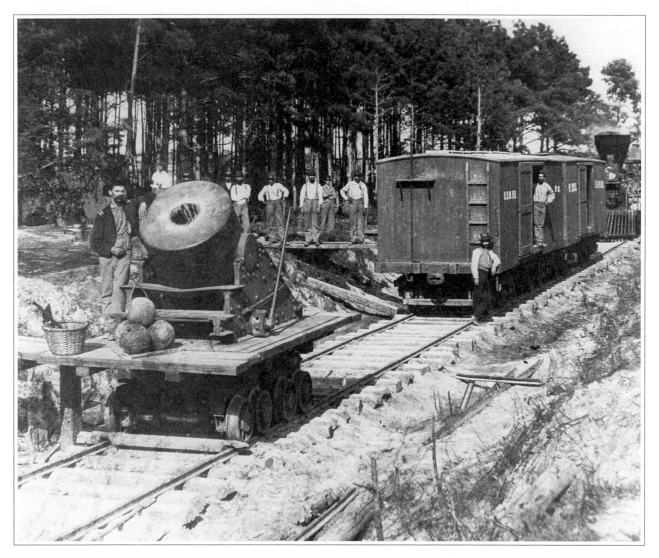

Union soldiers pose beside a mortar mounted on a railroad car in July 1864, during the siege of Petersburg, Virginia. Railroads played a critical role in the Civil War, and the superiority of the North's rail system was an important factor in its victory. It was appropriate, perhaps, that the battle for Petersburg, the last great struggle of the war, was over control of critical railroad lines. *(National Archives)*

do so in three ways: by levying taxes, issuing paper currency, and borrowing. Congress levied new taxes on almost all goods and services; and in 1861 the government levied an income tax for the first time, with rates that eventually rose to 10 percent on incomes above $5,000. But taxation raised only a small proportion of the funds necessary for financing the war, and strong popular resistance prevented the government from raising the rates. At least equally controversial was the printing of paper currency, or

"greenbacks." The new currency was backed not by gold or silver, but simply by the good faith and credit of the government (much like today's currency). The value of the greenbacks fluctuated according to the fortunes of the Northern armies. Early in 1864, with the war effort bogged down, a greenback dollar was worth only 39 percent of a gold dollar. Even at the close of the war, it was worth only 67 percent of a gold dollar. Because of the difficulty of making purchases with this uncertain currency, the government

■ **SENDING THE BOYS OFF TO WAR**
In this painting by Thomas Nast, New York's Seventh Regiment parades down Broadway in April 1861, to the cheers of exuberant, patriotic throngs, shortly before departing to fight in what most people then assumed would be a brief war. Thomas Nast is better known for his famous political cartoons of the 1870s. *(Seventh Regiment Armory, New York City)*

used greenbacks sparingly. The Treasury issued only $450 million worth of paper currency—a small proportion of the cost of the war but enough to produce significant inflation.

By far the largest source of financing for the war was loans from the American people. In previous wars, the government had sold bonds only to banks and to a few wealthy investors. Now, however, the Treasury persuaded ordinary citizens to buy over $400 million worth of bonds—the first example of mass financing of a war in American history. Still, bond purchases by individuals constituted only a small part of the government's borrowing, which in the end totaled $2.6 billion. Most of the loans came from banks and large financial interests.

Raising the Union Armies

Over 2 million men served in the Union armed forces during the course of the Civil War. But at the beginning of 1861, the regular army of the United States consisted of only 16,000 troops, many of them stationed in the West to protect white settlers from Indians. So the Union, like the Confederacy, had to raise its army mostly from scratch. Lincoln called for an increase of 23,000 in the regular army, but the bulk of the fighting, he knew, would have to be done by volunteers in state militias. When Congress convened in July 1861, it authorized enlisting 500,000

volunteers for three-year terms (as opposed to the customary three-month terms).

This voluntary system of recruitment produced adequate forces only briefly. After the first flush of enthusiasm for the war, enlistments declined. By March 1863, Congress was forced to pass a national draft law. Virtually all young adult males were eligible to be drafted; but a man could escape service by hiring someone to go in his place or by paying the government a fee of $300. Only about 46,000 men were ever actually conscripted, but the draft greatly increased voluntary enlistments.

To a people accustomed to a remote and inactive national government, conscription was strange and ominous. Opposition to the law was widespread, particularly among laborers, immigrants, and Democrats opposed to the war (known as "Peace Democrats"). Occasionally it erupted into violence. Demonstrators against the draft rioted in New York City for four days in July 1863, after the first names were selected for conscription. Over 100 people died. Irish workers were at the center of the violence. They were angry because black strikebreakers had been used against them in a recent longshoremen's strike; and they blamed African Americans generally for the war, which they thought was being fought for the benefit of slaves who would soon be competing with white workers for jobs. The rioters lynched a number of African Americans, burned

HANGING A NEGRO IN CLARKSON STREET.

■ **THE NEW YORK CITY DRAFT RIOT, 1863**
Opposition to the Civil War draft was widespread in the North and in July 1863 produced a violent four-day uprising in New York City in which as many as 100 people died. The riot began on July 13 with a march by 4,000 men, mostly poor Irish laborers, who were protesting the provisions by which some wealthy people could be exempted from conscription. "Rich man's war, poor man's fight," the demonstrators cried (just as some critics of the war chanted at times in the South). Many New Yorkers also feared that the war would drive black workers north to compete for their jobs. The demonstration turned violent when officials began drawing names for the draft. The crowd burned the draft building and then split into factions. Some rioters attacked symbols of wealth such as exclusive shops and mansions. Others terrorized black neighborhoods and lynched some residents. This contemporary engraving depicts one such lynching. Only by transferring five regiments to the city from Gettysburg (less than two weeks after the great battle there) was the government able to restore order. *(The Granger Collection)*

down homes and businesses (mostly those of free blacks), and even destroyed an orphanage for African-American children. Only the arrival of federal troops subdued the rioters.

Wartime Politics

When Abraham Lincoln arrived in Washington early in 1861, many politicians—noting his lack of national experience and his folksy, unpretentious manner—considered him a minor politician from the prairies, a man whom the real leaders of his party would easily control. But the new president moved quickly to establish his own authority. He assembled a cabinet representing every faction of the Republican Party and every segment of Northern opinion—men of exceptional prestige and influence and in some cases arrogance, several of whom believed that they, not Lincoln, should be president. Lincoln moved boldly as well to use the war powers of the presidency, ignoring inconvenient parts of the Constitution because, he said, it would be foolish to lose the whole by being afraid to disregard a part. He sent troops into battle without asking Congress for a declaration of war. (Lincoln insisted on calling the conflict a domestic insurrection, which required no formal declaration of war; to ask for a declaration would, he believed, constitute implicit recognition of the Confederacy as an independent nation.) He increased the size of the regular army without receiving legislative authority to do so. He unilaterally proclaimed a naval blockade of the South.

Lincoln's greatest political problem was the widespread popular opposition to the war, mobilized by factions in the Democratic Party. The Peace Democrats (or, as their enemies called them, "Copperheads") feared that agriculture and the Northwest were losing influence to industry and the East and that Republican nationalism was eroding states' rights. Lincoln used extraordinary methods to suppress them. He ordered military arrests of civilian dissenters and suspended the right of habeas corpus (the right of an arrested person to a speedy trial). At first, Lincoln used these methods only in sensitive areas such as the border states; but in 1862, he proclaimed that all persons who discouraged enlistments or engaged in disloyal practices were subject to martial law. In all, more than 13,000 persons were arrested and imprisoned for varying periods. The most prominent Copperhead in the country—Clement L. Vallandigham, a member of Congress from Ohio—was seized by military authorities and exiled to the Confederacy after he made a speech claiming that the purpose of the war was to free the blacks and enslave the whites. Lincoln defied all efforts to curb his authority to suppress opposition. He even defied the Supreme Court. When Chief Justice Taney issued a writ *(Ex parte Merryman)* requiring him to release an imprisoned Maryland secessionist leader, Lincoln simply ignored it. (After the war, in 1866, the Supreme Court ruled in *Ex parte Milligan* that military trials in areas where the civil courts existed were unconstitutional.)

The presidential election of 1864 occurred, therefore, in the midst of considerable political dissension. The Republicans had suffered heavy losses in the congressional elections of 1862, and in response leaders of the party tried to create a broad coalition of all the groups that supported the war. They called the new organization the Union Party, but in reality it was little more than the Republican Party and a small faction of War Democrats. The Union Party nominated Lincoln for another term as president and Andrew Johnson of Tennessee, a War Democrat who had opposed his state's decision to secede, for the vice presidency.

The Democrats nominated George B. McClellan, a celebrated former Union general who had been relieved of his command by Lincoln, and adopted a platform denouncing the war and calling for a truce. McClellan repudiated that demand, but the Democrats were clearly the peace party in the campaign, trying to profit from growing war weariness and from the Union's discouraging military position in the summer of 1864.

At this crucial moment, however, several Northern military victories, particularly the capture of Atlanta, Georgia, early in September, rejuvenated Northern morale and boosted Republican prospects. Lincoln won reelection comfortably, with 212 electoral votes to McClellan's 21; the president carried every state except Kentucky, New Jersey, and Delaware. But Lincoln's lead in the popular vote was a more modest 10 percent. Had Union victories not occurred when they did, and had Lincoln not made special arrangements to allow Union troops to vote, the Democrats might have won.

The Politics of Emancipation

Despite their surface unity in 1864 and their general agreement on most economic matters, the Republicans disagreed sharply on the issue of slavery. Radicals—led in Congress by such men as Representative Thaddeus Stevens of Pennsylvania and Senators Charles Sumner of Massachusetts and Benjamin Wade of Ohio—wanted to use the war to abolish slavery immediately and completely. Conservatives favored a slower, more gradual, and, they believed, less disruptive process for ending slavery; in the beginning, at least, they had the support of the president.

Despite Lincoln's cautious view of emancipation, momentum began to gather behind it early in the war. In 1861, Congress passed the Confiscation Act, which declared that all slaves used for "insurrectionary" purposes (that is, in support of the Confederate military effort) would be considered freed. Subsequent laws in the spring of 1862 abolished slavery in the District of Columbia and in the western territories, and compensated owners. In July 1862, the Radicals pushed through Congress the second Confiscation Act, which declared free the slaves of persons aiding and supporting the insurrection (whether or not the slaves themselves were doing so) and authorized the president to employ African Americans, including freed slaves, as soldiers.

As the war progressed, much of the North seemed slowly to accept emancipation as a central war aim; nothing less, many believed, would justify the enormous sacrifices of the struggle. As a result, the Radicals increased their influence within the Republican Party—a development that did not go unnoticed by the president, who decided to seize the leadership of the rising antislavery sentiment himself.

On September 22, 1862, after the Union victory at the Battle of Antietam, the president announced his intention to use his war powers to issue an executive order freeing all slaves in the Confederacy. And on January 1, 1863, he formally signed the Emancipation Proclamation, which declared forever free slaves in all areas of the Confederacy except those already under Union control: Tennessee, western Virginia, and southern Louisiana. The proclamation did not apply to the border slave states, which had never seceded from the Union and therefore were not subject to the president's war powers.

The immediate effect of the proclamation was limited, since it applied only to slaves still under Confederate control. But the document was of great importance nevertheless, because it clearly and irrevocably established that the war was being fought not only to preserve the Union but also to eliminate slavery. Eventually, as federal armies occupied much of the South, the proclamation became a practical reality and led directly to the freeing of thousands of slaves. Even in areas not directly affected by the proclamation, the antislavery impulse gained strength. By the end of the war, slavery had been abolished in two Union slave states—Maryland and Missouri—and in three Confederate states occupied by Union forces—Tennessee, Arkansas, and Louisiana. The final step came in 1865, when Congress approved and the necessary states ratified the Thirteenth Amendment, abolishing slavery as an institution in all parts of the United States. After more than two centuries, legalized slavery finally ceased to exist in the United States.

African Americans and the Union Cause

About 186,000 emancipated blacks served as soldiers, sailors, and laborers for the Union forces, joining a significant number of free blacks from the North. The services of African Americans to the Union military were significant in many ways, not least because of the substantial obstacles many blacks had to surmount in order to enlist.

In the first months of the war, African Americans were largely excluded from the military. A few black regiments eventually took shape in some of the Union-occupied areas of the Confederacy, largely because they were a ready source of manpower in these defeated regions. But once Lincoln issued the Emancipation Proclamation, black enlistment increased rapidly and the Union military began actively to recruit African-American soldiers and sailors in both the North and, where possible, the South.

Some of these men were organized into fighting units, of which the best known was probably the Fifty-fourth Massachusetts infantry, which (like most black regiments) had a white commander: Robert Gould Shaw, a member of an aristocratic Boston family. Shaw and more than half his regiment died during a battle near Charleston, South Carolina, in the summer of 1863.

Most black soldiers, however, were assigned menial tasks behind the lines, such as digging trenches and transporting water. Even though fewer blacks than whites died in combat, the black mortality rate was actually higher than the rate for white soldiers because so many black soldiers died of disease from working long, arduous hours in unsanitary conditions. Conditions for blacks and whites were unequal in other ways as well. African-American soldiers were paid a third less than were white soldiers (until Congress changed the law in mid-1864). Black fighting men captured by the Confederates were, unlike white prisoners, not returned to the North in exchange for Southern soldiers being returned to the

■ **AFRICAN AMERICAN TROOPS**
Although most of the black soldiers who enlisted in the Union army during the Civil War performed non-combat jobs behind the lines, there were also black combat regiments—members of one of which are pictured here—who fought with great success and valor in critical battles. *(Library of Congress)*

South. They were sent back to their masters (if they were escaped slaves) or often executed. In 1864, Confederate soldiers killed over 260 African Americans after capturing them in Tennessee.

The War and Economic Development

The Civil War did not, as some historians used to claim, transform the North from an agrarian to an industrial society. Industrialization was already far advanced when the war began, and in some areas, the war actually retarded growth—by cutting manufacturers off from their Southern markets and sources of raw material, and by diverting labor and resources to military purposes.

On the whole, however, the war sped the economic development of the North. That was in part a result of the political dominance of the Republican Party and its promotion of nationalistic economic legislation. But it was also because the war itself required the expansion of certain sectors of the economy. Coal production increased by nearly 20 percent during the war. Railroad facilities improved—mainly through the adoption of a standard gauge (track width) on new lines. The loss of farm labor to the military forced many farmers to increase the mechanization of agriculture.

The war was a difficult experience for many American workers. Industrial laborers experienced a substantial loss of purchasing power, as prices in the North rose by more than 70 percent during the war while wages rose only about 40 percent. That was partly because liberalized immigration laws permitted a flood of new workers into the labor market and helped keep wages low. It was also because the increasing mechanization of production eliminated the jobs of many skilled workers. One result of these hardships was a substantial increase in union membership in many industries and the creation of several national unions, for coal miners, railroad engineers, and others—organizations bitterly opposed and rigorously suppressed by employers.

Women, Nursing, and the War

Women found themselves, either by choice or by necessity, thrust into new and often unfamiliar roles during the war. They took over positions vacated by men and worked as teachers, retail sales clerks, office workers, and mill and factory hands. They were responding not only to the needs of employers for additional labor, but to their own, often desperate, need for money. With husbands and fathers away in the army, many women were left destitute—particularly since military pay was low and erratic.

Above all, women entered nursing, a field previously dominated by men. The U.S. Sanitary Commission, an organization of civilian volunteers led by Dorothea Dix, mobilized large numbers of female nurses to serve in field hospitals. By the end of the war, women were the dominant force in nursing; by the end of the century, nursing had become an almost entirely female profession. Female nurses not only cared for patients but performed other tasks considered appropriate for women: cooking, cleaning, and laundering.

Female nurses encountered considerable resistance from male doctors, many of whom considered women too weak for medical work and who, in any case, found the sight of women taking care of strange men inappropriate. The Sanitary Commission tried to counter such arguments by attributing to nursing many of the domestic ideals that American society attributed to women's work in the home. Women as nurses were to play the same maternal, nurturing, instructive role they played as wives and mothers. The commission was, according to its own literature, "a great artery that bears the people's love to the army." Just as women cared for sick people at home, so they could—and must—do so in the military hospitals. "The right of woman to her sphere, which includes housekeeping, cooking, and nursing, has never been disputed," one Sanitary Commission official insisted. But not all women who worked for the commission were content with a purely maternal role; some challenged the dominance of men in the organization and even stood up against doctors whom they considered incompetent, increasing the resentment felt toward them by many men. In the end, though, the work of female nurses was so indispensable to the military that the complaints of male doctors were irrelevant.

Nurses, and many other women, found the war a liberating experience, in which (as one Sanitary Commission nurse later wrote) the American woman "had developed potencies and possibilities of which she had been unaware and which surprised her, as it did those who witnessed her marvelous achievement." Some women, especially those who had been

committed to feminist causes earlier, came to see the war as an opportunity to win support for their own goals. Elizabeth Cady Stanton and Susan B. Anthony, who together founded the National Woman's Loyal League in 1863, worked simultaneously for the abolition of slavery and the awarding of suffrage to women. Clara Barton, who was active during the war in collecting and distributing medical supplies and who later became an important figure in the nursing profession (and a founder of the American Red Cross), said in 1888: "At the war's end, woman was at least fifty years in advance of the normal position which continued peace would have assigned her." That may have been a considerable exaggeration; but it captured the degree to which many women looked back on the war as a crucial moment in the redefinition of female roles and in the awakening of a sense of independence and new possibilities.

Whatever nursing may have done for the status of women, it had an enormous impact on the medical profession and on the treatment of wounded soldiers during the war. The U.S. Sanitary Commission not only organized women to serve at the front, it also funneled medicine and supplies to badly overtaxed field hospitals. The commission also (as its name suggests) helped spread ideas about the importance of sanitary conditions in hospitals and clinics and probably contributed to the relative decline of death by disease in the Civil War. Nevertheless, twice as many soldiers died of diseases—malaria, dysentery,

typhoid, gangrene, and others—as died in combat during the war. Even minor injuries could lead to fatal infections.

THE MOBILIZATION OF THE SOUTH

Early in February 1861, representatives of the seven states that had seceded from the Union met at Montgomery, Alabama, to create a new Southern nation. When Virginia seceded several months later, the government of the Confederacy moved to Richmond—one of the few Southern cities large enough to house a national government.

Many Southerners boasted loudly of the differences between their new nation and the nation they had left. Those differences were real. But there were also important similarities between the Union and the Confederacy, which became particularly clear as the two sides mobilized for war: similarities in their political systems, in the methods they used for financing the war and conscripting troops, and in the way they fought.

The Confederate Government

The Confederate constitution was almost identical to the Constitution of the United States, with several significant exceptions: It explicitly acknowledged the sovereignty of the individual states (although not the right of secession), and it specifically sanctioned slavery and made its abolition (even by one of the states) practically impossible.

The constitutional convention at Montgomery named a provisional president and vice president: Jefferson Davis of Mississippi and Alexander H. Stephens of Georgia, who were later chosen by the general electorate, without opposition, for six-year terms. Davis had been a moderate secessionist before the war; Stephens had argued against secession. The Confederate government, like the Union government, was dominated throughout the war by moderate leaders. Also like the Union, it was dominated less by the old aristocracy of the East than by the newer aristocrats of the West, of whom Davis was the most prominent example.

Davis was, in the end, an unsuccessful president. He was a reasonably able administrator and the dominating figure in his government, encountering little interference from the generally tame members of his unstable cabinet and serving as his own secretary of war. But he rarely provided genuinely national leadership. He spent too much time on routine items; and unlike Lincoln, he displayed a punctiliousness about legal and constitutional niceties inappropriate to the needs of a new nation at war. One shrewd Confederate official wrote: "All the revolutionary vigor is with the enemy. . . . With us timidity—hair splitting."

There were no formal political parties in the Confederacy, but its congressional and popular politics were rife with dissension nevertheless. Some white Southerners (and of course most African Americans who were aware of the course of events) opposed secession and war altogether. Many white people in poorer "backcountry" and "upcountry" regions, where slavery was limited, refused to recognize the new Confederate government or to serve in the Southern army; some worked or even fought for the Union. Most white Southerners supported the war, but as in the North many were openly critical of the government and the military, particularly as the tide of battle turned against the South and the Confederate economy decayed.

Money and Manpower

Financing the Confederate war effort was a monumental and ultimately impossible task. It involved creating a national revenue system in a society unaccustomed to significant tax burdens. It depended on a small and unstable banking system that had little capital to lend. Because most wealth in the South was invested in slaves and land, liquid assets were scarce; and the Confederacy's only specie—seized from U.S. mints located in the South—was worth only about $1 million.

The Confederate Congress tried at first not to tax the people directly but to requisition funds from the individual states. But most of the states were also unwilling to tax their citizens and paid their shares, when they paid them at all, with bonds or notes of dubious worth. In 1863, therefore, the congress enacted an income tax—which planters could pay "in kind" (as a percentage of their produce). But taxation never provided the Confederacy with very much revenue; it produced only about 1 percent of the government's total income. Borrowing was not much more successful. The Confederate government issued bonds in such vast amounts that the public lost faith in them and stopped buying them, and efforts to borrow money in Europe using cotton as collateral fared no better.

As a result the Confederacy had to pay for the war through the least stable, most destructive form of financing: paper currency, which it began issuing in 1861. By 1864, the Confederacy had issued the staggering total of $1.5 billion in paper money, more than twice what the Union had produced. And unlike the Union, the Confederacy did not establish a uniform currency system; the national government, states, cities, and private banks all issued their own notes, producing widespread chaos and confusion. The result was a disastrous inflation, far worse than anything the North experienced. Prices in the North rose 80 percent in the course of the war; in the South they rose 9,000 percent, with devastating effects on the new nation's morale.

Like the United States, the Confederacy first raised a military by calling for volunteers. And as in the North, by the end of 1861 voluntary enlistments were declining. In April 1862, therefore, the congress enacted a Conscription Act, which subjected all white males between the ages of eighteen and thirty-five to military service for three years. As in the North, a draftee could avoid service if he furnished a substitute. But since the price of substitutes was high, the provision aroused such opposition from poorer whites that it was repealed in

■ CONFEDERATE VOLUNTEERS
Young Southern soldiers posed for this photograph in 1861, shortly before the first Battle of Bull Run. The Civil War was the first major military conflict in the age of photography, and it launched the careers of many of America's early photographers. *(Cook Collection, Valentine Museum)*

1863. Even more controversial was the exemption from the draft of one white man on each plantation with twenty or more slaves, a provision that caused smaller farmers to complain: "It's a rich man's war but a poor man's fight." Many more white Southerners were exempted from military service than Northerners.

Even so, conscription worked for a time. At the end of 1862, about 500,000 men were in the Confederate military. (A total of approximately 900,000 served in the course of the entire war.) That number did not include the many slave men and women recruited by the military to perform such services as cooking, laundry, and manual labor, hence freeing additional white manpower for fighting. (Only late in the war, when the military situation was becoming desperate, was there any effort to involve slaves in combat.) After 1862, however, conscription began producing fewer men—in part because the Union had by then begun to seize large areas of the Confed-

eracy and thus had cut off much of the population from conscription or recruitment. The armed forces steadily decreased in size.

As 1864 opened, the government faced a critical manpower shortage. In a desperate move, the Confederate Congress began trying to draft men as young as seventeen and as old as fifty. But in a nation suffering from intense war weariness, where many had concluded that defeat was inevitable, nothing could attract or retain an adequate army any longer. In 1864-1865 there were 100,000 desertions. In a frantic final attempt to raise men, the congress authorized the conscription of 300,000 slaves, but the war ended before the government could attempt this incongruous experiment.

States' Rights Versus Centralization

The greatest source of division in the South, however, was not differences of opinion over the war, but the doctrine of states' rights. States' rights had become such a cult among many white Southerners that they resisted virtually all efforts to exert national authority, even those necessary to win the war. States' rights enthusiasts obstructed the conduct of the war in many ways. They restricted Davis's ability to impose martial law and suspend habeas corpus. They obstructed conscription. Recalcitrant governors such as Joseph Brown of Georgia and Zebulon M. Vance of North Carolina tried at times to keep their own troops apart from the Confederate forces and insisted on hoarding surplus supplies for their own states' militias.

But the Confederate government did make substantial strides in centralizing power in the South. By the end of the war, the Confederate bureaucracy was larger than its counterpart in Washington. The national government experimented, successfully for a time, with a "food draft"—which permitted soldiers to feed themselves by seizing crops from farms in their path. The government impressed slaves, often over the objections of their owners, to work as laborers on military projects. The Confederacy seized control of the railroads and shipping; it imposed regulations on industry; it limited corporate profits. States' rights sentiment was a significant handicap, but the South nevertheless took dramatic steps in the direction of centralization—becoming in the process increasingly like the region whose institutions it was fighting to escape.

Economic and Social Effects of the War

The war had a devastating effect on the economy of the South. It cut off Southern planters and producers from the markets in the North on which they had depended; it made the sale of cotton overseas much more difficult; it robbed farms and industries that did not have large slave populations of a male work force, leaving some of them unable to function effectively. While in the North production of all goods, agricultural and industrial, increased somewhat during the war, in the South it declined by more than a third.

Most of all, perhaps, the fighting itself wreaked havoc on the Southern economy. Almost all the major battles of the war occurred within the Confederacy; both armies spent most of their time on Southern soil. As a result of the savage fighting, the South's already inadequate railroad system was nearly destroyed; much of its most valuable farmland, and many of its most successful plantations, were ruined by Union troops (especially in the last year of the war).

Once the Northern naval blockade became effective, the South experienced massive shortages of almost everything. The region was overwhelmingly agricultural, but since it had concentrated so single-mindedly on producing cotton and other export crops, it did not grow enough food to meet its own needs. And despite the efforts of women and slaves to keep farms functioning, the departure of white male workers seriously diminished the region's ability to keep up what food production there had been. Large numbers of doctors were conscripted to serve the needs of the military, leaving many communities without any medical care. Blacksmiths, carpenters, and other craftsmen were similarly in short supply.

As the war continued, the shortages, the inflation, and the suffering created increasing instability in Southern society. There were major food riots, some led by women, in Georgia, North Carolina, and Alabama in 1863, as well as a large demonstration in Richmond that quickly turned violent. Resistance to conscription, food impressment, and taxation in-

■ **ATLANTA AFTER SHERMAN**
General William Tecumseh Sherman passed through Atlanta during his famous 1864 "March to the Sea" and, as in almost all the southern communities through which he moved, burned much of the city to the ground. When the people of Atlanta begged him not to set fire to the city, Sherman replied to them, "War is cruelty, and you cannot refine it . . . You might as well appeal against the thunderstorm as against the terrible hardships of war. They are inevitable." In this photograph, residents of the city stand amid the rubble after Sherman had moved on.
(Special Collections, Hill Memorial Library, Louisiana State University Libraries)

creased throughout the Confederacy, as did hoarding and black-market commerce.

In economic terms, in other words, the war affected the South very differently from the way it affected the North. In other respects, however, the war transformed Confederate society in many of the same ways that it was changing the society of the Union. It was particularly significant for Southern women. Because so many men left the farms and plantations to fight, the task of keeping families together and maintaining agricultural production fell increasingly to women. Slaveowners' wives often became responsible for managing large slave work forces; the wives of more modest farmers learned to plow fields and harvest crops. Substantial numbers of females worked in government agencies in Richmond. Even larger numbers chose nursing, both in hospitals and in temporary facilities set up to care for wounded soldiers. Others became schoolteachers.

The long-range results of the war for Southern women are more difficult to measure but equally profound. The experience of the 1860s almost certainly forced many women to question the prevailing Southern assumption that females were unsuited for certain activities, that they were not fit to participate actively in the public sphere. A more concrete legacy was the decimation of the male population and the creation of a major gender imbalance in the region. After the war, there were many thousands more women in the South than men. In Georgia, for example, women outnumbered men by 36,000 in 1870; in North Carolina by 25,000. The result, of course, was a large number of unmarried or widowed women who, both during and after the war, had no choice but to find employment—thus, by necessity rather than choice, expanding the number of acceptable roles for women in Southern society.

Even before emancipation, the war had far-reaching effects on the lives of slaves. Confederate leaders were even more terrified of slave revolts during the war than they had been in peacetime, and they enforced slave codes and other regulations with particular severity. Even so, many slaves—especially those near the front—found ways to escape their masters and cross behind Union lines in search of freedom. Those who had no realistic avenue for escape seemed, to their owners at least, to be particularly resistant to authority during the war. That was in part because on many plantations, the masters and overseers for whom they were accustomed to working

were away at war; they found it easier to resist the authority of the women and boys left behind to manage the farms.

STRATEGY AND DIPLOMACY

Militarily, the initiative in the Civil War lay mainly with the North, since it needed to defeat the Confederacy while the South needed only to avoid defeat. Diplomatically, however, the initiative lay with the South. It needed to enlist the recognition and support of foreign governments; the Union wanted only to preserve the status quo.

The Commanders

The most important Union military commander was Abraham Lincoln, whose previous military experience consisted only of brief service in his state militia during the Black Hawk War. Lincoln was a successful commander in chief because he realized that numbers and resources were on his side, and because he took advantage of the North's material advantages. He realized, too, that the proper objective of his armies was the destruction of the Confederate armies and not the occupation of Southern territory. It was important that Lincoln had a good grasp of strategy, because many of his generals did not. The problem of finding adequate commanders for the troops in the field plagued him throughout the first three years of the war.

From 1861 to 1864, Lincoln tried time and again to find a chief of staff capable of orchestrating the Union war effort. He turned first to General Winfield Scott, the aging hero of the Mexican War. But Scott was unprepared for the magnitude of the new conflict and retired on November 1, 1861. Lincoln replaced him with the young George B. McClellan, commander of the Union armies in the East, the Army of the Potomac; but the proud, arrogant McClellan had a wholly inadequate grasp of strategy and in any case returned to the field in March 1862. For most of the rest of the year, Lincoln had no chief of staff at all. And when he finally appointed General Henry W. Halleck to the post, he found him an ineffectual strategist who left all substantive decision making to the president. Not until March 1864 did Lincoln finally find a general he trusted to command

BASEBALL AND THE CIVIL WAR

Long before the great urban stadiums, long before the lights and the cameras and the multimillion dollar salaries, long before the Little Leagues and the high school teams, baseball was the most popular game in America. And during the Civil War, it was a treasured pastime for soldiers, and for thousands of men (and some women) behind the lines, in both North and South.

Baseball was not invented by Abner Doubleday, who probably never even saw the game. The legend that it was came many years later from Albert G. Spalding, a patriotic sporting-goods manufacturer eager to prove that the game had purely American origins and to dispel the notion that it came from England. In fact, baseball was derived from a variety of earlier games, especially the English pastimes of cricket and rounders. American baseball took its own distinctive form beginning in the 1840s, when Alexander Cartwright, a shipping clerk, formed the New York Knickerbockers, laid out a diamond-shaped field with four bases, and declared that batters with three strikes were out and that teams with three outs were retired.

Cartwright moved west in search of gold in 1849, ultimately grew rich, and settled finally in Hawaii (where he brought the game to Americans in the Pacific). But the game did not languish in his absence. Henry Chadwick, an English-born journalist, developed his own passion for baseball in the late 1840s and spent much of the next decade popularizing baseball (and regularizing its rules). "Our ambition," he said, was "that of endeavoring to establish a national game." It was also to keep baseball a sport for the "best classes," for gentlemen—a goal that was already lost before it was even uttered. By 1860, baseball was being played by col-

lege students and Irish workers, by urban elites and provincial farmers, by people of all classes and ethnic groups from New England to Louisiana. It was also attracting the attention of women. Students at Vassar College formed "ladies'" teams in the 1860s. And in Philadelphia, free black men formed the first of what was to become a great network of African-American baseball teams, the Pythians. From the beginning, they were barred from playing against most white teams.

When young men donned their uniforms of blue and gray and marched off to war in 1861, some took their bats and balls with them. Almost from the start of the fighting, soldiers in both armies took advantage of idle moments to lay out baseball diamonds and organize games. There were games in prison camps; games on the White House lawn (where Union soldiers were sometimes billeted); and games on battlefields that were sometimes interrupted by gunfire and cannon. "It is astonishing how indifferent a person can become to danger," a soldier wrote home to Ohio in 1862. "The report of musketry is heard but a very little distance from us, . . . yet over there on the other side of the road is most of our company, playing Bat Ball." After a skirmish in Texas, another Union soldier lamented that, in addition to casualties, his company had lost "the only baseball in Alexandria, Texas."

Legend has it that in Hilton Head, South Carolina—occupied by Union soldiers very early in the war—two teams of New York volunteers played a game in front of more than 40,000 spectators. Far from discouraging baseball, military commanders—and the United States Sanitary Commission, the Union army's medical arm—actively

encouraged the game during the war. It would, they believed, help keep up the soldiers' morale.

Away from the battlefield, baseball continued to flourish (even if diminished by the departure of so many young men to the war). In New York, still the leading baseball city in the nation, games between local teams continued to draw crowds of ten or twenty thousand. The National Associaton of Baseball Players (founded in 1859) had recruited ninety-one clubs in ten northern states by 1865; a North Western Association of Baseball Players, organized in Chicago in 1865, indicated that the game was becoming well established in the West as well. And in Brooklyn during the war, William Cammeyer drained a skating pond on his property, built a board fence around it, and created the first enclosed baseball field in America—the Union grounds. He charged 10 cents admission. The professionalization of the game was underway.

But for all the commercialization and spectacle that came to be associated with baseball in the years after the Civil War, the game remained for many Americans what it was to millions of young men fighting in the most savage war in the nation's history—an American passion that at times, even if briefly, erased the barriers dividing groups from one another. "Officers and men forget, for a time, the differences in rank," a Massachusetts private wrote in 1863, "and indulge in the invigorating sport with a school-boy's ardor."

■ **ULYSSES S. GRANT**
One observer said of Grant (seen here posing for a photograph during the Wilderness campaign of 1864): "He habitually wears an expression as if he had determined to drive his head through a brick wall, and was about to do it." It was an apt metaphor for Grant's military philosophy, which relied on constant, unrelenting assault. One result was that Grant was willing to fight when other Northern generals held back. Another was that Grant presided over some of the worst carnage of the Civil War. *(Library of Congress)*

the war effort: Ulysses S. Grant, who shared Lincoln's belief in making enemy armies and resources, not enemy territory, the target of military efforts. Lincoln gave Grant a relatively free hand, but the general always submitted at least the broad outlines of his plans to the president for advance approval.

Lincoln's (and later Grant's) handling of the war effort faced constant scrutiny from the Committee on the Conduct of the War, a joint investigative committee of the two houses of Congress and the most powerful voice the legislative branch has ever had in formulating war policies. Established in December 1861 and chaired by Senator Benjamin F. Wade of Ohio, it complained constantly of the insufficient ruthlessness of Northern generals, which Radicals on the committee attributed (largely inaccurately) to a secret sympathy among the officers for slavery. The committee's efforts often seriously interfered with the conduct of the war.

Southern command arrangements centered on President Davis, who unlike Lincoln was a trained professional soldier but who, also unlike Lincoln, failed ever to create an effective command system. Early in 1862, Davis named General Robert E. Lee as his principal military adviser. But in fact, Davis had no intention of sharing control of strategy with anyone. After a few months, Lee left Richmond to command forces in the field, and for the next two years Davis planned strategy alone. In February 1864, he named General Braxton Bragg as a military adviser; but Bragg never provided much more than technical advice. Not until February 1865 did the Confederate Congress create the formal position of general in chief. Davis named Lee to the post but made clear that he expected to continue to make all basic decisions. In any case, the war ended before this last command structure had time to take shape.

At lower levels of command, men of markedly similar backgrounds controlled the war in both the North and the South. Many of the professional officers on both sides were graduates of the United States Military Academy at West Point and the United States Naval Academy at Annapolis, and thus had been trained in similar ways. Many were closely acquainted, even friendly, with their counterparts on the other side. And all were imbued with the classic, eighteenth-century models of warfare that the service academies still taught. The most successful officers were those who, like Grant and William Tecumseh Sherman, were able to see beyond their academic training and envision a new kind of warfare in which destruction of resources was as important as battlefield tactics.

Amateur officers played an important role in both armies as commanders of volunteer regiments. In both North and South, such men were usually economic or social leaders in their communities who appointed themselves officers and rounded up troops to lead. This system was responsible for recruiting considerable numbers of men into the armies of the two nations. Only occasionally, however, did it produce officers of real ability.

■ **ROBERT E. LEE**

Lee was a moderate by the standards of Southern politics in the 1850s. He opposed secession and was ambivalent about slavery. But he could not bring himself to break with his region, and he left the U.S. army to lead Confederate forces beginning in 1861. He was (and remains) the most revered of all the white Southern leaders of the Civil War. For decades after his surrender at Appomattox, he was a symbol to white Southerners of the "Lost Cause." *(Bettmann)*

The Role of Sea Power

The Union had an overwhelming advantage in naval power, and it gave its navy two important roles in the war. One was enforcing a blockade of the Southern coast, which the president ordered on April 19, 1861. The other was assisting the Union armies in field operations.

The blockade of the South was never fully effective, but it had a major impact on the Confederacy nevertheless. The United States Navy could generally keep oceangoing ships out of Confederate ports. For a time, small blockade runners continued to slip through. But gradually, federal forces tightened the blockade by seizing the ports themselves. The last important port in Confederate hands—Wilmington, North Carolina—fell to the Union early in 1865.

The Confederates made bold attempts to break the blockade with new weapons. Foremost among them was an ironclad warship, constructed by plating with iron a former United States frigate, the *Merrimac,* which the Yankees had scuttled in Norfolk harbor when Virginia seceded. On March 8, 1862, the refitted *Merrimac,* renamed the *Virginia,* left Norfolk to attack a blockading squadron of wooden ships at nearby Hampton Roads. It destroyed two of the ships and scattered the rest. But the Union government had already built ironclads of its own. And one of them, the *Monitor,* arrived off the coast of Virginia only a few hours after the *Virginia's* dramatic foray. The next day, it met the *Virginia* in the first battle between ironclad ships. Neither vessel was able to sink the other, but the *Monitor* put an end to the *Virginia's* raids and preserved the blockade. The Confederacy experimented as well with other naval innovations, such as small torpedo boats and hand-powered submarines. But despite occasional small successes with these new weapons, the South never managed to overcome the Union's naval advantages.

As a supporter of land operations, the Union navy was particularly important in the western theater of war—the vast region between the Appalachian Mountains and the Mississippi River—where the major rivers were navigable by large vessels. The navy transported supplies and troops and joined in attacking Confederate strong points. With no significant navy of its own, the South could defend only with fixed land fortifications, which proved no match for the mobile land-and-water forces of the Union.

Europe and the Disunited States

Judah P. Benjamin, the Confederate secretary of state for most of the war, was a clever and intelligent man, but he lacked strong convictions and confined most of his energy to routine administrative tasks. William Seward, his counterpart in Washington, gradually became one of the great American secretaries of state. He had invaluable assistance from Charles Francis Adams, the American minister to London, who had inherited the considerable diplomatic talents of his father, John Quincy Adams, and his grandfather, John Adams.

At the beginning of the war, the ruling classes of England and France, the two nations whose support was most crucial to both sides, were generally sympathetic to the Confederacy, for several reasons. The two nations imported much Southern cotton for their textile industries; they were eager to weaken the United States, an increasingly powerful commercial rival; and some admired the supposedly aristocratic social order of the South, which they believed resembled the hierarchical structures of their own societies. But France was unwilling to take sides in the conflict unless England did so first. And in England, the government was reluctant to act because there was powerful popular support for the Union. Important English liberals such as John Bright and Richard Cobden considered the war a struggle between free and slave labor and urged their followers to support the Union cause. The politically conscious but largely unenfranchised workers in Britain expressed their sympathy for the North frequently and unmistakably—in mass meetings, in resolutions, and through their champions in Parliament. After Lincoln issued the Emancipation Proclamation, these groups worked particularly avidly for the Union.

Southern leaders hoped to counter the strength of the British antislavery forces by arguing that access to Southern cotton was vital to the English and French textile industries. But this "King Cotton diplomacy," on which the Confederacy had staked so many of its hopes, was a failure. English manufacturers had a surplus of both raw cotton and finished goods on hand in 1861 and could withstand a temporary loss of access to American cotton. Later, as the supply of cotton began to diminish, both England and France managed to keep at least some of their mills open by importing cotton from Egypt, India, and other sources. Equally important, English workers, the people most seriously threatened by the cotton shortage, did not clamor to have the blockade broken. Even the 500,000 English textile workers thrown out of jobs as a result of mill closings continued to support the North. In the end, therefore, no European nation offered diplomatic recognition to the Confederacy or intervened in the war. No nation wanted to antagonize the United States unless the Confederacy seemed likely to win, and the South never came close enough to victory to convince its potential allies to support it.

Even so, there was considerable tension, and on occasion near hostilities, between the United States and Britain, beginning in the first days of the war. Great Britain declared itself neutral as soon as the fighting began, followed by France and other nations. The Union government was furious. Neutrality implied that the two sides to the conflict had equal stature, but Washington was insisting that the conflict was simply a domestic insurrection, not a war between two legitimate governments.

A more serious crisis, the so-called Trent affair, began in late 1861. Two Confederate diplomats, James M. Mason and John Slidell, had slipped through the then ineffective Union blockade to Havana, Cuba, where they boarded an English steamer, the *Trent,* for England. Waiting in Cuban waters was the American frigate *San Jacinto,* commanded by the impetuous Charles Wilkes. Acting without authorization, Wilkes stopped the British vessel, arrested the diplomats, and carried them in triumph to Boston. The British government demanded the release of the prisoners, reparations, and an apology. Lincoln and Seward, aware that Wilkes had violated maritime law and unwilling to risk war with England, spun out the negotiations until American public opinion had cooled off, then released the diplomats with an indirect apology.

A second diplomatic crisis produced problems that lasted for years. Unable to construct large vessels itself, the Confederacy bought six ships, known as commerce destroyers, from British shipyards. The best known of them were the *Alabama,* the *Florida,* and the *Shenandoah.* The United States protested that this sale of military equipment to a belligerent violated the laws of neutrality, and the protests became the basis, after the war, of damage claims by the United States against Great Britain (see p. 526).

The American West and the War

Most of the states and territories of the American West, about which there had been so much controversy in the years leading up to the Civil War, were far removed from the major fighting. But they played a continuing political, diplomatic, and military part in the conflict nevertheless.

Except for Texas, which joined the Confederacy, all the western states and territories remained officially loyal to the Union—but not without controversy and conflict. Southerners and Southern sympathizers were active throughout the West encouraging secession and attempting to enlist both white settlers and Indians to support the Confederacy. And in some places, there was actual combat between Unionists and secessionists.

There was particularly vicious fighting in Kansas and Missouri, the scene of so much bitterness before the war. The same pro-slavery and free-state forces who had fought one another in the 1850s continued to do so, with even more deadly results. William C. Quantrill, an Ohio native who had spent much of his youth in the West, became a captain in the Confederate army after he organized a band of guerrilla fighters (mostly teenage boys) with which he terrorized areas around the Kansas-Missouri border. Quantrill and his band were an exceptionally murderous group, notorious for killing almost everyone in their path. Their most infamous act was a siege of Lawrence, Kansas, during which they slaughtered 150 civilians, adults and children alike. Quantrill finally died at the hands of Union troops shortly after the end of the war.

Union sympathizers in Kansas, organized in bands known as the Jayhawkers, were only marginally less savage, as they moved across western Missouri exacting reprisals for the actions of Quantrill and other Confederate guerrillas. One Jayhawk unit was commanded by the son of John Brown and the brother of Susan B. Anthony, men who brought the fervor of abolitionists to their work. Even without a major battle, the border areas of Kansas and Missouri were among the bloodiest and most terrorized places in the United States during the Civil War.

Not long after the war began, Confederate agents tried to negotiate alliances with the Five Civilized Tribes living in Indian Territory (later Oklahoma), in hopes of recruiting their support against Union forces in the West. The Indians themselves were divided. Some wanted to support the South, both because they resented the way the United States government had treated them and because some tribal leaders were themselves slaveholders. But other Indians supported the North out of a general hostility to slavery (both in the South and in their own nation).

One result of these divisions was something of a civil war within Indian Territory itself. Another was that Indian regiments fought for both the Union and the Confederacy during the war. But the tribes themselves never formally allied themselves with either side.

CAMPAIGNS AND BATTLES

In the absence of direct intervention by the European powers, the two contestants in America were left to resolve the conflict between themselves. They did so in four long years of bloody combat that produced more carnage than any war in American history, before or since. More than 618,000 Americans died in the Civil War, far more than the 115,000 who perished in World War I or the 318,000 who died in World War II; more, indeed, than died in all other American wars prior to Vietnam combined. There were nearly 2,000 deaths for every 100,000 of population during the Civil War. In World War I, the comparable figure was 109 deaths; in World War II, 241 deaths.

Despite the gruesome cost, the Civil War has become the most romanticized and the most intently studied of all American wars. In part, that is because the conflict produced—in addition to terrible fatalities—a series of military campaigns of classic strategic interest and a series of military leaders who displayed unusual brilliance and daring.

The Opening Clashes, 1861

The Union and the Confederacy fought their first major battle of the war in northern Virginia. A Union army of over 30,000 men under the command of General Irvin McDowell was stationed just outside Washington. About thirty miles away, at the town of Manassas, was a slightly smaller Confederate army under P. G. T. Beauregard. If the Northern army could destroy the Southern one, Union leaders believed, the war might end at once. In mid-July, McDowell marched his inexperienced troops toward Manassas. Beauregard moved his troops behind Bull Run, a small stream north of Manassas, and called for reinforcements, which reached him the day before the battle. The two armies were now approximately the same size.

On July 21, in the First Battle of Bull Run, or First Battle of Manassas, McDowell almost succeeded in dispersing the Confederate forces. But the Southerners stopped a last strong Union assault and then began a savage counterattack. The Union troops, exhausted after hours of hot, hard fighting, suddenly panicked. They broke ranks and retreated

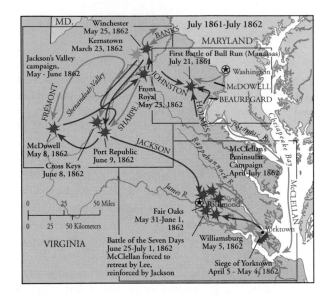

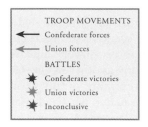

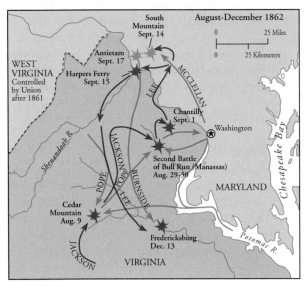

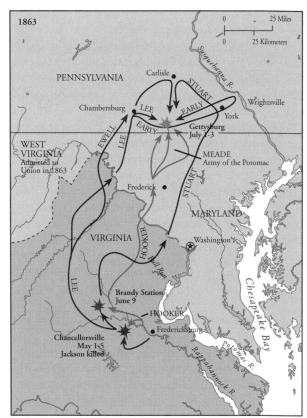

■ **THE VIRGINIA THEATER, 1861–1863**
Confederate armies thwarted Union hopes for a quick victory in Virginia, Maryland, and Pennsylvania. Throughout 1862, the overcautious George McClellan squandered opportunities to break the Confederate armies. The fiercely fought battles at Bull Run, Antietam, and Fredericksburg were among the largest and most deadly in American history.

chaotically. McDowell was unable to reorganize them, and he had to order a retreat to Washington— a disorderly withdrawal complicated by the presence along the route of many civilians who had ridden down from the capital, picnic baskets in hand, to watch the battle from nearby hills. The Confederates, as disorganized by victory as the Union forces were

by defeat, and short of supplies and transportation, did not pursue. The battle was a severe blow to Union morale and to the president's confidence in his officers. It also dispelled the illusion that the war would be a quick one.

Elsewhere in 1861, Union forces were achieving some small but significant victories. In Missouri, rebel forces gathered behind Governor Claiborne Jackson and other state officials who wanted to secede from the Union. Nathaniel Lyon, who commanded a small regular army force in St. Louis, moved his troops into southern Missouri to face the secessionists. On August 10, at the Battle of Wilson's Creek, he was defeated and killed—but not before he had seriously weakened the striking power of the Confederates. Union forces were subsequently able to hold most of the state.

Meanwhile, a Union force under George B. McClellan moved east from Ohio into western Virginia. By the end of 1861, it had "liberated" the anti-secession mountain people of the region. They created their own state government loyal to the Union and were admitted to the Union as West Virginia in 1863. The occupation of western Virginia was of limited military value, since the mountains cut the area off from the rest of Virginia. It was, however, an important symbolic victory for the North.

The Western Theater

After the battle at Bull Run, military operations in the East settled into a long and frustrating stalemate. The first decisive operations in 1862 occurred, therefore, in the western theater. Union forces were trying to seize control of the southern part of the Mississippi River, which would divide the Confederacy and give the North easy transportation into the heart of the South. Northern soldiers advanced on the southern Mississippi from both the north and south, moving downriver from Kentucky and upriver from the Gulf of Mexico toward New Orleans.

In April, a Union squadron of ironclads and wooden vessels commanded by David G. Farragut gathered in the Gulf of Mexico, then smashed past weak Confederate forts near the mouth of the Mississippi, and from there sailed up to New Orleans, which was virtually defenseless because the Confederate high command had expected the attack to come from the north. The city surrendered on April 25—the first major Union victory and an important turning point in the war. From then on, the mouth of the Mississippi was closed to Confederate trade; and the South's largest city and most important banking center was in Union hands.

Farther north in the western theater, Confederate troops under the command of Albert Sidney Johnston were stretched out in a long defensive line centered at two forts in Tennessee, Fort Henry and Fort Donelson, on the Tennessee and Cumberland Rivers

respectively. But the forts were located well behind the main Southern flanks, a fatal weakness that Union commanders recognized and exploited. Early in 1862, Ulysses S. Grant attacked Fort Henry, whose defenders, awed by the ironclad riverboats accompanying the Union army, surrendered with almost no resistance on February 6. Grant then moved both his naval and ground forces to Fort Donelson, where the Confederates put up a stronger fight but finally, on February 16, had to surrender. By cracking the Confederate center, Grant had gained control of river communications and forced Confederate forces out of Kentucky and half of Tennessee.

With about 40,000 men, Grant now advanced south along the Tennessee River to seize control of railroad lines vital to the Confederacy. From Pittsburg Landing, he marched to nearby Shiloh, Tennessee, where a force almost equal to his own, commanded by Albert Sidney Johnston and P. G. T. Beauregard, caught him by surprise. The result was the Battle of Shiloh, April 6–7. In the first day's fighting (during which Johnston was killed), the Southerners drove Grant back to the river. But the next day, reinforced by 25,000 fresh troops, Grant recovered the lost ground and forced Beauregard to withdraw. After the narrow Union victory at Shiloh, Northern forces occupied Corinth, Mississippi, the hub of several important railroads, and established control of the Mississippi River as far south as Memphis.

Braxton Bragg, now in command of the Confederate army in the West, gathered his forces at Chattanooga, in eastern Tennessee, which the Confederacy still controlled. He hoped to win back the rest of the state and then move north into Kentucky. But first he had to face a Union army (commanded by Don Carlos Buell and later by William S. Rosecrans), whose assignment was to capture Chattanooga. The two armies maneuvered for advantage inconclusively in northern Tennessee and southern Kentucky for several months until they finally met, December 31–January 2, in the Battle of Murfreesboro, or Stone's River. Bragg was forced to withdraw to the south, his campaign a failure. By the end of 1862, Union forces had made considerable progress in the West. But the major conflict remained in the East, where they were having much less success.

The Virginia Front, 1862

Union operations were being directed in 1862 by George B. McClellan, commander of the Army of the Potomac and the most controversial general of the

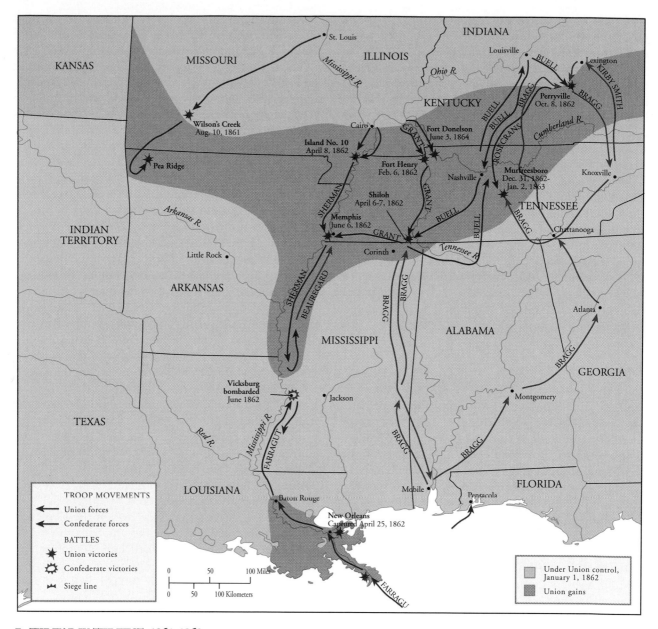

■ THE WAR IN THE WEST, 1861-1863

While Union armies met frustration in the East, the western theater proved to be a different story. David Farragut's Union ironclads captured New Orleans in April of 1862, while Ulysses S. Grant forced Confederate forces out of Kentucky and half of Tennessee. After a narrow Union victory at Shiloh, the North gained control of the Mississippi River as far south as Memphis. By the end of 1862, the Union forces had made considerable progress in the West, and catapulted Grant to fame.

war. McClellan was a superb trainer of men, but he often appeared reluctant to commit his troops to battle. Opportunities for important engagements came and went, and McClellan seemed never to take advantage of them—claiming always that his preparations were not yet complete or that the moment was not right.

During the winter of 1861–1862, McClellan concentrated on training his army of 150,000 men near Washington. Finally, he designed a spring campaign whose purpose was to capture the Confederate capital at Richmond. But instead of heading overland directly toward Richmond, McClellan chose a complicated, roundabout route that he thought would

circumvent the Confederate defenses. The navy would carry his troops down the Potomac to a peninsula east of Richmond, between the York and James Rivers. The army would approach the city from there. It became known as the Peninsular campaign.

McClellan began the campaign with only part of his army. Approximately 100,000 men accompanied him down the Potomac. Another 30,000—under General Irvin McDowell—remained behind to protect Washington. McClellan insisted that Washington was safe as long as he was threatening Richmond, and finally persuaded Lincoln to promise to send him the additional men. But before the president could do so, a Confederate army under Thomas J. ("Stonewall") Jackson changed his plans. Jackson staged a rapid march north through the Shenandoah Valley, as if he were planning to cross the Potomac and attack Washington. Alarmed, Lincoln dispatched McDowell's corps to head off Jackson. In the brilliant Valley campaign of May 4–June 9, 1862, Jackson defeated two separate Union forces and slipped away before McDowell could catch him.

Meanwhile, Confederate troops under Joseph E. Johnston were attacking McClellan's advancing army outside Richmond. But in the two-day Battle of Fair Oaks, or Seven Pines (May 31–June 1), they could not repel the Union forces. Johnston, badly wounded, was replaced by Robert E. Lee, who then recalled Stonewall Jackson from the Shenandoah Valley. With a combined force of 85,000 to face McClellan's 100,000, Lee launched a new offensive, known as the Battle of the Seven Days (June 25–July 1). Lee wanted to cut McClellan off from his base on the York River and then destroy the isolated Union army. But McClellan fought his way across the peninsula and set up a new base on the James. There, with naval support, the Army of the Potomac was safe.

McClellan was now only twenty-five miles from Richmond, with a secure line of water communications, and thus in a good position to renew the campaign. Time and again, however, he found reasons for delay. Instead of replacing McClellan with a more aggressive commander, Lincoln finally ordered the army to move to northern Virginia and join a smaller force under John Pope. The president hoped to begin a new offensive against Richmond on the direct overland route that he himself had always preferred.

As the Army of the Potomac left the peninsula by water, Lee moved north with the Army of Northern Virginia to strike Pope before McClellan could join him. Pope was as rash as McClellan was cautious, and he attacked the approaching Confederates without waiting for the arrival of all of McClellan's troops. In the ensuing Second Battle of Bull Run, or Second Battle of Manassas (August 29–30), Lee threw back the assault and routed Pope's army, which fled to Washington. With hopes for an overland campaign against Richmond now in disarray, Lincoln removed Pope from command and put McClellan in charge of all the Union forces in the region.

Lee soon went on the offensive again, heading north through western Maryland, and McClellan moved out to meet him. McClellan had the good luck to get a copy of Lee's orders, which revealed that a part of the Confederate army, under Stonewall Jackson, had separated from the rest to attack Harpers Ferry. But instead of attacking quickly before the Confederates could recombine, McClellan stalled and gave Lee time to pull most of his forces together behind Antietam Creek, near the town of Sharpsburg. There, on September 17, in the bloodiest single-day engagement of the war, McClellan's 87,000-man army repeatedly attacked Lee's force of 50,000, with enormous casualties on both sides. Six thousand soldiers died, and 17,000 sustained injuries. Late in the day, just as the Confederate line seemed ready to break, the last of Jackson's troops arrived from Harpers Ferry to reinforce it. McClellan might have broken through with one more assault. Instead, he allowed Lee to retreat into Virginia. Technically, Antietam was a Union victory, but in reality, it was an opportunity squandered. In November, Lincoln finally removed McClellan from command for good.

McClellan's replacement, Ambrose E. Burnside, was a short-lived mediocrity. He tried to move toward Richmond by crossing the Rappahannock at Fredericksburg, the strongest defensive point on the river. There, on December 13, he launched a series of attacks against Lee, all of them bloody, all of them hopeless. After losing a large part of his army, Burnside withdrew to the north bank of the Rappahannock. He was relieved at his own request.

1863: Year of Decision

At the beginning of 1863, General Joseph Hooker was in command of the still formidable Army of the Potomac, whose 120,000 troops remained north of the Rappahannock, opposite Fredericksburg. But despite his reputation as a fighter (his popular nickname was "Fighting Joe"), Hooker showed little resolve as he launched his own campaign in the spring. Taking part of his army, Hooker crossed the river above Fredericksburg and moved toward the town and Lee's army. But at the last minute, he apparently lost his nerve and drew back to a defensive position in a desolate area of brush and scrub trees known as the Wilderness. Lee had only half as many men as Hooker did, but he boldly divided his forces for a dual assault on the Union army. In the Battle of Chancellorsville, May 1–5, Stonewall Jackson attacked the Union right and Lee himself charged the front. Hooker barely managed to escape with his army. Lee had defeated the Union objectives, but he had not destroyed the Union army. And his ablest officer, Jackson, was fatally wounded during the battle.

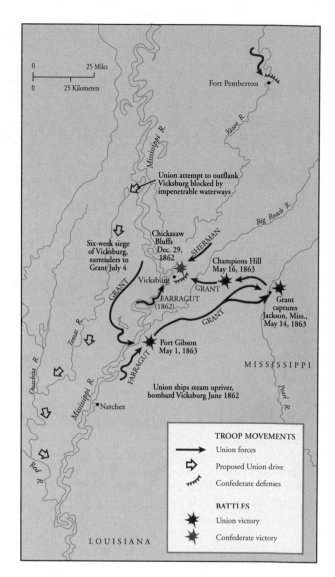

■ **ASSAULT ON VICKSBURG, MAY–JULY 1863**
In the spring of 1863, Ulysses S. Grant drove at Vicksburg, one of the Confederacy's two remaining strongholds on the southern Mississippi River. Vicksburg was well protected to the north and west as well as along the river, but in May, Grant boldly moved men and supplies to an area south of the city. On July 4, 1863, after a six-week siege, the starving residents of Vicksburg surrendered. The capture of Vicksburg and Port Hudson in Louisiana gave the Union control of the entire Mississippi River.

While the Union forces were suffering repeated frustrations in the East, they were continuing to win important victories in the West. In the spring of 1863, Ulysses S. Grant was driving at Vicksburg, Mississippi, one of the Confederacy's two remaining strongholds on the southern Mississippi River. Vicksburg was well protected, surrounded by rough country on the north and low, marshy ground on the west, and with good artillery coverage of the river itself. But in May, Grant

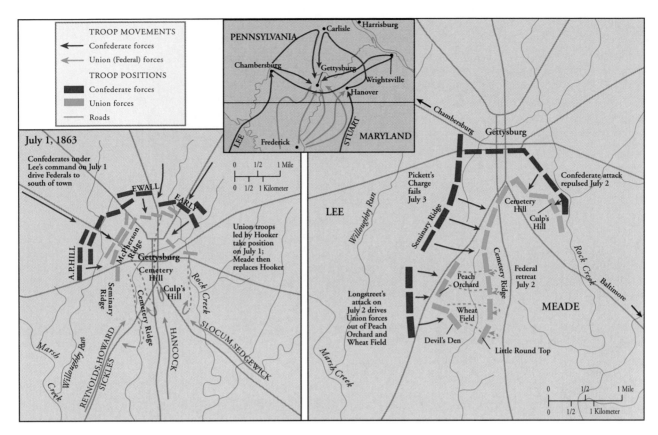

■ THE BATTLE OF GETTYSBURG, JULY 1–3, 1863

Gettysburg was the crucial battle of the Civil War. Lee hoped that an invasion of the North would relieve the Union threat to Richmond and enable the Confederate army to supply itself from the rich Pennsylvania countryside. Lee and 75,000 Confederates met General George C. Meade and 90,000 Union soldiers at the small town of Gettysburg, Pennsylvania, on July 1, 1863. When the battle ended, the Union army had suffered over 23,000 casualties, and at least one-third of Lee's men were dead, wounded, or missing. Lee was forced to retreat to Virginia, and the Confederacy was never again able to threaten Northern territory.

boldly moved men and supplies—overland and by water—to an area south of the city, where the terrain was better. He then attacked Vicksburg from the rear. Six weeks later, on July 4, Vicksburg—whose residents were by then literally starving as a result of a prolonged siege—surrendered. At almost the same time, the other Confederate strong point on the river, Port Hudson, Louisiana, also surrendered—to a Union force that had moved north from New Orleans. The Union had achieved one of its basic military aims: control of the whole length of the Mississippi. The Confederacy was split in two, with Louisiana, Arkansas, and Texas cut off from the other seceded states. The victories on the Mississippi were one of the great turning points of the war.

Early in the siege of Vicksburg, Lee proposed an invasion of Pennsylvania, which would, he argued, divert Union troops north and remove the pressure on the lower Mississippi. Further, he argued, if he could win a major victory on Northern soil, England and France

might come to the Confederacy's aid. The war-weary North might even quit the war before Vicksburg fell.

In June 1863, Lee moved up the Shenandoah Valley into Maryland and then entered Pennsylvania. The Union Army of the Potomac, commanded first by Hooker and then by George C. Meade, also moved north, parallel with the Confederates' movement, staying between Lee and Washington. The two armies finally encountered one another at the small town of Gettysburg, Pennsylvania. There, on July 1–3, 1863, they fought the most celebrated battle of the war.

Meade's army established a strong, well-protected position on the hills south of the town. The confident and combative Lee attacked, even though his army was outnumbered 75,000 to 90,000. His first assault on the Union forces on Cemetery Ridge failed. A day later he ordered a second, larger effort. In what is remembered as Pickett's Charge, a force of 15,000 Confederate soldiers advanced for almost a mile across open country while being swept by

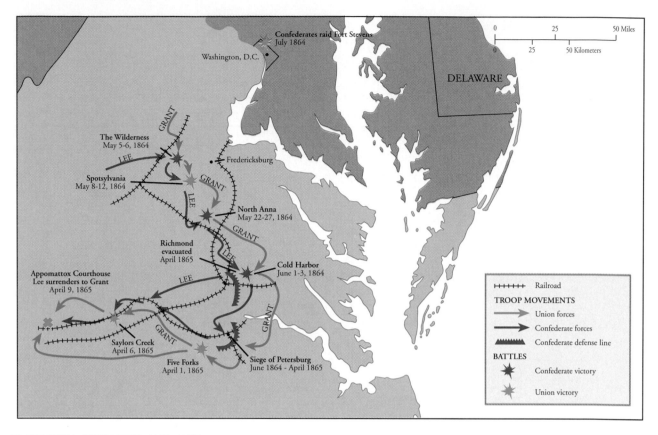

■ **VIRGINIA CAMPAIGNS, 1864-1865**
Under General Grant, the Army of the Potomac launched a relentless attack on Lee's army beginning in May 1864. Grant pursued Lee through the Wilderness area of northern Virginia, paused for a prolonged siege of Petersburg from June 1864 to April 1865, then pressed on against Lee's diminished army. Unable to find supplies, blocked from meeting Joseph Johnston's army in North Carolina, Lee surrendered to Grant at Appomattox Courthouse on April 9, 1865.

Union fire. Only about 5,000 made it up the ridge, and this remnant finally had to surrender or retreat. By now Lee had lost nearly a third of his army. On July 4, the same day as the surrender of Vicksburg, he withdrew from Gettysburg—another major turning point in the war. Never again were the weakened Confederate forces able to seriously threaten Northern territory.

Before the end of the year, there was a third important turning point, this one in Tennessee. After occupying Chattanooga on September 9, Union forces under William Rosecrans began an unwise pursuit of Bragg's retreating Confederate forces. Bragg was waiting for them just across the Georgia line, with reinforcements from Lee's army. The two armies engaged in the Battle of Chickamauga (September 19–20), one of the few battles in which the Confederates enjoyed a numerical superiority (70,000 to 56,000). Union forces could not break the Confederate lines and retreated back to Chattanooga.

Bragg now began a siege of Chattanooga itself, seizing the heights nearby and cutting off fresh supplies to the Union forces. Grant came to the rescue. In the Battle of Chattanooga (November 23–25), the reinforced Union army drove the Confederates back into Georgia. Northern troops then occupied most of eastern Tennessee. Union forces had now achieved a second important objective: control of the Tennessee River. Four of the eleven Confederate states were now effectively cut off from the Southern nation. No longer could the Confederacy hope to win independence through a decisive military victory. They could hope to win only by holding on and exhausting the Northern will to fight.

The Last Stage, 1864–1865

By the beginning of 1864, Ulysses S. Grant had become general in chief of all the Union armies. At long last, the president had found a commander whom he

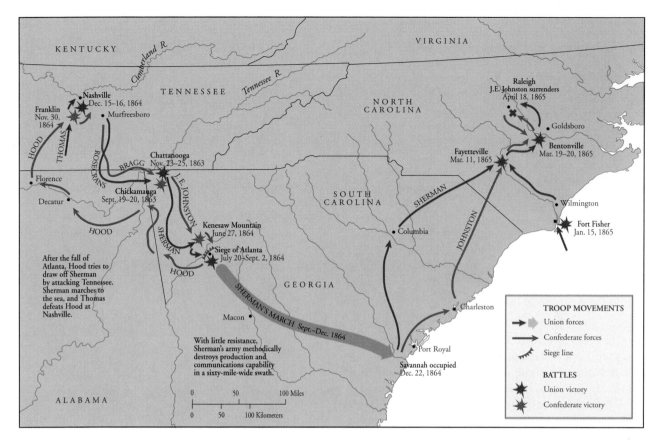

■ SHERMAN'S MARCH TO THE SEA, 1864–1865

While Grant wore down Lee in Virginia, General William T. Sherman initiated his relentless and devastating march across Georgia. Joseph Johnston's Confederate army was unable to prevent Union forces from taking Atlanta on September 2, 1864; nor could it stop Sherman's "March to the Sea" in the fall of 1864. After capturing Savannah in time for Christmas, Sherman continued his march by moving north through the Carolinas. Johnston finally surrendered on April 18, 1865, near Durham, North Carolina.

could rely on to pursue the war doggedly and tenaciously. Grant was not a subtle strategic or tactical general; he believed in using the North's overwhelming advantage in troops and material resources to overwhelm the South. He was not afraid to absorb massive casualties as long as he was inflicting similar casualties on his opponents.

Grant planned two great offensives for 1864. In Virginia, the Army of the Potomac (technically under Meade's command, but really now under Grant's) would advance toward Richmond and force Lee into a decisive battle. In Georgia, the western army, under William T. Sherman, would advance eastward toward Atlanta and destroy the remaining Confederate force further south, which was now under the command of Joseph E. Johnston. The northern campaign began when the Army of the Potomac, 115,000 strong, plunged into the rough, wooded Wilderness area of northwestern Virginia in pursuit of Lee's 75,000-man army. After avoiding an engagement for

several weeks, Lee turned Grant back in the Battle of the Wilderness (May 5–7). But Grant was undeterred. Without stopping to rest or reorganize, he resumed his march toward Richmond. He met Lee again in the bloody, five-day Battle of Spotsylvania Court House, in which 12,000 Union troops and a large but unknown number of Confederates died or were wounded. Despite the enormous losses, Grant kept moving. But victory continued to elude him. Lee kept his army between Grant and the Confederate capital and on June 1–3 repulsed the Union forces again, just northeast of Richmond, at Cold Harbor. The monthlong Wilderness campaign had cost Grant 55,000 men (killed, wounded, and captured) to Lee's 31,000. And Richmond still had not fallen.

Grant now changed his strategy. He moved his army east of Richmond, bypassing the capital altogether, and headed south toward the railroad center at Petersburg. If he could seize Petersburg, he could cut off the capital's communications with the rest of

■ MOBILE BAY, 1864

This painting by Robert Weir portrays a famous naval battle at the entrance to Mobile Bay between a Union Sloop-of War, the *U.S.S. Richmond,* part of a fleet commanded by Admiral David Farragut, and a Confederate ironclad, the *C.S.S. Tennessee.* Although Confederate mines were scattered across the entrance to the harbor, Farragut ordered his ships into battle with the memorable command: "Damn the torpedoes! Full speed ahead!" The Union forces defeated the Confederate flotilla and three weeks later captured the forts defending the harbor—thus removing from Confederate control the last port on the Gulf Coast available to the blockade runners who were attempting to supply the South's war needs.

(Mariners' Museum, Newport News, Virginia)

the Confederacy. But Petersburg had strong defenses; and once Lee came to the city's relief, the assault became a prolonged siege, which lasted nine months. In Georgia, meanwhile, Sherman was facing a less ferocious resistance. With 90,000 men, he confronted Confederate forces of 60,000 under Johnston, who was unwilling to risk a direct engagement. As Sherman advanced, Johnston tried to delay him by maneuvering. The two armies fought only one real battle—at Kennesaw Mountain, northwest of Atlanta, on June 27—where Johnston scored an impressive victory. Even so, he was unable to stop the Union advance toward Atlanta. President Davis replaced Johnston with the combative John B. Hood, who twice daringly attacked Sherman's army but accomplished nothing except seriously weakening his own forces. Sherman took Atlanta on September 2. News of the victory electrified the North and helped unite the previously divided Republican Party behind President Lincoln.

Hood now tried unsuccessfully to draw Sherman out of Atlanta by moving back up through Tennessee and threatening an invasion of the North. Sherman did not take the bait. But he did send Union troops to reinforce Nashville. In the Battle of Nashville on December 15–16, 1864, Northern forces practically destroyed what was left of Hood's army.

Meanwhile, Sherman had left Atlanta to begin his soon-to-be-famous March to the Sea. Living off the land, destroying supplies it could not use, his army cut a sixty-mile-wide swath of desolation across Georgia. "War is all hell," Sherman had once said. By

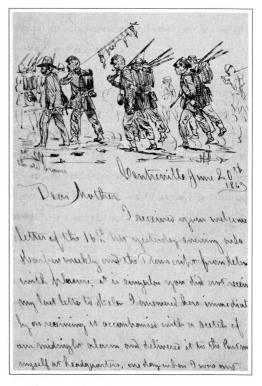

■ A LETTER FROM THE FRONT

Charles Wellington Reed, a nineteen-year-old soldier who was also a talented artist, sent illustrated letters to the members of his family throughout the war. In this 1863 letter to his mother, he portrays the Ninth Massachusetts Battery leaving Centreville, Virginia on its way to Gettysburg. Two weeks later, Reed fought in the famous battle and eventually received the Congressional Medal of Honor for his bravery there. "Such a shrieking, hissing, seathing I never dreamed was imaginable," he wrote of the fighting at the time. *(Manuscript Division, Library of Congress)*

that he meant not that war is a terrible thing to be avoided, but that it should be made as horrible and costly as possible for the opponent. He sought not only to deprive the Confederate army of war materials and railroad communications but also to break the will of the Southern people, by burning towns and plantations along his route. By December 20, he had reached Savannah, which surrendered two days later. Sherman offered it to President Lincoln as a Christmas gift. Early in 1865, having left Savannah largely undamaged, Sherman continued his destructive march northward through South Carolina. He was virtually unopposed until he was well inside North Carolina, where a small force under Johnston could do no more than cause a brief delay.

In April 1865, Grant's Army of the Potomac—still engaged in the prolonged siege at Petersburg—finally captured a vital railroad junction southwest of the town. Without rail access to the South, cut off from other Confederate forces, Lee could no longer hope to defend Richmond. With the remnant of his army, now about 25,000 men, Lee began moving west in the forlorn hope of finding a way around the Union forces so he could head south and link up with Johnston in North Carolina. But the Union army pursued him and blocked his escape route. Finally recognizing that further bloodshed was futile, Lee arranged to meet Grant at a private home in the small town of Appomattox Courthouse, Virginia. There, on April 9, he surrendered what was left of his forces. Nine days later, near Durham, North Carolina, Johnston surrendered to Sherman.

In military terms, at least, the long war was now effectively over, even though Jefferson Davis refused to accept defeat. He fled south from Richmond and was finally captured in Georgia. A few Southern diehards continued to fight, but even their resistance collapsed before long. Well before the last shot was fired, the difficult process of reuniting the shattered nation had begun.

CONCLUSION

The American Civil War began with high hopes and high ideals on both sides. In both the North and the South, thousands of men enthusiastically enlisted in local regiments; marched down the streets of their towns and cities dressed in uniforms of blue or gray to the cheers of family, friends, and neighbors; and went off to war. Four years later, over 600,000 of them were dead and many more maimed and traumatized for life. A fight for "principles" and "ideals"—a fight few people had thought would last more than a few months—had become one of the longest wars, and by far the bloodiest war, in American history, before or since.

During the first two years of fighting, the Confederate forces seemed to have all the advantages. They were fighting on their own soil. Their troops seemed more committed to the cause than those of the North. Their commanders were exceptionally talented, while Union forces were for a time erratically led. Gradually, however, the Union's advantages began to assert themselves. It had a stabler political system led by one of the greatest leaders in the nation's history (as opposed to the Confederacy's untested government led by a relatively weak president). It had a much larger population, a far more developed industrial economy, superior financial institutions, and a better railroad system. By the middle of 1863, the tide of war had changed; and over the next two years, Union forces gradually wore down the Confederate armies before finally triumphing in 1865.

The North's victory was not just a military one. The war strengthened the North's economy, giving a spur to industry and railroad development. It greatly weakened the South's, by destroying millions of dollars of property and depleting the region's young male population. Southerners had gone to war in part because of their fears of growing Northern dominance. The war itself, ironically, confirmed and strengthened that dominance. There was no doubt by 1865 that the future of the United States lay in the growth of industry and commerce, which would occur for many years primarily outside the South.

But most of all, the Civil War was a victory for the millions of African-American slaves, over whose plight the conflict had largely begun in the first place. The war produced Abraham Lincoln's epochal Emancipation Proclamation and, later, the Thirteenth Amendment to the Constitution, which abolished slavery altogether. It also encouraged hundreds of thousands of slaves literally to free themselves, to desert their masters and seek refuge behind Union lines—at times to fight in the Union armies. The future of the freed slaves was not to be an easy one, but three and a half million people who had once lived in bondage emerged from the war as free men and women.

Significant Events

1860	South Carolina secedes from Union
1861	Ten more Southern states secede
	Confederate States of America formed
	Jefferson Davis named president of Confederacy
	Conflict at Fort Sumter, South Carolina (April 12–14), begins Civil War
	George B. McClellan appointed commander of Army of the Potomac and army chief of staff
	Union blockades Confederate coast
	Trent affair imperils U.S. relations with Britain
	First Battle of Bull Run
1862	Battle of Shiloh (April 6–7)
	Union forces capture New Orleans
	Second Battle of Bull Run (August 29–30)
	Battle of Antietam (September 17)
	Battle of Fredericksburg (December 13)
	McClellan removed as chief of staff and, later, from command of Army of the Potomac
	Robert E. Lee named commander of Confederate armies
	Homestead Act and Morrill Land Grant Act passed
	Union Pacific Railroad chartered
	Confederacy enacts military draft
	Republicans experience heavy losses in congressional elections
1863	Lincoln issues Emancipation Proclamation (January 1)
	Battle of Chancellorsville (May 1–5)
	Battle of Gettysburg (July 1–3)
	Vicksburg surrenders (July 4)
	Battle of Chattanooga (November 23–25)
	Union enacts military draft
	Antidraft riots break out in New York City
	South experiences food riots
	West Virginia admitted to Union
1864	Grant named commander of Union armies
	Battle of the Wilderness (May 5–7)
	Petersburg, Virginia, besieged
	Sherman captures Atlanta (September 2)
	Sherman's "March to the Sea" begins
	Lincoln reelected president
	Central Pacific Railroad chartered
1865	Lee surrenders to Grant at Appomattox Courthouse (April 9)
	Thirteenth Amendment, abolishing slavery, ratified

FOR FURTHER REFERENCE

Suggested Readings   James McPherson, *Battle Cry of Freedom* (1988) is a fine general history the Civil War. Shelby Foote, *The Civil War: A Narrative,* 3 vols. (1958–1974) emphasizes the military history of the war with literary grace and power. David Donald, *Lincoln* (1995) is the best modern biography of the sixteenth president. James M. McPherson, *Abraham Lincoln and the Sec-* *ond American Revolution* (1990) offers provocative reflections on the life and significance of Lincoln. Douglas Southall Freeman, *Robert E. Lee,* 4 vols. (1934–1935) and William McFeely, *Grant* (1981) are the leading biographies of the two most important Civil War generals. Emory Thomas, *The Confederate Nation* (1979) is a fine one-volume history of the Confederacy. Ira Berlin et al., eds.,

Free At Last: A Documentary History of Slavery, Freedom and the Civil War (1992) is a superb compilation of primary sources from slaves and slaveowners relating to the demise of slavery during the Civil War years. Ira Berlin et al., *Slaves No More: Three Essays on Emancipation and the Civil War* (1992), the companion volume to the documents in *Free At Last,* argues that slaves and freedmen played an active role in destroying slavery and redefining freedom. Catherine Clinton and Nina Silber, *Divided Houses* (1992) is a collection of essays in the "new social history" from various historians demonstrating the importance of gender to the history of the Civil War.

Films   (The best source for information on how to find these and other films is *Bowker's Complete Video Directory*—3 volumes.) *The Civil War* (1989) is Ken Burns's award-winning, nine-episode epic documentary. *Civil War Journal,* focuses on the private stories within the great conflict. *The American Story, No. 11: The Eve of Conflict, No. 12: The Blue and the Grey,* and *No. 13: The Road to Appomattox* (1985) explore the Civil War from Lincoln's election to the end of the war. *Civil War Legends* (1989) includes biographies of Robert E. Lee, Stonewall Jackson, Ulysses S. Grant and Abraham Lincoln. *The Civil War: Anguish of Emancipation* (1972) reenacts the events confronting Abraham Lincoln as he prepared to issue the Emancipation Proclamation. *The Fifty-Fourth Massachusetts,* from the Arts & Entertainment Network Civil War Series, illuminates the history of Massachusetts's famous regiment of African-American soldiers. *Clara Barton* (1995) traces the life of a woman who became a nurse during the Civil War and was instrumental in establishing the American Red Cross.

Internet Resources   (For up-to-date URL addresses and links to these and other websites, consult the McGraw-Hill history site at http://www.mhhe.com/socsience/history/usa/link/linktop.htm) *U.S. Civil War Center* offers hundreds of links to information about the Civil War, including documents, maps, photographs, and information about specific battles and units. *Rare Map Collection–American Civil War* provides contemporary battlefield and other maps of the 1860s. *Abraham Lincoln Online* has hundreds of links to Lincoln sites. *The Avalon Project at the Yale Law School: The Confederate States of America* contains documents in the history of the Confederacy. *The Valley of the Shadow* is an excellent gateway into the story of the Civil War as seen by the people of two communities in the Great Valley of the United States: Franklin County, Pennsylvania, and Augusta County, Virginia. *Images of Battle* contains letters written by soldiers during the Civil War. *Civil War Photographs, 1861–1865* provides photographs of officers, troops, and battlefields. Most of these photographs were by Mathew Brady. *Lest We Forget—The Civil War* has selections on the history of African-American soldiers in the Civil War. *Arguing the Point* contains Currier & Ives images of the Civil War era, including the elections preceding the war.

BIBLIOGRAPHY

General Studies   Bruce Catton, *This Hallowed Ground* (1956). James M. McPherson, *What They Fought For, 1861–1865* (1994); *Ordeal by Fire,* rev. ed. (1985). Allan Nevins, *The War for the Union,* 4 vols. (1959–1971). James G. Randall and David Donald, *The Civil War and Reconstruction,* rev. ed. (1969).

The Secession Crisis   William L. Barney, *The Road to Secession* (1972); *The Secessionist Impulse: Alabama and Mississippi in 1860* (1974). Steven A. Channing, *Crisis of Fear* (1970). Daniel W. Crofts, *Reluctant Confederates: Upper South Unionists in the Secession Crisis* (1989). Richard N. Current, *Lincoln and the First Shot* (1963). Michael P. Johnson, *Toward a Patriarchal Republic* (1977). David Potter, *Lincoln and His Party in the Secession Crisis* (1942). Kenneth M. Stampp, *And the War Came* (1950).

Lincoln   LaWanda Cox, *Lincoln and Black Freedom* (1981). David Donald, *Lincoln Reconsidered: Essays on the Civil War Era,* 2nd ed. (1956). Mark E. Neely, *The Fate of Liberty: Abraham Lincoln and Civil Liberties* (1991); *The Last Best Hope of Earth: Abraham Lincoln and the Promise of America* (1993). Stephen B. Oates, *With Malice Toward None: The Life of Abraham Lincoln* (1979). Phillip Shaw Pauldan, *The Presidency of Abraham Lincoln* (1994). Merrill D. Peterson, *Lincoln in American Memory* (1994). James G. Randall, *Lincoln the President,* 4 vols. (1945–1955), the final volume completed by Richard N. Current. Benjamin Thomas, *Abraham Lincoln* (1952). T. Harry Williams, *Lincoln and the Radicals* (1941); *Lincoln and His Generals* (1952).

Politics and Society in the North   Daniel Aaron, *The Unwritten War* (1973). Iver Bernstein, *The New York City Draft Riots* (1990). John P. Bugardt, ed., *Civil War Nurse* (1980). Adrian Cook, *The Armies of the Streets: The New York City Draft Riots of 1863* (1974). David Donald, *Charles Sumner and the Rights of Man* (1970). Martin Duberman, *Charles Francis Adams* (1961). Eric Foner, *Politics and Ideology in the Age of the Civil War* (1980). George Fredrickson, *The Inner Civil War: Northern Intellectuals and the Crisis of the Union* (1965). J. Matthew Gallman, *The North Fights the Civil War: The Home Front*

(1994). Paul G. Gates, *Agriculture and the Civil War* (1965). Wood Gray, *The Hidden Civil War* (1942). Alvin M. Josephy, Jr., *The Civil War in the American West* (1991). Frank L. Klement, *The Copperheads in the Middle West* (1960); *Dark Lanterns: Secret Political Societies, Conspiracies, and Treason Trials in the Civil War* (1984). Elizabeth D. Leonard, *Yankee Women: Gender Battles in the Civil War* (1994). James H. Moorhead, *American Apocalypse: Yankee Protestants and the Civil War* (1978). Grace Palladino, *Another Civil War: Labor, Capital, and the State in Anthracite Regions of Pennsylvania, 1840-1868* (1990). Philip Shaw Paludan, *"A People's Contest": The Union and the Civil War, 1861-1868* (1988). Mitchell Reid, *The Vacant Chair: The Northern Soldier Leaves Home* (1993). Susan M. Reverby, *Ordered to Care: The Dilemma of American Nursing, 1850-1945* (1987). Glyndon Van Deusen, *William Henry Seward* (1967). Wendy Hamand Venet, *Neither Ballots nor Bullets: Women Abolitionists and the Civil War* (1991). Edmund Wilson, *Patriotic Gore* (1962).

African Americans and Emancipation   Ira Berlin, Leslie Rowland, et al., eds., *Freedom: A Documentary History of Emancipation, 1861-1867,* Series I–II (1982-1993). John W. Blassingame, *Black New Orleans* (1973). Dudley T. Cornish, *The Sable Arm: Negro Troops in the Union Army* (1966). Joseph T. Glatthaar, *Forged in Battle: The Civil War Alliance of Black Soldiers and White Officers* (1990). Peter Kolchin, *First Freedom* (1972). Ervin Jordan, Jr., *Black Confederates and Afro-Yankees in Civil War Virginia* (1995). Leon Litwack, *Been in the Storm So Long: The Aftermath of Slavery* (1979). David Long, *The Jewel of Liberty: Abraham Lincoln's Re-Election and the End of Slavery* (1994). James M. McPherson, *The Struggle for Equality* (1964); *The Negro's Civil War* (1965). Clarence L. Mohr, *On the Threshold of Freedom: Masters and Slaves in Civil War Georgia* (1986).

The Confederacy   Thomas B. Alexander and Richard E. Beringer, *The Anatomy of the Confederate Congress* (1972). Stephen V. Ash, *When the Yankees Came: Conflict and Chaos in the Occupied South, 1861-1865* (1995). William Davis, *"A Government of Our Own": The Making of the Confederacy* (1994). *Jefferson Davis* (1978). Paul D. Escott, *After Secession* (1978); *Slavery Remembered* (1979); *Many Excellent People* (1985). Drew Gilpin Faust, *The Creation of Confederate Nationalism* (1988); *Mothers of Invention: Women of the Slaveholding South in the American Civil War* (1996). William Marvel, *Andersonville: The Last Depot* (1994). George C. Rable, *The Confederate Republic: A Revolution Against Politics* (1994). James L. Roark, *Masters Without Slaves: Southern Planters in the Civil War and Reconstruction* (1978). Charles P.

Roland, *The Confederacy* (1960). Hudson Strode, *Jefferson Davis,* 3 vols. (1955-1964). Daniel E. Sutherland, *Seasons of War: The Ordeal of a Southern Community, 1861-1865* (1995). Emory Thomas, *The Confederacy as a Revolutionary Experience* (1971); *The Confederate State of Richmond* (1971). Bell I. Wiley, *The Life of Johnny Reb* (1943); *The Plain People of the Confederacy* (1943). C. Vann Woodward, ed., *Mary Chesnut's Civil War* (1982). W. Buck Yearns, *The Confederate Congress* (1960).

Diplomacy   Stuart L. Bernath, *Squall Across the Atlantic: American Civil War Prize Cases and Diplomacy* (1970). David P. Crook, *Diplomacy During the American Civil War* (1975); *The North, the South, and the Powers, 1861-1865* (1974). Howard Jones, *Union in Peril: The Crisis over British Intervention in the Civil War* (1992). Gordon H. Warren, *Fountain of Discontent: The Trent Affair and Freedom of the Seas* (1981).

Military Histories   Richard E. Beringer et al., *Why the South Lost the Civil War* (1986). John Carpenter, *Ulysses S. Grant* (1976). Bruce Catton, *Mr. Lincoln's Army* (1951); *Glory Road* (1952); *A Stillness at Appomattox* (1954); *America Goes to War* (1958); *Banners at Shenandoah* (1956); *Grant Moves South* (1960). Thomas L. Connelly, *The Marble Man* (1977). Burke Davis, *Sherman's March* (1980). David Donald, ed., *Why the North Won the Civil War* (1960). Michael Fellman, *Inside War: The Guerrilla Conflict in Missouri During the American Civil War* (1989). Shelby Foote, *The Civil War: A Narrative,* 3 vols. (1958-1974). Douglas Southall Freeman, *Robert E. Lee,* 4 vols. (1934-1935). Gary W. Gallagher, *Chancellorsville: The Battle and Its Aftermath* (1996). Kent Gramm, *Gettysburg* (1994). Herman Hattaway and Archer Jones, *How the North Won* (1983). Archer Jones et al., *Why the South Lost the Civil War* (1986). Alvin M. Josephy, *The Civil War in the American West* (1991). Lee Kennett, *Marching Through Georgia: The Story of Soldiers and Civilians During Sherman's Campaign* (1995). Gerald F. Linderman, *Embattled Courage: The Experience of Combat in the American Civil War* (1987). James M. McPherson, *What They Fought For, 1861-1865* (1994). John Niven, *Gideon Welles, Lincoln's Secretary of the Navy* (1973). Charles Royster, *The Destructive War: William Tecumseh Sherman, Stonewall Jackson, and the Americans* (1991). Stephen W. Sears, *George B. McClellan: The Young Napoleon* (1988); *Landscape Turned Red: The Battle of Antietam* (1983). Emory Thomas, *Robert E. Lee* (1995). Jeffry Wert, *General James Longstreet* (1993). Kenneth P. Williams, *Lincoln Finds a General,* 4 vols. (1949-1952). T. Harry Williams, *McClellan, Sherman, and Grant* (1962); *P. G. T. Beauregard, Napoleon in Gray* (1955).

FROM THE PLANTATION TO THE SENATE.

Chapter Fifteen

RECONSTRUCTION AND THE NEW SOUTH

Few periods in the history of the United States have produced as much bitterness or created such enduring controversy as the era of Reconstruction—the years following the Civil War when Americans attempted to reunite their shattered nation. Those who lived through Reconstruction viewed it in sharply different ways. To many white Southerners, it was a vicious and destructive experience—a time when vindictive Northerners inflicted humiliation and revenge on the prostrate South and unnecessarily delayed a genuine reunion of the sections. Northern defenders of Reconstruction, in contrast, argued that their policies were the only way to keep unrepentant Confederates from restoring Southern society as it had been before the war; without forceful federal intervention, it would be impossible to stop the reemergence of a backward aristocracy and the continued subjugation of former slaves; there would be no way, in other words, to prevent the same sectional problems that had produced the Civil War in the first place.

To most African Americans at the time, and to many people of all races since, Reconstruction was notable for other reasons. Neither a vicious tyranny, as white Southerners charged, nor a thoroughgoing reform, as many Northerners claimed, it was, rather, a small but important first step in the effort by former slaves to secure civil rights and economic power. Reconstruction did not provide African Americans with either the legal protections or the material resources to assure them anything like real equality. And when it came to an end, finally, in the late 1870s—as a result of an economic crisis, a lack of political will in the North, and organized, at times violent, resistance by white Southerners—the freed slaves found themselves abandoned by the federal government to face a system of economic peonage and legal subordination alone. For the remainder of the nineteenth century, those blacks who continued to live in what came to be known as the New South were unable effectively to resist oppression. And yet for all its shortcomings, Reconstruction did help African Americans create institutions and legal precedents that they carried with them into the twentieth century and that became the basis for later efforts to win freedom and equality.

■ **A RECONSTRUCTION-ERA TRIBUTE TO THE ELECTION OF AFRICAN AMERICANS TO CONGRESS**
From left to right: Sen. Hiram R. Revels, Rep. Benjamin S. Turner, the Rev. Richard Allen, Frederick Douglass, Rep. Josiah T. Walls, Rep. Joseph H. Rainy, and writer William Wells Brown.
(Library of Congress)

☙

THE PROBLEMS OF PEACEMAKING

In 1865, as it became clear that the war was almost over, no one in Washington knew quite what to do. Abraham Lincoln could not negotiate a treaty with

■ **RICHMOND, 1865**
By the time Union forces captured Richmond in early 1865, the Confederate capital had been under siege for months and much of the city lay in ruins, as this photograph reveals. On April 4, President Lincoln, accompanied by his son Tad, visited Richmond. As he walked through the streets of the shattered city, hundreds of former slaves emerged from the rubble to watch him pass. "No triumphal march of a conqueror could have equalled in moral sublimity the humble manner in which he entered Richmond," a black soldier serving with the Union army wrote. "It was a great deliverer among the delivered. No wonder tears came to this eyes." *(Library of Congress)*

the defeated government; he continued to insist that the Confederate government had no legal right to exist. Yet neither could he simply readmit the Southern states into the Union as if nothing had happened.

The Aftermath of War and Emancipation

What happened to the South in the Civil War was a catastrophe with no parallel in America's experience as a nation. The region in 1865 was a desolate place. Towns had been gutted, plantations burned, fields neglected, bridges and railroads destroyed. Many white Southerners, stripped of their slaves through emancipation and stripped of the capital they had invested in now worthless Confederate bonds and currency, had almost no personal property. Many families had to rebuild their fortunes without the help of

adult males. Some white Southerners faced starvation and homelessness.

More than 258,000 Confederate soldiers had died in the war—more than 20 percent of the adult white male population of the region; thousands more returned home wounded or sick. Almost all surviving white Southerners had lost people close to them in the fighting. A cult of ritualized mourning developed throughout the region in the late 1860s, particularly among white women—many of whom wore mourning clothes (and even special mourning jewelry) for two years or longer. At the same time, white Southerners began to romanticize the "Lost Cause" and its leaders, and to look back nostalgically at the South as it had existed before the terrible disruptions of war. Such Confederate heroes as Robert E. Lee, Stonewall Jackson, and (later) Jefferson Davis were treated with

■ **A MONUMENT TO THE CONFEDERATE DEAD**
This monument in the town square of Greenwood, South
Carolina, was typical of many such memorials erected all across
the South in the aftermath of the Civil War. They served to
commemorate the soldiers who had died in the struggle, but also
to remind white southerners of what was by the 1870s already
widely known and romanticized as the "Lost Cause." *(Museum of
the Confederacy, Richmond, Virginia)*

extraordinary reverence, almost as religious figures.
Communities throughout the South built elaborate
monuments to their war dead in town squares. The
tremendous sense of loss that pervaded the white
South reinforced the determination of many whites
to protect what remained of their now-vanished
world.

If conditions were bad for many Southern whites,
they were far worse for most Southern blacks—the
4 million men and women emerging from bondage.
Some of them had also seen service during the war—

as servants to Confederate officers or as teamsters
and laborers for the Southern armies. Nearly 200,000
had fought for the Union, and 38,000 had died. Others had worked as spies or scouts for Union forces in
the South. Many more had flocked to the Union lines
to escape slavery. Even before Emancipation, thousands of slaves in many parts of the South had taken
advantage of wartime disruptions to leave their owners and move off in search of freedom. As soon as the
war ended, hundreds of thousands more former
slaves—young and old, healthy and sick—left their
plantations. But most had nowhere to go. Many of
them trudged to the nearest town or city, roamed the
countryside camping at night on the bare ground, or
gathered around Union occupation forces, hoping
for assistance. Virtually none, of course, owned any
land or property. Most had no possessions except
the clothes they wore.

In 1865, in short, Southern society was in disarray.
Blacks and whites, men and women faced a future of
great uncertainty. Yet people of both races faced this
future with some very clear aspirations. For both
blacks and whites, Reconstruction became a struggle
to define the meaning of freedom. But the former
slaves and the defeated whites had very different
conceptions of what freedom meant.

Competing Notions of Freedom

For African Americans, freedom meant above all an
end to slavery and to all the injustices and humiliation they associated with it. But it also meant the acquisition of rights and protections that would allow
them to live as free men and women in the same way
white people did. "If I cannot do like a white man,"
one African-American man told his former master, "I
am not free."

Blacks differed with one another on how to
achieve that freedom. Some demanded a redistribution of economic resources, especially land, because,
as a convention of Alabama freedmen put it in a formal resolution, "The property which they hold was
nearly all earned by the sweat of our brows." Others
asked simply for legal equality, confident that given
the same opportunities as white citizens they could
advance successfully in American society.

But whatever their particular demands, virtually all
former slaves were united in their desire for independence from white control. Freed from slavery, blacks
throughout the South began almost immediately to

■ **A FREEDMANS' BUREAU SCHOOL**
African American students and teachers stand outside a school for former slaves, one of many run by the Freedman's Bureau throughout the defeated Confederacy in the first years after the war. *(U.S. Military History Institute, Carlisle, Pennsylvania. Photo by Jim Enos)*

create autonomous African-American communities. They pulled out of white-controlled churches and established their own. They created fraternal, benevolent, and mutual aid societies. When they could, they began their own schools.

For most white Southerners, freedom meant something very different. It meant the ability to control their own destinies without interference from the North or the federal government. And in the immediate aftermath of the war, they attempted to exercise this version of freedom by trying to restore their society to its antebellum form. Slavery had been abolished in the former Confederacy by the Emancipation Proclamation, and everywhere else (as of December 1865) by the Thirteenth Amendment. But many white planters wanted to continue slavery in an altered form by keeping black workers legally tied to the plantations. When these white Southerners fought for what they considered freedom, they were fighting above all to preserve local and regional autonomy and white supremacy.

The federal government kept troops in the South after the war to preserve order and protect the freedmen. In March 1865, Congress established the Freed-

men's Bureau, an agency of the army directed by General Oliver O. Howard. The Freedmen's Bureau distributed food to millions of former slaves. It established schools staffed by missionaries and teachers who had been sent to the South by Freedmen's Aid Societies and other private and church groups in the North. It made modest efforts to settle blacks on lands of their own. (The bureau also offered considerable assistance to poor whites, many of whom were similarly destitute and homeless after the war.) But the Freedmen's Bureau was not a permanent solution. It had authority to operate for only one year; and in any case it was far too small to deal effectively with the enormous problems facing southern society. By the time the war ended, other proposals for reconstructing the defeated South were emerging.

Issues of Reconstruction

The terms by which the southern states rejoined the Union had important implications for both major political parties. The Republican victories in 1860 and 1864 had been a result in large part of the division of the Democratic Party and, later, the removal of the South from the electorate. Readmitting the South, leaders of both parties believed, would reunite the Democrats and weaken the Republicans. In addition, the Republican Party had taken advantage of the South's absence from Congress to pass a program of nationalistic economic legislation—railroad subsidies, protective tariffs, banking and currency reforms, and other measures to benefit northern business leaders and industrialists. Should the Democratic Party regain power with heavy southern support, these programs would be in jeopardy. Complicating these practical questions were emotional concerns. Many northerners believed the South should be punished in some way for the suffering and sacrifice its rebellion had caused. Many northerners believed, too, that the South should be transformed, made over in the North's urbanized image—its supposedly backward, feudal, undemocratic society civilized and modernized.

Even among the Republicans in Congress, there was considerable disagreement about the proper approach to Reconstruction—disagreement that reflected the same factional division (between the party's Conservatives and Radicals) that had created disputes over emancipation during the war. Conservatives insisted that the South accept the abolition of slavery, but proposed few other conditions for the readmission of the seceded states. The Radicals, led by Representative Thaddeus Stevens of Pennsylvania and Senator Charles Sumner of Massachusetts, urged that the civil and military leaders of the Confederacy be punished, that large numbers of Southern whites be disenfranchised, that the legal rights of blacks be protected, and that the property of wealthy white Southerners who had aided the Confederacy be confiscated and distributed among the freedmen. Some Radicals favored granting suffrage to the former slaves. Others hesitated, since few Northern states permitted blacks to vote. Between the Radicals and the Conservatives stood a faction of uncommitted Republicans, the Moderates, who rejected the punitive goals of the Radicals but supported extracting at least some concessions from the South on black rights.

Plans for Reconstruction

President Lincoln's sympathies lay with the Moderates and Conservatives of his party. He believed that a lenient Reconstruction policy would encourage southern unionists and other former Whigs to join the Republican Party and would thus prevent the readmission of the South from strengthening the Democrats. More immediately, the southern unionists could become the nucleus of new, loyal state governments in the South. Lincoln was not uninterested in the fate of the freedmen, but he was willing to defer questions about their future for the sake of rapid reunification.

Lincoln's Reconstruction plan, which he announced in December 1863, offered a general amnesty to white southerners—other than high officials of the Confederacy—who would pledge loyalty to the government and accept the elimination of slavery. Whenever 10 percent of the number of voters in 1860 took the oath in any state, those loyal voters could set up a state government. Lincoln also hoped to extend suffrage to those blacks who were educated, owned property, and had served in the Union army. Three southern states—Louisiana, Arkansas, and Tennessee, all under Union occupation—reestablished loyal governments under the Lincoln formula in 1864.

The Radical Republicans were astonished at the mildness of Lincoln's program. They persuaded Congress to deny seats to representatives from the three "reconstructed" states and refused to count the electoral vote of those states in the election of 1864. But for the moment, the Radicals were uncertain about what form their own Reconstruction plan should take.

Their first effort to resolve that question was the Wade-Davis Bill, passed by Congress in July 1864. It authorized the president to appoint a provisional governor for each conquered state. When a majority (not Lincoln's 10 percent) of the white males of the state pledged their allegiance to the Union, the governor could summon a state constitutional convention, whose delegates were to be elected by those who would swear (through the so-called Ironclad Oath) that they had never borne arms against the United States—another departure from Lincoln's plan. The new state constitutions would have to abolish slavery, disfranchise Confederate civil and military leaders, and repudiate debts accumulated by the state governments during the war. After a state had met these conditions, Congress would readmit it to the Union. Like the president's proposal, the Wade-Davis Bill left up to the states the question of political rights for blacks. Congress passed the bill a few days before it adjourned in 1864, and Lincoln disposed of it with a pocket veto. His action enraged the Radical leaders, and the pragmatic Lincoln became convinced he would have to accept at least some of the Radical demands. He began to move toward a new approach to Reconstruction.

The Death of Lincoln

What plan he might have produced no one can say. On the night of April 14, 1865, Lincoln and his wife attended a play at Ford's Theater in Washington. As they sat in the presidential box, John Wilkes Booth, a member of a distinguished family of actors and a man obsessed with aiding the Southern cause, entered the box from the rear and shot Lincoln in the head. The president was carried unconscious to a house across the street, where early the next morning, surrounded by family, friends, and political associates (among them a tearful Charles Sumner), he died.

The circumstances of Lincoln's death earned him immediate martyrdom. It also produced something close to hysteria throughout the North. There were accusations that Booth had acted as part of a great conspiracy—accusations that contained some truth. Booth did indeed have associates, one of whom shot and wounded Secretary of State Seward the night of

■ **ABRAHAM LINCOLN AND HIS SON TAD**
During the last difficult months of the Civil War, Lincoln often found relief from the strains of his office in the company of his young son, Thomas (known as "Tad"), shown here with his father in an 1864 photograph by Mathew Brady. Much has been written about Lincoln's turbulent family life. His wife, Mary Todd Lincoln, was apparently a moody and difficult woman, but the marriage seems generally to have been a happy one. The Lincolns did, however, experience a series of heartbreaking bereavements as three of their four sons died in childhood. Their second child, Edward, died in 1850 at the age of three; their third, "Willie," died of fever in 1862 at the age of eleven; Tad outlived his father by only a few years and died in 1871 at the age of eighteen. Robert Todd Lincoln, the president's eldest son, lived a long, successful, but not very happy life, during which he served as secretary of war, American minister to England, and president of the Pullman Railroad Car Company. *(Library of Congress)*

the assassination, another of whom abandoned at the last moment a scheme to murder Vice President Johnson. Booth himself escaped on horseback into the Virginia countryside, where, on April 26, he was cornered by Union troops and shot to death in a blazing barn. A military tribunal convicted eight other people of participating in the conspiracy (at least two of them on the basis of virtually no evidence). Four were hanged.

To many Northerners, however, the murder of the president seemed evidence of an even greater conspiracy—one masterminded and directed by the unrepentant leaders of the defeated South. Militant Republicans exploited such suspicions relentlessly for months, ensuring that Lincoln's death would help doom his plans for a relatively easy peace.

Johnson and "Restoration"

Leadership of the Moderates and Conservatives fell to Lincoln's successor, Andrew Johnson, who was not well suited, either by circumstance or personality, for the task. A Democrat until he had joined the Union ticket with Lincoln in 1864, he became a Republican president at a moment when partisan passions were growing. Johnson himself was an intemperate and tactless man, filled with resentments and insecurities. He was also openly hostile to the freed slaves and unwilling to support any plans that guaranteed them civil equality or enfranchisement. He once declared, "White men alone must manage the South."

Johnson revealed his plan for Reconstruction—or "Restoration," as he preferred to call it—soon after he took office, and he implemented it during the summer of 1865 when Congress was in recess. Like Lincoln, he offered amnesty to those Southerners who would take an oath of allegiance. (High-ranking Confederate officials and any white Southerner with land worth $20,000 or more would have to apply to the president for individual pardons. Johnson, a self-made man, apparently liked the thought of the great planter aristocrats humbling themselves before him.) In most other respects, however, his plan resembled that of the Wade-Davis Bill. For each state, the president appointed a provisional governor, who was to invite qualified voters to elect delegates to a constitutional convention. Johnson did not specify how many qualified voters were necessary, but he implied that he would require a majority (as had the Wade-Davis Bill). In order to win readmission to Congress, a state had to revoke its ordinance of secession, abolish slavery, ratify the Thirteenth Amendment, and repudiate the Confederate and state war debts. The final procedure before restoration was for a state to elect a state government and send representatives to Congress.

By the end of 1865, all the seceded states had formed new governments—some under Lincoln's plan, some under Johnson's—and were prepared to rejoin the Union as soon as Congress recognized them. But Radical Republicans vowed not to recognize the Johnson governments, just as they had previously refused to recognize the Lincoln regimes; for by now, northern opinion had become more hostile toward the South than it had been a year earlier when Congress passed the Wade-Davis Bill. Many northerners were disturbed by the apparent reluctance of some delegates to the southern conventions to abolish slavery, and by the refusal of all the conventions to grant suffrage to any blacks. They were astounded that states claiming to be "loyal" should elect prominent leaders of the recent Confederacy as state officials and representatives to Congress. Particularly hard to accept was Georgia's choice of Alexander H. Stephens, former Confederate vice president, as a United States senator.

RADICAL RECONSTRUCTION

Reconstruction under Johnson's plan—often known as "presidential Reconstruction"—continued only until Congress reconvened in December 1865. At that point, Congress refused to seat the senators and representatives of the states the president had "restored." Instead, it set up a new Joint Committee on Reconstruction to investigate conditions in the South and to help Congress create a Reconstruction policy of its own. The period of "congressional" or "Radical" Reconstruction had begun.

The Black Codes

Meanwhile, events in the South were driving Northern opinion even more toward the Radicals. Throughout the South in 1865 and early 1866, state legislatures were enacting sets of laws known as the Black Codes, modeled in many ways on the codes that had regulated free blacks in the prewar South. The laws were designed to reestablish planter control over black workers. Although there were variations from state to state, all the codes authorized local officials to apprehend unemployed blacks, fine them for vagrancy, and hire them out to private employers to satisfy the fine. Some of the codes forbade blacks to own or lease farms or to take any jobs other than as plantation workers or domestic servants. To much of the white South, the Black Codes were a realistic approach to a great social problem. To most of the North, and to most African Americans, they represented a return to slavery in all but name.

Congress's first response to the Black Codes was to extend the life of the Freedmen's Bureau and to widen its powers. It could now establish special courts for settling labor disputes, which could nullify work agreements forced on freedmen under the Black Codes. In April 1866, Congress struck again at the Black Codes by passing the First Civil Rights Act, which declared blacks to be citizens of the United States and empowered the federal government to intervene in state affairs when necessary to protect the rights of citizens. Johnson vetoed both the Freedmen's Bureau and civil rights bills, but Congress overrode both vetoes.

The Fourteenth Amendment

In April 1866, the Radicals acted again. The Joint Committee on Reconstruction submitted a proposed Fourteenth Amendment to the Constitution, which Congress approved in early summer and sent to the states for ratification. Eventually, it became one of the most important of all the provisions in the Constitution.

The amendment offered the first constitutional definition of American citizenship. Everyone born in the United States, and everyone naturalized, was automatically a citizen and entitled to equal protection of the laws by both state and national governments. There could be no other citizenship requirements. The amendment also imposed penalties—reduction of representation in Congress and on the electoral college—on states that denied suffrage to any adult male inhabitants. (This was the first time the Constitution made reference to gender, and the wording clearly reflected the prevailing view in Congress and elsewhere that the franchise was properly restricted to men.) Finally, it prohibited those who had taken an oath to support the Constitution (that is, members of Congress and other federal officials) and later had aided the Confederacy from holding any state or federal office unless two-thirds of Congress voted to pardon them. Congressional Radicals made it clear that

■ **THE MEMPHIS RACE RIOT, 1866**
Angry whites (shown here shooting down blacks) rampaged through the black neighborhoods of Memphis, Tennessee, during the first three days of May 1866, burning homes, schools, and churches and leaving forty-six people dead. Some claimed the riot was a response to strict new regulations protecting blacks that had been imposed on Tennessee by General George Stoneman, the military commander of the district; others argued that it was an attempt by whites to intimidate and control an African-American population that was trying to exercise its new freedom. Such riots were among the events that persuaded Radical Republicans in Congress to press for a harsher policy of Reconstruction.
(The Granger Collection)

if southern legislatures ratified the Fourteenth Amendment, their states would be readmitted to the Union. But only Tennessee did so. The refusal of the former Confederate states to ratify, along with the refusal of Kentucky and Delaware, denied the amendment the necessary approval of three-fourths of the states and temporarily derailed it.

In the meantime, however, the Radicals were growing stronger, in part because of northern anger at the South's and Johnson's recalcitrance. Bloody race riots broke out in 1866 in New Orleans, Memphis, and other southern cities in which angry whites rampaged through black neighborhoods, burning homes, schools, and churches. In Memphis, forty-six people, almost all blacks, died. Radicals cited the riots as evidence of the inadequacy of Johnson's policy.

In the 1866 congressional elections, Johnson campaigned actively for Conservative candidates, but he did his own cause more harm than good with his intemperate speeches. The voters returned an overwhelming majority of Republicans, most of them Radicals, to Congress. In the Senate, there were now 42 Republicans to 11 Democrats; in the House, 143 Republicans to 49 Democrats. (The South remained largely unrepresented in both chambers.) Nothing now prevented the Republicans in Congress from devising a Reconstruction plan of their own.

The Congressional Plan

The Radicals passed three Reconstruction bills early in 1867. Johnson vetoed them all, and Congress overrode him each time. Finally, nearly two years after the end of the war, the federal government had established a coherent plan for Reconstruction.

That two-year delay significantly affected the South's reaction to the program. In 1865, with the South reeling from its defeat and nearly prostrate, the federal government could probably have imposed almost any plan on the region without much resistance. But by 1867, the South had already begun to reconstruct itself under the reasonably generous terms Lincoln and Johnson had extended. Measures that might once have seemed moderate to most white southerners now seemed radical and tyrannical, and the congressional Reconstruction plan created deep resentments and continuing resistance.

Under the congressional plan, Tennessee, which had ratified the Fourteenth Amendment and had been readmitted by Johnson in 1866, was permitted to remain in the Union. But the Lincoln-Johnson governments of the other ten Confederate states were rejected. Those states were now combined into five military districts, each under a military commander who—in preparation for the readmission of the states—was to register qualified voters, defined as all adult black males and those white males who had

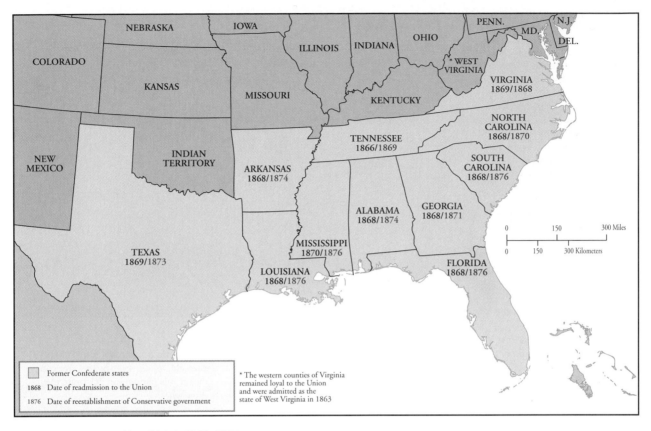

Former Confederate states

1868   Date of readmission to the Union

1876   Date of reestablishment of Conservative government

* The western counties of Virginia remained loyal to the Union and were admitted as the state of West Virginia in 1863

■ **POLITICAL RECONSTRUCTION, 1866–1877**
By the end of 1870, all the former Confederate states had been readmitted into the Union, but many white Southerners resented the new conditions imposed on them by the Radical Republicans in Congress and expressed in the Thirteenth, Fourteenth, and Fifteenth Amendments to the Constitution. Within a decade, the Republican Party had been ousted from power in every southern state, replaced by Conservative "Redeemer" governments, most of which combined white supremacy with a commitment to economic development.

not participated in the rebellion. After the completion of registration, voters would elect a convention to prepare a new state constitution, which had to include provisions for black suffrage. Once voters ratified the new constitution, states could hold elections for a government. Finally, if Congress approved the state's new constitution, if the state legislature ratified the Fourteenth Amendment, and if enough other states ratified it to make the amendment part of the Constitution, then the state was to be restored to the Union.

By 1868, seven more of the former Confederate states (Arkansas, North Carolina, South Carolina, Louisiana, Alabama, Georgia, and Florida) had fulfilled these conditions (including ratification of the Fourteenth Amendment, which now became part of the Constitution) and were readmitted to the Union. Conservative whites held up the return of Virginia

and Texas until 1869 and of Mississippi until 1870. By then, Congress had added an additional requirement for readmission: ratification of another constitutional amendment.

The Fifteenth Amendment

This was the Fifteenth Amendment, which forbade the states and the federal government to deny suffrage to any citizen on account of "race, color, or previous condition of servitude." Several northern and border states refused to approve it, and it was adopted only with the support of the southern states that had to ratify it in order to be readmitted to the Union.

The Fifteenth Amendment was important in theory, but in practice it had little effect on black suffrage for many years. It was, the historian Henry

■ **"AMERICAN CITIZENS (TO THE POLLS)"**
The artist T. W. Wood painted this watercolor of voters standing in line at the polls during the 1866 elections. A prosperous Yankee, a working-class Irishman, and a Dutch coach driver stand next to the newest addition to the American electorate: an African American, whose expression conveys his excitement at being able to join the community of voters. Wood meant this painting to celebrate the democratic character of American life after the Civil War. *(T. W. Wood Art Gallery, Vermont College, Montpelier)*

Adams once wrote, "more remarkable for what it does not than for what it does contain." The amendment guaranteed African Americans the right to vote, but not the right to hold public office. It did nothing to prohibit the literacy, property, and educational tests and the poll taxes that would be used by generations of white Southern leaders to prevent most blacks (and many poor whites) from voting.

Nor did the amendment make any reference to women. That was a particularly bitter blow to some feminists, because they had worked since the Civil War to ensure that any efforts to extend suffrage would link the black vote with the female vote. In 1866, Elizabeth Cady Stanton, Susan B. Anthony, Lucy Stone, and others had joined together in the Equal Rights Association, which worked to incorporate woman suffrage in state constitutions. In 1868, they created the Working Women's Association, which embraced a broad agenda of feminist and labor causes, including woman suffrage. And in 1869, Stanton and Anthony (now leading the National Woman Suffrage Association) opposed the Fifteenth Amendment because of its failure to include women

in its provisions and because, some said, it elevated black men over white women. Without woman suffrage, Stanton argued, political power would flow to "the lower orders of Chinese, Africans, Germans, and Irish, with their low ideals of womanhood." By opposing the Fifteenth Amendment, Stanton and Anthony alienated many more moderate feminists (among them Lucy Stone) and caused a final breakdown of the alliance between feminists and abolitionists, who had worked together so closely since the 1840s.

The limits of the Fifteenth Amendment reflected the politics of its principal sponsors. Southern Republicans and Northern Radicals did not want to guarantee universal suffrage, because they feared that in doing so they would assure former Confederates the right to vote. Many northern politicians, moreover, wanted to preserve voting restrictions in their own states. Some western states, for example, prohibited Chinese from voting, and several New England states retained property and literacy requirements. Republicans, in other words, wanted to expand their own electoral strength in the South (by enfranchising former slaves while disenfranchising former Confederates) without upsetting existing voting restrictions in the North, some of which also helped the Republicans.

Impeaching the President, Assaulting the Courts

To stop the president from interfering with their designs, Radicals in Congress passed two remarkable laws in 1867. One, the Tenure of Office Act, forbade the president to remove civil officials, including members of his cabinet, without the consent of the Senate. The principal purpose of the law was to protect the job of Secretary of War Edwin M. Stanton, the only Lincoln appointee still in the Cabinet, who was cooperating with the Radicals. The other law, the Command of the Army Act, prohibited the president from issuing military orders except through the commanding general of the army (General Grant), whose headquarters were to be in Washington and who could not be relieved or assigned elsewhere without the consent of the Senate.

President Johnson had long since ceased to be a serious obstacle to the passage of Radical legislation. But he was still the official charged with administering the Reconstruction programs, and as such, the Radicals believed, he was a serious impediment to their plans. Early in 1867 they began looking for a way to remove him. The only constitutional grounds for impeachment were "high crimes or misdemeanors." Republicans could find nothing on which to base such charges until Johnson gave them what they considered a plausible reason for action. He deliberately violated the Tenure of Office Act—in hopes of bringing a test case of the law before the courts. He dismissed Secretary of War Stanton even after Congress had refused to agree.

In the House of Representatives, elated Radicals impeached the president on eleven charges and sent them to the Senate for trial. The first nine counts dealt with the violation of the Tenure of Office Act. The tenth and eleventh charged Johnson with slandering Congress and with not enforcing the Reconstruction acts.

The trial before the Senate lasted through April and May 1868. The president's accusers argued that Johnson had defied Congress and was indeed guilty of high crimes and misdemeanors. His defenders claimed that he had acted properly in challenging what he considered an unconstitutional law. Radicals put heavy pressure on all the Republican senators, but the Moderates (who were losing faith in the Radical program) wavered. On the first three charges to come to a vote, seven Republicans joined the twelve Democrats to support acquittal. The vote was 35 to 19, one short of the constitutionally required two-thirds majority. After that, the Radicals dropped the impeachment effort.

The congressional Radicals also took action to stop the Supreme Court from interfering with their plans. In 1866, the Court had declared in *Ex parte Milligan* that military tribunals were unconstitutional in places where civil courts were functioning, a decision that seemed to threaten the system of military government the Congress was establishing in the South. Radicals immediately proposed legislation to require a two-thirds majority of the justices to overrule a law of Congress, to deny the Court jurisdiction in Reconstruction cases, to reduce its membership to three, and even to abolish it. The justices apparently took note. Over the next two years, the Court refused to accept jurisdiction in any cases involving Reconstruction. The bills affecting the Court never passed.

THE SOUTH IN RECONSTRUCTION

When white Southerners spoke bitterly in later years of the effects of Reconstruction, they referred most frequently to the governments Congress helped impose on them—governments they claimed were both incompetent and corrupt, that saddled the region with enormous debts, and that trampled on the rights of citizens. When black Southerners and their defenders condemned Reconstruction, in contrast, they spoke of the failure of the national and state governments to go far enough to guarantee freedmen even the most elemental rights of citizenship—a failure that resulted in a harsh new system of economic subordination. (See "Where Historians Disagree," pp. 530–532).

The Reconstruction Governments

In the ten states of the South that were reorganized under the congressional plan, approximately one-fourth of the white males were at first excluded from

■ **THE BURDENED SOUTH**

This Reconstruction-era cartoon expresses the South's sense of
its oppression at the hands of Northern Republicans. President
Grant (whose hat bears Abraham Lincoln's initials) rides in
comfort in a giant carpetbag, guarded by bayonet-wielding
soldiers, as the South staggers under the burden in chains. More
evidence of destruction and military occupations is visible in the
background. *(Culver)*

slavery and who hoped the Republican program of
internal improvements would help end their economic isolation. Despite their diverse social positions, scalawags shared a belief that the Republican
Party would serve their economic interests better
than the Democrats.

White men from the North also served as Republican leaders in the South. Critics of Reconstruction
referred to them pejoratively as "carpetbaggers,"
which conveyed an image of penniless adventurers
who arrived with all their possessions in a carpetbag
(a common kind of cheap suitcase covered with carpeting material). In fact, most of the so-called carpetbaggers were well-educated people of middle-class
origin, many of them doctors, lawyers, and teachers.
Most were veterans of the Union army who looked
on the South as a new frontier, more promising than
the West. They had settled there at war's end as
hopeful planters, or as business and professional
people.

But the most numerous Republicans in the South
were the black freedmen, most of whom had no previous experience in politics and who tried, therefore,
to build institutions through which they could learn
to exercise their power. In several states, African-
American voters held their own conventions to chart
their future course. One such "colored convention,"
as Southern whites called them, assembled in Alabama in 1867 and announced: "We claim exactly
the same rights, privileges and immunities as are enjoyed by white men—we ask nothing more and will
be content with nothing less." The black churches
freedmen created after emancipation, when they
withdrew from the white-dominated churches they
had been compelled to attend under slavery, also
helped give unity and political self-confidence to the
former slaves. African Americans played a significant
role in the politics of the Reconstruction South. They
served as delegates to the constitutional conventions.
They held public offices of practically every kind. Between 1869 and 1901, twenty blacks served in the
U.S. House of Representatives, two in the Senate
(Hiram Revels of Mississippi and Blanche K. Bruce of
Virginia). African Americans served, too, in state legislatures and in various other state offices. Southern
whites complained loudly (both at the time and for
generations to come) about "Negro rule" during Reconstruction, but no such thing ever actually existed
in any of the states. No black man was ever elected
governor of a southern state (although Lieutenant

voting or holding office. That produced black majorities among voters in South Carolina, Mississippi, and
Louisiana (states where blacks were also a majority of
the population), and in Alabama and Florida (where
they were not). But the government soon lifted most
suffrage restrictions so that nearly all white males
could vote. After that, Republicans maintained control only with the support of many Southern whites.

Critics called these Southern white Republicans
"scalawags." Many were former Whigs who had
never felt comfortable in the Democratic Party—
some of them wealthy (or once wealthy) planters or
businessmen interested in the economic development of the region. Others were farmers who lived
in remote areas where there had been little or no

■ **"THE COLORED NATIONAL CONVENTION"**
This engraving portrays one of many conventions organized by African Americans during Reconstruction, at which they hammered out demands for equal rights, economic opportunities, and education. This national convention took place in Nashville, Tennessee in April 1876. The picture appeared in *Frank Leslie's Illustrated Newspaper* a month later.
(The Newberry Library, Chicago, Illinois)

Governor P. B. S. Pinchback briefly performed gubernatorial duties in Louisiana). Blacks never controlled any of the state legislatures, although they held a majority in the lower house in South Carolina for a time. In the South as a whole, the percentage of black officeholders was always far lower than the percentage of blacks in the population.

The record of the Reconstruction governments is mixed. Critics at the time and since denounced them for corruption and financial extravagance, and there is some truth to both charges. Officeholders in many states enriched themselves through graft and other illicit activities. State budgets expanded to hitherto unknown totals, and state debts soared to previously undreamed-of heights. In South Carolina, for example, the public debt increased from $7 million to $29 million in eight years.

But the corruption in the South, real as it was, was hardly unique to the Reconstruction governments. Corruption was at least as rampant in the northern states. And in both North and South, it was a result of the same thing: a rapid economic expansion of government services (and revenues) that put new strains on (and new temptations before) elected officials everywhere. The end of Reconstruction did not end corruption in southern state governments. In many states, in fact, corruption increased.

And the state expenditures of the Reconstruction years were huge only in comparison with the meager budgets of the antebellum era. They represented an effort to provide the South with desperately needed services that antebellum governments had never offered: public education, public works programs, poor relief, and other costly new commitments. There were, to be sure, graft and extravagance in Reconstruction governments; there were also positive and permanent accomplishments.

Education

Perhaps the most important of those accomplishments was a dramatic improvement in southern education—an improvement that benefited both whites and blacks. In the first years of Reconstruction, much of the impetus for educational reform in the South came from outside groups—from the Freedmen's Bureau, from Northern private philanthropic organizations, from many Northern women, black and white, who traveled to the South to teach in freedmen's schools—and from southern blacks themselves. Over the opposition of many southern whites, who feared that education would give blacks "false notions of equality," these reformers established a large network of schools for former slaves—4,000 schools by 1870, staffed by 9,000 teachers (half of them black), teaching 200,000 students (about 12 percent of the total school-age population of the freedmen). In the 1870s, Reconstruction governments began to build a comprehensive public school system in the South. By 1876, more than half of all white children and about

40 percent of all black children were attending schools in the South. Several black "academies," offering more advanced education, also began operating. Gradually, these academies grew into an important network of black colleges and universities, which included such distinguished schools as Fisk and Atlanta Universities and Morehouse College.

Already, however, southern education was becoming divided into two separate systems, one black and one white. Early efforts to integrate the schools of the region were a dismal failure. The Freedmen's Bureau schools, for example, were open to students of all races, but almost no whites attended them. New Orleans set up an integrated school system under the Reconstruction government; again, whites almost universally stayed away. The one federal effort to mandate school integration—the Civil Rights Act of 1875—had its provisions for educational desegregation removed before it was passed. As soon as the Republican governments of Reconstruction were replaced, the new Southern Democratic regimes quickly abandoned all efforts to promote integration.

Landownership and Tenancy

The most ambitious goal of the Freedmen's Bureau, and of some Republican Radicals in Congress, was to make Reconstruction the vehicle for a fundamental reform of landownership in the South. The effort failed. In the last years of the war and the first years of Reconstruction, the Freedmen's Bureau did oversee the redistribution of substantial amounts of land to freedmen in a few areas—notably the Sea Islands of South Carolina and Georgia, and areas of Mississippi that had once belonged to the family of Jefferson Davis. By June 1865, the Bureau had settled nearly 10,000 black families on their own land—most of it drawn from abandoned plantations—arousing dreams among former slaves throughout the South of "forty acres and a mule." By the end of that year, however, the experiment was already collapsing. Southern plantation owners were returning and demanding the restoration of their property, and President Johnson was supporting their demands. Despite the resistance of the Freedmen's Bureau, the government eventually returned most of the confiscated land to the original white owners. Congress, moreover, never had much stomach for the idea of land redistribution. Very few Northern Republicans believed that the federal government had the right to confiscate property. Even so, distribution of landownership in the South changed considerably in the postwar years. Among whites, there was a striking decline in landownership, from 80 percent before the war to 67 percent by the end of Reconstruction. Some whites lost their land because of unpaid debt or increased taxes; some left the marginal lands they had owned to move to more fertile areas, where they rented. Among blacks, during the same period, the proportion who owned land rose from virtually none to more than 20 percent. Many black landowners acquired their property through hard work or luck or both. But some relied on assistance from white-dominated financial or philanthropic institutions. One of them was the Freedman's Bank, established in 1865 by antislavery whites in an effort to promote landownership among blacks. They persuaded thousands of freedmen to deposit their modest savings in the bank, but then invested heavily in unsuccessful enterprises. It was ill prepared, therefore, for the national depression of the 1870s and it failed in 1874.

Still, most blacks, and a growing minority of whites, did not own their own land during Reconstruction; and some who acquired land in the 1860s had lost it by the 1890s. These people worked for others in one form or another. Many black agricultural laborers—perhaps 25 percent of the total—simply worked for wages. Most, however, became tenants of white landowners—working their own plots of land and paying their landlords either a fixed rent or a share of their crop (See pp. 539–540.).

The new system represented a repudiation by blacks of the gang-labor system of the antebellum plantation, in which slaves had lived and worked together under the direction of a master. As tenants and sharecroppers, blacks enjoyed at least a physical independence from their landlords and had the sense of working their own land, even if in most cases they could never hope to buy it. But tenantry also benefited landlords in some ways, relieving them of any responsibility for the physical well-being of their workers.

Incomes and Credit

In some respects, the postwar years were a period of remarkable economic progress for African Americans. If the material benefits they had received under slavery are calculated as income, then prewar blacks

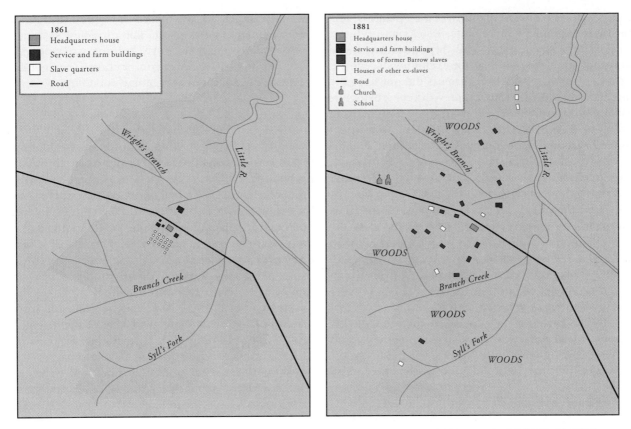

■ **THE SOUTHERN PLANTATION BEFORE AND AFTER EMANCIPATION: BARROW PLANTATION, OGLETHORPE COUNTY, GEORGIA**
Emancipation altered the individual and community lives of former slaves. On the Barrow Plantation, the dispersal of housing on the post-emancipation plantation reveals the freedmen's desire to escape the direct control and supervision of their former master. The construction of a church and a school on the Barrow plantation after emancipation demonstrates the former slaves' efforts to build new communal institutions that might help them forge a new life in freedom.

had earned about a 22 percent share of the profits of the plantation system. By the end of Reconstruction, they were earning 56 percent. Measured another way, the per capita income of southern blacks rose 46 percent between 1857 and 1879, while the per capita income of southern whites declined 35 percent. This represented one of the most significant redistributions of income in American history.

But these figures are somewhat misleading. For one thing, while the black share of profits was increasing, the total profits of southern agriculture were declining—a result of the dislocations of the war and a reduction in the world market for cotton. For another thing, while blacks were earning a greater return on each hour of labor than they had under slavery, they were working fewer hours. Women and children were less likely to labor in the fields than in the past. Adult men tended to work

shorter days. In all, the black labor force worked about one-third fewer hours during Reconstruction than it had been compelled to work under slavery—a reduction that brought the working schedule of blacks roughly into line with that of white farm laborers. Nor did the income redistribution of the postwar years lift many blacks out of poverty. Black per capita income rose from about one-quarter of white per capita income to about one-half in the first few years after the war. And after this initial increase, it rose hardly at all.

For blacks and poor whites alike, whatever gains there might have been as a result of land and income redistribution were often overshadowed by the ravages of the crop-lien system. Few of the traditional institutions of credit in the South—the "factors" and banks—returned after the war. In their stead emerged a new system of credit, centered in large part on local country stores, some of them owned by planters, others by independent merchants. Blacks and whites, landowners and tenants—all depended on these stores for such necessities as food, clothing, seed, and farm implements. And since farmers did not have the same steady cash flow as other workers, customers usually had to rely on credit from these merchants in order to purchase what they needed. Most local stores had no competition (and went to great lengths to ensure that things stayed that way). As a result, they were able to set interest rates as high as 50 or 60 percent. Farmers had to give the merchants a lien (or claim) on their crops as collateral for the loans (thus the term "crop-lien system," generally used to describe Southern farming in this period). Farmers who suffered a few bad years in a row, as often happened, could become trapped in a cycle of debt from which they could never escape.

This burdensome credit system had a number of effects on the region, almost all of them unhealthy. One was that some blacks who had acquired land during the early years of Reconstruction gradually lost it as they fell into debt. So, to a lesser extent, did white small landowners. Another was that Southern farmers became almost wholly dependent on cash crops—and most of all on cotton—because only such marketable commodities seemed to offer any possibility of escape from debt. Thus Southern agriculture, never sufficiently diversified even in the best of times, became more one-dimensional than ever. The relentless planting of cotton, moreover, was contributing to an exhaustion of the soil. The crop-lien system, in other words, was not only helping to impoverish small farmers; it was also contributing to a general decline in the Southern agricultural economy.

The African-American Family in Freedom

One of the most striking features of the black response to Reconstruction was the effort to build or rebuild family structures and to protect them from the interference they had experienced under slavery. A major reason for the rapid departure of so many blacks from plantations was the desire to find lost relatives and reunite families. Thousands of African Americans wandered through the South—often over vast distances—looking for husbands, wives, children, or other relatives from whom they had been separated. In the few black newspapers that circulated in the South, there were many advertisements by people searching for information about their relatives. Former slaves rushed to have marriages, previously without legal standing, sanctified by church and law. Black families resisted living in the former slave quarters and moved instead to small cabins scattered widely across the countryside, where they could enjoy at least some privacy.

Within the black family, the definition of male and female roles quickly came to resemble that within white families. Many women and children

■ **"A VISIT FROM THE OLD MISTRESS"** Winslow Homer's 1876 painting of an imagined visit by a southern white woman to a group of her former slaves was an effort to convey something of the tension in relations between the races in the South during Reconstruction. The women, once intimately involved in one another's lives, look at each other guardedly, carefully maintaining the space between them. White southerners attacked the painting for portraying white and black women on a relatively equal footing. Some black southerners criticized it for depicting poor rural African Americans instead of the more prosperous professional blacks who were emerging in southern cities. "There were plenty of well-dressed negroes if he would but look for them," one wrote. *(National Museum of American Art Smithsonian Institution. Gift of William T. Evans/Art Resource, NY)*

ceased working in the fields. Such work, they believed, was a badge of slavery. Instead, many women restricted themselves largely to domestic tasks—cooking, cleaning, gardening, raising children, attending to the needs of their husbands. Some black husbands refused to allow their wives to work as servants in white homes. "When I married my wife I married her to wait on me," one freedman told a former master who was attempting to hire his wife as a servant. "She got all she can do right here for me and the children."

Still, middle-class notions of domesticity were often difficult to sustain in the impoverished circumstances of most former slaves. Economic necessity required many black women to engage in income-producing activities, including activities that they

■ **AFRICAN-AMERICAN WORK AFTER SLAVERY**
Black men and women engaged in a wide range of economic activities in the aftermath of slavery. But discrimination by white Southerners and the former slaves' own lack of education limited most of them to relatively menial jobs. Many black women (including this former slave) earned money for their families by working as "washer women," doing laundry for white people. *(Historic New Orleans Collection)*

and their husbands resisted because they reminded them of slavery: working as domestic servants, taking in laundry, or helping in the field. By the end of Reconstruction, half of all black women over the age of sixteen were working for wages. And unlike white working women, most black female income-earners were married.

THE GRANT ADMINISTRATION

Exhausted by the political turmoil of the Johnson administration, American voters in 1868 yearned for a strong, stable figure to guide them through the troubled years of Reconstruction. They did not find one. Instead, they turned trustingly to General Ulysses S. Grant, the hero of the war and, by 1868, a revered national idol. Grant was a failure as president. During his two terms in office, he faced problems that would have taxed the abilities of a master of statecraft. Grant, however, was a dull and unimaginative man with few political skills and little vision.

The Soldier President

Grant could have had the nomination of either party in 1868. But believing that Republican Reconstruction policies were more attuned to public opinion than the Democratic alternatives, he accepted the Republican nomination. The Democrats nominated former governor Horatio Seymour of New York. The campaign was an exceptionally bitter one, in large part because the Democrats, desperate to revive their party's declining fortunes, chose to make opposition to Reconstruction and an open defense of white supremacy the basis of their appeal. The Ku Klux Klan (see p. 527), in the meantime, terrorized Southern Republicans, both black and white, in an effort to discourage them from voting. One member of Congress from Arkansas and three members of the South Carolina legislature were assassinated in the violence and terror that accompanied the campaign in the South.

The 1868 election was also the first in which Northern capitalists united behind the Republicans, making the party the principal defender of industrial growth in American politics, as it would remain for several generations. It was also in 1868 that the so-called Stalwarts established their dominance within the party. Fervently committed to the economic interests of Northern capitalists, they worked from within to shift the party's concerns away from issues related to the South and the freedmen and toward industrialization.

Grant's victory in the end was surprisingly narrow, an indication, perhaps, of how unpopular Reconstruction was already becoming. He carried twenty-six states to Seymour's eight. But Grant's popular majority was a scant 310,000 votes, a result of 500,000 black votes in the reconstructed states of the South.

Grant entered the White House with no political experience of any kind, and his performance in office was clumsy and ineffectual from the start. Except for Hamilton Fish, whom Grant appointed secretary of state and who served for eight years with great distinction, most members of the cabinet were as dull and inept as the president. Grant relied chiefly, and increasingly, on the machine leaders in the party—the group most ardently devoted to the spoils system. Grant used the spoils system even more blatantly than most of his predecessors. And in doing so, he provoked the opposition of Senator Charles Sumner and other Republican leaders, who joined with reformers to agitate for a new civil service system to limit the president's appointive powers. Nothing came of their efforts. Grant soon attracted the hostility of other Republicans as well. Many Northerners were growing disillusioned with Reconstruction, disgusted by stories of corruption, extravagance, and incompetence in the South. They opposed Grant's continuing support of Radical programs there. Some Republicans suspected (correctly) that there was corruption in the Grant administration itself. Still others criticized Grant because he did not support a tariff reduction.

The Liberal Republicans

By the end of Grant's first term, a substantial faction of the party—those who called themselves Liberal Republicans—had come to oppose what they called "Grantism." They had many disagreements with the president, but among the most important was their distaste for the way he used the patronage system to reward political cronies. They agitated, therefore, for a civil service system, which would limit the president's powers of appointment and, presumably, raise the quality of those working in government. Such

scholarly journalists as E. L. Godkin of *The Nation* and George William Curtis of *Harper's Weekly* argued that the government should base its appointments not on services to the party but on fitness for office as determined by competitive examinations, as the British government already was doing. Grant reluctantly agreed to establish a civil service commission, which Congress authorized in 1871, to devise a system of hiring based on merit. It proposed a set of rules that Grant seemed to approve; but the president was not really much interested in reform, and even if he had been he could not have persuaded his followers to accept a new system that would undermine the very basis of party loyalty—patronage. Nothing came of the commission's work.

Debate over civil service reform remained one of the leading political issues of the next three decades. The debate involved more than simply an argument over patronage and corruption. It also reflected basic differences of opinion over who was fit to serve in public life. Middle-class reformers were saying, implicitly, that only educated, middle-class people (the "best men") should be permitted access to government office. Their concerns grew in large part out of their alarm over the character of those who served in the Reconstruction governments and their fear that the growing immigrant population of the North would produce similarly unfit leaders there. As Charles Francis Adams, Jr., one of the leaders of the Liberal Republicans, once said: "Universal suffrage can only mean in plain English the government of ignorance and vice:—it means a European, and especially Celtic proletariat on the Atlantic coast, an African proletariat on the shores of the Gulf, and a Chinese proletariat on the Pacific." Civil service reform would, in short, help limit the power of democracy to debase public life.

Those opposing civil service reform included not just party leaders but immigrants, workers, some farmers, and others. They argued that the establishment of an elite corps of civil servants would be undemocratic. It would exclude them from participation in government and restrict power to the upper classes. That was precisely what the reformers hoped to do.

In 1872, hoping to prevent Grant's reelection, the Liberal Republicans deserted the party and nominated their own presidential candidate: Horace Greeley, veteran editor and publisher of the *New York Tribune*. The Democrats, somewhat reluctantly,

their positions as Union Pacific stockholders to steer large and fraudulent contracts to their construction company, in the process bilking the Union Pacific (and the federal government, which provided large subsidies to the railroad) of millions. To prevent investigations, the directors had transferred some Crédit Mobilier stock to key members of Congress. But in 1872, Congress did investigate and revealed that some highly placed Republicans—including Schuyler Colfax, now Grant's vice president—had accepted stock.

One dreary episode followed another in Grant's second term. Benjamin H. Bristow, Grant's third Treasury secretary, discovered that some of his officials and a group of distillers operating as a "whiskey ring" were cheating the government out of taxes by filing false reports. Among those involved was the president's private secretary, Orville E. Babcock. Then a House investigation revealed that William W. Belknap, secretary of war, had accepted bribes to retain a white employee on an Indian reservation in office; it became known as the "Indian ring." Other, lesser scandals added to the growing impression that "Grantism" had brought rampant corruption to government.

■ **THE GRANT SCANDALS**
This hostile cartoon suggests the growing popular discontent at the many scandals plaguing the Grant administration in its last years. Although the president himself was never proved to have been involved in any illegality, the scandals damaged his reputation nevertheless and helped thwart his hope of winning a third term as president. *(Bettmann)*

named Greeley their candidate as well, hoping that the alliance with the Liberals would enable them to defeat Grant. But the effort was in vain. Grant won a substantial victory, polling 286 electoral votes and 3,597,000 popular votes to Greeley's 66 and 2,834,000. Greeley had carried only two Southern states and four border states. Three weeks later, apparently crushed by his defeat, Greeley died.

The Grant Scandals

During the 1872 campaign, the first of a series of political scandals came to light that would plague Grant and the Republicans for the next eight years. It involved the Crédit Mobilier, a French-owned construction company that had helped build the Union Pacific Railroad. The heads of Crédit Mobilier had used

The Greenback Question

Compounding Grant's, and the nation's, problems was the financial crisis known as the Panic of 1873. It began with the failure of a leading investment banking firm, Jay Cooke and Company, which had invested too heavily in postwar railroad building. There had been panics before—in 1819, 1837, and 1857—but this was the worst one yet. The depression it produced lasted four years.

Debtors now pressured the government to inflate the currency, which would have made it easier for them to pay their debts. More specifically, they urged the government to redeem its war bonds with "greenbacks"—paper currency of the sort issued during the Civil War—which would increase the amount of money in circulation, lower the value of the dollar, and hence reduce the value of their debts. But Grant and most Republicans favored a "sound" currency—based solidly on gold reserves—which would favor the interests of banks and other creditors by keeping the dollar, and hence the value of the debts owed to them, high.

The greenback question would not go away. For one thing, there was the approximately $356 million in paper currency issued during the Civil War that was still in circulation. And in 1873, when the Supreme Court ruled in *Knox* v. *Lee* that greenbacks were legal, the Treasury issued more in response to the panic. The following year, Congress voted to raise the total further. But Grant, under pressure from eastern financial interests, vetoed the measure—over the loud objections of many Republicans.

In 1875, Republican leaders in Congress, in an effort to crush the greenback movement for good, passed the Specie Resumption Act. This law provided that after January 1, 1879, the greenback dollars, whose value constantly fluctuated, would be redeemed by the government and replaced with new certificates, firmly pegged to the price of gold. The law satisfied creditors, who had worried that debts would be repaid in debased paper currency. But "resumption" did nothing for debtors, because the gold-based money supply was not able to expand enough to help them.

In 1875, the greenbackers, as the inflationists were called, formed their own political organization: the National Greenback Party. It was active in the next three presidential elections, but it failed to gain widespread support. It did, however, keep the money issue alive. And in the 1880s, the greenback forces began to merge with another, more powerful group of currency reformers—those who favored silver as the basis of currency—to help produce a political movement that would ultimately attain enormous strength. The question of the proper composition of the currency was to remain one of the most controversial and enduring issues in late-nineteenth-century American politics.

Republican Diplomacy

The Johnson and Grant administrations achieved their greatest successes in foreign affairs. The accomplishments were the work not of the presidents themselves, who displayed little aptitude for diplomacy, but of two talented secretaries of state: William H. Seward, who had served Lincoln, and Hamilton Fish, who served throughout the two terms of the Grant administration.

An ardent expansionist and advocate of a vigorous foreign policy, Seward acted with as much daring as the demands of Reconstruction politics and the Republican Party's hatred of President Johnson would permit. Seward agreed to a Russian offer to sell Alaska to the United States for $7.2 million. Only with great difficulty was he able to persuade Congress to authorize the purchase, and he faced criticism from many who considered Alaska a useless frozen wasteland and called it "Seward's Folly." But Seward knew that Alaska was an important fishing center and a potential source of valuable resources such as gold. In 1867, Seward also engineered the American annexation of the tiny Midway Islands west of Hawaii.

In contrast with its sometimes shambling course in domestic politics, the diplomatic performance of the Grant administration under Hamilton Fish was generally decisive and firm. Fish was in many ways the personification of northeastern conservatism and, while officially a Republican, had opposed virtually all the party's Reconstruction policies. But he was a skilled and effective diplomat. His first major challenge was resolving a burning controversy with England. Many Americans believed that the British government had violated the neutrality laws during the Civil War by permitting English shipyards to build ships (among them the *Alabama*) for the Confederacy. American demands that England pay for the damage these vessels had caused became known as the "*Alabama* claims."

Seward had tried to settle the *Alabama* claims through the Johnson-Clarendon Convention of 1869, which would have submitted the matter to arbitration. But the Senate rejected the convention because it contained no British apology. In 1871, Fish succeeded in forging a new agreement: the Treaty of Washington, which provided for international arbitration of the claims and in which Britain expressed regret for the escape of the *Alabama* from England.

THE ABANDONMENT OF RECONSTRUCTION

As the North grew increasingly preoccupied with its own political and economic problems, interest in Reconstruction began to wane. The Grant administration continued to protect Republican governments in the South, but less because of any interest in ensuring the position of freedmen than because of a desire to prevent the reemergence of a strong Democratic Party in the region. But even the presence of federal troops was not enough to prevent white Southerners from overturning the Reconstruction regimes. By the time Grant left office, Democrats had taken back (or, as white Southerners liked to put it, "redeemed") the governments of seven of the eleven former Confederate states. For three other states—South Carolina, Louisiana, and Florida—the end of Reconstruction had to wait for the withdrawal of the last federal troops in 1876, a withdrawal that was the result of a long process of political bargaining and compromise at the national level. (One former Confederate state, Tennessee, had never been part of the Reconstruction process.)

The Southern States "Redeemed"

In the states where whites constituted a majority— the states of the upper South—overthrowing Republican control was relatively simple. By 1872, all but a handful of Southern whites had regained suffrage. Now a clear majority of the electorate, they needed only to organize and vote for their candidates.

In other states, where blacks were a majority or the populations of the two races were almost equal, whites used intimidation and violence to undermine the Reconstruction regimes. Secret societies—the Ku Klux Klan, the Knights of the White Camellia, and others—used terrorism to frighten or physically bar blacks from voting or otherwise exercising citizenship. Paramilitary organizations—the Red Shirts and White Leagues—armed themselves to "police" elections and worked to force all white males to join the Democratic Party and to exclude all blacks from meaningful political activity.

The Ku Klux Klan was the largest and most effective of these organizations. Formed in 1866 and led by former Confederate General Nathan Bedford Forrest, it gradually absorbed many of the smaller terrorist organizations. Its leaders devised rituals, costumes, secret languages, and other airs of mystery to create a bond among its members and make it seem even more terrifying to those it was attempting to intimidate. The Klan's "midnight rides"—bands of men clad in white sheets and masks, their horses covered with white robes and with hooves muffled— created terror in black communities throughout the South.

Many white Southerners considered the Klan and the other secret societies and paramilitary groups proud, patriotic societies. Together such groups served, in effect, as a military force (even if a decentralized and poorly organized one) continuing the battle against Northern rule. They worked in particular to advance the interests of those with the most to gain from a restoration of white supremacy—above all the planter class and the Southern Democratic Party. Even stronger than the Klan in discouraging black political power, however, was the simple weapon of economic pressure. Some planters refused to rent land to Republican blacks; storekeepers refused to extend them credit; employers refused to give them work.

The Ku Klux Klan Acts

The Republican Congress tried for a time to turn back this new wave of white repression. In 1870 and 1871, they passed two Enforcement Acts, also known as the Ku Klux Klan Acts, which were in many ways the most radical measures of the era. The Enforcement Acts prohibited the states from discriminating against voters on the basis of race and gave the federal government power to supersede the state courts and prosecute violations of the law. It was the first time the federal government had ever claimed the power to prosecute crimes by individuals under federal law. Federal district attorneys were now empowered to take action against conspiracies to deny African Americans such rights as voting, holding office, and serving on juries. The new laws also authorized the president to use the military to protect civil rights and to suspend the right of habeas corpus (the right of individuals to be freed from jail unless they are formally charged with a crime) when violations of the rights seemed particularly egregious. In October 1871, President Grant used this provision of the law when he declared a "state of lawlessness" in nine counties in South Carolina and sent in federal troops to occupy the area. Hundreds of suspected Klan members were arrested; some were held for long periods without trial; some were eventually convicted under the law and sent to jail.

The Enforcement Acts were seldom used as severely as they were in South Carolina, but they were effective in the effort by blacks and Northern whites to weaken the Klan. By 1872, Klan violence against blacks was in decline throughout the region.

Waning Northern Commitment

The Ku Klux Klan Acts marked the peak of Republican commitment to enforce the new rights Reconstruction and was extending to black citizens. But that commitment did not last for very long. Southern blacks were gradually losing the support of many of their former backers in the North. As early as 1870, after the adoption of the Fifteenth Amendment, some reformers convinced themselves that their long campaign on behalf of black people was now over; that with the vote, blacks ought to be able to take care of themselves. Over the next several years, former Radical leaders such as Charles Sumner and Horace Greeley now began calling themselves Liberals, cooperating with Democrats, and at times outdoing even the Democrats in denouncing what they viewed as black and carpetbag misgovernment. Within the South itself, many white Republicans joined the Liberals and eventually moved into the Democratic Party.

The Panic of 1873 further undermined support for Reconstruction. This economic crisis spurred Northern industrialists and their allies to find an explanation for the poverty and instability around them. They found it in a new idea known as "Social Darwinism" (see p.528), a harsh theory that argued that individuals who failed did so because of their own weakness and "unfitness." Those influenced by Social Darwinism came to view the large number of unemployed vagrants in the North as irredeemable misfits. They took the same view of poor blacks in the South. Social Darwinism also encouraged a broad critique of government intervention in social and economic life, which further weakened commitment to the Reconstruction program. Support for land redistribution, never great, waned quickly after 1873. So did willingness to spend money from the depleted federal treasury to aid the freedmen. State and local governments also found themselves short of funds, and rushed to cut back on social services—which in the South meant the end of almost all services to the former slaves.

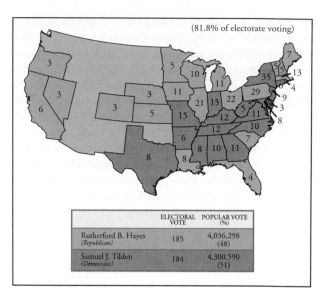

(81.8% of electorate voting)

	ELECTORAL VOTE	POPULAR VOTE (%)
Rutherford B. Hayes *(Republican)*	185	4,036,298 (48)
Samuel J. Tilden *(Democratic)*	184	4,300,590 (51)

■ **ELECTION OF 1876**

Although Samuel Tilden won the popular vote by a substantial margin in the presidential election of 1876, the electoral vote resulted in a deadlock. A special electoral commission awarded Hayes all the disputed electoral votes, thereby throwing the election to him. Once in office, however, the Republican Hayes attempted to mollify white Southern Democrats by withdrawing federal troops from the South and effectively abandoning the effort to improve the lives of black people in the South.

In the congressional elections of 1874, the Democrats won control of the House of Representatives for the first time since 1861. Grant took note of the changing temper of the North and made use of military force to prop up the Republican regimes that were still standing in the South. By the end of 1876, only three states were left in the hands of the Republicans—South Carolina, Louisiana, and Florida. In state elections that year, Democrats (after using terrorist tactics) claimed victory in all three. But the Republicans challenged the results and claimed victory as well, and they were able to remain in office because of the presence of federal troops. Without federal troops, it was now clear, the last of the Republican regimes would quickly fall.

The Compromise of 1877

Grant had hoped to run for another term in 1876, but most Republican leaders—shaken by recent Democrat successes, afraid of the scandals with which Grant was associated, and concerned about the president's failing health—resisted. Instead, they sought a candidate not associated with the problems of the Grant years, one who might entice Liberals back and unite the party again. They settled on Rutherford B. Hayes, a former Union army officer, governor, and congressman, champion of civil service reform. The Democrats united behind Samuel J. Tilden, the reform governor of New York who had been instrumental in overthrowing the corrupt Tweed Ring of New York City's Tammany Hall.

Although the campaign was a bitter one, there were few differences of principle between the candidates, both of whom were conservatives committed to moderate reform. The November election produced an apparent Democratic victory. Tilden carried the South and several large Northern states, and his popular margin over Hayes was nearly 300,000 votes. But disputed returns from Louisiana, South Carolina, Florida, and Oregon, whose total electoral vote was 20, threw the election in doubt. Tilden had undisputed claim to 184 electoral votes, only one short of a majority. But Hayes could still win if he managed to receive all 20 disputed votes.

The Constitution had established no method to determine the validity of disputed returns. It was clear that the decision lay with Congress, but it was not clear with which house or through what method. (The Senate was Republican, the House, Democratic.) Members of each party naturally supported a solution that would yield them the victory.

Finally, late in January 1877, Congress tried to break the deadlock by creating a special electoral commission to judge the disputed votes. The commission was to be composed of five senators, five representatives, and five justices of the Supreme Court. The congressional delegation would consist of five Republicans and five Democrats. The Court delegation would include two Republicans, two Democrats, and an independent. But the independent seat ultimately went to a justice whose real sympathies were with the Republicans. The commission voted along straight party lines, 8 to 7, awarding every disputed vote to Hayes. Congress accepted their verdict on March 2. Two days later, Hayes was inaugurated.

Behind the resolution of the deadlock however, lay a series of elaborate compromises among leaders of both parties. When a Democratic filibuster threat-

ened to derail the commission's report, Republican Senate leaders met secretly with Southern Democratic leaders to work out terms by which the Democrats would allow the election of Hayes. According to traditional accounts, Republicans and Southern Democrats met at Washington's Wormley Hotel. In return for a Republican pledge that Hayes would withdraw the last federal troops from the South, thus permitting the overthrow of the last Republican governments there, the Southerners agreed to abandon the filibuster.

Actually, the story behind the "Compromise of 1877" is somewhat more complex. Hayes was already on record favoring withdrawal of the troops, so Republicans needed to offer more than that if they hoped for Democratic support. The real agreement, the one that won over the Southern Democrats, was reached well before the Wormley meeting. As the price of their cooperation, the Southern Democrats (among them some former Whigs) exacted several pledges from the Republicans in addition to withdrawal of the troops: the appointment of at least one Southerner to the Hayes cabinet, control of federal patronage in their areas, generous internal improvements, and federal aid for the Texas and Pacific Railroad. Many powerful Southern Democrats supported industrializing their region. They believed Republican programs of federal support for business would aid the South more than the states' rights policies of the Democrats.

In his inaugural address, Hayes announced that the South's most pressing need was the restoration of "wise, honest, and peaceful local self-government"—a signal that he planned to withdraw federal troops and let white Democrats take over the state governments. That statement, and Hayes's subsequent actions, supported the widespread charges that he was paying off the South for acquiescing in his election and strengthened those who referred to him as "his Fraudulency." Hayes tried to counter such charges by projecting an image of stern public (and private) rectitude. But the election had already created such bitterness that even Hayes's promise to serve only one term could not mollify his critics.

The president and his party had hoped to build up a "new Republican" organization in the South drawn from Whiggish conservative white groups and committed to some modest acceptance of African-American rights. But all such efforts failed.

RECONSTRUCTION

Debate over the nature of Reconstruction—not only among historians, but among the public at large—has created so much controversy over the decades that one scholar, writing in 1959, described the issue as a "dark and bloody ground." Among historians, the passions of the debate have to some extent subsided since then; but in the popular mind, Reconstruction continues to raise "dark and bloody" images.

For many years, a relatively uniform and highly critical view of Reconstruction prevailed among historians, a reflection of broad currents in popular thought. By the late nineteenth century, most white Americans in both the North and the South had come to believe that few real differences any longer divided the sections, that the nation should strive for a genuine reconciliation. And most white Americans believed as well in the superiority of their race, in the inherent unfitness of blacks for political or social equality. Out of this mentality was born the first major historical interpretation of Reconstruction, through the work of William A. Dunning. In *Reconstruction, Political and Economic* (1907), Dunning portrayed Reconstruction as a corrupt outrage perpetrated on the prostrate South by a vicious and vindictive cabal of Northern Republican Radicals. Reconstruction governments were based on "bayonet rule." Unscrupulous and self-aggrandizing carpetbaggers flooded the South to profit from the misery of the defeated region. Ignorant, illiterate blacks were thrust into positions of power for which they were entirely unfit. The Reconstruction experiment, a moral abomination from its first moments, survived only because of the determination of the Republican Party to keep itself in power. (Some later writers, notably Howard K. Beale, added an economic motive—to protect Northern business interests.) Dunning and his many students (who together formed what became known as the "Dunning school") compiled state-by-state evidence to show that the legacy of Reconstruction was corruption, ruinous taxation, and astronomical increases in the public debt.

The Dunning school not only shaped the views of several generations of historians. It also reflected and helped to shape the views of much of the public. Popular depictions of Reconstruction for years to come (as first the 1915 film *The Birth of a Nation* and then the 1936 book and 1939 movie *Gone With the Wind* illustrated) portrayed the era as one of tragic exploitation of the South by the North. Even today, many white southerners and many others continue to accept the basic premises of the Dunning interpretation. Among historians, however, the old view of Reconstruction has gradually lost credibility.

The great African-American scholar W. E. B. Du Bois was among the first to challenge the Dunning view in a 1910 article and, later, in a 1935 book, *Black Reconstruction*. To him, Reconstruction politics in the Southern states had been an effort on the part of the masses, black and white, to create a more democratic society. The misdeeds of the Reconstruction governments, he claimed, had been greatly exaggerated, and their achievements overlooked. The governments had been expensive, he insisted, because they had tried to provide public education and other public services on a scale never before attempted in the South. But Du Bois's use of Marxist theory in his work caused many historians to dismiss his argument; and it remained for a group of less radical, white historians to shatter the Dunning image of Reconstruction.

(U.S. Military History Institute, Carlisle, Pennsylvania. Photo by Jim Enos)

In the 1940s, historians such as C. Vann Woodward, David Herbert Donald, Thomas B. Alexander, and others began to reexamine the Reconstruction governments in the South and to suggest that their records were not nearly as bad as most historians had previously assumed. They also looked at the Radical Republicans in Congress and suggested that they had not been motivated by vindictiveness and partisanship alone. By the early 1960s, a new view of Reconstruction was emerging from these efforts, a view whose appeal to historians grew stronger with the emergence of the "Second Reconstruction," the civil rights movement. The revisionist approach was summarized by John Hope Franklin in *Reconstruction After the Civil War* (1961) and Kenneth Stampp in *The Era of Reconstruction* (1965), which claimed that the postwar Republicans had been engaged in a genuine, if flawed, effort to solve the problem of race in the South by providing much-needed protection to the freedmen. The Reconstruction governments, for all their faults, had been bold experiments in interracial politics. The congressional Radicals were not saints, but they had displayed a genuine concern for the rights of slaves. Andrew Johnson was not a martyred defender of the Constitution, but an inept, racist politician who resisted reasonable compromise and brought the government to a crisis. There had been no such thing as "bayonet rule" or "Negro rule" in the South. Blacks had played only a small part in Reconstruction governments and had generally acquitted themselves well. The Reconstruction regimes had, in fact, brought important progress to the South, establishing the region's first public school system and other important social changes. Corruption in the South had been no worse than corruption in the North at that time. What was tragic about Reconstruction, the revisionist view claimed, was not what it did to Southern whites but what it did not do for Southern blacks. By stopping short of the reforms necessary to ensure blacks genuine equality, Reconstruction had consigned them to more than a century of injustice and discrimination.

In recent years scholars have begun to question the revisionist view—not in an effort to revive the old Dunning interpretation, but in an attempt to draw attention to those things Reconstruction in fact achieved. Eric Foner, in *Nothing but Freedom* (1983) and *Reconstruction: America's Unfinished Revolution* (1988) concluded that what is striking about the American experience in this context is not how little was accomplished, but how far the former slaves moved toward freedom and independence in a short time, and how large a role African Americans themselves played in shaping

(continued)

Reconstruction. During Reconstruction, blacks won a certain amount of legal and political power in the South; and even though they held that power only temporarily, they used it for a time to strengthen their economic and social positions and to win a position of limited but genuine independence. Through Reconstruction they won, if not equality, a measure of individual and community autonomy, building blocks of the freedom that emancipation alone had not guaranteed.

Historians writing from the perspective of African American and women's history have made related arguments. Leon Litwack's *Been in the Storm So Long* (1979) maintained that former slaves used the relative latitude they enjoyed under Reconstruction to build a certain independence for themselves within Southern society. They strengthened their churches; they reunited their families; they refused to work in the "gang labor" system of the plantations and forced the creation of a new labor system in which they had more control over their own lives. Amy Dru Stanley and Jacqueline Jones have both argued that the freed slaves displayed considerable independence in constructing their households on their own terms and asserting their control over family life, reproduction, and work. Women in particular sought the opportunity, according to Jacqueline Jones in *Labor of Love, Labor of Sorrow* (1985), "to labor on behalf of their own families and kin within the protected spheres of household and community."

Although many white Southern leaders sympathized with Republican economic policies, popular resentment of Reconstruction was so deep that supporting the party was politically impossible. At the same time, the withdrawal of federal troops signaled that the national government was giving up its attempts to control Southern politics and to improve the lot of blacks in Southern society.

The Legacy of Reconstruction

Reconstruction made some important contributions to the efforts of former slaves to achieve dignity and equality in American life. And it was not as disastrous an experience for Southern whites as most believed at the time. But Reconstruction was in the end largely a failure. For in those years the United States failed in its first serious effort to resolve its oldest and deepest social problem—the problem of race. What was more, the experience so disappointed, disillusioned, and embittered white Americans that it would be nearly a century before they would try again in any serious way.

Why did this great assault on racial injustice not achieve more? In part, it was because of the weaknesses and errors of the people who directed it. But in greater part, it was because attempts to produce solutions ran up against conservative obstacles so deeply embedded in the nation's life that they could not be dislodged. Veneration of the Constitution sharply limited the willingness of national leaders to infringe on the rights of states and individuals. A profound respect for private property and free enterprise prevented any real assault on economic privilege in the South. Above all, perhaps, a pervasive belief among many of even the most liberal whites that African Americans were inherently inferior served as an obstacle to equality. Given the context within which Americans of the 1860s and 1870s were working, what is surprising, perhaps, is not that Reconstruction did so little, but that it did even as much as it did.

Considering the odds confronting them, therefore, African Americans had reason for pride in the gains they were able to make during Reconstruction. And future generations had reason for gratitude for two great charters of freedom—the Fourteenth and Fifteenth Amendments to the Constitution—which, although largely ignored at the time, would one day serve as the basis for a "Second Reconstruction" that would renew the drive to bring freedom and equality to all Americans.

THE NEW SOUTH

The agreement between southern Democrats and northern Republicans that helped settle the disputed election of 1876 was supposed to be the first step toward developing a stable, permanent Republican Party in the South. In that respect, at least, it failed. In the years following the end of Reconstruction, white southerners established the Democratic Party as the only viable political organization for the region's whites. Even so, the South did change in the years after Reconstruction in some of the ways the framers of the Compromise of 1877 had hoped.

The "Redeemers"

By the end of 1877—after the last withdrawal of federal troops—every southern state government had been "redeemed." That is, political power had been restored to white Democrats. Many white southerners rejoiced at the restoration of what they liked to call "home rule." But in reality, political power in the region was soon more restricted than at any time since the Civil War. Once again, the South fell under the control of a powerful, conservative oligarchy, whose members were known variously as the "Redeemers" (to themselves and their supporters) or the "Bourbons" (a term for aristocrats used by some of their critics).

In a few places, this post-Reconstruction ruling class was much the same as the ruling class of the antebellum period. In Alabama, for example, the old planter elite—despite challenges from new merchant and industrial forces—retained much of its former power and continued largely to dominate the state for decades. In most areas, however, the Redeemers constituted a genuinely new ruling class. They were merchants, industrialists, railroad developers, and financiers. Some of them were former planters, some of them northern immigrants who had become absorbed into the region's life, some of them ambitious, upwardly mobile white southerners from the region's lower social tiers.

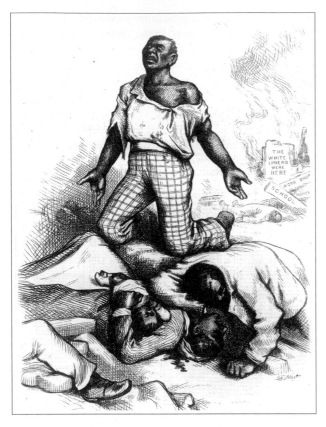

■ **"IS *THIS* A REPUBLICAN FORM OF GOVERNMENT?"**
The New York artist and cartoonist Thomas Nast marked the end
of Reconstruction in 1876 with this biting cartoon in *Harper's
Weekly,* expressing his dismay at what he considered the nation's
betrayal of the former slaves, who still had not received adequate
guarantees of their rights. The caption of the cartoon continued:
"Is *this* protecting life, liberty, or property? Is *this* equal protection
of the laws?" *(The Newberry Library, Chicago, Illinois)*

They combined a commitment to "home rule" and
social conservatism with a commitment to economic development.

The various Bourbon governments of the New
South behaved in many respects quite similarly to one
another. Conservatives had complained that the Reconstruction governments fostered widespread corruption, but the Redeemer regimes were, if anything,
even more awash in waste and fraud. (In this, they
were little different from governments in every region
of the country.) At the same time, virtually all the new
Democratic regimes lowered taxes, reduced spending,
and drastically diminished state services—including

many of the most important accomplishments of
Reconstruction. In one state after another, for example, state support for public school systems was reduced or eliminated. "Schools are not a necessity," an
economy-conscious governor of Virginia commented.

By the late 1870s, significant dissenting groups
were challenging the Bourbons: protesting the cuts
in services and denouncing the commitment of the
Redeemer governments to paying off the prewar and
Reconstruction debts in full, at the original (usually
high) rates of interest. In Virginia, for example, a vigorous "Readjuster" movement emerged, demanding
that the state revise its debt payment procedures so
as to make more money available for state services.
In 1879, the Readjusters won control of the legislature, and in the next few years they captured the
governorship and a U.S. Senate seat. Other states produced similar movements, some of them adding demands as well for greenbacks, debt relief, and other
economic reforms. (A few such independent movements included significant numbers of blacks in their
ranks, but all consisted primarily of lower-income
whites.) By the mid-1880s, however, conservative
southerners—largely by exploiting racial prejudice—
had effectively destroyed most of the dissenting
movements.

Industrialization and the "New South"

Many white southern leaders in the post-Reconstruction era hoped to see their region become the
home of a vigorous industrial economy. The South
had lost the war, many argued, because its economy had been unable to compete with the modernized manufacturing capacity of the North. Now the
region must "out-Yankee the Yankees" and build a
"New South." Henry Grady, editor of the *Atlanta
Constitution,* and other prominent spokesmen for
a New South seldom challenged white supremacy,
but they did advocate other important changes in
southern values. Above all, they promoted the
virtues of thrift, industry, and progress—qualities
that prewar southerners had often denounced in
northern society. "We have sown towns and cities
in the place of theories," Grady boasted to a New
England audience in the 1880s, "and put business
above politics. . . . We have fallen in love with
work." But even the most fervent advocates of the
New South creed were generally unwilling to break

entirely with the southern past. That was evident in, among other things, the popular literature of the region. At the same time that white southern writers were extolling the virtues of industrialization in newspaper editorials and speeches, they were painting nostalgic portraits of the Old South in their literature. Few southerners advocated a literal return to the old ways, but most whites eagerly embraced romantic talk of the "Lost Cause." And they responded warmly to the local-color fiction of such writers as Joel Chandler Harris, whose folk tales—the most famous being *Uncle Remus* (1880)—portrayed the slave society of the antebellum years as a harmonious world marked by engaging dialect and close emotional bonds between the races. The writer Thomas Nelson Page similarly extolled the old Virginia aristocracy. The growing popularity of minstrel shows also reflected the romanticization of the old South (see pp. 536–537). The white leaders of the New South, in short, faced their future with one foot still in the past.

Even so, New South enthusiasts did help southern industry expand dramatically in the years after Reconstruction and become a more important part of the region's economy than ever before. Most visible was the growth in textile manufacturing, which increased ninefold in the last twenty years of the century. In the past, southern planters had usually shipped their cotton out of the region to manufacturers in the North or in Europe. Now textile factories appeared in the South itself—many of them drawn to the region from New England by the abundance of water power, the ready supply of cheap labor, the low taxes, and the accommodating conservative governments. The tobacco-processing industry, similarly, established an important foothold in the region, largely through the work of James B. Duke of North Carolina, whose American Tobacco Company established for a time a virtual monopoly over the processing of raw tobacco into marketable materials. In the lower South, and particularly in Birmingham, Alabama, the iron (and, later, steel) industry grew rapidly. By 1890, the southern iron and steel industry represented nearly a fifth of the nation's total capacity.

Railroad development increased substantially in the post-Reconstruction years—at a rate far greater than that of the nation at large. Between 1880 and 1890, trackage in the South more than doubled.

And the South took a major step toward integrating its transportation system with that of the rest of the country when, in 1886, it changed the gauge (width) of its trackage to correspond with the standards of the North. No longer would it be necessary for cargoes heading into the South to be transferred from one train to another at the borders of the region. Yet southern industry developed within strict limits, and its effects on the region were never even remotely comparable to the effects of industrialization on the North. The southern share of national manufacturing doubled in the last twenty years of the century, to 10 percent of the total. But that percentage was the same the South had claimed in 1860; the region, in other words, had done no more than regain what it had lost during the war and its aftermath. The region's per capita income increased 21 percent in the same period. But at the end of the century, average income in the South was only 40 percent of that in the North; in 1860 it had been more than 60 percent. And even in those areas where development had been most rapid—textiles, iron, railroads—much of the capital had come from the North. In effect, the South was developing a colonial economy.

The growth of industry in the South required the region to recruit a substantial industrial work force for the first time. From the beginning, a high percentage of the factory workers (and an especially high percentage of textile workers) were women. Heavy male casualties in the Civil War had helped create a large population of unmarried women who desperately needed employment. Factories also hired entire families, many of whom were moving into towns from failed farms. Hours were long (often as much as twelve hours a day) and wages were far below the northern equivalent; indeed one of the greatest attractions of the South to industrialists was that employers were able to pay workers there as little as one-half what northern workers received. Life in most mill towns was rigidly controlled by the owners and managers of the factories. They rigorously suppressed attempts at protest or union organization. Company stores sold goods to workers at inflated prices and issued credit at exorbitant rates (much like country stores in agrarian areas), and mill owners ensured that no competitors were able to establish themselves in the community. At the same time, however, the

THE MINSTREL SHOW

The minstrel show was one of the most popular forms of entertainment in America in the second half of the nineteenth century. It was also a testament to the high awareness of race (and the high level of racism) in American society both before and after the Civil War. At the same time, however, African-American performers themselves formed their own minstrel shows and transformed them, at least to a degree, into vehicles for training black entertainers and developing important new forms of music and dance.

Before and during the Civil War, minstrel shows consisted almost entirely of white performers who blackened their faces with cork and presented grotesque stereotypes of the slave culture of the American South. Among the most popular of the stumbling, ridiculously ignorant characters invented for these shows were such figures as "Zip Coon" and "Jim Crow" (whose name later resurfaced as a label for late nineteenth-century segregation laws). A typical minstrel show presented a group of seventeen or more men seated in a semicircle facing the audience. The man in the center ran the show, played the straight man for the jokes of others, and led the music—lively dances and sentimental ballads played on banjos, castanets, and other instruments and sung by soloists or the entire group.

The shows were popular in the South, but they were particularly popular in the North, where black life was less familiar and more exotic and where white audiences (who, whatever their views of slavery, generally held a low opinion of African-Americans) reveled in the demeaning portrayals of slaves. White minstrel performers were so invested in portraying the stupidity and inferiority of blacks that they lashed out savagely at abolitionists and antislavery activists and, during the Civil War, portrayed black soldiers as incompetents and cowards—creating a military stereotype as insulting and inaccurate as the stereotypes they had used to portray slaves.

After the Civil War, white minstrels began to expand their repertoire. Drawing from the famous and successful freak shows of P. T. Barnum and other entertainment entrepreneurs, some began to include Siamese twins, bearded ladies, and even a supposedly 8-foot, 2-inch "Chinese giant" in their shows. They also incorporated sex, both by including women in some shows and, even more popularly, by recruiting female impersonators. One of the most successful minstrel performers of the 1870s was Francis Leon, who delighted crowds with his portrayal of a flamboyant "prima donna."

One reason white minstrels began to move in these new directions was that they were now facing competition from black performers, who could provide more authentic versions of black music, dance, and humor, and bring more talent to the task. The Georgia Minstrels, organized in 1865, was one of the first all-black minstrel troupes, and it had great success in attracting white audiences in the Northeast for several years. By the 1870s, touring African-American minstrel groups were numerous. The black minstrels used many of the conventions of the white shows. There were dances, music, comic routines, and sentimental recitations. Some black performers even chalked their faces to make

■ MINSTRELSY AT HIGH TIDE

The Primrose & West minstrel troupe—a lavish and expensive entertainment that drew large crowds in the 1800s—was one of many companies to offer this brand of entertainment to eager audiences all over the country. Although minstrelsy began with white musicians performing in black face, the popularity of real African-American minstrels encouraged the impresarios of the troupe to include groups of white and black performers alike.

(© Collection of the New York Historical Society)

themselves look as dark as the white black-face performers with whom they were competing. Black minstrels sometimes denounced slavery (at least indirectly) and did not often speak demeaningly of the capacities of their race. But they could not entirely escape caricaturing African-American life as they struggled to meet the expectations of their white audiences.

While the black minstrel shows had few openly political aims, they did help develop some important forms of African-American entertainment and transform them into a part of the national culture. Black minstrels introduced new forms of dance, derived from the informal traditions of slavery and black community life: the "buck and wing," the "stop time," and the "Virginia essence," which established the foundations for the tap and jazz dancing of the early twentieth century. They also improvised musically and began experimenting with forms that over time contributed to the growth of ragtime, jazz, and rhythm and blues.

(continued)

■ **THE ELECTRIC 3 MINSTRELS**
For every large troupe such as Primrose & West there were dozens of smaller traveling minstrel bands such as Calley, Haley, and Callan's shown here on the road in the 1880s. In concert, these men performed in exaggerated blackface. Posing for photographs, they tried to exhibit sober, middle-class respectability.
(Brown Brothers)

Eventually, black minstrelsy—like its white counterpart—evolved into other forms of theater, including the beginnings of serious black drama. At Ambrose Park in Brooklyn in the 1890s, for example, the celebrated black comedian Sam Lucas (a veteran of the minstrel circuit) starred in the play *Darkest America,* which one black newspaper later described as a "delineation of Negro life, carrying the race through all their historical phases from the plantation, into reconstruction days and finally painting our people as they are today, cultured and accomplished in the social graces, [holding] the mirror faithfully up to nature."

But interest in the minstrel show did not die altogether. In 1927, Hollywood released *The Jazz Singer,* the first feature film with sound. It was about the career of a white minstrel performer, and its star was one of the most popular singers of the twentieth century: Al Jolson, whose career had begun on the black-face minstrel circuit years before.

conditions of the mill town helped create a strong sense of community and solidarity among workers (even if they seldom translated such feelings into militancy).

Some industries, textiles for example, offered virtually no opportunities to African American workers. Others—tobacco, iron, and lumber, among others— did provide some employment for blacks, usually the most menial and lowest-paid positions. Some mill towns, therefore, were places where black and white culture came into close contact. That proximity contributed less to the growth of racial harmony than to the determination of white leaders to take additional measures to protect white supremacy.

At times, industrialization proceeded on the basis of no wage-paying employment at all. Through the "convict-lease" system, southern states leased gangs of convicted criminals to private interests as a cheap labor supply. The system exposed the convicts to brutal and at times fatal mistreatment. It paid them nothing (the leasing fees went to the states, not the workers). And it denied employment in railroad construction and other projects to the free labor force.

Tenants and Sharecroppers

Despite significant growth in southern industry, the region remained primarily agrarian. The most important economic reality in the post-Reconstruction South, therefore, was the impoverished state of agriculture. The 1870s and 1880s saw an acceleration of the trends that had begun in the immediate postwar years: the imposition of systems of tenantry and debt peonage on much of the region; the reliance on a few cash crops rather than on a diversified agricultural system; and increasing absentee ownership of valuable farmlands (many of them purchased by merchants and industrialists who paid little attention to whether the land was being properly used). During Reconstruction, perhaps a third or more of the farmers in the South were tenants; by 1900 the figure had increased to 70 percent. That was in large part the result of the crop-lien system that had emerged in the aftermath of the Civil War. Farmers who owned their own land often lost it as merchants seized it for payment of liens. Farmers who rented could never accumulate enough capital to buy land.

Tenantry took several forms. Farmers who owned tools, equipment, and farm animals—or who had the money to buy them—usually paid an annual cash rent for their land. But many farmers (including most black ones) had no money or equipment at all. Landlords would supply them with land, a crude house, a few tools, seed, and sometimes a mule. In return, farmers would promise the landlord a large share of the annual crop—hence the term "sharecropping." After paying their landlords and their local furnishing merchants (who were often the same people), sharecroppers seldom had anything left to sell on their own. The crop-lien system was one of several factors contributing to a particularly harsh social and economic transformation of the southern backcountry, the piney woods and mountain regions where cotton and slavery had always been rare and where farmers lived ruggedly independent lives. Subsistence agriculture had long been the norm in these areas; but as indebtedness grew, many farmers now had to grow cash crops such as cotton instead of the food crops they had traditionally cultivated in order to make enough money to pay off their loans.

But the transformation of the backcountry was a result of other factors as well. Many backcountry residents had traditionally subsisted by raising livestock, which had roamed freely across the landscape. In the 1870s, as commercial agriculture began to intrude into these regions, many communities began to pass "fence laws," which required farmers to fence in their animals (as opposed to fencing off their crops, as had once been the custom). There were widespread protests against the new laws, and at times violent efforts to resist them. But the existence of the open range (which had once been as much a part of life in the backcountry South as it was in the American West) could not survive the spread of commercial agriculture. Increasingly, therefore, opportunities for families to live largely self-sufficiently were declining. At the same time, opportunities for profiting within the market remained slim. The people of the backcountry, perhaps even more than other groups for whom agriculture had always been a business, felt the pain of losing their economic independence. They would be among the most important constituents for the populist protests of the 1880s and 1890s.

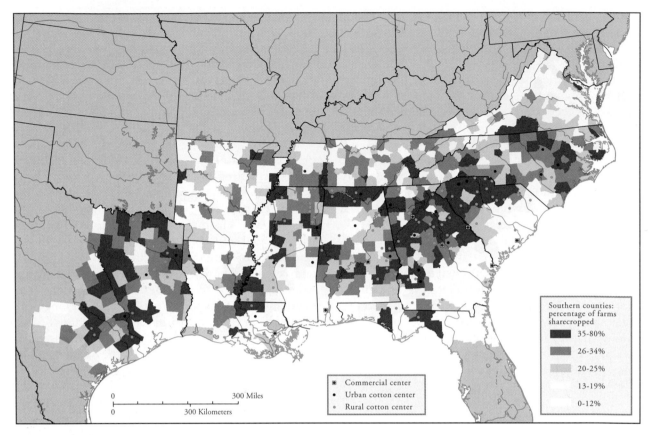

■ THE CROP-LIEN SYSTEM: THE SOUTH IN 1880

After the Civil War, more and more southern farmers became tenants and sharecroppers, both in black belt and upcountry regions. This development emerged in large part because of a new crop-lien system that transferred land ownership from farmers to merchants. The crop-lien system also shifted southern agriculture even more toward the production of cotton and undermined opportunities for families of small farmers to preserve their economic independence.

The crop-lien system was particularly devastating to southern blacks, few of whom owned their own land to begin with. These economic difficulties were compounded by social and legal discrimination, which in the post-Reconstruction era began to take new forms and to inspire new responses.

African Americans and the New South

The "New South creed" was not the property of whites alone. Many African Americans were attracted to the vision of progress and self-improvement as well. Some blacks succeeded in elevating themselves into a distinct middle class—economically inferior to the white middle class, but nevertheless significant. These were former slaves (and, as the decades passed, their offspring) who managed to acquire property, establish small businesses, or enter professions. A few blacks accumulated substantial fortunes by establishing banks and insurance companies for their race. One of those was Maggie Lena, a black woman who became the first female bank president in the United States when she founded the St. Luke Penny Savings Bank in Richmond in 1903. Most middle-class blacks experienced more modest gains by becoming doctors, lawyers, nurses, or teachers serving members of their own race.

A cardinal tenet of this rising group of blacks was that education was vital to the future of their race. With the support of northern missionary societies and, to a far lesser extent, a few southern state governments, they expanded the network of black col-

■ **TUSKEGEE INSTITUTE, 1881**
From these modest beginnings, Booker T. Washington's Tuskegee Institute in Alabama became the preeminent academy offering technical and industrial training to black men. It deliberately deemphasized the traditional liberal arts curricula of most colleges. Washington considered such training an unnecessary frill and encouraged his students to work on developing practical skills. *(Bettmann)*

leges and institutes that had taken root during Reconstruction into an important educational system.

The chief spokesman for this commitment to education, and for a time the major spokesman for his race as a whole, was Booker T. Washington, founder and president of the Tuskegee Institute in Alabama. Born into slavery, Washington had worked his way out of poverty after acquiring an education (at Virginia's famous Hampton Institute). He urged other blacks to follow the same road to self-improvement.

Washington's message was both cautious and hopeful. African Americans should attend school, learn skills, and establish a solid footing in agriculture and the trades. Industrial, not classical, education should be their goal. Blacks should, moreover, refine their speech, improve their dress, and adopt habits of thrift and personal cleanliness; they should, in short, adopt the standards of the white middle class. Only thus, he claimed, could they win the respect of the white population, the prerequisite for any larger social gains. Blacks should forgo agitating for political rights, he said, and concentrate on self-improvement and preparation for equality.

In a famous speech in Georgia in 1895, Washington outlined a philosophy of race relations that became widely known as the Atlanta Compromise. "The wisest among my race understand," he said, "that the agitation of questions of social equality is the extremest folly." Rather, blacks should engage in "severe and constant struggle" for economic gains; for, as he explained, "no race that has anything to contribute to the markets of the world is long in any degree ostracized." If blacks were ever to win the rights and privileges of citizenship, they must first show that they were "prepared for the exercise of these privileges." Washington offered a powerful challenge to those whites who wanted to discourage African Americans from acquiring an education or winning any economic gains. He helped awaken the interest of a new generation to the possibilities for self-advancement through self-improvement. But his message was also an implicit promise that blacks would not challenge the system of seg-regation that whites were then in the process of erecting.

The Birth of Jim Crow

Few white Southerners had ever accepted the idea of racial equality. That the former slaves acquired any legal and political rights at all after emancipation was in large part the result of federal support. That support all but vanished after 1877. Federal troops withdrew. Congress lost interest. And the Supreme Court effectively stripped the Fourteenth and Fifteenth Amendments of much of their significance. In the so-called civil rights cases of 1883, the Court ruled that the Fourteenth Amendment prohibited state governments from discriminating against people because of race but did not restrict private organizations or individuals from doing so. Thus railroads, hotels, theaters, and the like could legally practice segregation.

Eventually, the Court also validated state legislation that institutionalized the separation of the races. In *Plessy* v. *Ferguson* (1896), a case involving a Louisiana law that required separate seating arrangements for the races on railroads, the Court held that separate accommodations did not deprive blacks of equal rights if the accommodations were equal, a decision that survived for years as part of the legal basis of segregated schools. In *Cumming* v. *County Board of Education* (1899), the Court ruled that laws estab-

lishing separate schools for whites were valid even if there were no schools for blacks comparable to the white schools from which they were excluded.

Even before these decisions, white southerners were working to strengthen white supremacy and to separate the races to the greatest extent possible. One illustration of this movement from subordination to segregation was black voting rights. In some states, disfranchisement had begun almost as soon as Reconstruction ended. But in other areas, black voting continued for some time after Reconstruction—largely because conservative whites believed they could control the black electorate and use it to beat back the attempts of poor white farmers to take control of the Democratic Party. In the 1890s, however, franchise restrictions became much more rigid. During those years, some small white farmers began to demand complete black disfranchisement—both because of racial prejudice and because they objected to the black vote being used against them by the Bourbons. At the same time, many members of the conservative elite began to fear that poor whites might unite politically with poor blacks to challenge them. They too began to support further franchise restrictions.

In devising laws to disfranchise black males (black females, like white women, had never voted), the southern states had to find ways to evade the Fifteenth Amendment, which prohibited states from denying anyone the right to vote because of race. Two devices emerged before 1900 to accomplish this goal. One was the poll tax or some form of property qualification; few blacks were prosperous enough to meet such requirements. Another was the "literacy" or "understanding" test, which required voters to demonstrate an ability to read and to interpret the Constitution. Even those African Americans who could read had difficulty passing the difficult test white officials gave them. Such restrictions were often applied unequally. Literacy tests for whites, for example, were sometimes much easier than those for blacks. Even so, the laws affected poor white voters as well as blacks. By the late 1890s, the black vote had decreased by 62 percent, the white vote by 26 percent. One result was that some states passed so-called grandfather laws, permitting men who could not meet the literacy and property qualifications to be enfranchised if their ancestors had voted before

THE ORIGINS OF SEGREGATION

Not until after World War II, when the emergence of the civil rights movement forced white Americans to confront the issue of racial segregation, did historians pay much attention to the origins of the institution. Most had assumed that the separation of the races had emerged naturally and even inevitably out of the abolition of slavery. It had been a response to the failure of Reconstruction, the weakness and poverty of the African-American community, and the pervasiveness of white racism. It was (as W. J. Cash argued in his classic and controversial 1941 study, *The Mind of the South*) the way things had always been.

The first major challenge to these assumptions, indeed the first serious scholarly effort to explain the origins of segregation, was C. Vann Woodward's *The Strange Career of Jim Crow* published in 1956. Not only was it important in reshaping scholarship. It had a significant political impact as well. As a southern liberal, Woodward was eager to refute assumptions that segregation was part of an unchanging and unchangeable southern tradition. He wanted to convince scholars that the history of the South had been one of sharp discontinuities; and he wanted to convince a larger public that the racial institutions they considered part of a long, unbroken tradition were in fact the product of a particular set of historical circumstances.

In the aftermath of emancipation, and indeed for two decades after Reconstruction, Woodward argued, race relations in the South had remained relatively fluid. Blacks and whites did not often interact as equals, certainly, but black southerners enjoyed a degree of latitude in social and even political affairs that they would subsequently lose. Blacks and whites often rode together in the same railroad cars, ate in the same restaurants, used the same public facilities. African Americans voted in significant numbers. Blacks and whites considered a number of different visions of how the races should live together, and as late as 1890 it was not at all clear which of those visions would prevail. By the end of the nineteenth century, however, a great wave of racist legislation—the Jim Crow laws, which established the basis of segregation—had hardened race relations and destroyed the gentler alternatives that many whites and blacks had considered viable only a few years before. The principal reason, Woodward argued, was the Populist political insurgency of the 1890s, which mobilized blacks and whites alike and which frightened many white southerners into thinking that African Americans might soon be a major political power in the region. Southern conservatives, in particular, used the issue of white supremacy to attack the Populists and to prevent blacks from forming an alliance with them. The result was disfranchisement and segregation.

Woodward's argument suggested that laws are important in shaping social behavior—that laws had made segregation and, by implication, other laws could unmake it. Not all historians agreed. A more pessimistic picture of segregation emerged in 1965 from Joel Williamson's study of South Carolina, *After Slavery*. Williamson argued that the laws of the 1890s

(continued)

did not mean very much, that they simply ratified a set of conditions that had been firmly established by the end of Reconstruction. As early as the mid-1870s, Williamson claimed, the races had already begun to live in two separate societies. Blacks had constructed their own churches, schools, businesses, and neighborhoods; whites had begun to exclude blacks from white institutions. The separation was partly a result of pressure and coercion from whites, partly a result of the desire of blacks to develop their own, independent culture. Whatever the reasons, however, segregation was largely in place by the end of the 1870s, continuing in a different form a pattern of racial separation established under slavery. The laws of the 1890s did little more than codify an already established system.

In the same year that Williamson published his argument, Leon Litwack joined the debate, even if somewhat indirectly, with the publication of *North of Slavery*. Litwack revealed the existence of widespread segregation, supported by an early version of Jim Crow laws, in the North before the Civil War. In almost every northern state, he revealed, free blacks experienced a kind of segregation not very different from what freed slaves would experience in the South after the Civil War. A few years later, Ira Berlin argued in *Slaves Without Masters* (1974) that in the antebellum South, too, white people had created a wide range of discriminatory laws aimed at free blacks and ensuring segregation. The postbellum regime of Jim Crow, such works suggested, emerged naturally out of well-established precedents from before the Civil War, in both the North and the South.

Other scholars have challenged all these interpretations by attempting to link the rise of legal segregation to changing social and economic circumstances in the South. Howard Rabinowitz's *Race Relations in the Urban South* (1978) linked the rise of segregation to the new challenge of devising a form of race relations suitable to life in the growing southern cities, into which rural blacks were moving in substantial numbers. The creation of separate public facilities—schools, parks, waiting rooms, etc.—was not so much an effort to drive blacks out of white facilities; they had never had access to those facilities, and few whites had ever been willing to consider granting them access. It was, rather, an attempt to create for a black community that virtually all whites agreed must remain essentially separate a set of facilities where none had previously existed. Without segregation, in other words, urban blacks would have had no schools or parks at all. The alternative to segregation, Rabinowitz suggested, was not integration, but exclusion.

In the early 1980s, a number of scholars began examining segregation anew in light of the rising American interest in South Africa, whose system of apartheid seemed to them to be similar in many ways to the by then largely dismantled Jim Crow system in the South. John Cell's *The Highest Stage of White Supremacy* (1982) used the comparison to construct a revised explanation of how segregation emerged in the American South. Like Rabinowitz, he considered the increasing urbanization of the region the principal factor. But he ascribed different motives to those whites who promoted the rise of Jim Crow. The segregation laws, Cell argued, were a continuation of an

unchanging determination by southern whites to retain control over the black population. What had shifted was not their commitment to white supremacy but the things necessary to preserve it. The emergence of large black communities in urban areas and of a significant black labor force in factories presented a new challenge to white southerners. In the city, blacks and whites were in more direct competition than they had been in the countryside. There was more danger of social mixing. The city therefore required different, and more rigidly institutionalized, systems of control. The Jim Crow laws were a response not just to an enduring commitment to white supremacy, but to a new reality that required white supremacy to move to its "highest stage," where it would have a rigid legal and institutional basis.

Reconstruction began, thus barring the descendants of slaves from the polls while allowing poor whites access to them. In many areas, however, ruling elites were quite content to see poor whites, a potential source of opposition to their power, barred from voting.

The Supreme Court proved as compliant in ruling on the disfranchising laws as it was in dealing with the civil rights cases. The Court eventually voided the grandfather laws, but it validated the literacy test (in the 1898 case of *Williams* v. *Mississippi*) and displayed a general willingness to let the southern states define their own suffrage standards as long as evasions of the Fifteenth Amendment were not too glaring.

Laws restricting the franchise and segregating schools were only part of a network of state statutes—known as the Jim Crow laws—that by the first years of the twentieth century had institutionalized an elaborate system of segregation reaching into almost every area of southern life. Blacks and whites could not ride together in the same railroad cars, sit in the same waiting rooms, use the same washrooms, eat in the same restaurants, or sit in the same theaters. Blacks had no access to many public parks, beaches, and picnic areas; they could not be patients in many hospitals. Much of the new legal structure did no more than confirm what had already been widespread social practice in the South since well before the end of Reconstruction. But the Jim Crow laws also stripped blacks of many of the modest social, economic, and political gains they had made in the more fluid atmosphere of the late nineteenth century. They served, too, as a means for whites to retain control of social relations between the races in the newly growing cities and towns of the South, where traditional patterns of deference and subjugation were more difficult to preserve than in the countryside. What had been maintained by custom in the rural South was to be maintained by law in the urban South.

More than legal efforts were involved in this process. The 1890s witnessed a dramatic increase in white violence against blacks, which, along with the Jim Crow laws, served to inhibit black agitation for equal rights. The worst such violence—lynching of blacks by white mobs, either because the victims were accused of crimes or because they had seemed somehow to violate their proper station—reached appalling levels. In the nation as a whole in the 1890s, there was an average of 187 lynchings each year, more than 80 percent of them in the South. The vast majority of victims were black.

The most celebrated lynchings occurred in cities and towns, where large, well-organized mobs—occasionally with the tacit cooperation of local authorities—seized black prisoners from the jails and hanged them in great public rituals. Such public lynchings were often planned well in advance and elaborately organized. They attracted large audiences from surrounding regions. Entire families traveled many miles to witness the spectacles. But such great public lynchings were relatively rare. Much more frequent, and more dangerous to blacks because less visible or predictable, were lynchings performed by small vigilante mobs, often composed of friends or relatives of the victim (or supposed victim) of a crime. Those involved in lynchings often saw their actions as a legitimate form of law enforcement; and indeed, some victims of lynchings had in fact committed crimes. But lynchings were also a means by which whites controlled the black population through terror and intimidation. Thus, some lynch mobs killed blacks whose only "crime" had been presumptuousness. Others chose as victims outsiders in the community, whose presence threatened to disturb the normal pattern of race relations. Black men who had made any sexual advances toward white women (or who white men thought had done so) were particularly vulnerable to lynchings; the fear of black sexuality, and the unspoken fear among many men that white women might be attracted to that sexuality, was always an important part of the belief system that supported segregation. Whatever the reasons or circumstances, the victims of lynch mobs were denied the protection of the laws and the opportunity to prove their innocence.

The rise of lynchings shocked the conscience of many white Americans in a way that other forms of racial injustice did not. Almost from the start there was a substantial anti-lynching movement. In 1892 Ida B. Wells, a committed black journalist, launched

■ **A LYNCH MOB, 1893**
A large, almost festive crowd gathers to watch the lynching of a black man accused of the murder of a three-year-old white girl. Lynchings remained frequent in the South until as late as the 1930s, but they reached their peak in the 1890s and the first years of the twentieth century. Lynchings such as this one—published well in advance and attracting whole families who traveled great distances to see them— were relatively infrequent. Most lynchings were the work of smaller groups, operating with less visibility. *(Library of Congress)*

what became an international anti-lynching move- ment with a series of impassioned articles after the lynching of three of her friends in Memphis, Ten- nessee, her home. The movement gradually gathered strength in the first years of the twentieth century, attracting substantial support from whites in both the North and South (particularly from white women). Its goal was a federal anti-lynching law, which would allow the national government to do what state and local governments in the South were generally unwilling to do: punish those responsible for lynchings.

But the substantial white opposition to lynchings in the South stood as an exception to the general white support for suppression of African Americans. Indeed, just as in the antebellum period, the shared commitment to white supremacy helped dilute class animosities between poorer whites and the Bourbon oligarchies. Economic issues tended to play a sec- ondary role to race in southern politics, distracting people from the glaring social inequalities that af- flicted blacks and whites alike. The commitment to white supremacy, in short, was a burden for poor whites as well as for blacks.

Significant Events

1863	Lincoln announces preliminary Reconstruction plan
1864	Louisiana, Arkansas, and Tennessee readmitted to Union under Lincoln plan
	Wade-Davis Bill passed
1865	Lincoln assassinated (April 14); Andrew Johnson becomes president
	Johnson tries to readmit rest of Confederate states to Union
	Black Codes enacted in South
	Freedmen's Bureau established
	Congress reconvenes (December) and refuses to admit Southern representatives; creates Joint Committee on Reconstruction
1866	Freedmen's Bureau Act renewed
	Congress approves Fourteenth Amendment; most Southern states reject it
	Republicans gain in congressional elections
	Ex parte Milligan challenges Radicals' Reconstruction plans
	Ku Klux Klan formed in South
1867	Military Reconstruction Act (and two supplementary acts) outlines congressional plan of Reconstruction
	Tenure of Office Act and Command of the Army Act restrict presidential power
	Southern states establish Reconstruction governments under congressional plan
	U.S. purchases Alaska
1868	Most Southern states readmitted to Union under congressional plan
	Andrew Jackson impeached but not convicted
	Fourteenth Amendment ratified
	Ulysses S. Grant elected president
1869	Congress passes Fifteenth Amendment
	First "redeemer" governments elected in South
1870	Last Southern states readmitted to Union
	"Enforcement acts" passed
1871	*Alabama* claims settled
1872	Liberal Republicans defect
	Grant reelected president
1873	Commercial and financial panic disrupts economy
1875	Specie Resumption Act passed
	"Whiskey ring" scandal discredits Grant administration
1877	Rutherford B. Hayes elected president after disputed election
	Last federal troops withdrawn from South after Compromise of 1877
	Last Southern states "redeemed"
1879	Readjusters win control of Virginia legislature
1880	Joel Chandler Harris publishes *Uncle Remus*
1883	Supreme Court upholds segregation in private institutions
1890s	"Jim Crow" laws passed throughout South
	Lynchings increase in South
1895	Booker T. Washington outlines Atlanta Compromise
1896	*Plessy* v. *Ferguson* upholds "separate but equal" racial facilities
1898	*Williams* v. *Mississippi* validates literacy tests for voting

CONCLUSION

Reconstruction, long remembered by many white Americans as a vindictive outrage or a tragic failure, was in fact a profoundly important moment in American history. Despite the bitter political battles in Washington and throughout the South, culminating in the unsuccessful effort to impeach President Andrew Johnson, the most important result of the effort to reunite the nation after its long and bloody war was a reshaping of the lives of ordinary people in all regions of the nation.

In the North, Reconstruction solidified the power of the Republican Party and ensured that public policy would support the continued growth of an advanced industrial economy. The rapid growth of the northern economy continued and accelerated, drawing more and more of its residents into an expanding commercial world.

In the South, Reconstruction did more than simply bring slavery to an end. It fundamentally rearranged the relationship between the region's white and black citizens. Only for a while did Reconstruction permit African Americans to participate actively and effectively in southern politics. After a few years of widespread black voting and significant black office-holding, the forces of white supremacy forced most African Americans to the margins of the southern political world, where they would mostly remain until the 1960s.

But in other ways, the lives of southern blacks changed dramatically. Overwhelmingly, they left the plantations. Some sought work in towns and cities. Some left the region altogether. But the great majority began farming on small farms of their own—not as landowners, except in rare cases, but as tenants and sharecroppers on land owned by whites. The result was a form of economic bondage, driven by debt, only scarcely less oppressive than the legal bondage of slavery. But within this system, African Americans managed to carve out a much larger sphere of social and cultural activity than they had ever been able to create under slavery. Black churches organized in great numbers. African-American schools emerged in some communities, and black colleges began to appear in the region. Some former slaves owned businesses and flourished. In southern cities and towns, a fledgling black middle class began to emerge.

The system of tenantry, which emerged in the course of Reconstruction, continued after its end to dominate the southern economy. Strenuous efforts by "New South" advocates to advance industry and commerce in the region produced significant results in a few areas. But the South on the whole remained what it had always been, an overwhelmingly rural society with a sharply defined class structure. It was also a region with a deep commitment among its white citizens to the subordination of African Americans—a commitment solidified in the 1890s and the early twentieth century when white southerners erected an elaborate legal system of segregation (the "Jim Crow" laws). The promise of the great Reconstruction amendments to the Constitution—the Fourteenth and Fifteenth—remained largely unfulfilled in the South as the century drew to its close.

FOR FURTHER REFERENCE

Suggested Readings Eric Foner, *Reconstruction: America's Unfinished Revolution, 1863-1877* (1988), the most important modern synthesis of Reconstruction scholarship, emphasizes the radicalism of Reconstruction and the agency of freedpeople in the process of political and economic renovation. Thomas Holt, *Black over White: Negro Political Leadership in South Carolina During Reconstruction* (1977) examines Reconstruction in the state where black political power reached its apex. C. Vann Woodward, *Origins of the New South* (1951), still the leading work on the history of the South after Reconstruction after forty years, argues that a rising middle class sdefined the economic and political transformation of the New South. Edward Ayers, *The Promise of the New South* (1992) offers a rich portrait of social and cultural life in the New South. Steven Hahn, *The Roots of Southern Populism: Yeoman Farmers and the Transformation of the Georgia Upcountry* (1983) argues that southern farmers experienced an erosion of autonomy in the years after the Civil War, and their increasing discontent with market relations helped produce the populist revolt of the 1890s. C. Vann Woodward, *The Strange Career of Jim Crow* (rev. 1974) claims that segregation emerged only gradually across the South after Reconstruction. The "Woodward Thesis" has been challenged by, among others, Joel Williamson, *After Slavery: The Negro in South Carolina During Reconstruction* (1965); John W. Cell, *The Highest Stage of White Supremacy: The Origins of Segregation in South Africa and the American South* (1982); and Howard N. Rabinowitz, *Race Relations in the Urban South, 1865–1890* (1978).

Films   (The best source for information on how to find these and other films is *Bowker's Complete Video Directory*—3 volumes.) *The American Story, No. 14: Reconstruction* and *No. 14: Rebuilding the Union* (1985) details the effects of Lincoln's assassination and the course of Reconstruction under the Grant administration. *Reconstructing the South,* featuring Eric Foner, highlights the difficult social, political, and economic adjustments of the postwar era. *Reconstruction & Segregation 1870–1910* (1996) follows race relations from the assassination of Lincoln through the rise of the Ku Klux Klan and the imposition of Jim Crow. *The Civil War: Promise of Reconstruction* (1972) focuses on the Port Royal "experiment" in South Carolina.

Internet Resources   (For up-to-date URL addresses and links to these and other websites, consult the McGraw-Hill history site at http://www.mhhe.com/socscience/history/usa/link/linktop.htm) *The Freedmen and Southern Society Project* is an important ongoing archival exploration in the history of emancipation, with links to documents. *The Souls of Black Folk by W. E. B. Du Bois* is the full-text of the 1903 work. *Uncle Remus (1881)* is the test of the famous Joel Chandler Harris novel.

BIBLIOGRAPHY

Reconstruction   General Studies W. E. B. Du Bois, *Black Reconstruction* (1935). John Hope Franklin, *Reconstruction After the Civil War* (1961). Rembert Patrick, *The Reconstruction of the Nation* (1967). Kenneth M. Stampp, *The Era of Reconstruction, 1865–1877* (1965).

Early Reconstruction   Richard H. Abbott, *The First Southern Strategy: The Republican Party and the South, 1855–1877* (1986). Louis S. Gerteis, *From Contraband to Freedman* (1973). Willie Lee Rose, *Rehearsal for Reconstruction: The Port Royal Experiment* (1964). Brooks D. Simpson, *Let Us Have Peace: Ulysses S. Grant and the Politics of War and Reconstruction, 1861–1868* (1991).

Congressional Reconstruction   Herman Belz, *A New Birth of Freedom* (1976); *Emancipation and Equal Rights* (1978). Michael Les Benedict, *A Compromise of Principle: Congressional Republicans and Reconstruction, 1863–1869* (1974); *The Impeachment and Trial of Andrew Johnson* (1973). Richard Franklin Bensel, *Yankee Leviathan: The Origins of Central State Authority in America, 1859–1877* (1990). William R. Brock, *An American Crisis* (1963). Fawn Brodie, *Thaddeus Stevens* (1959). La Wanda Cox and John H. Cox, *Politics, Principles, and Prejudice, 1865–1867* (1963). Richard N. Current, *Old Thad Stevens* (1942). David Donald, *Charles Sumner and the Rights of Man* (1970); *The Politics of Reconstruction* (1965). Charles Fairman, *Reconstruction and Reunion* (1971). William Gillette, *The Right to Vote* (1965). Harold Hyman, *A More Perfect Union* (1973). Stanley Kutler, *The Judicial Power and Reconstruction Politics* (1968). Eric McKitrick, *Andrew Johnson and Reconstruction* (1960). Mark W. Summers, *Railroads, Reconstruction, and the Gospel of Prosperity* (1984). Hans L. Trefousse, *The Radical Republicans* (1963); *The Impeachment of a President* (1975); *Andrew Johnson: A Biography* (1989).

The South in Reconstruction   Roberta Alexander, *North Carolina Faces the Freedmen: Race Relations During Presidential Reconstruction, 1865–1867* (1985). James D. Anderson, *The Education of Blacks in the South* (1989). Dan Carter, *When the War Was Over: The Failure of Self-Reconstruction in the South, 1865–1867* (1985). Richard N. Current, *Those Terrible Carpetbaggers*

gers (1988). Barbara Fields, *Slavery and Freedom on the Middle Ground* (1985). Eric Foner, *Nothing but Freedom: Emancipation and Its Legacy* (1983). William Gillette, *Retreat from Reconstruction, 1869–1879* (1980); *The Right to Vote: Politics and Passage of the Fifteenth Amendment* (1969). William C. Harris, *The Day of the Carpetbagger: Republican Reconstruction in Mississippi, 1867–1875* (1979). Robert Higgs, *Competition and Coercion: Blacks in the American Economy, 1865–1914* (1977). Elizabeth Jacoway, *Yankee Missionaries in the South* (1979). Jacqueline Jones, *Soldiers of Light and Love: Northern Teachers and Georgia Blacks, 1865–1873* (1980); *Labor of Love, Labor of Sorrow: Black Women, Work, and the Family from Slavery to the Present* (1985). Peter Kolchin, *First Freedom: The Responses of Alabama's Blacks to Emancipation* (1972). Leon Litwack, *Been in the Storm So Long: The Aftermath of Slavery* (1979). Richard Lowe, *Republicans and Reconstruction in Virginia, 1865–1870* (1991). Peyton McCrary, *Abraham Lincoln and Reconstruction* (1978). William S. McFeely, *Yankee Stepfather: General O. O. Howard and the Freedmen* (1968). Edward Miller, Jr., *Gullah Statesman: Robert Smalls from Slavery to Congress, 1839–1915* (1995). *Carl Moneyhon,* The Impact of the Civil War and Reconstruction on Arkansas (1994). Michael Perman, *Reunion Without Compromise* (1973); *The Road to Redemption: Southern Politics, 1869–1979* (1984). L. N. Powell, *New Masters: Northern Planters During the Civil War and Reconstruction* (1980). Roger L. Ransom and Richard Sutch, *One Kind of Freedom: The Economic Consequences of Emancipation* (1977). C. Peter Ripley, *Slaves and Freedmen in Civil War Louisiana* (1976). Julie Saville, *The Work of Reconstruction: From Slave to Wage Laborer in South Carolina, 1860–1870* (1994). Crandall A. Shifflett, *Patronage and Poverty in the Tobacco South: Louisa County, Virginia, 1860–1900* (1982). Joel G. Taylor, *Louisiana Reconstructed* (1974). Allen Trelease, *White Terror: The Ku Klux Klan Conspiracy and Southern Reconstruction* (1967). Michael Wayne, *The Reshaping of Plantation Society: The Natchez District* (1983). Vernon Wharton, *The Negro in Mississippi, 1865–1890* (1965). Sarah Wiggins, *The Scalawag in Alabama Politics, 1865–1881* (1977).

The Grant Administration Ari Hoogenboom, *Outlawing the Spoils* (1961). William McFeely, *Grant* (1981). K. I. Polakoff, *The Politics of Inertia* (1973). John G. Sproat, *"The Best Men"* (1968). Margaret S. Thompson, *The "Spider Web": Congress and Lobbying in the Age of Grant* (1985). Irwin Unger, *The Greenback Era* (1964). C. Vann Woodward, *Reunion and Reaction* (1951).

The New South Orville Vernon Burton, *In My Father's House Are Many Mansions: Family and Community in Edgefield, South Carolina* (1985). Orville Vernon Burton and Robert C. McMath, Jr., eds., *Toward a New South? Studies in Post-Civil War Southern Communities* (1982). W. J. Cash, *The Mind of the South* (1941). Paul Gaston, *The New South Creed* (1970). J. Morgan Kousser and James M. McPherson, eds., *Region, Race, and Reconstruction* (1982). John Solomon Otto, *Southern Agriculture During the Civil War Era, 1860–1880* (1994). Howard Rabinowitz, *The First New South, 1865–1920* (1992). John Reps, *Cities of the Mississippi* (1994). Edward Royce, *The Origins of Southern Sharecropping* (1993). Jonathan Wiener, *Social Origins of the New South: Alabama, 1860–1885* (1978). C. Vann Woodward, *The Burden of Southern History* (rev., 1968); *American Counterpoint* (1971); *Thinking Back* (1986); *The Future of the Past* (1989).

Politics in the New South Kenneth E. Davison, *The Presidency of Rutherford B. Hayes* (1972). Carl Degler, *The Other South: Southern Dissenters in the Nineteenth Century* (1974). Vincent P. DeSantis, *Republicans Face the Southern Question: The New Departure Years, 1877–1897* (1959). Sheldon Hackney, *Populism to Progressivism in Alabama* (1959). Stanley P. Hirshson, *Farewell to the Bloody Shirt: Northern Republicans and the Southern Negro* (1962). V. O. Key, Jr., *Southern Politics and the Nation* (1949). J. Morgan Kousser, *The Shaping of Southern Politics: Suffrage Restriction and the Establishment of the One-Party South, 1880–1910* (1974). David Potter, *The South and the Concurrent Majority* (1972). Harold Woodman, *New South-New Law* (1995). C. Vann Woodward, *Reunion and Reaction* (1951); *Tom Watson: Agrarian Rebel* (1938).

Race, Economics, and Social Structure W. Fitzhugh Brundage, *Lynching in the New South: Georgia and Virginia, 1880–1930* (1993). David Carlton, *Mill and Town in South Carolina, 1880–1920* (1982). Melvin Greenhut and W. Tate Whitman, eds., *Essays in Southern Economic Development* (1964). Robert Dykstra, *Bright Radical Star: Black Freedom and White Supremacy on the Hawkeye Frontier* (1993). Janette Thomas Greenwood, *Bittersweet Legacy: The Black and White "Better Classes" in Charlotte, 1850–1910* (1994). Steven Hahn and Jonathan Prude, eds., *The Countryside in the Age of Capitalist Transformation* (1985). Jacquelyn Dowd Hall et al., *Like a Family: The Making of a Southern Cotton Mill World* (1987). Louis R. Harlan, *Booker T. Washington: The Making of a Black Leader, 1856–1901* (1972); *Booker T. Washington: The Wizard of Tuskegee: 1901–1915* (1983). Robert Higgs, *Competition and*

Coercion: Blacks in the American Economy, 1865–1914 (1977). Melton A. McLaurin, *Paternalism and Protest: Southern Cotton Mill Workers and Organized Labor* (1971). James M. McPherson, *The Abolitionist Legacy: From Reconstruction to the NAACP* (1975). August Meier, *Negro Thought in America* (1963). Cynthia Neverdon-Morton, *Afro-American Women of the South and the Advancement of the Race, 1895–1925* (1989). David Oshinsky, *Worse Than Slavery: Parchman Prison and the Ordeal of Jim Crow Justice* (1996). Roger Ransom and Richard Sutch, *One Kind of Freedom* (1977). Elliott M. Rudwick, *W. E. B. DuBois: Propagandist of Negro Protest* (rev., 1969). Altina L. Waller, *Feud: Hatfields, McCoys, and Social Changes: Appalachia, 1860–1900* (1988). Joel Williamson, *After Slavery* (1965); *The Crucible of Race: Black-White Relations in the American South Since Emancipation* (1985); *A Rage for Order* (1986, an abridgment of *The Crucible of Race*). Gavin Wright, *Old South, New South: Revolutions in the Southern Economy Since the Civil War* (1986).

APPENDICES

THE UNITED STATES

CANADA

MAINE

NESOTA

Lake Superior

MICHIGAN

Lake Huron

WISCONSIN

napolis
St. Paul

Burlington
Montpelier
Augusta
VT. N.H.
Portland
NEW YORK
Concord
Manchester
Albany
Boston
Rochester
Syracuse
Springfield
MASS
Worcester
R.I.
Buffalo
Hartford
Providence
CT.
New Haven
Bridgeport
Stamford
Newark
New York
Jersey City
Trenton
N.J.

Lake Ontario

Grand
Rapids
Flint
Sterling Heights
Warren
Lansing
Ann
Arbor
Detroit
Livonia
Lake Erie
PENN.
Allentown
Harrisburg
Philadelphia
Dover
DE.

Milwaukee
Madison
Rockford
OWA
Cedar
Rapids
Davenport
Moines
aha

South
Bend
Toledo
Cleveland
Akron
Youngstown
Pittsburgh
Baltimore
Annapolis
MD.

Chicago
Gary
Fort
Wayne
OHIO
WASHINGTON D.C.

ILLINOIS
Peoria
Urbana
Indianapolis
Columbus
Dayton
Cincinnati
W.VA.
Charleston
Richmond
Hampton
Norfolk
Newport News
Virginia Beach
Portsmouth
Chesapeake

Independence
Kansas City
Jefferson
City
Springfield
St. Louis
Louisville
INDIANA
Frankfort
Lexington
Roanoke
VA.

Evansville
KENTUCKY
Greensboro
Durham
Winston
Salem
Raleigh
N.C.

MISSOURI
Nashville
Knoxville
Asheville
Charlotte

ARKANSAS
TENNESSEE
Chattanooga
Greenville
Columbia

Memphis
S.C.

Little
Rock
Huntsville
Atlanta
Augusta
Charleston

Birmingham
Macon
Savannah

Shreveport
Montgomery
Columbus

LOUISIANA
Jackson
ALABAMA
GEORGIA

MISSISSIPPI
Biloxi
Pensacola
Tallahassee
Jacksonville

Baton Rouge
Mobile
FLORIDA

ont
New Orleans

Gulf of Mexico

Orlando

St. Petersburg
Tampa

Hialeah
Miami
Fort Lauderdale
Hollywood

*ATLANTIC
OCEAN*

URBAN POPULATION CENTERS	
▣	Over 5,000,000
■	1,000,000 - 5,000,000
⊡	500,000 - 1,000,000
○	100,000 - 500,000
●	Less than 100,00
☆	State Capitals

0   250   500 Miles

0   250   500 Kilometers

TOPOGRAPHICAL MAP OF THE UNITED STATES

PACIFIC OCEAN

Puget Sound

Coast Ranges
Willamette R.
Columbia R.
Cascade Range
Columbia Plateau
Snake R.
Columbia R.

Sacramento R.
Humboldt R.
Onyhee R.
Snake R.

San Joaquin R.
Central Valley
Coast Ranges
Death Valley
Mohave Desert
Colorado R.
Gila R.
Verde R.
Virgin R.
Sevier R.
Great Salt Lake
Green R.
Colorado R.
Colorado Plateau

Rocky Mountains
Marias R.
Missouri R.
Mills R.
Yellowstone R.
Bighorn
Tongue R.
Powder R.
Belle Fourche
Little Missouri R.
Black Hills
Cheyenne R.
N. Platte R.
Yampa R.
White R.
Laramie R.
Lodgepole Cr.
Niobrara R.
Loup R.
Platte
Republican
Smoky Hill R.

Gunnison R.
Rio Grande
Arkansas R.
Rocky Mountains
Pecos R.
Cimarron R.
N. Can.
Canadian R.
Rio Grande
Rio Grande
Nueces R.
Colorado R.
Braz
Red

Assiniboine
Missouri R.

45° 125° 120° 50° 115° 110° 105° 100°
40°
35°
30°
25°
20°

Inset (Hawaii / Alaska)

PACIFIC OCEAN
160° 155°
0 125 Miles

ARCTIC OCEAN
Brooks Range
Arctic Circle
Yukon R.
Alaska Range
Mt. McKinley
60°

PACIFIC OCEAN
BERING SEA
0 500 Miles
170° 180° 170° 160° 150° 140°

90°   85°   80°   75°   70°   65°

Lake Superior

Croix R.
Mississippi R.
Des Moines R.
Iowa R.
Cedar R.
Rock R.
Fox R.
Kankakee R.
Illinois R.
Wabash R.
Scioto R.

Lake Michigan
Lake Huron
Lake Erie
Lake Ontario

Mohawk R.
Hudson R.

Adirondack
Mts.

St. Lawrence R.

Kennebeck R.

Connecticut R.

Delaware R.
Allegheny R.
Susquehanna R.

Central   Plains

Missouri R.
Osage R.
Mississippi R.
Ohio R.
Tennessee R.

Ozark Plateau

White R.
Arkansas R.
Mississippi R.
Cumberland R.
Allegheny R.
Kanawha R.

Potomac R.

Mts.

*Shenandoah
Valley*
James R.

Chesapeake
Bay

Roanoke R.

Appalachian Mountain

Blue Ridge Mts.

Atlantic Coastal Plain

Saluda R.
Savannah R.

Yazoo R.
Ouachita R.
Tombigbee R.
Alabama R.
Chattahoochee R.
Altamaha R.

Red R.
Sabine R.
Pearl R.

Coastal   Plain

Galveston
Bay

Gulf of Mexico

*ATLANTIC
OCEAN*

0   250   500 Miles

0   250   500 Kilometers

THE WORLD

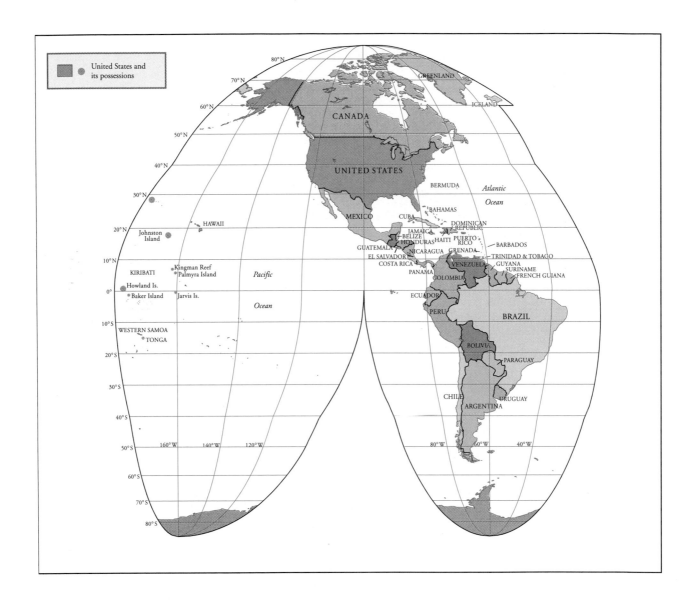

United States and
its possessions

80°N

70°N

GREENLAND

60°N

ICELAND

CANADA

50°N

40°N

UNITED STATES

30°N

BERMUDA

Atlantic

Ocean

HAWAII

BAHAMAS

20°N

Johnston
Island

MEXICO

CUBA

DOMINICAN
REPUBLIC

JAMAICA

PUERTO
RICO

BELIZE

HAITI

BARBADOS

10°N

Kingman Reef
Palmyra Island

GUATEMALA

HONDURAS

GRENADA

TRINIDAD & TOBAGO

KIRIBATI

EL SALVADOR

NICARAGUA

Pacific

COSTA RICA

VENEZUELA

GUYANA

Howland Is.

PANAMA

SURINAME

0°

COLOMBIA

FRENCH GUIANA

Baker Island

Jarvis Is.

Ocean

ECUADOR

10°S

PERU

BRAZIL

WESTERN SAMOA

TONGA

20°S

BOLIVIA

PARAGUAY

30°S

URUGUAY

CHILE

160°W

140°W

120°W

ARGENTINA

80°W

60°W

40°W

40°S

50°S

60°S

70°S

80°S

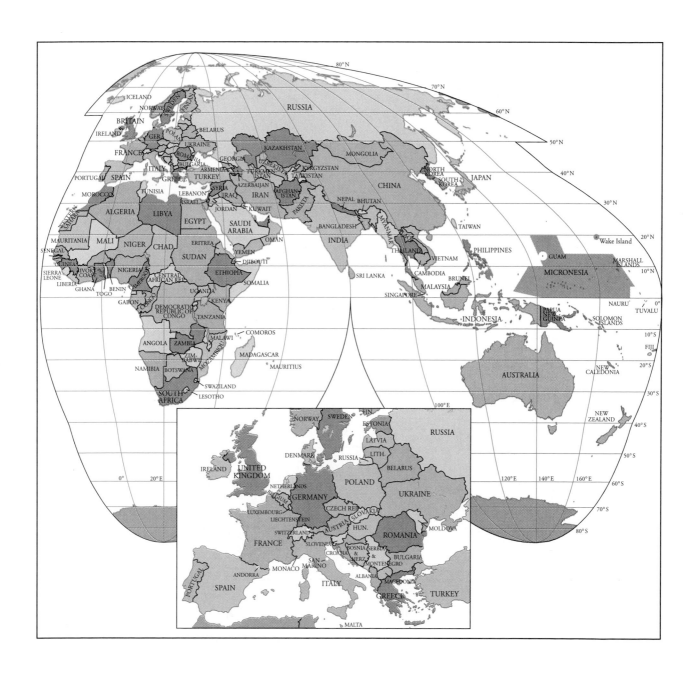

UNITED STATES TERRITORIAL EXPANSION, 1783–1898

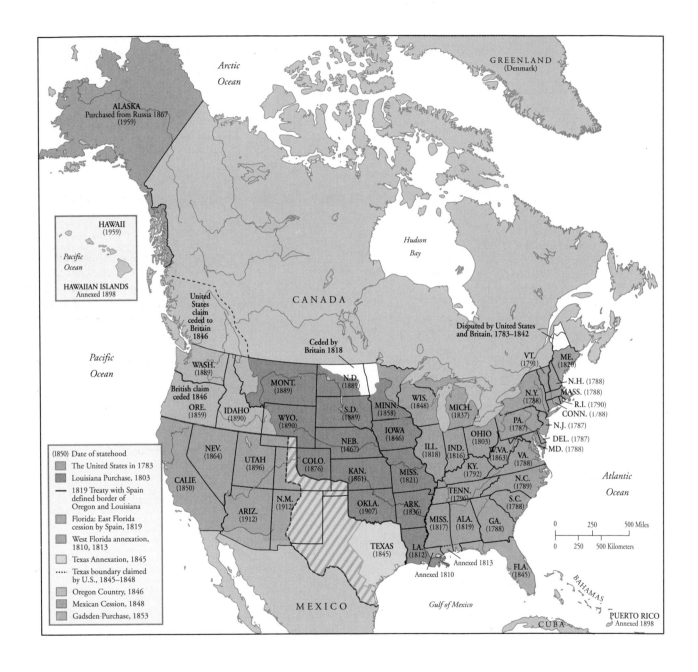

THE DECLARATION OF INDEPENDENCE

In Congress, July 4, 1776,

THE UNANIMOUS DECLARATION OF THE THIRTEEN UNITED STATES OF AMERICA

When, in the course of human events, it becomes necessary for one people to dissolve the political bands which have connected them with another, and to assume, among the powers of the earth, the separate and equal station to which the laws of nature and of nature's God entitle them, a decent respect to the opinions of mankind requires that they should declare the causes which impel them to the separation.

We hold these truths to be self-evident, that all men are created equal; that they are endowed by their Creator with certain unalienable rights; that among these, are life, liberty, and the pursuit of happiness. That, to secure these rights, governments are instituted among men, deriving their just powers from the consent of the governed; that, whenever any form of government becomes destructive of these ends, it is the right of the people to alter or to abolish it, and to institute a new government, laying its foundation on such principles, and organizing its powers in such form, as to them shall seem most likely to effect their safety and happiness. Prudence, indeed, will dictate that governments long established, should not be changed for light and transient causes; and, accordingly, all experience hath shown, that mankind are more disposed to suffer, while evils are sufferable, than to right themselves by abolishing the forms to which they are accustomed. But, when a long train of abuses and usurpations, pursuing invariably the same object, evinces a design to reduce them under absolute despotism, it is their right, it is their duty, to throw off such government and to provide new guards for their future security. Such has been the patient sufferance of these colonies, and such is now the necessity which constrains them to alter their former systems of government. The history of the present King of Great Britain is a history of repeated injuries and usurpations, all having, in direct object, the establishment of an absolute tyranny over these States. To prove this, let facts be submitted to a candid world:

He has refused his assent to laws the most wholesome and necessary for the public good.

He has forbidden his governors to pass laws of immediate and pressing importance, unless suspended in their operation till his assent should be obtained; and, when so suspended, he has utterly neglected to attend to them.

He has refused to pass other laws for the accommodation of large districts of people, unless those people would relinquish the right of representation in the legislature; a right inestimable to them, and formidable to tyrants only.

He has called together legislative bodies at places unusual, uncomfortable, and distant from the depository of their public records, for the sole purpose of fatiguing them into compliance with his measures.

He has dissolved representative houses repeatedly for opposing, with manly firmness, his invasions on the rights of the people.

He has refused, for a long time after such dissolutions, to cause others to be elected; whereby the legislative powers, incapable of annihilation, have returned to the people at large for their exercise; the state remaining, in the meantime, exposed to all the danger of invasion from without, and convulsions within.

He has endeavored to prevent the population of these States; for that purpose, obstructing the laws for naturalization of foreigners, refusing to pass others to encourage their migration hither, and raising the conditions of new appropriations of lands.

He has obstructed the administration of justice, by refusing his assent to laws for establishing judiciary powers.

He has made judges dependent on his will alone, for the tenure of their officers, and the amount and payment of their salaries.

He has erected a multitude of new offices, and sent hither swarms of officers to harass our people, and eat out their substance.

He has kept among us, in time of peace, standing armies, without the consent of our legislatures.

He has affected to render the military independent of, and superior to, the civil power.

He has combined, with others, to subject us to a jurisdiction foreign to our Constitution, and unacknowledged by our laws; giving his assent to their acts of pretended legislation:

For quartering large bodies of armed troops among us:

For protecting them by a mock trial, from punishment, for any murders which they should commit on the inhabitants of these States:

For cutting off our trade with all parts of the world:

For imposing taxes on us without our consent:

For depriving us, in many cases, of the benefit of trial by jury:

For transporting us beyond seas to be tried for pretended offences:

For abolishing the free system of English laws in a neighboring province, establishing therein an arbitrary government, and enlarging its boundaries, so as to render it at once an example and fit instrument for introducing the same absolute rule into these colonies:

For taking away our charters, abolishing our most valuable laws, and altering, fundamentally, the powers of our governments:

For suspending our own legislatures, and declaring themselves invested with power to legislate for use in all cases whatsoever.

He has abdicated government here, by declaring us out of his protection, and waging war against us.

He has plundered our seas, ravaged our coasts, burnt our towns, and destroyed the lives of our people.

He is, at this time, transporting large armies of foreign mercenaries to complete the works of death, desolation, and tyranny, already begun, with circumstances of cruelty and perfidy scarcely paralleled in the most barbarous ages, and totally unworthy the head of a civilized nation.

He has constrained our fellow citizens, taken captive on the high seas, to bear arms against their country, to become the executioners of their friends, and brethren, or to fall themselves by their hands.

He has excited domestic insurrections amongst us, and has endeavored to bring on the inhabitants of our frontiers, the merciless Indian savages, whose known rule of warfare is an undistinguished destruction of all ages, sexes, and conditions.

In every stage of these oppressions, we have petitioned for redress, in the most humble terms; our repeated petitions have been answered only by repeated injury. A prince, whose character is thus marked by every act which may define a tyrant, is unfit to be the ruler of a free people.

Nor have we been wanting in attention to our British brethren. We have warned them, from time to time, of attempts made by their legislature to extend an unwarrantable jurisdiction over us. We have reminded them of the circumstances of our emigration and settlement here. We have appealed to their native justice and magnanimity, and we have conjured them, by the ties of our common kindred, to disavow these usurpations, which would inevitably interrupt our connections and correspondence. They, too, have been deaf to the voice of justice and consanguinity. We must, therefore, acquiesce in the necessity, which denounces our separation, and hold them as we hold the rest of mankind, enemies in war, in peace, friends.

We, therefore, the representatives of the United States of America, in general Congress assembled, appealing to the Supreme Judge of the world for the rectitude of our intentions, do, in the name, and by the authority of the good people of these colonies, solemnly publish and declare, that these united colonies are, and of right ought to be, free and independent states: that they are absolved from all allegiance to the British Crown, and that all political connection between them and the state of Great Britain is, and ought to be, totally dissolved; and that, as free and independent states, they have full power to levy war, conclude peace, contract alliances, establish commerce, and to do all other acts and things which independent states may of right do. And, for the support of this declaration, with a firm reliance on the protection of Divine Providence, we mutually pledge to each other our lives, our fortunes, and our sacred honor.

The foregoing Declaration was, by order of Congress, engrossed, and signed by the following members:

JOHN HANCOCK

New Hampshire
Josiah Bartlett
William Whipple
Matthew Thornton

Massachusetts Bay
Samuel Adams
John Adams
Robert Treat Paine
Elbridge Gerry

Rhode Island
Stephen Hopkins
William Ellery

Connecticut
Robert Sherman
Samuel Huntington
William Williams
Oliver Wolcott

New York
William Floyd
Philip Livingston
Francis Lewis
Lewis Morris

New Jersey
Richard Stockton
John Witherspoon
Francis Hopkinson
John Hart
Abraham Clark

Pennsylvania
Robert Morris
Benjamin Rush
Benjamin Franklin
John Morton
George Clymer
James Smith
George Taylor
James Wilson
George Ross

Delaware
Caesar Rodney
George Read
Thomas McKean

Maryland
Samuel Chase
William Paca
Thomas Stone
Charles Carroll, of
Carrollton

Virginia
George Wythe
Richard Henry Lee
Thomas Jefferson
Benjamin Harrison
Thomas Nelson, Jr.
Francis Lightfoot Lee
Carter Braxton

North Carolina
William Hooper
Joseph Hewes
John Penn

South Carolina
Edward Rutledge
Thomas Heyward, Jr.
Thomas Lynch, Jr.
Arthur Middleton

Georgia
Button Gwinnett
Lyman Hall
George Walton

Resolved, That copies of the Declaration be sent to the several assemblies, conventions, and committees, or councils of safety, and to the several commanding officers of the continental troops; that it be proclaimed in each of the United States, at the head of the army.

THE CONSTITUTION OF THE UNITED STATES OF AMERICA[1]

We the People of the United States, in Order to form a more perfect Union, establish Justice, insure domestic Tranquility, provide for the common defence, promote the general Welfare, and secure the Blessings of Liberty to ourselves and our Posterity, do ordain and establish this CONSTITUTION for the United States of America.

ARTICLE 1

Section 1.

All legislative Powers herein granted shall be vested in a Congress of the United States, which shall consist of a Senate and House of Representatives.

Section 2.

The House of Representatives shall be composed of Members chosen every second Year by the People of the several States, and the Electors in each State shall have the Qualifications requisite for Electors of the most numerous Branch of the State Legislature.

No Person shall be a Representative who shall not have attained to the Age of twenty-five Years, and been seven Years a Citizen of the United States, and who shall not, when elected, be an Inhabitant of that State in which he shall be chosen.

[Representatives and direct Taxes[2] shall be apportioned among the several States which may be included within this Union, according to their respective Numbers, which shall be determined by adding to the whole Number of free Persons, including those bound to Service for a Term of Years, and excluding Indians not taxed, three fifths of all other Persons.][3] The actual Enumeration shall be made within three Years after the first Meeting of the Congress of the United States, and within every subsequent Term of ten Years, in such Manner as they shall by Law direct. The Number of Representatives shall not exceed one for every thirty Thousand, but each State shall have at Least one Representative; and until such enumeration shall be made, the State of New Hampshire shall be entitled to chuse three, Massachusetts eight, Rhode-Island and Providence Plantations one, Connecticut five, New York six, New Jersey four, Pennsylvania eight, Delaware one, Maryland six, Virginia ten, North Carolina five, South Carolina five, and Georgia three.

When vacancies happen in the Representation from any State, the Executive Authority thereof shall issue Writs of Election to fill such Vacancies.

The House of Representatives shall chuse their Speaker and other Officers; and shall have the sole Power of Impeachment.

Section 3.

The Senate of the United States shall be composed of two Senators from each State, chosen by the Legislature thereof, for six Years; and each Senator shall have one Vote.

Immediately after they shall be assembled in Consequence of the first Election, they shall be divided as equally as may be into three Classes. The Seats of the Senators of the first Class shall be vacated at the Expiration of the second Year, of the second Class at the Expiration of the fourth Year, and of the third Class at the Expiration of the sixth Year, so that one-third may be chosen every second Year; and if Vacancies happen by Resignation, or otherwise, during the Recess of the Legislature of any State, the Executive thereof may make temporary Appointments until the next Meeting of the Legislature, which shall then fill such Vacancies.

No Person shall be a Senator who shall not have attained to the Age of thirty Years, and been nine Years a Citizen of the United States, and who shall not, when elected, be an Inhabitant of that State for which he shall be chosen.

The Vice President of the United States shall be President of the Senate, but shall have no vote, unless they be equally divided.

The Senate shall chuse their other Officers, and also a President pro tempore, in the absence of the Vice President, or when he shall exercise the office of President of the United States.

The Senate shall have the sole Power to try all Impeachments. When sitting for that purpose they shall be on Oath

---

[1]This version, which follows the original Constitution in capitalization and spelling, was published by the United States Department of the Interior, Office of Education, in 1935.
[2]Altered by the Sixteenth Amendment.
[3]Negated by the Fourteenth Amendment.

or Affirmation. When the President of the United States is tried, the Chief Justice shall preside: And no person shall be convicted without the Concurrence of two thirds of the Members present.

Judgment in Cases of Impeachment shall not extend further than to removal from Office, and disqualification to hold and enjoy any Office of honor, Trust, or Profit under the United States: but the Party convicted shall nevertheless be liable and subject to Indictment, Trial, Judgment, and Punishment, according to Law.

Section 4.

The Times, Places and Manner of holding Elections for Senators and Representatives, shall be prescribed in each State by the Legislature thereof; but the Congress may at any time by Law make or alter such Regulations, except as to the Places of Chusing Senators.

The Congress shall assemble at least once in every Year, and such Meeting shall be on the first Monday in December, unless they shall by Law appoint a different day.

Section 5.

Each House shall be the Judge of the Elections, Returns and Qualifications of its own Members, and a Majority of each shall constitute a Quorum to do Business; but a smaller number may adjourn from day to day, and may be authorized to compel the Attendance of absent Members, in such Manner, and under such Penalties, as each House may provide.

Each House may determine the Rules of its Proceedings, punish its Members for disorderly Behaviour, and, with the Concurrence of two thirds, expel a Member.

Each House shall keep a Journal of its Proceedings, and from time to time publish the same, excepting such Parts as may in their Judgment require Secrecy; and the Yeas and Nays of the Members of either House on any question shall, at the Desire of one fifth of those Present, be entered on the Journal.

Neither House, during the Session of Congress, shall, without the Consent of the other, adjourn for more than three days, nor to any other Place than that in which the two Houses shall be sitting.

Section 6.

The Senators and Representatives shall receive a Compensation for their Services, to be ascertained by Law, and paid out of the Treasury of the United States. They shall in all Cases, except Treason, Felony, and Breach of the Peace, be privileged from Arrest during their Attendance at the Session of their respective Houses, and in going to and returning from the same; and for any Speech or Debate in either House, they shall not be questioned in any other Place.

No Senator or Representative shall, during the Time for which he was elected, be appointed to any civil Office under the Authority of the United States, which shall have been created, or the Emoluments whereof shall have been increased, during such time; and no Person holding any Office under the United States shall be a Member of either House during his continuance in Office.

Section 7.

All Bills for raising Revenue shall originate in the House of Representatives; but the Senate may propose or concur with Amendments as on other bills.

Every Bill which shall have passed the House of Representatives and the Senate, shall, before it become a Law, be presented to the President of the United States; If he approve he shall sign it, but if not he shall return it, with his Objections, to that House in which it shall have originated, who shall enter the Objections at large on their Journal, and proceed to reconsider it. If after such Reconsideration two thirds of that House shall agree to pass the bill, it shall be sent, together with the objections, to the other House, by which it shall likewise be reconsidered, and if approved by two thirds of that House, it shall become a Law. But in all such Cases the Votes of both Houses shall be determined by Yeas and Nays, and the Names of the Persons voting for and against the Bill shall be entered on the Journal of each House respectively. If any Bill shall not be returned by the President within ten Days (Sundays excepted) after it shall have been presented to him, the Same shall be a Law, in like Manner as if he had signed it, unless the Congress by their Adjournment prevent its Return, in which Case it shall not be a Law.

Every Order, Resolution, or Vote to which the Concurrence of the Senate and House of Representatives may be necessary (except on a question of Adjournment) shall be presented to the President of the United States; and before the Same shall take Effect, shall be approved by him, or being disapproved by him, shall be repassed by two thirds of the Senate and House of Representatives, according to the Rules and Limitations prescribed in the Case of a Bill.

Section 8.

The Congress shall have Power To lay and collect Taxes, Duties, Imposts and Excises, to pay the Debts and provide for the common Defence and general Welfare of the United States; but all Duties, Imposts and Excises shall be uniform throughout the United States;

To borrow money on the credit of the United States;

To regulate Commerce with foreign Nations, and among the several States, and with the Indian Tribes;

To establish an uniform rule of Naturalization, and uniform Laws on the subject of Bankruptcies throughout the United States;

To coin Money, regulate the Value thereof, and of foreign Coin, and fix the Standard of Weights and Measures;

To provide for the Punishment of counterfeiting the Securities and current Coin of the United States;

To establish Post Offices and post Roads;

To promote the Progress of Science and useful Arts, by securing for limited Times to Authors and Inventors the exclusive Right to their respective Writings and Discoveries;

To constitute Tribunals inferior to the Supreme Court;

To define and punish Piracies and Felonies committed on the high Seas, and Offenses against the Law of Nations;

To declare War, grant Letters of Marque and Reprisal, and make Rules concerning Captures on Land and Water;

To raise and support Armies, but no Appropriation of Money to that Use shall be for a longer Term than two Years;

To provide and maintain a Navy;

To make Rules for the Government and Regulation of the land and naval forces;

To provide for calling forth the Militia to execute the Laws of the Union, suppress Insurrections and repel Invasions;

To provide for organizing, arming, and disciplining the Militia, and for governing such Part of them as may be employed in the Service of the United States, reserving to the States respectively, the Appointment of the Officers, and the Authority of training the Militia according to the discipline prescribed by Congress;

To exercise exclusive Legislation in all Cases whatsoever, over such District (not exceeding ten Miles square) as may, by Cession of particular States, and the acceptance of Congress, become the Seat of the Government of the United States, and to exercise like Authority over all Places purchased by the Consent of the Legislature of the State in which the Same shall be, for the Erection of Forts, Magazines, Arsenals, Dockyards, and other needful Buildings;—And

To make all Laws which shall be necessary and proper for carrying into Execution for foregoing Powers, and all other Powers vested by this Constitution in the Government of the United States, or in any Department or Officer thereof.

Section 9.

The Migration or Importation of such Persons as any of the States now existing shall think proper to admit, shall not be prohibited by the Congress prior to the Year one thousand eight hundred and eight, but a tax or duty may be imposed on such Importation, not exceeding ten dollars for each Person.

The privilege of the Writ of Habeas Corpus shall not be suspended, unless when in Cases of Rebellion or Invasion the public Safety may require it.

No bill of Attainder or ex post facto Law shall be passed.

No capitation, or other direct, Tax shall be laid unless in Proportion to the Census or Enumeration herein before directed to be taken.

No Tax or Duty shall be laid on Articles exported from any State.

No Preference shall be given by any Regulation of Commerce or Revenue to the Ports of one State over those of another: nor shall Vessels bound to, or from, one State, be obliged to enter, clear, or pay Duties in another.

No Money shall be drawn from the Treasury, but in Consequence of Appropriations made by Law; and a regular Statement and Account of the Receipts and Expenditures of all public Money shall be published from time to time.

No Title of Nobility shall be granted by the United States: An no Person holding any Office of Profit or Trust under them, shall, without the Consent of the Congress, accept of any present, Emolument, Office, or Title, of any kind whatever, from any King, Prince, or foreign State.

Section 10.

No State shall enter into any Treaty, Alliance, or Confederation; grant Letters of Marque and Reprisal; coin Money; emit Bills of Credit; make any Thing but gold and silver Coin a Tender in Payment of Debts; pass any Bill of Attainder, ex post facto Law, or Law impairing the Obligation of Contracts, or grant any Title of Nobility.

No State shall, without the Consent of the Congress, lay any Imposts or Duties on Imports or Exports, except what may be absolutely necessary for executing its inspection Laws; and the net Produce of all Duties and Imposts, laid by any State on Imports or Exports, shall be for the use of the Treasury of the United States; and all such Laws shall be subject to the Revision and Control of the Congress.

No state shall, without the Consent of Congress, lay any duty of Tonnage, keep Troops, or Ships of War in time of Peace, enter into any Agreement or Compact with another State, or with a foreign Power, or engage in War, unless actually invaded, or in such imminent Danger as will not admit of delay.

ARTICLE II

Section 1.

The executive Power shall be vested in a President of the United States of America. He shall hold his Office during the Term of four years, and, together with the Vice President, chosen for the same Term, be elected, as follows:

Each State shall appoint, in such Manner as the Legislature thereof may direct, a Number of Electors, equal to the whole Number of Senators and Representatives to which the State may be entitled in the Congress: but no Senator or Representative, or Person holding an Office of Trust or Profit under the United States, shall be appointed an Elector.

[The Electors shall meet in their respective States, and vote by Ballot for two persons, of whom one at least shall not be an Inhabitant of the same State with themselves. And they shall make a List of all the Persons voted for, and of the Number of Votes for each; which List they shall sign and certify, and transmit sealed to the Seat of the Government of the United States, directed to the President of the Senate. The President of the Senate shall, in the Presence of the Senate and House of Representatives, open all the Certificates, and the Votes shall then be counted. The Person having the greatest Number of Votes shall be the President, if such Number be a Majority of the whole Number of Electors appointed; and if there be more than one who have such Majority, and have an equal Number of Votes, then the House of Representatives shall immediately chuse by Ballot one of them for President; and if no Person have a Majority, then from the five highest on the list the said House shall in like Manner chuse the President. But in chusing the President, the Votes shall be taken by States, the Representation from each State having one Vote; a quorum for this Purpose shall consist of a Member or Members from two-thirds of the States, and a Majority of all the States shall be necessary to a Choice. In every Case, after the Choice of the President, the Person having the greatest Number of Votes of the Electors shall be the Vice President. But if there should remain two or more who have equal votes, the Senate shall chuse from them by Ballot the Vice President.][4]

The Congress may determine the Time of chusing the Electors, and the Day on which they shall give their Votes; which Day shall be the same throughout the United States.

No person except a natural-born Citizen, or a Citizen of the United States, at the time of the Adoption of this Constitution, shall be eligible to the Office of President; neither shall any Person be eligible to that Office who shall not have attained to the Age of thirty-five years, and been fourteen Years a Resident within the United States.

In Case of the Removal of the President from Office, or of his Death, Resignation, or Inability to discharge the Powers and Duties of the said Office, the same shall devolve on the Vice President, and the Congress may by Law provide for the Case of Removal, Death, Resignation, or Inability, both of the President and Vice President, declaring what Officer shall then act as President, and such Officer shall act accordingly, until the disability be removed, or a President shall be elected.

The President shall, at stated Times, receive for his Services a Compensation, which shall neither be increased nor diminished during the Period for which he shall have been elected, and he shall not receive within that Period any other Emolument from the United States, or any of them.

Before he enter on the execution of his Office, he shall take the following Oath or Affirmation:—"I do solemnly swear (or affirm) that I will faithfully execute the Office of President of the United States, and will, to the best of my Ability, preserve, protect, and defend the Constitution of the United States."

Section 2.

The President shall be Commander in Chief of the Army and Navy of the United States, and of the Militia of the several States, when called into the actual Service of the United States; he may require the Opinion, in writing, of the principal Officer in each of the executive Departments, upon any subject relating to the Duties of their respective Offices, and he shall have Power to Grant Reprieves and Pardons for Offenses against the United States, except in Cases of Impeachment.

He shall have Power, by and with the Advice and Consent of the Senate, to make Treaties, provided two-thirds of the Senators present concur; and he shall nominate, and by and with the Advice and Consent of the Senate, shall appoint Ambassadors, other public Ministers and Consuls. Judges of the supreme Court, and all other Officers of the United States, whose Appointments are not herein otherwise provided for, and which shall be established by Law: but the Congress may by Law vest the Appointment of such inferior Officers, as they think proper, in the President alone, in the Courts of Law, or in the Heads of Departments.

---

[4]Revised by the Twelfth Amendment.

The President shall have Power to fill up all Vacancies that may happen during the Recess of the Senate, by granting Commissions which shall expire at the End of their next Session.

Section 3.

He shall from time to time give to the Congress Information of the State of the Union, and recommend to their Consideration such Measures as he shall judge necessary and expedient; he may, on extraordinary occasions, convene both Houses, or either of them, and in Case of Disagreement between them, with respect to the Time of Adjournment, he may adjourn them to such Time as he shall think proper; he shall receive Ambassadors and other public Ministers; he shall take care that the Laws be faithfully executed, and shall Commission all the Officers of the United States.

Section 4.

The President, Vice President and all civil Officers of the United States, shall be removed from Office on Impeachment for, and Conviction of, Treason, Bribery, or other high Crimes and Misdemeanors.

ARTICLE III

Section 1.

The judicial Power of the United States, shall be vested in one supreme Court, and in such inferior Courts as the Congress may from time to time ordain and establish. The Judges, both of the supreme and inferior Courts, shall hold their Offices during good Behaviour, and shall, at stated Times, receive for their Services, a Compensation, which shall not be diminished during their Continuance in Office.

Section 2.

The judicial Power shall extend to all Cases, in Law and Equity, arising under this Constitution, the Laws of the United States, and Treaties made, or which shall be made, under their Authority;—to all Cases affecting ambassadors, other public ministers and consuls;—to all cases of admiralty and maritime Jurisdiction;—to Controversies to which the United States shall be a Party;—to Controversies between two or more States;—between a State and Citizens of another State;[5]—between Citizens of different States—between Citizens of the same State claiming Lands under Grants of different States, and between a State, or the Citizens thereof, and foreign States, Citizens, or Subjects.

In all Cases affecting Ambassadors, other public Ministers and Consuls, and those in which a State shall be Party, the supreme Court shall have original Jurisdiction. In all the other Cases before mentioned, the supreme Court shall have appellate Jurisdiction, both as to Law and Fact, with such Exceptions, and under such Regulations as the Congress shall make.

The trial of all Crimes, except in Cases of Impeachment, shall be by Jury; and such Trial shall be held in the State where the said Crimes shall have been committed; but when not committed within any State, the Trial shall be at such Place or Places as the Congress may by Law have directed.

Section 3.

Treason against the United States, shall consist only in levying War against them, or in adhering to their Enemies, giving them Aid and Comfort. No Person shall be convicted of Treason unless on the Testimony of two Witnesses to the same overt Act, or on Confession in open Court.

The Congress shall have power to declare the Punishment of Treason, but no Attainder of Treason shall work Corruption of Blood, or Forfeiture except during the Life of the Person attained.

ARTICLE IV

Section 1.

Full Faith and Credit shall be given in each State to the public Acts, Records, and judicial Proceedings of every State. And the Congress may by general Laws prescribe the Manner in which such Acts, Records and Proceedings shall be proved, and the Effect thereof.

Section 2.

The Citizens of each State shall be entitled to all Privileges and Immunities of Citizens in the several States.

A Person charged in any State with Treason, Felony, or other Crime, who shall flee from Justice, and be found in another State, shall on demand of the executive Authority of the State from which he fled, be delivered up, to be removed to the State having Jurisdiction of the crime.

No Person held to Service or Labour in one State, under the Laws thereof, escaping into another, shall, in

---

[5]Qualified by the Eleventh Amendment.

Consequence of any Law or Regulation therein, be discharged from such Service or Labour, but shall be delivered up on Claim of the Party to whom such Service or Labour may be due.

Section 3.

New States may be admitted by the Congress into this Union; but no new State shall be formed or erected within the Jurisdiction of any other State; nor any State be formed by the Junction of two or more States, or parts of States, without the Consent of the Legislatures of the States concerned as well as of the Congress.

The Congress shall have Power to dispose of and make all needful Rules and Regulations respecting the Territory or other Property belonging to the United States; and nothing in this Constitution shall be so construed as to Prejudice any Claims of the United States, or of any particular State.

Section 4.

The United States shall guarantee to every State in this Union a Republican Form of Government, and shall protect each of them against Invasion; and on Application of the Legislature, or of the Executive (when the Legislature cannot be convened) against domestic violence.

ARTICLE V

The Congress, whenever two-thirds of both Houses shall deem it necessary, shall propose Amendments to this Constitution, or, on the Application of the Legislatures of two-thirds of the several States, shall call a Convention for proposing Amendments, which, in either Case, shall be valid to all Intents and Purposes, as part of this Constitution, when ratified by the Legislatures of three-fourths of the several States, or by Conventions in three-fourths thereof, as the one or the other Mode of Ratification may be proposed by the Congress; Provided that no Amendment which may be made prior to the Year One thousand eight hundred and eight shall in any Manner affect the first and fourth Clauses in the Ninth Section of the first Article; and that no State, without its Consent, shall be deprived of its equal Suffrage in the Senate.

ARTICLE VI

All Depts contracted and Engagements entered into, before the Adoption of this Constitution, shall be as valid against the United States under this Constitution, as under the Confederation.

This Constitution, and the Laws of the United States which shall be made in Pursuance thereof; and all Treaties made, or which shall be made, under the Authority of the United States, shall be the supreme Law of the Land; and the Judges in every State shall be bound thereby, any Thing in the Constitution or Laws of any State to the Contrary notwithstanding.

The Senators and Representatives before mentioned, and the Members of the several State Legislatures, and all executive and judicial Officers, both of the United States and of the several States, shall be bound by Oath or Affirmation to support this Constitution; but no religious Tests shall ever be required as a qualification to any Office or public Trust under the United States.

ARTICLE VII

The Ratification of the Conventions of nine States shall be sufficient for the Establishment of this Constitution between the States so ratifying the same.

Done in convention by the Unanimous Consent of the States present the Seventeenth Day of September in the Year of our Lord one thousand seven hundred and Eighty seven, and of the Independence of the United States of America the Twelfth. In Witness whereof We have hereunto subscribed our Names.[6]

George Washington
President and deputy from Virginia

New Hampshire
John Langdon
Nicholas Gilman

Massachusetts
Nathaniel Gorham
Rufus King

Connecticut
William Samuel Johnson
Roger Sherman

New York
Alexander Hamilton

New Jersey
William Livingston
David Brearley
William Paterson
Jonathan Dayton

Pennsylvania
Benjamin Franklin
Thomas Mifflin
Robert Morris
George Clymer
Thomas FitzSimons
Jared Ingersoll
James Wilson
Gouverneur Morris

[6]These are the full names of the signers, which in some cases are not the signatures on the document.

Delaware
George Read
Gunning Beford, Jr.
John Dickinson
Richard Bassett
Jacob Broom

Maryland
James McHenry
Daniel of St. Thomas Jenifer
Daniel Carroll

Virginia
John Blair
James Madison, Jr.

North Carolina
William Blount
Richard Dobbs Spaight
Hugh Williamson

South Carolina
John Rutledge
Charles Cotesworth
    Pinckney
Charles Pinckney
Pierce Butler

Georgia
William Few
Abraham Baldwin

Articles in Addition to, and Amendment of, the Constitution of the United States of America, Proposed by Congress, and Ratified by the Legislatures of the Several States, Pursuant to the Fifth Article of the Original Constitution[7]

[ARTICLE I]

Congress shall make no law respecting an establishment of religion, or prohibiting the free exercise thereof; or abridging the freedom of speech, or of the press; or the right of the people peaceably to assemble, and to petition the Government for a redress of grievances.

[ARTICLE II]

A well regulated Militia, being necessary to the security of a free State, the right of the people to keep and bear Arms shall not be infringed.

[ARTICLE III]

No Soldier shall, in time of peace, be quartered in any house, without the consent of the Owner, nor in time of war, but in a manner to be prescribed by law.

---

[7]This heading appears only in the joint resolution submitting the first ten amendments.

[ARTICLE IV]

The right of the people to be secure in their persons, houses, papers, and effects, against unreasonable searches and seizures, shall not be violated, and no Warrants shall issue, but upon probable cause, supported by Oath or affirmation, and particularly describing the place to be searched, and the persons or things to be seized.

[ARTICLE V]

No person shall be held to answer for a capital or otherwise infamous crime, unless on a presentment or indictment of a Grand Jury, except in cases arising in the land or naval forces, or in the Militia, when in actual service in time of War or public danger; nor shall any person be subject for the same offence to be twice put in jeopardy of life or limb; nor shall be compelled in any criminal case to be a witness against himself, nor be deprived of life, liberty, or property, without due process of law; nor shall private property be taken for public use, without just compensation.

[ARTICLE VI]

In all criminal prosecutions, the accused shall enjoy the right to a speedy and public trial, by an impartial jury of the State and district wherein the crime shall have been committed, which district shall have been previously ascertained by law, and to be informed of the nature and cause of the accusation; to be confronted with the witnesses against him; to have compulsory process for obtaining witnesses in his favour, and to have the Assistance of Counsel for his defence.

[ARTICLE VII]

In suits at common law, where the value in controversy shall exceed twenty dollars, the right of trial by jury shall be preserved, and no fact tried by a jury, shall be otherwise reexamined in any Court of the United States, than according to the rules of the common law.

[ARTICLE VIII]

Excessive bail shall not be required, nor excessive fines imposed, nor cruel and unusual punishments inflicted.

[ARTICLE IX]

The enumeration of the Constitution, of certain rights, shall not be construed to deny or disparage others retained by the people.

[ARTICLE X]

The powers not delegated to the United States by the Constitution, nor prohibited by it to the States, are reserved to the States respectively, or to the people.
[Amendments I-X, in force 1791.]

[ARTICLE XI][8]

The Judicial power of the United States shall not be construed to extend to any suit in law or equity, commenced or prosecuted against one of the United States by Citizens of another State, or by Citizens or Subjects of any Foreign State.

[ARTICLE XII][9]

The Electors shall meet in their respective States and vote by ballot for President and Vice-President, one of whom, at least, shall not be an inhabitant of the same State with themselves; they shall name in their ballots the person voted for as President, and in distinct ballots the person voted for as Vice-President, and they shall make distinct lists of all persons voted for as President, and of all persons voted for as Vice-President, and of the number of votes for each, which lists they shall sign and certify, and transmit sealed to the seal of the government of the United States, directed to the President of the Senate;—The President of the Senate shall, in the presence of the Senate and House of Representatives, open all the certificates and the votes shall then be counted;—The person having the greatest number of votes for President, shall be the President, if such number be a majority of the whole number of Electors appointed; and if no person have such majority, then from the persons having the highest numbers not exceeding three on the list of those voted for as President, the House of Representatives shall choose immediately, by ballot, the President. But in choosing the President, the votes shall be taken by states, the representation from each state having one vote; a quorum for this purpose shall consist of a member or members from two-thirds of the states, and a majority of all the states shall be necessary to a choice. And if the House of Representatives shall not choose a President whenever the right of choice shall devolve upon them, before the fourth day of March next following, then the Vice-President shall act as President, as in the case of the death or other constitutional disability of the President.—The person having the greatest number of votes as Vice-President, shall be the Vice-President, if such number be a majority of the whole number of Electors appointed, and if no person have a majority, then from the two highest numbers on the list, the Senate shall choose the Vice-President; a quorum for the purpose shall consist of two-thirds of the whole number of Senators, and a majority of the whole number shall be necessary to a choice. But no person constitutionally ineligible to the office of President shall be eligible to that of Vice-President of the United States.

[ARTICLE XIII][10]

Section 1.

Neither slavery nor involuntary servitude, except as a punishment for crime whereof the party shall have been duly convicted, shall exist within the United States, or any place subject to their jurisdiction.

Section 2.

Congress shall have power to enforce this article by appropriate legislation.

[ARTICLE XIV][11]

Section 1.

All persons born or naturalized in the United States, and subject to the jurisdiction thereof, are citizens of the United States and of the State wherein they reside. No State shall make or enforce any law which shall abridge the privileges or immunities of citizens of the United States; nor shall any State deprive any person of life, liberty, or property, without due process of law; nor deny to any person within its jurisdiction the equal protection of the laws.

---

[8]Adopted in 1798.
[9]Adopted in 1804.

[10]Adopted in 1865.
[11]Adopted in 1868.

Section 2.

Representatives shall be apportioned among the several States according to their respective numbers, counting the whole number of persons in each State, excluding Indians not taxed. But when the right to vote at any election for the choice of electors for President and Vice-President of the United States, Representatives in Congress, the Executive and Judicial officers of a State, or the members of the Legislature thereof, is denied to any of the male inhabitants of such State, being twenty-one years of age, and citizens of the United States, or in any way abridged, except for participation in rebellion, or other crime, the basis of representation therein shall be reduced in the proportion which the number of such male citizens shall bear to the whole number of male citizens twenty-one years of age in such State.

Section 3.

No person shall be a Senator or Representative in Congress, or elector of President and Vice-President, or hold any office, civil or military, under the United States, or under any State, who, having previously taken an oath, as a member of Congress, or as an officer of the United States, or as a member of any State legislature, or as an executive or judicial officer of any State, to support the Constitution of the United States, shall have engaged in insurrection or rebellion against the same, or given aid or comfort to the enemies thereof. But Congress may be a vote of two-thirds of each House, remove such disability.

Section 4.

The validity of the public debt of the United States, authorized by law, including debts incurred for payment of pensions and bounties for services in suppressing insurrection or rebellion, shall not be questioned. But neither the United States nor any State shall assume or pay any debts or obligation incurred in aid of insurrection or rebellion against the United States, or any claim for the loss or emancipation of any slave; but all such debts, obligations, and claims shall be held illegal and void.

Section 5.

The Congress shall have the power to enforce, by appropriate legislation, the provisions of this article.

[ARTICLE XV][12]

Section 1.

The right of citizens of the United States to vote shall not be denied or abridged by the United States or by any State on account of race, color, or previous condition of servitude—

Section 2.

The Congress shall have power to enforce this article by appropriate legislation.

[ARTICLE XVI][13]

The Congress shall have power to lay and collect taxes on incomes, from whatever source derived, without apportionment among the several States, and without regard to any census or enumeration.

[ARTICLE XVII][14]

The Senate of the United States shall be composed of two Senators from each State, elected by the people thereof, for six years; and each Senator shall have one vote. The electors in each State shall have the qualifications requisite for electors of the most numerous branch of the State legislatures.

When vacancies happen in the representation of any State in the Senate, the executive authority of such State shall issue writs of election to fill such vacancies: *Provided,* That the legislature of any State may empower the executive thereof to make temporary appointments until the people fill the vacancies by election as the legislature may direct.

This amendment shall not be so constructed as to affect the election or term of any Senator chosen before it becomes valid as part of the Constitution.

[ARTICLE XVIII][15]

Section 1.

After one year from the ratification of this article the manufacture, sale, or transportation of intoxicating liquors within, the importation thereof into, or the exportation thereof from the United States and all territory

---

[12]Adopted in 1870.
[13]Adopted in 1913.
[14]Adopted in 1913.
[15]Adopted in 1918.

subject to the jurisdiction thereof for beverage purposes is hereby prohibited.

Section 2.

The Congress and the several States shall have concurrent power to enforce this article by appropriate legislation.

Section 3.

This article shall be inoperative unless it shall have been ratified as an amendment to the Constitution by the legislatures of the several States, as provided in the Constitution,within seven years from the date of the submission hereof to the States by the Congress.

[ARTICLE XIX][16]

The right of citizens of the United States to vote shall not be denied or abridged by the United States or by any State on account of sex.

Congress shall have power to enforce this article by appropriate legislation.

[ARTICLE XX][17]

Section 1.

The terms of the President and Vice-President shall end at noon on the 20th day of January, and the terms of Senators and Representatives at noon on the 3d day of January, of the years in which such terms would have ended if this article had not been ratified; and the terms of their successors shall then begin.

Section 2.

The Congress shall assemble at least once in every year, and such meeting shall begin at noon on the 3d day of January, unless they shall by law appoint a different day.

Section 3.

If, at the time fixed for the beginning of the term of the President, the President elect shall have died, the Vice-President elect shall become President. If a President shall not have been chosen before the time fixed for the beginning of his term or if the President elect shall have failed to qualify, then the Vice-President elect shall act as President until a President shall have qualified; and the Congress may by law provide for the case wherein neither a President elect nor a Vice-President elect shall have qualified, declaring who shall then act as President, or the manner in which one who is to act shall be selected, and such person shall act accordingly until a President or Vice-President shall have qualified.

Section 4.

The Congress may by law provide for the case of the death of any of the persons from whom the House of Representatives may choose a President whenever the right of choice shall have developed upon them, and for the case of the death of any of the persons from whom the Senate may choose a Vice-President whenever the right of choice shall have developed upon them.

Section 5.

Sections 1 and 2 shall take effect on the 15th day of October following the ratification of this article.

Section 6.

This article shall be inoperative unless it shall have been ratified as an amendment to the Constitution by the legislatures of three-fourths of the several States within seven years from the date of its submission.

[ARTICLE XXI][18]

Section 1.

The eighteenth article of amendment to the Constitution of the United States is hereby repealed.

Section 2.

The transportation or importation into any State, Territory, or possession of the United States for delivery or use therein of intoxicating liquors, in violation of the laws thereof, is hereby prohibited.

Section 3.

This article shall be inoperative unless it shall have been ratified as an amendment to the Constitution by conventions in the several States, as provided in the Constitution, within seven years from the date of the submission hereof to the States by the Congress.

[16]Adopted in 1920.
[17]Adopted in 1933.

[18]Adopted in 1933.

[ARTICLE XXII][19]

No person shall be elected to the office of the President more than twice, and no person who has held the office of President, or acted as President, for more than two years of a term to which some other person was elected President shall be elected to the office of the President more than once.

But this Article shall not apply to any person holding the office of President when this Article was proposed by the Congress, and shall not prevent any person who may be holding the office of President, or acting as President, during the term within which this Article becomes operative from holding the office of President or acting as President during the remainder of such term.

This article shall be inoperative unless it shall have been ratified as an amendment to the Constitution by the legislatures of three-fourths of the several states within seven years from the date of its submission to the states by the Congress.

[ARTICLE XXIII][20]

Section 1.

The District constituting the seat of Government of the United States shall appoint in such manner as the Congress may direct:

A number of electors of President and Vice-President equal to the whole number of Senators and Representatives in Congress to which the District would be entitled if it were a State, but in no event more than the least populous State; they shall be in addition to those appointed by the States, but they shall be considered, for the purposes of the election of President and Vice-President, to be electors appointed by a State; and they shall meet in the District and perform such duties as provided by the twelfth article of amendment.

Section 2.

The Congress shall have power to enforce this article by appropriate legislation.

[ARTICLE XXIV][21]

Section 1.

The right of citizens of the United States to vote in any primary or other election for President or Vice President, for electors for President or Vice President, or for Senator or Representative in Congress, shall not be denied or abridged by the United States or any state by reason of failure to pay any poll tax or other tax.

Section 2.

The Congress shall have the power to enforce this article by appropriate legislation.

[ARTICLE XXV][22]

Section 1.

In case of the removal of the President from office or of his death or resignation, the Vice President shall become President.

Section 2.

Whenever there is a vacancy in the office of the Vice President, the President shall nominate a Vice President who shall take office upon confirmation by a majority vote of both Houses of Congress.

Section 3.

Whenever the President transmits to the President Pro Tempore of the Senate and the Speaker of the House of Representatives his written declaration that he is unable to discharge the powers and duties of his office, and until he transmits to them a written declaration to the contrary, such powers and duties shall be discharged by the Vice President as Acting President.

Section 4.

Whenever the Vice President and a majority of either the principal officers of the executive departments or of such other body as Congress may by law provide, transmit to

---

[19]Adopted in 1961.
[20]Adopted in 1961.

[21]Adopted in 1964.
[22]Adopted in 1967.

the President Pro Tempore of the Senate and the Speaker of the House of Representatives their written declaration that the President is unable to discharge the powers and duties of his office, the Vice President shall immediately assume the powers and duties of the office as Acting President.

Thereafter, when the President transmits to the President Pro Tempore of the Senate and the Speaker of the House of Representatives his written declaration that no inability exists, he shall resume the powers and duties of his office unless the Vice President and a majority of either the principal officers of the executive departments or of such other body as Congress may by law provide, transmit within four days to the President Pro Tempore of the Senate and the Speaker of the House of Representatives their written declaration that the President is unable to discharge the powers and duties of his office. Thereupon Congress shall decide the issue, assembling within forty-eight hours for that purpose if not in session. If the Congress, within twenty-one days after receipt of the latter written declaration, or, if Congress is not in session, within twenty-one days after Congress is required to assemble, determines by two-thirds vote of both Houses that the President is unable to discharge the powers and duties of his office, the Vice President shall continue to discharge the same as Acting President; otherwise, the President shall resume the powers and duties of his office.

[ARTICLE XXVI][23]

Section 1.

The right of citizens of the United States, who are eighteen years of age or older, to vote shall not be denied or abridged by the United States or by any State on account of age.

Section 2.

The Congress shall have power to enforce this article by appropriate legislation.

[AMENDMENT XXVII][24]

No law varying the compensation for the services of Senators and Representatives shall take effect until an election of Representatives shall have intervened.

---

[23]Adopted in 1971.
[24]Adopted in 1992.

PRESIDENTIAL ELECTIONS

Year	Candidates	Parties	Popular Vote	Percentage of Popular Vote	Electoral Vote	Percentage of Voter Participation
1789	**GEORGE WASHINGTON (Va.)***				69	
	John Adams				34	
	Others				35	
1792	**GEORGE WASHINGTON (Va.)**				132	
	John Adams				77	
	George Clinton				50	
	Others				5	
1796	**JOHN ADAMS (Mass.)**	Federalist			71	
	Thomas Jefferson	Democratic-Republican			68	
	Thomas Pinckney	Federalist			59	
	Aaron Burr	Dem.-Rep.			30	
	Others				48	
1800	**THOMAS JEFFERSON (Va.)**	Dem.-Rep.			73	
	Aaron Burr	Dem.-Rep.			73	
	John Adams	Federalist			65	
	C. C. Pinckney	Federalist			64	
	John Jay	Federalist			1	
1804	**THOMAS JEFFERSON (Va.)**	Dem.-Rep.			162	
	C. C. Pinckney	Federalist			14	
1808	**JAMES MADISON (Va.)**	Dem.-Rep.			122	
	C. C. Pinckney	Federalist			47	
	George Clinton	Dem.-Rep.			6	
1812	**JAMES MADISON (Va.)**	Dem.-Rep.			128	
	De Witt Clinton	Federalist			89	
1816	**JAMES MONROE (Va.)**	Dem.-Rep.			183	
	Rufus King	Federalist			34	
1820	**JAMES MONROE (Va.)**	Dem.-Rep.			231	
	John Quincy Adams	Dem.-Rep.			1	
1824	**JOHN Q. ADAMS (Mass.)**	Dem.-Rep.	108,740	30.5	84	26.9
	Andrew Jackson	Dem.-Rep.	153,544	43.1	99	
	William H. Crawford	Dem.-Rep.	46,618	13.1	41	
	Henry Clay	Dem.-Rep.	47,136	13.2	37	
1828	**ANDREW JACKSON (Tenn.)**	Democratic	647,286	56.0	178	57.6
	John Quincy Adams	National Republican	508,064	44.0	83	
1832	**ANDREW JACKSON (Tenn.)**	Democratic	687,502	55.0	219	55.4
	Henry Clay	National Republican	530,189	42.4	49	
	John Floyd	Independent			11	
	William Wirt	Anti-Mason	33,108	2.6	7	
1836	**MARTIN VAN BUREN (N.Y.)**	Democratic	765,483	50.9	170	57.8
	W. H. Harrison	Whig			73	
	Hugh L. White	Whig	739,795	49.1	26	
	Daniel Webster	Whig			14	
	W. P. Magnum	Independent			11	

*State of residence at time of election.

Year	Candidates	Parties	Popular Vote	Percentage of Popular Vote	Electoral Vote	Percentage of Voter Participation
1840	**WILLIAM H. HARRISON (Ohio)**	Whig	1,274,624	53.1	234	80.2
	Martin Van Buren	Democratic	1,127,781	46.9	60	
	J. G. Birney	Liberty	7,069		—	
1844	**JAMES K. POLK (Tenn.)**	Democratic	1,338,464	49.6	170	78.9
	Henry Clay	Whig	1,300,097	48.1	105	
	J. G. Birney	Liberty	62,300	2.3	—	
1848	**ZACHARY TAYLOR (La.)**	Whig	1,360,967	47.4	163	72.7
	Lewis Cass	Democratic	1,222,342	42.5	127	
	Martin Van Buren	Free-Soil	291,263	10.1	—	
1852	**FRANKLIN PIERCE (N.H.)**	Democratic	1,601,117	50.9	254	69.6
	Winfield Scott	Whig	1,385,453	44.1	42	
	John P. Hale	Free-Soil	155,825	5.0	—	
1856	**JAMES BUCHANAN (Pa.)**	Democratic	1,832,955	45.3	741	78.9
	John C. Frémont	Republican	1,339,932	33.1	114	
	Millard Fillmore	American	871,731	21.6	8	
1860	**ABRAHAM LINCOLN (Ill.)**	Republican	1,865,593	39.8	180	81.2
	Stephen A. Douglas	Democratic	1,382,713	29.5	12	
	John C. Breckinridge	Democratic	848,356	18.1	72	
	John Bell	Union	592,906	12.6	39	
1864	**ABRAHAM LINCOLN (Ill.)**	Republican	2,213,655	55.0	212	73.8
	George B. McClellan	Democratic	1,805,237	45.0	21	
1868	**ULYSSES S. GRANT (Ill.)**	Republican	3,012,833	52.7	214	78.1
	Horatio Seymour	Democratic	2,703,249	47.3	80	
1872	**ULYSSES S. GRANT (Ill.)**	Republican	3,597,132	55.6	286	71.3
	Horace Greeley	Democratic; Liberal Republican	2,834,125	43.9	66	
1876	**RUTHERFORD B. HAYES (Ohio)**	Republican	4,036,298	48.0	185	81.8
	Samuel J. Tilden	Democratic	4,300,590	51.0	184	
1880	**JAMES A. GARFIELD (Ohio)**	Republican	4,454,416	48.5	214	79.4
	Winfield S. Hancock	Democratic	4,444,952	48.1	155	
1884	**GROVER CLEVELAND (N.Y.)**	Democratic	4,874,986	48.5	219	77.5
	James G. Blaine	Republican	4,851,981	48.2	182	
1888	**BENJAMIN HARRISON (Ind.)**	Republican	5,439,853	47.9	233	79.3
	Grover Cleveland	Democratic	5,540,309	48.6	168	
1892	**GROVER CLEVELAND (N.Y.)**	Democratic	5,556,918	46.1	277	74.7
	Benjamin Harrison	Republican	5,176,108	43.0	145	
	James B. Weaver	People's	1,041,028	8.5	22	
1896	**WILLIAM McKINLEY (Ohio)**	Republican	7,104,779	51.1	271	79.3
	William J. Bryan	Democratic- People's	6,502,925	47.7	176	
1900	**WILLIAM McKINLEY (Ohio)**	Republican	7,207,923	51.7	292	73.2
	William J. Bryan	Dem.-Populist	6,358,133	45.5	155	
1904	**THEODORE ROOSEVELT (N.Y.)**	Republican	7,623,486	57.9	336	65.2
	Alton B. Parker	Democratic	5,077,911	37.6	140	
	Eugene V. Debs	Socialist	402,283	3.0	—	
1908	**WILLIAM H. TAFT (Ohio)**	Republican	7,678,098	51.6	321	65.4
	William J. Bryan	Democratic	6,409,104	43.1	162	
	Eugene V. Debs	Socialist	420,793	2.8	—	

Year	Candidates	Parties	Popular Vote	Percentage of Popular Vote	Electoral Vote	Percentage of Voter Participation
1912	**WOODROW WILSON (N.J.)**	Democratic	6,293,454	41.9	435	58.8
	Theodore Roosevelt	Progressive	4,119,538	27.4	88	
	William H. Taft	Republican	3,484,980	23.2	8	
	Eugene V. Debs	Socialist	900,672	6.0	—	
1916	**WOODROW WILSON (N.J.)**	Democratic	9,129,606	49.4	277	61.6
	Charles E. Hughes	Republican	8,538,221	46.2	254	
	A. L. Benson	Socialist	585,113	3.2	—	
1920	**WARREN G. HARDING (Ohio)**	Republican	16,152,200	60.4	404	49.2
	James M. Cox	Democratic	9,147,353	34.2	127	
	Eugene V. Debs	Socialist	919,799	3.4	—	
1924	**CALVIN COOLIDGE (Mass.)**	Republican	15,725,016	54.0	382	48.9
	John W. Davis	Democratic	8,386,503	28.8	136	
	Robert M. LaFollette	Progressive	4,822,856	16.6	13	
1928	**HERBERT HOOVER (Calif.)**	Republican	21,391,381	58.2	444	56.9
	Alfred E. Smith	Democratic	15,016,443	40.9	87	
	Norman Thomas	Socialist	267,835	0.7	—	
1932	**FRANKLIN D. ROOSEVELT (N.Y.)**	Democratic	22,821,857	57.4	472	56.9
	Herbert Hoover	Republican	15,761,841	39.7	59	
	Norman Thomas	Socialist	881,951	2.2	—	
1936	**FRANKLIN D. ROOSEVELT (N.Y.)**	Democratic	27,751,597	60.8	523	61.0
	Alfred M. Landon	Republican	16,679,583	36.5	8	
	William Lemke	Union	882,479	1.9	—	
1940	**FRANKLIN D. ROOSEVELT (N.Y.)**	Democratic	27,244,160	54.8	449	62.5
	Wendell L. Willkie	Republican	22,305,198	44.8	82	
1944	**FRANKLIN D. ROOSEVELT (N.Y.)**	Democratic	25,602,504	53.5	432	55.9
	Thomas E. Dewey	Republican	22,006,285	46.0	99	
1948	**HARRY S. TRUMAN (Mo.)**	Democratic	24,105,695	49.5	304	53.0
	Thomas E. Dewey	Republican	21,969,170	45.1	189	
	J. Strom Thurmond	State-Rights Democratic	1,169,021	2.4	38	
	Henry A. Wallace	Progressive	1,156,103	2.4	—	
1952	**DWIGHT D. EISENHOWER (N.Y.)**	Republican	33,936,252	55.1	442	63.3
	Adlai E. Stevenson	Democratic	27,314,992	44.4	89	
1956	**DWIGHT D. EISENHOWER (N.Y.)**	Republican	35,575,420	57.6	457	60.6
	Adlai E. Stevenson	Democratic	26,033,066	42.1	73	
	Other	—	—		1	
1960	**JOHN F. KENNEDY (Mass.)**	Democratic	34,227,096	49.9	303	62.8
	Richard M. Nixon	Republican	34,108,546	49.6	219	
	Other	—	—		15	
1964	**LYNDON B. JOHNSON (Tex.)**	Democratic	43,126,506	61.1	486	61.7
	Barry M. Goldwater	Republican	27,176,799	38.5	52	
1968	**RICHARD M. NIXON (N.Y.)**	Republican	31,770,237	43.4	301	60.6
	Hubert H. Humphrey	Democratic	31,270,533	42.7	191	
	George Wallace	American Indep.	9,906,141	13.5	46	
1972	**RICHARD M. NIXON (N.Y.)**	Republican	47,169,911	60.7	520	55.2
	George S. McGovern	Democratic	29,170,383	37.5	17	
	Other	—	—		1	
1976	**JIMMY CARTER (Ga.)**	Democratic	40,828,587	50.0	297	53.5
	Gerald R. Ford	Republican	39,147,613	47.9	241	
	Other	—	1,575,459	2.1	—	
1980	**RONALD REAGAN (Calif.)**	Republican	43,901,812	50.7	489	52.6
	Jimmy Carter	Democratic	35,483,820	41.0	49	
	John B. Anderson	Independent	5,719,722	6.6	—	
	Ed Clark	Libertarian	921,188	1.1	—	

Year	Candidates	Parties	Popular Vote	Percentage of Popular Vote	Electoral Vote	Percentage of Voter Participation
1984	**RONALD REAGAN (Calif.)**	Republican	54,455,075	59.0	525	53.3
	Walter Mondale	Democratic	37,577,185	41.0	13	
1988	**GEORGE BUSH (Texas)**	Republican	47,946,422	54.0	426	50.2
	Michael S. Dukakis	Democratic	41,016,429	46.0	112	
1992	**WILLIAM J. CLINTON (Ark.)**	Democratic	44,908,233	43.3	370	55.2
	George Bush	Republican	39,102,282	37.7	168	
	Ross Perot	Independent	19,721,433	19.0	—	
1996	**WILLIAM J. CLINTON (Ark.)**	Democratic	47,401,185	49.3	379	
	Robert Dole	Republican	39,197,469	40.7	159	49.0
	Ross Perot	Reform	8,085,294	8.4	—	

VICE PRESIDENTS AND CABINET MEMBERS

The Washington Administration (1789–1797)

Vice President	John Adams	1789–1797
Secretary of State	Thomas Jefferson	1789–1793
	Edmund Randolph	1794–1795
	Timothy Pickering	1795–1797
Secretary of Treasury	Alexander Hamilton	1789–1795
	Oliver Wolcott	1795–1797
Secretary of War	Henry Knox	1789–1794
	Timothy Pickering	1795–1796
	James McHenry	1796–1797
Attorney General	Edmund Randolph	1789–1793
	William Bradford	1794–1795
	Charles Lee	1795–1797
Postmaster General	Samuel Osgood	1789–1791
	Timothy Pickering	1791–1794
	Joseph Habersham	1795–1797

The John Adams Administration (1797–1801)

Vice President	Thomas Jefferson	1797–1801
Secretary of State	Timothy Pickering	1797–1800
	John Marshall	1800–1801
Secretary of Treasury	Oliver Wolcott	1797–1800
	Samuel Dexter	1800–1801
Secretary of War	James McHenry	1797–1800
	Samuel Dexter	1800–1801
Attorney General	Charles Lee	1797–1801
Postmaster General	Joseph Habersham	1797–1801
Secretary of Navy	Benjamin Stoddert	1798–1801

The Jefferson Administration (1801–1809)

Vice President	Aaron Burr	1801–1805
	George Clinton	1805–1809
Secretary of State	James Madison	1801–1809
Secretary of Treasury	Samuel Dexter	1801
	Albert Gallatin	1801–1809
Secretary of War	Henry Dearborn	1801–1809
Attorney General	Levi Lincoln	1801–1805
	Robert Smith	1805
	John Breckinridge	1805–1806
	Caesar Rodney	1807–1809
Postmaster General	Joseph Habersham	1801
	Gideon Granger	1801–1809
Secretary of Navy	Robert Smith	1801–1809

The Madison Administration (1809–1817)

Vice President	George Clinton	1809–1813
	Elbridge Gerry	1813–1817
Secretary of State	Robert Smith	1809–1811
	James Monroe	1811–1817
Secretary of Treasury	Albert Gallatin	1809–1813
	George Campbell	1814
	Alexander Dallas	1814–1816
	William Crawford	1816–1817
Secretary of War	William Eustis	1809–1812
	John Armstrong	1813–1814
	James Monroe	1814–1815
	William Crawford	1815–1817
Attorney General	Caesar Rodney	1809–1811
	William Pinkney	1811–1814
	Richard Rush	1814–1817
Postmaster General	Gideon Granger	1809–1814
	Return Meigs	1814–1817
Secretary of Navy	Paul Hamilton	1809–1813
	William Jones	1813–1814
	Benjamin Crowninshield	1814–1817

The Monroe Administration (1817–1825)

Vice President	Daniel Tompkins	1817–1825
Secretary of State	John Quincy Adams	1817–1825
Secretary of Treasury	William Crawford	1817–1825
Secretary of War	George Graham	1817
	John C. Calhoun	1817–1825
Attorney General	Richard Rush	1817
	William Wirt	1817–1825
Postmaster General	Return Meigs	1817–1823
	John McLean	1823–1825
Secretary of Navy	Benjamin Crowninshield	1817–1818
	Smith Thompson	1818–1823
	Samuel Southard	1823–1825

The John Quincy Adams Administration (1825-1829)

Vice President	John C. Calhoun	1825-1829
Secretary of State	Henry Clay	1825-1829
Secretary of Treasury	Richard Rush	1825-1829
Secretary of War	James Barbour	1825-1828
	Peter Porter	1828-1829
Attorney General	William Wirt	1825-1829
Postmaster General	John McLean	1825-1829
Secretary of Navy	Samuel Southard	1825-1829

The Jackson Administration (1829-1837)

Vice President	John C. Calhoun	1829-1833
	Martin Van Buren	1833-1837
Secretary of State	Martin Van Buren	1829-1831
	Edward Livingston	1831-1833
	Louis McLane	1833-1834
	John Forsyth	1834-1837
Secretary of Treasury	Samuel Ingham	1829-1831
	Louis McLane	1831-1833
	William Duane	1833
	Roger B. Taney	1833-1834
	Levi Woodbury	1834-1837
Secretary of War	John H. Eaton	1829-1831
	Lewis Cass	1831-1837
	Benjamin Butler	1837
Attorney General	John M. Berrien	1829-1831
	Roger B. Taney	1831-1833
	Benjamin Butler	1833-1837
Postmaster General	William Barry	1829-1835
	Amos Kendall	1835-1837
Secretary of Navy	John Branch	1829-1831
	Levi Woodbury	1831-1834
	Mahlon Dickerson	1834-1837

The Van Buren Administration (1837-1841)

Vice President	Richard M. Johnson	1837-1841
Secretary of State	John Forsyth	1837-1841
Secretary of Treasury	Levi Woodbury	1837-1841
Secretary of War	Joel Poinsett	1837-1841
Attorney General	Benjamin Butler	1837-1838
	Felix Grundy	1838-1840
	Henry D. Gilpin	1840-1841
Postmaster General	Amos Kendall	1837-1840
	John M. Niles	1840-1841
Secretary of Navy	Mahlon Dickerson	1837-1838
	James Paulding	1838-1841

The William Harrison Administration (1841)

Vice President	John Tyler	1841
Secretary of State	Daniel Webster	1841
Secretary of Treasury	Thomas Ewing	1841
Secretary of War	John Bell	1841
Attorney General	John J. Crittenden	1841
Postmaster General	Francis Granger	1841
Secretary of Navy	George Badger	1841

The Tyler Administration (1841-1845)

Vice President	None	
Secretary of State	Daniel Webster	1841-1843
	Hugh S. Legaré	1843
	Abel P. Upshur	1843-1844
	John C. Calhoun	1844-1845
Secretary of Treasury	Thomas Ewing	1841
	Walter Forward	1841-1843
	John C. Spencer	1843-1844
	George Bibb	1844-1845
Secretary of War	John Bell	1841
	John C. Spencer	1841-1843
	James M. Porter	1843-1844
	William Wilkins	1844-1845
Attorney General	John J. Crittenden	1841
	Hugh S. Legaré	1841-1843
	John Nelson	1843-1845
Postmaster General	Francis Granger	1841
	Charles Wickliffe	1841
Secretary of Navy	George Badger	1841
	Abel P. Upshur	1841
	David Henshaw	1843-1844
	Thomas Gilmer	1844
	John Y. Mason	1844-1845

The Polk Administration (1845-1849)

Vice President	George M. Dallas	1845-1849
Secretary of State	James Buchanan	1845-1849
Secretary of Treasury	Robert J. Walker	1845-1849
Secretary of War	William L. Marcy	1845-1849

Attorney General	John Y. Mason	1845–1846
	Nathan Clifford	1846–1848
	Isaac Toucey	1848–1849
Postmaster General	Cave Johnson	1845–1849
Secretary of Navy	George Bancrocft	1845–1846
	John Y. Mason	1846–1849

The Taylor Administration (1849–1850)

Vice President	Millard Fillmore	1849–1850
Secretary of State	John M. Clayton	1849–1850
Secretary of Treasury	William Meredith	1849–1850
Secretary of War	George Crawford	1849–1850
Attorney General	Reverdy Johnson	1849–1850
Postmaster General	Jacob Collamer	1849–1850
Secretary of Navy	William Preston	1849–1850
Secretary of Interior	Thomas Ewing	1849–1850

The Fillmore Administration (1850–1853)

Vice President	None	
Secretary of State	Daniel Webster	1850–1852
	Edward Everett	1852–1853
Secretary of Treasury	Thomas Corwin	1850–1853
Secretary of War	Charles Conrad	1850–1853
Attorney General	John J. Crittenden	1850–1853
Postmaster General	Nathan Hall	1850–1852
	Sam D. Hubbard	1852–1853
Secretary of Navy	William A. Graham	1850–1852
	John P. Kennedy	1852–1853
Secretary of Interior	Thomas McKennan	1850
	Alexander Stuart	1850–1853

The Pierce Administration (1853–1857)

Vice President	William R. King	1853–1857
Secretary of State	William L. Marcy	1853–1857
Secretary of Treasury	James Guthrie	1853–1857
Secretary of War	Jefferson Davis	1853–1857

Attorney General	Caleb Cushing	1853–1857
Postmaster General	James Campbell	1853–1857
Secretary of Navy	James C. Dobbin	1853–1857
Secretary of Interior	Robert McClelland	1853–1857

The Buchanan Administration (1857–1861)

Vice President	John C. Breckinridge	1857–1861
Secretary of State	Lewis Cass	1857–1860
	Jeremiah S. Black	1860–1861
Secretary of Treasury	Howell Cobb	1857–1860
	Philip Thomas	1860–1861
	John A. Dix	1861
Secretary of War	John B. Floyd	1857–1861
	Joseph Holt	1861
Attorney General	Jeremiah S. Black	1857–1860
	Edwin M. Stanton	1860–1861
Postmaster General	Aaron V. Brown	1857–1859
	Joseph Holt	1859–1861
	Horatio King	1861
Secretary of Navy	Isaac Toucey	1857–1861
Secretary of Interior	Jacob Thompson	1857–1861

The Lincoln Administration (1861–1865)

Vice President	Hannibal Hamlin	1861–1865
	Andrew Jackson	1865
Secretary of State	William H. Seward	1861–1865
Secretary of Treasury	Salmon P. Chase	1861–1864
	William P. Fessenden	1864–1865
	Hugh McCulloch	1865
Secretary of War	Simon Cameron	1861–1862
	Edwin M. Stanton	1862–1865
Attorney General	Edward Bates	1861–1864
	James Speed	1864–1865
Postmaster General	Horatio King	1861
	Montgomery Blair	1861–1864
	William Dennison	1864–1865
Secretary of Navy	Gideon Welles	1861–1865
Secretary of Interior	Caleb B.Smith	1861–1863
	John P. Usher	1863–1865

The Andrew Johnson Administration (1865–1869)

Vice President	None	
Secretary of State	William H. Seward	1865–1869
Secretary of Treasury	Hugh McCulloch	1865–1869
Secretary of War	Edwin M. Stanton Ulysses S. Grant Lorenzo Thomas John M. Schofield	1865–1867 1867–1868 1868 1868–1869
Attorney General	James Speed Henry Stanbery William M. Evarts	1865–1866 1866–1868 1868–1869
Postmaster General	William Dennison Alexander Randall	1865–1866 1866–1869
Secretary of Navy	Gideon Welles	1865–1869
Secretary of Interior	John P. Usher James Harlan Orville H. Browning	1865 1865–1866 1866–1869

The Grant Administration (1869–1877)

Vice President	Schuyler Colfax Henry Wilson	1869–1873 1873–1877
Secretary of State	Elihu B. Washburne Hamilton Fish	1869 1869–1877
Secretary of Treasury	George S. Boutwell William Richardson Benjamin Bristow Lot M. Morrill	1869–1873 1873–1874 1874–1876 1876–1877
Secretary of War	John A. Rawlins William T. Sherman William W. Belknap Alphonso Taft James D. Cameron	1869 1869 1869–1876 1876 1876–1877
Attorney General	Ebenezer Hoar Amos T. Ackerman G. H. Williams Edwards Pierrepont Alphonso Taft	1869–1870 1870–1871 1871–1875 1875–1876 1876–1877
Postmaster General	John A. J. Creswell James W. Marshall Marshall Jewell James N. Tyner	1869–1874 1874 1874–1876 1876–1877
Secretary of Navy	Adolph E. Borie George M. Robeson	1869 1869–1877
Secretary of Interior	Jacob D. Cox Columbus Delano Zachariah Candler	1869–1870 1870–1875 1875–1877

The Hayes Administration (1877–1881)

Vice President	William A. Wheeler	1877–1881
Secretary of State	William M. Evarts	1877–1881
Secretary of Treasury	John Sherman	1877–1881
Secretary of War	George W. McCrary Alex Ramsey	1877–1879 1879–1881
Attorney General	Charles Devens	1877–1881
Postmaster General	David M. Key Horace Maynard	1877–1880 1880–1881
Secretary of Navy	Richard W. Thompson Nathan Goff, Jr.	1877–1880 1881
Secretary of Interior	Carl Schurz	1877–1881

The Garfield Administration (1881)

Vice President	Chester A. Arthur	1881
Secretary of State	James G. Blaine	1881
Secretary of Treasury	William Windom	1881
Secretary of War	Robert T. Lincoln	1881
Attorney General	Wayne MacVeagh	1881
Postmaster General	Thomas L. James	1881
Secretary of Navy	William H. Hunt	1881
Secretary of Interior	Samuel J. Kirkwood	1881

The Arthur Administration (1881–1885)

Vice President	None	
Secretary of State	F. T. Frelinghuysen	1881–1885
Secretary of Treasury	Charles J. Folger Walter Q. Gresham Hugh McCulloch	1881–1884 1884 1884–1885
Secretary of War	Robert T. Lincoln	1881–1885
Attorney General	Benjamin H. Brewster	1881–1885
Postmaster General	Timothy O. Howe Walter Q. Gresham Frank Hatton	1881–1883 1883–1884 1884–1885

Secretary of Navy	William H. Hunt	1881–1882
	William E. Chandler	1882–1885
Secretary of Interior	Samuel J. Kirkwood	1881–1882
	Henry M. Teller	1882–1885

The Cleveland Administration (1885–1889)

Vice President	Thomas A. Hendricks	1885–1889
Secretary of State	Thomas F. Bayard	1885–1889
Secretary of Treasury	Daniel Manning	1885–1887
	Charles S. Fairchild	1887–1889
Secretary of War	William C. Endicott	1885–1889
Attorney General	Augustus H. Garland	1885–1889
Postmaster General	William F. Vilas	1885–1888
	Don M. Dickinson	1888–1889
Secretary of Navy	William C. Whitney	1885–1889
Secretary of Interior	Lucius Q. C. Lamar	1885–1888
	William F. Vilas	1888–1889
Secretary of Agriculture	Norman J. Colman	1889

The Benjamin Harrison Administration (1889–1893)

Vice President	Levi P. Morton	1889–1893
Secretary of State	James G. Blaine	1889–1892
	John W. Foster	1892–1893
Secretary of Treasury	William Windom	1889–1891
	Charles Foster	1891–1893
Secretary of War	Redfield Proctor	1889–1891
	Stephen B. Elkins	1891–1893
Attorney General	William H. H. Miller	1889–1891
Postmaster General	John Wanamaker	1889–1893
Secretary of Navy	Benjamin F. Tracy	1889–1893
Secretary of Interior	John W. Noble	1889–1893
Secretary of Agriculture	Jeremiah M. Rusk	1889–1893

The Cleveland Administration (1893–1897)

Vice President	Adlai E. Stevenson	1893–1897
Secretary of State	Walter Q. Gresham	1893–1895
	Richard Olney	1895–1897
Secretary of Treasury	John G. Carlisle	1893–1897
Secretary of War	Daniel S. Lamont	1893–1897
Attorney General	Richard Olney	1893–1895
	James Harmon	1895–1897
Postmaster General	Wilson S. Bissell	1893–1895
	William L. Wilson	1895–1897
Secretary of Navy	Hilary A. Herbert	1893–1897
Secretary of Interior	Hoke Smith	1893–1896
	David R. Francis	1896–1897
Secretary of Agriculture	Julius S. Morton	1893–1897

The McKinley Administration (1897–1901)

Vice President	Garret A. Hobart	1897–1901
	Theodore Roosevelt	1901
Secretary of State	John Sherman	1897–1898
	William R. Day	1898
	John Hay	1898–1901
Secretary of Treasury	Lyman J. Gage	1897–1901
Secretary of War	Russell A. Alger	1897–1899
	Elihu Root	1899–1901
Attorney General	Joseph McKenna	1897–1898
	John W. Griggs	1898–1901
	Philander C. Knox	1901
Postmaster General	James A. Gary	1897–1898
	Charles E. Smith	1898–1901
Secretary of Navy	John D. Long	1897–1901
Secretary of Interior	Cornelius N. Bliss	1897–1899
	Ethan A. Hitchcock	1899–1901
Secretary of Agriculture	James Wilson	1897–1901

The Theodore Roosevelt Administration (1901–1909)

Vice President	Charles Fairbanks	1905–1909
Secretary of State	John Hay	1901–1905
	Elihu Root	1905–1909
	Robert Bacon	1909
Secretary of Treasury	Lyman J. Gage	1901–1902
	Leslie M. Shaw	1902–1907
	George B. Cortelyou	1907–1909
Secretary of War	Elihu Root	1901–1904
	William H. Taft	1904–1908
	Luke E. Wright	1908–1909

Attorney General	Philander C. Knox	1901–1904
	William H. Moody	1904–1906
	Charles J. Bonaparte	1906–1909
Postmaster General	Charles E. Smith	1901–1902
	Henry C. Payne	1902–1904
	Robert J. Wynne	1904–1905
	George B. Cortelyou	1905–1907
	George von L. Meyer	1907–1909
Secretary of Navy	John D. Long	1901–1902
	William H. Moody	1902–1904
	Paul Morton	1904–1905
	Charles J. Bonaparte	1905–1906
	Victor H. Metcalf	1906–1908
	Truman H. Newberry	1908–1909
Secretary of Interior	Ethan A. Hitchcock	1901–1907
	James R. Garfield	1907–1909
Secretary of Agriculture	James Wilson	1901–1909
Secretary of Labor and Commerce	George B. Cortelyou	1903–1904
	Victor H. Metcalf	1904–1906
	Oscar S. Straus	1906–1909
	Charles Nagel	1909

The Taft Administration (1909–1913)

Vice President	James S. Sherman	1909–1913
Secretary of State	Philander C. Knox	1909–1913
Secretary of Treasury	Franklin MacVeagh	1909–1913
Secretary of War	Jacob M. Dickinson	1909–1911
	Henry L. Stimson	1911–1913
Attorney General	George W. Wickersham	1909–1913
Postmaster General	Frank H. Hitchcock	1909–1913
Secretary of Navy	George von L. Meyer	1909–1913
Secretary of Interior	Richard A. Ballinger	1909–1911
	Walter L. Fisher	1991–1913
Secretary of Agriculture	James Wilson	1909–1913
Secretary of Labor and Commerce	Charles Nagel	1909–1913

The Wilson Administration (1913–1921)

Vice President	Thomas R. Marshall	1913–1921
Secretary of State	William J. Bryan	1913–1915
	Robert Lansing	1915–1920
	Bainbridge Colby	1920–1921
Secretary of Treasury	William G. McAdoo	1913–1918
	Carter Glass	1918–1920
	David F. Houston	1920–1921
Secretary of War	Lindley M. Garrison	1913–1916
	Newton D. Baker	1916–1921
Attorney General	James C. McReyolds	1913–1914
	Thomas W. Gregory	1914–1919
	A. Mitchell Palmer	1919–1921
Postmaster General	Albert S. Burleson	1913–1921
Secretary of Navy	Josephus Daniels	1913–1921
Secretary of Interior	Franklin K. Lane	1913–1920
	John B. Payne	1920–1921
Secretary of Agriculture	David F. Houston	1913–1920
	Edwin T. Meredith	1920–1921
Secretary of Commerce	William C. Redfield	1913–1919
	Joshua W. Alexander	1919–1921
Secretary of Labor	William B. Wilson	1913–1921

The Harding Administration (1921–1923)

Vice President	Calvin Coolidge	1921–1923
Secretary of State	Charles E. Hughes	1921–1923
Secretary of Treasury	Andrew Mellon	1921–1923
Secretary of War	John W. Weeks	1921–1923
Attorney General	Harry M. Daugherty	1921–1923
Postmaster General	Will H. Hays	1921–1922
	Hubert Work	1922–1923
	Harry S. New	1923
Secretary of Navy	Edwin Denby	1921–1923
Secretary of Interior	Albert B. Fall	1921–1923
	Hubert Work	1923
Secretary of Agriculture	Henry C. Wallace	1921–1923
Secretary of Commerce	Herbert C. Hoover	1921–1923
Secretary of Labor	James J. Davis	1921–1923

The Coolidge Administration (1923–1929)

Vice President	Charles G. Dawes	1925–1929
Secretary of State	Charles E. Hughes	1923–1925
	Frank B. Kellogg	1925–1929

Secretary of Treasury	Andrew Mellon	1923–1929
Secretary of War	John W. Weeks	1923–1925
	Dwight F. Davis	1925–1929
Attorney General	Harry M. Daugherty	1923–1924
	Harlan F. Stone	1924–1925
	John G. Sargent	1925–1929
Postmaster General	Harry S. New	1923–1929
Secretary of Navy	Edwin Derby	1923–1924
	Curtis D. Wilbur	1924–1929
Secretary of Interior	Hubert Work	1923–1928
	Roy O. West	1928–1929
Secretary of Agriculture	Henry C. Wallace	1923–1924
	Howard M. Gore	1924–1925
	William M. Jardine	1925–1929
Secretary of Commerce	Herbert C. Hoover	1923–1928
	William F. Whiting	1928–1929
Secretary of Labor	James J. Davis	1923–1929

The Hoover Administration (1929–1933)

Vice President	Charles Curtis	1929–1933
Secretary of State	Henry L. Stimson	1929–1933
Secretary of Treasury	Andrew Mellon	1929–1932
	Ogden L. Mills	1932–1933
Secretary of War	James W. Good	1929
	Patrick J. Hurley	1929–1933
Attorney General	William D. Mitchell	1929–1933
Postmaster General	Walter F. Brown	1929–1933
Secretary of Navy	Charles F. Adams	1929–1933
Secretary of Interior	Ray L. Wilbur	1929–1933
Secretary of Agriculture	Arthur M. Hyde	1929–1933
Secretary of Commerce	Robert P. Lamont	1929–1932
	Roy D. Chapin	1932–1933
Secretary of Labor	James J. Davis	1929–1930
	William N. Doak	1930–1933

The Franklin D. Roosevelt Administration (1933–1945)

Vice President	John Nance Garner	1933–1941
	Henry A. Wallace	1941–1945
	Harry S. Truman	1945

Secretary of State	Cordell Hull	1933–1944
	Edward R. Stettinius, Jr.	1944–1945
Secretary of Treasury	William H. Woodin	1933–1934
	Henry Morgenthau, Jr.	1934–1945
Secretary of War	George H. Dern	1933–1936
	Henry A. Woodring	1936–1940
	Henry L. Stimson	1940–1945
Attorney General	Homer S. Cummings	1933–1939
	Frank Murphy	1939–1940
	Robert H. Jackson	1940–1941
	Francis Biddle	1941–1945
Postmaster General	James A. Farley	1933–1940
	Frank C. Walker	1940–1945
Secretary of Navy	Claude A. Swanson	1933–1940
	Charles Edison	1940
	Frank Knox	1940–1944
	James V. Forrestal	1944–1945
Secretary of Interior	Harold L. Ickes	1933–1945
Secretary of Agriculture	Henry A. Wallace	1933–1940
	Claude R. Wickard	1940–1945
Secretary of Commerce	Daniel C. Roper	1933–1939
	Harry L. Hopkins	1939–1940
	Jesse Jones	1940–1945
	Henry A. Wallace	1945
Secretary of Labor	Frances Perkins	1933–1945

The Truman Administration (1945–1953)

Vice President	Alben W. Barkley	1949–1953
Secretary of State	Edward R. Stettinius, Jr.	1945
	James F. Byrnes	1945–1947
	George C. Marshall	1947–1949
	Dean G. Acheson	1949–1953
Secretary of Treasury	Fred M. Vinson	1945–1946
	John W. Snyder	1946–1953
Secretary of War	Robert P. Patterson	1945–1947
	Kenneth C. Royall	1947
Attorney General	Tom C. Clark	1945–1949
	J. Howard McGrath	1949–1952
	James P. McGranery	1952–1953
Postmaster General	Frank C. Walker	1945
	Robert E. Hannegan	1945–1947
	Jesse M. Donaldson	1947–1953
Secretary of Navy	James V. Forrestal	1945–1947
Secretary of Interior	Harold L. Ickes	1945–1946
	Julius A. Krug	1946–1949
	Oscar L. Chapman	1949–1953

Secretary of Agriculture	Clinton P. Anderson	1945–1948
	Charles F. Brannan	1948–1953
Secretary of Commerce	Henry A. Wallace	1945–1946
	W. Averell Harriman	1946–1948
	Charles W. Sawyer	1948–1953
Secretary of Labor	Lewis B. Schwellenbach	1945–1948
	Maurice J. Tobin	1948–1953
Secretary of Defense	James V. Forrestal	1947–1949
	Louis A. Johnson	1949–1950
	George C. Marshall	1950–1951
	Robert A. Lovett	1951–1953

The Eisenhower Administration (1953–1961)

Vice President	Richard M. Nixon	1953–1961
Secretary of State	John Foster Dulles	1953–1959
	Christian A. Herter	1959–1961
Secretary of Treasury	George M. Humphrey	1953–1957
	Robert B. Anderson	1957–1961
Attorney General	Herbert Brownell, Jr.	1953–1958
	William P. Rogers	1958–1961
Postmaster General	Arthur E. Summerfield	1953–1961
Secretary of Interior	Douglas McKay	1953–1956
	Freed A. Seaton	1956–1961
Secretary of Agriculture	Ezra T.Benson	1953–1961
Secretary of Commerce	Sinclair Weeks	1953–1958
	Lewis L. Strauss	1958–1959
	Frederick H. Mueller	1959–1961
Secretary of Labor	Martin P. Durkin	1953
	James P. Mitchell	1953–1961
Secretary of Defense	Charles E. Wilson	1953–1957
	Neil H. McElroy	1957–1959
	Thomas S. Gates Jr.	1959–1961
Secretary of Health, Education, and Welfare	Oveta Culp Hobby	1953–1955
	Marion B. Folsom	1955–1958
	Arthur S. Flemming	1958–1961

The Kennedy Administration (1961–1963)

Vice President	Lyndon B. Johnson	1961–1963
Secretary of State	Dean Rusk	1961–1963
Secretary of Treasury	C. Douglas Dillon	1961–1963
Attorney General	Robert F. Kennedy	1961–1963
Postmaster General	J. Edward Day	1961–1963
	John A. Gronouski	1963
Secretary of Interior	Stewart L. Udall	1961–1963
Secretary of Agriculture	Orville L. Freeman	1961–1963
Secretary of Commerce	Luther H. Hodges	1961–1963
Secretary of Labor	Arthur J. Goldberg	1961–1962
	W. Willard Wirtz	1962–1963
Secretary of Defense	Robert S. McNamara	1961–1963
Secretary of Health, Education, and Welfare	Abraham A. Ribicoff	1961–1962
	Anthony J. Celebrezze	1962–1963

The Lyndon Johnson Administration (1963–1969)

Vice President	Hubert H. Humphrey	1965–1969
Secretary of State	Dean Rusk	1963–1969
Secretary of Treasury	C. Douglas Dillon	1963–1965
	Henry H. Fowler	1965–1969
Attorney General	Robert F. Kennedy	1963–1964
	Nicholas Katzenbach	1965–1966
	Ramsey Clark	1967–1969
Postmaster General	John A.Gronouski	1963–1965
	Lawrence F. O'Brien	1965–1968
	Marvin Watson	1968–1969
Secretary of Interior	Stewart L. Udall	1963–1969
Secretary of Agriculture	Orville L. Freeman	1963–1969
Secretary of Commerce	Luther H. Hodges	1963–1964
	John T. Connor	1964–1967
	Alexander B. Trowbridge	1967–1968
	Cyrus R. Smith	1968–1969
Secretary of Labor	W. Willard Wirtz	1963–1969
Secretary of Defense	Robert F. McNamara	1963–1968
	Clark Clifford	1968–1969
Secretary of Health, Education, and Welfare	Anthony J. Celebrezze	1963–1965
	John W. Gardner	1965–1968
	Wilbur J. Cohen	1968–1969
Secretary of Housing and Urban Development	Robert C. Weaver	1966–1969
	Robert C. Wood	1969
Secretary of Transportation	Alan S. Boyd	1967–1969

The Nixon Administration (1969-1974)

Vice President	Spiro T. Agnew	1969-1973
	Gerald R. Ford	1973-1974
Secretary of State	William P.Rogers	1969-1973
	Henry S. Kissinger	1973-1974
Secretary of Treasury	David M. Kennedy	1969-1970
	John B. Connally	1971-1972
	George P. Shultz	1972-1974
	William E. Simon	1974
Attorney General	John N. Mitchell	1969-1972
	Richard G. Kleindienst	1972-1973
	Elliot L. Richardson	1973
	William B. Saxbe	1973-1974
Postmaster General	Winton M. Blount	1969-1971
Secretary of Interior	Walter J. Hickel	1969-1970
	Rogers Morton	1971-1974
Secretary of Agriculture	Clifford M. Hardin	1969-1971
	Earl L. Butz	1971-1974
Secretary of Commerce	Maurice H. Stans	1969-1972
	Peter G. Peterson	1972-1973
	Frederick B. Dent	1973-1974
Secretary of Labor	George P. Shultz	1969-1970
	James D. Hodgson	1970-1973
	Peter J. Brennan	1973-1974
Secretary of Defense	Melvin R. Laird	1969-1973
	Elliot L. Richardson	1973
	James R. Schlesinger	1973-1974
Secretary of Health, Education, and Welfare	Robert H. Finch	1969-1970
	Elliot L. Richardson	1970-1973
	Caspar W. Weinberger	1973-1974
Secretary of Housing and Urban Development	George Romney	1969-1973
	James T. Lynn	1973-1974
Secretary of Transportation	John A. Volpe	1969-1973
	Claude S. Brinegar	1973-1974

The Ford Administration (1974-1977)

Vice President	Nelson A. Rockefeller	1974-1977
Secretary of State	Henry A. Kissinger	1974-1977
Secretary of Treasury	William E. Simon	1974-1977
Attorney General	William Saxbe	1974-1975
	Edward Levi	1975-1977
Secretary of Interior	Rogers Morton	1974-1975
	Stanley K. Hathaway	1975
	Thomas Kleppe	1975-1977
Secretary of Agriculture	Earl L. Butz	1974-1976
	John A. Knebel	1976-1977
Secretary of Commerce	Frederick B. Dent	1974-1975
	Rogers Morton	1975-1976
	Elliot L. Richardson	1976-1977
Secretary of Labor	Peter J. Brennan	1974-1975
	John T. Dunlop	1975-1976
	W. J. Usery	1976-1977
Secretary of Defense	James R. Schlesinger	1974-1975
	Donald Rumsfeld	1975-1977
Secretary of Health, Education, and Welfare	Caspar Weinberger	1974-1975
	Forrest D. Mathews	1975-1977
Secretary of Housing and Urban Development	James T. Lynn	1974-1975
	Carla A. Hills	1975-1977
Secretary of Transportation	Claude Brinegar	1974-1975
	William T. Colemn	1975-1977

The Carter Administration (1977-1981)

Vice President	Walter F. Mondale	1977-1981
Secretary of State	Cyrus R. Vance	1977-1980
	Edmund Muskie	1980-1981
Secretary of Treasury	W. Michael Blumenthal	1977-1979
	G. William Miller	1979-1981
Attorney General	Griffin Bell	1977-1979
	Benjamin R. Civiletti	1979-1981
Secretary of Interior	Cecil D. Andrus	1977-1981
Secretary of Agriculture	Robert Bergland	1977-1981
Secretary of Commerce	Juanita M. Kreps	1977-1979
	Philip M. Klutznick	1979-1981
Secretary of Labor	F. Ray Marshall	1977-1981
Secretary of Defense	Harold Brown	1977-1981
Secretary of Health, Education and Welfare	Joseph A. Califano	1977-1979
	Patricia R. Harris	1979
Secretary of Health and Human Services	Patricia R. Harris	1979-1981
Secretary of Education	Shirley M. Hufstedler	1979-1981
Secretary of Housing and Urban Development	Patricia R. Harris	1977-1979
	Moon Landrieu	1979-1981
Secretary of Transportation	Brock Adams	1977-1979
	Neil E. Goldschmidt	1979-1981
Secretary of Energy	James R. Schlesinger	1977-1979
	Charles W. Duncan	1979-1981

The Reagan Administration (1981-1989)

Vice President	George Bush	1981-1989
Secretary of State	Alexander M. Haig	1981-1982
	George P. Shultz	1982-1989

Secretary of Treasury	Donald Regan	1981–1985
	James A. Baker III	1985–1988
	Nicholas F. Brady	1988–1989
Attorney General	William F. Smith	1981–1985
	Edwin A. Meese III	1985–1988
	Richard Thornburgh	1988–1989
Secretary of Interior	James Watt	1981–1983
	William P. Clark, Jr.	1983–1985
	Donald P. Hodel	1985–1989
Secretary of Agriculture	John Block	1981–1986
	Richard E. Lyng	1986–1989
Secretary of Commerce	Malcolm Baldridge	1981–1987
	C. William Verity, Jr.	1987–1989
Secretary of Labor	Raymond Donovan	1981–1985
	William Brock	1985–1987
	Ann D. McLaughlin	1987–1989
Secretary of Defense	Caspar Weinberger	1981–1987
	Frank C. Carlucci	1987–1989
Secretary of Health and Human Services	Richard Schweiker	1981–1983
	Margaret Heckler	1983–1985
	Otis R. Bowen	1985–1989
Secretary of Education	Terrel H. Bell	1981–1985
	William J. Bennett	1985–1988
	Laura F. Cavazos	1988–1989
Secretary of Housing and Urban Development	Samuel Pierce	1981–1989
Secretary of Transportation	Drew Lewis	1981–1983
	Elizabeth Dole	1983–1987
	James H. Burnley	1987–1989
Secretary of Energy	James Edwards	1981–1982
	Donald P. Hodel	1982–1985
	John S. Herrington	1984–1989

The Bush Administration (1989–1993)

Vice President	J. Danforth Quayle	1989–1993
Secretary of State	James A. Baker III	1989–1992
	Lawrence S. Eagleburger	1992–1993
Secretary of Treasury	Nicholas F. Brady	1989–1993
Attorney General	Richard Thornburgh	1989–1991
	William P. Barr	1991–1993
Secretary of Interior	Manuel Lujan	1989–1993
Secretary of Agriculture	Clayton K. Yeutter	1989–1991
	Edward Madigan	1991–1993
Secretary of Commerce	Robert A. Mosbacher	1989–1992
	Barbara H. Franklin	1992–1993
Secretary of Labor	Elizabeth Dole	1989–1991
	Lynn M. Martin	1991–1993

Secretary of Defense	Richard B. Cheney	1989–1993
Secretary of Health and Human Services	Louis W. Sullivan	1989–1993
Secretary of Education	Laura F. Cavazos	1989–1991
	Lamar Alexander	1991–1993
Secretary of Housing and Urban Development	Jack F. Kemp	1989–1993
Secretary of Transportation	Samuel K. Skinner	1989–1992
	Andrew H. Card	1992–1993
Secretary of Energy	James D. Watkins	1989–1993
Secretary of Veterans Affairs	Edward J. Derwinski	1989–1993

The Clinton Administration (1993–   )

Vice President	Albert Gore, Jr.	1993–
Secretary of State	Warren M. Christopher	1993–1997
	Madeleine Albright	1997–
Secretary of Treasury	Lloyd M. Bentsen, Jr.	1993–1995
	Robert E. Rubin	1995–
Attorney General	Janet Reno	1993–
Secretary of Interior	Bruce Babbitt	1993–
Secretary of Agriculture	Mike Espy	1993–1995
	Daniel R. Glickman	1995–
Secretary of Commerce	Ronald H. Brown	1993–1996
	William M. Daley	1997–
Secretary of Labor	Robert B. Reich	1993–1997
	Alexis M. Herman	1997–
Secretary of Defense	Les Aspin	1993–1994
	William Perry	1994–1996
	William S. Cohen	1996–
Secretary of Health and Human Services	Donna E. Shalala	1993–
Secretary of Education	Richard W. Riley	1993–
Secretary of Housing and Urban Development	Henry G. Cisneros	1993–1997
	Andrew Cuomo	1997–
Secretary of Energy	Hazel R. O'Leary	1993–1997
	Federico Pena	1997–
Secretary of Transportation	Federico Pena	1993–1997
	Rodney Slates	1997–
Secretary of Veterans Affairs	Jesse Brown	1993–

POPULATION OF THE UNITED STATES, 1790–1996

Year	Population	Percent Increase	Population per Square Mile	Percent Urban/ Rural	Percent White/ Nonwhite	Median Age
1790	3,929,214		4.5	5.1/94.9	80.7/19.3	NA
1800	5,308,483	35.1	6.1	6.1/93.9	81.1/18.9	NA
1810	7,239,881	36.4	4.3	7.3/92.7	81.0/19.0	NA
1820	9,638,453	33.1	5.5	7.2/92.8	81.6/18.4	16.7
1830	12,866,020	33.5	7.4	8.8/91.2	81.9/18.1	17.2
1840	17,069,453	32.7	9.8	10.8/89.2	83.2/16.8	17.8
1850	23,191,876	35.9	7.9	15.3/84.7	84.3/15.7	18.9
1860	31,443,321	35.6	10.6	19.8/80.2	85.6/14.4	19.4
1870	39,818,449	26.6	13.4	25.7/74.3	86.2/13.8	20.2
1880	50,155,783	26.0	16.9	28.2/71.8	86.5/13.5	20.9
1890	62,947,714	25.5	21.2	35.1/64.9	87.5/12.5	22.0
1900	75,994,575	20.7	25.6	39.6/60.4	87.9/12.1	22.9
1910	91,972,266	21.0	31.0	45.6/54.4	88.9/11.1	24.1
1920	105,710,620	14.9	35.6	51.2/48.8	89.7/10.3	25.3
1930	122,775,046	16.1	41.2	56.1/43.9	89.8/10.2	26.4
1940	131,669,275	7.2	44.2	56.5/43.5	89.8/10.2	29.0
1950	150,697,361	14.5	50.7	64.0/36.0	89.5/10.5	30.2
1960	179,323,175	18.5	50.6	69.9/30.1	88.6/11.4	29.5
1970	203,302,031	13.4	57.4	73.5/26.5	87.6/12.4	28.0
1980	226,545,805	11.4	64.0	73.7/26.3	86.0/14.0	30.0
1990	248,718,000	9.8	70.3	77.5/22.5	83.8/16.2	32.9
1996	265,284,000	6.6	74.9	NA/NA	82.1/17.9	NA

NA = Not Available.

EMPLOYMENT, 1870–1996

Year	Number of Workers (in millions)	Male/Female Employment Ratio	Percentage of Workers in Unions
1870	12.5	85/15	—
1880	17.4	85/15	—
1890	23.3	83/17	—
1900	29.1	82/18	3
1910	38.2	79/21	6
1920	41.6	79/21	12
1930	48.8	78/22	7
1940	53.0	76/24	27
1950	59.6	72/28	25
1960	69.9	68/32	26
1970	82.1	63/37	25
1980	108.5	58/42	23
1985	108.9	57/43	19
1990	118.8	55/45	16
1996	126.7	54/46	14.5

PRODUCTION, TRADE, AND FEDERAL SPENDING/DEBT, 1790–1996

Year	Gross National Product (GNP) (in billions $)	Balance of Trade (in billions $)	Federal Budget (in billions $)	Federal Surplus/Deficit (in billions $)	Federal Debt (in billions $)
1790	—	–3	.004	+0.00015	.076
1800	—	–20	.011	+0.0006	.083
1810	—	–18	.008	+0.0012	.053
1820	—	–4	.018	–0.0004	.091
1830	—	+3	.015	+0.100	.049
1840	—	+25	.024	–0.005	.004
1850	—	–26	.040	+0.004	.064
1860	—	–38	.063	–0.01	.065
1870	7.4	–11	.310	+0.10	2.4
1880	11.2	+92	.268	+0.07	2.1
1890	13.1	+87	.318	+0.09	1.2
1900	18.7	+569	.521	+0.05	1.2
1910	35.3	+273	.694	–0.02	1.1
1920	91.5	+2,880	6.357	+0.3	24.3
1930	90.7	+513	3.320	+0.7	16.3
1940	100.0	–3,403	9.6	–2.7	43.0
1950	286.5	+1,691	43.1	–2.2	257.4
1960	506.5	+4,556	92.2	+0.3	286.3
1970	992.7	+2,511	196.6	+2.8	371.0
1980	2,631.7	+24,088	579.6	–59.5	914.3
1985	4,087.7	–148,480	946.3	–212.3	1,827.5
1990	5,764.9	–101,012	1,251.8	–220.5	4,064.6
1996	7,567.1	–165,095	1,572.4	–145.6	5,207.3

Illustrations

Maps

Charts

Index

Note: Some pages are in *italics* and are preceded by letters. These refer to (*i*) illustrations and their captions, (*m*) maps, and (*c*) charts.

War of the Spanish Succession, 65

Warr, Lord De La, 39

Warren, Mercy Otis, 142, 225

Washington, Booker T., 541

Washington, D.C.: building of, 238–39; establishment of as capital, 206; slavery in, 446, 447; War of 1812 and burning of, i257

Washington, George: American Revolution, 157, 158–59, 167, 168, 171–72; cabinet members, A-28; Constitution and, 195, 202; death of, 224; French and Indian War, 122; Mount Vernon, i194, i211; as president, 203, 206, 210; retirement from office, 211; slavery and, 177; War of 1812, 256

Washington, Martha, 171, i211

Washington, Treaty of (1871), 526

Washington Temperance Society, 408–9

Water, and American environment, 335–37

Water power, and industry, 335–37

Watson, Harry, 297

Watt, James, 229, 232

Wayne, Gen. Anthony, i159, 181

Wealth, distribution of and Industrial Revolution, 351–53

Weather, and colonial almanacs, 106

Webster, Daniel: Bank of United States, 308–9; Compromise of 1850, 448; contract law, 279; land speculation, 315; Revolt of New England, 256; as secretary of state, 319; Webster-Hayne debate, 301–2; Whig Party, 313

Webster, Noah, 225

Webster-Ashburton Treaty (1842), 319

Webster-Hayne Debate (1830), 301–2

Weems, Mason, 225

Weir, Robert, i500

Weld, Theodore Dwight, 417, 420

Wells, Ida B., 546–47

Wesley, Charles, 103

Wesley, John, 103, 226

West: British policy on colonial expansion, m129; canal building, 334; chronology of expansion, A-8; Civil War and, 490–91, m494; Eastern images of, 273; economy of and urban growth before Civil War, 328; education, 411; expansion in 1840s, 429–37; expansionism in Jefferson era and conflicts with Native Americans, 250–52; Lewis and Clark expedition, 246–47; nationalism in years following War of 1812, 269–73; politics and conflict in 1840s, 437–42; Proclamation of 1763, 127–28; removal of Native Americans from South and, 306–8; slavery controversy of 1840s and 1850s, 265, 450–53; social and geographic mobility, 353; voting rights, 293. See also Northwest; Ohio; Pacific northwest

West Africa: preIslamic cultures prior to beginning of slave trade, 23–24; rice production, 89

West Country (England), 33

Western Union Telegraph Company, 341

West Indies: English colonization of, 46; France and, 244; slave trade and, 84; tobacco, 40; triangular trade, i26, 93; witchcraft accusations in New England and servants from, 98. See also Caribbean

West Virginia, and Civil War, m469, 493

We the People (McDonald, 1958), 200

Wheelwright, John, 56

Whigs: in Jackson era, 311–13; Kansas-Nebraska Act, 451; slavery and "Conscience," 449; Tyler presidency and, 318–19; westward expansion in 1840s, 437

Whirling Thunder (Sauk), i304

Whiskey Rebellion (1794), 208, i209

Whiskey ring scandal, 525

White, Hugh Lawson, 313

White, John, i7, 32

White Leagues, 527

White Over Black (Jordan, 1968), 82

White supremacy, in New South, 542, 547. See also Ku Klux Klan

Whitman, Marcus and Narcissa, 435

Whitman, Walt, 401

Whitney, Eli, 230–31, 344

Wide, Wide World, The (Warner, 1850), 422–23

Wilderness, and literature of antebellum period, 401. See also Nature

Wilderness, Battle of (1864), 499

Wilentz, Sean, 297

Wilkes, Charles, 490

Wilkie, William, i356

Wilkinson, Gen. James, 246, 247

Willard, Emma, 415

William (joint sovereign of England with Mary), 68, 121

William and Mary College, 105

Williams, Roger, m54, 55

Williams v. Mississippi (1898), 546

Williamson, Joel, 543–44

Wilmot, David, 442

Wilmot Proviso (1846), 442

Wilson, Henry, 471

Winsor, Joshua, i91

Winthrop, John, 52–53, 55, 56

Wisconsin: Fugitive Slave Act, 449; immigration in 1840s and 1850s, 331

Witchcraft, in New England, 98–99

Within the Plantation Household (Fox-Genovese, 1988), 385

Witness trees, 184

Wolfe, James, 123

Wollstonecraft, Mary, 172

Woman in the Nineteenth Century (Fuller, 1844), 405

Women: American Revolution and, 142, 143, 171–73; Civil War and, 480–81, 485; class in antebellum South, 379–80; colonial Chesapeake and, 40, 79–80; colonial New England and, 80–81; cult

of domesticity, 357–58; education of, 222–23, 357, 379–80, i399, 411; household industries in colonial North, 90; as indentured servants in colonies, 77; Iroquois society, 7; Jackson era and reduction in rights of, 297; labor in New South and, 535; labor unions and, 351; literacy in colonial period, 105; middle class in early 1800s, 354; as midwives, 224; migrations to West and, 436–37; plantations in southern colonies, 94; Puritan society, 56; Quakers and, 63; Reconstruction and African-American, 522–23, 532; reform and homes for "friendless," 414; religious revivalism and, i227, 228, 408; sentimental novels of antebellum period, 422–23; Separatists and Protestant Reformation, 28; Shakers and, 405; slavery and, 96, 385, 386, 394, 395; textile industry and, 346–48; West African societies, 24; witchcraft accusations and, 99. See also Childbearing and child rearing; Family; Feminism; Gender; Women's suffrage movement

Women's suffrage movement: Fifteenth Amendment and, 516; Seneca Falls convention of 1848, 415

Wood, Gordon, 155, 201

Woods, Peter, 83

Woodward, C. Vann, 531, 543

Woolen Act of 1699, 90

Wool trade, and England, 25, 26

Worcester v. Georgia (1832), 281, 305, m306

Workhouses, 414

Working class: employment of women and, 358; industrial revolution in England, 229–30. See also Class

Working Women's Association, 516

World antislavery convention (London, 1840), 414

World War I, deaths in compared to Civil War, 491

World War II, death in compared to Civil War, 491

Wright, Mother Lucy, 405

XYZ Affair, 213

Yale, Elihu, 105

Yale University, 105, 226

Yancey, William L., 389

Yazoo Land Companies, 279

Yellow fever, 244

Yorktown, Battle of (1781), 168

Young, Brigham, 406

"Young America" (Democratic Party), 449–50

Young Mill-Wright's and Miller's Guide, The (Evans, 1795), 230

Yucatán, and Mayan civilization, 4

Zenger, John Peter, 109